Summer Jobs in the USA

2003

Australia • Canada • Mexico • Singapore • Spain • United Kingdom • United States

About The Thomson Corporation and Peterson's

With revenues of US$7.2 billion, The Thomson Corporation (www.thomson.com) is a leading global provider of integrated information solutions for business, education, and professional customers. Its Learning businesses and brands (www.thomsonlearning.com) serve the needs o individuals, learning institutions, and corporations with products and services for both tradition and distributed learning.

Peterson's, part of The Thomson Corporation, is one of the nation's most respected provi lifelong learning online resources, software, reference guides, and books. The Education Supersite℠ at www.petersons.com—the Internet's most heavily traveled education reso has searchable databases and interactive tools for contacting U.S.-accredited institution programs. In addition, Peterson's serves more than 105 million education consumers an

For more information, contact Peterson's, 2000 Lenox Drive, Lawrenceville, NJ 08648; 800-338-3282; or find us on the World Wide Web at www.petersons.com/about.

Peterson's makes every reasonable effort to obtain accurate, complete, and timely data from reliable sources. Nevertheless, Peterson's and the third-party data suppliers make no representation or warranty, either expressed or implied, as to the accuracy, timeliness, or completeness of the data or the results to be obtained from using the data, including, but not limited to, its quality, performance, merchantability, or fitness for a particular purpose, non-infringement or otherwise.

Neither Peterson's nor the third-party data suppliers warrant, guarantee, or make any representations that the results from using the data will be successful or will satisfy users' requirements. The entire risk to the results and performance is assumed by the user.

ISSN 1064-6701
ISBN 0-7689-0946-5

Printed in Canada

10 9 8 7 6 5 4 3 2 1 04 03 02

CONTENTS

How to Use This Book 1

Looking for a Summer Job? 4
by Shirley J. Longshore

Look Into Summer Jobs Carefully 10

International Applicants for Summer Employment in the U.S. 11
by Elizabeth Chazottes

Working for the National Park Service 21

Do You Want to Work Temporarily in Canada? 35

State-by-State Listings 39

Canada and Countries Outside North America 357

Category Index 368

Employer Index 373

Job Types Index 378

HOW TO USE THIS BOOK

What are you going to do to make this summer special? You already have a good start. *Summer Jobs in the USA 2003* is an indispensable catalog of interesting and enriching summer work experiences for students or anyone looking for summer employment. You'll find detailed, up-to-date information on more than 50,000 positions offered across the country and abroad—from counselors, instructors, and lifeguards to theater stagehands, wilderness guides, and office clerical workers. The list is long, and many of these jobs require little or no previous experience.

Search by Your Interests

There are many different ways you can use *Summer Jobs in the USA 2003* to find the right work opportunity:

- If your primary consideration is the geographic location of a job (if, for instance, you'd like to spend the summer working near your hometown or in a particular area of the country), you can turn directly to the **State-by-State Listings**, where employers are listed alphabetically by state.
- The **Canada and Countries Outside North America** section features summer employment opportunities in Canada and elsewhere. This section profiles eighteen employers offering hundreds of summer jobs to young adults.
- If you're interested in working at a U.S. national park, turn to **Working for the National Park Service** to learn about job opportunities for U.S. citizens at National Park Service sites in regions throughout the country.

Another way you can put *Summer Jobs in the USA 2003* to work for you is by looking for jobs according to the services they provide. The opportunities featured in this book are divided into fifteen main areas, which are listed in the **Category Index** at the back of the book. If you know, for instance, that you want to work at an amusement or theme park, the **Category Index** lists all such employers that are featured in the book. Use the following list of categories as your guide:

Accommodations and Food Services
Agriculture, Forestry, Fishing, and Hunting
Ambulatory Health Care Services
Amusement and Theme Parks
Business and Professional Organizations
Educational Services
Nature Parks and Environmental Organizations
Performing Arts Companies
Professional, Scientific, and Technical Services
Public Administration
Recreation Industries
Recreational and Vacation Camps
Religious Organizations

Retail Trade
Social Assistance

Of course, if you already know the name of the employer you want to contact, you can simply turn to the **Employer Index** for a page reference to the description of that employer's job opportunities.

If you're interested in knowing what kinds of jobs are most readily available, turn to the **Job Types Index**. It lists the most frequently cited job types in the book and the facilities that offer them.

Read the Employer Profiles

Once you have found an employer that interests you, you can read about the opportunities provided. The **General Information** section of each profile provides details about the location, size, focus, and special features of the facility. You can check the **Profile of Summer Employees** to get an idea of who your coworkers might be. **Employment Information** includes descriptions of available jobs as well as important details about when positions are available, salaries, and special requirements. Any **Benefits,** such as meals, laundry facilities, health insurance, or the possibility of college credit, and **Preemployment Training,** such as leadership skills or accident prevention and safety, are also noted. The **Contact** paragraph provides you with information on how the employer wants you to apply for a position and the application deadline.

International applicants for any of the positions found in this guide should pay special attention to valuable information found in the **Employment Information** section. If international students are encouraged to apply for available positions, a sentence stating such will appear at the end of this section, along with any special application procedures required of international applicants, such as referral through an agency designed to handle these applications.

The data in this book were collected in the spring and summer of 2002 from employers eager to fill staff vacancies with high-quality, motivated workers. A representative of each employer completed a questionnaire to describe the job opportunities to be offered specifically for the summer of 2003, but more than likely in subsequent summers as well. In some cases, additional information was obtained through secondary research. Since the data were collected in 2002, you should check with the employer before applying for or accepting a position to verify that all information in the profiles is still accurate and up-to-date. A phone call to the contact person listed in the profile or a visit to the employer's Web site (address is in the **Contact** section) will provide you with even more information about the employer and the type of employment that is available. Peterson's does not assume responsibility for the hiring policies or actions of these employers.

Learn How to Apply

Summer Jobs in the USA 2003 features five articles that provide additional help in your search for a summer job. If you are just learning how to apply for a summer job, be sure to read "Looking for a Summer Job?" "Look Into Summer Jobs Carefully" provides valuable information for those pursuing summer work as a salesperson. International job hunters are strongly urged to read "International Applicants for Summer Employment in the U.S." "Working for the National Park Service" gives you all the information you'll need if you're a U.S. citizen considering a summer job at a U.S. National Park Service site; the article tells you about the positions offered, job requirements, participating sites, and application contacts. "Do You Want to Work Temporarily in Canada?" tells you the steps you need to take before you begin a summer job in Canada; the article outlines procedures you and your Canadian employer must follow for you to receive employment authorization.

Remember, all of the employers listed in this book are actively looking for your help—they are waiting for your application! We hope that this book will help make your summer a fun, interesting, and profitable experience.

Abbreviation Chart

The following are abbreviations commonly used in this book:

ACA	American Camping Association
AHSE	Association for Horsemanship Safety and Education
ALS	Advanced Life Saving
ARC	American Red Cross
BUNAC	British University North American Club
CAA	Camp Archery Association
CIT	Counselor-in-Training
CPR	Cardiopulmonary Resuscitation
EMR	Educationally Mentally Retarded
EMT	Emergency Medical Technician
EOE	Equal Opportunity Employer
HSA	Horsemanship Safety Association
ICCP	International Camp Counselors Program
IDC	Instructor Development Center
LD	Learning Disabled
LPN	Licensed Practical Nurse
NAUI	National Association of Underwater Instructors
NRA	National Rifle Association
PADI	Professional Association of Diving Instructors
RN	Registered Nurse
SASE	Self-addressed, stamped envelope
SCI	Small-Craft Instructor
SLS	Senior Life Saving
WSI	Water Safety Instructor

LOOKING FOR A SUMMER JOB?

by Shirley J. Longshore

As an older teenager or young adult concerned about your future, working at a job—for pay or not—is an important, if not mandatory, summer undertaking. If you've never done it, looking for a job may seem intimidating, but it's not. Hundreds of thousands of young people *do* find interesting and rewarding jobs every summer.

Many young adults turn to summer employment not only to pay for college expenses but also to earn spending money or even to help out their families. Competition for these jobs can be stiff, but keep in mind that summer employment can provide the background you'll need to compete aggressively both with other college-bound students when applying to schools *and* with other job seekers when looking for a full-time job. Guidance counselors, admissions officers, and corporate human-resource managers look for college and job applications that display outside activities, work experiences, and additional credentials. A good summer job record is a plus that colleges and employers now routinely expect to see.

"Strong academics are not enough any more," says a college admissions officer at a small university in Georgia. "We're looking very hard at what else students are doing, how they use their time, and what other skills they are acquiring. Even the less competitive colleges are becoming much more demanding in evaluating prospective students." If you don't need to earn money, working as a volunteer will also give you a competitive edge.

Get Started Now

Landing the summer job that will add to the bottom line in your bank book and bolster your resume is harder than it used to be. The competition can be tough, but you can overcome the obstacles. To increase your chances for success, you must be willing to work at mounting an organized, targeted job search; the sooner you get started, the better!

"The key is to start early," emphasizes the personnel director of a large state park that employs many young people each summer. "You can't wait until May and then see what's around, because there truly won't be anything left. I see this over and over. We have all of our hiring done, and then we get call after call and letter after letter from panicked, although qualified, students who are just applying much too late." A job seeker fortunate enough to get his or her application in early and who is hired also has the opportunity to ensure a somewhat more secure summer job situation throughout the rest of high school or college; those who prove

---

Shirley J. Longshore is a writer, editor, and communications consultant. Her articles about business, work, and education have appeared in national publications.

themselves valuable will likely have first crack at getting the job back the following summer. To help you with your search, this book lists nearly 800 U.S. and Canadian employers who are looking for qualified, hard-working people to fill specific openings on their staffs.

Prepare Your Resume and Cover Letter

Your resume should be limited to one page and must communicate your strong points by detailing relevant experience and describing your background. It should present you in a way that will interest an employer enough to arrange an interview.

"I had a student this year who said he didn't have to be convinced that a summer job was important, but he didn't have a clue how to begin looking for one," says a guidance counselor at a large public high school in Florida. "High school students look at me like I'm from outer space when I tell them that, first, they should write a resume. They say things like: 'What would I put on it? I have no real skills; I've never done much of anything. A resume is for older people looking for real jobs.' But when we look at the clubs they have participated in, after-school activities, volunteer work, and baby-sitting jobs, we can often work up quite a list together. It gives young people an idea of what they have to offer an employer."

Everyone has the makings of a resume in their background—even those just starting out. You simply have to look at your past thoroughly. Don't overlook any activities that could enhance your credentials. Don't forget the computer knowledge you gained in school. Do you teach Sunday school? Have you worked in your town's recreation program? Do you assist in a shelter for the homeless or collect newspapers for recycling? All of these activities require skills that can be translated into proven experience for an employer. At the very least, participating in these kinds of activities will show that you are focused, well-rounded, community-minded, responsible, and trustworthy.

A resume should also list people who will give you good recommendations. (Before listing anyone as a reference, check to make sure he or she is willing to be listed.) To prepare a reference list, create a separate page with your name, address, and phone number followed by the names, addresses, and phone numbers of 2 to 4 people who will verify your skills and testify to the qualities that will convince the employer to hire you.

You may want to tailor your resume to appeal to a particular employer—using a computer makes this easy. Perhaps you are intrigued by a counselor's job at an academic-oriented camp. The resume for that position should contain an item that mentions that you put the skill you show in math to good use tutoring a third-grader after school. Phrase the item: "Demonstrated maturity and responsibility tutoring third-grade student in math in after-school sessions." With this entry on your resume, you are showcasing both a skill at an academic subject and experience working with a younger person. If you're using a computer, this item can easily be deleted from the resume you'll send in application to a job that doesn't involve academics or supervising children.

Your resume should also include items mentioning any athletics training you have had, such as swimming lessons, ballet classes, and team memberships. These activities demand those qualities employers look for—self-discipline, high energy, dedication, and a desire for self-improvement.

A college student from Massachusetts didn't think his experience as head cook for the school's international club's dinners was very important. "I just did it for fun," the student admitted. "But then I saw an opening for an assistant chef at a lodge for the summer between my junior and senior years, and I realized I could parlay that experience into a job. It worked."

The best resume is one that is straightforward and clearly presented. If you're composing one for the first time, you should take advantage of the knowledge of older siblings or friends—talk with them and ask to see their resumes. Remember, it must state relevant information about you and your skills.

This is where a strong cover letter comes into play. A cover letter serves as your introduction to a potential employer and, hopefully, will interest him or her enough to want to read your resume. A cover letter should draw the reader's attention to those experiences that best relate to the qualifications required for a particular job. For example, if a camp is looking for counselors to lead activities, your letter should mention your involvement in school plays (an item on your resume) and suggest that this experience would enable you to confidently instruct campers in drama or in a stage production. Although a cover letter should be brief and to the point, it doesn't hurt to help the resume reader along by flagging pertinent information. Sell yourself!

My Resume Is Ready—Now What?

After you've identified your skills and written your resume, you need to consider what you want to get out of your summer job. Ask yourself: What do I enjoy doing? What am I really good at? What would I like to learn more about? What work experience would enhance my chances at future opportunities? Do I love to be outdoors in the summer, or do I really prefer the air-conditioned comfort of an office? Is this the time to go far away from home, or would I rather stay close by? Do I need to make money? Keep in mind that some jobs may be too costly for you. If you need to earn money to cover college expenses, for instance, you may not want your pay to be eaten away by transportation and room-and-board costs.

After answering the questions above, turn to the **Category Index** to zero in on the kinds of opportunities that make sense for you. The listings go beyond what you'll find in your local community through the usual pavement-pounding, want-ad-answering, asking-around methods. The jobs in this guide are located all over. Some may be in your geographic area, and others may be hundreds or thousands of miles away. Included are camps, resorts, summer theaters, conservation and environmental programs, lodges, ranches, conference and training centers, national parks, and amusement and theme parks that normally hire many young people for each busy summer season. The possibilities are endless, so you don't have to worry about ending up in a job in which you have little interest.

Keep in mind that many summer employers provide on-site training in the particular skills needed for their jobs, so don't be discouraged if your skills don't match exactly. These people are generally looking for qualities other than direct experience—motivation, interest, and the desire to learn. When you read about a position, *read between the lines* to see what kind of employee is really being sought.

Winning Interviews

Once you have contacted the employers you'd like to work for, think about how you'll present yourself at interviews. An interview may take place over the phone or in a face-to-face meeting. In either case, it's an opportunity for you and the employer to get a better sense of each other.

Remember, an interview goes both ways. It is also an opportunity for you to ask any questions and to decide whether you really want the job. You may want to ask about specific duties, hours, pay, what benefits are provided (such as room and board), and when hiring decisions will be made. Always write a brief, sincere thank-you note to follow up an interview, even if it was very short or conducted by telephone.

It's important to dress appropriately for an in-person interview. Bring with you any credentials that are required (e.g., working papers, birth certificate, school records, or Social Security card). If you don't have a Social Security card, you can, and should, get one right away. You can start the process by calling 800-772-1213, the nationwide toll-free number for Social Security information.

Finding a good summer job opportunity is not an impossible task. There are jobs out there. You have a good shot at landing one if you prepare your resume, start going after the jobs you know about early, and present yourself both on paper and in person in the best possible light.

Sample Cover Letter

ANNE MEREDITH

421 South Street
Apartment 2C
City Line, NJ 07685
821-663-4121

218 Tower Hall
State University
Brighton, PA 62451
580-341-6840

January 4, 2003

Name of person in charge, title
Name of camp or resort
Street address
Town, state, zip code

Dear Mr. or Ms. (last name):

I saw the listing describing your summer program in Summer Jobs in the USA 2003. It states that you are hiring a Waterfront Director, a summer position for which I would like to apply.

As you will see from the attached resume, I am qualified for such a position. I taught swimming, was a lifeguard, coached a swim team, and swam on my high school team for four years. I was named to the Junior Varsity Swim Team at State University in both my freshman and sophomore years.

I am experienced at supervising and teaching both adults and children in swimming and waterfront safety. I enjoy working with people and sharing my expertise with them. Your summer program sounds like one in which my skills would be fully utilized.

I would appreciate the opportunity to explore this position with you further. I would be happy to talk with you by telephone or to arrange a personal interview during my winter break, which is until the end of this month.

Thank you for your consideration. I look forward to hearing from you soon. You can reach me at my home number in City Line until January 27th.

Sincerely,

Anne Meredith

Sample Resume

ANNE MEREDITH

421 South Street
Apartment 2C
City Line, NJ 07685
821-663-4121

218 Tower Hall
State University
Brighton, PA 62451
580-341-6840

EDUCATION:
State University, Brighton, PA
Expected date of graduation, 2004
Major: Biology GPA: 3.4 Degree track: B.S.

HONORS:
Dean's List, first semester, State University
Science Scholar Award, City Line High School
State Merit Scholarship Winner

EXPERIENCE:
Head Lifeguard/Swimming Coach
River Edge Athletic Club, Edgeton, NJ
Summer 2001 and 2002
Responsibilities included scheduling and overseeing the summer staff of ten lifeguards and serving as one of two coaches for the club's competitive children's swim team (35 members). I also gave private swimming lessons to club members.

Lifeguard
YWCA, City Line, NJ; Winter 2000–2001

Swimming Instructor/Lifeguard
River Edge Athletic Club; Summer 2000 and 1999

Assistant Swimming Instructor (3- to 5-year-olds)
YWCA, City Line, NJ; Summer 1998

Day Camp Helper (9- and 10-year-olds)
YWCA, City Line, NJ; Summer 1997

ACTIVITIES:
Swim Team, Junior Varsity, State University, 2001–2002
Glee Club, State University, 2001–2002
Swim Team, YWCA, City Line, NJ, 1999–2000
Captain, 1999–2000
Junior-Senior Chorus, City Line High School, 1998–2000
Youth Group, St. John's Church, 1998–2001
President, 2001
Springvale Nursing Home, volunteer visitor, 2000–2001

SKILLS:
Red Cross Certification, Lifesaving
Fluent in Spanish
Teaching experience with children and adults
Computer skills: Microsoft Word

LOOK INTO SUMMER JOBS CAREFULLY

Some newspaper ads promise great summer jobs for students—offering travel and good pay. Many of these summer jobs require long hours of selling and traveling in car pools in a van and sharing cheap motels with others on the sales team.

To entice you to sign up, some of these companies offer examples of students who made big money selling for them. But such promises of huge earnings often are misleading because the companies use examples of students who also were paid commissions to recruit others to join the company. People who just sell the company's products earn a great deal less and often do it under less than ideal working conditions.

Moreover, because students often are hired as independent contractors, the company assumes no responsibility for its actions. It likewise may provide no unemployment insurance or Workers' Compensation benefits.

It is your responsibility to know the laws about selling in the state in which you are working. For example, if you get arrested for not having a state transient merchant's license, it would probably be your responsibility to get yourself out of jail—not the company's.

Your ability to sell and your personal motivation will determine how much money you make. Some students have complained that they could have earned more money working at a minimum-wage restaurant job based on the number of hours they spent selling.

Be sure to check out any company before you sign up for a job. Some unscrupulous companies make students work long hours for little pay in dangerous communities. Some of these same companies put their recruits through emotional and physical abuse.

Before you sign up:

- Ask the company detailed questions about the working conditions and income potential.
- Ask what will happen if you get injured on the job or need to quit in the middle of the summer.
- Ask the company how you will get home in case of an emergency.
- Ask how and when you will be paid and what room and board accommodations the company will provide.

Reprinted with the permission of the North Dakota Attorney General's Office, Consumer Protection Division.

INTERNATIONAL APPLICANTS FOR SUMMER EMPLOYMENT IN THE U.S.

by Elizabeth Chazottes

Nothing is more exciting and rewarding than an international summer job in the United States. International students have been spending their summers in the U.S. for years to learn American methods of business, to perfect their English skills, and to make international connections that last a lifetime. There are more opportunities today than ever before, but you must be well informed. Take the time to learn about your options and which opportunities will best meet your needs. The better prepared you are, the more successful your experience will be. All international students interested in coming to the U.S. for a summer job should make sure they are clear on what they can and cannot do in the workplace on the type of visa they receive to come to the U.S.

In an effort to provide guidance that is as accurate as possible for students from outside the United States, each employer listed in *Summer Jobs in the USA 2003* has been asked if applications will be accepted from international students. Peterson's has also asked if the employer is willing to undertake the necessary steps—either directly with the U.S. Immigration and Naturalization Service (INS) or through an educational exchange organization—to make it possible for the student to secure a proper U.S. visa that will allow him or her to complete the program and legally receive a salary or stipend, if applicable, while in the United States.

There are significant penalties for employers who hire foreign nationals illegally. Foreign nationals can be deported and barred from returning to the United States for violating their visa status. If an employer in the United States offers you a summer job, make certain that both you *and* the employer know and follow the requirements of U.S. law *before* you leave home.

Passports

In order to get a U.S. visa that permits summer employment, you must have a valid passport from your own country. Your passport must be valid for six months beyond the date on which you expect to leave the United States. A number of countries have special "passport validity" agreements with the United States under which a passport is considered to be valid for six months beyond the expiration date

---

Elizabeth Chazottes is the Executive Director and CEO of the Association for International Practical Training and has written numerous articles on international training, overseas employment, and international human resources issues.

stated in the passport. In order to avoid last-minute problems, you should contact U.S. consular officials as early as possible to determine the exact requirement for your country.

Visas

Unlike many countries, the United States does not issue work permits or residence permits or require police registration. Instead, what an individual may or may not do while in the United States depends entirely on the specific type of visa granted. As a result, the United States has the world's most complex visa system—there are currently forty-six different kinds of nonimmigrant visas! Please note that although an individual may be a full-time student in his or her own country, a "student" visa for admission to the United States applies only to people attending an American school for full-time study. Therefore, the three kinds of student visas (F-1, J-1, and M) cannot be used by a student coming to the United States uniquely for a summer job experience.

As a general rule, there are only four U.S. visas that are likely to be suitable for students coming to the United States for summer employment:

H-2B "Temporary Worker": U.S. companies may use this visa to temporarily employ skilled or unskilled foreign nationals when they have a temporary need and there are no qualified U.S. workers available. There is a two-step process involved that must be initiated by the U.S. employer. First, the employer must request a "temporary labor" certification from the state employment service office serving the area in which the proposed employment is to be offered. Once the state office processes the temporary labor certification, the request must then be forwarded to the U.S. Department of Labor's regional office so that a final determination can be made. The employer has to demonstrate: (a) that a real job exists (i.e., not a job made up to suit the particular background of the foreign national); (b) that substantial efforts have been made to fill the job with a U.S. citizen; (c) that no qualified U.S. citizens can be found for the job; and (d) that the job to be filled is of a one-time, seasonal, peak-load, or intermittent nature. Once the labor certification is approved, a visa petition must then be filed by the employer with the INS. There are also annual limits on the number of H-2B admissions permitted. Once the limit is attained, no new petitions are accepted by INS until the next fiscal year (October 1). This process can be rather lengthy, so it should be initiated well in advance by the U.S. employer.

H-3 "Trainee": This visa is used by U.S. companies to bring foreign employees to the U.S. to participate in established company training programs. The U.S. employer must submit the H-3 application to the Immigration Service District Office that covers the area in which the person will work. The application must include a detailed training plan to show what the trainee will do in the U.S., including how much time will be spent in "classroom and other instruction" and how much time will be devoted to "on-the-job training." Information on the position the individual will fill when he or she returns to his or her home country is also required. The company must demonstrate that the training is provided with the intent to employ the individual abroad upon completion of training or to provide skills that will increase the value of the individual to a foreign business. Any productive work must be incidental to the training program. The employer must also show that the training program provides knowledge or experience that is unavailable in the individual's own country.

J-1 "Exchange Visitor": J-1 visa programs are managed by approved organizations or sponsors, such as U.S. government agencies, schools and universities, hospitals, companies, and private nonprofit educational exchange organizations. The Bureau of Educational and Cultural Affairs of the U.S. Department of State, formerly the U.S. Information Agency, has authority over these programs. There are fourteen different J-1 categories, each with its own specific rules and regulations. Among these categories are those that permit international high school students, university students, trainees, au pairs, and researchers to participate in programs in the U.S. Each sponsor is granted a "program description" that specifies the activities that are permitted for participants in the sponsor's program.

Of the fourteen J-1 categories, the "trainee" category is suitable for most international students coming to the U.S. for summer jobs. J-1 trainees can come to the U.S. to receive training in their field for periods of up to eighteen months. A detailed training program must be prepared by the U.S. host employer, specifying the objectives and skills to be learned as well as the length of time required to complete the program. A trainee cannot replace a U.S. worker but comes to the U.S. to acquire skills and knowledge in U.S. methodology.

The number of trainee programs has grown over the years. Two of the long-standing trainee exchange organizations for students are the International Association of Students in Economics and Business Management (AIESEC)—for business and economics students—and the International Association for the Exchange of Students for Technical Experience (IAESTE)—for students in technical fields. The Council on International Educational Exchange (CIEE) is the largest of the student trainee programs, followed by the Association for International Practical Training (AIPT), which brings in students and professionals from some eighty countries annually. Other programs are also available that deal primarily with trainees from specific countries or regions of the world or specific industries. Some U.S. universities also run trainee programs.

There are three additional J-1 categories that may also be of interest to students who desire a work experience in the U.S.: Summer Travel/Work, Camp Counselor, and Au Pair.

Several organizations have been granted J-1 authorizations for "summer travel/work" programs. These permit university students to work in any job they may find during the summer months (November to February for students from the Southern Hemisphere). No extensions of visas are permitted, and changes to other J-1 visa categories are not allowed. Preplacement is required for 50 percent of the participants, and students should check with the U.S. sponsoring organization about specific requirements. The Council on International Educational Exchange (CIEE) is the largest of these programs, but several other programs also operate summer travel/work programs.

The second type of additional J-1 visa is for placements in summer camps for camp counselor experience. Participants must be at least 18 years old. Placements are limited to a maximum of four months and must be for genuine camp counseling assignments in accredited U.S. camps. The YMCA, Camp America, Summer Camp USA, and InterExchange operate several of the better-known camp counselor programs.

The third is the au pair category. Au pair programs allow participants to live with and participate in the home life of an American host family while providing child-care services and attending a U.S. postsecondary educational institution. The au pair participant cannot provide child-care services for more than 45 hours per week. All participants must register and attend classes offered by an accredited U.S. postsecondary institution. Au pairs must be between the ages of 18 and 26, be secondary school graduates or the equivalent, and be proficient in spoken English.

In some cases, an individual coming to the United States on the J-1 visa may be subject to something called the "two-year foreign residence requirement." Some countries have asked the U.S. government to establish a "skills list" for its citizens. If the person's field is included on the skills list for his or her country, that means that this particular skill is greatly needed in the home country, and it will generally be necessary for the individual to return to his or her country after completing a program in the U.S. Someone subject to this residence requirement must return to his or her home country for a minimum of two years before coming back to the United States on most of the nonimmigrant visas or as a "permanent resident." Most European countries do not have skills lists, but many other countries do. If the ability to return to the United States within a two-year period after training is of concern, you should get specific information regarding this from U.S. consular officials. Also, participants who receive funding from the sending foreign government or the U.S. government may also be subject to the two-year residency requirement.

J-1 PROGRAM SPONSORS

Trainee Exchange Programs

AIESEC National Staff
135 West 50th Street, 17th Floor
New York, New York 10020
212-757-3774
Fax: 212-757-4062
E-mail: aiesec@us.aiesec.org
www.us.aiesec.org

American-Scandinavian Foundation
58 Park Avenue
New York, New York 10016
212-879-9779
Fax: 212-249-3444
E-mail: info@mscan.org
www.amscan.org

Association for International Practical Training (AIPT) and IAESTE–U.S.
10400 Little Patuxent Parkway, Suite 250
Columbia, Maryland 21044-3519
410-997-2200
410-992-3924
Fax: 410-992-3924
E-mail: aipt@aipt.org
www.aipt.org

CDS International, Inc.
871 United Nations Plaza, 15th Floor
New York, New York 10017-1814
212-497-3500
Fax: 212-497-3535
E-mail: info@cdsintl.org
www.cdsintl.org

CIEE: Council on International Educational Exchange
633 Third Avenue, 20th Floor
New York, New York 10017-6706
212-822-2600
800-40-study
Fax: 212-822-2779
E-mail: info@councilexchanges.org
www.ciee.org

InterExchange, Inc.
161 Sixth Avenue
New York, New York 10013
212-924-0446
Fax: 212-924-0575
E-mail: info@interexchange.org
www.interexchange.org

YMCA International Program Services
5 West 63rd Street
New York, New York 10023
212-727-8800
Fax: 212-727-8814
E-mail: ips@ymcanyc.org

Agricultural and Agribusiness Trainee Programs

MAST International
240 VoTech Building
1954 Buford Avenue
Saint Paul, Minnesota 55108-6197
612-624-3740
Fax: 612-625-7031
E-mail: mast@tc.umn.edu
www.mast.coafes.umn.edu/index2.htm

Ohio International Agricultural and Horticultural Intern Program
700 Ackerman Road, Suite 360
Columbus, Ohio 43202-1559
614-292-7720
Fax: 614-688-8611
E-mail: mchrisma@postbox.acs.ohio-state.edu

Summer Travel/Work Programs

CIEE: Council on International Educational Exchange
(see address in previous list)

InterExchange, Inc.
(see address in previous list)

YMCA International Program Services
(see address in previous list)

Au Pair Programs

Au Pair in America
River Plaza
9 West Broad Street
Stamford, Connecticut 06902
800-928-7247
E-mail: aupair.info@aifs.com
www.aupairinamerica.com

EF Au Pair
EF Center Boston
One Education Street
Cambridge, Massachusetts 02141
800-333-6056
Fax: 617-619-1001
E-mail: efaupair.operations@ef.com
www.efaupair.org

InterExchange Au Pair
(see address for InterExchange, Inc. in previous list)

Camp Counselor Programs

Camp America
9 West Broad Street
Stamford, Connecticut 06902-3788
800-727-2437
Fax: 203-399-5590

InterExchange—Camp USA Program
(see address in previous list)

International Camp Counselor Program—YMCA
(see address in previous list)

Summer Camp USA
BUNAC
P.O. Box 430
Southbury, Connecticut 06488
800-GO-BUNAC
203-264-0901
E-mail: info@bunacusa.org
www.bunac.org

Q "International Cultural Exchange Visitor": The Q visa allows the U.S. employer to apply to INS for permission to hire a person over 18 years of age from another country for a period of not more than fifteen months. The purpose of the program is for the international participant to work or train and to share or demonstrate his or her own culture with Americans. A frequently cited example of a major Q employer is the EPCOT Center at Walt Disney World in Florida. Another example would be a museum or a department of a museum devoted to the art and culture of the student's home country.

The "cultural component" must be an integral part of the employment or training offered. The employer must demonstrate that the individual to be hired is fully able to communicate with Americans about his or her culture as well as being fully qualified for the work aspects of the position. Substantial documentation is required as part of the employer's application.

Visa Procedures

If an employer's applications for an H-2B, H-3, or Q visa are successful, the District Office of the Immigration and Naturalization Service will advise the U.S. Embassy in the student's country. The student can then obtain the visa and travel to the U.S. In the case of the J-1 visa, the sponsoring organization that is arranging the program issues a U.S. government document called an IAP-66 (a Certificate of Eligibility). The IAP-66, which is sent to the student, is used to apply for the J-1 visa in his or her own country.

Upon entering the United States, the admitting Immigration Inspector issues a Form I-94 (Arrival/Departure Record) to H-2B, H-3, and Q visa holders that notes the specific visa granted and the date when the "Permit to Stay" expires. J-1 visa holders are issued a Permit to Stay with the notation "D/S" (for duration of status). This means that J-1 trainees may remain in the U.S. as long as they are engaged in their training program or until the end date of their IAP-66, plus thirty days. The I-94 form (and IAP-66 for the J-1 trainee) is the only documentation needed for the student to proceed to the workplace and take up the assignment.

Employment Eligibility Verification

U.S. law requires employers to examine documentation proving that persons hired are either citizens of the United States or noncitizens legally authorized for employment during their stay in the United States.

Essentially, the law requires that within three business days after a person is hired, the employer must *physically examine* documentation that (a) establishes proof of the new employee's identity and (b) establishes that the person is either a U.S. citizen or is a noncitizen who has the legal right to be employed in the United States. The law requires that a record of the verification process be maintained in the employer's files for a period of three years after the date of hiring. For this purpose, the INS has developed the I-9 form.

Virtually all kinds of employment are covered, from a full-time job with a large employer such as IBM to selling hamburgers part-time at the local McDonald's. Certainly, all of the jobs listed in *Summer Jobs in the USA 2003* will require you and your employer to complete the I-9 form. The I-9 form is in two parts. The top half must be filled out by the employee—you. You then present the form, together with your documentation, to your employer, who will complete the bottom half of the form.

Social Security Number

In most cases, you will need to obtain a Social Security number. It is widely used in the United States as a basic identification number—and in most automated payroll systems, in university enrollment systems, and for transactions such as opening a bank account.

Individuals entering the U.S. on the F, J, M, and Q visas are usually exempt from the U.S. Social Security tax, but those entering on other visas (such as H-2B or H-3) can expect to have the tax withheld from their pay. Even if you are exempt from paying Social Security tax, you will still need to obtain a Social Security number.

Social Security regulations require that you apply in person, and it is advised that you do this shortly after arrival. Normally, numbers are issued within a few weeks.

It will be important for you to provide full documentation that clearly shows you have a visa that permits employment. The Social Security official to whom you submit your application will want to see your passport, your I-94 form, visa documents (such as the triplicate copy of the IAP-66), and any documents related to your work placement. If you do not present the proper documentation, a Social Security card marked "Not Valid for Employment" will be issued. If this happens, you will not be able to receive a salary or stipend during the program. If you have any problems getting your Social Security card, you should contact your sponsoring organization for assistance.

Income Tax

As a general rule, individuals coming to the United States on any of the visas discussed in this article will be subject to U.S. income tax (and possibly state and local income tax) on the money they earn while in the country. H-2B workers are required to obtain a Certificate of Compliance, or Sailing Permit, before departure from the U.S. The Sailing Permit is evidence that they have paid whatever taxes may be due the U.S. government. H-3, J-1, and Q visa holders are exempt from this requirement. However, they are not exempt from filing an income tax return. Between January 1 and April 15 of the year following your employment, you will have to submit an income tax return (Form 1040EZ or Form 1040) to the IRS. The 1040EZ is used if you have no dependents, earned less than $50,000 of income, and have no travel expense deductions. If you have remained in the country from one year to the next, you also must submit a Form 8843 to verify your nonresident status. Tax regulations and procedures are not simple, and you should seek help from your employer and/or your sponsoring organization if you are participating in a J-1 program. You may also wish to secure a copy of IRS Publication 519, *U.S. Tax Guide for Aliens*, which is available free of charge from the Internal Revenue Service. Forms are available online at www.irs.ustreas.gov/prod/forms_pubs/.

Full-Time Students at U.S. Schools

Individuals enrolled at U.S. colleges and universities for full-time academic study are usually admitted on the basis of the F-1 (student), M-1 (student), or student category of the J-1 visa. In each case, summer employment may be possible before graduation, after graduation, or both. When such employment may take place, the length of time allowed and what the employment is called (practical training, curricular practical training, academic training) depend on the specific visa and circumstances of the individual student. A number of schools in the United States offer academic courses—usually known as cooperative education programs—that combine periods of study with periods of practical training employment. Under certain conditions, students from other countries who are enrolled as regular, full-time students in a cooperative education program are allowed to undertake the practical training assignments (usually paid) in the same manner as American students. For information on enrollment in cooperative education programs and the American colleges and universities that offer these opportunities, contact:

Cooperative Education & Internship Association
4190 S. Highland Drive, Suite 211
Salt Lake City, Utah 84124
Telephone: 801-984-2026
Fax: 801-984-2027
www.ceainc.org

Whether enrolled in a cooperative education program, either before or after graduation, and regardless of the type of visa (M-1, F-1, or J-1), the student remains under the legal sponsorship of his or her college, university, or (in the case of some J-1 students) Exchange Visitor Program sponsor. Therefore, students should seek assistance from the international student adviser at their school.

Visa Violations or Overstays

In recent years, U.S. immigration laws have become more restrictive. All international visitors, trainees, and temporary work visa holders should make sure that they fully understand their responsibilities under the particular visa they use to enter the U.S. It is extremely important that you know exactly what you are permitted to do on the type of visa you have been granted and how long you are permitted to remain in the United States. If you have any questions about this, please check with your program sponsor, employer, or the INS. If your program ends early, you are not permitted to remain in the United States. You must either return home upon completion of your work program or take the steps necessary to legally remain in the United States. There are severe penalties for foreign nationals who overstay their visas or who violate their status. You could be barred from returning to the U.S. for ten years or longer if you violate your visa status, even unintentionally.

In Conclusion

Most countries have very strict regulations regarding employment for noncitizens in order to protect job opportunities for their own citizens. The United States is no different. What is different, however, is the U.S. system of visas and the rules and regulations that apply to each type (and subtype) of visa. The process of acquiring the proper visa takes a good deal of time (sometimes as long as four to six months) and can often be frustrating and confusing. Therefore, it is important to plan ahead and contact prospective employers as early as possible so that the employer has sufficient time to undertake the paperwork involved. If you have applied to or have been accepted by a "trainee" program, make sure that the employer knows the name of the organization, because each sponsoring organization has its own internal procedures that must be followed. Prepare well in advance, ask lots of questions, and make sure you understand what needs to be done. If you do your research and begin early, you will soon be on your way to a fulfilling work experience in the United States.

WORKING FOR THE NATIONAL PARK SERVICE

Since its inception in 1916, the National Park Service has been dedicated to the preservation and management of this country's outstanding natural, historical, and recreational areas. Today the National Park Service encompasses more than 370 sites across the United States and in Guam, Puerto Rico, and the Virgin Islands. There are parks of great natural beauty and grandeur, such as the Grand Canyon and Yellowstone; parks that preserve the nation's cultural and historical treasures, such as Mesa Verde, the Statue of Liberty, and Gettysburg Battlefield; and parks of significant recreational value along seashores, lakeshores, and riverways that provide opportunities for outdoor activities and relaxation, such as Assateague Island and Lake Mead. The National Park Service is a bureau of the U.S. Department of the Interior; it should not be confused with the U.S. Forest Service of the Department of Agriculture.

Every year, millions of people from the United States and abroad visit our national park areas. To protect park resources and to serve the public, the National Park Service employs a permanent workforce and an essential seasonal workforce. Seasonals are hired every year to help permanent staff at many National Park Service parks and offices. The variety of positions available may surprise you: campground rangers, fee collectors, tour guides, naturalists, landscape architects, firefighters, laborers, law enforcement rangers, lifeguards, carpenters, clerks, historians; persons are hired for these seasonal jobs and more. Whatever the job, seasonal employees have the opportunity to learn more about the National Park Service and its mission.

Competition for seasonal jobs is keen. The number of applicants far outnumbers the positions available every year, particularly at larger, well-known parks. Some positions are filled by experienced seasonal employees who have worked previously for the National Park Service. And, Office of Personnel Management regulations require that veterans of the United States Armed Forces may be given preference among applicants. In the summer season, when most seasonal employees are hired, employment opportunities are extremely competitive.

About Seasonal Jobs

PAY: Many seasonal positions require irregular hours of work, including weekends, holidays, and evenings. Entry-level grades for National Park Service seasonal positions generally range from the GS-3 to GS-7. GS levels indicate the rate of pay for most federal government positions. For current salary information for these grades, check with any federal agency or the Office of Personnel Management in that geographic area where you desire employment. Prevailing local wages govern certain positions, such as laborer, maintenance, and skilled trades and crafts.

WG levels indicate the rate of pay: the higher the WG number, the higher the wage. WG wages are paid on an hourly basis with a standard work week of 40 hours. Overtime may be required; additional compensation is provided for extra hours worked. GS levels and WG levels are not equivalent.

UNIFORMS: Most seasonal park rangers and maintenance personnel are required to wear the official Park Service uniform; specific requirements and ordering information are contained in the employment package forwarded to successful applicants. For those positions requiring a uniform, an allowance is allotted that *partially* covers its cost.

HOUSING: Address specific questions about housing, area living conditions, and similar matters to the park or office where you desire employment. Seasonal employee housing may or may not be available.

EQUAL EMPLOYMENT OPPORTUNITY: The National Park Service is an Equal Opportunity employer. Selection for positions will be made solely on the basis of merit, fitness, and qualifications, without regard to race, sex, color, creed, age, marital status, national origin, sexual orientation, nondisqualifying handicap conditions, or any other nonmerit factors.

GENERAL INFORMATION ON APPLYING

The NPS has a centralized recruitment program for seasonal hiring. In addition, some parks may choose to hire directly. For information on these and other seasonal job opportunities, visit the Office of Personnel Management's Web page: www.usajobs.opm.gov. Information can also be accessed through the NPS Web page on the Internet (www.nps.gov and go to InfoZone for employment information).

CENTRALIZED SEASONAL RECRUITMENT: For information, including the list of parks hiring through the centralized recruitment program, contact the National Park Service's Seasonal Employment Program office. The address is: Seasonal Employment Program, Human Resources Office, National Park Service, 1849 C Street, NW, Mail Stop 2225, Washington, D.C. 20240; telephone: 877-554-4550; Web site: http://www.sep.nps.gov. At this Web site, applicants can also apply online. Applicants may also apply using a paper application by first calling the seasonal office or checking the Web site for vacant positions, and then requesting an application by providing the park name(s) and the vacancy announcement number(s) for the position(s) for which they wish to apply.

SEASONAL POSITIONS

PARK RANGER

Grades: GS-3, GS-4, GS-5, GS-7

Duties

Duties vary greatly from position to position and may include providing visitor services; interpreting a park's natural, historic, or archeological features through talks, guided walks, and demonstrations; working at an information desk; planning and implementing resource management programs, including fire control; performing search-and-rescue activities; providing for the public's safety through law enforcement; collecting fees; firefighting; lifeguarding; and radio dispatching.

Qualifications

GS-3: 6 months of general experience and 3 months of specialized experience that demonstrates the knowledge, skills, and abilities necessary to perform the job duties **or** 1 year of college (30 semester hours with 6 semester hours of natural sciences, social sciences, park and recreation management, and other disciplines related to management and protection of park resources, both natural and cultural).

GS-4: 6 months of general experience and 6 months of specialized experience that demonstrates the knowledge, skills, and abilities necessary to perform the job duties **or** 2 years of college (60 semester hours with 12 semester hours of natural sciences, social sciences, park and recreation management, and other disciplines related to management and protection of park resources, both natural and cultural).

GS-5: 1 year of specialized experience equivalent to the GS-4 level **or** 4 years of college leading to a bachelor's degree (120 semester hours with 24 semester hours of natural sciences, social sciences, park and recreation management, and other disciplines related to management and protection of park resources, both natural and cultural).

GS-7: 1 year of specialized experience equivalent to the GS-5 or GS-6 level **or** 1 full academic year of graduate education related to the management and protection of park resources or superior academic achievement.

How to Apply

For centralized recruitment, call the Seasonal Employment Office at 1-877-554-4550 for a listing of current vacancies and an application package, or check their Web site at http://www.sep.nps.gov for current vacancies and apply online. For information on other seasonal job opportunities, contact the personnel office in the geographic area in which you want to work, or visit the Office of Personnel Management's Web page (www.usajobs.opm.gov) or the NPS Web page (www.nps.gov and go to InfoZone for employment information).

PARK GUIDE

Grades: GS-3 through GS-5

Duties

Provides guided tours, gives formal talks on natural and historic features, answers questions, and provides miscellaneous services to visitors.

Requirements

GS-3: 6 months general experience **or** 1 year of college (30 semester hours with 6 semester hours in American history, science, or public speaking).

GS-4: 6 months of general experience and 6 months of specialized experience **or** 1 year as a Park Guide, GS-3 **or** 2 years of college (60 semester hours with 12 semester hours in American history, science, or public speaking).

GS-5: 1 year of specialized experience **or** 1 year as a Guide, GS-4 **or** 4 years of college leading to a bachelor's degree (120 semester hours with 24 semester hours in American history, science, or public speaking).

How to Apply

For centralized recruitment, call the Seasonal Employment Office at 1-877-554-4550 for a listing of current vacancies and an application package, or check their Web site at http://www.sep.nps.gov for current vacancies and apply online. For information on other seasonal job opportunities, contact the personnel office in the geographic area in which you want to work or visit the Office of Personnel Management's Web page (www.usajobs.opm.gov) or the NPS Web page (www.nps.gov and go to InfoZone for employment information).

VISITOR USE ASSISTANT

Grades: GS-4, GS-5

Duties

Collects and accounts for fees and provides miscellaneous services and information to visitors.

Requirements

GS-4: 1 year of general experience **or** 1 year as a Visitor Use Assistant, GS-3 **or** 2 years of college (60 semester hours).

GS-5: 1 year of specialized experience **or** 1 year as a Visitor Use Assistant, GS-4 **or** 4 years of college (120 semester hours).

How to Apply

For centralized recruitment, call the Seasonal Employment Office at 877-554-4550 for a listing of current vacancies and an application package or check their Web site at www.sep.nps.gov for current vacancies and apply online. For information on other seasonal job opportunities, contact the personnel office in the geographic area in which you want to work or visit the Office of Personnel Management's Web page (www.usajobs.opm.gov) or the NPS Web page (www.nps.gov and go to InfoZone for employment information).

RECREATIONAL AID/ASSISTANT

Grades: GS-3 through GS-6

Duties

Guards and manages beach and swimming areas and performs lifesaving and rescue work as needed for persons in rivers, lakes, and oceans. Positions are located at national recreation areas, seashores, and lakeshores.

Qualifications

GS-3: 6 months of general experience **or** 1 year of college.

GS-4: 6 months of general experience and 6 months specialized experience **or** 2 years of college (60 semester hours with 12 semester hours of courses related to recreation).

GS-5: 1 year of specialized experience equivalent to the GS-4 level **or** 4 years of college leading to a bachelor's degree (120 semester hours with 24 semester hours or a degree in recreation or physical education).

GS-6: 1 year of specialized experience equivalent to the GS-5 level.

How to Apply

Contact the personnel office in the geographic area in which you want to work, or visit the Office of Personnel Management's Web page (www.usajobs.opm.gov) or the NPS Web page (www.nps.gov and go to InfoZone for employment information).

BIOLOGICAL TECHNICIAN

Grades: GS-4, GS-5

Duties

Assists researchers and management staff in collecting and analyzing data on flora and fauna in parks.

Qualifications

GS-4: 6 months of general experience and 6 months specialized experience **or** 2 years of college (60 semester hours with 12 semester hours in biology, chemistry, statistics, entomology, animal husbandry, botany, physics, agriculture, and mathematics with 6 of those directly related to the position to be filled).

GS-5: 1 year of specialized experience equivalent to the GS-4 level **or** 4 years of college leading to a bachelor's degree (120 semester hours with 24 semester hours or a degree in biology, chemistry, statistics, entomology, animal husbandry, botany, physics, agriculture, or mathematics with 6 of those directly related to the position to be filled).

How to Apply

For centralized recruitment, call the Seasonal Employment Office at 1-877-554-4550 for a listing of current vacancies and an application package, or check their Web site at www.sep.nps.gov for current vacancies and apply online. Contact the personnel office in the geographic area in which you want to work, or visit the Office of Personnel Management's Web page (www.usajobs.opm.gov) or the NPS Web page (www.nps.gov and go to InfoZone for employment information).

FORESTRY TECHNICIAN

Grades: GS-4, GS-5

Duties

Assists in fire control, prevention, and suppression work on park lands.

Qualifications

GS-4: 6 months of general experience and 6 months of specialized experience **or** 4 seasons of specialized experience **or** 2 years of college (60 semester hours with 12 semester hours in forestry, agriculture, crop or plant science, range management or conservation, wildlife management, and other related fields).

GS-5: 1 year of specialized experience equivalent to the GS-4 level **or** 4 years of college leading to a bachelor's degree (120 semester hours with 24 semester hours or a degree in forestry, agriculture, crop or plant science, range management or conservation, wildlife management, or other related field).

How to Apply

Contact the personnel office in the geographic area in which you want to work, or visit the Office of Personnel Management's Web page (www.usajobs.opm.gov) or the NPS Web page (www.nps.gov and go to InfoZone for employment information).

ARCHITECTURE AND LANDSCAPE ARCHITECTURE

Grades: GS-4 and above

Duties

Produces drawings of structures of historical, architectural, landscape, engineering industrials, and maritime significance; prepares field notes; develops and edits measured drawings.

Qualifications

GS-4: 2 years of study (60 semester hours with 12 semester hours in architecture and landscape architecture).

GS-5: 4 years of study leading to a bachelor's degree, with major study or 24 semester hours in architecture or landscape architecture.

GS-7 and above: currently working toward a master's or doctoral degree in architecture or landscape architecture.

How to Apply

Contact Summer Program Administrator, HABS/HAER, National Park Service, 1849 C Street, NW, Washington, D.C. 20240. Submit a personal qualifications statement (resume, SF-171, or OF-612), letter of recommendation from a faculty member or employer familiar with your work, and samples indicating drafting ability (copies of sketches, lettering, and precision drafting).

HISTORIAN

Grades: GS-5, GS-7, and above

Duties

Conducts research using primary and secondary sources to produce inventories and reports on specific sites, structures, or technical processes.

Qualifications

A graduate degree in architectural history, landscape architecture, history of technology, American civilization, historic preservation, or a related field is preferred; a B.A. is required.

How to Apply

Contact Summer Program Administrator, HABS/HAER, National Park Service, 1849 C Street, NW, Washington, D.C. 20240. Submit a personal qualifications statement (resume, SF-171, or OF-612), letter of recommendation from a faculty member or employer familiar with your work, and (a) a paper demonstrating primary research in architectural history, landscape architecture, or history of technology or (b) a paper focusing on an aspect of the built environment.

CLERICAL

Grades: GS-1 through GS-4

Duties

Performs duties of receptionist, administrative clerk, clerk-typist, and data entry. The number of jobs available is limited.

Qualifications

GS-1: no education or experience required.

GS-2: 3 months of experience **or** high school graduate.
GS-3: 6 months of experience **or** 1 year of college (30 semester hours).
GS-4: 1 year of experience **or** 2 years of college (60 semester hours).
For typing positions, must be able to type 40 words per minute.

How to Apply

Contact the personnel office in the geographic area in which you want to work, or visit the Office of Personnel Management's Web page (www.usajobs.opm.gov) or the NPS Web page (www.nps.gov and go to InfoZone for employment information).

LABORER

Grades: WG-2 through WG-4

Duties

Performs manual outdoor work on trails and for forestry programs; other park maintenance activities, such as cleaning campgrounds; and similar work in which physical labor must be performed.

Qualifications

Ability to perform the job duties, including necessary physical requirements.

How to Apply

Contact the personnel office in the geographic area in which you want to work, or visit the Office of Personnel Management's Web page (www.usajobs.opm.gov) or the NPS Web page (www.nps.gov and go to InfoZone for employment information).

MAINTENANCE, TRADES, AND CRAFTS

Grades: WG-5 and above

Duties

Performs skilled and semi-skilled trades work: carpenter, mechanic, sawyer (woodsworker), trail maintenance worker, motor vehicle operation, and other similar positions.

Qualifications

Helper- to journeyman-level proficiency usually required.

How to Apply

Contact the personnel office in the geographic area in which you want to work, or visit the Office of Personnel Management's Web page (www.usajobs.opm.gov) or the NPS Web page (www.nps.gov and go to InfoZone for employment information).

OTHER EMPLOYMENT OPPORTUNITIES

Other types of positions may be available in National Park Service parks and offices. Contact the park or office where you are interested in working for information. In addition, hotels, lodges, restaurants, stores, transportation services, marinas, and many other visitor facilities in National Parks may have positions available. These facilities are operated by private companies and individuals called park concessioners who recruit and hire their own employees. These are not federal government positions. Concessioners usually pay the minimum wage set by the state in which their operation is located. Although some pay a small bonus at the end of the season, they do not pay or make arrangements for travel to and from the parks. The National Park Service Regional Office for the geographic region in which you want to work, or the park itself, can provide names and addresses of concessioners. Contact the concessioner for applications and information about concession jobs, salaries, and working and living conditions.

NATIONAL PARK SERVICE REGIONAL OFFICES AND SITES

ALASKA REGION

Alagnak Wild River
Aniakchak National Monument and Preserve
Bering Land Bridge National Preserve
Cape Krusenstern National Monument
Denali National Park and Preserve
Gates of Arctic National Park and Preserve
Glacier Bay National Park and Preserve
Katmai National Park and Preserve
Kenai Fjords National Park
Klondike Gold Rush National Historical Park
Kobuk Valley National Park
Lake Clark National Park and Preserve
Noatak National Preserve
Sitka National Historical Park
Wrangell-St. Elias National Park and Preserve
Yukon-Charley Rivers National Preserve

For information about seasonal employment opportunities in this region, contact: National Park Service, 2525 Gambell Street, Anchorage, Alaska 99503; telephone: 907-257-2526.

INTERMOUNTAIN REGION

COLORADO PLATEAU CLUSTER

Arches National Park
Aztec Ruins National Monument
Bryce Canyon National Park
California National Historical Trail (Salt Lake City)
Canyon de Chelly National Monument
Canyonlands National Park
Capitol Reef National Park
Cedar Breaks National Monument
Chaco Culture National Historical Park
Colorado National Monument
Dinosaur National Monument
El Malpais National Monument
El Morro National Monument
Fossil Butte National Monument
Glen Canyon National Recreation Area
Golden Spike National Historic Site
Grand Canyon National Park
Grand Staircase-Escalante National Monument
Hovenweep National Monument
Hubbell Trading Post National Historic Site
Mesa Verde National Park
Mormon Pioneer National Historical Trail (Salt Lake City)

Oregon National Historical Trail (Salt Lake City)
Pony Express National Historical Trail (Salt Lake City)
Natural Bridges National Monument
Navajo National Monument
Petrified Forest National Park
Pipe Spring National Monument
Rainbow Bridge National Monument
Sunset Crater Volcano National Monument
Timpanogos Cave National Monument
Walnut Canyon National Monument
Wupatki National Monument
Yucca House National Monument
Zion National Park

ROCKY MOUNTAIN CLUSTER

Bent's Old Fort National Historic Site
Bighorn Canyon National Recreation Area
Black Canyon of the Gunnison National Monument
Curecanti National Recreation Area
Devils Tower National Monument
Florissant Fossil Beds National Monument
Fort Laramie National Historic Site
Glacier National Park
Grand Teton National Park
Grant-Kohrs Ranch National Historic Site
Great Sand Dunes National Monument
John D. Rockefeller, Jr. Memorial Parkway
Little Bighorn Battlefield National Monument
Rocky Mountain National Park
Yellowstone National Park

SOUTHWEST CLUSTER

Alibates Flint Quarrie National Monument
Amistad National Recreation Area
Bandelier National Monument
Big Bend National Park
Big Thicket National Preserve
Capulin Volcano National Monument
Carlsbad Cavern National Park
Casa Grande Ruins National Monument
Chamizal National Monument
Chickasaw National Recreation Area
Chiricahua National Monument
Coronado National Monument
Fort Bowie National Historic Site
Fort Union National Monument
Fort Davis National Historic Site
Gila Cliff Dwellings National Monument
Glorieta Battlefield
Guadalupe Mountains National Park
Hohokam Pima National Monument
Lake Meredith National Recreation Area
Lyndon B. Johnson National Historical Park
Montezuma Castle National Monument
Organ Pipe Cactus National Monument
Padre Island National Seashore
Palo Alto Battlefield National Historic Site
Pecos National Historical Park
Petroglyph National Monument
Rio Grand Wild and Scenic River
Saguaro National Park
Salinas Pueblo Missions National Monument
San Antonio Missions National Historical Park
Sante Fe National Historical Trail (Santa Fe)
Trail of Tears National Historic Trail (Santa Fe)
Tonto National Monument
Tumacacori National Historical Park
Tuzigoot National Monument
White Sands National Monument

For information about seasonal employment opportunities in this region, contact: National Park Service, P.O. Box 25287, 12795 West Alameda Parkway, Denver, Colorado, 80225; telephone: 303-969-2020.

MIDWEST REGION

GREAT LAKES CLUSTER

Apostle Islands National Lakeshore
Cuyahoga Valley National Recreation Area
Dayton Aviation Heritage National Historical Park
George Rogers Clark National Historical Park
Grand Portage National Monument
Hopewell Culture National Historical Park
Ice Age National Scenic Trail
Indiana Dunes National Lakeshore
Isle Royale National Park
James A. Garfield National Historic Site
Keweenaw National Historical Park
Lewis & Clark National Historical Trail
Lincoln Boyhood National Monument

Lincoln Home National Historic Site
Mississippi National River and Recreation Area
North Country National Scenic Trail
Perry's Victory and International Peace Memorial
Pictured Rocks National Lakeshore
Sleeping Bear Dunes National Lakeshore
St. Croix/Lower St. Croix National Scenic Riverways
Voyageurs National Park
William Howard Taft National Historic Site

GREAT PLAINS CLUSTER

Agate Fossil Beds National Monument
Arkansas Post National Monument
Badlands National Park
Brown vs. Board of Education National Historic Site
Buffalo National River
Effigy Mounds National Monument
Fort Larned National Historic Site
Fort Smith National Historic Site
Fort Scott National Historic Site
Fort Union Trading Post National Historic Site
George Washington Carver National Monument
Harry S Truman National Historic Site
Herbert Hoover National Historic Site
Homestead National Monument of America
Hot Springs National Park
Jewel Cave National Monument
Jefferson National Expansion Memorial
Knife River Indian Villages National Historic Site
Missouri National Recreational River
Mount Rushmore National Monument
Niobrara National Scenic Riverway
Ozark National Scenic Riverways
Pea Ridge National Military Park
Pipestone National Monument
Scotts Bluff National Monument
Theodore Roosevelt National Park
Ulysses S. Grant National Historic Site
Wilson's Creek National Battlefield
Wind Cave National Park

For information about seasonal employment opportunities in this region, contact: National Park Service, 1709 Jackson Street, Omaha, Nebraska 68102; telephone: 402-221-3456.

NATIONAL CAPITAL REGION

NATIONAL CAPITAL CLUSTER

Antietam National Battlefield
Antietam National Cemetery
Arlington House, The Robert E. Lee Memorial
Baltimore-Washington Parkway
Battleground National Cemetery
Catoctin Mountain Park
Chesapeake and Ohio Canal National Historical Park
Clara Barton National Historic Site
Clara Barton Parkway
Constitution Gardens
Ford's Theatre National Historic Site
Fort Washington Park
Francis Scott Key Memorial
Franklin Delano Roosevelt Memorial Park
Frederick Douglass National Historic Site
George Washington Memorial Parkway
Greenbelt Park
Harpers Ferry National Historical Park
Kahlil Gibran Memorial Garden
Korean War Veterans Memorial
Lincoln Memorial
Lyndon Baines Johnson Memorial Grove on the Potomac
Manassas National Battlefield Park
Mary McLeod Bethune Memorial
Mary McLeod Bethune Council House National Historic Site
Monocacy National Battlefield
National Capital Parks
National Mall
National Law Enforcement Officers Memorial
Pennsylvania Avenue National Historic Site
Piscataway Park
Potomac Heritage National Scenic Trail
Prince William Forest Park
Rock Creek Park
Rock Creek Parkway
Suitland Parkway
Theodore Roosevelt Island
Thomas Jefferson Memorial
United States Navy Memorial
Vietnam Veterans Memorial
Vietnam Woman's Memorial
Washington Monument

White House
Wolf Trap Farm Park

For information about seasonal employment opportunities in this region, contact: National Park Service, 1100 Ohio Drive, SW, Washington, D.C. 20242; telephone: 202-619-7256.

NORTHEAST REGION

ALLEGHENY AND CHESAPEAKE CLUSTER

Allegheny Portage Railroad National Historic Site
Appomattox Court House National Historical Park
Assateague Island National Seashore
Bluestone National Scenic River
Booker T. Washington National Monument
Colonial National Historical Park
Delaware & Lehigh Navigation Canal National Heritage Corridor Commission
Delaware Water Gap National Recreation Area
Edgar Allen Poe National Historic Site
Eisenhower National Historic Site
Fort McHenry National Monument and Historic Shrine
Fort Necessity National Battlefield
Fredericksburg and Spotsylvania County Battlefields Memorial National Military Park
Friendship Hill National Historic Site
Gauley River National Recreation Area
George Washington Birthplace National Monument
Gettysburg National Military Park
Gloria Dei National Historic Site
Great Egg Harbor National Scenic and Recreational River
Hampton National Historic Site
Hopewell Furnace National Historical Park
Independence National Historical Park
Johnstown Flood National Monument
Maggie Walker National Historic Site
New Jersey Coastal Heritage Trail Route
New River Gorge National River
Petersburg National Battlefield
Pinelands National Reserve
Richmond National Battlefield Park
Shenandoah National Park
Southwestern Pennsylvania Heritage Preservation Commission
Steamtown National Historic Site
Thaddeus Kosciuszko National Monument
Thomas Stone National Historic Site
Upper Delaware National Scenic and Recreational River
Valley Forge National Historical Park

For information about seasonal employment opportunities in this cluster of the region, contact: National Park Service, U.S. Custom House, 200 Chestnut Street, Philadelphia, Pennsylvania 19106; telephone: 215-597-4972.

NEW ENGLAND CLUSTER

Acadia National Park
Adams National Historic Site
Blackstone River Valley National Heritage Conservation Corridor
Boston African-American National Historic Site
Boston National Historical Park
Cape Cod National Seashore
Castle Clinton National Monument
Edison National Historic Site
Eleanor Roosevelt National Historic Site
Farmington Wild and Scenic River
Federal Hall National Monument
Fire Island National Seashore
Fort Stanwix National Monument
Frederick Law Olmsted National Historic Site
Gateway National Recreation Area
General Grant National Monument
Hamilton Grange National Monument
Home of Franklin D. Roosevelt National Historic Site
John F. Kennedy National Historic Site
Longfellow National Historic Site
Lowell National Historical Park
Maine Acadian Culture Preservation Commission

Marsh-Billings National Historical Park
Martin Van Buren National Historic Site
Minute Man National Historical Park
Morristown National Historical Park
Quinebaug-Shetucket National Heritage Corridor
Roger Williams National Monument
Roosevelt Campobello International Park
Sagamore Hill National Historic Site
Saint Paul's Church National Historic Site
Saint Croix Island International Historic Site
Saint-Gaudens National Historic Site
Salem Maritime National Historic Site
Saratoga National Historical Park
Saugus Iron Works National Historic Site
Springfield Armory National Historic Site
Statue of Liberty/Ellis Island National Monuments
Theodore Roosevelt Birthplace National Historic Site
Theodore Roosevelt Inaugural National Historic Site
Touro Synagogue National Historic Site
Vanderbilt Mansion National Historic Site
Weir Farm National Historic Site
Wildcat Brook Wild and Scenic River
Women's Rights National Historical Park

For information about seasonal employment opportunities in this cluster of the region, contact: National Park Service, 15 State Street, Boston, Massachusetts 02109; telephone: 617-223-5101.

PACIFIC WEST REGION

COLUMBIA CASCADES CLUSTER

Big Hole National Battlefield
City of Rocks National Reserve
Coulee Dam National Recreation Area
Crater Lake National Park
Craters of the Moon National Monument
Ebey's Landing National Reserve
Fort Vancouver National Historic Site
Fort Clatsop National Monument
Hagerman Fossil Beds National Monument
John Day Fossil Beds National Monument
Klondike Gold Rush National Historical Park
Lake Chelan National Recreation Area
Mount Rainier National Park
Nez Perce National Historical Park
North Cascades National Park
Olympic National Park
Oregon Caves National Monument
Ross Lake National Recreation Area
San Juan Island National Historical Park
Whitman Mission National Historic Site

For information about seasonal employment opportunities in this cluster of the region, contact: National Park Service, 909 First Avenue, Seattle, Washington 98104-1060; telephone: 206-220-4053.

PACIFIC GREAT BASIN CLUSTER

Cabrillo National Monument
Channel Islands National Park
Death Valley National Park
Devils Postpile National Monument
Eugene O'Neill National Historic Site
Fort Point National Historic Site
Golden Gate National Recreation Area
Great Basin National Park
John Muir National Historic Site
Joshua Tree National Park
Juan Bautista De Anza National Heritage Trail
Kings Canyon National Park
Lake Mead National Recreation Area
Lassen Volcanic National Park
Lava Beds National Monument
Manzanar National Historic Site
Mojave National Preserve
Muir Woods National Monument
Pinnacles National Monument
Point Reyes National Seashore
Redwood National and State Parks
San Francisco Maritime National Historical Park
Santa Monica Mountains National Recreation Area
Sequoia National Park
Whiskeytown-Shasta-Trinity National Recreation Area
Yosemite National Park

For information about seasonal employment opportunities in this cluster of the region, contact: National Park Service, 600 Harrison Street, Suite 600, San Francisco, California 94107; telephone: 415-427-1300, option 2.

PACIFIC ISLANDS CLUSTER
American Memorial Park
Haleakala National Park
Hawaii Volcanoes National Park
Kalaupapa National Historic Site
Kaloko-Honokohau National Historical Park
Pu'uhonua O Honaunau National Historical Park
Puukohola Heiau National Historic Site
The National Park of American Samoa
USS Arizona Memorial
War in the Pacific National Historical Park

For information about seasonal employment opportunities in this cluster of the region, contact: National Park Service, 300 Ala Moana Boulevard, Suite 6305, P.O. Box 50165, Honolulu, Hawaii 96850; telephone: 808-541-2693.

SOUTHEAST REGION

APPALACHIAN CLUSTER
Abraham Lincoln Birthplace National Historic Site
Andrew Johnson National Historic Site
Big South Fork National River and National Recreation Area
Blue Ridge Parkway
Carl Sandburg Home National Historic Site
Chickamauga & Chattanooga National Military Park
Cowpens National Battlefield
Cumberland Gap National Historical Park
Fort Donelson National Battlefield
Great Smoky Mountains National Park
Guilford Courthouse National Military Park
Kings Mountain National Military Park
Little River Canyon National Preserve
Mammoth Cave National Park
Ninety Six National Historic Site
Obed Wild and Scenic River
Overmountain Victory National Historic Trail
Russell Cave National Monument
Stones River National Battlefield

ATLANTIC COAST CLUSTER
Andersonville National Historic Site
Canaveral National Seashore
Cape Hatteras National Seashore
Cape Lookout National Seashore
Castillo de San Marcos National Monument
Charles Pinckney National Historic Site
Chattahoochee River National Recreation Area
Congaree Swamp National Monument
Cumberland Island National Seashore
Fort Caroline National Monument
Fort Frederica National Monument
Fort Mantanzas National Monument
Fort Pulaski National Monument
Fort Raleigh National Historic Site
Fort Sumter National Monument
Horseshoe Bend National Military Park
Jimmy Carter National Historic Site
Kennesaw Mountain National Battlefield Park
Martin Luther King, Jr. National Historic Site
Moores Creek National Battlefield
Ocmulgee National Monument
Timucuan Ecological and Historic Preserve
Tuskegee Institute National Historic Site
Wright Brothers National Monument

GULF COAST CLUSTER
Big Cypress National Preserve
Biscayne National Park
Brices Cross Roads National Battlefield Site
Buck Island Reef National Monument
Cane River Creole National Historical Park and Heritage Area
Christiansted National Historic Site
DeSoto National Monument
Dry Tortugas National Park
Everglades National Park
Gulf Islands National Seashore
Jean Lafitte National Historical Park and Preserve

Working for the National Park Service

Natchez National Historical Park
Natchez Trace Parkway
New Orleans Jazz National Historical Park
Poverty Point National Monument
Salt River Bay National Historical Park
San Juan National Historic Site
Shiloh National Military Park
Tupelo National Battlefield
Vicksburg National Military Park
Virgin Islands National Park

For information about seasonal employment opportunities in this field area, contact: National Park Service, Atlanta Federal Center, 1924 Building, 100 Alabama Street, SW, Atlanta, Georgia 30303; telephone: 404-562-3296.

Information in this article is supplied by the National Park Service.

DO YOU WANT TO WORK TEMPORARILY IN CANADA?

WHAT YOU NEED TO KNOW

If you wish to work temporarily in Canada, you will likely be required to have an **employment authorization.** An employment authorization is issued by an immigration officer after a Human Resources Centre approves your job offer.

This article outlines what you and your employer must do *before* you arrive in Canada. For additional advice, contact the Canadian Embassy, High Commission, or Consulate General near you.

Additional procedures may be required if you wish to work in Quebec. For further information, contact the Canadian Embassy abroad.

WHAT YOUR EMPLOYER MUST DO

Your employer must give details of your job offer to a Human Resources Centre. An employment counselor will check to determine if your offer of employment meets the prevailing wages and working conditions for the occupation concerned. A check will also be made to see if the job cannot be filled by a suitably qualified and available Canadian or permanent resident. If these conditions are met, the Human Resources Centre will approve your job offer. They will then issue a confirmation of offer of employment and send this to the Canadian Embassy, High Commission, or Consulate in your country.

The employer will be provided with a copy of the confirmation of offer of employment, to be forwarded to you. Your employer is responsible for arranging your workers' compensation and medical coverage when you arrive in Canada.

Some jobs may be exempt from Human Resources Centre approval, and either the centre or a visa office at a Canadian embassy or consulate can advise you on this.

WHAT YOU MUST DO

The Canadian visa office near you will contact you upon receipt of your confirmation of offer of employment. You may be asked to go to an interview or to send some information by mail. You may also be asked to have a medical checkup, which you will have to pay for yourself. If you qualify and have all the necessary documents, you will receive an employment authorization and will possibly have a separate visitor visa placed in your passport.

The employment authorization will state that you can work at a specific job for a specific period of time for a specific employer. You will need to produce the authorization when you arrive in Canada, as well as your passport, visa (if issued), and airline tickets.

There is a processing fee when you submit an application for an employment authorization. There are no refunds if your application is refused. Please request the brochure on immigration fees by calling Public Enquiries or ask an immigration officer for fee information.

Different procedures exist for citizens or permanent residents of the United States. You should seek clarification from the nearest Canadian embassy or consulate; general procedures are stated later in this article.

An employment authorization will not be issued to you to come to Canada to look for work. *It is valid only for the specific job, the specific amount of time, and the employer stated on the form.*

When You Arrive in Canada

When you arrive at the port of entry to Canada, show your confirmation of offer of employment, your employment authorization, and other papers to an immigration officer. You will be given forms to fill out so that you can get a Social Insurance Number (SIN). These forms and proper identification, such as a birth certificate, should be taken to a counselor at a Human Resources Centre, who can help you if you have trouble filling them out. When you receive your SIN card, you will have to give your number to your employer.

Your employment authorization is not a contract. Your job can be ended by you or your employer at any time. However, if your duties change or the job is to be extended, you must contact immigration right away, before the expiry date of your current authorization. You can do this by calling the Citizenship and Immigration Call Centre at 888-242-2100.

Some Workers Can Apply at a Port of Entry

Most foreign workers must apply for employment authorization outside of Canada, but if you are a resident of the United States, Greenland, or St. Pierre and Miquelon, you can apply for an employment authorization when you arrive at a port of entry to Canada. To apply this way, you must produce your confirmation of offer of employment and other papers when you arrive at the port of entry. Remember that you must find out what papers you will need *before* arriving in Canada. Check with the Canadian Embassy, High Commission, or Consulate General.

Remember

- There is a nonrefundable fee to process a request for an employment authorization.
- Most foreign workers must get their employment authorizations before arriving in Canada. Visitors *cannot* obtain employment authorization while in Canada.
- You must follow the terms of your employment authorization while in Canada. If you do not, you may be asked to leave the country.
- Human Resources Centre staff in Canada and Canadian government representatives in your home country cannot help you find a job.
- If you want to work temporarily or if you have further questions about working in Canada, contact the nearest Canadian Embassy, High Commission, or Consulate.

- This is not a legal document. For precise, legal information consult the Immigration Act and Regulations.

Produced by Communications Branch, Citizenship and Immigration Canada. Reproduced with the permission of Citizenship and Immigration Canada and Public Works and Government Services Canada, 2000. For more information, please visit http://www.cic.gc.ca.

ALABAMA

CAMP LANEY FOR BOYS

916 WEST RIVER ROAD
MENTONE, ALABAMA 35984

General Information Traditional summer camp for boys ages 8-14 with a ropes course, archery, riflery, horseback, tennis, team sports, swimming, canoeing and mountain biking. Optional activities include rock climbing and white water rafting. Established in 1959. 120-acre facility located 58 miles from Chattanooga, Tennessee. Features: beautiful river; mountain bike trails; climbing wall; extensive ropes course; surrounding woods; 3 tennis courts.

Profile of Summer Employees Total number: 55; typical ages: 19–22. 100% men; 5% high school students; 95% college students. Nonsmokers preferred.

Employment Information Openings are from June 1 to August 4. Jobs available: ▶ 3–4 *horseback staff* (minimum age 18) experienced with horses (or training provided) at $2100–$3000 per season ▶ 7–9 *ropes course staff* (minimum age 18) training is provided; paid at $2100–$2700 per season ▶ *waterfront staff* (minimum age 18) Red Cross lifeguarding training provided at $2100–$2800 per season. Applicants must submit formal organization application, three personal references. An in-person interview is required. International applicants accepted; must apply through a recognized agency.

Benefits and Preemployment Training Free housing, free meals, health insurance, willing to provide letters of recommendation, willing to complete paperwork for educational credit, willing to act as a professional reference, and opportunity to attend seminars/workshops. Preemployment training is required and includes accident prevention and safety, first aid, CPR, interpersonal skills, leadership skills.

Contact Associate Director, Camp Laney for Boys, PO Box 289, Mentone, Alabama 35984. Telephone: 800-648-2919. Fax: 256-634-4098. E-mail: info@camplaney.com. World Wide Web: http://www.camplaney.com. Contact by e-mail, phone, or through World Wide Web site. Application deadline: continuous.

CAMP SKYLINE

4888 ALABAMA HIGHWAY 117
MENTONE, ALABAMA 35984

General Information Residential camp located on top of Lookout Mountain serving 275–315 girls. Campers select a "six-a-day" schedule from more than 20 activities. Established in 1947. 80-acre facility located 50 miles from Chattanooga, Tennessee. Features: river access; three oval riding rings; western trails; hut row cabins; triplex; lodge, Riverside Hotel; large gymnasium; arts and crafts building; tennis, volleyball, basketball courts; circus; spacious dining hall.

Profile of Summer Employees Total number: 115–125; typical ages: 18–24. 5% men; 95% women; 6% minorities; 10% high school students; 90% college students; 2% retirees; 2% non-U.S. citizens; 5% local applicants. Nonsmokers preferred.

Employment Information Openings are from June 7 to August 4. Jobs available: ▶ 10–20 *Christian leadership instructors* (minimum age 18) ▶ 4–6 *canoeing instructors* (minimum age 18) ▶ 10–15 *cheerleading/flag twirling/baton twirling instructors* (minimum age 16) ▶ 8–10 *circus staff* (minimum age 18) ▶ 10 *fine and performing arts instructors (music, dance, arts and crafts, and drama)* (minimum age 16) ▶ 10–12 *lifeguards and swimming instructors* (minimum age 16) with WSI certification ▶ 2–3 *nature specialists* (minimum age 18) ▶ 3–4 *riflery instructors* (minimum age 18) ▶ 15–20 *ropes course instructors for climbing tower* (minimum age 18)

▶ 8–10 *sports instructors* (minimum age 16) including archery, tennis, swimming, diving, horseback riding, and gymnastics. Applicants must submit formal organization application, four personal references. An in-person interview is recommended, but a telephone interview is acceptable. International applicants accepted; must obtain own visa, obtain own working papers, apply through a recognized agency.

Benefits and Preemployment Training Free housing, free meals, willing to provide letters of recommendation, and on-the-job training. Preemployment training is required and includes accident prevention and safety, first aid, CPR, leadership skills.

Contact Sally C. Johnson, Director, Camp Skyline, PO Box 287, Mentone, Alabama 35984. Telephone: 800-448-9279. Fax: 256-634-3018. E-mail: info@campskyline.com. World Wide Web: http://www.campskyline.com. Contact by e-mail, fax, mail, phone, or through World Wide Web site. Application deadline: continuous.

THE SOUTHWESTERN COMPANY, ALABAMA

See The Southwestern Company on page 302 for complete description.

STUDENT CONSERVATION ASSOCIATION (SCA), ALABAMA

See Student Conservation Association (SCA), New Hampshire on page 209 for complete description.

ALASKA

A CHRISTIAN MINISTRY IN THE NATIONAL PARKS–ALASKA

See A Christian Ministry in the National Parks–Maine on page 122 for complete description.

ALASKA STATE PARKS VOLUNTEER PROGRAM

550 WEST 7TH AVENUE, SUITE 1380
ANCHORAGE, ALASKA 99501-3561

General Information Program offering volunteer positions in state parks throughout the state of Alaska. Established in 1970. 3,300,000-acre facility. Features: wilderness; wildlife.

Profile of Summer Employees Total number: 184; typical ages: 18–70. 45% college students; 50% retirees; 5% local applicants.

Employment Information Openings are from May 15 to October 15. Winter break positions also offered. Jobs available: ▶ 6 *backcountry ranger assistants* (minimum age 18) with outdoor experience, good physical condition, familiarity with hand and power tools, and some education in natural resources at $200–$300 per month ▶ 15 *natural history interpreters* (minimum age 18) with outdoor experience, good people skills, and some education in natural resources at $200–$300 per month ▶ 5 *park caretakers* (minimum age 18) with outdoor experience, good people skills, good physical condition at $200–$300 per month ▶ 20 *ranger assistants* (minimum age 18) with outdoor experience, good people skills, good physical condition, and some education in natural resources at $100–$300 per month ▶ 15 *trail crew* (minimum age 18) with outdoor experience, good physical condition, familiar with hand and power tools, and some education in natural resources at $200–$300 per month. Applicants must submit a formal organization application, letter of interest, resume, personal reference, letter of recommendation. A telephone interview is required.

Benefits and Preemployment Training Free housing, on-the-job training, willing to complete paperwork for educational credit, and expense allowance for food. Preemployment training is required.

Contact Lynn Blessington, Volunteer Coordinator, Alaska State Parks Volunteer Program. Telephone: 907-269-8708. Fax: 907-269-8907. E-mail: volunteer@dnr.state.ak.us. World Wide Web: http://www.dnr.state.ak.us/parks/vip. Contact by e-mail, fax, mail, phone, or through World Wide Web site. Application deadline: April 1.

AMERICA & PACIFIC TOURS, INC. (A&P)

430 K STREET
ANCHORAGE, ALASKA 99510

General Information Japanese land operator for Japanese tourists providing planned, individualized, and special guided trips of Alaska. Established in 1970. Features: main office; boys' condominium (1); girls' condominium (1); Fairbanks office; Tokyo, Japan office; Palmer Land only Alaska.

Profile of Summer Employees Total number: 15. 50% men; 50% women; 90% college students; 50% non-U.S. citizens; 50% local applicants. Nonsmokers preferred.

Employment Information Openings are from June 1 to September 30. Winter break and year-round positions also offered. Jobs available: ▶ 1 *accounting* (minimum age 22) with accounting skills at $1800–$2000 per month ▶ 1–2 *bookkeepers* (minimum age 23) with ability to speak Japanese and English at $1800–$1900 per year ▶ 10–15 *tour guides and office workers* (minimum age 20) with current driver's license and fluency in Japanese (salary depends upon experience as guide) at $1400–$3000 per month. Applicants must submit a letter of interest, resume. A telephone interview is required. International applicants accepted.

Benefits and Preemployment Training On-the-job training and willing to complete paperwork for educational credit. Preemployment training is optional.

Contact Keizo Sugimoto, President, America & Pacific Tours, Inc. (A&P), PO Box 10-1068, Anchorage, Alaska 99510. Telephone: 907-272-9401. Fax: 907-272-0251. E-mail: aptours@alaska.com. World Wide Web: http://www.aptoursalaska.com. Contact by e-mail, fax, or phone. Application deadline: continuous.

CAMP TOGOWOODS

WASILLA, ALASKA 99654

General Information Residential program of traditional camping activities for girls ages 7–15. Established in 1958. 260-acre facility located 50 miles from Anchorage. Features: freshwater lake; wooded setting; low ropes course; hiking trails.

Profile of Summer Employees Total number: 26–28; typical ages: 18–50. 100% women; 24% minorities; 95% college students; 10% non-U.S. citizens; 38% local applicants.

Employment Information Openings are from June to August. Jobs available: ▶ 1 *art director* (minimum age 21) at $2200 per season ▶ 1 *assistant director* (minimum age 21) at $2200 per season ▶ 2 *cooks* (minimum age 18) at $2000 per season ▶ 12 *counselors* (minimum age 21) first aid and CPR certifications required at $2000 per season ▶ 1 *environmental education director* (minimum age 21) at $2200 per season ▶ 1 *food service director* (minimum age 21) at $2200 per season ▶ 1 *health care director* (minimum age 21) with RN license or EMT and current CPR certification at $2200 per season ▶ 2 *lifeguards* (minimum age 18) with lifeguard certification (waterfront lifeguarding preferred) at $2000 per season ▶ 1 *waterfront director* (minimum age 21) with WSI certification, lifeguard training, and waterfront lifeguarding at $2200 per season ▶ 4 *wilderness counselors* (minimum age 21) with wilderness trip-leading experience preferred; wilderness first aid and CPR required at $2000 per season ▶ 1 *wilderness program director* (minimum age 21) with experience leading wilderness trips at $2200 per season. Applicants must submit formal organization application, three personal references. An in-person interview is recommended, but a telephone interview is acceptable. International applicants accepted; must apply through a recognized agency.

Benefits and Preemployment Training Free housing, free meals, health insurance, willing to provide letters of recommendation, on-the-job training, willing to complete paperwork for educational credit, and willing to act as a professional reference. Preemployment training is required and includes accident prevention and safety, interpersonal skills, leadership skills, supervision training.

Contact Kelly Feder, Camp Director, Girl Scouts Susitna Council, Camp Togowoods, HC 30, Box 5400, Wasilla, Alaska 99687. Telephone: 907-376-1310. Fax: 907-376-1358. E-mail: camptogo@alaska.net. World Wide Web: http://www.girlscouts.ak.org. Contact by e-mail, fax, mail, or phone. Application deadline: continuous.

KATMAILAND INC.

4125 AIRCRAFT DRIVE
ANCHORAGE, ALASKA 99502

General Information Katmailand Inc. operates three lodges and a restaurant in Katmail National Park. Established in 1949. 4-acre facility. Features: wooded setting; photography; hiking; kayaking; fishing; scenic mountains.

Profile of Summer Employees Total number: 58; typical ages: 22–38. 70% men; 30% women; 85% college students; 15% local applicants.

Employment Information Openings are from May 20 to September 20. Jobs available: ▶ *administrators/auditors/front desk staff* with extensive bookkeeping experience; responsibilities include: front desk operation, customer service, cash handling, credit cards, and ten key and typing 40 wpm ▶ *assistant chef/head chef* must assist in prep work, baking, stocking, cleaning, and other assigned tasks ▶ *auditor* ▶ *bartender* ▶ *bus drivers* (minimum age 25) must have Commercial Driver's License allowing operation of school bus with multiple passengers, good communication skills, and good physical condition ▶ *dishwasher* ▶ *driver/laborers* (minimum age 25) responsibilities include cleaning of facility, float planes, dumping garbage daily, greeting guests at airport or pier, loading luggage; must have customer service skills and Commercial Driver's License ▶ *head maintenance* must have knowledge of carpentry, plumbing, and welding skills; requires well rounded background ▶ *house supervisor* oversees housekeeping, bartender, and storekeeper ▶ 5–10 *housekeepers/food service workers* (minimum age 18) must clean guest's cabins, do laundry, wait tables during meal hours, bus tables, help in kitchen, and have ability to lift 40 pounds, customer service at $5.65 per hour ▶ *inn keeper* must oversee all kitchen operations, including ordering, inventory, quality control, special diet requests; clean guest cabins, wait tables, and bus ▶ *sport fishing guides* with extensive fishing experience, knowledge of fly-fishing, casting, trolling, fly-tying, and spin fishing, boat handling skills and maintenance experience. Must have OUPC six pack license and three years Alaska guiding experience ▶ *storekeeper* responsibilities include: inventory control, pricing, stocking, display, daily reports, balancing cash, and being in charge of rental equipment. Should have knowledge of fishing. Applicants must submit a formal organization application, three personal references, three letters of recommendation. A telephone interview is required. International applicants accepted; must obtain own visa, obtain own working papers.

Benefits and Preemployment Training Free housing, free meals, on-the-job training, and airfare from Anchorage to Lodge. Preemployment training is required and includes accident prevention and safety, first aid, CPR.

Contact Jim Albert, Brooks Lodge Manager, Katmailand Inc., 4125 Aircraft Drive, Anchorage, Alaska 99502. E-mail: job@katmailand.com. World Wide Web: http://www.katmailand.com. Contact by e-mail, mail, or through World Wide Web site. Application deadline: continuous.

THE SOUTHWESTERN COMPANY, ALASKA

See The Southwestern Company on page 302 for complete description.

STUDENT CONSERVATION ASSOCIATION (SCA), ALASKA

See Student Conservation Association (SCA), New Hampshire on page 209 for complete description.

ARIZONA

A CHRISTIAN MINISTRY IN THE NATIONAL PARKS–ARIZONA

See A Christian Ministry in the National Parks–Maine on page 122 for complete description.

GRAND CANYON NATIONAL PARK LODGES

PO BOX 699
GRAND CANYON, ARIZONA 86023

General Information National park concessioner providing all hotel, restaurant, retail, and transportation services on the south rim of the Grand Canyon. Established in 1903. 640-acre facility located 90 miles from Flagstaff. Features: Grand Canyon; San Francisco Peaks; Sedona/Red Rock Wilderness Area; Kendrick Mountain Wilderness Area; Lake Powell/NRA; Lake Havasu.

Profile of Summer Employees Total number: 1,220; typical ages: 18–42. 50% men; 50% women; 30% minorities; 20% college students; 20% retirees; 10% non-U.S. citizens; 30% local applicants.

Employment Information Openings are from February 15 to October 20. Year-round positions also offered. Jobs available: ▶ 30–40 *cafeteria workers* (minimum age 18) at $6 per hour ▶ 15–25 *cashiers* (minimum age 18) with experience cashiering in food service at $6 per hour ▶ 10–15 *cooks' helpers* (minimum age 18) with some food service experience at $6.35 per hour ▶ 20–30 *cooks-I,II,III* (minimum age 18) with a minimum of 6 months restaurant and cooking experience at $6.50–$10 per hour ▶ 80–100 *guest room attendants* (minimum age 18) at $6 per hour ▶ 15–25 *guest service agents* (minimum age 18) with hotel front desk or previous customer service experience at $6.50 per hour ▶ 10–12 *hosts/hostesses* (minimum age 15) with a minimum of 6 months restaurant experience at $6 per hour ▶ 50–70 *kitchen/utility personnel* (minimum age 18) at $6 per hour ▶ 40–50 *retail clerks* (minimum age 18) with cashier and/or retail sales experience at $6 per hour. Applicants must submit formal organization application. An in-person interview is recommended, but a telephone interview is acceptable. International applicants accepted; must apply through a recognized agency.

Benefits and Preemployment Training Housing at a cost, meals at a cost, formal training, possible full-time employment, health insurance, names of contacts, on-the-job training, willing to complete paperwork for educational credit, opportunity to attend seminars/workshops, and living in a National Park. Preemployment training is required and includes accident prevention and safety, general information about company and park.

Contact Patrice Armstrong, Staffing Manager, Grand Canyon National Park Lodges. Telephone:

928-638-2343. Fax: 928-638-2361. E-mail: jobs@grandcanyonlodges.com. Contact by e-mail, fax, mail, or phone. Application deadline: continuous.

ORME SUMMER CAMP
1000 ORME ROAD
MAYER, ARIZONA 86333

General Information Residential coed camp serving up to 200 campers with a wide variety of indoor and outdoor activities, including mountain biking, horseback riding, and desert survival/ rock climbing. Established in 1929. 40,000-acre facility located 70 miles from Phoenix. Features: swimming pool; complete gymnasium with weight room; riflery range; high desert climate; 40,000 acres for horseback riding; fully equipped boarding school campus.

Profile of Summer Employees Total number: 45; typical ages: 19–24. 50% men; 50% women; 2% minorities; 10% high school students; 80% college students; 1% retirees; 18% non-U.S. citizens; 10% local applicants. Nonsmokers preferred.

Employment Information Openings are from June 1 to August 14. Jobs available: ▶ 5–10 *general counselors* (minimum age 19) with driver's license and some experience at $1300–$1400 per season ▶ 1–2 *horsemanship staff* (minimum age 21) with driver's license and extensive experience with horses and children at $1400–$1600 per season ▶ 1–2 *outdoor adventure/ survival instructors* (minimum age 21) with Outward Bound or NOLS completion or equivalent and driver's license at $1500–$1600 per season ▶ 1 *photo journalist* (minimum age 19) with experience with digital camera and basic computer competency at $1300–$1400 per season ▶ 1–2 *pool assistants* (minimum age 19) with WSI and lifeguard certification at $1300–$1400 per season ▶ 1 *riflery instructor* (minimum age 19) with driver's license and riflery safety courses at $1500–$1600 per season ▶ 1–3 *senior counselors* (minimum age 20) with one year of college completed, driver's license, and experience working with children in camp setting at $1500–$1600 per season. Applicants must submit formal organization application, writing sample, three personal references, three letters of recommendation. A telephone interview is required. International applicants accepted; must obtain own visa, obtain own working papers, apply through a recognized agency.

Benefits and Preemployment Training Free housing, free meals, willing to provide letters of recommendation, on-the-job training, willing to act as a professional reference, and travel reimbursement. Preemployment training is required and includes accident prevention and safety, first aid, CPR, interpersonal skills, leadership skills.

Contact Mr. Doug Bartlett, Director, Orme Summer Camp, HC 63, Box 3040, Mayer, Arizona 86333. Telephone: 928-632-7601. Fax: 928-632-7605. E-mail: dbartlett@ormeschool.org. World Wide Web: http://www.ormecamp.org. Contact by e-mail, fax, mail, or phone. Application deadline: March 15.

THE SOUTHWESTERN COMPANY, ARIZONA

See The Southwestern Company on page 302 for complete description.

STIVERS STAFFING SERVICES–ARIZONA

See Stivers Staffing Services–Illinois on page 110 for complete description.

STUDENT CONSERVATION ASSOCIATION (SCA), ARIZONA

See Student Conservation Association (SCA), New Hampshire on page 209 for complete description.

ARKANSAS

NOARK GIRL SCOUT CAMP

ROUTE 3
HUNTSVILLE, ARKANSAS 72740

General Information Residential Girl Scout camp serving approximately 100 girls ages 8–17 weekly. Program includes a balance of traditional and innovative activities. Established in 1967. 1,039-acre facility located 30 miles from Fayetteville. Features: trail system; scenic Ozarks; basketball/tennis courts.

Profile of Summer Employees Total number: 25; typical ages: 18–25. 3% men; 97% women; 5% minorities; 30% high school students; 70% college students; 15% non-U.S. citizens; 85% local applicants. Nonsmokers preferred.

Employment Information Openings are from June 9 to August 2. Jobs available: ▶ 1 *assistant camp director* (minimum age 21) with leadership and Girl Scouts and residential camp/child care experience at $180 per week ▶ 1 *business manager* (minimum age 21) with experience in record keeping, buying, and inventory control; driver's license required at $160 per week ▶ 1 *canoe trip leader* (minimum age 21) with lifeguard certification and river canoeing experience at $160 per week ▶ 1 *head cook* (minimum age 21) with experience cooking for large groups at $200–$250 per week ▶ 1 *health supervisor* (minimum age 21) with RN, LPN, or EMT license at $250 per week ▶ 12 *unit counselors* (minimum age 18) with experience in child care and camping at $150 per week ▶ 4 *unit leaders* (minimum age 21) with experience in leadership, child care, and camping at $160 per week ▶ 1 *waterfront director* (minimum age 21) with WSI and lifeguard certification and ability to teach children, supervise instructors, keep records, and organize large groups; should have canoeing and pool management experience at $170 per week ▶ 1 *wrangler* (minimum age 18) with Western riding instruction and horse experience at $150 per week. Applicants must submit formal organization application, three personal references, drug test, state criminal background check. An in-person interview is recommended, but a telephone interview is acceptable. International applicants accepted; must apply through a recognized agency.

Benefits and Preemployment Training Free housing, free meals, formal training, health insurance, willing to provide letters of recommendation, names of contacts, on-the-job training, willing to complete paperwork for educational credit, and willing to act as a professional reference.

Contact Betty Perkins, Camp Director, Noark Girl Scout Camp, PO Box 6353, Harrison, Arkansas 72764. Telephone: 479-750-2442. Fax: 479-750-4699. World Wide Web: http://www.nwark.com/noarkgs. Contact by mail or phone. Application deadline: continuous.

THE SOUTHWESTERN COMPANY, ARKANSAS

See The Southwestern Company on page 302 for complete description.

STUDENT CONSERVATION ASSOCIATION (SCA), ARKANSAS

See Student Conservation Association (SCA), New Hampshire on page 209 for complete description.

CALIFORNIA

ACADEMY BY THE SEA/CAMP PACIFIC

2605 CARLSBAD BOULEVARD
CARLSBAD, CALIFORNIA 92008

General Information Non-profit, private camp that hires camp counselors, teachers, and administrative staff. Established in 1943. 16-acre facility located 35 miles from San Diego. Features: ocean front campus; 4 tennis courts; ocean front recreation center; swimming pool; dormitories; athletic fields.

Profile of Summer Employees Total number: 100; typical ages: 20–40. 60% men; 40% women; 2% high school students; 30% college students; 20% non-U.S. citizens; 10% local applicants. Nonsmokers preferred.

Employment Information Openings are from June 15 to August 5. Jobs available: ▶ 1–12 *camp counselors* (minimum age 21) at $2100–$2500 per season ▶ 10–20 *teachers* (minimum age 21) must have degree at $3000–$3500 per season. Applicants must submit formal organization application, letter of interest, resume, academic transcripts, two personal references, letter of recommendation. An in-person interview is required. International applicants accepted; must apply through a recognized agency.

Benefits and Preemployment Training Free housing, free meals, possible full-time employment, willing to provide letters of recommendation, names of contacts, on-the-job training, and willing to act as a professional reference. Preemployment training is required and includes accident prevention and safety, first aid, CPR, interpersonal skills, leadership skills.

Contact Lori Adlfinger, Associate Director, Academy by the Sea/Camp Pacific, PO Box 3000, Carlsbad, California 92018. Fax: 760-729-1574. E-mail: info@abts.com. World Wide Web: http://www.abts.com. Contact by e-mail, fax, or mail. Application deadline: continuous.

A CHRISTIAN MINISTRY IN THE NATIONAL PARKS–CALIFORNIA

See A Christian Ministry in the National Parks–Maine on page 122 for complete description.

ADVATECH PACIFIC, INC.

2015 PARK AVENUE, SUITE 8
REDLANDS, CALIFORNIA 92373

General Information Engineering and development firm specializing in support of aerospace and defense industries. Conducts engineering analysis and develops engineering applications software. Established in 1995. Located 60 miles from Los Angeles.

Profile of Summer Employees Total number: 20; typical ages: 21–24. 50% minorities; 100% college students. Nonsmokers required.

Employment Information Year-round positions also offered. Jobs available: ▶ 1 *administrative assistant* with Microsoft Office experience and a friendly manner at $6–$10 per hour ▶ 1–2 *engineering assistants* with engineering background with structures, design, or fluids at $10–$20 per hour ▶ 1–2 *marketing/finance assistants* with excellent verbal and writing skills; multilingual desirable at $6–$10 per hour ▶ 1–2 *programming assistants* with background in C++, GUI, UNIX, and Motif desirable at $10–$20 per hour. Applicants must submit resume. An in-person interview is required.

Benefits and Preemployment Training Possible full-time employment, on-the-job training, and willing to act as a professional reference.

Contact Sheila Snider, Administrator, Advatech Pacific, Inc., 2015 Park Avenue, Suite 8, Redlands, California 92373. Fax: 909-798-9368. E-mail: info@advatechpacific.com. World Wide Web: http://www.advatechpacific.com. Contact by e-mail, fax, or through World Wide Web site. Application deadline: continuous.

ADVENTURE CITY
10120 BEACH BOULEVARD
STANTON, CALIFORNIA 90680

General Information Small child amusement park with rides. Established in 1994. 3-acre facility located 1 mile from Anaheim. Features: 9 adult and child capacity rides; food service; rock climbing wall; children's theater; petting farm; game room.

Profile of Summer Employees Total number: 90–100; typical ages: 16–75. 40% men; 60% women; 50% minorities; 40% high school students; 40% college students; 5% retirees; 5% non-U.S. citizens; 20% local applicants. Nonsmokers required.

Employment Information Openings are from January to December. Year-round positions also offered. Jobs available: ▶ 5–10 *food service staff* (minimum age 16) with friendly, outgoing personality at $6.75 per hour ▶ 5–10 *ride operators* (minimum age 18) with friendly, outgoing personality at $6.75 per hour. Applicants must submit a formal organization application, resume, two letters of recommendation. An in-person interview is required.

Benefits and Preemployment Training Possible full-time employment, on-the-job training, willing to complete paperwork for educational credit, and reduced cost meals. Preemployment training is required and includes accident prevention and safety, interpersonal skills, leadership skills.

Contact Human Resources, Adventure City. Telephone: 714-236-9300. Fax: 714-236-9762. E-mail: adventurecity@prodigy.net. World Wide Web: http://www.adventurecity.com. Contact by phone. Application deadline: continuous.

ADVENTURE CONNECTION, INC.
986 LOTUS ROAD
LOTUS, CALIFORNIA 95651

General Information River trips for children and adults ages 7 and up. Established in 1983. 25-acre facility located 45 miles from Sacramento. Features: river-side camp; volleyball court.

Profile of Summer Employees Total number: 30; typical ages: 20–50. 50% men; 50% women; 20% minorities; 35% college students; 15% retirees; 10% non-U.S. citizens; 50% local applicants.

Employment Information Openings are from April 1 to October 15. Spring break positions also offered. Jobs available: ▶ 1 *food packer/ordering staff* (minimum age 18) with driver's license (noncommercial license acceptable); training provided; paid at $7–$10 per hour ▶ 25 *river guides* (minimum age 18) with experience guiding or completion of guide school; first aid/CPR at $60–$110 per day. Applicants must submit a formal organization application, resume, personal reference, letter of recommendation. An in-person interview is recommended, but a telephone interview is acceptable. International applicants accepted.

Benefits and Preemployment Training Free housing, formal training, willing to provide letters of recommendation, on-the-job training, willing to complete paperwork for educational credit, willing to act as a professional reference, and opportunity to attend seminars/workshops. Preemployment training is required and includes accident prevention and safety, first aid, CPR, interpersonal skills, leadership skills, swiftwater rescue, natural and human history, interpretive training.

Contact Nate Rangel, President, Adventure Connection, Inc., PO Box 475, Coloma, California 95613. Telephone: 800-556-6060. Fax: 530-626-9268. E-mail: getwet@raftcalifornia.com. World

Wide Web: http://www.raftcalifornia.com. Contact by e-mail, fax, mail, or phone. Application deadline: continuous.

ALPINE CONFERENCE CENTER
PO BOX 155, 415 CLUBHOUSE DRIVE
BLUE JAY, CALIFORNIA 92317

General Information An Evangelical Christian camp serving youth and churches. Established in 1957. 46-acre facility located 20 miles from San Bernardino. Features: wooded setting; dorm style housing; heated pool; ropes course; Indian village; recreational facilities.

Profile of Summer Employees Total number: 90; typical ages: 17–25. 50% men; 50% women; 10% minorities; 20% high school students; 50% college students; 20% local applicants. Nonsmokers required.

Employment Information Openings are from March 1 to August 31. Jobs available: ▶ 15–18 *counselors* (minimum age 18) at $150 per week ▶ 4–5 *facilities staff* (minimum age 16) at $150 per week ▶ 4–6 *food services staff* (minimum age 16) with Food Handlers Certificate at $150 per week ▶ 1 *gift shop/retail salesperson* (minimum age 18) at $150 per week ▶ 2 *healthcare providers* (minimum age 18) upper classman in nursing, LVN, EMT, RN at $250 per week ▶ 4 *lifeguards* (minimum age 16) with life saving certificate at $160 per week ▶ 1 *office assistant* (minimum age 18) at $150 per week ▶ 4–6 *outdoor adventure instructors* (minimum age 18) at $55 per day ▶ 2 *program assistants* (minimum age 18) at $175 per week. Applicants must submit a formal organization application, three personal references, certificate specialization if required for position, i.e., lifeguard. An in-person interview is recommended, but a telephone interview is acceptable. International applicants accepted; must obtain own visa, obtain own working papers.

Benefits and Preemployment Training Free housing, free meals, formal training, possible full-time employment, willing to provide letters of recommendation, on-the-job training, willing to complete paperwork for educational credit, and willing to act as a professional reference.

Contact Terri Watson, Human Resources Assistant, Alpine Conference Center. Telephone: 909-337-6287. Fax: 909-337-2574. E-mail: alpinecc@alpine-cc.org. World Wide Web: http://alpine-cc.org. Contact by e-mail, fax, mail, phone, or through World Wide Web site. Application deadline: continuous.

AMERICAN ADVENTURES
PO BOX 1338
GARDENA, CALIFORNIA 90249

General Information Adventure camping and hostelling tours for international passengers throughout the USA, Canada, and Mexico.

Profile of Summer Employees 50% men; 50% women; 20% minorities; 50% college students; 5% non-U.S. citizens; 5% local applicants.

Employment Information Openings are from May to September. Jobs available: ▶ 75 *tour leaders/drivers* (minimum age 23) with strong leadership and driving skills and knowledge of history/culture and current events of North America (foreign language and first aid skills helpful) at $1100 per month. Applicants must submit letter of interest, resume. International applicants accepted; must obtain own visa, obtain own working papers, apply through a recognized agency.

Benefits and Preemployment Training Free housing, formal training, on-the-job training, willing to complete paperwork for educational credit, and travel reimbursement. Preemployment training is required and includes accident prevention and safety, interpersonal skills, leadership skills.

Contact Ken Roberts, Recruiting and Training Manager, AmeriCan Adventures. Telephone: 800-345-8777. Fax: 310-719-1478. E-mail: personnel@premiereops.com. World Wide Web: http://www.americanadventures.com. Contact by e-mail or mail. Application deadline: continuous.

BAR 717 RANCH/CAMP TRINITY

STAR ROUTE BOX 150
HAYFORK, CALIFORNIA 96041

General Information Coed ranch offering horsemanship, swimming, hiking, crafts, animal care, ranch work projects, pottery, and the teaching of responsibility. Established in 1930. 450-acre facility located 80 miles from Redding. Features: located on pristine river; surrounded by acres of pristine forest; barn with 30 horses; miles of trails for horseback riding and hikes; extensive crafts facility; large gardens.

Profile of Summer Employees Total number: 50; typical ages: 16–60. 50% men; 50% women; 10% minorities; 5% high school students; 90% college students; 5% retirees; 10% non-U.S. citizens; 10% local applicants. Nonsmokers required.

Employment Information Openings are from June 20 to September 1. Jobs available: ▶ 30 *counselors* (minimum age 20) 2 years of college completed (or equivalent work experience), lifesaving, first aid/CPR, wilderness first aid at $210–$245 per week ▶ 6–10 *junior counselors* (minimum age 18) lifesaving, first aid/CPR at $185–$195 per week ▶ 4–6 *kitchen staff members* (minimum age 16) at $185 per week. Applicants must submit formal organization application, two personal references. An in-person interview is recommended, but a telephone interview is acceptable. International applicants accepted; must obtain own visa, obtain own working papers, apply through a recognized agency.

Benefits and Preemployment Training Housing at a cost, meals at a cost, willing to provide letters of recommendation, on-the-job training, willing to complete paperwork for educational credit, and willing to act as a professional reference. Preemployment training is required and includes accident prevention and safety, first aid, CPR, interpersonal skills, leadership skills.

Contact Gretchen Collard, Staff Director, Bar 717 Ranch/Camp Trinity, Star Route Box 150, Hayfork, California 96041. Telephone: 530-628-5992. Fax: 530-628-9392. E-mail: gretchen@bar717.com. World Wide Web: http://www.bar717.com. Contact by e-mail, fax, mail, phone, or through World Wide Web site. Application deadline: May 15.

BASSETT-MARTIN TENNIS CAMP

PO BOX 64335
LOS ANGELES, CALIFORNIA 90064

General Information Tennis camp for boys and girls ages 8–18 of all different ability levels. Established in 1972. 8-acre facility located 100 miles from Los Angeles. Features: 12 tennis courts; pool; game room and climbing wall; roller blade rink; soccer field; golfing range.

Profile of Summer Employees Total number: 17; typical ages: 20–30. 65% men; 35% women; 50% minorities; 85% college students; 10% non-U.S. citizens; 75% local applicants. Nonsmokers preferred.

Employment Information Openings are from June 15 to September 1. Jobs available: ▶ 10–15 *tennis camp counselors* (minimum age 18) with CPR certification, tennis teaching experience, and good swimming skills; must be at least 19 and no longer in high school due to NCAA rules; at $300–$400 per week. Applicants must submit a formal organization application, resume, personal reference, 3 or 4 personal references. An in-person interview is recommended, but a telephone interview is acceptable. International applicants accepted.

Benefits and Preemployment Training Free housing, free meals, willing to provide letters of recommendation, on-the-job training, willing to complete paperwork for educational credit, and willing to act as a professional reference.

Contact Billy Martin, Director, Bassett-Martin Tennis Camp, PO Box 64335, Los Angeles, California 90064. Telephone: 310-475-5853. Fax: 310-475-5853. E-mail: bmartin@athletics.ucla.edu. World Wide Web: http://www.bmtennis.com. Contact by e-mail, fax, mail, phone, or through World Wide Web site. Application deadline: June 15.

CAMP JCA SHALOM
34342 MULHOLLAND HIGHWAY
MALIBU, CALIFORNIA 90265

General Information Residential Jewish camp offering a warm, supportive atmosphere for campers ages 7–17. Established in 1961. 135-acre facility located 40 miles from Los Angeles. Features: wooded setting in mountains; ropes course; swimming pool; archery range.

Profile of Summer Employees Total number: 60; typical age: 18. 50% men; 50% women; 10% minorities; 20% high school students; 78% college students; 10% non-U.S. citizens; 70% local applicants. Nonsmokers preferred.

Employment Information Openings are from June to August. Spring break and winter break positions also offered. Jobs available: ▶ 1 *Jewish education director* (minimum age 21) with knowledge of Jewish traditions, culture, history, and entertainment, as well as the ability to develop and lead camp-wide programs, including all-day Shabbat programs at $1000–$3000 per season ▶ 1–5 *bus drivers* (minimum age 18) with current Class B California driver's license and a clean driving record (knowledge of mountain driving extremely helpful) at $1000–$3000 per season ▶ 40–60 *counselors* (minimum age 18) at $1000–$3000 per season ▶ 1–4 *registered nurses* with RN and ability to run the infirmary, supervise nurse's aide, and interact well with parents at $1000–$3000 per season ▶ 1 *ropes course leader* (minimum age 21) with ability to lead groups through high and low elements at $1000–$3000 per season ▶ 1 *song leader* with ability to lead camp-wide singing of American and Hebrew folk songs, highly spirited nature, and guitar-playing skills at $1000–$3000 per season ▶ 5 *swimming and water safety instructors* with CPR, ALS, and WSI certifications at $1000–$3000 per season ▶ 2 *teen travel leaders* (minimum age 21) with college degree, knowledge of outdoors (experience with children essential), and current first aid and CPR certification at $1000–$3000 per season ▶ 3–4 *unit heads* (minimum age 21) with college degree, three years of camping experience, and good Jewish program skills (graduate training or social work experience helpful) at $1000–$3000 per season. Applicants must submit formal organization application, three personal references, three letters of recommendation. An in-person interview is recommended, but a telephone interview is acceptable. International applicants accepted; must apply through a recognized agency.

Benefits and Preemployment Training Free housing and on-the-job training. Preemployment training is optional and includes accident prevention and safety, interpersonal skills, leadership skills.

Contact Mr. Stu Dang, Director, Camp JCA Shalom, 34342 Mulholland Highway, Malibu, California 90265. Telephone: 818-889-5500. Fax: 818-889-5132. World Wide Web: http://www.shalominstitute.com. Contact by mail or phone. Application deadline: continuous.

CAMP LA JOLLA
176 C AVENUE
CORONADO, CALIFORNIA 92118

General Information Weight-loss/fitness camp for ages 8 and older serving separate age and gender groups in fitness, sports, nutrition, behavior modification, field trips, beach visits, theater arts and arts and crafts; emphasis on healthy lifestyle. Established in 1979. 50-acre facility located 10 miles from San Diego. Features: beachside location; numerous athletic fields; outdoor swimming pool; 35 million dollar workout facility; university dormitories–suite style.

Profile of Summer Employees Total number: 86. 20% men; 80% women; 25% minorities; 5% high school students; 95% college students; 30% local applicants. Nonsmokers required.

Employment Information Openings are from June 14 to August 25. Year-round positions also offered. Jobs available: ▶ *aerobics instructors* at $900–$1600 per season ▶ 3 *behavior modification specialists* at $900–$1600 per season ▶ 15 *counselors* at $900–$1600 per season ▶ 10 *exercise specialists* with WSI and lifeguard certification at $900–$1600 per season ▶ 2 *nurses* with RN, EMT, or LPN license at $2000–$2600 per season ▶ 3 *nutritionists* at $900–$1600 per season ▶ 10 *personal trainers* at $900–$1600 per season ▶ *tennis instructors* at $900–$1600 per season. Applicants must submit a formal organization application, personal reference, letter of recommendation. An in-person interview is recommended, but a telephone interview is acceptable.

Benefits and Preemployment Training Free housing, free meals, willing to provide letters of recommendation, on-the-job training, willing to complete paperwork for educational credit, willing to act as a professional reference, and internship opportunities available. Preemployment training is required and includes accident prevention and safety, first aid, interpersonal skills, leadership skills.

Contact Nancy Lenhart, Director, Camp La Jolla, 176 C Avenue, Coronado, California 92118. Telephone: 800-825-8746. Fax: 619-435-8188. E-mail: camplj@aol.com. World Wide Web: http://www.camplajolla.com. Contact by e-mail, fax, mail, phone, or through World Wide Web site. Application deadline: June 1.

CAMP LAKOTA
11220 DOROTHY LANE
FRAZIER PARK, CALIFORNIA 93225

General Information Residential camp serving 140 girls ages 7–17 weekly and emphasizing traditional activities, horsemanship, and Girl Scout programs. Established in 1949. 58-acre facility located 75 miles from Los Angeles. Features: pine forest setting; strong equestrian program; heated swimming pool; adjacent to National Forest.

Profile of Summer Employees Total number: 40; typical ages: 18–35. 5% men; 95% women; 30% minorities; 5% high school students; 95% college students; 20% non-U.S. citizens; 2% local applicants. Nonsmokers preferred.

Employment Information Openings are from June 1 to August 25. Year-round positions also offered. Jobs available: ▶ 1 *assistant cook* (minimum age 18) at $165–$190 per week ▶ 1 *head cook* (minimum age 21) with food preparation experience at $235–$265 per week ▶ 1 *health supervisor* (minimum age 21) with RN license (preferred); EMT or LVN at $295–$315 per week ▶ 3 *kitchen staff members* (minimum age 16) at $120–$191 per week ▶ 1 *leadership director* (minimum age 21) with experience as a camp counselor or equivalent at $165–$195 per week ▶ 1 *maintenance person* (minimum age 21) with driver's license at $162–$186 per week ▶ 1 *pool director* (minimum age 18) with lifeguard, CPR, and standard first aid certification; WSI preferred at $164–$186 per week ▶ 1 *program director* (minimum age 21) camp experience required at $200–$230 per week ▶ 1 *riding director* (minimum age 21) with AHA certification or equivalent (preferred) at $210–$235 per week ▶ 15 *unit counselors* (minimum age 18) at $150–$185 per week ▶ 7 *unit leaders* (minimum age 21) at $165–$195 per week ▶ 2–3 *wranglers* (minimum age 16) with horse experience at $160–$187 per week. Applicants must submit formal organization application, three personal references. International applicants accepted; must apply through a recognized agency.

Benefits and Preemployment Training Free housing, free meals, health insurance, willing to provide letters of recommendation, on-the-job training, and willing to complete paperwork for educational credit. Preemployment training is required and includes accident prevention and safety, first aid, CPR, interpersonal skills, leadership skills, program skills, group building activities.

Contact Connie Scharff, Outdoor Program/Property Director, Camp Lakota, 9421 Winnetka Avenue, Chatsworth, California 91311. Telephone: 818-886-1801 EXT. 31. Fax: 818-407-4840. E-mail: cscharff@sfvgsc.org. World Wide Web: http://www.sfvgsc.org. Contact by e-mail, fax, mail, phone, or through World Wide Web site. Application deadline: continuous.

CASTILLEJA SCHOOL
1310 BRYANT STREET
PALO ALTO, CALIFORNIA 94301

General Information All-girls, day school grades 6-12 and summer day camp with full enrichment program. Established in 1907. Affiliated with National Association of Independent Schools,

Secondary School Admission Test Board. 5-acre facility located 30 miles from San Francisco. Features: competitive pool; beautiful campus; theater; full gymnasium; excellent dining services.
Profile of Summer Employees Total number: 25; typical ages: 19–30. 20% men; 80% women; 33% minorities; 75% college students; 98% local applicants.
Employment Information Openings are from June 12 to August 9. Jobs available: ▶ 23–26 *camp counselors* with one year out of high school at $3200 per season ▶ *lifeguards/counselors* with current lifeguard certification at $3200 per season. Applicants must submit a formal organization application, three personal references. An in-person interview is recommended, but a telephone interview is acceptable. International applicants accepted; must obtain own visa, obtain own working papers.
Benefits and Preemployment Training Free meals, willing to provide letters of recommendation, willing to complete paperwork for educational credit, and willing to act as a professional reference. Preemployment training is required and includes accident prevention and safety, first aid, CPR, interpersonal skills, leadership skills, the culture of the program.
Contact Nancy Nagramada, Camp Director, Castilleja School. Telephone: 650-328-3160 Ext. 109. Fax: 650-326-8036. E-mail: nancy_nagramada@castilleja.org. World Wide Web: http://www.castilleja.org. Contact by e-mail, phone, or through World Wide Web site. Application deadline: continuous.

CENTER FOR TALENTED YOUTH/JOHNS HOPKINS UNIVERSITY–LOYOLA MARYMOUNT UNIVERSITY

LOS ANGELES, CALIFORNIA

See Center for Talented Youth/Johns Hopkins University on page 145 for complete description.

CENTER FOR TALENTED YOUTH/JOHNS HOPKINS UNIVERSITY–MIRMAN SCHOOL

WEST LOS ANGELES, CALIFORNIA

See Center for Talented Youth/Johns Hopkins University on page 145 for complete description.

CENTER FOR TALENTED YOUTH/JOHNS HOPKINS UNIVERSITY–PEPPERDINE UNIVERSITY

MALIBU, CALIFORNIA

See Center for Talented Youth/Johns Hopkins University on page 145 for complete description.

CENTER FOR TALENTED YOUTH/JOHNS HOPKINS UNIVERSITY–STANFORD UNIVERSITY

PALO ALTO, CALIFORNIA

See Center for Talented Youth/Johns Hopkins University on page 145 for complete description.

CENTER FOR TALENTED YOUTH/JOHNS HOPKINS UNIVERSITY–UNIVERSITY OF CALIFORNIA, SANTA CRUZ

SANTA CRUZ, CALIFORNIA

See Center for Talented Youth/Johns Hopkins University on page 145 for complete description.

CYBERCAMPS–CHAPMAN UNIVERSITY

ORANGE, CALIFORNIA

See Cybercamps–University of Washington on page 335 for complete description.

CYBERCAMPS–CONCORDIA UNIVERSITY
IRVINE, CALIFORNIA

See Cybercamps–University of Washington on page 335 for complete description.

CYBERCAMPS–DEANZA COLLEGE
CUPERTINO, CALIFORNIA

See Cybercamps–University of Washington on page 335 for complete description.

CYBERCAMPS–MENLO COLLEGE
ATHERTON, CALIFORNIA

See Cybercamps–University of Washington on page 335 for complete description.

CYBERCAMPS–UCLA
LOS ANGELES, CALIFORNIA

See Cybercamps–University of Washington on page 335 for complete description.

CYBERCAMPS–UC SAN DIEGO (UCSD)
LA JOLLA, CALIFORNIA

See Cybercamps–University of Washington on page 335 for complete description.

CYBERCAMPS–UNIVERSITY OF CALIFORNIA AT BERKELEY
BERKELEY, CALIFORNIA

See Cybercamps–University of Washington on page 335 for complete description.

CYBERCAMPS–WEST VALLEY COLLEGE
SARATOGA, CALIFORNIA

See Cybercamps–University of Washington on page 335 for complete description.

DOUGLAS RANCH CAMPS
33200 EAST CARMEL VALLEY ROAD
CARMEL VALLEY, CALIFORNIA 93924

General Information Private, traditional, residential summer camp for 120 children ages 7–14. Structured program in horseback riding, swimming, archery, tennis, riflery, and crafts. Focus is on improving social skills, leadership, and confidence in a positive and fun environment. Established in 1925. 120-acre facility located 15 miles from Carmel. Features: large oval pool; central lodge and dining hall; 4 tennis courts; private hiking and riding trails; shady oak trees on hillside; 15 miles to ocean.

Profile of Summer Employees Total number: 45; typical ages: 19–24. 45% men; 55% women; 15% minorities; 85% college students; 5% retirees; 10% non-U.S. citizens; 20% local applicants. Nonsmokers required.

Employment Information Openings are from June 13 to August 25. Jobs available: ▶ 2–5 *archery instructors* (minimum age 18) with camp, school, or archery team experience and at least one year of college completed at $2100–$2700 per season ▶ 2–5 *crafts instructors* (minimum age 18) with experience working with children, teaching and/or experience with arts and crafts, and at least one year of college completed at $2100–$2700 per season ▶ 30–32 *general counselors* (minimum age 18) with experience working with children, general experience in at least 1 activity (riding, swimming, tennis, archery, riflery, crafts, ballsports); at least one year of college completed at $2100–$2700 per season ▶ 2–3 *kitchen assistants* (minimum age 18) with experience in general food preparation and dishwashing, and at least one year of college completed at $2200–$2750 per season ▶ 4–10 *riding instructors* (minimum age 18) with experience giving riding lessons, teaching children, riding, saddling, and/or general horse care; at least one year of college completed at $2200–$2750 per season ▶ 2–5 *riflery instructors* (minimum age 18) with camp, school, or riflery team experience and at least one year of college completed at $2100–$2700 per season ▶ 4–10 *swimming instructors* (minimum age 18) with WSI and/or lifeguard certification; experience on club or team, and at least one year of college completed at $2200–$2750 per season ▶ 2–5 *tennis instructors* (minimum age 18) with experience on tennis team, club, or in teaching and at least one year of college completed at $2100–$2700 per season. Applicants must submit formal organization application, two personal references, two letters of recommendation. An in-person interview is recommended, but a telephone interview is acceptable. International applicants accepted; must apply through a recognized agency.

Benefits and Preemployment Training Free housing, free meals, formal training, health insurance, willing to provide letters of recommendation, on-the-job training, willing to complete paperwork for educational credit, willing to act as a professional reference, and CPR and first aid certification. Preemployment training is required and includes accident prevention and safety, first aid, CPR, interpersonal skills, leadership skills, child psychology and development, team building.

Contact Mrs. Kristen Smith, Assistant Director, Douglas Ranch Camps, 33200 East Carmel Valley Road, Carmel Valley, California 93924. Telephone: 831-659-2761. Fax: 831-659-5690. E-mail: director@douglascamp.com. World Wide Web: http://www.douglascamp.com. Contact by e-mail, fax, mail, phone, or through World Wide Web site. Application deadline: continuous.

DRAKESBAD GUEST RANCH

END OF WARNER VALLEY ROAD
CHESTER, CALIFORNIA 96020

General Information Rustic guest ranch in the heart of Lassen Volcanic National Park. Established in 1974. 100-acre facility located 120 miles from Reno, Nevada. Features: National Park setting; hot spring pool; horse stable; no electricity or television; hiking trails; fishing stream.

Profile of Summer Employees Total number: 22; typical ages: 20–26. 15% men; 85% women; 10% minorities; 80% college students; 5% retirees; 75% non-U.S. citizens; 10% local applicants. Nonsmokers preferred.

Employment Information Openings are from June 1 to October 15. Jobs available: ▶ 2–3 *grill cooks* (minimum age 18) with cooking, food safety, and sanitation experience at $8–$9 per hour ▶ 5–6 *housekeepers/groundskeepers/waitstaff/children's program staff/kitchen maintenance* (minimum age 18) with knowledge of children's games and crafts at $7–$8 per hour ▶ 1–2 *kitchen help/food staff* (minimum age 18) at $7–$8 per hour ▶ 1 *kitchen maintenance staff* (minimum age 18) at $7–$8 per hour ▶ 1 *maintenance/groundskeeper* (minimum age 18) with technical skills at $7–$8 per hour ▶ 3–4 *store clerks/cashiers* (minimum age 18) with driver's license at $7–$8 per hour ▶ 3–4 *waitstaff* (minimum age 18) at $7–$8 per hour ▶ 1–2 *wranglers* (minimum age 21) with first aid and CPR certification; 5 years horsemanship, 2 years stable hand experience at $7–$8 per hour. Applicants must submit letter of interest, resume, photograph, e-mail address, Web site application (preferred). An in-person interview is recommended, but a telephone interview is acceptable. International applicants accepted; must apply through a recognized agency.

Benefits and Preemployment Training Housing at a cost, meals at a cost, willing to provide letters of recommendation, and on-the-job training. Preemployment training is required and includes accident prevention and safety, CPR, interpersonal skills.

Contact Ed Fiebiger, Ranch Host, Drakesbad Guest Ranch, 2150 North Main Street, Red Bluff, California 96080. Fax: 530-529-4511. E-mail: billie@goldrush.com. World Wide Web: http://www.drakesbad.com. Contact by e-mail or through World Wide Web site. Application deadline: March 15.

EASTER SEALS CAMP HARMON

430 WEST GRANT STREET
HEALDSBURG, CALIFORNIA 95448

General Information Non-profit organization residential summer camp serving children and adults with disabilities. Established in 1964. 11-acre facility located 60 miles from San Francisco. Features: near San Francisco; Redwood forest; one half-hour from Pacific Ocean.

Profile of Summer Employees Total number: 50; typical ages: 18–22. 35% men; 65% women; 10% minorities; 80% college students; 40% non-U.S. citizens; 10% local applicants. Nonsmokers required.

Employment Information Openings are from June 2 to August 18. Jobs available: ▶ 10–30 *camp counselors* prefer experience with disabled at $200 per week ▶ 2 *camp nurses* (minimum age 25) RN at $1000 per week. Applicants must submit formal organization application, three letters of recommendation. An in-person interview is recommended, but a telephone interview is acceptable. International applicants accepted; must apply through a recognized agency.

Benefits and Preemployment Training Free housing, free meals, willing to provide letters of recommendation, on-the-job training, willing to complete paperwork for educational credit, willing to act as a professional reference, and opportunity to attend seminars/workshops. Preemployment training is required and includes accident prevention and safety, CPR, interpersonal skills, leadership skills, training in caring for disabled.

Contact Jane Carr, Camp Director, Easter Seals Camp Harmon. E-mail: janecarres@aol.com. World Wide Web: http://www.es-cc.org. Contact by e-mail or mail. Application deadline: continuous.

ELITE EDUCATIONAL INSTITUTE

4009 WILSHIRE BOULEVARD, #200
LOS ANGELES, CALIFORNIA 90010

General Information Academic enrichment and college preparation. Established in 1985.

Profile of Summer Employees Total number: 200; typical ages: 25–35. 70% men; 30% women. Nonsmokers preferred.

Employment Information Openings are from June 20 to August 25. Jobs available: ▶ 10–20 *SAT-verbal, math/junior high verbal, math instructors* (minimum age 25) teaching experience required at $20–$35 per hour. Applicants must submit a formal organization application, letter of interest, resume.

Benefits and Preemployment Training Formal training, possible full-time employment, health insurance, willing to provide letters of recommendation, and opportunity to attend seminars/ workshops. Preemployment training is optional and includes teacher training.

Contact Wonna Kim, Program Director, Elite Educational Institute, 4009 Wilshire Bouldevard #200, Los Angeles, California 90010. Fax: 213-365-1253. E-mail: wonna.kim@eliteprep.com. World Wide Web: http://eliteprep.com. Contact by e-mail or fax. Application deadline: continuous.

EMANDAL–A FARM ON A RIVER

16500 HEARST ROAD
WILLITS, CALIFORNIA 95490

General Information Coeducational residential camp for 70 youngsters ages 6–16 for the first half of the summer; a family vacation farm for 45–55 people of all ages for the second half. Established in 1965. 1,000-acre facility located 160 miles from San Francisco. Features: wild river; farm; organic garden; oaks, firs, madrones; home-made bread; rustic cabins.

Profile of Summer Employees Total number: 30; typical ages: 18–30. 50% men; 50% women; 1% minorities; 10% high school students; 80% college students; 1% retirees; 10% non-U.S. citizens; 10% local applicants. Nonsmokers required.

Employment Information Openings are from June 7 to September 7. Jobs available: ▶ 15–22 *camp counselors (June–July)* (minimum age 18) at $1000 per season ▶ 3–6 *environmental* *education naturalists (March–June)* (minimum age 21) at $190 per week ▶ 8 *family camp workers (July–August)* (minimum age 16) at $190 per week ▶ 2 *farm workers (until Thanksgiving)* (minimum age 20) at $190 per week ▶ *gardener's apprentice (volunteer from April–November)* ▶ 2 *gardeners (entire summer)* (minimum age 22) at $190 per week ▶ 1 *pickle maker (August–October)* (minimum age 20) at $190 per week. Applicants must submit formal organization application, two personal references. A telephone interview is required. International applicants accepted; must obtain own working papers, apply through a recognized agency.

Benefits and Preemployment Training Free housing, free meals, formal training, health insurance, willing to provide letters of recommendation, on-the-job training, willing to complete paperwork for educational credit, willing to act as a professional reference, and opportunity to attend seminars/workshops. Preemployment training is required and includes accident prevention and safety, first aid, CPR, interpersonal skills, leadership skills.

Contact Tamara Adams, Director, Emandal–A Farm on a River, 16500 Hearst Road, Willits, California 95490. Telephone: 707-459-5439. Fax: 707-459-1808. E-mail: emandal@pacific.net. World Wide Web: http://www.emandal.com. Contact by e-mail, fax, mail, phone, or through World Wide Web site. Application deadline: continuous.

GIRL SCOUTS OF THE SAN FERNANDO VALLEY

9421 WINNETKA AVENUE
CHATSWORTH, CALIFORNIA 91311

General Information Non-profit organization serving the girls of the San Fernando Valley. 58-acre facility located 80 miles from Los Angeles. Features: forest setting; mountainous terrain; horseback riding; heated swimming pool; rustic living; tripping and leadership programs.

Profile of Summer Employees Total number: 35; typical ages: 18–25. 2% men; 98% women; 15% minorities; 2% high school students; 96% college students; 40% non-U.S. citizens; 50% local applicants.

Employment Information Openings are from June 13 to June 25. Jobs available: ▶ 1–5 *cooks/lifeguard* (minimum age 18) lifeguard certification and previous experience at $1700–$3200 per season ▶ 10–22 *unit counselors* (minimum age 18) previous child care experience preferred at $1900–$2150 per season ▶ 3–5 *wrangler/riding instructors* (minimum age 18) horseback instructional experience needed at $2000–$3900 per season. Applicants must submit formal organization application, three personal references. An in-person interview is recommended, but a telephone interview is acceptable. International applicants accepted; must apply through a recognized agency.

Benefits and Preemployment Training Free housing, free meals, formal training, health insurance, willing to provide letters of recommendation, on-the-job training, willing to complete paperwork for educational credit, willing to act as a professional reference, and opportunity to attend seminars/workshops. Preemployment training is required and includes accident prevention and safety, first aid, CPR, leadership skills, Program and Risk management training.

Contact Connie Scharf, Program/Property Director, Girl Scouts of the San Fernando Valley. Telephone: 818-886-1801 Ext. 31. Fax: 818-407-4840. E-mail: camplakota@sfvgsc.org. World Wide Web: http://www.sfvgsc.org. Contact by e-mail, fax, phone, or through World Wide Web site. Application deadline: continuous.

GIRL SCOUTS OF TIERRA DEL ORO

3005 GOLD CANAL DRIVE
RANCHO CORDOVA, CALIFORNIA 95670

General Information Nonprofit organization for girls. Established in 1921. 176-acre facility located 90 miles from Stockton. Features: wooded setting; canoe lake; rustic; swimming lake; archery; 5000 foot elevation.

Profile of Summer Employees Total number: 45; typical ages: 18–27. 1% men; 99% women;

30% minorities; 1% high school students; 98% college students; 1% retirees; 10% non-U.S. citizens; 70% local applicants. Nonsmokers required.

Employment Information Openings are from June 3 to August 18. Jobs available: ▶ 1 *assistant camp director* (minimum age 21) with administrative, supervisory and camp experience, knowledge of Girl Scout program; Class B driver's license required at $72–$75 per day ▶ 1 *assistant cook* (minimum age 19) with experience preparing food for large groups at $61–$63 per day ▶ 19 *assistant unit leaders* (minimum age 18) with experience in camping and/or group leadership at $46–$48 per day ▶ 1 *business manager* (minimum age 21) with business and purchasing experience; Class B driver's license required at $50–$53 per day ▶ 1 *health supervisor* (minimum age 21) with state license or registered as an MD, PA, RN, LVN, or EMT; current first aid training and CPR at $84–$89 per day ▶ 3 *kitchen assistants* (minimum age 16) with some kitchen experience, dishwashing helpful at $43–$45 per day ▶ 1 *kitchen manager* (minimum age 21) with menu planning ability and experience cooking for large groups (100 plus) at $75–$78 per day ▶ 1 *leadership assistant* (minimum age 19) with previous camp experience, skills in activity programming, teen communication, camp craft, and supervision; valid driver's license at $48–$51 per day ▶ 1 *leadership director* (minimum age 21) with previous camp experience, skills in activity programming, teen communication, camp craft, and supervision; valid driver's license at $50–$53 per day ▶ *maintenance support* (minimum age 18) with a valid driver's license, carpentry, plumbing and electrical aptitude; willingness to take direction at $53–$55 per day ▶ 1 *program manager* (minimum age 21) with supervisory and camp experience required; knowledge of Girl Scout program at $56–$59 per day ▶ 3 *program specialists (arts and crafts, science and nature, archery)* (minimum age 19) with extensive knowledge and experience related to the specific program area at $48–$51 per day ▶ 2 *trip adventure leaders* (minimum age 21) with extensive outdoor skills and backpacking experience; certification as EMT in wilderness first aid, or willingness to obtain at $50–$53 per day ▶ 1 *trip coordinator* (minimum age 21) with California/equivalent Class B driver's license, or willingness to obtain; previous camp experience at $48–$51 per day ▶ 3 *unit leaders* (minimum age 21) with experience with children in groups; supervisory experience (preferred); valid driver's license at $48–$51 per day ▶ 3 *waterfront assistants* (minimum age 18) with current lifeguard, First Aid and CPR certifications; canoeing experience helpful at $48–$51 per day ▶ 1 *waterfront director* (minimum age 21) with current Water Safety Instructor, lifeguard, First Aid and CPR certifications; canoeing skills, supervisory and waterfront experience at $51–$54 per day. Applicants must submit formal organization application, three personal references. An in-person interview is recommended, but a telephone interview is acceptable. International applicants accepted; must apply through a recognized agency.

Benefits and Preemployment Training Free housing, free meals, formal training, health insurance, on-the-job training, and opportunity to attend seminars/workshops. Preemployment training is required and includes accident prevention and safety, first aid, CPR, interpersonal skills, leadership skills, songs, games, lifeguarding (occasionally).

Contact Joy Galloway, Camp Director, Girl Scouts of Tierra del Oro. Telephone: 916-638-4475. Fax: 916-638-8452. E-mail: joy_galloway@tdogs.org. World Wide Web: http://www.tdogs.org. Contact by e-mail, fax, mail, phone, or through World Wide Web site. Application deadline: continuous.

GRIFFITH PARK BOYS CAMP

4730 CRYSTAL SPRINGS DRIVE
LOS ANGELES, CALIFORNIA 90027

General Information Camp for boys, ages 6-14, arts and crafts, climbing wall, high ropes course, athletic field, pool, 16 heated-air conditioned cabins, dining hall, kitchen. Established in 1926. Features: 32 foot climbing wall; high ropes course; archery range; swimming pool; athletic field; arts and crafts area.

Profile of Summer Employees Total number: 35–50; typical ages: 18–30. 99% men; 1% women;

85% minorities; 1% high school students; 99% college students; 100% local applicants. Nonsmokers preferred.

Employment Information Openings are from June 13 to August 31. Jobs available: ▶ *camp counselors* (minimum age 18) at $260–$350 per week. Applicants must submit a formal organization application. An in-person interview is required.

Benefits and Preemployment Training Free housing, free meals, willing to provide letters of recommendation, on-the-job training, and willing to complete paperwork for educational credit. Preemployment training is required and includes accident prevention and safety, first aid, CPR, interpersonal skills, leadership skills.

Contact Roger Williams, Camp Director, Griffith Park Boys Camp. Telephone: 323-664-0571. Fax: 323-913-4170. Contact by fax, mail, or phone. Application deadline: June 15.

HAMLIN CAMPS

2129 VALLEJO STREET
SAN FRANCISCO, CALIFORNIA 94123

General Information Urban-adventure day camp located in wooded national park inside city of San Francisco. Established in 1997. Features: climbing wall; wooded setting; set in national park; location in San Francisco.

Profile of Summer Employees Total number: 25; typical ages: 15–30. 33% men; 67% women; 40% minorities; 50% high school students; 40% college students; 5% non-U.S. citizens; 60% local applicants. Nonsmokers preferred.

Employment Information Openings are from June 15 to August 25. Jobs available: ▶ 3–6 *group counselors* (minimum age 18) at $300–$400 per week. Applicants must submit a formal organization application, two personal references. An in-person interview is recommended, but a telephone interview is acceptable. International applicants accepted; must obtain own visa, obtain own working papers.

Benefits and Preemployment Training Formal training, possible full-time employment, willing to provide letters of recommendation, on-the-job training, and willing to act as a professional reference. Preemployment training is required and includes accident prevention and safety, leadership skills.

Contact Tyler Fonarow, Director, Hamlin Camps. Telephone: 415-561-3085. Fax: 412-674-5418. E-mail: camp@hamlin.org. World Wide Web: http://www.hamlin.org. Contact by e-mail, fax, or phone. Application deadline: continuous.

HUNEWILL GUEST RANCH

TWIN LAKES ROAD
BRIDGEPORT, CALIFORNIA 93517

General Information Guest ranch accommodating 45–55 guests weekly. Established in 1931. 4,800-acre facility located 120 miles from Reno, Nevada. Features: lush mountain meadows; surrounding mountains; mountain lakes nearby; 180 horses; 26 rooms; Victorian-style ranch house and dining room.

Profile of Summer Employees Total number: 20; typical ages: 18–25. 25% men; 75% women; 5% high school students; 80% college students; 15% local applicants. Nonsmokers required.

Employment Information Openings are from May 15 to October 1. Jobs available: ▶ 1 *breakfast/pastry chef* (minimum age 18) with experience baking for groups at $457 per week ▶ 3 *cabin staff members* (minimum age 18) with ability to work quickly and eye for neatness at $381.46–$423.77 per week ▶ 1 *cook* with cooking experience or cooking school certification at $2080–$2100 per month ▶ 1 *gardener* (minimum age 18) with experience with lawn mowers, some landscaping, and an aptitude for gardening at $381–$423 per week ▶ 1 *kitchen janitorial* (minimum age 18) physically able to do manual labor and have an eye for neatness at $381–$423 per week ▶ 1 *maintenance person* (minimum age 18) with general plumbing, electrical, and carpentry ability, including fence building and some work with livestock at $381.46–$423.77 per week ▶ 2 *waiters/waitresses* (minimum age 18) with experience at $411–$457 per week ▶ 3–6 *wranglers* (minimum age 18) with extensive horse experience and good people skills at $381–$423 per week. Applicants must submit resume, three personal references, three letters of recommendation. A telephone interview is required. International applicants accepted; must obtain own visa, obtain own working papers, apply through a recognized agency.

Benefits and Preemployment Training Meals at a cost, free housing, willing to provide letters of recommendation, and on-the-job training.

Contact Betsy Hunewill Elliott, Assistant Manager, Hunewill Guest Ranch, 205 Hunewill Lane, Wellington, Nevada 89444. Telephone: 702-465-2238. World Wide Web: http://www.hunewillranch.com. Contact by mail, phone, or through World Wide Web site. Application deadline: continuous.

IDYLLWILD ARTS SUMMER PROGRAM

PO BOX 38
IDYLLWILD, CALIFORNIA 92549

General Information Non-profit educational organization that offers intensive summer instruction to students of all ages and abilities. Established in 1946. 205-acre facility located 110 miles from Los Angeles. Features: mountain campus; state of the art film studio; new art gallery; large dance studios; air conditioned practice rooms; modern dormitories.

Profile of Summer Employees Total number: 350; typical ages: 19–25. 40% men; 60% women; 20% minorities; 95% college students; 10% local applicants. Nonsmokers preferred.

Employment Information Openings are from June 20 to August 25. Jobs available: ▶ 30–35 *resident counselors* (minimum age 19) with 1 year of college at $165 per week ▶ 5–6 *teaching assistants* (minimum age 21) with visual arts background teaching experience at $165 per week ▶ 4–6 *tech assistants* (minimum age 19) with theater tech experience at $165 per week. Applicants must submit a formal organization application, resume, three personal references. A telephone interview is required. International applicants accepted; must obtain own visa, obtain own working papers.

Benefits and Preemployment Training Free housing, free meals, willing to provide letters of recommendation, on-the-job training, willing to complete paperwork for educational credit, willing to act as a professional reference, opportunity to attend seminars/workshops, and Workers Compensation, Cal SDI. Preemployment training is required and includes accident prevention and safety, first aid, CPR, interpersonal skills, leadership skills.

Contact Emma Showalter, Assistant Director, Idyllwild Arts Summer Program. Telephone: 909-659-2171 Ext. 369. Fax: 909-659-5463. E-mail: iasumpro@aol.com. World Wide Web: http://www.idyllwildarts.org. Contact by e-mail, fax, mail, or phone. Application deadline: March 15.

JAMESON RANCH CAMP

GLENNVILLE, CALIFORNIA 93226

General Information Jameson Ranch Camp connects children to a self-sufficient ranch lifestyle where campers grow some of the food and help with the farm animals. Established in 1934. 520-acre facility located 40 miles from Bakersfield. Features: 5000-ft. elevation in Sierras; mountain setting; closest neighbors 4 miles away; property borders National Forest; freshwater lake with great fishing; cattle ranch.

Profile of Summer Employees Total number: 30; typical ages: 19–55. 50% men; 50% women; 20% minorities; 90% college students; 5% retirees; 10% non-U.S. citizens; 5% local applicants. Nonsmokers required.

Employment Information Openings are from June 10 to August 26. Jobs available: ▶ 1 *archery instructor* (minimum age 19) with archery experience at $2700 per season ▶ 2 *crafts instructors* (minimum age 19) with crafts or art experience at $2700 per season ▶ 1 *drama instructor* (minimum age 19) with some theater background at $2700 per season ▶ 1 *head cook* (minimum age 21) with experience in the field at $2700 per season ▶ 2 *horse instructors* (minimum age 19) with Western riding and bareback riding experience at $2700 per season ▶ 1 *horse vaulting* *instructor* (minimum age 19) with some horse vaulting experience at $2700 per season ▶ 2 *kitchen persons* (minimum age 19) with some food service experience at $2700 per season ▶ 4 *lifeguards* (minimum age 19) with ALS certification or equivalent at $2700 per season ▶ 1 *mountain biking instructor* (minimum age 19) with good technique in mountain biking and bike maintenance skills required at $2700 per season ▶ 1 *photography instructor* (minimum age 19) with darkroom and photo composition experience required at $2700 per season ▶ 1 *riflery instructor* (minimum age 19) with riflery and hunter's safety experience at $2700 per season ▶ 1 *rock climbing instructor* (minimum age 19) with technical expertise and extensive climbing experience at $2700 per season ▶ 2 *swimming instructors* (minimum age 19) with WSI certification and lifeguard certification at $2700 per season. Applicants must submit formal organization application, letter of interest, resume, four personal references. An in-person interview is recommended, but a telephone interview is acceptable. International applicants accepted; must apply through a recognized agency.

Benefits and Preemployment Training Free housing, free meals, formal training, willing to provide letters of recommendation, on-the-job training, willing to complete paperwork for educational credit, and willing to act as a professional reference. Preemployment training is required and includes accident prevention and safety, interpersonal skills, leadership skills.

Contact Ross Jameson, Owner/Director, Jameson Ranch Camp, PO Box 459, Glennville, California 93226. Telephone: 661-536-8888. Fax: 661-536-8896. E-mail: thejamesons@jamesonranchcamp.com. World Wide Web: http://www.jamesonranchcamp.com. Contact by e-mail, fax, mail, phone, or through World Wide Web site. Application deadline: continuous.

LE CAMP FRAN&CCAIS EN CALIFORNIE

210 POST STREET, SUITE 502
SAN FRANCISCO, CALIFORNIA 94108

General Information Non-profit French language and culture summer camp for children 7–13 and teens 14–17. Established in 1998. Features: wooded setting; near Pacific Ocean; rustic environment.

Profile of Summer Employees Total number: 10; typical ages: 18–25. 20% men; 80% women; 100% college students; 80% non-U.S. citizens; 20% local applicants. Nonsmokers preferred.

Employment Information Openings are from July 1 to July 24. Jobs available: ▶ 3–5 *counselors* (minimum age 18) with French language skills. Applicants must submit a formal organization application, resume, letter of recommendation. A telephone interview is required. International applicants accepted.

Benefits and Preemployment Training Free housing, free meals, willing to provide letters of recommendation, on-the-job training, willing to complete paperwork for educational credit, willing to act as a professional reference, and travel reimbursement. Preemployment training is required and includes accident prevention and safety, first aid, CPR, interpersonal skills, leadership skills.

Contact Etienne Vallee, Camp Director, Le Camp Français en Californie. Telephone: 415-477-3667. Fax: 415-477-3669. E-mail: info@lecamp.org. World Wide Web: http://www.lecamp.org. Contact by e-mail, fax, mail, phone, or through World Wide Web site. Application deadline: continuous.

RAWHIDE RANCH

PO BOX 216
BONSALL, CALIFORNIA 92003

General Information Camp that teaches children how to ride horses and take care of farm animals. Established in 1964. 36-acre facility located 13 miles from Escondido. Features: old western town setting; vaulting arena; horseback riding arena; covered arena and rodeo arena; over 40 horses and ponies; teepees, covered wagons, and a fort dormitory.

Profile of Summer Employees Total number: 48; typical ages: 18–25. 20% men; 80% women;

80% college students; 15% non-U.S. citizens; 5% local applicants. Nonsmokers preferred.
Employment Information Openings are from June 9 to August 24. Jobs available: ▶ 10–12 *program staff* (minimum age 18) at $6.75 per hour ▶ 36 *summer camp counselors* (minimum age 18) at $1800 per season. Applicants must submit formal organization application, three personal references, 3 job references. An in-person interview is recommended, but a telephone interview is acceptable. International applicants accepted; must apply through a recognized agency.
Benefits and Preemployment Training Free housing, free meals, possible full-time employment, on-the-job training, and willing to complete paperwork for educational credit. Preemployment training is required and includes leadership skills, animal care skills.
Contact Paul Tate, Co-Director, Rawhide Ranch. Telephone: 760-758-0083. Fax: 760-758-0440. E-mail: paul@rawhideranch.com. World Wide Web: http://www.rawhideranch.com. Contact through World Wide Web site. Application deadline: continuous.

SANTA CATALINA SCHOOL SUMMER CAMP
1500 MARK THOMAS DRIVE
MONTEREY, CALIFORNIA 93940

General Information Residential and day camp for girls ages 8–14 with an emphasis on performing and fine arts and athletics. Established in 1953. 35-acre facility located 90 miles from San Jose. Features: 6 tennis courts; heated swimming pool; modern dormitories; library; weight room; computer labs.
Profile of Summer Employees Total number: 50; typical ages: 18–24. 100% women; 20% minorities; 100% college students. Nonsmokers required.
Employment Information Openings are from June 15 to July 30. Jobs available: ▶ 18 *counselors* (minimum age 18) with one year of college completed at $1350–$1550 per season. Applicants must submit a formal organization application, two letters of recommendation. A telephone interview is required.
Benefits and Preemployment Training Free housing, free meals, willing to provide letters of recommendation, and on-the-job training.
Contact Ms. Peggy Aoto, Director of Summer Programs, Santa Catalina School Summer Camp, 1500 Mark Thomas Drive, Monterey, California 93940. Telephone: 408-655-9386. Fax: 408-649-3056. E-mail: summercamp@santacatalina.org. World Wide Web: http://www.santacatalina.org. Contact by e-mail, mail, or phone. Application deadline: continuous.

SARATOGA SPRINGS PICNIC, CAMPGROUNDS, AND DAY CAMP
22801 BIG BASIN HIGHWAY
SARATOGA, CALIFORNIA 95070

General Information Full-service corporate picnic facility serving 50-2000 guests daily. Services include catering, beverages, an entertainment package, and a summer camp serving children ages 7-12. Established in 1972. 14-acre facility located 10 miles from San Jose. Features: wooded setting; 2 year-round streams; fabulous barbecued food; RV and tent campsites; 6 private picnic groves; general store/arcade.
Profile of Summer Employees Total number: 40–50; typical age: 14. 25% minorities; 60% high school students; 15% college students; 5% retirees; 95% local applicants.
Employment Information Openings are from May 1 to October 31. Jobs available: ▶ 10–15 *barbecue cooks* (minimum age 18) at $10–$15 per hour ▶ 1 *lifeguard supervisor* (minimum age 18) with supervisory experience; 2 years lifeguarding experience; certifications at $10–$13 per hour ▶ 4–8 *lifeguards* (minimum age 16) with lifeguard certification at $10–$13 per hour ▶ 5–10 *maintenance/parking attendants* (minimum age 14) at $7.25–$12 per hour ▶ 1 *recreation director* (minimum age 18) with ability to supervise, schedule, manage employees at $12–$16 per hour ▶ 15–20 *recreation leaders* (minimum age 14) at $6.75–$12 per hour ▶ 2–4 *recreation*

supervisors (minimum age 18) at $8–$12 per hour. Applicants must submit a formal organization application. An in-person interview is required. International applicants accepted; must obtain own visa.

Benefits and Preemployment Training Free meals, formal training, possible full-time employment, willing to provide letters of recommendation, and on-the-job training. Preemployment training is required and includes training is available only for certain positions.

Contact Mimi Giannini, Director of Human Resources, Saratoga Springs Picnic, Campgrounds, and Day Camp. Telephone: 408-867-3016. Fax: 408-867-0766. E-mail: mimi@saratoga-springs.com. World Wide Web: http://www.saratoga-springs.com. Contact by e-mail, fax, mail, or phone. Application deadline: continuous.

SHAFFER'S HIGH SIERRA CAMP

248 SAN MARIN DRIVE
NOVATO, CALIFORNIA 94945

General Information Non-competitive, largely team-based wilderness adventure program for boys and girls ages 9-16; activities include sailing, kayaking, rock climbing, backpacking, mountain biking, archery, volleyball, ropes course, drama, and arts and crafts. Established in 2000. 22-acre facility located 35 miles from Truckee, California. Features: tipis and cabins; setting in Tahoe National Forest; over 70 mountain lakes; on peaceful headwaters of North Yuba River; miles of hiking/biking trails.

Profile of Summer Employees Total number: 25; typical ages: 19–28. 50% men; 50% women; 5% minorities; 75% college students; 20% non-U.S. citizens; 80% local applicants. Nonsmokers required.

Employment Information Openings are from January 1 to May 15. Jobs available: ▶ 1–2 *archery specialists/counselors* (minimum age 19) with current first aid/CPR certification; relevant experience; 18 year-olds with 1 year of college are also eligible at $250–$300 per week ▶ 1–2 *arts/crafts specialists/counselors* (minimum age 19) with current first aid/CPR certification and arts/crafts experience; 18 year-olds with 1 year of college are also eligible at $250–$300 per week ▶ 1–2 *drama/theatre arts specialists/counselors* (minimum age 19) with current first aid and CPR certification; relevant experience; 18 year-olds with 1 year of college are also eligible at $250–$300 per week ▶ 1–2 *games specialists (volleyball, frisbee, golf, group games)/ counselors* (minimum age 19) with current first aid/CPR certification; relevant experience; 18 year-olds with 1 year of college are also eligible at $250–$300 per week ▶ 1–2 *lakefront specialists/counselors* (minimum age 19) with current CPR/first aid certification; open water lifeguard certification; sailing kayaking, windsurfing experience; 18 year-olds with 1 year of college are also eligible at $275–$300 per week ▶ 2–3 *mountain biking specialists/counselors* (minimum age 19) with current first aid and CPR certification and basic bike repair/maintenance skills; 18 year-olds with 1 year of college are also eligible at $250–$300 per week ▶ 1 *program director* (minimum age 23) with experience in the position or as an assistant director; current CPR and first aid certification required at $500–$700 per week ▶ 2–4 *rock climbing/ropes course specialists/counselors* (minimum age 19) with current first aid/CPR certification; relevant experience; 18 year-olds with 1 year of college are also eligible at $250–$300 per week ▶ 1–2 *waterfront specialists/counselors* (minimum age 19) with current first aid/CPR certification and lifeguard certification; 18 year-olds with 1 year of college are also eligible at $275–$300 per week. Applicants must submit formal organization application, three personal references. A telephone interview is required. International applicants accepted; must apply through a recognized agency.

Benefits and Preemployment Training Free housing, free meals, willing to provide letters of recommendation, on-the-job training, willing to complete paperwork for educational credit, willing to act as a professional reference, and opportunity to attend seminars/workshops. Preemployment training is required and includes accident prevention and safety, interpersonal skills, leadership skills.

Contact Lisa Shaffer, Director, Shaffer's High Sierra Camp. Telephone: 415-897-0316. Fax: 415-897-0316. E-mail: highsierracamp@hotmail.com. World Wide Web: http://www.highsierracamp.com. Contact by e-mail. Application deadline: continuous.

THE SOUTHWESTERN COMPANY, CALIFORNIA

See The Southwestern Company on page 302 for complete description.

STEVENSON SCHOOL SUMMER CAMP

3152 FOREST LAKE ROAD
PEBBLE BEACH, CALIFORNIA 93953

General Information Residential and day summer camp for children aged 10-15. Established in 1972. Located 5 miles from Monterey. Features: golf courses; ocean; pool; tennis courts; high school dormitories; close to Big Sur.

Profile of Summer Employees Total number: 40; typical ages: 18–35. 55% men; 45% women; 80% college students; 1% non-U.S. citizens; 3% local applicants. Nonsmokers preferred.

Employment Information Openings are from January 1 to March 1. Jobs available: ▶ 5–15 *camp counselors* must be high school graduate at $1700–$3000 per season. Applicants must submit a formal organization application, letter of interest, personal reference. A telephone interview is required. International applicants accepted; must obtain own visa, obtain own working papers.

Benefits and Preemployment Training Free housing and free meals.

Contact Ellen Meranze, Director of Summer Camp, Stevenson School Summer Camp, 3152 Forest Lake Road, Pebble Beach, California 93953. Fax: 831-625-5208. E-mail: summercamp@rlstevenson.org. World Wide Web: http://www.rlstevenson.org. Contact by e-mail. Application deadline: March 1.

STIVERS STAFFING SERVICES–CALIFORNIA

See Stivers Staffing Services–Illinois on page 110 for complete description.

STUDENT CONSERVATION ASSOCIATION (SCA), CALIFORNIA

See Student Conservation Association (SCA), New Hampshire on page 209 for complete description.

SUMMER DISCOVERY AT UCLA

UNIVERSITY OF CALIFORNIA, LOS ANGELES
LOS ANGELES, CALIFORNIA 90024

General Information Precollege enrichment program for high school students at University of California, Los Angeles. Established in 1986. Features: sport facilities; beaches; mountains; lakes; major cities nearby; college towns.

Profile of Summer Employees Total number: 50; typical ages: 21–35. 45% men; 55% women; 10% minorities; 60% college students. Nonsmokers required.

Employment Information Openings are from June 20 to August 25. Jobs available: ▶ 50 *resident counselors* (minimum age 21) with experience working with high school students/children at $200 per week. Applicants must submit a formal organization application, resume, three personal references. An in-person interview is required. International applicants accepted; must obtain own visa, obtain own working papers.

Benefits and Preemployment Training Free housing, free meals, possible full-time employment, on-the-job training, willing to complete paperwork for educational credit, willing to act as a professional reference, and travel reimbursement. Preemployment training is required and includes accident prevention and safety, CPR, leadership skills.

Contact Jason Walley, Admissions Director, Summer Discovery at UCLA, 1326 Old Northern Boulevard, Roslyn, New York 11576. Telephone: 516-621-3939. Fax: 516-625-3438. E-mail: staff@summerfun.com. World Wide Web: http://www.summerfun.com. Contact by e-mail, fax, phone, or through World Wide Web site. Application deadline: continuous.

THUNDERBIRD RANCH
9455 HIGHWAY 128
HEALDSBURG, CALIFORNIA 95448

General Information Private independent camp with traditional camp activities and a complete horse mastership program "Where the fun never sets". Established in 1962. 600-acre facility located 15 miles from Santa Rosa. Features: western theme; pool; Russian River; oak trees; ranch setting; covered wagons/railroad caboose.

Profile of Summer Employees Total number: 16; typical ages: 19–25. 50% men; 50% women; 5% high school students; 45% college students; 45% non-U.S. citizens; 5% local applicants. Nonsmokers required.

Employment Information Openings are from June 9 to August 12. Jobs available: ▶ 3 *Western riding instructors (equine)* (minimum age 18) with experience in riding at $2700 per season ▶ 10–12 *camp counselors* (minimum age 18) with first aid, CPR, lifeguarding and ability to assist in activities at $2000–$2700 per season. Applicants must submit formal organization application, resume, two personal references, two letters of recommendation. An in-person interview is recommended, but a telephone interview is acceptable. International applicants accepted; must apply through a recognized agency.

Benefits and Preemployment Training Free housing, free meals, on-the-job training, willing to complete paperwork for educational credit, and willing to act as a professional reference. Preemployment training is required and includes accident prevention and safety, interpersonal skills.

Contact Bruce Johnson, Owner/Director, Thunderbird Ranch. Telephone: 707-433-3729. Fax: 707-433-2960. E-mail: alexvalley@aol.com. Contact by e-mail, fax, mail, or phone. Application deadline: continuous.

UCLA BRUIN TENNIS CAMP
PO BOX 64335
LOS ANGELES, CALIFORNIA 90064

General Information Tennis camp for boys and girls ages 8–18 of all different ability levels. Established in 1994. 30-acre facility. Features: swimming pool; game room; movie room; track; basketball court; 12 lighted tennis courts.

Profile of Summer Employees Total number: 30; typical ages: 19–27. 60% men; 40% women; 40% minorities; 90% college students; 10% non-U.S. citizens; 80% local applicants. Nonsmokers preferred.

Employment Information Openings are from June 15 to September 1. Winter break positions also offered. Jobs available: ▶ 8–10 *tennis camp counselors* (minimum age 19) with CPR certification, tennis instruction experience, and good swimming skills; cannot be in high school due to NCAA rules at $300–$400 per week. Applicants must submit resume, three personal references, three letters of recommendation. An in-person interview is recommended, but a telephone interview is acceptable. International applicants accepted; must obtain own visa.

Benefits and Preemployment Training Free housing, free meals, willing to provide letters of recommendation, on-the-job training, and willing to act as a professional reference. Preemployment training is required and includes accident prevention and safety, first aid, interpersonal skills, leadership skills.

Contact Bill Martin, Director, UCLA Bruin Tennis Camp, PO Box 64335, Los Angeles, California 90064. Telephone: 310-475-5853. Fax: 310-475-5853. E-mail: bmartin@athletics.ucla.edu. World

Wide Web: http://www.uclabruins.com. Contact by e-mail, fax, mail, phone, or through World Wide Web site. Application deadline: June 15.

WALTON'S GRIZZLY LODGE SUMMER CAMP

PO BOX 519
PORTOLA, CALIFORNIA 96122

General Information Residential, traditional summer camp for children. Established in 1926. 50-acre facility located 45 miles from Reno. Features: private lake; ropes course; historic lodge; horseback riding; arts and crafts; water sports.

Profile of Summer Employees Total number: 50; typical ages: 18–25. 50% men; 50% women; 100% college students. Nonsmokers preferred.

Employment Information Openings are from January 2 to April 15. Jobs available: ▶ 12–20 *general group counselors* (minimum age 18) at $260 per week. Applicants must submit a formal organization application, three personal references. An in-person interview is recommended, but a telephone interview is acceptable.

Benefits and Preemployment Training Free housing, free meals, formal training, willing to provide letters of recommendation, on-the-job training, willing to complete paperwork for educational credit, willing to act as a professional reference, and travel reimbursement. Preemployment training is required and includes accident prevention and safety, interpersonal skills, leadership skills.

Contact Adam Stein, Director, Walton's Grizzly Lodge Summer Camp, 510 West Main Street, Grass Valley, California 95945. Telephone: 530-274-9577. Fax: 530-274-9677. E-mail: wgl4u@aol.com. World Wide Web: http://www.grizzlylodge.com. Contact by phone. Application deadline: April 15.

YES TO JOBS

PO BOX 3390
LOS ANGELES, CALIFORNIA 90078

General Information Organization providing paid internships for minority high school students in the entertainment industry for ten weeks. Established in 1987.

Profile of Summer Employees Total number: 150; typical ages: 16–18. 50% men; 50% women; 98% minorities; 100% high school students.

Employment Information Openings are from June 10 to August 31. Jobs available: ▶ 100–150 *YES interns* (minimum age 16) must be a minority high school student with interest in entertainment or media. Applicants must submit formal organization application, resume, academic transcripts, letter of recommendation, statement of interest. An in-person interview is recommended, but a telephone interview is acceptable.

Benefits and Preemployment Training Willing to provide letters of recommendation, on-the-job training, willing to act as a professional reference, and opportunity to attend seminars/workshops. Preemployment training is required and includes interpersonal skills, leadership skills.

Contact Program Manager, YES TO JOBS. Telephone: 310-358-4923. Fax: 310-358-4330. E-mail: yestojobs@aol.com. World Wide Web: http://www.yestojobs.org. Contact by e-mail, mail, or through World Wide Web site.

YMCA CAMP SURF

106 CARNATION AVENUE
IMPERIAL BEACH, CALIFORNIA 91932

General Information Residential oceanside camp serving groups and individuals for summer camp, outdoor education, teen leadership, youth retreats, mission projects to Mexico, and beach tent camping. Established in 1969. 40-acre facility located 2 miles from San Diego. Features:

beach camping; guarded ocean waterfront; salt marsh reserve; 13 wooden cabins; outdoor dining deck; nearby town pier.

Profile of Summer Employees Total number: 60; typical ages: 19–28. 25% minorities; 5% high school students; 70% college students; 1% retirees; 30% non-U.S. citizens; 20% local applicants. Nonsmokers required.

Employment Information Openings are from June 1 to September 1. Year-round positions also offered. Jobs available: ▶ 30–40 *camp counselors* (minimum age 18) with first aid and CPR certification; (lifeguard training helpful) at $180–$240 per week ▶ 5–6 *coordinators* (minimum age 21) with leadership experience, Class B license, and lifeguard training at $240–$300 per week ▶ 1 *health services coordinator* (minimum age 21) with first aid, CPR, BLS, and EMT certification at $3000–$3600 per season ▶ 8–12 *ocean lifeguards* (minimum age 18) with lifeguarding and Basic Life Support certification at $180–$240 per week ▶ 1 *photographer/technology support* (minimum age 21) with basic photography and Web design experience at $180–$240 per week. Applicants must submit formal organization application, letter of interest, resume, personal reference, three letters of recommendation. An in-person interview is recommended, but a telephone interview is acceptable. International applicants accepted; must apply through a recognized agency.

Benefits and Preemployment Training Free housing, free meals, willing to provide letters of recommendation, on-the-job training, willing to complete paperwork for educational credit, willing to act as a professional reference, and opportunity to attend seminars/workshops. Preemployment training is required and includes accident prevention and safety, first aid, CPR, interpersonal skills, leadership skills, lifeguard training.

Contact Zayanne Thompson, Senior Program Director, YMCA Camp Surf, 106 Carnation Avenue, Imperial Beach, California 91932. Telephone: 619-423-5850. Fax: 619-423-4141. E-mail: campsurf@ymca.org. World Wide Web: http://www.camp.ymca.org/. Contact by e-mail, fax, mail, phone, or through World Wide Web site. Application deadline: continuous.

YOSEMITE CONCESSION SERVICES CORPORATION

PO BOX 578
YOSEMITE NATIONAL PARK, CALIFORNIA 95389

General Information Main concessionaire for Yosemite National Park, providing all aspects of guest services. 100 miles from Fresno. Features: wooded setting; high sierra lakes; steep granite walls; waterfalls; meadows.

Profile of Summer Employees Total number: 1,800; typical ages: 18–25. 50% men; 50% women; 17% minorities; 1% high school students; 41% college students; 6% non-U.S. citizens; 52% local applicants.

Employment Information Openings are from March 1 to October 30. Year-round positions also offered. Jobs available: ▶ 20 *buspeople* (minimum age 18) with restaurant experience at $6.75 per hour ▶ 25 *cooks* (minimum age 18) with experience in the field at $9–$10 per hour ▶ 25 *custodians* (minimum age 18) at $6.75 per hour ▶ 150 *food service utility staff* (minimum age 18) at $6.75 per hour ▶ 25 *front desk personnel* (minimum age 18) with cash handling and computer experience at $7 ▶ 20 *hosts/hostesses* (minimum age 18) with restaurant experience at $7 per hour ▶ 50–75 *kitchen utility staff* (minimum age 18) at $6.75 per hour ▶ 14 *lifeguards* (minimum age 18) with CPR for Professional Rescuer, BFA, lifeguard certification, and Title 22 at $7.07 per hour ▶ 250 *roomkeepers* (minimum age 18) at $6.75 per hour ▶ 100 *sales clerks* (minimum age 18) with cash handling experience at $7 per hour ▶ 20 *waitresses/waiters* (minimum age 18) with restaurant experience at $6.75 per hour. Applicants must submit formal organization application. International applicants accepted; must obtain own visa, obtain own working papers, apply through a recognized agency.

Benefits and Preemployment Training Housing at a cost, meals at a cost, possible full-time employment, health insurance, on-the-job training, and opportunity to attend seminars/workshops. Preemployment training is required and includes accident prevention and safety, first aid, CPR, interpersonal skills, leadership skills, AHLA certification (American hotel and lodging association). **Contact** Debbie Brown, Recruiting Manager, Yosemite Concession Services Corporation. Telephone: 209-372-1133. Fax: 209-372-1050. E-mail: dbrown@dncinc.com. World Wide Web: http://www.yosemitepark.com. Contact by fax, mail, phone, or through World Wide Web site. Application deadline: continuous.

COLORADO

A CHRISTIAN MINISTRY IN THE NATIONAL PARKS–COLORADO

See A Christian Ministry in the National Parks–Maine on page 122 for complete description.

ANDERSON WESTERN COLORADO CAMPS, LTD.

7177 COLORADO RIVER ROAD
GYPSUM, COLORADO 81637

General Information Residential coed camp serving 125 campers per session. Children are given daily choices of noncompetitive activities. Wilderness pioneer camp for 14-17 year olds emphasizes out-of-camp trips. Established in 1962. 200-acre facility located 140 miles from Denver. Features: Colorado River; climbing wall; ropes course; cliffs for rappelling; creek; pond.
Profile of Summer Employees Total number: 40; typical ages: 19–22. 50% men; 50% women; 25% minorities; 3% high school students; 60% college students; 5% retirees; 15% non-U.S. citizens; 20% local applicants. Nonsmokers required.
Employment Information Openings are from May 12 to August 20. Year-round positions also offered. Jobs available: ▶ 20 *camp counselors* with two years of college preferred at $975–$1200 per season ▶ 2 *cooks* at $2500–$7000 per season ▶ 4 *lodge/grounds staff members* (minimum age 16) at $975–$1200 per season ▶ *nurse* with RN certification at $200–$400 per week ▶ 1 *rafting director* (minimum age 21) with rafting ability, organizational skills, and teaching skills ▶ 1 *riding instructor* (minimum age 21) at $1200–$1500 per season ▶ 3 *wranglers* with knowledge of horses at $975–$1200 per season. Applicants must submit a formal organization application, writing sample, three personal references. An in-person interview is recommended, but a telephone interview is acceptable. International applicants accepted; must obtain own visa, obtain own working papers.
Benefits and Preemployment Training Free housing, free meals, formal training, possible full-time employment, willing to provide letters of recommendation, names of contacts, on-the-job training, willing to complete paperwork for educational credit, willing to act as a professional reference, and travel reimbursement. Preemployment training is required and includes accident prevention and safety, first aid, CPR, interpersonal skills, leadership skills.
Contact Christopher Porter, Director, Anderson Western Colorado Camps, Ltd., 7177 Colorado River Road, Gypsum, Colorado 81637. Telephone: 970-524-7766. Fax: 970-524-7107. E-mail: andecamp@rof.net. World Wide Web: http://www.andersoncamps.com. Contact by e-mail, fax, mail, phone, or through World Wide Web site. Application deadline: continuous.

BAR NI RANCH

6614 HIGHWAY 12, STONEWALL GAP
WESTON, COLORADO 81091

General Information Private guest ranch with 15–35 guests per week; gentle, resistance-free horse training and riding; quarter horse breeding; ranch-style, health conscious, and gourmet meals; hiking, fishing, ninety percent repeat guests, conservation easement, and a fabulous staff. Established in 1946. 36,000-acre facility located 35 miles from Trinidad. Features: Sangre de Cristo Mountain range; 13,000 and 14,000-foot mountain peaks; 36,000 acres of forests, meadows, and alpine basins; environmentally protected setting; 7 streams and 5 ponds; abundant wildlife: elk, deer, wild turkey, bear, eagles.

Profile of Summer Employees Total number: 12–14; typical ages: 18–50. 50% men; 50% women; 10% minorities; 10% high school students; 30% college students; 40% local applicants. Nonsmokers preferred.

Employment Information Openings are from April 15 to November 15. Year-round positions also offered. Jobs available: ▶ 1 *baker* (minimum age 18) with some experience and a love for baking at $900 per month ▶ 1 *chef* (minimum age 18) with cooking school certification preferred at $1500 per month ▶ 2–4 *cook's helpers/waitstaff/child care/lawn care* (minimum age 18) at $900 per month ▶ 2 *housekeepers* (minimum age 18) at $900 per month ▶ 2 *mechanics/general ranch help* (minimum age 18) with large and small engine mechanical skills at $1000 per month ▶ 2 *wranglers/general ranch help* (minimum age 18) with CPR and first aid certification desirable and experience at $1000 per month. Applicants must submit a formal organization application, resume, 3 work references. A telephone interview is required.

Benefits and Preemployment Training Free housing, free meals, possible full-time employment, on-the-job training, and willing to complete paperwork for educational credit.

Contact Tom Perry, Ranch Manager, Bar NI Ranch, 6614 Highway 12, Weston, Colorado 81091. Fax: 719-868-2708. E-mail: barniranch@aol.com. Contact by fax or mail. Application deadline: continuous.

BLAZING ADVENTURES
BOX 5068, 48 UPPER VILLAGE MALL
SNOWMASS VILLAGE, COLORADO 81615

General Information Organization providing outdoor adventure tours. Established in 1969. Located 10 miles from Aspen. Features: mountains; rivers; national forest; summer resort.

Profile of Summer Employees Total number: 100; typical ages: 22–40. 55% men; 45% women; 15% college students; 80% local applicants.

Employment Information Openings are from May 1 to September 1. Jobs available: ▶ *adventure guides* (minimum age 21) at $9–$11 per hour ▶ 3 *group coordinators* (minimum age 20) at $9–$12 per hour ▶ 10 *office staff* (minimum age 20) at $9–$11 per hour ▶ 10 *sales and marketing coordination reservation interns* (minimum age 20) at $9–$11 per hour. Applicants must submit formal organization application, 3-4 letters of recommendations, 3-4 personal references. A telephone interview is required. International applicants accepted; must obtain own visa, obtain own working papers, apply through a recognized agency.

Benefits and Preemployment Training Formal training, possible full-time employment, willing to provide letters of recommendation, on-the-job training, willing to complete paperwork for educational credit, and willing to act as a professional reference. Preemployment training is required and includes first aid, CPR, interpersonal skills, leadership skills.

Contact Teresa Haller, Controller, Blazing Adventures, Box 5068, Snowmass Village, Colorado 81615. Telephone: 970-923-4544. Fax: 970-923-4994. E-mail: blazing@rof.net. World Wide Web: http://www.blazingadventures.com. Contact by e-mail, fax, mail, or phone. Application deadline: continuous.

CENTRAL CITY OPERA
621 17TH STREET, SUITE 1601
DENVER, COLORADO 80293

General Information Opera house that produces three mainstage productions per summer between late June and early August. Established in 1932. Features: Rocky Mountains.

Profile of Summer Employees Total number: 150; typical ages: 18–25. 50% men; 50% women;

20% minorities; 85% college students; 20% local applicants. Nonsmokers preferred.

Employment Information Openings are from May 29 to August 19. Jobs available: ▶ 1 *assistant house manager* (minimum age 22) at $200 per week ▶ 2–3 *costume shop assistants and dressers* (minimum age 22) at $200 per week ▶ 1 *festival coordinator* (minimum age 25) with supervisory experience at $415 per week ▶ 1 *gardener* (minimum age 18) at $200 per week ▶ 4 *gift shop assistants and gift shop manager* (minimum age 22) with previous experience in retail (manager) at $200 per week ▶ 1 *house manager* (minimum age 26) with supervisory experience at $400 per week ▶ 2–3 *music librarians* (minimum age 18) with ability to read music at $200 per week ▶ 2 *office assistants* (minimum age 18) at $200 per week ▶ 3 *production assistants (stage management)* (minimum age 22) with ability to read music at $200 per week ▶ 1 *properties intern* (minimum age 22) at $200 per week ▶ 1 *public relations assistant* (minimum age 22) at $200 per week ▶ 2–3 *van drivers* (minimum age 22) with ability to drive 15-passenger van on mountain roads and in city of Denver; clean driving record at $200 per week. Applicants must submit a formal organization application, letter of interest, resume, three personal references, three letters of recommendation, a writing sample (required for one position). An in-person interview is recommended, but a telephone interview is acceptable. International applicants accepted; must obtain own visa, obtain own working papers.

Benefits and Preemployment Training Free housing, willing to provide letters of recommendation, on-the-job training, willing to complete paperwork for educational credit, willing to act as a professional reference, and travel reimbursement.

Contact Karen T. Federing, Festival Manager, Central City Opera, 621 17th Street, Suite 1601, Denver, Colorado 80293. Telephone: 303-292-6500. Fax: 303-292-4958. E-mail: kfedering@centralcityopera.org. World Wide Web: http://www.centralcityopera.org. Contact by e-mail, fax, mail, or phone. Application deadline: April 1.

CHELEY COLORADO CAMPS
ESTES PARK, COLORADO 80517

General Information Residential camp serving 475 campers ages 9–17 for four-week sessions in a rigorous outdoor western adventure program. Established in 1921. 1,600-acre facility located 75 miles from Denver. Features: wooded setting; mountain streams; 14,000-foot peak; 5 western riding rings; historic log lodges; freshwater lake.

Profile of Summer Employees Total number: 210; typical ages: 19–70. 50% men; 50% women; 1% minorities; 90% college students; 15% retirees; 5% non-U.S. citizens; 20% local applicants. Nonsmokers required.

Employment Information Openings are from May 23 to August 29. Jobs available: ▶ 40 *cooks* (minimum age 19) with experience at $1600–$2200 per season ▶ 100 *counselors* (minimum age 19) with CPR/first aid certification at $1500–$1700 per season ▶ 10–12 *drivers* (minimum age 20) with clean driving record at $1500–$1800 per season ▶ 6 *nurses* (minimum age 24) with RN license at $2500 per season ▶ 4–6 *office staff members* (minimum age 19) with office experience at $1500–$1700 per season. Applicants must submit formal organization application, resume, three personal references, three letters of recommendation. A telephone interview is required. International applicants accepted; must apply through a recognized agency.

Benefits and Preemployment Training Free housing, free meals, formal training, health insurance, willing to provide letters of recommendation, on-the-job training, willing to complete paperwork for educational credit, willing to act as a professional reference, opportunity to attend seminars/workshops, and travel reimbursement. Preemployment training is required and includes accident prevention and safety, first aid, CPR, interpersonal skills, leadership skills, child behavior skills.

Contact Brooke Cheley, Staff Director, Cheley Colorado Camps, PO Box 6525, Denver, Colorado 80206. Telephone: 303-377-3616. Fax: 303-377-3605. E-mail: brooke@cheley.com. World Wide Web: http://www.cheley.com. Contact by e-mail, fax, mail, phone, or through World Wide Web site. Application deadline: continuous.

CHEROKEE PARK RANCH
436 CHEROKEE HILLS DRIVE
LIVERMORE, COLORADO 80536

General Information Summer guest ranch providing fun outdoor activities for the entire family and specializing in Western hospitality. Established in 1886. 300-acre facility located 180 miles from Denver. Features: heated swimming pool; hot tub; horseback riding; lake and river; Rocky Mountain location.

Profile of Summer Employees Total number: 22; typical ages: 20–24. 42% men; 58% women; 11% minorities; 90% college students; 12% local applicants. Nonsmokers preferred.

Employment Information Openings are from May 10 to September 30. Jobs available: ▶ 2 *children's counselors* (minimum age 19) with CPR/first aid and lifesaving certification; experience working with children preferred at $500 per month ▶ 1 *cook* (minimum age 19) with experience cooking for large groups preferred at $1000 per month ▶ 5 *housekeepers/waitresses/waiters* (minimum age 19) at $450 per month ▶ 1 *prep cook/dishwasher* (minimum age 19) with kitchen experience preferred at $425–$450 per month ▶ 1 *secretary* (minimum age 19) with office/clerical experience preferred at $500 per month ▶ 1 *wrangler* (minimum age 19) with CPR certification (preferred); experience with horses and tack and Western riding at $500 per month. Applicants must submit a formal organization application, three personal references, photograph. A telephone interview is required. International applicants accepted; must obtain own visa, obtain own working papers.

Benefits and Preemployment Training Free housing, free meals, willing to provide letters of recommendation, on-the-job training, willing to act as a professional reference, and gratuity pool. Preemployment training is required and includes first aid, CPR.

Contact Christine Prince, Owner, Cherokee Park Ranch, 436 Cherokee Hills Drive, Livermore, Colorado 80536. Telephone: 800-628-0949. Fax: 970-493-5802. E-mail: ccpranch@gateway.net. World Wide Web: http://www.ranchweb.com/cherokeepark. Contact by e-mail, mail, or phone. Application deadline: January 15.

THE COLORADO MOUNTAIN RANCH
10063 GOLD HILL ROAD
BOULDER, COLORADO 80302

General Information Day camp serving approximately 200 boys and girls ages 7-17 and enjoyed by other clientele as a mountain retreat. Established in 1947. 200-acre facility. Features: pine and aspen forests and wildflower meadows; snowy peak vistas; lodge and cabins; heated swimming pool; horse and foot trails; dirt basketball and volleyball.

Profile of Summer Employees Total number: 45; typical ages: 19–25. 40% men; 60% women; 10% minorities; 90% college students; 5% non-U.S. citizens. Nonsmokers preferred.

Employment Information Openings are from June 5 to August 15. Jobs available: ▶ 1 *Indian lore instructor* (minimum age 18) at $1550 per season ▶ 1 *administrative assistant* at $1700 per season ▶ 1 *archery instructor* (minimum age 18) with experience in the field at $1550 per season ▶ 1 *arts and crafts instructor* (minimum age 18) at $1550 per season ▶ 3 *bus drivers* (minimum age 18) with commercial driver's license; training and certification given at $1850 per season ▶ 10 *day-camp counselors* (minimum age 18) at $1550 per season ▶ 1 *drama/creative writing/newspaper instructor* (minimum age 18) at $1550 per season ▶ 2 *gymnastics instructors* (minimum age 18) at $1550 per season ▶ 1 *head cook/kitchen manager* (minimum age 21) with experience in menu planning, food ordering, and staff management at $3500 per season ▶ 2 *kitchen workers* (minimum age 18) at $1850 per season ▶ 2 *maintenance staff* (minimum age 18) at $1850 per season ▶ 1 *office staff* (minimum age 18) at $1700–$1850 per season ▶ 2 *outcamp/hiking/backpacking/outdoor living/nature instructors* (minimum age 21) at $1550 per season ▶ 1 *riflery instructor* (minimum age 18) with experience in the field at $1550 per season ▶ 1 *ropes course instructor* (minimum age 18) at $1550 per season ▶ 2 *swimming instructors* (minimum age 18) with one required to have WSI certification and both required to have LGT certification at $1600 per season ▶ 8 *wranglers* (minimum age 18) at $1700 per season. Applicants must submit a formal organization application, three personal references and/or letters of recommendation. A telephone interview is required. International applicants accepted; must obtain own visa, obtain own working papers.

Benefits and Preemployment Training Free housing, free meals, willing to provide letters of recommendation, on-the-job training, willing to complete paperwork for educational credit, willing to act as a professional reference, and opportunity to attend seminars/workshops. Preemployment training is required and includes accident prevention and safety, first aid, CPR, interpersonal skills, leadership skills.

Contact Lynn Walker, Director, The Colorado Mountain Ranch, 10063 Gold Hill Road, Boulder, Colorado 80302. Telephone: 800-267-9573. E-mail: office@coloradomountainranch.com. World Wide Web: http://www.coloradomountainranch.com. Contact by e-mail, mail, phone, or through World Wide Web site. Application deadline: May 1.

COLORADO TRAILS RANCH

12161 CR 240
DURANGO, COLORADO 81301

General Information Full service, family-oriented guest ranch offering cabin accommodations, meals, and a full activity program including horseback riding, fishing, marksmanship, sports and more. Established in 1960. 500-acre facility. Features: mountain location; heated pool; beautiful lodge; excellent children's program; excellent riding program; excellent fishing program.

Profile of Summer Employees Total number: 40; typical ages: 19–25. 40% men; 60% women; 95% college students; 5% non-U.S. citizens; 5% local applicants. Nonsmokers preferred.

Employment Information Openings are from May to October. Jobs available: ▶ 3–4 *counselors* (minimum age 18) with horse experience required; experience with children and teens preferred ▶ 4 *general staff (floaters)* (minimum age 18) with flexible attitude and willingness to help where needed ▶ 4 *housekeepers* (minimum age 18) ▶ 4 *kitchen staff* (minimum age 18) with kitchen experience preferred ▶ 3 *maintenance staff* (minimum age 18) with general maintenance experience preferred ▶ 7 *waitstaff* (minimum age 18) with serving experience preferred ▶ 7–8 *wranglers* (minimum age 18) with extensive horse experience. Applicants must submit formal organization application, three personal references, three letters of recommendation, optional riding video for wranglers and counselors. An in-person interview is recommended, but a telephone interview is acceptable. International applicants accepted; must obtain own visa, obtain own working papers, apply through a recognized agency.

Benefits and Preemployment Training Free housing, free meals, willing to provide letters of recommendation, on-the-job training, willing to complete paperwork for educational credit, willing to act as a professional reference, and opportunity to participate in ranch activities.

Contact Jane Giese, Assistant Manager, Colorado Trails Ranch, 12161 CR 240, Durango, Colorado 81301. Telephone: 970-247-5055. Fax: 970-385-7372. E-mail: cotranch@aol.com. World Wide Web: http://www.coloradotrails.com. Contact by e-mail, fax, mail, phone, or through World Wide Web site. Application deadline: continuous.

COLVIG SILVER CAMPS

9665 FLORIDA ROAD
DURANGO, COLORADO 81301

General Information Outdoor adventure camp located in natural surroundings; mix of traditional summer camp activities and wilderness adventure. Established in 1969. 600-acre facility located 250 miles from Albuquerque, New Mexico. Features: rustic setting; creek running through site; Ponderosa Forest; 3 ponds; National Forest access; proximity to high alpine and desert areas.

Profile of Summer Employees Total number: 45–55; typical ages: 18–25. 50% men; 50% women; 90% college students; 5% local applicants. Nonsmokers required.

Employment Information Openings are from June 2 to August 9. Jobs available: ▶ 1 *arts and* *crafts director* (minimum age 21) with first aid and CPR certification, supervisory experience and experience with all types of arts and crafts at $1200 per season ▶ 6–10 *assistant counselors/ trip leaders* (minimum age 18) with first aid and CPR certification; additional consideration for lifeguarding and wilderness first aid; should have experience with children and wilderness skills at $1000 per season ▶ 20 *head counselors/trip leaders* (minimum age 21) with first aid and CPR certification; additional consideration for lifeguarding and wilderness first aid; should have experience with children and wilderness skills at $1100 per season ▶ 1 *head wrangler* (minimum age 21) with first aid and CPR certification; experience with horses and Western riding instruction at $1900 per season ▶ 1 *nurse* (minimum age 21) with RN license, CPR certification, and pediatric/summer camp experience at $2500–$3000 per season. Applicants must submit a formal organization application, three personal references. A telephone interview is required.

Benefits and Preemployment Training Free housing, free meals, formal training, willing to provide letters of recommendation, on-the-job training, willing to complete paperwork for educational credit, willing to act as a professional reference, and laundry, workmen's compensation insurance. Preemployment training is required and includes accident prevention and safety, interpersonal skills, leadership skills, individual program area and wilderness training, wilderness first aid.

Contact Amie Podolsky, Program Director, Colvig Silver Camps, 9665 Florida Road, Durango, Colorado 81301. Telephone: 970-247-2564. Fax: 970-247-2547. E-mail: colvigsilvercamps@compuserve.com. World Wide Web: http://www.colvigsilvercamps.com. Contact by e-mail, fax, mail, phone, or through World Wide Web site. Application deadline: continuous.

CROSS BAR X YOUTH RANCH

2111 COUNTY ROAD 222
DURANGO, COLORADO 81303

General Information Christian camp for low income and inner city youth. Established in 1977. 149-acre facility. Features: lake; trails; obstacle course; basketball court; horseback riding.

Profile of Summer Employees Typical ages: 18–22. 50% men; 50% women; 90% college students. Nonsmokers required.

Employment Information Openings are from May 27 to August 11. Jobs available: ▶ *activities coordinator* with experience in backpacking, mountain biking, and leadership at $50–$100 per week ▶ 1 *cook* with ability to cook for 50 people ▶ 8 *counselors* (minimum age 18) with general understanding of the Bible and strong Christian commitment at $50–$160 per week. Applicants must submit a formal organization application, five personal references. International applicants accepted; must obtain own visa, obtain own working papers.

Benefits and Preemployment Training Free housing, free meals, formal training, on-the-job training, and willing to complete paperwork for educational credit. Preemployment training is required and includes accident prevention and safety, first aid, CPR, interpersonal skills, leadership skills.

Contact Nick Brothers, Director, Cross Bar X Youth Ranch, 2111 County Road 222, Durango, Colorado 81303. Telephone: 970-259-2716. Fax: 970-259-8006. E-mail: crossbar@frontier.net. World Wide Web: http://www.crossbarxcamp.org. Contact by e-mail, mail, phone, or through World Wide Web site. Application deadline: May 15.

CYBERCAMPS–UNIVERSITY OF DENVER

DENVER, COLORADO

See Cybercamps–University of Washington on page 335 for complete description.

DEER HILL EXPEDITIONS

PO BOX 180
MANCOS, COLORADO 81328

General Information Wilderness and service programming in the American Southwest, for coed groups ages 13-19; rafting, canoeing, backpacking, rock climbing, service with Native

Americans, and conservation service; Association for Experiential Education Accredited. Established in 1985. 160-acre facility located 30 miles from Durango. Features: outfitting store; back country pantry; staff cabins; kitchen and dining facilities; hot showers; pond.

Profile of Summer Employees Total number: 40; typical ages: 18–35. 50% men; 50% women; 5% minorities; 15% college students; 5% non-U.S. citizens; 15% local applicants. Nonsmokers preferred.

Employment Information Openings are from June to August. Jobs available: ▶ 5–10 *basecamp support staff* (minimum age 18) with a desire to work in a fast paced outdoor environment at $25 per day ▶ 30–40 *field leaders* (minimum age 21) with Wilderness First Responder and extensive experience leading youth in the wilderness for extended periods of time at $25–$85 per day ▶ 2–4 *interns (available year-round)* (minimum age 18) weekly stipend plus free room and board. Applicants must submit a formal organization application, letter of interest, resume. International applicants accepted; must obtain own visa, obtain own working papers.

Benefits and Preemployment Training Free housing, free meals, formal training, possible full-time employment, willing to provide letters of recommendation, on-the-job training, willing to complete paperwork for educational credit, and willing to act as a professional reference. Preemployment training is required and includes accident prevention and safety, interpersonal skills, leadership skills, rafting, backpacking, and rock climbing.

Contact Bradley Hoessle, Staff Manager, Deer Hill Expeditions. Telephone: 800-533-7221. Fax: 970-533-7221. E-mail: staff@deerhillexpeditions.com. World Wide Web: http://www.deerhillexpeditions.com. Contact by e-mail, fax, mail, phone, or through World Wide Web site. Application deadline: February 1.

DROWSY WATER RANCH

PO BOX 147 J
GRANBY, COLORADO 80446

General Information Mountain dude ranch serving 60 guests weekly. Established in 1977. 600-acre facility located 110 miles from Denver. Features: mountains; horses; entertainment; Colorado River.

Profile of Summer Employees Total number: 27; typical ages: 18–50. 48% men; 52% women; 15% high school students; 75% college students; 1% non-U.S. citizens; 5% local applicants. Nonsmokers required.

Employment Information Openings are from May 1 to September 30. Jobs available: ▶ 3 *assistant cooks* with experience in the field at $875 per month ▶ 2 *counselors* with first aid certification and experience in the field at $875 per month ▶ 2 *dishwashers* at $875 per month ▶ 1 *head chef* with experience in the field at $1700–$2000 per month ▶ 8 *horse wranglers/trail guides* with first aid certification and experience in the field at $1400 per month ▶ 6 *housekeeping staff members/wait persons* at $875 per month ▶ 3 *maintenance staff members* at $875 per month ▶ 1 *office person* with experience in the field at $875 per month. Applicants must submit formal organization application, letter of interest, resume, personal reference. A telephone interview is required. International applicants accepted; must obtain own visa, obtain own working papers, apply through a recognized agency.

Benefits and Preemployment Training Free housing, free meals, possible full-time employment, on-the-job training, and willing to complete paperwork for educational credit. Preemployment training is optional and includes accident prevention and safety, first aid, CPR, leadership skills.

Contact Randy Sue Fosha, Owner, Drowsy Water Ranch, PO Box 147 J, Granby, Colorado 80446. Telephone: 970-725-3456. Fax: 970-725-3611. E-mail: dwrken@aol.com. World Wide Web: http://www.drowsywater.com. Contact by e-mail, fax, mail, phone, or through World Wide Web site. Application deadline: continuous.

EAGLE LAKE CAMP–COLORADO
3820 NORTH 30TH STREET
COLORADO SPRINGS, COLORADO 80904

General Information 4 camps including wilderness adventure, horsemanship, mountain and road biking, resident experiences. Serves more than 2000 campers ages 8-18 each summer. Established in 1957. 330-acre facility. Features: located in Pikes National Forest; 10-acre freshwater lake; zipline; covered basketball courts; cabins and teepees; waterslide.

Profile of Summer Employees Total number: 125; typical ages: 19–28. 50% men; 50% women; 10% minorities; 90% college students; 10% local applicants. Nonsmokers required.

Employment Information Openings are from May 20 to August 15. Jobs available: ▶ 65 *counselors* with one year of college and CPR/SFA certification at $1000 per season ▶ 2 *emergency medical technicians* with EMT basic training at $1000 per season ▶ 1 *food service staff member* at $1000 per season ▶ 5 *maintenance staff members* with experience at $1000 per season ▶ 2 *office administration staff members* at $1000 per season ▶ 3 *registered nurses* at $1000–$1400 per season ▶ 1 *transportation director* (minimum age 21) with first aid/CPR certifications at $1000 per season ▶ 1 *videographer* with experience in the field at $1000 per season. Applicants must submit a formal organization application, two personal references. A telephone interview is required. International applicants accepted; must obtain own visa, obtain own working papers.

Benefits and Preemployment Training Free housing, free meals, health insurance, willing to provide letters of recommendation, on-the-job training, willing to complete paperwork for educational credit, and willing to act as a professional reference. Preemployment training is required and includes accident prevention and safety, interpersonal skills, leadership skills.

Contact Mark Heffentrager, On-Site Director, Eagle Lake Camp–Colorado, PO Box 6000, Colorado Springs, Colorado 80934. Telephone: 719-472-1260. Fax: 719-623-0148. E-mail: mark_heffentrager@navigators.org. World Wide Web: http://www.eaglelake.org. Contact through World Wide Web site. Application deadline: continuous.

ECHO CANYON RIVER EXPEDITIONS
45000 U.S. HIGHWAY 50 WEST
CAÑON CITY, COLORADO 81212

General Information Professional white-water river outfitter offering guided river trips ranging from mild to wild to more than 20,000 guests per year. Established in 1978. 4-acre facility located 8 miles from Canon City.

Profile of Summer Employees Total number: 75; typical age: 24. 60% men; 40% women; 10% minorities; 2% high school students; 65% college students; 4% retirees; 20% local applicants.

Employment Information Openings are from April to September. Jobs available: ▶ 10 *bus drivers* with CDL license for Colorado, pre-employment drug/alcohol test, and physical at $200–$400 per week ▶ 10 *customer service representatives* with guest service experience (preferred) at $200–$400 per week ▶ 15 *river guides* with standard first aid and CPR certification and river guide experience or completion of our training program (fee charged) at $200–$800 per week.

Benefits and Preemployment Training Preemployment training is required and includes accident prevention and safety, interpersonal skills, leadership skills.

Contact Andy Neinas, Echo Canyon River Expeditions. Telephone: 719-275-3154. E-mail: echocanyon@amigo.net. World Wide Web: http://www.raftecho.com. Contact by e-mail, mail, phone, or through World Wide Web site. Application deadline: applications by April 1 preferred.

ELK MOUNTAIN RANCH
13300 COUNTY ROAD 185B
BUENA VISTA, COLORADO 81211

General Information Guest ranch serving 35 guests. A true Western vacation experience offering weekly packages from June through the end of September. Established in 1981. 5-acre

facility located 90 miles from Colorado Springs. Features: highest elevation in Colorado (9,500 feet); family-oriented; very remote setting; horseback riding through unspoiled wilderness; white-water rafting; hot tub.
Profile of Summer Employees Total number: 14; typical ages: 19–27. 50% men; 50% women; 100% college students. Nonsmokers required.
Employment Information Openings are from May 15 to September 30. Jobs available: ▶ 1 *assistant cook* with service- and quality-oriented personality at $650 per month plus gratuities ▶ 1 *children's counselor* with experience, love of children 4-7, familiarity with horses, and first aid/CPR preferred at $575 per month plus gratuities ▶ 1 *cook* with high-quality service and love of great food at $800 per month plus gratuities ▶ 1 *general maintenance person* with knowledge of minor repairs, groundskeeping, and vehicle maintenance at $575 per month plus gratuities ▶ 5 *waitstaff/housekeeping personnel/dishwashers* with service- and quality-oriented personality at $575 per month plus gratuities ▶ 6 *wranglers* with experience riding and/or instructing horsemanship and basic knowledge of horses (care, feeding, and grooming) and good people skills; first aid/CPR preferred at $575 per month plus gratuities. Applicants must submit a formal organization application, three personal references. A telephone interview is required.
Benefits and Preemployment Training Free housing, free meals, willing to provide letters of recommendation, on-the-job training, willing to complete paperwork for educational credit, willing to act as a professional reference, and gratuities. Preemployment training is required and includes first aid, CPR.
Contact Sue Murphy, Co-Owner, Elk Mountain Ranch, PO Box 910, Buena Vista, Colorado 81211. Telephone: 800-432-8812. Fax: 719-539-4430. E-mail: info@elkmtn.com. World Wide Web: http://www.elkmtn.com. Contact by e-mail, mail, phone, or through World Wide Web site. Application deadline: May 1.

ESTES VALLEY RESORTS
6120 HIGHWAY 7
ESTES PARK, COLORADO 80517

General Information Resort, conference center, and ranch providing lodging, entertainment, and meals. Established in 1947. 85-acre facility located 80 miles from Denver.
Profile of Summer Employees Total number: 150. 50% men; 50% women.
Employment Information Openings are from May 15 to September 15. Year-round positions also offered. Jobs available: ▶ 5 *children's counselors* (minimum age 18) at $6.50 per hour ▶ 4–6 *front desk attendants* (minimum age 18) at $8 per hour ▶ 7 *livery staff/wranglers* (minimum age 18) with experience with horses at $6.50 per hour ▶ 5 *recreation staff* (minimum age 18) at $6.50 per hour ▶ *various positions* (minimum age 18) ▶ 15 *waitresses* (minimum age 18) at $3–$6 per hour. Applicants must submit a formal organization application. A telephone interview is required.
Benefits and Preemployment Training Housing at a cost, meals at a cost, formal training, possible full-time employment, on-the-job training, and willing to complete paperwork for educational credit.
Contact Deborah Vallia, Human Resources Officer, Estes Valley Resorts, 6120 Highway 7, Estes Park, Colorado 80517. Telephone: 970-577-3416. Fax: 970-577-3414. E-mail: humanres@aspenlodge.net. World Wide Web: http://www.estesvalleyresorts.com. Contact by e-mail, fax, mail, phone, or through World Wide Web site. Application deadline: continuous.

FLYING G RANCH
400 SOUTH BROADWAY
DENVER, COLORADO 80209

General Information Residential camp serving approximately 750 girls ages 9-17 throughout the summer. Established in 1946. 365-acre facility. Features: Rocky Mountain setting; surrounded by National Forest; rustic housing-tents; dry-cool climate.

Profile of Summer Employees Total number: 40; typical ages: 19–23. 1% men; 99% women; 15% minorities; 1% high school students; 90% college students; 1% retirees; 17% non-U.S. citizens; 50% local applicants. Nonsmokers preferred.

Employment Information Openings are from May 22 to August 8. Jobs available: ▶ 1 *administrative assistant* (minimum age 21) with skill in several program areas, business experience, and summer camp experience at $140–$170 per week ▶ 1 *arts and crafts specialist* (minimum age 18) with ability to teach craft activities to a variety of age levels at $140–$170 per week ▶ 1 *assistant camp director/program director* (minimum age 21) with first responder/EMT certification (can obtain after hire); successful administrative/supervisory experience (preferably in a camp); skill in several program specialties at $165–$250 per week ▶ 18 *assistant unit leaders* (minimum age 18) with experience working with children and/or camp experience at $140–$160 per week ▶ 2 *challenge course instructors* (minimum age 18) with training and employment in different levels of challenge courses and first aid and CPR certifications at $140–$170 per week ▶ 1 *health supervisor* (minimum age 21) with RN or LPN license; recent first aid training; school/camp work with children preferred at $300–$400 per week ▶ 8 *horseback riding counselors* (minimum age 18) with training in Western riding, at least 2 years riding experience, and first aid and CPR certifications at $150–$170 per week ▶ 1 *horseback riding director* (minimum age 21) with ability to teach, train, and supervise campers and staff in horsemanship; should have Western riding background and at least 5 years experience in horsemanship training, preferably with children; first aid and CPR certifications at $200–$275 per week ▶ 1 *nature specialist* (minimum age 18) with experience working with children in nature awareness and outdoor appreciation activities at $140–$170 per week ▶ 1 *outdoor skill specialist* (minimum age 18) with knowledge of hiking, backpacking, compass use, and cooking at $140–$170 per week ▶ 6 *unit leaders* (minimum age 21) with supervisory skills, experience working with children including camp counseling or leadership techniques, and first aid and CPR certifications at $160–$180 per week. Applicants must submit formal organization application, three personal references. An in-person interview is recommended, but a telephone interview is acceptable. International applicants accepted; must apply through a recognized agency.

Benefits and Preemployment Training Free housing, free meals, formal training, health insurance, willing to provide letters of recommendation, on-the-job training, willing to complete paperwork for educational credit, willing to act as a professional reference, opportunity to attend seminars/workshops, travel reimbursement, and health/accident insurance. Preemployment training is required and includes accident prevention and safety, first aid, CPR, interpersonal skills, leadership skills, legal issues relevant to dealing with children, behavior management, leave no trace principles.

Contact Rhonda Mickelson, Camp Administrator, Flying G Ranch, PO Box 9407, Denver, Colorado 80209-0407. Telephone: 303-778-8774 Ext. 281. Fax: 303-733-6345. E-mail: rhondam@gsmhc.org. Contact by e-mail, fax, mail, or phone. Application deadline: continuous.

FLYING G RANCH, TOMAHAWK RANCH–GIRL SCOUTS MILE HI COUNCIL

400 SOUTH BROADWAY, PO BOX 9407
DENVER, COLORADO 80209-0407

General Information Traditional overnight camp programs focusing on enhancing self-esteem, social relationships, outdoor skills, and leadership development.

Employment Information Openings are from June 1 to August 10. Jobs available: ▶ 2 *administrative assistants* (minimum age 21) with first aid certification, valid driver's license, business and administrative experience, skill in several program specialties, college degree or equivalent work experience at $150–$175 per week ▶ 2 *assistant camp directors/program directors* (minimum age 21) with first aid certification, administrative and supervisory experience, planning and implementing outdoor programs, skill in several program specialties, college degree or equivalent experience, valid driver's license at $175–$250 per week ▶ 36 *assistant* *counselors* (minimum age 18) with experience with children, first aid training, experience as camper or camp leader, at least one year of college or equivalent post-high school work experience at $145–$155 per week ▶ 2 *backpacking instructors* (minimum age 21) with experience teaching backpacking to children in camp setting, taking children on backpacking trips or equivalent, ability to carry backpack and walk long distances, first aid training, one year of college or equivalent wilderness first responder certification at $160–$180 per week ▶ 2 *business managers/assistant day camp directors* (minimum age 21) with administrative experience; valid driver's license, automobile, and auto insurance; first aid and CPR training; one year of college or equivalent at $260–$300 per week ▶ 2 *campcraft instructors* (minimum age 18) with experience teaching campcraft skills, ability to carry a backpack and walk long distances, first aid, one year or more college experience or equivalent at $145–$160 per week ▶ 2 *challenge course instructors* (minimum age 21) with first aid certification, experience working with children, one year or more college experience or equivalent, ability to teach children in informal resident camp setting, documented challenge course experience at $145–$180 per week ▶ 12 *counselors* (minimum age 21) with experience in camp counseling, team leader, first aid certification, 3 years or more college experience or equivalent post-high school work, organizational skills at $160–$180 per week ▶ 2 *craft instructors* (minimum age 18) with first aid certification, at least one year of college or equivalent work experience at $140–$180 per week ▶ 1 *dance/drama instructor* (minimum age 18) with first aid training, at least one year of college or equivalent work experience at $140–$170 per week ▶ 1 *farm instructor* (minimum age 18) with experience feeding and caring for farm animals, one year or more college experience or equivalent work experience, first aid training at $145–$160 per week ▶ 2 *handymen* (minimum age 18) with driver's license and acceptable driving record, strong communication skills at $180–$260 per week ▶ *health supervisor* (minimum age 21) must be registered RN or LPN, first aid training, experience working with children, valid driver's license at $375–$475 per week ▶ 7 *horseback riding counselors* (minimum age 18) with instructional western riding experience, organized camp experience, experience with horses, first aid training, one year or more college experience or equivalent work experience at $150–$170 per week ▶ 1 *horseback riding director* (minimum age 21) with western riding skills, ability to teach riding skills to kids, first aid and CPR training; salary based on experience at $185–$225 per week ▶ 2 *nature instructors* (minimum age 18) with experience working with children in outdoor activities, one year or more college experience or equivalent work experience, first aid skills at $140–$180 per week ▶ 2 *sports instructors* (minimum age 18) with first aid certification, one year or more college experience, certification or training in archery, teaching variety of sports to children at $145–$160 per week. Applicants must submit a formal organization application, three personal references. An in-person interview is recommended, but a telephone interview is acceptable.

Benefits and Preemployment Training Free housing, free meals, health insurance, on-the-job training, willing to complete paperwork for educational credit, opportunity to attend seminars/workshops, and accident insurance, time off, end-of-season bonus, travel allowance. Preemployment training is required and includes accident prevention and safety, interpersonal skills, leadership skills, discipline policies, camp procedures, emergency procedures.

Contact Rhonda Mickelson, Camp Administrator, Flying G Ranch, Tomahawk Ranch–Girl Scouts Mile Hi Council, PO Box 9407, Denver, Colorado 80209-0407. Telephone: 303-778-0109 Ext. 281. Fax: 303-733-6345. E-mail: rhondam@gsmhc.org. World Wide Web: http://www.girlscoutsmilehi.org. Contact by e-mail or phone. Application deadline: May 15.

GENEVA GLEN CAMP, INC.

PO BOX 248, 5793 SANTA CLARA ROAD
INDIAN HILLS, COLORADO 80454

General Information Private co-ed residence camp offering traditional program activities, rich tradition of THEME programming emphasizing American Heritage, Knighthood, and World Friendship. Established in 1922. 485-acre facility located 25 miles from Denver. Features:

heated pool; ropes course; climb wall; horses; perfect climate; social atmosphere.

Profile of Summer Employees Total number: 95; typical ages: 18–23. 50% men; 50% women; 10% minorities; 30% high school students; 45% college students; 25% local applicants. Nonsmokers required.

Employment Information Openings are from June 9 to August 10. Jobs available: ▶ 1 *assistant nurse* (minimum age 21) EMT or nursing student, some medical experience at $2500 per season ▶ 10–20 *counselors* (minimum age 19) with experience (helpful) and sincere desire to live with kids at $1250 per season ▶ 1–2 *registered nurses* (minimum age 21) with Colorado RN license or reciprocity at $3500 per season. Applicants must submit a formal organization application. A telephone interview is required.

Benefits and Preemployment Training Free housing, free meals, formal training, health insurance, willing to provide letters of recommendation, on-the-job training, willing to complete paperwork for educational credit, willing to act as a professional reference, opportunity to attend seminars/workshops, and travel reimbursement. Preemployment training is required and includes accident prevention and safety, first aid, CPR, interpersonal skills, leadership skills.

Contact Ken Atkinson, Director, Geneva Glen Camp, Inc. Telephone: 303-697-4621. E-mail: ggcamp@genevaglen.org. World Wide Web: http://www.genevaglen.org. Contact by e-mail, mail, or phone. Application deadline: April 15.

LONGACRE EXPEDITIONS, COLORADO

TAYLOR PARK, COLORADO

General Information Adventure travel program in Colorado for teenagers, emphasizing group living skills, physical challenges, and fun. Challenging programs place equal emphasis on physical accomplishment and emotional growth. Established in 1981. 60-acre facility located 20 miles from Crested Butte. Features: old lodge in Colorado.

Profile of Summer Employees Total number: 20; typical ages: 21–30. 50% men; 50% women; 10% minorities; 40% college students; 30% local applicants. Nonsmokers required.

Employment Information Openings are from June 15 to August 15. Jobs available: ▶ 8 *assistant trip leaders* (minimum age 21) with WFR and CPR certification, and good driving record at $252–$300 per week ▶ 1 *mountaineering instructor* (minimum age 21) with good driving record, WFR, and CPR at $300–$400 per week ▶ 1 *rock climbing instructor* (minimum age 21) with good driving record, WFR, and CPR at $300–$400 per week ▶ 3 *support and logistics staff members* (minimum age 21) with good driving record, CPR, and WFR at $180–$240 per week. Applicants must submit a formal organization application, letter of interest, resume, three personal references. An in-person interview is recommended, but a telephone interview is acceptable. International applicants accepted; must obtain own visa, obtain own working papers.

Benefits and Preemployment Training Free housing, free meals, willing to provide letters of recommendation, on-the-job training, willing to complete paperwork for educational credit, willing to act as a professional reference, and pro-deal purchase program. Preemployment training is required and includes accident prevention and safety, interpersonal skills, leadership skills.

Contact Meredith Schuler, Director, Longacre Expeditions, Colorado, 4030 Middle Ridge Road, Newport, Pennsylvania 17074-8110. Telephone: 717-567-6790. Fax: 717-567-3955. E-mail: merry@longacreexpeditions.com. World Wide Web: http://www.longacreexpeditions.com. Contact by e-mail, fax, mail, phone, or through World Wide Web site. Application deadline: continuous.

NORTH FORK GUEST RANCH

55395 HIGHWAY 285, PO BOX B
SHAWNEE, COLORADO 80475

General Information Small ranch offering a weekly family-oriented vacation. All-inclusive package (meals, activities, and lodging) with lots of personal attention and Western fun. Established in 1985. 520-acre facility located 50 miles from Denver. Features: horseback riding; fly fishing; swimming pool; fishing pond and river; mountain setting.

Profile of Summer Employees Total number: 22; typical ages: 19–29. 40% men; 60% women; 90% college students; 10% local applicants. Nonsmokers required.

Employment Information Openings are from April 1 to November 1. Jobs available: ▶ 3 *activity personnel/maintenance/drivers* (minimum age 19) with good driving record and people skills at $600–$700 per month ▶ 3 *cooks* (minimum age 19) must enjoy cooking; no formal training needed at $600–$700 per month ▶ 3 *kids' counselors* (minimum age 19) with WSI/ lifeguard certification; CPR and first aid training (preferred); genuine love for small children at $600–$700 per month ▶ 6 *waitresses/waiters and cabin staff members* (minimum age 19) with food service experience preferred, must have good people skills at $600–$700 per month ▶ 8 *wranglers* (minimum age 19) with CPR/first aid training, experience with horses, and good people skills at $600–$700 per month. Applicants must submit formal organization application, letter of recommendation. A telephone interview is required. International applicants accepted; must obtain own visa, obtain own working papers, apply through a recognized agency.

Benefits and Preemployment Training Free housing, free meals, possible full-time employment, willing to provide letters of recommendation, on-the-job training, willing to complete paperwork for educational credit, and willing to act as a professional reference.

Contact Karen May, Co-Owner/Manager, North Fork Guest Ranch, PO Box B, Shawnee, Colorado 80475. Telephone: 800-843-7895. Fax: 303-838-1549. E-mail: northforkranch@ worldnet.att.net. World Wide Web: http://www.northforkranch.com. Contact by e-mail, fax, mail, phone, or through World Wide Web site. Application deadline: continuous.

POULTER COLORADO CAMPS

STEAMBOAT SPRINGS, COLORADO 80477

General Information Residential camp and adventure programs serving 80 campers (ages 8–18) per session with group dynamics and outdoor education emphasis. There are frequent wilderness excursions. Established in 1966. 180-acre facility located 160 miles from Denver. Features: athletic fields; picturesque wooded setting; climbing wall; natural hot springs; cabins.

Profile of Summer Employees Total number: 30; typical ages: 19–34. 43% men; 57% women; 10% minorities; 15% high school students; 71% college students; 5% non-U.S. citizens. Nonsmokers required.

Employment Information Openings are from June 10 to August 20. Jobs available: ▶ 6 *assistant counselors* (minimum age 18) with first aid/CPR required; wilderness first aid preferred at $850–$1000 per season ▶ 3 *cooks* (minimum age 17) with first aid/CPR and experience cooking for large groups at $1000–$3000 per season ▶ 1 *nurse* (minimum age 21) with RN license, first aid, and CPR required (wilderness first aid preferred); camp experience or work with youth preferred at $2000–$3000 per season ▶ 12 *senior counselors/trip leaders* (minimum age 21) with wilderness first aid/CPR required; lifeguard training (preferred); and experience working with youth at $1300–$1400 per season ▶ 4–8 *wilderness instructors* (minimum age 21) with Wilderness First Responder/EMT and CPR; technical skills and teaching experience at $1600–$2000 per season ▶ 3 *wranglers* (minimum age 19) with first aid/CPR; strong horsemanship and teaching skills; and experience leading Western riding at $1000–$2000 per season. Applicants must submit formal organization application, three personal references, three letters of recommendation. An in-person interview is recommended, but a telephone interview is acceptable. International applicants accepted; must apply through a recognized agency.

Benefits and Preemployment Training Free housing, free meals, formal training, willing to provide letters of recommendation, on-the-job training, willing to complete paperwork for educational credit, and willing to act as a professional reference.

Contact Jay B. Poulter, Director, Poulter Colorado Camps, PO Box 772947-P, Steamboat Springs, Colorado 80477. Telephone: 970-879-4816. Fax: 800-860-3587. E-mail: poulter@poultercamps. com. World Wide Web: http://www.poultercamps.com. Contact by e-mail, mail, phone, or through

World Wide Web site. Application deadline: continuous.

ROCKY MOUNTAIN PARK COMPANY (THE TRAIL RIDGE STORE)

ROCKY MOUNTAIN NATIONAL PARK
ESTES PARK, COLORADO 80517

General Information Facility providing high-quality gifts and food service to national park visitors. 1-acre facility. Features: concession located within Rocky Mountain National Park; located on Trail Ridge Road at elevation of 12,000 feet; 350 miles of hiking trails; dormitory located close to town; flora and fauna; wildlife.

Profile of Summer Employees Total number: 75; typical ages: 19–22. 40% men; 60% women; 4% minorities; 75% college students; 25% retirees; 5% non-U.S. citizens; 2% local applicants.

Employment Information Openings are from May 21 to October 11. Jobs available: ▶ 2 *food supervisors* with experience in the field at $900–$1100 per month ▶ 20 *gift shop sales clerks* with outgoing and energetic personality at $800–$900 per month ▶ 5 *merchandising assistants* with three months of merchandising experience or six credit hours in color and design at $800–$1000 per month ▶ 4 *parking attendants* with outgoing and patient personality at $800–$900 per month ▶ 3 *sales supervisors* with experience in the field at $900–$1100 per month ▶ 21 *snack bar assistants* with outgoing and energetic personality at $800–$900 per month ▶ 7 *stockroom assistants* with ability to perform heavy lifting at $800–$900 per month. Applicants must submit formal organization application, two personal references. A telephone interview is required. International applicants accepted; must obtain own visa, obtain own working papers, apply through a recognized agency.

Benefits and Preemployment Training Housing at a cost, meals at a cost, willing to provide letters of recommendation, on-the-job training, willing to complete paperwork for educational credit, and willing to act as a professional reference.

Contact Walt Poole, General Manager, Rocky Mountain Park Company (The Trail Ridge Store), PO Box 2680, Estes Park, Colorado 80517. Telephone: 970-586-3097. Fax: 970-586-8590. E-mail: jobs@rockymountainpark.com. World Wide Web: http://www.foreverresorts.com. Contact by e-mail, fax, mail, phone, or through World Wide Web site. Application deadline: most applicants are hired by April 15.

ROCKY MOUNTAIN VILLAGE

2644 ALVARADO ROAD
EMPIRE, COLORADO 80438

General Information Nonprofit organization that provides camping services for children and adults with physical and/or mental disabilities. Established in 1951. Located 40 miles from Denver. Features: mountains; pond; stream.

Profile of Summer Employees Total number: 10; typical ages: 18–25. 45% men; 55% women; 5% minorities; 15% high school students; 75% college students; 10% non-U.S. citizens; 10% local applicants.

Employment Information Openings are from May 27 to August 13. Year-round positions also offered. Jobs available: ▶ 1 *activities director* (minimum age 18) at $2125 per season ▶ 1 *arts and crafts instructor* (minimum age 18) at $2125 per season ▶ 1 *assistant cook* (minimum age 19) at $2300–$2600 per season ▶ 1 *athletics specialist* (minimum age 18) at $2125 per season ▶ 14 *boys counselors* (minimum age 18) at $2125 per season ▶ 1 *computer specialist* (minimum age 18) with knowledge of MAC and IBM; assistive technology experience preferred at $2125 per season ▶ 14 *girls counselors* (minimum age 18) at $2125 per season ▶ 1 *horseback specialist* (minimum age 18) with therapeutic riding experience at $2125 per season ▶ 3 *kitchen helpers* (minimum age 16) at $175 per week ▶ 3 *maintenance helpers* (minimum age 16) at $175 per week ▶ 1 *photography specialist* (minimum age 18) at $2125 per season ▶ 2 *pool specialists* (minimum age 18) with WSI/advanced lifesaving certification at $2125 per season ▶ 1 *public* *relations specialist* (minimum age 18) with PR/journalism experience at $2125 per season ▶ 2 *registered nurses* (minimum age 21) at $700 per week ▶ 1 *trip specialist* (minimum age 21) with outdoor camping experience and first aid/CPR certification at $2125 per season. Applicants must submit formal organization application, three personal references, one writing sample (required for public relations specialist position). An in-person interview is recommended, but a telephone interview is acceptable. International applicants accepted; must apply through a recognized agency.

Benefits and Preemployment Training Free housing, free meals, formal training, willing to provide letters of recommendation, on-the-job training, and willing to complete paperwork for educational credit. Preemployment training is required and includes accident prevention and safety, first aid, CPR, interpersonal skills, leadership skills, providing personal care for people with disabilities.

Contact Ms. Melissa Huber, Assistant Director, Rocky Mountain Village, PO Box 115, Empire, Colorado 80438. Telephone: 303-569-2333. Fax: 303-569-3857. E-mail: huberm@cess.org. World Wide Web: http://www.eastersealsco.org. Contact by e-mail, fax, mail, phone, or through World Wide Web site. Application deadline: before May (preferred).

SANBORN WESTERN CAMPS

PO BOX 167
FLORISSANT, COLORADO 80816

General Information Boys and girls camps serving ages 8-16 in 2 five-week sessions. Established in 1948. 6,000-acre facility located 35 miles from Colorado Springs. Features: 2 riding stables; science interpretive center; 3 ponds; 17½-inch telescope; 2 heated and filtered pools; 4 tennis courts.

Profile of Summer Employees Total number: 120; typical ages: 20–25. 50% men; 50% women; 20% minorities; 100% college students; 5% non-U.S. citizens. Nonsmokers preferred.

Employment Information Openings are from June 1 to August 25. Jobs available: ▶ 8 *arts and crafts instructors* (minimum age 20) with experience in the field at $1500 per season ▶ 20 *backpacking instructors* (minimum age 20) with experience in the field at $1500 per season ▶ 8 *campcraft instructors* (minimum age 20) with experience in the field at $1500 per season ▶ 8 *canoeing instructors* (minimum age 20) with experience in the field at $1500 per season ▶ 4–6 *cooks* (minimum age 18) with experience in the field at $1800–$2000 per season ▶ 4 *drama instructors* (minimum age 20) with experience in the field at $1500 per season ▶ 10 *ecology instructors* (minimum age 20) with experience in the field at $1500 per season ▶ 60 *general counselors* (minimum age 20) with interest and experience in working with children at $1500 per season ▶ 4 *geology instructors* (minimum age 20) with experience in the field at $1500 per season ▶ 10 *mountaineering instructors* (minimum age 20) with experience in the field at $1500 per season ▶ 4 *nurses* (minimum age 22) with RN license and experience at $2500–$3000 per season ▶ 12 *riding instructors* (minimum age 20) with experience in the field at $1500 per season ▶ 8 *rock climbing instructors* (minimum age 20) with experience in the field at $1500 per season ▶ 8 *sports instructors* (minimum age 20) with experience in the field at $1500 per season ▶ 8 *swimming instructors* (minimum age 20) with lifeguard training and experience in the field at $1500 per season ▶ 8 *tennis instructors* (minimum age 20) with experience in the field at $1500 per season. Applicants must submit a formal organization application, letter of interest, resume, four letters of recommendation. An in-person interview is recommended, but a telephone interview is acceptable. International applicants accepted; must obtain own visa.

Benefits and Preemployment Training Free housing, free meals, formal training, willing to provide letters of recommendation, on-the-job training, and willing to complete paperwork for educational credit. Preemployment training is required and includes accident prevention and safety, first aid, CPR, interpersonal skills, leadership skills.

Contact Mike MacDonald, Director, Boys Camp, Sanborn Western Camps, 2000 Old Stage Road, PO Box 167, Florissant, Colorado 80816. Telephone: 719-748-3341. Fax: 719-748-3259.

E-mail: info@sanbornwesterncamps.com. World Wide Web: http://www.sanbornwesterncamps.com. Contact by e-mail, mail, or phone. Application deadline: continuous.

THE SOUTHWESTERN COMPANY, COLORADO

See The Southwestern Company on page 302 for complete description.

STIVERS STAFFING SERVICES–COLORADO

See Stivers Staffing Services–Illinois on page 110 for complete description.

STUDENT CONSERVATION ASSOCIATION (SCA), COLORADO

See Student Conservation Association (SCA), New Hampshire on page 209 for complete description.

TOMAHAWK RANCH

DENVER, COLORADO 80209

General Information Residential camp serving approximately 1,500 girls ages 6-17 throughout the summer. Established in 1953. 480-acre facility. Features: Rocky Mountain setting; surrounded by National Forest; cabins and tents.

Profile of Summer Employees Total number: 40; typical ages: 19–23. 1% men; 99% women; 15% minorities; 1% high school students; 90% college students; 1% retirees; 17% non-U.S. citizens; 50% local applicants.

Employment Information Openings are from June 1 to August 8. Jobs available: ▶ 1 *administrative assistant* (minimum age 21) with skill in several program areas, summer camp experience, and clean driving record at $150–$175 per week ▶ 1 *arts and crafts instructor* (minimum age 18) with ability to teach craft activities to a variety of age levels at $140–$160 per week ▶ 1 *assistant camp director/program director* (minimum age 21) with first responder/EMT certification (can obtain after hire); successful administrative/supervisory experience (preferably in a camp); skill in several program specialties at $200–$250 per week ▶ 18 *assistant unit leaders* (minimum age 18) with experience working with children and/or camp experience at $140–$150 per week ▶ 1 *dance and drama instructor* (minimum age 18) with ability to teach music, dance, puppetry, or theater to groups of children at $140–$160 per week ▶ 1 *farm instructor* (minimum age 18) with ability to care for small farm animals and teach programs at $140–$160 per week ▶ 1 *health supervisor* (minimum age 21) with RN or LPN license; recent first aid training; school/camp work with children preferred at $300–$400 per week ▶ 1 *nature instructor* (minimum age 18) with experience working with children in nature awareness and outdoor appreciation activities at $140–$160 per week ▶ 1 *outdoor skills instructor* (minimum age 18) with knowledge of hiking, backpacking, compass use, and cooking at $140–$160 per week ▶ 1 *sports/archery instructor* (minimum age 18) with certification in archery instruction or proven teaching experience with children and ability to teach games and non-competitive sports at $140–$160 per week ▶ 6 *unit leaders* (minimum age 21) with supervisory skills, experience working with children including camp counseling or leadership techniques, and first aid and CPR certifications at $160–$180 per week. Applicants must submit formal organization application, three personal references. An in-person interview is recommended, but a telephone interview is acceptable. International applicants accepted; must obtain own visa, apply through a recognized agency.

Benefits and Preemployment Training Free housing, free meals, health insurance, willing to provide letters of recommendation, on-the-job training, willing to complete paperwork for educational credit, willing to act as a professional reference, opportunity to attend seminars/workshops, and health/accident insurance, travel allowance. Preemployment training is required and includes accident prevention and safety, interpersonal skills, leadership skills, legal issues relevant to dealing with children.

Contact Angela Langhus, Camp Administrator, Tomahawk Ranch, PO Box 9407, Denver, Colorado 80209-0407. Telephone: 303-778-8774. Fax: 303-733-6345. E-mail: angelal@gsmhc.org. Contact by e-mail, fax, mail, or phone. Application deadline: continuous.

TUMBLING RIVER RANCH
PO BOX 30
GRANT, COLORADO 80448

General Information Guest ranch serving families. Established in 1940. 200-acre facility located 62 miles from Denver. Features: wilderness area; 9,200-12,000-foot mountains; remote area; rustic and very comfortable; family-oriented atmosphere; fly fishing.

Profile of Summer Employees Total number: 30; typical ages: 19–40. 50% men; 50% women; 75% college students. Nonsmokers preferred.

Employment Information Openings are from May 1 to October 1. Year-round positions also offered. Jobs available: ▶ 2 *assistant cooks* (minimum age 19) ▶ 1 *baker* (minimum age 19) with bed and breakfast experience ▶ 8–12 *cabin staff/waitstaff* (minimum age 19) with willingness to alternate jobs weekly ▶ 3 *children's counselors* (minimum age 19) with horseman skills and first aid certification ▶ 2 *cooks* (minimum age 19) commercial kitchen experience ▶ 1 *fly-fishing guide* (minimum age 19) must have guiding experience ▶ 3 *general maintenance personnel* (minimum age 19) ▶ 1 *secretary* (minimum age 19) ▶ 7 *wranglers* (minimum age 19) with horseman skills and first aid/CPR certification. Applicants must submit formal organization application, letter of interest, resume, writing sample, two personal references, 3-4 work references. International applicants accepted; must obtain own visa, obtain own working papers, apply through a recognized agency.

Benefits and Preemployment Training Free housing, free meals, formal training, possible full-time employment, willing to provide letters of recommendation, on-the-job training, willing to complete paperwork for educational credit, and willing to act as a professional reference.

Contact Mary Dale Gordon, Owner, Tumbling River Ranch, PO Box 30, Grant, Colorado 80448. Telephone: 800-654-8770. Fax: 303-838-5133. E-mail: info@tumblingriver.com. World Wide Web: http://www.tumblingriver.com. Contact by e-mail, fax, mail, phone, or through World Wide Web site. Application deadline: continuous.

VAIL RESORTS
PO BOX 7
VAIL, COLORADO 81658

General Information Owners and operators of Vail, Beaver Creek, Keystone, and Breckenridge ski resorts. near Denver. Features: Rocky Mountains of Colorado; rivers; golf courses; national forests.

Profile of Summer Employees Total number: 2,500; typical ages: 21–25. 60% men; 40% women.

Employment Information Jobs available: ▶ *adventure ridge attraction attendant* at $9 per hour ▶ *childcare staff members* at $8–$9 per hour ▶ *day camp attendants* at $8–$9 per hour ▶ *food service personnel* at $8–$9 per hour ▶ *golf course staff members* at $8–$9 per hour ▶ *grounds/maintenance persons* at $8–$9 per hour ▶ *hospitality positions* at $8–$9 per hour ▶ *lift-operations personnel* (minimum age 18) at $8–$9 per hour ▶ *outdoor mountain, indoor hotel, ticket sales, food and beverage* (minimum age 18) with guest service skills at $8–$9 per hour. Applicants must submit a formal organization application. An in-person interview is recommended, but a telephone interview is acceptable. International applicants accepted; must obtain own visa.

Benefits and Preemployment Training Housing at a cost, meals at a cost, formal training, possible full-time employment, health insurance, on-the-job training, willing to complete paperwork for educational credit, and ski pass in winter; free bike haul in summer. Preemployment training is required and includes accident prevention and safety, interpersonal skills, leadership skills.

Contact Sabrina Coufal, Recruiting Coordinator, Vail Resorts. Telephone: 970-845-2461. Fax: 970-845-2473. E-mail: vbcjobs@vailresorts.com. World Wide Web: http://www.snow.com. Contact by e-mail, fax, mail, phone, or through World Wide Web site. Application deadline: continuous.

VISTA VERDE RANCH

PO BOX 465
STEAMBOAT SPRINGS, COLORADO 80477

General Information Upscale dude ranch with a wide variety of activities and adventures in both summer and winter. Established in 1975. 500-acre facility located 150 miles from Denver. Features: secluded setting; surrounded by forest; adjacent to continental divide; elegantly furnished accommodations; on-property streams and ponds; wonderful vistas.

Profile of Summer Employees Total number: 35; typical ages: 20–25. 50% men; 50% women; 95% college students; 5% non-U.S. citizens. Nonsmokers preferred.

Employment Information Openings are from May 1 to October 31. Winter break positions also offered. Jobs available: ▶ 2–4 *fishing/hiking guides* with knowledge of fly-fishing and biology at $400 per month plus tips ▶ 2–4 *housekeepers/ranch hands* with at least 1 year of college at $400 per month plus tips ▶ 3–4 *kid's wranglers* one year of college, experience working with children, and horse experience at $400 per month plus tips ▶ 2–4 *waitstaff* with 1 year of college and previous serving experience at $400 per month plus tips ▶ 3–4 *wranglers* one year of college and extensive horse experience at $400 per month plus tips. Applicants must submit formal organization application, letter of interest, resume, five personal references, photo. A telephone interview is required. International applicants accepted; must obtain own visa, obtain own working papers, apply through a recognized agency.

Benefits and Preemployment Training Free housing, free meals, possible full-time employment, on-the-job training, willing to complete paperwork for educational credit, and willing to act as a professional reference. Preemployment training is required and includes accident prevention and safety, first aid, CPR, interpersonal skills, outdoor skills, guest relations.

Contact Mark Sortum, Staff Manager, Vista Verde Ranch, PO Box 465, Steamboat Springs, Colorado 80477. Telephone: 800-526-7433. Fax: 970-879-1413. E-mail: vvranch@cs.com. World Wide Web: http://www.vistaverde.com. Contact by e-mail, fax, mail, phone, or through World Wide Web site. Application deadline: January 1.

WINTER PARK RESORT

PO BOX 36
WINTER PARK, COLORADO 80482

General Information Mountain resort offering a variety of mountain bike and hiking trails, an alpine slide, an indoor and outdoor climbing wall, and an 18-hole mini golf course. Established in 1940. 3,000-acre facility located 67 miles from Denver. Features: mountain setting; mountain biking; hiking; music festivals; rodeos; outdoor activities.

Profile of Summer Employees Total number: 100; typical ages: 18–25. 60% men; 40% women; 50% college students; 10% non-U.S. citizens; 40% local applicants.

Employment Information Openings are from June 1 to September 5. Spring break, winter break, and year-round positions also offered. Jobs available: ▶ 35–40 *summer program attendants* (minimum age 18) with high school diploma or GED at $8.75 per hour. Applicants must submit formal organization application. An in-person interview is recommended, but a telephone interview is acceptable. International applicants accepted; must obtain own visa, obtain own working papers, apply through a recognized agency.

Benefits and Preemployment Training Housing at a cost, possible full-time employment, health insurance, and on-the-job training. Preemployment training is required and includes accident prevention and safety, first aid, CPR, interpersonal skills.

Contact Recruiting Office, Winter Park Resort, Box 36, Winter Park, Colorado 80482. Telephone: 970-726-1536. Fax: 303-892-5823. E-mail: wpjobs@mail.skiwinterpark.com. World Wide Web: http://www.skiwinterpark.com. Contact by e-mail, fax, mail, phone, or through World Wide Web site. Application deadline: interviews are usually conducted mid-April but applications are accepted through the summer.

YMCA OF THE ROCKIES–CAMP CHIEF OURAY
PO BOX 648
GRANBY, COLORADO 80446-0648

General Information Residential camp dedicated to helping children grow in spirit, mind, and body. Programs for teens include backpacking, leadership training, rafting, and mountain biking. Established in 1907. 5,150-acre facility located 80 miles from Denver. Features: challenge course; reservoir; wooded setting; frisbee golf course; biathlon range; teepee village.
Profile of Summer Employees Total number: 75; typical ages: 19–30. 50% men; 50% women; 1% minorities; 1% high school students; 98% college students; 1% retirees; 1% non-U.S. citizens. Nonsmokers required.
Employment Information Openings are from May 19 to August 21. Jobs available: ▶ 46 *cabin counselors* (minimum age 18) with CPR and first aid certification at $155–$165 per week ▶ 4 *dishwashers* (minimum age 16) with CPR and FA at $150 per week ▶ 2 *nurses* (minimum age 21) with RN at $400–$600 per week ▶ 5 *riding staff members* (minimum age 19) with CPR and FA; experience with horses and teens at $160–$200 per week ▶ 10 *support staff members* (minimum age 21) with CPR and FA at $155–$175 per week ▶ 15 *wilderness adventure staff* (minimum age 20) with CPR and FA; backpacking, rafting, mountain biking, and experience working with teens at $160–$200 per week. Applicants must submit formal organization application, three personal references. A telephone interview is required. International applicants accepted; must obtain own visa, obtain own working papers, apply through a recognized agency.
Benefits and Preemployment Training Free housing, free meals, health insurance, willing to provide letters of recommendation, on-the-job training, willing to complete paperwork for educational credit, and willing to act as a professional reference. Preemployment training is required and includes accident prevention and safety, first aid, CPR, interpersonal skills, leadership skills.
Contact Trueman Hoffmeister, Camp Director, YMCA of the Rockies–Camp Chief Ouray, PO Box 648, Granby, Colorado 80446-0648. Telephone: 970-887-2152 Ext. 4174. Fax: 303-449-6781. E-mail: chiefouray@aol.com. Contact by e-mail, fax, mail, or phone. Application deadline: continuous.

YMCA OF THE ROCKIES ESTES PARK CENTER
2515 TUNNEL ROAD
ESTES PARK, COLORADO 80511-2550

General Information Large Christian-oriented family resort and conference center offering a day camp and serving an average of 3,500 family and conference guests daily during the summer months. Established in 1907. 850-acre facility located 60 miles from Denver. Features: located next to Rocky Mountain National Park; property surrounded by majestic mountains; variety of recreational activities.
Profile of Summer Employees Total number: 500; typical ages: 18–82. 45% men; 55% women; 8% minorities; 5% high school students; 45% college students; 25% retirees; 17% non-U.S. citizens; 20% local applicants.
Employment Information Openings are from January 1 to December 31. Spring break positions also offered. Jobs available: ▶ 12 *craft shop instructors* (minimum age 18) with artistic talent and/or experience with arts and crafts at $155 per week ▶ 60 *day camp/adventure camp counselors* (minimum age 21) with first aid/CPR and training and/or practical experience in education/day camp work/childcare at $155 per week ▶ 8 *family programmers* (minimum age

18) who should enjoy working with families planning activities; first aid/CPR preferred at $155 per week ▶ 105 *food service workers* (minimum age 18) with ability to carry 40 pounds up to 20 feet at $155 per week ▶ 12 *front desk clerks* (minimum age 18) with computer and public relations skills at $155 per week ▶ 80 *housekeeping staff members* (minimum age 18) with ability to carry up to 30 pounds up/downstairs and to move furniture at $155 per week ▶ 11 *lifeguards* with lifeguard certification (Red Cross or YMCA), first aid, and CPR at $155 per week ▶ 12 *maintenance workers* (minimum age 18) with good driving record at $155 per week ▶ 2 *miniature golf and roller skating rink attendants* (minimum age 18) with ability to lift 60 pounds up to 4 feet at $155 per week ▶ 3 *resident assistants* (minimum age 21) with good driving record and at least one year experience as a college resident assistant at $205 per week. Applicants must submit formal organization application, telephone interview for day camp/ outdoor education/ rock climbing positions; 3 personal references (forms provided) or 3 letters of recommendation. International applicants accepted; must obtain own visa, obtain own working papers, apply through a recognized agency.

Benefits and Preemployment Training Free housing, free meals, possible full-time employment, on-the-job training, willing to complete paperwork for educational credit, and willing to act as a professional reference. Preemployment training is required and includes accident prevention and safety, interpersonal skills, leadership skills.

Contact JoAnne Wilkinson, Human Resources Assistant, YMCA of the Rockies Estes Park Center, 2515 Tunnel Road, Estes Park, Colorado 80511-2550. Telephone: 970-586-3341 Ext. 1013. Fax: 970-577-8322. E-mail: jwilkinson@ymcarockies.org. World Wide Web: http://www.ymcarockies.org. Contact by e-mail, fax, mail, phone, or through World Wide Web site. Application deadline: continuous.

YMCA OF THE ROCKIES, SNOW MOUNTAIN RANCH

PO BOX 169
WINTER PARK, COLORADO 80482

General Information A year-round YMCA conference center and family resort accommodating up to 2,100 guests per day. Owned by YMCA of the Rockies. Established in 1907. 5,150-acre facility located 90 miles from Denver. Features: located in beautiful Rocky Mountains; indoor swimming pool; tennis; trail system for hiking and mountain biking; basketball courts; climbing wall.

Profile of Summer Employees Total number: 225; typical ages: 19–22. 40% men; 60% women; 15% minorities; 1% high school students; 62% college students; 10% retirees; 25% non-U.S. citizens; 2% local applicants. Nonsmokers preferred.

Employment Information Openings are from May 26 to August 22. Spring break, winter break, and year-round positions also offered. Jobs available: ▶ 1 *chaplain's assistant* (minimum age 18) with valid driver's license at $155 per week ▶ 1–2 *conference associates* (minimum age 18) with office and/or guest relations experience preferred at $155 per week ▶ 7 *conference services staff members* (minimum age 18) with valid driver's license at $155 per week ▶ 7 *crafts shop instructors* (minimum age 18) at $155 per week ▶ 2 *family programs assistants* (minimum age 18) with first aid and CPR certification at $155 per week ▶ 47 *food service personnel* (minimum age 18) at $155 per week ▶ 10–12 *front desk attendants* (minimum age 18) at $155 per week ▶ 65 *housekeeping personnel* (minimum age 18) at $155 per week ▶ 1 *human resources associate* (minimum age 18) with valid driver's license; interest in human resources as a career preferred at $155 per week ▶ 4–5 *janitorial crew* (minimum age 18) at $155 per week ▶ 15 *lifeguards* (minimum age 18) with American Red Cross lifeguard, first aid, and CPR certification or equivalent at $165 per week ▶ 8 *maintenance personnel* (minimum age 18) with valid driver's license at $155 per week ▶ 2 *recreation attendants* (minimum age 18) with first aid and CPR certification at $155 per week ▶ 2 *retail sales personnel* (minimum age 18) at $155 per week ▶ 2 *staff activities coordinators* (minimum age 18) at $155 per week ▶ 11 *youth program and early childhood counselors* (minimum age 18) with CPR and first aid certification at $155

per week. Applicants must submit a formal organization application, three letters of recommendation. International applicants accepted; must obtain own visa, obtain own working papers.
Benefits and Preemployment Training Free housing, free meals, formal training, possible full-time employment, willing to provide letters of recommendation, on-the-job training, willing to complete paperwork for educational credit, and extensive seasonal staff activities. Preemployment training is required and includes accident prevention and safety, customer service.
Contact Jeni Fuqua, Human Resources Director, YMCA of the Rockies, Snow Mountain Ranch, PO Box 169, Winter Park, Colorado 80482. Telephone: 970-887-2152. Fax: 303-449-6781. E-mail: hbrodofsky@ymcarockies.org. World Wide Web: http://www.ymcarockies.org. Contact by e-mail, fax, mail, phone, or through World Wide Web site. Application deadline: continuous.

CONNECTICUT

AWOSTING AND CHINQUEKA CAMPS
BANTAM, CONNECTICUT 06750

General Information Residential camps serving 150 boys and 150 girls in programs of two to eight weeks. There are two separate campuses 4 miles apart that have daily coed programs as well as coed evening activities. Established in 1900. 200-acre facility located 10 miles from Torrington. Features: large 3½-mile long lake; cabins with facilities; wooded setting; 1,000-foot elevations with great weather; more than 100 watercraft; go-kart and minibike tracks.
Profile of Summer Employees Total number: 85; typical ages: 19–30. 50% men; 50% women; 10% minorities; 80% college students; 5% retirees; 30% non-U.S. citizens; 5% local applicants. Nonsmokers required.
Employment Information Openings are from June 17 to August 18. Jobs available: ▶ 2 *archery instructors* (minimum age 19) with NAA certification (clinic available) at $1350–$2200 per season ▶ 3 *arts and crafts instructors* (minimum age 19) with experience teaching or assisting instruction at $1350–$2200 per season ▶ 4 *black-and-white photography/video/filming instructors* (minimum age 19) with knowledge of equipment at $1350–$2200 per season ▶ 2 *ceramics/clay instructors* (minimum age 19) with pottery wheel and kiln firing knowledge at $1350–$2200 per season ▶ 4 *computers and journalism staff members* (minimum age 19) with ability to operate Apple and IBM computers and experience in the field at $1350–$2200 per season ▶ 3 *dance/theater/music instructors* (minimum age 19) with some stage and music background at $1350–$2200 per season ▶ 2 *fencing instructors* (minimum age 19) with some coaching background at $1350–$2200 per season ▶ 2 *go-cart/minibike/and quads personnel* (minimum age 20) with knowledge of equipment and racing at $1350–$2200 per season ▶ 2 *golf instructors* (minimum age 19) with experience at $1350–$2200 per season ▶ 3 *gymnastics instructors* (minimum age 19) with coach certification and experience in the field at $1350–$2200 per season ▶ 6 *kitchen aides* (minimum age 20) with food service experience at $1800–$2300 per season ▶ 2 *laundry workers* with some laundry experience at $1800–$2200 per season ▶ 2 *maintenance personnel* (minimum age 21) with background in painting, carpentry, grounds maintenance, electrical, and plumbing at $2200–$2800 per season ▶ 2 *mountain biking instructors* (minimum age 19) with off-road biking experience at $1350–$2200 per season ▶ 2 *nurses or first aid persons* (minimum age 21) with RN, LPN, EMT, or standard first aid and CPR certification at $2500–$4000 per season ▶ 2 *outdoor camping and hiking staff members* (minimum age 21) with first aid/CPR and experience in Outward Bound/scouting at $1350–$2200 per

season ▶ 2–4 *ropes instructors* (minimum age 20) with certification in ACCT, prior experience with rappelling and zipline (training and certification clinic is available) at $1350–$2200 per season ▶ 6 *small-craft instructors* (minimum age 19) with certification in one or more of the following: canoeing, sailing, kayaking, or boating (clinic available) at $1450–$2300 per season ▶ 6 *sports instructors* (minimum age 19) with background in one or more of the following: softball, soccer, tennis, or golf (varsity level or coaching) at $1350–$2200 per season ▶ 6 *swimming instructors* (minimum age 19) with WSI, LGT, or LGTI certification (clinic available) at $1450–$2300 per season ▶ 3 *waterskiing instructors* (minimum age 19) with LGT and CPR certification, teaching experience, and Coast Guard boating license at $1350–$2200 per season ▶ 2 *woodworking instructors* (minimum age 20) with teaching or assisting woodworking experience; background in woodworking as a hobby; and ability with wood, tools, and machines at $1350–$2200 per season. Applicants must submit formal organization application, personal reference, two letters of recommendation, copies of any certifications. An in-person interview is recommended, but a telephone interview is acceptable. International applicants accepted; must apply through a recognized agency.

Benefits and Preemployment Training Free housing, free meals, willing to provide letters of recommendation, on-the-job training, willing to complete paperwork for educational credit, opportunity to attend seminars/workshops, and travel reimbursement. Preemployment training is required and includes accident prevention and safety, first aid, CPR, interpersonal skills, leadership skills.

Contact Oscar Ebner, Director, Awosting and Chinqueka Camps, 4 Breezy Hill, Harwinton, Connecticut 06791. Telephone: 860-485-9566. Fax: 860-485-1681. E-mail: info@awosting.com. World Wide Web: http://www.awosting.com. Contact by e-mail, fax, mail, phone, or through World Wide Web site. Application deadline: continuous.

BUCK'S ROCK PERFORMING AND CREATIVE ARTS CAMP

59 BUCK'S ROCK ROAD
NEW MILFORD, CONNECTICUT 06776

General Information Creative arts camp primarily devoted to the development of talents and the potential of boys and girls ages 11–16. Established in 1943. 165-acre facility located 75 miles from New York, New York. Features: wooded setting; Olympic-size pool; more than 30 art studios of the highest standard; glass blowing facility; 75 miles from New York City; 5 performance sites.

Profile of Summer Employees Total number: 230; typical ages: 21–39. 50% men; 50% women; 10% minorities; 66% college students; 20% non-U.S. citizens; 5% local applicants. Nonsmokers preferred.

Employment Information Openings are from June 20 to August 20. Jobs available: ▶ 2–3 *batik instructors* (minimum age 21) at $1500–$1800 per season ▶ 4–6 *dining room staff members* (minimum age 18) at $1500–$1800 per season ▶ 2–4 *farming instructors* (minimum age 21) at $1500–$1800 per season ▶ 16–26 *guidance counselors* (minimum age 21) at $1500–$1800 per season ▶ 8–15 *kitchen staff members* (minimum age 19) at $1500–$1800 per season ▶ 6–10 *maintenance staff members* (minimum age 19) at $1500–$1800 per season ▶ 8–16 *music instructors* (minimum age 21) at $1500–$1800 per season ▶ 2–4 *office assistants* (minimum age 21) at $1500–$1800 per season ▶ 2–3 *registered nurses* (minimum age 25) with RN or LPN license at $1500–$2500 per season ▶ 2–4 *sculpture instructors* (minimum age 21) at $1500–$1800 per season ▶ 4–8 *sewing instructors* (minimum age 21) at $1500–$1800 per season ▶ 4–8 *silversmithing instructors* (minimum age 21) at $1500–$1800 per season ▶ 1–2 *sports instructors* (minimum age 21) at $1500–$1800 per season ▶ 4–7 *stage design and construction personnel* (minimum age 21) at $1500–$1700 per season ▶ 2–4 *videotaping instructors* (minimum age 21) at $1500–$1800 per season ▶ 2–4 *waterfront staff members* (minimum age 21) with WSI and ARC certifications at $1500–$1850 per season ▶ 3–5 *weaving instructors* (minimum age 21) at $1500–$1800 per season ▶ 5–9 *woodworking instructors* (minimum age 21) at $1500–$1800 per season. Applicants must submit formal organization application, resume, portfolio, three personal references, slides of art work in SASE. An in-person interview is recommended, but a telephone interview is acceptable. International applicants accepted; must apply through a recognized agency.

Benefits and Preemployment Training Free housing, free meals, formal training, health insurance, willing to provide letters of recommendation, on-the-job training, willing to act as a professional reference, and laundry service. Preemployment training is required and includes first aid, general orientation to the program.

Contact Ms. Laura Morris, Director, Buck's Rock Performing and Creative Arts Camp. Telephone: 860-354-5030. Fax: 860-354-1355. E-mail: bucksrock@mindspring.com. World Wide Web: http://www.bucksrockcamp.com. Contact by e-mail, fax, mail, phone, or through World Wide Web site. Application deadline: continuous.

CAMP JEWELL YMCA

PROCK HILL ROAD
COLEBROOK, CONNECTICUT 06021

General Information Full-featured coeducational residential camp with teen adventure trips, year-round environmental education, and team building. Established in 1901. 540-acre facility located 35 miles from Hartford. Features: located in the Berkshire Mountains; 55 acre private lake; unique and innovated; indoor bouldering room; giant slide; rope swing.

Profile of Summer Employees Total number: 155; typical ages: 16–65. 50% men; 50% women; 10% minorities; 5% high school students; 85% college students; 1% retirees; 10% non-U.S. citizens; 25% local applicants. Nonsmokers required.

Employment Information Openings are from June 14 to August 17. Year-round positions also offered. Jobs available: ▶ 4 *aquatic program specialists* at $1600–$2300 per season ▶ 30 *cabin counselors* with one year of college completed at $1775–$1850 per season ▶ 3 *crafts program specialists* at $1600–$2500 per season ▶ 1 *drama program specialist* at $1600–$2200 per season ▶ 1 *leader-in-training director* at $2400–$2600 per season ▶ 4 *leader-in-training staff* at $2000–$2150 per season ▶ 2 *naturalists* at $1600–$2500 per season ▶ 2 *ropes course directors* with experience in the field at $1750–$2500 per season ▶ 2 *sailing program specialists* at $1600–$2300 per season ▶ 15 *teen trip leaders* at $1700–$2400 per season ▶ 2 *tennis program specialists* at $1600–$2200 per season ▶ 6 *village directors* with experience in the field at $1800–$2500 per season ▶ 1 *waterfront director* with lifeguard/WSI certification and experience in the field at $1700–$3500 per season. Applicants must submit formal organization application, three personal references, drug screening (provided by camp). An in-person interview is recommended, but a telephone interview is acceptable. International applicants accepted; must apply through a recognized agency.

Benefits and Preemployment Training Free housing, free meals, and health insurance.

Contact Paul Kamin, Camp Director, Camp Jewell YMCA, Prock Hill Road, Colebrook, Connecticut 06021. Telephone: 860-379-2782. Fax: 860-379-8715. E-mail: paul.kamin@ghymca.org. World Wide Web: http://www.ghymca.org. Contact by e-mail, fax, mail, phone, or through World Wide Web site. Application deadline: continuous.

CAMP SLOANE YMCA, INC.

124 INDIAN MOUNTAIN ROAD, PO BOX 1950
LAKEVILLE, CONNECTICUT 06039-1950

General Information Not-for-profit, independent YMCA camp in northwest Connecticut Berkshire Mountains. Established in 1928. 250-acre facility located 130 miles from New York,

New York. Features: lake; pool; high/low ropes; climbing wall; indoor/outdoor stage at Performing Arts Building; tent living.
Profile of Summer Employees Total number: 155; typical ages: 17–25. 45% men; 55% women; 20% minorities; 10% high school students; 85% college students; 30% non-U.S. citizens; 5% local applicants. Nonsmokers preferred.
Employment Information Openings are from June 14 to August 17. Year-round positions also offered. Jobs available: ▶ 80 *counselors* (minimum age 18) at $1100–$1400 per season ▶ 35 *supervisors* (minimum age 21) with certifications as needed at $1800–$2000 per season. Applicants must submit formal organization application, writing sample, two personal references. A telephone interview is required. International applicants accepted; must apply through a recognized agency.
Benefits and Preemployment Training Free housing, free meals, willing to provide letters of recommendation, willing to complete paperwork for educational credit, and willing to act as a professional reference. Preemployment training is required and includes accident prevention and safety, CPR, interpersonal skills, leadership skills.
Contact Kathleen H. Woods, Director of Camping Services, Camp Sloane YMCA, Inc., PO Box 1950, Lakeville, Connecticut 06039. Telephone: 860-435-2557. Fax: 860-435-2599. E-mail: staff@camp-sloane.org. World Wide Web: http://www.camp-sloane.org. Contact by e-mail, fax, mail, or phone. Application deadline: continuous.

CAMP WASHINGTON
190 KENYON ROAD
LAKESIDE, CONNECTICUT 06758

General Information Episcopal, coeducational summer resident and day camp serving a diverse population of campers from Connecticut. Traditional and specialty programs available: tripping program with backpacking, canoeing/kayaking, mountain biking; theater week; choir camp; inner-city day camp; family camps. Established in 1917. 300-acre facility located 25 miles from Waterbury. Features: private pond for swimming; 300 private woodland acres; Adirondack shelter on property for primitive camp set up; 8 dormitory-style cabins (heated with indoor plumbing); easy train access to New York City; located in foothills of Berkshire Mountains in historic Litchfield County.
Profile of Summer Employees Total number: 50–60; typical ages: 18–28. 50% men; 50% women; 15% minorities; 20% high school students; 80% college students; 10% non-U.S. citizens; 90% local applicants. Nonsmokers required.
Employment Information Openings are from June to August. Jobs available: ▶ 1 *counselor-in-training coordinator* (minimum age 21) with experience facilitating young people (ages 16-17) in leadership positions, prior camp work or school equivalent at $1500–$2000 per season ▶ 16–18 *general counselors* (minimum age 18) with experience working with children at $1300–$1500 per season ▶ 2 *head counselors* (minimum age 21) with ability to work with staff, campers, and community in a conflict and behavior management position; ability to conduct staff meetings at $1500–$2000 per season ▶ 1 *nurse* (minimum age 21) with RN or LPN license (valid in Connecticut) at $3000 per season ▶ 5–6 *program coordinators* (minimum age 19) with ability to teach a specific activity, facilitate program area, supervise staff, program inventory and order, and evaluate program at $1500–$1800 per season ▶ 7 *waterfront staff* (minimum age 18) with WSI certification and lifeguard training at $2000–$2500 per season ▶ 6–7 *wilderness trip staff* (minimum age 21) with ability to lead 10-14 day primitive camping trips in the areas of backpacking, canoeing, kayaking, and mountain biking, good communication skills are a must at $1800–$2000 per season. Applicants must submit formal organization application, three personal references, criminal record background check. An in-person interview is recommended, but a telephone interview is acceptable. International applicants accepted; must apply through a recognized agency.
Benefits and Preemployment Training Free housing, free meals, formal training, possible full-time employment, willing to provide letters of recommendation, on-the-job training, willing

to complete paperwork for educational credit, willing to act as a professional reference, and opportunity to attend seminars/workshops.

Contact LéAnn Cassidy, Camp Director, Camp Washington, 190 Kenyon Road, Lakeside, Connecticut 06758. Telephone: 860-567-9623. Fax: 860-567-3037. E-mail: leanncassidy@mailcity.com. World Wide Web: http://www.campwashington.org. Contact by e-mail, fax, mail, or phone. Application deadline: continuous.

CHANNEL 3 KIDS CAMP

73 TIMES FARM ROAD
ANDOVER, CONNECTICUT 06232

General Information Camp for underprivileged children. Established in 1910. 365-acre facility located 18 miles from Hartford. Features: woods; cabins; river; swimming pools; trails; campsites.

Profile of Summer Employees Total number: 50; typical ages: 18–30. 50% men; 50% women; 35% minorities; 75% college students; 15% non-U.S. citizens; 60% local applicants.

Employment Information Openings are from June 15 to August 18. Jobs available: ▶ 1 *archery instructor* with archery safety course certification at $2000–$2800 per season ▶ 2 *athletics instructors* (minimum age 18) good with children at $1700–$2500 per season ▶ 8 *counselors* with two years of organizational camp experience and college junior or senior status at $1500–$2000 per season ▶ 1 *creative crafts instructor* (minimum age 18) with child-handicraft experience and college junior or senior status at $2000–$2800 per season ▶ 1 *environmental education instructor* (minimum age 18) with interest and experience in nature, and college junior or senior status at $1700–$2500 per season ▶ 1 *health care director* with American Red Cross first aid, BLS, and CPR certification at $2800–$3300 per season ▶ 1 *swimming director* with lifeguard training and WSI, American Red Cross BLS, and CPR certification at $2700–$2900 per season ▶ 2 *swimming instructors* (minimum age 18) with LG/CPR; WSI and American Red Cross ALS certification (preferred) *at $2000–$2500 per season. Applicants must submit formal organization application, three personal references. An in-person interview is recommended, but a telephone interview is acceptable. International applicants accepted; must obtain own visa, apply through a recognized agency.*

Benefits and Preemployment Training Free housing, free meals, health insurance, willing to provide letters of recommendation, on-the-job training, and willing to complete paperwork for educational credit. Preemployment training is required and includes accident prevention and safety, first aid, CPR, interpersonal skills, leadership skills.

Contact David Meizels, Director, Channel 3 Kids Camp, 73 Times Farm Road, Andover, Connecticut 06232. Telephone: 860-742-2267. Fax: 860-742-3298. E-mail: ch3cc@aol.com. World Wide Web: http://www.channel3kidscamp.org. Contact by e-mail, fax, mail, phone, or through World Wide Web site. Application deadline: continuous.

CHOATE ROSEMARY HALL

333 CHRISTIAN STREET
WALLINGFORD, CONNECTICUT 06492

General Information Secondary school with summer enrichment programs. Established in 1916. 400-acre facility located 15 miles from Hartford. Features: small college-like campus; air-conditioned classrooms; air-conditioned dining hall; 24 tennis courts and pool; close to major cities and attractions; 56,000-volume library.

Profile of Summer Employees Total number: 100. 50% men; 50% women; 100% college students. Nonsmokers preferred.

Employment Information Openings are from June 27 to August 1. Jobs available: ▶ 25–30 *teaching interns* at $2,300 to $2,400 per 5-week session. Applicants must submit two letters of recommendation. International applicants accepted.

Benefits and Preemployment Training Free housing, free meals, willing to provide letters of

recommendation, and on-the-job training. Preemployment training is required.
Contact Jim Irzyk, Director of Summer Program, Choate Rosemary Hall, 333 Christian Street, Wallingford, Connecticut 06492. Telephone: 203-697-2365. Fax: 203-697-2519. E-mail: jirzyk@choate.edu. World Wide Web: http://www.choate.edu/summer. Contact by e-mail or through World Wide Web site. Application deadline: February 31.

CYBERCAMPS–UNIVERSITY OF HARTFORD

HARTFORD, CONNECTICUT

See Cybercamps–University of Washington on page 335 for complete description.

SJ RANCH, INC.

130 SANDY BEACH ROAD
ELLINGTON, CONNECTICUT 06029

General Information Residential camp offering extensive riding and horse care programs for 48 girls ages 7–15. Established in 1956. 100-acre facility located 20 miles from Hartford. Features: 3 riding rings; cross-country course; lake; tennis and basketball courts; rustic cedar cabins; dining hall and recreation hall.
Profile of Summer Employees Total number: 15; typical ages: 18–35. 1% men; 99% women; 10% high school students; 90% college students; 5% non-U.S. citizens; 10% local applicants. Nonsmokers required.
Employment Information Openings are from June 18 to August 26. Jobs available: ▶ *crafts, kitchen, general, and sports staff members* (minimum age 18) at $1600–$1700 per season ▶ *kitchen and general counselors* (minimum age 18) at $1600–$1700 per season ▶ 4–5 *riding counselors* (minimum age 18) with one year of college completed; should be experienced riders; teaching experience helpful; at $1600–$2100 per season ▶ *swimming counselor* (minimum age 20) with lifeguard training and FPR/CPR certification at $1900–$2100 per season ▶ 2 *swimming instructors* (minimum age 18) with WSI certification at $1600–$1700 per season. Applicants must submit formal organization application, three personal references. An in-person interview is recommended, but a telephone interview is acceptable. International applicants accepted; must obtain own visa, obtain own working papers, apply through a recognized agency.
Benefits and Preemployment Training Free housing, free meals, formal training, willing to provide letters of recommendation, on-the-job training, willing to complete paperwork for educational credit, willing to act as a professional reference, and riding instructors may attend seminars/workshops. Preemployment training is required and includes accident prevention and safety, interpersonal skills, leadership skills, working with children, teaching skills.
Contact Pat Haines, Director, SJ Ranch, Inc., 130 Sandy Beach Road, Ellington, Connecticut 06029. Telephone: 860-872-4742. Fax: 860-870-4914. E-mail: sjranch@erols.com. Contact by e-mail, mail, or phone. Application deadline: continuous.

THE SOUTHWESTERN COMPANY, CONNECTICUT

See The Southwestern Company on page 302 for complete description.

STUDENT CONSERVATION ASSOCIATION (SCA), CONNECTICUT

See Student Conservation Association (SCA), New Hampshire on page 209 for complete description.

SUNRISE RESORT

ROUTE 151, PO BOX 415
MOODUS, CONNECTICUT 06469

General Information Summer resort catering to families, day outing groups, music festivals, and weddings. Established in 1916. 140-acre facility located 20 miles from Hartford. Features:

50 x 100- foot pool; Salmon River; mountain biking; horseback riding; rural setting.

Profile of Summer Employees Total number: 125; typical ages: 17–24. 40% men; 60% women; 5% minorities; 40% high school students; 20% college students; 5% retirees; 28% non-U.S. citizens; 75% local applicants.

Employment Information Openings are from May 15 to October 15. Jobs available: ▶ 3–5 *housekeeping staff* (minimum age 19) at $3500–$4500 per season ▶ 2–3 *kitchen help* (minimum age 19) at $3500–$4500 per season ▶ 2–3 *lifeguards* (minimum age 19) with lifesaving and CPR; WSI certification preferred at $3500–$4500 per season ▶ 1–3 *office personnel* (minimum age 19) with typing ability at $3500–$4500 per season ▶ 1 *tennis instructor* (minimum age 19) at $3500–$4500 per season ▶ 10–12 *waiters/waitresses* (minimum age 19) at $3500–$4500 per season. Applicants must submit a formal organization application. A telephone interview is required. International applicants accepted; must obtain own visa.

Benefits and Preemployment Training Housing at a cost, possible full-time employment, willing to provide letters of recommendation, on-the-job training, willing to complete paperwork for educational credit, willing to act as a professional reference, and room and board at $40 per week. Preemployment training is optional.

Contact Jim Johnson, Director, Sunrise Resort, PO Box 415, Moodus, Connecticut 06469. Telephone: 860-873-8681. Fax: 860-873-8681. E-mail: suntimes@connix.com. World Wide Web: http://www.sunriseresort.com. Contact by e-mail, fax, mail, phone, or through World Wide Web site. Application deadline: April 15.

TENNIS: EUROPE

73 ROCKRIDGE LANE
STAMFORD, CONNECTICUT 06903

General Information Takes teams of junior players to international tennis tournaments, allowing them to gain valuable experience in match play and providing them with intercultural educational experiences. There are 12 teams in Europe and 3 teams in North America. Established in 1973.

Profile of Summer Employees Typical ages: 21–45. 50% men; 50% women; 5% minorities; 33% college students; 5% non-U.S. citizens. Nonsmokers required.

Employment Information Openings are from June 22 to August 15. Jobs available: ▶ 22 *tennis coaches/chaperones* (minimum age 21) with ability to coach tennis at high school varsity or ranked players' levels and must serve as chaperone to students during travel; all positions require extensive travel and no positions are in Connecticut; 22 positions for Europe and 6 in North America at $400 to $550 per trip. Applicants must submit a formal organization application, letter of interest, resume, four personal references. An in-person interview is recommended, but a telephone interview is acceptable. International applicants accepted; must obtain own visa.

Benefits and Preemployment Training Free housing, free meals, possible full-time employment, willing to provide letters of recommendation, names of contacts, on-the-job training, willing to complete paperwork for educational credit, willing to act as a professional reference, and domestic travel reimbursement ($100); while on trip, organization pays all airfare and other travel expenses. Preemployment training is required and includes accident prevention and safety, interpersonal skills, leadership skills.

Contact Dr. Martin Vinokur, Director, TENNIS: EUROPE, 73 Rockridge Lane, Stamford, Connecticut 06903. Telephone: 203-322-9803. Fax: 203-322-0089. E-mail: tenniseuro@aol.com. World Wide Web: http://www.tenniseurope.com. Contact by e-mail, fax, mail, phone, or through World Wide Web site. Application deadline: preferred deadline March 15, later applications accepted.

UNITED CEREBRAL PALSY ASSOCIATION OF GREATER HARTFORD

301 GREAT NECK ROAD
WATERFORD, CONNECTICUT 06385

General Information Residential camping program serving individuals with physical disabilities, ages 8-adult, during a nine-week summer program. Established in 1957. 5-acre facility located 5 miles from New London. Features: beachfront facility; community outings; basketball courts; heated, fully equipped cabins; horseback riding; gardens and horticulture.

Profile of Summer Employees Total number: 23; typical ages: 18–35. 30% men; 70% women; 20% minorities; 1% high school students; 60% college students; 1% non-U.S. citizens; 40% local applicants.

Employment Information Openings are from June 17 to August 17. Jobs available: ▶ 1 *activity leader* (minimum age 21) with creativity, experience in recreation activities (preferred), and ability to work with others at $2500–$2700 per season ▶ 14 *general counselors* (minimum age 18) with dedication and maturity, willingness to learn, and experience working with disabled persons (preferred) at $2500–$2700 per season. Applicants must submit a formal organization application, two personal references, two letters of recommendation, physical, background check, drug test, copy of high school diploma or GED. An in-person interview is recommended, but a telephone interview is acceptable. International applicants accepted.

Benefits and Preemployment Training Free housing, free meals, formal training, names of contacts, on-the-job training, and willing to complete paperwork for educational credit. Preemployment training is required and includes accident prevention and safety, first aid, CPR, interpersonal skills, leadership skills, bloodborne pathogens information, abuse and neglect prevention, lifting and transferring, disability sensitivity.

Contact Shannon Credit, Program Coordinator, United Cerebral Palsy Association of Greater Hartford, 80 Whitney Street, Hartford, Connecticut 06105. Telephone: 860-236-6201. Fax: 860-236-6205. Contact by fax, mail, or phone. Application deadline: continuous.

DELAWARE

CHESAPEAKE BAY GIRL SCOUT COUNCIL

501 SOUTH COLLEGE AVENUE
NEWARK, DELAWARE 19713

General Information Residential and day camps serving girls ages 5–17 during June, July, and August. 265-acre facility located 60 miles from Wilmington. Features: swimming pool; waterfront (river); wooded property; tennis courts; nature trails.

Profile of Summer Employees Total number: 30; typical ages: 18–23. 5% men; 95% women; 10% minorities; 80% college students; 20% non-U.S. citizens; 50% local applicants. Nonsmokers preferred.

Employment Information Openings are from June 14 to August 11. Jobs available: ▶ 7 *aquatics assistants* (minimum age 18) with lifeguard certification; Red Cross waterfront module; certification in advanced lifesaving or WSI, first aid, CPR, and windsurfing/sailing/canoeing experience preferred (one or all) at $1200–$1350 per season ▶ 1 *pool director* (minimum age 21) with WSI (preferred), Red Cross Advanced Lifesaving, first aid/CPR certification, and experience working in a camp setting at $1500–$1650 per season ▶ 10 *unit counselors* (minimum age 18) with children/camp experience preferred at $1100–$1300 per season ▶ 6 *unit leaders* (minimum age 21) with training in Girl Scout program or camp counseling and experience

preferred at $1300–$1500 per season. Applicants must submit formal organization application, three personal references, three letters of recommendation, criminal history check (fingerprinting). An in-person interview is recommended, but a telephone interview is acceptable. International applicants accepted; must apply through a recognized agency.
Benefits and Preemployment Training Free housing, free meals, formal training, willing to provide letters of recommendation, on-the-job training, willing to complete paperwork for educational credit, willing to act as a professional reference, and first aid and CPR training provided. Preemployment training is required and includes accident prevention and safety, first aid, CPR, interpersonal skills, leadership skills, Girl Scout outdoor skills.
Contact Mrs. Peg Reynolds, Director of Outdoor Programs, Chesapeake Bay Girl Scout Council, 501 South College Avenue, Newark, Delaware 19713. Telephone: 302-456-7150. Fax: 302-456-7188. E-mail: preynolds@cbgsc.org. World Wide Web: http://www.cbgsc.org. Contact by e-mail, fax, or phone. Application deadline: continuous.

CHILDREN'S BEACH HOUSE, INC.
1800 BAY AVENUE
LEWES, DELAWARE 19958

General Information Private nonprofit residential camp for Delaware children, ages 6–12, with speech, hearing, and/or mild orthopedic disabilities. 23 children attend each 4-week session (2 sessions per summer). Established in 1936. 6-acre facility located 5 miles from Rehoboth Beach. Features: beach front on Delaware Bay; in-ground pool; semi-private rooms for staff with bathroom; near state park; near resort town.
Profile of Summer Employees Total number: 25; typical ages: 18–25. 50% men; 50% women; 80% college students; 20% local applicants.
Employment Information Openings are from June 8 to August 19. Jobs available: ▶ 2 *program counselors (arts and crafts)* (minimum age 18) with experience working with special needs children; should be flexible, creative, energetic and multi-task oriented at $2600 per season ▶ 2 *program counselors (environmental studies)* (minimum age 18) with background in environmental studies and experience working with special needs children; should be flexible, creative, energetic, and multi-task oriented at $2600 per season ▶ 2 *program counselors (waterfront)* (minimum age 18) with lifeguarding/WSI certification and experience working with special needs children; should be flexible, creative, energetic, and multi-task oriented at $2600 per season. Applicants must submit a formal organization application, three personal references, biographical sketch. An in-person interview is recommended, but a telephone interview is acceptable.
Benefits and Preemployment Training Free housing, free meals, willing to provide letters of recommendation, on-the-job training, willing to complete paperwork for educational credit, and willing to act as a professional reference. Preemployment training is required and includes accident prevention and safety, first aid, CPR, interpersonal skills, leadership skills, behavior management program.
Contact Diane O'Hara, Program Director, Children's Beach House, Inc., 1800 Bay Avenue, Lewes, Delaware 19958. Fax: 302-645-9467. E-mail: inquirysrp@cbhinc.org. Contact by e-mail or mail. Application deadline: continuous.

FUNLAND
6 DELAWARE AVENUE
REHOBOTH BEACH, DELAWARE 19971

General Information Amusement park providing family entertainment. Established in 1962. 2-acre facility located 30 miles from Dover. Features: rides for children and adults; games; arcade.
Profile of Summer Employees Total number: 80; typical ages: 16–22. 50% men; 50% women;

5% minorities; 40% high school students; 60% college students; 5% non-U.S. citizens; 50% local applicants. Nonsmokers preferred.

Employment Information Openings are from May 15 to September 15. Jobs available: ▶ 80 *ride and game attendants* (minimum age 16) at $6.90 per hour plus performance bonus ($1.00 per hour potential); wages increase during last 3 weeks of season. Applicants must submit formal organization application, letter of interest, resume, letter of recommendation. An in-person interview is recommended, but a telephone interview is acceptable. International applicants accepted; must apply through a recognized agency.

Benefits and Preemployment Training Free meals, formal training, willing to provide letters of recommendation, on-the-job training, and free housing or housing at cost (possible). Preemployment training is required and includes accident prevention and safety.

Contact Steve Hendricks, Vice President/Personnel Manager, Funland, 7055 Red Top Road, Harrisburg, Pennsylvania 17111. Telephone: 302-227-2785. Fax: 717-566-6599. E-mail: srhfunland@cs.com. World Wide Web: http://www.funlandrehoboth.com. Contact by e-mail, fax, mail, phone, or through World Wide Web site. Application deadline: continuous.

THE SOUTHWESTERN COMPANY, DELAWARE

See The Southwestern Company on page 302 for complete description.

STUDENT CONSERVATION ASSOCIATION (SCA), DELAWARE

See Student Conservation Association (SCA), New Hampshire on page 209 for complete description.

VIKING GOLF THEME & WATERPARK

CORNER OF ROUTE 1 AND ROUTE 54
FENWICK ISLAND, DELAWARE 19944

General Information Amusement/theme park with mini-golf, go-kart track, waterslides, activity pools, and food shops. Established in 1984. 2-acre facility located 120 miles from Washington, DC. Features: one block from beach; bayside; located on 10-mile island; new 2800-square-foot themed activity pool; 6 waterslides; boardwalk concessions.

Profile of Summer Employees Total number: 40–50; typical ages: 15–29. 50% men; 50% women; 30% high school students; 40% college students; 10% non-U.S. citizens; 30% local applicants. Nonsmokers preferred.

Employment Information Openings are from May 14 to September 30. Jobs available: ▶ 10 *amusement ride attendants/GoKart operators* (minimum age 16) with English fluency; paid $7 to $9 per hour; bonus at end of season if work performance meets requirements ▶ 15–25 *food shop attendants* (minimum age 15) with short order cooking skills (a plus but not required for all shops) at $6.15 to $9 per hour; bonus at end of season if work performance meets requirements ▶ 6 *miniature golf attendants* (minimum age 16) with English fluency; paid $6.25 to $9 per hour; bonus at end of season if work performance meets requirements ▶ 20–30 *waterpark lifeguards* (minimum age 16) with CPR and lifeguard certification preferred at $7 to $9 per hour; bonus at end of season if work performance meets requirements. Applicants must submit a formal organization application. An in-person interview is recommended, but a telephone interview is acceptable. International applicants accepted; must obtain own working papers.

Benefits and Preemployment Training Meals at a cost, willing to provide letters of recommendation, names of contacts, on-the-job training, and willing to act as a professional reference. Preemployment training is optional and includes interpersonal skills, job-specific training.

Contact Jon Andersen, Vice President, Viking Golf Theme & Waterpark, 11004 Trappe Creek Road, Berlin, Maryland 21811. Telephone: 302-539-1644. Fax: 302-537-1551. Contact by fax, mail, or phone. Application deadline: continuous.

DISTRICT OF COLUMBIA

AMERICAN RED CROSS NATIONAL HEADQUARTERS

1730 E STREET, NW
WASHINGTON, DISTRICT OF COLUMBIA 20006

General Information A humanitarian organization that provides relief to victims of disasters and helps people prevent, prepare for, and respond to emergencies. Established in 1881.

Employment Information Openings are from June 1 to August 30. Jobs available: ▶ 10–30 *Presidential Interns for racial/ethnic minority college students* must be enrolled in undergraduate or graduate program at $9.40 per hour. Applicants must submit a letter of interest, resume. A telephone interview is required. International applicants accepted; must obtain own visa, obtain own working papers.

Benefits and Preemployment Training Formal training, possible full-time employment, willing to provide letters of recommendation, on-the-job training, willing to complete paperwork for educational credit, willing to act as a professional reference, and opportunity to attend seminars/workshops.

Contact Jennifer Carino, Diversity Associate, American Red Cross National Headquarters. E-mail: carinoj@usa.redcross.org. World Wide Web: http://www.redcross.org. Contact by e-mail or through World Wide Web site. Application deadline: March 1.

CYBERCAMPS–GEORGETOWN UNIVERSITY

WASHINGTON, DISTRICT OF COLUMBIA

See Cybercamps–University of Washington on page 335 for complete description.

THE SOUTHWESTERN COMPANY, DISTRICT OF COLUMBIA

See The Southwestern Company on page 302 for complete description.

STUDENT CONSERVATION ASSOCIATION (SCA), DISTRICT OF COLUMBIA

See Student Conservation Association (SCA), New Hampshire on page 209 for complete description.

SUMMER DISCOVERY AT GEORGETOWN

GEORGETOWN UNIVERSITY
WASHINGTON, DISTRICT OF COLUMBIA 20057

General Information Precollege enrichment program for high school students at Georgetown University. Established in 1994. Features: sport facilities; beaches; mountains; lakes; major cities nearby; college towns.

Profile of Summer Employees Total number: 20; typical ages: 21–35. 10% minorities; 60% college students; 2% non-U.S. citizens. Nonsmokers required.

Employment Information Openings are from June 20 to August 25. Jobs available: ▶ 20 *resident counselors* (minimum age 21) with experience working with high school students/children at $125–$400 per week. Applicants must submit a formal organization application, resume, personal reference. An in-person interview is required. International applicants accepted; must obtain own visa, obtain own working papers.

Benefits and Preemployment Training Free housing and on-the-job training. Preemployment training is required and includes accident prevention and safety, CPR, leadership skills.
Contact Jason Walley, Admissions Director, Summer Discovery at Georgetown, 1326 Old Northern Boulevard, Roslyn, New York 11576. Telephone: 516-621-3939. Fax: 516-625-3438. E-mail: staff@summerfun.com. World Wide Web: http://www.summerfun.com. Contact by e-mail or phone. Application deadline: continuous.

FLORIDA

A CHRISTIAN MINISTRY IN THE NATIONAL PARKS–FLORIDA

See A Christian Ministry in the National Parks–Maine on page 122 for complete description.

ACTIONQUEST
PO BOX 5517
SARASOTA, FLORIDA 34277

General Information Live-aboard sailing and diving certification voyages for 13-19 year olds. Waterskiing, windsurfing, and marine biology available. No experience necessary. Established in 1986. Features: locations in British Virgin Islands, Mediterranean, Leeward Islands, Galapagos, Australia, and South Pacific; 12 50-foot sailing yachts.
Profile of Summer Employees Total number: 40; typical age: 28. 60% men; 40% women; 50% college students; 10% non-U.S. citizens. Nonsmokers required.
Employment Information Openings are from June 10 to August 20. Year-round positions also offered. Jobs available: ▶ 12 *PADI diving instructors* with PADI instructor-level certification and/or USCG license at $2200 per season ▶ *emergency medical technician* with PADI instructor certification or USCG license or windsurfing/sailing/waterski instruction skills at $1000 per season ▶ *marine science instructors* with PADI scuba instructor-level certification at $2200 per season ▶ 12 *sailing instructors* should be United States Coast Guard licensed or British Yachtmasters at $3000 per season ▶ *windsurfing instructors* with certification in field at $1000 per season. Applicants must submit a formal organization application, letter of interest, resume, two personal references. A telephone interview is required. International applicants accepted.
Benefits and Preemployment Training Free housing, free meals, willing to provide letters of recommendation, and travel reimbursement.
Contact James Stoll, Director, ActionQuest, PO Box 5517, Sarasota, Florida 34277. Telephone: 941-924-2115. Fax: 941-924-6075. E-mail: info@actionquest.com. World Wide Web: http://www.actionquest.com. Contact by e-mail, fax, mail, phone, or through World Wide Web site. Application deadline: continuous.

CAMP BLUE RIDGE
BOX 2888
MIAMI, FLORIDA 33140

General Information Residential camp with an average of 200 campers providing athletics, waterfront, roller hockey, paintball, arts and crafts, rappelling, horseback riding, and waterskiing activities. Established in 1969. 212-acre facility. Features: freshwater lake and pool; roller hockey rink; rappelling tower; recreation hall and game room; go-cart track; tennis courts.

Profile of Summer Employees Total number: 85; typical ages: 19–40. 50% men; 50% women; 5% high school students; 80% college students; 50% non-U.S. citizens; 50% local applicants. Nonsmokers required.
Employment Information Openings are from June 15 to August 15. Jobs available: ▶ 4 *arts and crafts instructors* at $1000–$1200 per season ▶ 10 *athletics instructors* at $1000–$1200 per season ▶ 6 *dance and drama instructors* at $1000–$1200 per season ▶ 1 *martial arts instructor* at $1000–$1200 per season ▶ 3 *rappelling instructors* at $1000–$1500 per season ▶ 12 *swimming, boating, all-waterfront, and skiing instructors* at $1000–$1500 per season. Applicants must submit formal organization application, personal reference. A telephone interview is required. International applicants accepted; must apply through a recognized agency.
Benefits and Preemployment Training Free housing and free meals. Preemployment training is required and includes accident prevention and safety, first aid, CPR, leadership skills.
Contact Joey Waldman, Director, Camp Blue Ridge, PO Box 2888, Miami Beach, Florida 33140. Telephone: 305-538-3434. Fax: 305-532-3152. E-mail: campcbr@aol.com. Contact by e-mail, fax, mail, or phone. Application deadline: continuous.

CAMP THUNDERBIRD
909 EAST WELCH ROAD
APOPKA, FLORIDA 32712

General Information Residential camp designed exclusively to benefit children and adults who have a developmental disability. Campers participate in traditional camping activities which help increase the camper's level of independence and self-esteem. 20-acre facility located 15 miles from Orlando. Features: freshwater lake; wooded setting; air-conditioned dorms; ropes challenge course; private staff recreation room; close to local attractions and beaches.
Profile of Summer Employees Total number: 70; typical ages: 18–40. 25% men; 75% women; 17% minorities; 60% college students; 50% non-U.S. citizens; 35% local applicants.
Employment Information Openings are from June 14 to August 14. Jobs available: ▶ 6 *activity leaders* (minimum age 18) with experience leading a specific activity ▶ 30 *cabin counselors* with experience working with the mentally retarded ▶ 2–3 *camp nurses* with Florida nursing license (1 RN, 2 LPNs) ▶ 4 *head counselors* (minimum age 21) with experience working at summer camps; supervisory experience preferred ▶ 2 *kitchen staff members* with experience ▶ 3 *swimming pool staff members* (minimum age 18) with WSI and lifeguard certification. Applicants must submit formal organization application, three personal references, three letters of recommendation. An in-person interview is recommended, but a telephone interview is acceptable. International applicants accepted; must obtain own visa, obtain own working papers, apply through a recognized agency.
Benefits and Preemployment Training Free housing, free meals, willing to provide letters of recommendation, on-the-job training, willing to complete paperwork for educational credit, and possible free admission to local attractions (Disney, Universal Studios, Sea World, and more). Preemployment training is required and includes accident prevention and safety, first aid, CPR, interpersonal skills, leadership skills.
Contact Greg Giraulo, Program Director, Camp Thunderbird, 909 East Welch Road, Apopka, Florida 32712. Telephone: 407-889-8088. Fax: 407-889-8072. E-mail: ggiraulo@questinc.org. World Wide Web: http://www.questinc.org. Contact by e-mail, fax, mail, phone, or through World Wide Web site. Application deadline: continuous.

SABIN-MULLOY-GARRISON TENNIS CAMP
11550 LASTCHANCE ROAD
CLERMONT, FLORIDA 34711

General Information Residential camp for boys and girls who have an interest in competitive tennis. Established in 1961. 5-acre facility located 30 miles from Orlando. Features: freshwater lake; 5 tennis courts; wooded setting; trips to Orlando area attractions; sanctioned tennis tournaments; waterskiing.

Profile of Summer Employees Total number: 3; typical ages: 19–23. 50% men; 50% women; 25% minorities; 75% college students; 25% non-U.S. citizens; 25% local applicants. Nonsmokers required.

Employment Information Openings are from July to August. Jobs available: ▶ *cook* (minimum age 19) at $800–$1000 per month ▶ 2–3 *tennis instructors* (minimum age 19) at $800–$1000 per month. Applicants must submit resume, two personal references, two letters of recommendation. International applicants accepted; must obtain own visa, obtain own working papers.

Benefits and Preemployment Training Free housing and free meals.

Contact Dickey W. Garrison, Owner, Sabin-Mulloy-Garrison Tennis Camp, 11550 Lastchance Road, Clermont, Florida 34711. Telephone: 352-394-3543. Fax: 352-394-3543. E-mail: smgtennis@yahoo.com. Contact by e-mail, fax, mail, or phone. Application deadline: continuous.

SEACAMP ASSOCIATION, INC.

1300 BIG PINE AVENUE
BIG PINE KEY, FLORIDA 33043

General Information A private not-for-profit coed camp located in the middle of the Florida Keys National Marine Sanctuary, offering a residential marine science/SCUBA program for teens 12–17, and a day camp marine science program for youth 10–13. Established in 1963. 8-acre facility located 150 miles from Miami. Features: located on a peninsula; on Cupon Bight Aquatic Preserve; near coral reefs; on an island; mangrove habitats; shallow bay.

Profile of Summer Employees Total number: 105; typical ages: 19–26. 50% men; 50% women; 3% minorities; 42% college students; 18% non-U.S. citizens. Nonsmokers preferred.

Employment Information Jobs available: ▶ *administrative staff* ▶ *arts and crafts coordinator* ▶ *cabin counselors* (minimum age 19) with interest in teaching teens about the marine environment; must be comfortable in the water with strong boating and aquatic skills; SCUBA preferred; strong interest/experience in sailing or windsurfing; must live with group of campers, participate in all camp functions and assist in supervision as assigned ▶ *day camp counselors* (minimum age 21) with ability to assist or teach in courses; experience working with 10-13 year old children; valid driver's license with excellent driving record required, participation in all camp functions and camper supervision ▶ *photographer* ▶ *registered nurse* ▶ *science, SCUBA, sailing, and windsurfing instructors* with interest in teaching teens about marine environment ▶ *unit leaders* (minimum age 21) with ability to supervise counselors and activities, plan evening programs and special events, teach and assist in courses; valid driver's license with excellent driving record required. Applicants must submit formal organization application, resume, academic transcripts, three personal references, employment verification(s); portfolio for photo instructor only. A telephone interview is required. International applicants accepted; must apply through a recognized agency.

Benefits and Preemployment Training Free housing, free meals, and formal training. Preemployment training is required and includes accident prevention and safety, first aid, CPR, interpersonal skills, leadership skills, captains workshop, lifeguarding, NAUI Skindiving Instructor and dive resume (if SCUBA certified) and more.

Contact Assistant Camp Director, Seacamp Personnel Department, Seacamp Association, Inc. Telephone: 305-872-2331. Fax: 305-872-2555. E-mail: seacamp2002@aol.com. World Wide Web: http://seacamp.org. Contact by e-mail or mail. Application deadline: continuous.

SEA WORLD OF FLORIDA

7007 SEA HARBOR DRIVE
ORLANDO, FLORIDA 32821

General Information Marine life theme park, open year-round, designed to entertain and educate guests offers employees an enthusiastic, imaginative, and intellectually stimulating atmosphere.

Established in 1973. Features: new water coaster ride; simulator ride; animal shows (marine life); close to downtown Orlando; close to sister properties Busch Gardens and Adventure Island.
Profile of Summer Employees Typical ages: 16–24. 50% men; 50% women; 30% high school students; 20% college students; 10% retirees; 40% non-U.S. citizens.
Employment Information Openings are from May 15 to September 5. Spring break, winter break, and year-round positions also offered. Jobs available: ▶ *buspersons* at $6.65 per hour ▶ *counter persons* at $6.65 per hour ▶ *dishwashers* at $6.65 per hour ▶ *gift shop personnel* with ability to operate cash register, assist guests, and stock shelves at $6.65 per hour ▶ *kitchen staff* at $6.65 per hour ▶ *landscape personnel* with ability to work with a wide variety of plant material and design beds, plus maintain drainage and irrigation (some experience preferred) at $6.90–$7.70 per hour ▶ *lifeguards* at $7–$7.95 per hour ▶ *operations, crowd and traffic control personnel* with desire to maintain park cleanliness and assist at information center at $6.65 per hour ▶ *prep cooks* at $6.65–$7.50 per hour ▶ *swim gear staff* at $6.65 per hour ▶ *ticket sellers* with cash handling experience at $6.65 per hour ▶ *tour guides* (minimum age 18) with ability to narrate at animal exhibits throughout the park and conduct educational tours at $6–$7 per hour ▶ *waiters/waitresses* at $4.70 per hour plus gratuity ▶ *warehouse personnel* at $7.10–$7.50 per hour. Applicants must submit formal organization application. International applicants accepted; must obtain own visa, obtain own working papers, apply through a recognized agency.
Benefits and Preemployment Training Meals at a cost, formal training, possible full-time employment, on-the-job training, opportunity to attend seminars/workshops, and opportunity to purchase health insurance; free meals for food service employees. Preemployment training is required and includes accident prevention and safety, CPR, interpersonal skills, leadership skills.
Contact Christine Runnells, Manager of Employment, Sea World of Florida, 7007 Sea Harbor Drive, Orlando, Florida 32821. Fax: 407-363-2615. Contact by fax. Application deadline: continuous.

THE SOUTHWESTERN COMPANY, FLORIDA

See The Southwestern Company on page 302 for complete description.

SPORTS INTERNATIONAL–JAGUARS

JACKSONVILLE, FLORIDA

See Sports International, Inc. on page 147 for complete description.

STUDENT CONSERVATION ASSOCIATION (SCA), FLORIDA

See Student Conservation Association (SCA), New Hampshire on page 209 for complete description.

GEORGIA

CAMP BARNEY MEDINTZ

4165 HIGHWAY 129 NORTH
CLEVELAND, GEORGIA 30528-2309

General Information Residential camp serving 900 campers ages 8–16 during two 4-week sessions. Camp also offers Wonder Weeks, serving second and third graders during four 2-week

sessions, and Chalutzim, serving children ages 9–16 with special needs during a four-week session. Established in 1963. 500-acre facility located 75 miles from Atlanta. Features: 2 lakes; 30 stall equestrian center; climbing wall; swimming pool; high ropes course; tennis courts.
Profile of Summer Employees Total number: 200; typical ages: 18–24. 50% men; 50% women; 5% minorities; 28% high school students; 66% college students; 20% non-U.S. citizens; 65% local applicants.
Employment Information Openings are from June to August. Jobs available: ▶ 50 *counselors* (minimum age 18) at $750–$1500 per season ▶ 9 *horseback staff members* with first aid certificate at $750–$2000 per season ▶ 14 *nature crafts staff members* (minimum age 18) with CPR and first aid certification at $750–$2200 per season ▶ 2 *song leaders* at $1200–$2500 per season ▶ 10 *special-needs staff members* at $800–$1800 per season ▶ 2 *theater directors* at $1200–$2300 per season ▶ 15 *waterfront staff members* (minimum age 18) with LGT, WSI, CPR, and first aid certification at $750–$2200 per season. Applicants must submit formal organization application, three letters of recommendation. An in-person interview is recommended, but a telephone interview is acceptable. International applicants accepted; must apply through a recognized agency.
Benefits and Preemployment Training Free housing, free meals, formal training, willing to provide letters of recommendation, on-the-job training, and willing to complete paperwork for educational credit. Preemployment training is required and includes accident prevention and safety, first aid, CPR, interpersonal skills, leadership skills.
Contact Mark Balser, Associate Director, Camp Barney Medintz, 5342 Tilly Mill Road, Atlanta, Georgia 30338-4499. Telephone: 770-396-3250. Fax: 770-481-0101. E-mail: summer@campbarney.org. World Wide Web: http://www.campbarney.org. Contact by e-mail, fax, mail, phone, or through World Wide Web site. Application deadline: continuous.

CAMP WOODMONT FOR BOYS AND GIRLS ON LOOKOUT MOUNTAIN

1339 YANKEE ROAD
CLOUDLAND, GEORGIA 30731

General Information Residential summer camp serving up to 80 boys and girls ages 6–14 for one- to two-week sessions; wholesome, fun activities emphasizing nature. Established in 1981. 170-acre facility located 28 miles from Chattanooga, Tennessee. Features: small lake; swimming pool; challenge trail and climbing tower; recreation/dining hall; cabins with central bathhouses; pavilion; gym.
Profile of Summer Employees Total number: 10–20; typical ages: 18–35. 50% men; 50% women; 2% high school students; 98% college students; 100% local applicants. Nonsmokers required.
Employment Information Openings are from June 4 to August 10. Jobs available: ▶ 10 *counselors* (minimum age 18) current CPR/FA certification required; LGT and experience preferred at $1000–$2200 per season ▶ 2 *swimming instructors* (minimum age 18) with LGT/WSI certification at $950–$2000 per season. Applicants must submit a formal organization application, resume, two writing samples, three personal references. An in-person interview is recommended, but a telephone interview is acceptable. International applicants accepted; must obtain own visa, obtain own working papers.
Benefits and Preemployment Training Free housing, free meals, formal training, willing to provide letters of recommendation, on-the-job training, willing to complete paperwork for educational credit, willing to act as a professional reference, and opportunity to attend seminars/workshops. Preemployment training is required and includes accident prevention and safety, interpersonal skills, leadership skills.
Contact Jane Bennett, Camp Director, Camp Woodmont for Boys and Girls on Lookout Mountain, 2339 Welton Place, Dunwoody, Georgia 30338. Telephone: 770-457-0862. E-mail: campdirector@

campwoodmont.com. World Wide Web: http://www.campwoodmont.com. Contact by e-mail, mail, phone, or through World Wide Web site. Application deadline: continuous.

THE SOUTHWESTERN COMPANY, GEORGIA

See The Southwestern Company on page 302 for complete description.

STUDENT CONSERVATION ASSOCIATION (SCA), GEORGIA

See Student Conservation Association (SCA), New Hampshire on page 209 for complete description.

HAWAII

LONGACRE EXPEDITIONS, HAWAII

HAWAII

General Information Adventure travel program in Hawaii for teenagers, emphasizing group living skills and physical challenges. Established in 1981.

Profile of Summer Employees Total number: 6; typical ages: 23–30. 50% men; 50% women; 100% college students. Nonsmokers required.

Employment Information Openings are from June 30 to July 30. Jobs available: ▶ 4 *assistant leaders* (minimum age 21) with scuba certification, WFR, CPR, and lifeguard training at $252–$300 per week. Applicants must submit a formal organization application, letter of interest, resume, three personal references. An in-person interview is recommended, but a telephone interview is acceptable. International applicants accepted; must obtain own visa, obtain own working papers.

Benefits and Preemployment Training Free housing, free meals, willing to provide letters of recommendation, on-the-job training, willing to complete paperwork for educational credit, willing to act as a professional reference, and pro-deal purchase program. Preemployment training is required and includes accident prevention and safety, interpersonal skills, leadership skills.

Contact Meredith Schuler, Director, Longacre Expeditions, Hawaii, 4030 Middle Ridge Road, Newport, Pennsylvania 17074-8110. Telephone: 717-567-6790. Fax: 717-567-3955. E-mail: longacre@longacreexpeditions.com. World Wide Web: http://www.longacreexpeditions.com. Contact by e-mail, fax, mail, phone, or through World Wide Web site. Application deadline: continuous.

THE SOUTHWESTERN COMPANY, HAWAII

See The Southwestern Company on page 302 for complete description.

STUDENT CONSERVATION ASSOCIATION (SCA), HAWAII

See Student Conservation Association (SCA), New Hampshire on page 209 for complete description.

IDAHO

EPLEY'S WHITEWATER ADVENTURES
BOX 987
MCCALL, IDAHO 83638

General Information River rafting on Salmon River offering adventures to groups of up to 100 people on short trips. Also offers overnight trips for 2–24 people. Established in 1962. 1-acre facility located 150 miles from Boise. Features: River of No Return; free flowing river with no dams; wildlife; very deep canyon; large sandy beaches; Class III river run.

Profile of Summer Employees Total number: 18; typical ages: 18–28. 80% men; 20% women; 75% college students; 25% local applicants. Nonsmokers required.

Employment Information Openings are from May 1 to September 15. Jobs available: ▶ 4–6 *food service, laundry and office staff, and shuttle drivers* (minimum age 18) with Red Cross, first aid, and CPR (training provided); experience preferred at $750–$1000 per month ▶ 12–15 *river guides* (minimum age 18) with Red Cross, first aid, and CPR; training provided for license at $750–$1200 per month. Applicants must submit formal organization application, letter of interest, resume, portfolio, three personal references, letter of recommendation. An in-person interview is recommended, but a telephone interview is acceptable. International applicants accepted; must obtain own visa, obtain own working papers, apply through a recognized agency.

Benefits and Preemployment Training Free housing, free meals, formal training, willing to provide letters of recommendation, on-the-job training, willing to complete paperwork for educational credit, and laundry service. Preemployment training is optional and includes accident prevention and safety, first aid, CPR, leadership skills.

Contact Ted Epley, Owner, Epley's Whitewater Adventures, Box 987, McCall, Idaho 83638. Telephone: 208-634-5173. Fax: 208-634-5270. World Wide Web: http://www.epleys.com. Contact by fax, mail, or phone. Application deadline: applications accepted December 1 through March 31.

HIDDEN CREEK RANCH
7600 EAST BLUE LAKE ROAD
HARRISON, IDAHO 83833

General Information Guest ranch conducting six-day programs with daily scheduled activities including horseback riding, rodeo, mountain biking, pond fishing, trap shooting, archery, hiking, boat tours, Native American activities, and activities for fitness, mind, body, and spirit well-being. Established in 1992. 570-acre facility located 35 miles from Coeur d'Alene. Features: 100 horses; 40 mountain bikes; abundant wildlife; spring-fed pond and hot tubs in a private mountain valley; ropes challenge course; 7000-square foot lodge and 6 guest cabins; tipi village and 2 sweat lodges; trails overlook Coeur d'Alene chain of lakes.

Profile of Summer Employees Total number: 36; typical ages: 18–60. 50% men; 50% women; 1% minorities; 10% college students; 1% non-U.S. citizens; 1% local applicants.

Employment Information Openings are from April 1 to September 30. Jobs available: ▶ 1 *assistant cook* (minimum age 18) with standard first aid/CPR certification and kitchen experience at $500 per month plus room and board; $500 per month bonus payable at end of contract ▶ 1 *baker* (minimum age 18) with standard first aid/CPR certification and kitchen and baking experience at $500 per month plus room and board; $500 per month bonus payable at end of contract ▶ 3–4 *children's counselors* (minimum age 18) with standard first aid/CPR certification and child care or camp experience at $500 per month plus room and board; $500 per month bonus payable at end of contract ▶ 2 *children's wranglers* (minimum age 18) with standard first aid/CPR certification, child care or camp experience, and horse background at $500 per month plus room and board; $500 per month bonus payable at end of contract ▶ 6 *housekeeping/waitstaff members* (minimum age 18) with standard first aid/CPR certification at $500 per month plus room and board; $500 per month bonus payable at end of contract ▶ 1 *kitchen assistant/prep/dishwasher* (minimum age 18) with standard first aid/CPR certification and kitchen experience at $500 per month plus room and board; $500 per month bonus payable at end of contract ▶ 4 *maintenance staff* (minimum age 18) with standard first aid/CPR certification; grounds maintenance, construction, and mechanical background at $500 per month plus room and board; $500 per month bonus payable at end of contract ▶ 2 *office/waitstaff* (minimum age 18) with standard first aid/CPR certification and office experience at $500 per month plus room and board; $500 per month bonus payable at end of contract ▶ 7 *wranglers* (minimum age 18) with standard first aid/CPR certification and horse background at $500 per month plus room and board; $500 per month bonus payable at end of contract. Applicants must submit formal organization application, video detailing horsemanship skills for wrangler applicants. A telephone interview is required. International applicants accepted; must obtain own visa, obtain own working papers, apply through a recognized agency.

Benefits and Preemployment Training Free housing, free meals, willing to provide letters of recommendation, on-the-job training, willing to complete paperwork for educational credit, willing to act as a professional reference, and participation in guest activities on days off and time off; housing is not available for couples or families.

Contact Cindy Loe, Head of Human Resources, Hidden Creek Ranch. Telephone: 208-689-3209. Fax: 208-689-9115. E-mail: jobs@hiddencreek.com. World Wide Web: http://www.hiddencreek.com. Contact by e-mail, fax, mail, phone, or through World Wide Web site. Application deadline: applications in November or December are preferred.

MYSTIC SADDLE RANCH

STATE HIGHWAY 75
STANLEY, IDAHO 83278

General Information Program offering pack trips, trail rides, and fall hunting trips. Established in 1980. Located 130 miles from Boise. Features: Sawtooth Wilderness nearby; inside a national recreation area; rural historic area; 3 freshwater lakes nearby; 270 miles of trail; fly-fishing abounds.

Profile of Summer Employees Total number: 17; typical ages: 18–70. 80% men; 20% women; 60% college students; 20% retirees; 20% local applicants. Nonsmokers required.

Employment Information Openings are from June 1 to November 15. Year-round positions also offered. Jobs available: ▶ 1–3 *cooks/house helpers* (minimum age 18) at $1100–$1800 per month ▶ *corral manager* (minimum age 18) with no Fish and Game violations at $1100–$1800 per month ▶ 2–6 *fall hunting guides* (minimum age 18) with no Fish and Game violations at $1100–$1800 per month ▶ 2–10 *horse packers* (minimum age 18) with no Fish and Game violations at $1100–$1800 per month ▶ 2–10 *trail ride guides* (minimum age 18) with no Fish and Game violations at $1100–$1800 per month. Applicants must submit a formal organization application, three personal references, valid first aid card. An in-person interview is recommended, but a telephone interview is acceptable.

Benefits and Preemployment Training Housing at a cost, meals at a cost, possible full-time employment, willing to provide letters of recommendation, on-the-job training, willing to complete paperwork for educational credit, willing to act as a professional reference, and workmen's compensation insurance.

Contact Deb Bitton, Owner, Mystic Saddle Ranch, Stanley, Idaho 83278. Telephone: 208-774-3591. Fax: 208-774-3455. E-mail: info@mysticsaddleranch.com. World Wide Web: http://www.mysticsaddleranch.com. Contact by e-mail, fax, mail, phone, or through World Wide Web site. Application deadline: continuous.

REDFISH LAKE LODGE

BOX 9

STANLEY, IDAHO 83278

General Information Family-oriented rustic lodge on a lake in the Sawtooth Mountains with restaurant, marina, and general store. Established in 1930. 20-acre facility located 150 miles from Boise. Features: freshwater lake; Sawtooth Mountains; white-water rafting; mountain biking; hiking; Salmon River.

Profile of Summer Employees Total number: 60; typical ages: 18–28. 50% men; 50% women; 1% minorities; 10% high school students; 85% college students; 5% retirees; 50% local applicants. Nonsmokers preferred.

Employment Information Openings are from May 1 to October 10. Jobs available: ▶ 1 *bartender* (minimum age 19) at $700 to $900 per month plus room and board ▶ 4 *buspersons* (minimum age 16) at $772 per month plus room and board ▶ 8 *cooks* with one year of restaurant line experience at $772 to $1000 per month plus room and board ▶ 3 *dishwashers* at $772 to $800 per month plus room and board ▶ 4 *front desk personnel* (minimum age 18) at $772 to $900 per month plus room and board ▶ 8 *housekeepers* (minimum age 17) at $772 per month plus room and board ▶ 3 *maintenance personnel* (minimum age 18) at $772 to $900 per month plus room and board ▶ 5 *marina personnel* (minimum age 20) at $772 to $900 per month plus room and board ▶ 2 *service station personnel* (minimum age 50) with maintenance experience (helpful); retired couple (preferred) at $772 to $900 per month plus room and board ▶ 4 *store personnel* (minimum age 19) at $772 to $900 per month plus room and board ▶ 7 *waitresses/waiters* (minimum age 19) 2 to 3 years serving experience at $570 per month plus room and board. Applicants must submit a formal organization application, three personal references. An in-person interview is recommended, but a telephone interview is acceptable. International applicants accepted; must obtain own visa, obtain own working papers.

Benefits and Preemployment Training Housing at a cost, meals at a cost, willing to provide letters of recommendation, on-the-job training, willing to complete paperwork for educational credit, willing to act as a professional reference, and end-of-job bonus, possible internships.

Contact Jeff Clegg, Manager, Redfish Lake Lodge, Box 43, Jerome, Idaho 83338. Telephone: 208-774-3536. Fax: 208-774-3546. E-mail: hr@redfishlake.com. World Wide Web: http://www.redfishlake.com. Contact by e-mail, mail, or through World Wide Web site. Application deadline: continuous.

THE SOUTHWESTERN COMPANY, IDAHO

See The Southwestern Company on page 302 for complete description.

STUDENT CONSERVATION ASSOCIATION (SCA), IDAHO

See Student Conservation Association (SCA), New Hampshire on page 209 for complete description.

ILLINOIS

CAMP ALGONQUIN
1889 CARY ROAD
ALGONQUIN, ILLINOIS 60102

General Information A non-profit retreat and educational facility offering a variety of programs designed to serve adults, youth and families, providing summer residential camp sessions to youth, mothers and children and senior adults experiencing financial hardship.

Employment Information Openings are from June to August. Jobs available: ▶ 1 *aquatics director* (minimum age 18) with supervisory skills, American Red Cross lifeguard certification, four-year degree (desirable) at $1900–$2200 per season ▶ 1 *arts and crafts director* with skills in arts and crafts, group leadership and/or teaching experience with groups, ability to work with others to plan activities, two-year degree at $1700 per season ▶ 20 *cabin counselors* (minimum age 18) must have high school diploma at $1550–$1950 per season ▶ 1 *camp nurse* (minimum age 21) with RN at $2160–$5200 per season ▶ 6 *food service assistants* with high school diploma, work or volunteer experience at $1450–$1700 per season ▶ 3 *lifeguards* (minimum age 18) with high school diploma, experience in canoeing and boating at $1600–$1940 per season ▶ 2 *medical aides* (minimum age 18) with two-year degree at $1600–$1925 per season ▶ 1 *outdoor education specialist* (minimum age 18) with group leadership and/or teaching experience with groups, two-year degree at $1640–$1975 per season ▶ 1 *outdoor living skills instructor* with two-year degree or 2 years of college experience at $1640–$1975 per season ▶ 1 *sports and game specialist* (minimum age 18) with group leadership and teaching skills at $1640–$1975 per season. Applicants must submit formal organization application, resume. International applicants accepted; must apply through a recognized agency.

Benefits and Preemployment Training Housing at a cost and career development opportunities, staff lounge, paid time-off after each session, paid internship and field placement. Preemployment training is required and includes accident prevention and safety, first aid, CPR, interpersonal skills, leadership skills.

Contact Richard Morris, Director, Camp Algonquin. Telephone: 847-658-8212. Fax: 847-658-8431. World Wide Web: http://www.campalgonquin.org. Contact by fax, phone, or through World Wide Web site. Application deadline: continuous.

CAMP CEDAR POINT
1327 CAMP CEDAR POINT LANE
MAKANDA, ILLINOIS 62958

General Information Girl Scout residential camp serving 150 girls weekly for both Girl Scouts and nonmembers ages 6–17. Established in 1953. 250-acre facility located 115 miles from St. Louis, Missouri. Features: freshwater lake; wooded setting; platform tents/hogans; located within National Wildlife Refuge; rolling hills; sandstone rock formations.

Profile of Summer Employees Total number: 45; typical ages: 18–25. 5% men; 95% women; 10% minorities; 9% high school students; 90% college students; 5% non-U.S. citizens; 40% local applicants. Nonsmokers required.

Employment Information Openings are from June 1 to August 4. Jobs available: ▶ 1 *arts/crafts instructor* (minimum age 18) with experience in the field at $200 per week ▶ 15 *assistant unit leaders/counselors* (minimum age 18) with experience working with children at $200 per week ▶ 1 *environmental education instructor* (minimum age 18) with experience in the field at $200 per week ▶ 1 *head lifeguard* (minimum age 18) with lifeguarding certification at $215 per week ▶ 3 *junior counselors* (minimum age 16) with previous Camp Cedar Point experience at $75–$90 per week ▶ 1 *junior lifeguard* (minimum age 16) with lifeguard certification at $90 per week ▶ 5 *lifeguards* (minimum age 18) with lifeguarding certification at $200 per week ▶ 1 *nurse* (minimum age 21) with Illinois RN, LPN, or PA license at $350 per week ▶ 1 *program director* (minimum age 21) with experience at $300 per week ▶ 8 *unit leaders/counselors* (minimum age 21) with experience working with children at $215 per week ▶ 1 *waterfront coordinator* (minimum age 21) with lifeguarding certification; supervisory experience preferred at $250 per week. Applicants must submit a formal organization application, three personal references. An in-person interview is recommended, but a telephone interview is acceptable. International applicants accepted; must obtain own visa, obtain own working papers.

Benefits and Preemployment Training Free housing, free meals, formal training, willing to provide letters of recommendation, on-the-job training, willing to complete paperwork for educational credit, willing to act as a professional reference, and CPR/first aid certification. Preemployment training is required and includes accident prevention and safety, first aid, CPR, interpersonal skills, leadership skills.

Contact Kate Fogg, Camp Director, Camp Cedar Point, Girl Scouts of Shagbark Council, 304 North 14th Street, Herrin, Illinois 62948. Telephone: 618-942-3164. Fax: 618-942-7153. E-mail: kfogg@shagbark.org. World Wide Web: http://www.shagbark.org. Contact by e-mail, fax, mail, or phone. Application deadline: continuous.

CAMP TAPAWINGO

ROUTE 5, BOX 15
METAMORA, ILLINOIS 61548

General Information Residential camp serving 120 Girl Scouts and non-Girl Scouts per week. Established in 1951. 640-acre facility located 15 miles from Peoria. Features: pool; lake; wooded setting.

Profile of Summer Employees Total number: 20–25; typical ages: 18–22. 100% women; 1% minorities; 98% college students; 5% non-U.S. citizens; 15% local applicants. Nonsmokers preferred.

Employment Information Openings are from June 1 to August 17. Jobs available: ▶ 1 *business manager* (minimum age 21) at $180–$200 per week ▶ 3 *canoe instructors* (minimum age 18) with canoe experience and lifeguard certification at $160–$180 per week ▶ 1 *health supervisor* (minimum age 21) with RN, LPN, or EMT license at $200–$220 per week ▶ 1 *older girl program supervisor* (minimum age 21) with camp leadership experience and experience working with girls 13-17 at $175–$195 per week ▶ 1 *riding instructor* (minimum age 21) with experience in beginning and intermediate Western riding at $200–$220 per week ▶ 12–15 *unit counselors* (minimum age 18) at $160–$180 per week ▶ 5 *unit leaders* (minimum age 21) at $175–$195 per week ▶ 1 *waterfront assistant* (minimum age 18) with lifeguard certification at $160–$180 per week ▶ 1 *waterfront supervisor* (minimum age 21) with lifeguard certification and canoeing background at $180–$200 per week. Applicants must submit formal organization application, 2-3 personal references, 2-3 letters of recommendation. A telephone interview is required. International applicants accepted; must apply through a recognized agency.

Benefits and Preemployment Training Free housing, free meals, health insurance, willing to provide letters of recommendation, on-the-job training, willing to complete paperwork for educational credit, and willing to act as a professional reference. Preemployment training is required and includes accident prevention and safety, first aid, CPR, leadership skills.

Contact Lara Campbell, Director of Program and Properties, Camp Tapawingo, 1103 West Lake, Peoria, Illinois 61614. Telephone: 309-688-8671 Ext. 24. Fax: 309-688-7358. E-mail: campbell@girlscouts-kickapoocouncil.org. World Wide Web: http://girlscouts-kickapoocouncil.org. Contact by e-mail, fax, mail, or phone. Application deadline: continuous.

CENTER FOR AMERICAN ARCHEOLOGY

PO BOX 366
KAMPSVILLE, ILLINOIS 62053

General Information Nonprofit organization that provides public outreach and educational programs about archaeology. Established in 1953. Located 80 miles from St. Louis, Missouri. Features: rural environment; outdoor classroom; library; dormitories.

Profile of Summer Employees Total number: 30; typical ages: 21–30. 40% men; 60% women; 100% college students.

Employment Information Openings are from June 14 to July 20. Jobs available: ▶ 2 *field assistant/chaperones* (minimum age 21) with field experience, valid driver's license, and excellent interpersonal skills at $5–$6 per hour. Applicants must submit a letter of interest, resume, three personal references. An in-person interview is recommended, but a telephone interview is acceptable.

Benefits and Preemployment Training Free housing, free meals, willing to provide letters of recommendation, willing to complete paperwork for educational credit, willing to act as a professional reference, and opportunity to attend seminars/workshops. Preemployment training is required and includes program training (education programs).

Contact Mary Pirkl, Director of Education, Center for American Archeology. Telephone: 618-653-4316. Fax: 618-653-4232. E-mail: caa@caa-archaeology.org. World Wide Web: http://www.caa-archeology.org. Contact by e-mail, fax, or phone. Application deadline: application deadline in late spring.

CYBERCAMPS–BARAT COLLEGE OF DEPAUL UNIVERSITY

LAKE FOREST, ILLINOIS

See Cybercamps–University of Washington on page 335 for complete description.

CYBERCAMPS–BENEDICTINE UNIVERSITY

LISLE, ILLINOIS

See Cybercamps–University of Washington on page 335 for complete description.

CYBERCAMPS–CONCORDIA UNIVERSITY

RIVER FOREST, ILLINOIS

See Cybercamps–University of Washington on page 335 for complete description.

CYBERCAMPS–DEPAUL UNIVERSITY

CHICAGO, ILLINOIS

See Cybercamps–University of Washington on page 335 for complete description.

DISCOVERY DAY CAMP

BOX 753
LINCOLNSHIRE, ILLINOIS 60069

General Information Private day camp serving children ages 4-14 on Chicago's North Shore. Emphasis on helping children to feel good about themselves through noncompetitive activities: swimming, sports, and fine arts. Established in 1984. Located 40 miles from Chicago. Features: 25 meter pool with diving; tennis court; air conditioned indoor space; low ropes course; fields for sports; drama stages and gymnastics platform.

Profile of Summer Employees Total number: 75; typical ages: 16–25. 45% men; 55% women; 10% high school students; 65% college students; 75% local applicants. Nonsmokers required.

Employment Information Openings are from June to August. Jobs available: ▶ 20–30 *group leaders/drivers* (minimum age 18) swimming, sports; paid at $1800–$3200 per season ▶ *special-*

ists: tennis, drama, dance, gymnastics, biking, music, arts and crafts (minimum age 18) with skill in area of specialty, paid at $1800–$3500 per season ▶ 1–3 *unit directors* must be college graduate; paid at $80–$150 per day. Applicants must submit a formal organization application, three personal references. An in-person interview is required.

Benefits and Preemployment Training Formal training, willing to provide letters of recommendation, on-the-job training, willing to complete paperwork for educational credit, willing to act as a professional reference, and opportunity to attend seminars/workshops. Preemployment training is required and includes accident prevention and safety, first aid, CPR, interpersonal skills, leadership skills, swimming.

Contact Ilise Schwartzwald, President, Discovery Day Camp. Telephone: 847-367-CAMP. Fax: 847-367-4202. E-mail: ilise@campdiscovery.com. World Wide Web: http://www.campdiscovery.com. Contact by e-mail, fax, phone, or through World Wide Web site.

THE SOUTHWESTERN COMPANY, ILLINOIS

See The Southwestern Company on page 302 for complete description.

SPORTS INTERNATIONAL–BEARS

DEERFIELD, ILLINOIS

See Sports International, Inc. on page 147 for complete description.

SPORTS INTERNATIONAL–RAMS

EDWARDSVILLE, ILLINOIS

See Sports International, Inc. on page 147 for complete description.

STIVERS STAFFING SERVICES–ILLINOIS

200 WEST MONROE
CHICAGO, ILLINOIS 60606

General Information National staffing service that places people in office support positions throughout the United States. Locations include: Arizona (Phoenix, Scottsdale, Temple); Colorado (Aurora, Denver); Indiana (Indianapolis); Kansas (Overland Park); Missouri (Des Peres, Kansas City, St. Ann, St. Louis, North Kansas City); Wisconsin (Milwaukee); California (Encino, Westwood, Los Angeles, Pasadena, San Diego, San Francisco); Illinois (Chicago, Deerfield, Des Plaines, Evanston, Oak Brook, Schaumburg, Fox Valley, Niles); Pennsylvania (Philadelphia, Pittsburgh, King of Prussia); Canada (Toronto). Established in 1945. Features: office settings; professional environments.

Profile of Summer Employees Total number: 2,000. 5% high school students; 60% college students; 10% retirees; 20% local applicants.

Employment Information Openings are from January to December. Year-round positions also offered. Jobs available: ▶ *clerk/typist* with six months office experience at $7–$10 per hour ▶ *customer service representative* with 6 months relevant experience at $8–$12 per hour ▶ *receptionist* with six months office experience at $7–$10 per hour. Applicants must submit a formal organization application, testing. An in-person interview is required.

Benefits and Preemployment Training Possible full-time employment, health insurance, willing to provide letters of recommendation, on-the-job training, and willing to act as a professional reference.

Contact Chris Goodfarb, Internet Manager, Stivers Staffing Services–Illinois, 1717 West Northern, #117, Phoenix, Arizona 85021. Telephone: 602-264-4580. Fax: 602-678-5649. E-mail: chrisg@stivers.com. World Wide Web: http://www.stivers.com. Contact by e-mail, fax, mail, phone, or through World Wide Web site. Application deadline: continuous.

STUDENT CONSERVATION ASSOCIATION (SCA), ILLINOIS

See Student Conservation Association (SCA), New Hampshire on page 209 for complete description.

INDIANA

CAMP LOGAN

303 EMS D14 LANE
SYRACUSE, INDIANA 46567

General Information Residential camp serving girls ages 7-17. Established in 1928. 200-acre facility located 50 miles from Fort Wayne. Features: freshwater lake; wooded setting; rustic dining lodge; natural wetland area; wetland observation platform; tent-cabin units.

Profile of Summer Employees Total number: 35; typical ages: 18–26. 5% men; 95% women; 5% minorities; 10% high school students; 75% college students; 15% non-U.S. citizens; 40% local applicants. Nonsmokers preferred.

Employment Information Openings are from June 6 to August 12. Jobs available: ▶ 3–4 *aquatic assistants* (minimum age 18) with lifeguard training and CPR/first aid certification and experience with children or teaching at $1620 per season ▶ 1 *aquatic manager* (minimum age 21) with CPR/first aid/lifeguard training/WSI certifications. Aquatic facility or program management experience. Teaching and supervisory experience. Certification or experience in canoeing, sailing, kayaking, rowing, or other boating activities at $1920 per season ▶ 1 *assistant director* (minimum age 25) with three years experience in camp setting, one year administration experience, and strong organizational, supervisory, and communication skills at $2100 per season ▶ 1 *business manager* (minimum age 21) with excellent organizational and communication skills. Experience in bookkeeping or accounting at $1920 per season ▶ 8–12 *counselors* (minimum age 18) with ability to work as part of a team. Experience or background with children, camping, or Girl Scouting at $1620 per season ▶ 1 *environmental education director* (minimum age 21) with leadership, organization, and communication skills, teaching experience, and environmental education/nature study knowledge at $1920 per season ▶ 3–4 *equestrian assistants* (minimum age 18) with ability to work as part of a team. Knowledge of horse care and western horseback riding. Experience with children or teaching at $1620 per season ▶ 1 *equestrian manager* (minimum age 21) with CHA/AAHS certification or extensive background in western horseback riding. Strong organizational and supervisory skills at $1920 per season ▶ 2–4 *food service assistants* (minimum age 18) with food service experience and excellent organizational skills at $1620 per season ▶ 1–2 *food service managers* (minimum age 21) with food service experience, excellent organizational skills, supervisory skills at $1920 per season ▶ 1 *health manager* (minimum age 21) with CPR and advanced first aid certifications, LPN/RN/EMT, and strong organizational and people skills at $1920 per season ▶ 1–2 *program coordinators* (minimum age 21) with first aid/CPR certifications, three years experience in camp setting or programming. Strong organizational and communication skills. Certification or experience in ropes course, teambuilding, primitive camping, tripping, environmental education, arts and crafts or other specialty area at $1920 per season ▶ 8–10 *senior counselors* (minimum age 21) with strong organizational and communication skills. Background in leadership and supervision. Experience in teaching and working with children. Camping and Girl Scout experience preferred at $1820 per season ▶ 1–2 *support services coordinators* (minimum age 18) with excellent organizational skills, ability to work with minimal supervision at $1620 per season. Applicants must submit

formal organization application, three personal references, copies of certifications. A telephone interview is required. International applicants accepted; must apply through a recognized agency.
Benefits and Preemployment Training Free housing, free meals, formal training, health insurance, willing to provide letters of recommendation, on-the-job training, willing to complete paperwork for educational credit, willing to act as a professional reference, and opportunity to attend seminars/workshops. Preemployment training is required and includes accident prevention and safety, first aid, CPR, interpersonal skills, leadership skills, child development and program skills.
Contact Deb Dilley, Director, Camp Logan, 203 EMS Lane D14, Syracuse, Indiana 46567. Telephone: 574-457-2841. Fax: 574-457-3021. E-mail: camplogan@hotmail.com. World Wide Web: http://www.gslimberlost.org. Contact by e-mail, fax, mail, phone, or through World Wide Web site. Application deadline: continuous.

CULVER SUMMER CAMPS
1300 ACADEMY ROAD, #138
CULVER, INDIANA 46511

General Information Six-week all-activity program followed by a two-week session of ten specialty camps. Established in 1902. 1,800-acre facility located 50 miles from South Bend. Features: Indiana's 2nd largest natural lake; 120 sail and power boats; hockey and ice skating facilities; 6 Piper Cherokee "140" aircraft; more than 100 horses; ropes/initiatives challenge courses.
Profile of Summer Employees Total number: 325; typical ages: 19–25. 60% men; 40% women; 5% minorities; 2% high school students; 40% college students; 5% retirees; 1% non-U.S. citizens; 10% local applicants. Nonsmokers preferred.
Employment Information Openings are from June 16 to August 23. Jobs available: ▶ *English instructor* with at least one year of experience and English teaching certification; competitive salary ▶ 3 *administrative assistants* with good typing, computer, phone, and organizational skills; competitive salary ▶ *aerobics instructor* with knowledge and experience in area; ability to work with children; competitive salary ▶ 4 *aquatics instructors* certificate in lifeguarding, CPR, first aid preferred; may obtain certifications prior to camp; WSI certification desirable; competitive salary ▶ *art instructor* with knowledge and teaching experience in the area; competitive salary ▶ 20 *assistant counselors* with one year of college, experience working with children, a sense of responsibility, and maturity; competitive salary ▶ 2 *athletic instructors* with knowledge and experience in the field and one year of teaching experience; competitive salary ▶ 7 *aviation flight instructors* with certification by FAA to give flying instruction and experience teaching children; competitive salary ▶ *computer instructor* with knowledge and experience teaching children in related area; competitive salary ▶ 35 *counselors* with at least one year of college and experience working with children; competitive salary ▶ 10 *dining hall assistants* with one year of college experience, responsible, mature young adult; competitive salary ▶ *driver's training experience instructor* with certification and at least one year teaching experience; competitive salary ▶ 5 *equitation instructors* with knowledge and experience teaching children equitation skills, basic care for animals; competitve salary ▶ *fencing instructor* with teaching experience and skills in epee, foil, and saber; competitive salary ▶ *golf instructors* with knowledge and teaching experience with children a plus; competitive salary ▶ *hockey instructor* with adequate knowledge and teaching experience in the field; competitive salary ▶ *ice skating instructor* with adequate knowledge and teaching experience in the area; competitive salary ▶ *math instructor* with at least one year experience and must be a certified math teacher; competitive salary ▶ *music instructor* with music/band teaching experience preferred; competitive salary ▶ *nurse assistant* with one year of college; responsible, mature young adult; competitive salary ▶ *photography instructor* with adequate knowledge, skills, and teaching experience in area; competitive salary ▶ *reading instructor* with teacher certification in related field and at least one year of experience; competitive salary ▶ *rifle instructor* with adequate knowledge and teaching experi-

ence in the field; competitive salary ▶ 1–5 *sailing instructors* with knowledge and experience teaching sailing in a variety of craft; competitive salary ▶ 2 *soccer instructors* with knowledge and experience in coaching; competitive salary ▶ 2 *tennis instructors* with knowledge and coaching experience in tennis; competitive salary ▶ *theater instructor* with adequate knowledge, skills, and teaching experience; competitive salary ▶ 3 *waterski instructors* with proficiency in teaching waterskiing and dealing with children; competitive salary. Applicants must submit formal organization application, three personal references. An in-person interview is recommended, but a telephone interview is acceptable. International applicants accepted; must obtain own working papers, apply through a recognized agency.

Benefits and Preemployment Training Free housing, free meals, willing to provide letters of recommendation, on-the-job training, willing to complete paperwork for educational credit, willing to act as a professional reference, and uniforms provided. Preemployment training is required and includes accident prevention and safety, first aid, CPR, interpersonal skills, leadership skills, lifeguard certification.

Contact Marc T. Read, Assistant Director, Culver Summer Camps, 1300 Academy Road, #138, Culver, Indiana 46511. Telephone: 800-221-2020. Fax: 574-842-8462. E-mail: summer@culver.org. World Wide Web: http://www.culver.org. Contact by e-mail, fax, mail, phone, or through World Wide Web site. Application deadline: continuous.

DUDLEY GALLAHUE VALLEY CAMPS

MORGANTOWN, INDIANA 46160

General Information Residential camp serving 128–140 campers weekly and biweekly. Established in 1912. 800-acre facility located 50 miles from Indianapolis. Features: freshwater lake; wooded setting; platform tents; hills.

Profile of Summer Employees Total number: 40; typical age: 18. 2% men; 98% women; 5% minorities; 5% high school students; 80% college students; 10% local applicants. Nonsmokers preferred.

Employment Information Openings are from June 1 to August 15. Jobs available: ▶ 24 *assistant unit leaders* with completion of group leadership, counselor-in-training, or leader-in-training course and experience in the field at $1400–$1700 per season ▶ 4 *cooks* should be able to provide records of necessary health exams required by Department of Health ▶ 1 *health supervisor* with state license or registration as a physician, physician's assistant, RN, LPN, paramedic, camp health director, or EMT; advanced first aid and/or CPR certification; emotional stability to meet emergencies; and knowledge of medicine and pesticide storage and use at $2000–$2500 per season ▶ 1 *horseback unit leader* with experience in leadership, outdoor, and program specialty training at $1600 per season ▶ 1 *trip unit leader* with leadership, outdoor, and program specialty training and work experience as a teacher or counselor of children at $1600 per season ▶ 8 *unit leaders* with experience in the field and first aid and lifesaving training, training in Girl Scout program, and management and organizational skills at $1600–$1900 per season ▶ 4 *waterfront assistants, canoe/sailing assistants* with current basic swimming instructor certification issued by the American Red Cross or equivalent from the YMCA at $1400 per season. Applicants must submit formal organization application, resume, two personal references, three letters of recommendation. An in-person interview is recommended, but a telephone interview is acceptable. International applicants accepted; must apply through a recognized agency.

Benefits and Preemployment Training Free housing, free meals, formal training, on-the-job training, and willing to complete paperwork for educational credit. Preemployment training is required and includes accident prevention and safety, first aid, CPR, interpersonal skills, leadership skills.

Contact Diana Keely, Outdoor Program Specialist, Dudley Gallahue Valley Camps, Hoosier Capital Girl Scout Council, 1800 North Meridian Street, Indianapolis, Indiana 46202-1433. Telephone: 317-924-3450 Ext. 155. Fax: 317-924-2976. E-mail: dkeely@gshcc.org. World Wide

Web: http://www.gshcc.org. Contact by e-mail, fax, mail, phone, or through World Wide Web site. Application deadline: continuous.

HOWE MILITARY SCHOOL SUMMER CAMP

PO BOX 191
HOWE, INDIANA 46746

General Information A residential camp serving boys ages 9-15 in a modified military setting, emphasizing leadership, sports and academics. Established in 1932. 50-acre facility located 30 miles from South Bend. Features: freshwater lake; wooded setting; cabins; basketball courts and baseball fields; full waterfront; tennis courts.

Profile of Summer Employees Total number: 40; typical ages: 18–55. 80% men; 20% women; 20% minorities; 50% high school students; 30% college students; 20% local applicants. Nonsmokers preferred.

Employment Information Openings are from June 23 to August 2. Jobs available: ▶ 2 *English instructors* (minimum age 19) with a major in teaching at $1800–$2000 per season ▶ 8–12 *cabin counselors* (minimum age 19) with one year of college completed at $1800–$2000 per season ▶ 2 *math instructors* (minimum age 19) with a major in teaching at $1800–$2000 per season ▶ 3–5 *waterfront staff members* (minimum age 18) with WSI or lifeguard certifications at $1600–$1800 per season. Applicants must submit a formal organization application, three personal references, three letters of recommendation. An in-person interview is required.

Benefits and Preemployment Training Free housing, free meals, formal training, possible full-time employment, willing to provide letters of recommendation, on-the-job training, willing to complete paperwork for educational credit, and willing to act as a professional reference. Preemployment training is required and includes accident prevention and safety, first aid, CPR, interpersonal skills, leadership skills.

Contact Duane Van Orden, Camp Director, Howe Military School Summer Camp, Howe Military School, Howe, Indiana 46746. Fax: 219-562-3678. E-mail: dvanorden@howemilitary.com. Contact by e-mail, fax, or mail. Application deadline: May 15.

THE SOUTHWESTERN COMPANY, INDIANA

See The Southwestern Company on page 302 for complete description.

SPORTS INTERNATIONAL–COLTS

RICHMOND, INDIANA

See Sports International, Inc. on page 147 for complete description.

STIVERS STAFFING SERVICES–INDIANA

See Stivers Staffing Services–Illinois on page 110 for complete description.

STUDENT CONSERVATION ASSOCIATION (SCA), INDIANA

See Student Conservation Association (SCA), New Hampshire on page 209 for complete description.

IOWA

CAMP COURAGEOUS OF IOWA
12007 190TH STREET
MONTICELLO, IOWA 52310-0418

General Information Year-round camp for children and adults with disabilities. Traditional camp activities such as swimming, canoeing, nature activities, and crafts are offered. Also adventure activities such as rock climbing, high ropes, and caving are available. Established in 1972. 70-acre facility located 35 miles from Cedar Rapids. Features: wooded setting; indoor pool; nature center; caves; bluffs to rock climb and rappel; staff dormitory.

Profile of Summer Employees Total number: 50; typical ages: 18–30. 30% men; 70% women; 3% minorities; 70% college students; 1% retirees; 10% non-U.S. citizens; 5% local applicants. Nonsmokers required.

Employment Information Openings are from May 18 to August 15. Year-round positions also offered. Jobs available: ▶ 2 *adventure specialists* (minimum age 18) with belaying training and experience leading rock climbing, rappelling, and high/low ropes; training can be provided at $240–$330 per week ▶ 15–20 *camp counselors* (minimum age 18) with a sincere desire to work with people with disabilities at $240–$330 per week ▶ 1 *canoeing specialist* with current lifeguard training certification and experience leading canoeing at $240–$330 per week ▶ 1 *crafts specialist* (minimum age 18) with experience with projects for people with disabilities at $240–$330 per week ▶ 1 *health staff assistant* (minimum age 18) with CPR and first aid training at $240 per week ▶ 1 *nature specialist* (minimum age 18) with experience leading nature activities and working with small farm animals at $240–$330 per week ▶ 1 *outdoor living skills specialist* (minimum age 18) with experience teaching outdoor living skills for people with disabilities at $240–$330 per week ▶ 1 *recreation specialist* (minimum age 18) with experience with recreational activities for people with disabilities at $240–$330 per week ▶ 1 *swimming specialist* (minimum age 18) with current lifeguard training certification at $240–$330 per week. Applicants must submit formal organization application, resume, three letters of recommendation, in-person interview (for year-round jobs), telephone interview acceptable for seasonal jobs; on-line applications available on Web site. International applicants accepted; must obtain own visa, obtain own working papers, apply through a recognized agency.

Benefits and Preemployment Training Free housing, free meals, formal training, possible full-time employment, willing to provide letters of recommendation, on-the-job training, willing to complete paperwork for educational credit, willing to act as a professional reference, and first aid/CPR training, restricted medical plan. Preemployment training is required and includes accident prevention and safety, first aid, CPR, interpersonal skills, leadership skills, behavior management, child and dependant adult abuse awareness.

Contact Jeanne Muellerleile, Camp Director, Camp Courageous of Iowa, 12007 190th Street, PO Box 418, Monticello, Iowa 52310-0418. Telephone: 319-465-5916 Ext. 206. Fax: 319-465-5919. E-mail: jmuellerleile@campcourageous.org. World Wide Web: http://www.campcourageous.org. Contact by e-mail, fax, mail, phone, or through World Wide Web site. Application deadline: continuous.

GIRL SCOUT CAMP TANGLEFOOT
14948 DOGWOOD AVENUE
CLEAR LAKE, IOWA 50428

General Information Residential summer camp serving 120 Girl Scouts weekly. Established in 1947. 50-acre facility. Features: freshwater lake; cabins and platform tents; prairie and wooded site; high ropes course; waterfront building and dock complex; new staff/program building.

Profile of Summer Employees Total number: 36; typical ages: 17–30. 5% men; 95% women; 1% minorities; 25% high school students; 70% college students; 1% non-U.S. citizens; 90% local applicants. Nonsmokers preferred.

Employment Information Openings are from June 1 to August 15. Jobs available: ▶ 1 *arts director* (minimum age 18) with driver's license at $1600–$1800 per season ▶ 1 *business manager* (minimum age 20) with computer (Win98) skills, some bookkeeping experience, and driver's license at $1600–$1800 per season ▶ 3 *food service staff members* (minimum age 18) at $1600–$1800 per season ▶ *health and wellness supervisor* (minimum age 21) with first aid, CPR (will train), driver's license, and health education and record keeping experience at $1800–$2000 per season ▶ 15 *program counselors* (minimum age 17) with LG, first aid, CPR (will offer additional training); driver's license preferred at $1200–$1800 per season ▶ 1 *program director* (minimum age 21) with organizational and supervisory skills, and driver's license at $1900–$2200 per season ▶ 1 *waterfront director* (minimum age 18) with Red Cross LG (LGI preferred), WSI, CPR, first aid, small craft safety, and driver's license at $1700–$1800 per season ▶ 5 *waterfront staff members* (minimum age 17) with Red Cross lifeguard training, WSI certification, and driver's license at $1300–$1600 per season. Applicants must submit formal organization application, three personal references, background check. An in-person interview is recommended, but a telephone interview is acceptable. International applicants accepted; must apply through a recognized agency.

Benefits and Preemployment Training Free housing, free meals, formal training, willing to provide letters of recommendation, on-the-job training, willing to complete paperwork for educational credit, willing to act as a professional reference, opportunity to attend seminars/workshops, and certification training. Preemployment training is required and includes accident prevention and safety, first aid, CPR, interpersonal skills, leadership skills, waterfront/small craft certification.

Contact C. L. Findley, Camp Director, Girl Scout Camp Tanglefoot, 14948 Dogwood Avenue, Clear Lake, Iowa 50428. Telephone: 641-357-2481. Fax: 641-357-7735. E-mail: cindy@niowagirlscouts.org. World Wide Web: http://www.niowagirlscouts.org. Contact by e-mail, fax, mail, phone, or through World Wide Web site. Application deadline: continuous.

THE SOUTHWESTERN COMPANY, IOWA

See The Southwestern Company on page 302 for complete description.

STUDENT CONSERVATION ASSOCIATION (SCA), IOWA

See Student Conservation Association (SCA), New Hampshire on page 209 for complete description.

KANSAS

MITCHELL HARVESTING

2298 NORTH ROAD I
ULYSSES, KANSAS 67880

General Information Harvests grain, wheat, barley, oats, and milo. Starts in Texas May 15 and works way north to Montana, then back to Colorado and Texas for fall harvest ending in November. Established in 1992. Located 200 miles from Amarillo, Texas. Features: beautiful,

vast wheat fields; historical sites; mountains; rolling hills; working outdoors; rural city setting.
Profile of Summer Employees Total number: 1; typical ages: 25–30. 90% men; 10% women; 20% high school students; 30% retirees; 50% local applicants. Nonsmokers preferred.
Employment Information Openings are from May 1 to November 1. Year-round positions also offered. Jobs available: ▶ 1 *combine operator* (minimum age 18) with farm background at $1000-$1400 per month plus bonus for full season ▶ 1–2 *truck drivers* (minimum age 18) with CDL or willing to obtain it at $1000-$1400 per month plus bonus for full season. An in-person interview is recommended, but a telephone interview is acceptable. International applicants accepted; must obtain own working papers.
Benefits and Preemployment Training Free housing, free meals, possible full-time employment, names of contacts, on-the-job training, opportunity to attend seminars/workshops, and travel reimbursement. Preemployment training is optional and includes accident prevention and safety, leadership skills.
Contact Tammi Mitchell, Co-Owner, Mitchell Harvesting, 2298 North Road I, Ulysses, Kansas 67880. Telephone: 620-424-1771. Fax: 620-424-1778. E-mail: mitchelt@pld.com. Contact by e-mail or phone. Application deadline: continuous.

THE SOUTHWESTERN COMPANY, KANSAS

See The Southwestern Company on page 302 for complete description.

STIVERS STAFFING SERVICES–KANSAS

See Stivers Staffing Services–Illinois on page 110 for complete description.

STUDENT CONSERVATION ASSOCIATION (SCA), KANSAS

See Student Conservation Association (SCA), New Hampshire on page 209 for complete description.

KENTUCKY

A CHRISTIAN MINISTRY IN THE NATIONAL PARKS–KENTUCKY

See A Christian Ministry in the National Parks–Maine on page 122 for complete description.

BEAR CREEK AQUATIC CAMP/GIRL SCOUTS OF KENTUCKIANA

LOUISVILLE, KENTUCKY

General Information Organization serving the needs of over 20,000 girls and 7,000 adult volunteers in 57 countries. Established in 1980. 183-acre facility located 40 miles from Paducah. Features: 183 acres of waterfront property; boating dock; swimming area; wooded setting; fresh water lake.
Profile of Summer Employees Total number: 25–30; typical ages: 18–26. 10% men; 90% women; 10% high school students; 80% college students; 10% non-U.S. citizens.
Employment Information Openings are from May 30 to August 8. Jobs available: ▶ 1 *assistant*

director with current lifeguard certification, bachelor's degree, and resident camping experience; salary varies depending on experience ▶ 3–5 *boating staff* (minimum age 18) with sailing, kayaking and canoeing experience; lifeguard certification; salary based on certifications and experience ▶ 1 *health supervisor* with EMT/LPN certification, camping experience desired; salary based on certifications and experience RN, EMT, LPN ▶ 10 *unit staff* (minimum age 18) must be experienced program leader with lifeguarding experience; Girl Scout experience desired; salary based on certifications and experience ▶ 2–4 *waterfront staff* (minimum age 18) with lifeguard/WSI certification desired; salary based on certifications and experience. Applicants must submit formal organization application, three personal references, (application available online through Web site). A telephone interview is required. International applicants accepted; must apply through a recognized agency.

Benefits and Preemployment Training Free housing, free meals, health insurance, willing to provide letters of recommendation, on-the-job training, willing to complete paperwork for educational credit, willing to act as a professional reference, opportunity to attend seminars/ workshops, and use of equipment; first aid; CPR; lifeguarding; and small craft safety training.

Contact Lisa Gunterman, Camping Administrator, Bear Creek Aquatic Camp/Girl Scouts of Kentuckiana, PO Box 32335, Louisville, Kentucky 40232-2335. Telephone: 502-636-0900. Fax: 502-634-0837. E-mail: lgunterman@kyanags.org. World Wide Web: http://www.kygirlscoutcamps.org. Contact by e-mail, phone, or through World Wide Web site. Application deadline: continuous.

CAMP PENNYROYAL/GIRL SCOUTS OF KENTUCKIANA

PO BOX 32335

LOUISVILLE, KENTUCKY 40232-2335

General Information Organization serving the needs of over 20,000 girls and 7,000 adult volunteers in 57 countries. Established in 1950. 200-acre facility located near Owensboro. Features: wooded setting; 8 acre lake; hiking trails; new lodge; tent and cabin units.

Profile of Summer Employees Total number: 35; typical ages: 18–26. 10% men; 90% women; 10% high school students; 80% college students; 10% non-U.S. citizens.

Employment Information Openings are from June 3 to August 10. Jobs available: ▶ 1 *assistant director* (minimum age 21) with resident camp experience, outdoor program experience, experience with children, administrative or supervisory experience desired at $3000–$4000 per season ▶ 2 *cooks* (minimum age 25) with experience as camp or school cook, good organizational skills, registered dietician preferred at $3000–$5000 per season ▶ 1 *program director* (minimum age 21) with experience in outdoor programming with children, resident camp experience, arts and craft experience at $1800–$2160 per season ▶ 15 *unit staff* (minimum age 18) with experience working with children, a desire to work in camp setting, and leadership experience (desired) at $1300–$2000 per season ▶ 5 *waterfront staff* (minimum age 18) with lifeguard certification, WSI desired at $1300–$2100 per season. Applicants must submit formal organization application, three personal references, (application available online through Web site). A telephone interview is required. International applicants accepted; must apply through a recognized agency.

Benefits and Preemployment Training Free housing, free meals, formal training, health insurance, willing to provide letters of recommendation, on-the-job training, willing to complete paperwork for educational credit, willing to act as a professional reference, and free use of equipment on time off; lifeguard, CPR, and first aid training. Preemployment training is required and includes accident prevention and safety, first aid, CPR, interpersonal skills, leadership skills, lifeguarding, small craft safety, first aid and CPR.

Contact Lisa Gunterman, Camping Administrator, Camp Pennyroyal/Girl Scouts of Kentuckiana. Telephone: 888-771-5170. Fax: 502-634-0837. E-mail: lgunterman@kyanags.org. World Wide Web: http://www.kygirlscoutcamps.org. Contact by e-mail, fax, phone, or through World Wide Web site. Application deadline: continuous.

CAMP WOODMEN OF THE WORLD

93 SCHWARTZ ROAD
MURRAY, KENTUCKY 42071

General Information Residential camp serving Woodmen of the World members ages 8–15; also a senior program serving adults ages 60 and over with a general camp program that provides transportation Monday and Friday. Established in 1983. 14-acre facility. Features: junior olympic swimming pool; 45-foot rappelling tower; 24-foot pool slide; 2 tennis courts; 6 cabins.

Profile of Summer Employees Total number: 25–30; typical ages: 18–25. 50% men; 50% women; 2% minorities; 30% high school students; 70% college students; 2% non-U.S. citizens; 40% local applicants.

Employment Information Openings are from May to August. Jobs available: ▶ 1 *archery instructor* (minimum age 18) with certification in field at $130 per week ▶ 1 *arts and crafts instructor* (minimum age 18) with experience in the field at $130 per week ▶ 1 *assistant cook* (minimum age 21) with quantity cooking skills at $150 per week ▶ 1 *food service staff–head cook* (minimum age 21) with quantity cooking skills at $175 per week ▶ 8–12 *general counselors* (minimum age 18) with experience in the field at $120 per week ▶ 2 *kitchen helpers* (minimum age 15) with basic kitchen assistance skills at $90 per week ▶ 1 *rifle instructor* (minimum age 21) with experience or NRA certification at $130 per week ▶ 2 *ropes course instructors* (minimum age 18) with certification or documented experience at $130 per week ▶ 1 *water safety instructor/ pool manager* (minimum age 21) with WSI certification (preferred) at $130 per week. Applicants must submit formal organization application, three personal references. An in-person interview is recommended, but a telephone interview is acceptable. International applicants accepted; must obtain own visa, obtain own working papers, apply through a recognized agency.

Benefits and Preemployment Training Free housing, free meals, health insurance, willing to provide letters of recommendation, names of contacts, on-the-job training, willing to complete paperwork for educational credit, and willing to act as a professional reference. Preemployment training is required and includes accident prevention and safety, first aid, CPR, leadership skills, lifeguard certification.

Contact Colleen Anderson, Camp Director, Camp Woodmen of the World, 401-A Maple Street, Murray, Kentucky 42071. Telephone: 270-753-4382. Fax: 270-753-4396. E-mail: campwow@ onemain.com. World Wide Web: http://www.campwow.net. Contact by e-mail, fax, phone, or through World Wide Web site. Application deadline: April 1.

LIFE ADVENTURE CAMP

1122 OAK HILL DRIVE
LEXINGTON, KENTUCKY 40505

General Information Primitive wilderness camp with weekly programs that serve 32–40 campers per session (ages 9–18) who are either emotionally or behaviorally challenged, or who are in need of enhanced self-esteem, cooperation, and team-building skills. Established in 1977. 600-acre facility. Features: wooded setting; 6 caves on site; large creek; tent camping.

Profile of Summer Employees Total number: 15; typical ages: 19–30. 31% men; 69% women; 5% high school students; 75% college students; 20% local applicants. Nonsmokers required.

Employment Information Openings are from May 28 to July 30. Jobs available: ▶ 12 *counselors* (minimum age 19) with first aid/CPR certification, one year of college or related work experience, some camping or outdoor experience, ability to live and work comfortably in a primitive outdoor setting, and some experience in a leadership role with children, preferably with children who have emotional and/or behavioral problems at $1600–$1800 per season ▶ 1 *food director* (minimum age 21) with experience with food management and valid driver's license at $1000–$1200 per season ▶ 1 *health supervisor* (minimum age 19) with first aid/CPR certification and valid driver's license at $1600–$1900 per season. Applicants must submit a formal organization application, three personal references, background check. An in-person interview is recommended, but a telephone interview is acceptable.

Benefits and Preemployment Training Free housing, free meals, formal training, willing to provide letters of recommendation, on-the-job training, willing to complete paperwork for educational credit, and willing to act as a professional reference. Preemployment training is required and includes accident prevention and safety, first aid, CPR, interpersonal skills, leadership skills, behavior management, crisis management.

Contact Keith Haas, Assistant Program Director, Life Adventure Camp, 1122 Oak Hill Drive, Lexington, Kentucky 40505. Telephone: 859-252-4733. Fax: 859-225-5115. E-mail: lac@lifeadventurecamp.org. World Wide Web: http://www.lifeadventurecamp.org. Contact by e-mail, mail, phone, or through World Wide Web site. Application deadline: April 30.

THE SOUTHWESTERN COMPANY, KENTUCKY

See The Southwestern Company on page 302 for complete description.

STUDENT CONSERVATION ASSOCIATION (SCA), KENTUCKY

See Student Conservation Association (SCA), New Hampshire on page 209 for complete description.

LOUISIANA

CAMP FIRE CAMP WI-TA-WENTIN

2126 OAK PARK BOULEVARD
LAKE CHARLES, LOUISIANA 70601

General Information Three-week day camp and two-week resident camp. Established in 1950. 96-acre facility. Located 13 miles from . Features: freshwater bay; wooded setting; rustic cabins; nature trails.

Profile of Summer Employees Total number: 24; typical ages: 18–25. 50% men; 50% women; 5% minorities; 20% high school students; 80% college students; 85% local applicants. Nonsmokers required.

Employment Information Openings are from June 7 to July 16. Year-round positions also offered. Jobs available: ▶ *canoeing instructor* (minimum age 19) at $600 per season ▶ *general counselors* (minimum age 17) at $500 per season ▶ *lifeguards* (minimum age 19) at $600 per season ▶ *program director* (minimum age 17) at $600 per season ▶ 1 *water safety instructor* (minimum age 19) at $500 per season. Applicants must submit a formal organization application, three personal references, two letters of recommendation. An in-person interview is recommended, but a telephone interview is acceptable. International applicants accepted.

Benefits and Preemployment Training Free housing, free meals, formal training, willing to provide letters of recommendation, on-the-job training, and willing to act as a professional reference. Preemployment training is required and includes accident prevention and safety, first aid, CPR.

Contact Katheleen M. Mayo, Director, Camp Fire Camp Wi-Ta-Wentin, 2126 Oak Park Boulevard, Lake Charles, Louisiana 70601. Telephone: 318-478-6550. Fax: 318-478-6551. E-mail: kmkmayo@bellsouth.net. World Wide Web: http://www.cfsowela.bigstep.com. Contact by e-mail, fax, mail, or phone. Application deadline: June 1.

THE SOUTHWESTERN COMPANY, LOUISIANA

See The Southwestern Company on page 302 for complete description.

STUDENT CONSERVATION ASSOCIATION (SCA), LOUISIANA

See Student Conservation Association (SCA), New Hampshire on page 209 for complete description.

MAINE

ACADIA CORPORATION

85 MAIN STREET, BOX 24
BAR HARBOR, MAINE 04609

General Information National park concessioner operating a restaurant and three gift shops in Acadia National Park and several shops in the town of Bar Harbor. Established in 1932. Located 18 miles from Ellsworth. Features: national park setting; near Atlantic Ocean; hiking, biking, and sailing activities available; busy resort community; tea and popovers on the lawn.

Profile of Summer Employees Total number: 150–175; typical ages: 18–70. 44% men; 56% women; 4% minorities; 1% high school students; 89% college students; 10% retirees; 2% non-U.S. citizens; 20% local applicants.

Employment Information Openings are from May 15 to October 26. Jobs available: ▶ 1 *bartender* (minimum age 18) with ability to operate service bar and cash register per hour at $5.50 per hour plus tips ▶ 5 *buspersons* (minimum age 18) with ability to lift and carry more than 25 pounds up to 100 times per day at $5.75 per hour plus tips ▶ 6 *hosts* (minimum age 18) with pleasant personality and calm demeanor to greet and seat customers and take reservations at $6.50 per hour plus tips ▶ 1–2 *housekeepers* (minimum age 18) with willingness to clean housing, offices, and restrooms at $9 per hour ▶ 15 *kitchen workers* (minimum age 18) with ability to run cold food line and bakery and to perform food prep work, dishwashing, cleaning and lifting and carrying more than 25 pounds up to 100 times per day at $8.50 per hour plus bonus ▶ 3 *lead cooks* (minimum age 18) with strong creative cooking skills, including saute and sauces, and two years of supervisory experience or equivalent at $9.50 per hour ▶ 3 *office clerks* (minimum age 18) with ability to perform work accurately, pay attention to detail, and type (must have valid driver's license) at $8 per hour ▶ 32 *shop clerks* (minimum age 18) with ability to perform various duties, including operating cash register, assisting with purchases, stocking and ordering merchandise, and orienting park visitors at $8 per hour ▶ 36 *waiters/waitresses* (minimum age 18) with pleasant personality, calm demeanor, and ability to lift and carry more than 25 pounds up to 100 times per day at $2.88 per hour plus tips ▶ 4 *warehouse clerks* (minimum age 18) with ability to maintain accurate records and pay attention to detail, clean driving record, valid driver's license; ability to frequently lift and carry up to 50 pounds at $8 per hour. Applicants must submit formal organization application, two personal references, letter of recommendation. A telephone interview is required. International applicants accepted; must obtain own visa, obtain own working papers, apply through a recognized agency.

Benefits and Preemployment Training Housing at a cost, meals at a cost, willing to provide letters of recommendation, and on-the-job training. Preemployment training is required and includes accident prevention and safety, interpersonal skills, information about camping policies and information about Acadia National Park and surrounding area.

Contact Rebecca Ghelli, Personnel, Acadia Corporation, PO Box 24, Bar Harbor, Maine 04609. Telephone: 207-288-5592. Fax: 207-288-2420. E-mail: acadia@acadia.net. World Wide Web: http://www.jordanpond.com. Contact by e-mail, fax, mail, or phone. Application deadline: continuous.

A CHRISTIAN MINISTRY IN THE NATIONAL PARKS–MAINE

10 JUSTIN'S WAY
FREEPORT, MAINE 04032

General Information Nonprofit interdenominational Christian ministry that places individuals in the national parks to work, witness, and conduct worship services and activities. Established in 1952. Features: National Parks; mountains; water; lakes; hiking opportunities.

Profile of Summer Employees Total number: 200–250; typical ages: 19–25. 40% men; 60% women; 10% minorities; 80% college students; 5% retirees; 5% local applicants.

Employment Information Openings are from January 1 to December 31. Year-round positions also offered. Jobs available: ▶ 20–30 *ministry staff leaders* (minimum age 18) with willingness to learn the following: leading worship, preaching, providing pastoral care, teaching, administration, and music at $1200–$2000 per three months ▶ 220–250 *ministry staff members* (minimum age 18) with abilities in leading bible studies, Christian education, drama, music, leading discussion groups, and offering recreation ideas at $1200–$2000 per three months ▶ 20–30 *ministry staff musicians* (minimum age 18) to provide music for weekly services of worship, lead choirs, and organize special musical events at $1200–$2000 per three months. Applicants must submit a formal organization application, three letters of recommendation. International applicants accepted; must obtain own visa, obtain own working papers.

Benefits and Preemployment Training Housing at a cost, meals at a cost, willing to provide letters of recommendation, and on-the-job training. Preemployment training is optional and includes interpersonal skills, leadership skills, ministry preparation.

Contact Rev. Richard P. Camp, Jr., Director, A Christian Ministry in the National Parks–Maine. Telephone: 207-865-6436. Fax: 207-865-6852. E-mail: acmnp@juno.com. World Wide Web: http://www.acmnp.com. Contact by e-mail, fax, mail, phone, or through World Wide Web site. Application deadline: continuous.

ALFORD LAKE CAMP

258 ALFORD LAKE ROAD
HOPE, MAINE 04847

General Information Residential camp for girls offering a multiactivity program for 175 girls ages 8–15. Extensive trip programs for girls and/or boys on the Appalachian Trail and in Great Britain offered, as well as exchange programs in Mexico, Japan, and Nova Scotia. Established in 1907. 416-acre facility located 10 miles from Camden. Features: freshwater lake; wooded setting; 4 tennis courts; library; stables and riding rings; climbing wall/high and low cable courses.

Profile of Summer Employees Total number: 90; typical ages: 17–25. 2% men; 98% women; 60% college students; 6% non-U.S. citizens. Nonsmokers required.

Employment Information Openings are from June 12 to August 18. Jobs available: ▶ 1 *archery instructor* (minimum age 18) National Archery Association Level 1 at $1500–$2200 per season ▶ 1–3 *canoeing instructors* (minimum age 18) with Red Cross canoeing (or equivalent) and American Red Cross Lifeguard Certification at $1500–$2200 per season ▶ 2 *climbing wall and high/low cable course instructors* (minimum age 18) with climbing experience at $1500–$2200 per season ▶ 1–2 *drama instructors* (minimum age 18) with teaching and production experience at $1500–$2200 per season ▶ 1–2 *gymnastics instructors* (minimum age 18) with teaching experience and certification or documentation at $1500–$2200 per season ▶ 2 *office personnel* (minimum age 20) with knowledge of computers, attention to detail, and telephone skills (essential) at $1000–$1800 per season ▶ 1–3 *outdoor explorations (campcraft and nature)* (minimum age 18) with Maine trip-leading certification, Wilderness First Aid and ARS Lifeguard Training Certification at $1500–$2200 per season ▶ 5 *riding instructors* (minimum age 18) with British Horse Society, Pony Club certification, or equivalent at $1500–$2200 per season ▶ 1–2 *sailboarding instructors* (minimum age 18) with sailboarding experience documentation and American Red Cross Lifeguard-Training Certification at $1500–$2200 per season ▶ 3–5 *sailing instructors* (minimum age 18) with Red Cross lifeguard training and sailing experience at $1500–$2200 per season ▶ 5–9 *swimming instructors* (minimum age 18) with WSI and American Red Cross lifeguard certification at $1500–$2200 per season ▶ 4 *tennis counselors* (minimum age 18) with teaching experience at $1500–$2200 per season ▶ 4 *trip leaders* (minimum age 21) with Maine Trip Leading Certification, Wilderness First Aid, LGT, CPR, first aid, and experience leading 2- to 3-day trips at $1500–$1800 per season. Applicants must submit formal organization application, three personal references. A telephone interview is required. International applicants accepted; must apply through a recognized agency.

Benefits and Preemployment Training Free housing, free meals, formal training, willing to provide letters of recommendation, on-the-job training, willing to complete paperwork for educational credit, and possible internship. Preemployment training is required and includes accident prevention and safety, interpersonal skills, leadership skills.

Contact Ms. Betsy Brayley, Alford Lake Camp, 5 Salt Marsh Way, Cape Elizabeth, Maine 04107. Telephone: 207-799-3005. Fax: 207-799-5044. E-mail: alc@alfordlake.com. Contact by e-mail, fax, mail, or phone. Application deadline: continuous.

CAMP AGAWAM

CRESCENT LAKE, 54 AGAWAM ROAD
RAYMOND, MAINE 04071

General Information Residential camp serving 125 boys ages 8–15 in a single 7-week session. There is also a 1-week session for 85 disadvantaged boys. Established in 1919. 115-acre facility located 35 miles from Portland. Features: freshwater lake; wooded setting; renovated screened cabins and bathrooms; new dining hall and main lodge; 4 new tennis courts; new basketball court; 2 new soccer fields; well-maintained facility.

Profile of Summer Employees Total number: 65; typical ages: 18–70. 90% men; 10% women; 5% minorities; 20% high school students; 80% college students; 10% non-U.S. citizens; 10% local applicants. Nonsmokers required.

Employment Information Openings are from June 10 to August 15. Jobs available: ▶ 1 *counselor/crafts instructor* (minimum age 18) with experience preferred at $1350–$1600 per season ▶ 1 *counselor/dramatics instructor* (minimum age 18) with acting classes, directing, and performing experience at $1350–$1600 per season ▶ 1 *counselor/woodworking instructor* (minimum age 19) at $1350–$2000 per season ▶ 2 *counselors/archery and riflery instructors* (minimum age 19) with NAA or NRA certification or equivalent at $1350–$1800 per season ▶ 4 *counselors/campcraft and trip leaders* with LGT, CPR/first aid, Maine Trip Leader certification, and Wilderness First Aid at $1350–$1600 per season ▶ 15 *counselors/sports instructors/coaches* with experience, including attending clinics at $1350–$1600 per season ▶ 4 *counselors/water sports instructors* (minimum age 18) with CPR, first aid, and WSI or LGT certification at $1350–$1750 per season ▶ *ropes course facilitator* (minimum age 19) with ropes course facilitator certification at $1350–$1750 per season ▶ *watercraft counselor (sailboards, sailboats, canoes, rowboats)* (minimum age 18) at $1350–$1600 per season. Applicants must submit a formal organization application, three personal references. An in-person interview is recommended, but a telephone interview is acceptable. International applicants accepted.

Benefits and Preemployment Training Free housing, free meals, formal training, willing to provide letters of recommendation, on-the-job training, willing to complete paperwork for educational credit, willing to act as a professional reference, and opportunity to attend seminars/workshops. Preemployment training is required and includes accident prevention and safety, first aid, CPR, interpersonal skills, leadership skills, child development.

Contact Scott Malm, Program Director, Camp Agawam, 30 Fieldstone Lane, Hanover, Massachusetts 02339. Telephone: 781-826-5913. Fax: 781-829-0208. E-mail: bowman@campagawam.org. World Wide Web: http://www.campagawam.org. Contact by e-mail, fax, mail, phone, or through World Wide Web site. Application deadline: continuous.

CAMP ANDROSCOGGIN

WAYNE, MAINE 04284

General Information Private residential camp serving 250 boys from the United States and abroad in one 8-week session. Established in 1907. 125-acre facility located 15 miles from Augusta. Features: freshwater lake; wooded setting; 12 tennis courts; 4 sports fields; 30 watercraft; indoor gymnasium.

Profile of Summer Employees Total number: 100; typical ages: 19–25. 90% men; 10% women; 80% college students; 10% non-U.S. citizens; 10% local applicants. Nonsmokers preferred.

Employment Information Openings are from June 17 to August 17. Jobs available: ▶ 1 *animation/video instructor* at $1250–$1750 per season ▶ 1 *archery instructor* at $1250–$1750 per season ▶ 4 *baseball instructors* at $1250–$1750 per season ▶ 4 *basketball instructors* at $1250–$1750 per season ▶ 1 *bicycling instructor* at $1250–$1750 per season ▶ 2 *canoeing instructors* at $1250–$1750 per season ▶ 1 *ceramics instructor* at $1250–$1750 per season ▶ 1 *crafts instructor* at $1250–$1750 per season ▶ 2 *drama instructors* at $1250–$1750 per season ▶ 1 *kayaking instructor* at $1250–$1750 per season ▶ 2 *lacrosse instructors* at $1250–$1750 per season ▶ 1 *nature instructor* at $1250–$1750 per season ▶ 2 *nurses* at $3000–$4000 per season ▶ 1 *photography instructor* at $1250–$1750 per season ▶ 1 *radio broadcasting instructor* at $1250–$1750 per season ▶ 1 *riflery instructor* at $1250–$1750 per season ▶ 4 *ropes course instructors* at $1250–$1750 per season ▶ 3 *sailing instructors* at $1250–$1750 per season ▶ 2 *secretaries* at $1750–$2250 per season ▶ 4 *soccer instructors* at $1250–$1750 per season ▶ 10 *swimming instructors* with WSI certification or lifeguard training at $1250–$1750 per season ▶ 10 *tennis instructors* at $1250–$1750 per season ▶ 4 *waterskiing instructors* at $1250–$1750 per season ▶ 1 *windsurfing instructor* at $1250–$1750 per season ▶ 1 *woodworking instructor* at $1250–$1750 per season. Applicants must submit formal organization application, letter of interest, three personal references. An in-person interview is recommended, but a telephone interview is acceptable. International applicants accepted; must apply through a recognized agency.

Benefits and Preemployment Training Free housing, free meals, willing to provide letters of recommendation, on-the-job training, willing to complete paperwork for educational credit, willing to act as a professional reference, and travel reimbursement. Preemployment training is required and includes accident prevention and safety, first aid, CPR, interpersonal skills, leadership skills.

Contact Peter Hirsch, Director, Camp Androscoggin, 601 West Street, Harrison, New York 10528. Telephone: 914-835-5800. Fax: 914-777-2718. E-mail: staff@campandro.com. World Wide Web: http://www.campandro.com. Contact by e-mail, fax, mail, phone, or through World Wide Web site. Application deadline: continuous.

CAMP ARCADIA

ROUTE 121
CASCO, MAINE 04015

General Information Residential camp for girls serving 160 campers for part of the season or seven full weeks concentrating on individual camper growth and development in a warm, family atmosphere. Established in 1916. 365-acre facility located 35 miles from Portland. Features: extensive freshwater lake frontage; 2 natural sandy beaches; sunny fields and pine woods; tennis courts; riding ring and stables.

Profile of Summer Employees Total number: 80; typical ages: 19–23. 10% men; 90% women; 5% minorities; 75% college students; 10% non-U.S. citizens. Nonsmokers preferred.

Employment Information Openings are from June 13 to August 19. Jobs available: ▶ 1 *archery instructor* at $1100–$1300 per season ▶ 2 *arts and crafts instructors* with silk-screening, block-printing, batik, drawing, and painting experience at $1500–$2200 per season ▶ 4 *canoeing instructors* (minimum age 19) with lifeguard training certification at $1500–$2000 per season ▶ 1 *ceramics instructor* with electric kiln and potter's wheel experience at $1500–$2000 per season ▶ *chef/baker* at a negotiable salary ▶ 2 *drama instructors* with driver's license and experience in children's drama, directing, lighting, and sets at $1500–$2200 per season ▶ 1 *environmental (nature) instructor* at $1500–$2500 per season ▶ 1 *gymnastics instructor* with rhythmic, floor, and low beam gymnastics experience at $1500–$2000 per season ▶ 1 *music instructor* with piano playing and camp song leadership ability at $1500–$2200 per season ▶ 2 *nurses* with RN license at a negotiable salary ▶ 2 *office workers* with 50 wpm typing and knowledge of computers at $1500–$2000 per season ▶ 1 *photography instructor* with black-and-white darkroom experience at $1500–$2000 per season ▶ 2 *riding instructors* with English balance seat-riding and stable management ability at $1500–$2000 per season ▶ 4 *sailing instructors* with lifeguard training and knowledge of racing at $1300–$2000 per season ▶ *swimming instructors* with WSI and lifeguard training certification at $1200–$1600 per season ▶ 4 *tennis instructors* with tennis team background at $1500–$2200 per season ▶ 3 *trip instructors* (minimum age 21) with driver's license at $1500–$2500 per season ▶ 2 *weaving instructors* with knowledge of floor, table, and hand looms at $1500–$1800 per season. Applicants must submit formal organization application, personal reference, letter of recommendation. An in-person interview is recommended, but a telephone interview is acceptable. International applicants accepted; must obtain own visa, obtain own working papers, apply through a recognized agency.

Benefits and Preemployment Training Free housing, free meals, formal training, health insurance, willing to provide letters of recommendation, names of contacts, on-the-job training, willing to complete paperwork for educational credit, willing to act as a professional reference, travel reimbursement, and free uniforms. Preemployment training is required and includes accident prevention and safety, first aid, CPR, leadership skills.

Contact Anne Henderson Fritts, Director, Camp Arcadia, PO Box 225, Pleasantville Road, New Vernon, New Jersey 07976. Telephone: 973-538-5409. Fax: 973-540-1555. Contact by fax, mail, or phone. Application deadline: continuous.

CAMP ENCORE-CODA FOR A GREAT SUMMER OF MUSIC, SPORTS, AND FRIENDS

STEARNS POND
SWEDEN, MAINE 04040

General Information Residential coed music and sports camp. Ensembles and private instruction in the areas of classical, jazz, and rock music as well as musical theater are featured. Established in 1950. 80-acre facility located 40 miles from Portland. Features: freshwater lake; wooded setting; 2 tennis courts; cabins; 28 pianos.

Profile of Summer Employees Total number: 75; typical ages: 17–60. 50% men; 50% women; 5% minorities; 10% high school students; 50% college students; 5% non-U.S. citizens; 5% local applicants. Nonsmokers required.

Employment Information Jobs available: ▶ 1 *arts and crafts counselor* (minimum age 19) at $1200–$1600 per season ▶ *assistant head counselor* (minimum age 21) with camp leadership experience, good organizational skills, and a college degree at $2000–$2500 per season ▶ *boating counselor* (minimum age 19) with LGT certification (ARC, Boy Scouts, Y, Ellis all acceptable) at $1400–$1800 per season ▶ *head counselor* with camp leadership experience, good organizational skills, and a college degree at $2500–$3000 per season ▶ 4 *land sports counselors* with CPR and first aid at $1200–$1600 per season ▶ 10 *music counselors* (minimum age 21) with solid performing skills on your instrument or voice. Ability to teach these skills to students aged 7-17. Prior teaching experience desired at $1400–$1700 per season ▶ 3 *piano accompanists* (minimum age 19) with excellent sight reading skills at $1200–$1700 per season ▶ 1–2 *sailing counselors* (minimum age 19) with LGT certification (ARC, Boy Scouts, Y, Ellis all acceptable) at $1400–$1800 per season ▶ 7 *swimming instructors* (minimum age 19) with LGT certification at $1300–$1800 per season ▶ 2 *tennis counselors* (minimum age 19) with CPR and first aid at $1100–$1600 per season ▶ 1 *waterfront director* (minimum age 21) with LGT/WSI certification; CPR, first aid; LGI preferred at $2300–$3000 per season. Applicants must submit formal organization application, three personal references. An in-person interview is recommended, but a telephone interview is acceptable. International applicants accepted; must apply through a recognized agency.

Benefits and Preemployment Training Free housing, free meals, formal training, willing to provide letters of recommendation, names of contacts, on-the-job training, willing to complete paperwork for educational credit, and willing to act as a professional reference. Preemployment training is required and includes accident prevention and safety, interpersonal skills, leadership skills.

Contact Ellen Donohue-Saltman, Director, Camp Encore-Coda for a Great Summer of Music, Sports, and Friends, 32 Grassmere Road, Brookline, Massachusetts 02467. Telephone: 617-325-1541. Fax: 617-325-7278. E-mail: ellen@encore-coda.com. World Wide Web: http://www.encore-coda.com. Contact by e-mail, fax, mail, phone, or through World Wide Web site. Application deadline: continuous.

CAMP HAWTHORNE

PLUMMER ROAD, PANTHER POND
RAYMOND, MAINE 04071

General Information Coed residential camp with visual and performing arts programs and noncompetitive sports. Established in 1919. 140-acre facility located 20 miles from Portland. Features: 2½ miles of shorefront; pristine lake; professional staff for theater, art, and movie-making; great sailing instruction.

Profile of Summer Employees Total number: 45; typical ages: 19–26. 50% men; 50% women; 15% minorities; 5% high school students; 80% college students; 5% non-U.S. citizens. Nonsmokers preferred.

Employment Information Openings are from June 18 to August 12. Jobs available: ▶ 2 *archery/riflery instructors* (minimum age 18) ▶ 2 *canoeing/boating instructors* (minimum age 18) with knowledge of canoeing, waterskiing, and small kayaks at $1300–$1600 per season ▶ 4 *creative arts teachers* (minimum age 18) ▶ 2 *drama instructors* (minimum age 18) at $1300–$1700 per season ▶ 6 *sailing instructors* (minimum age 18) with ability to rigg a sail (14- to 18-foot sailboat with 2 sails) at $1300–$1700 per season ▶ 6 *sports instructors* at $1400–$1700 per season ▶ 5 *swimming instructors* with lifeguard training or WSI certification at $1300–$1800 per season. Applicants must submit a formal organization application, letter of interest, resume. International applicants accepted; must obtain own visa.

Benefits and Preemployment Training Free housing, free meals, on-the-job training, travel reimbursement, and leadership skills, accident prevention and safety, first aid, and CPR training available.

Contact Ronald Furst, Owner, Camp Hawthorne, 10 Scotland Bridge Road, York, Maine 03909. Telephone: 207-363-1773. Fax: 207-363-1773. Contact by mail or phone. Application deadline: May 30.

CAMP LAUREL

ROUTE 41
READFIELD, MAINE 04355

General Information Camp welcoming 235 boys and 235 girls ages 8-15 from all over the United States as well as several other countries. Established in 1949. 150-acre facility located 15 miles from Augusta. Features: 4-mile lake; 15 tennis courts; 4000-square foot gymnastics building; 18 horses; cabins; 55-foot climbing tower.

Profile of Summer Employees Total number: 280; typical ages: 20–45. 50% men; 50% women; 75% college students; 3% non-U.S. citizens; 3% local applicants. Nonsmokers required.

Employment Information Openings are from June 1 to August 30. Jobs available: ▶ 2 *AM radio personalities* (minimum age 19) at $1600–$2200 per season ▶ 2 *archery instructors* (minimum age 19) at $1600–$2200 per season ▶ 2 *arts and crafts instructors* (minimum age 19) at $1600–$2200 per season ▶ 15 *athletics counselors* (minimum age 18) at $1600–$2200 per season ▶ 5 *ceramics instructors* (minimum age 18) at $1600–$2200 per season ▶ 3 *climbing and ropes course staff* (minimum age 18) at $1600–$2200 per season ▶ 3 *dance counselors* (minimum age 18) at $1600–$2200 per season ▶ 5 *fitness counselors* (minimum age 19) at $1600–$2200 per season ▶ 6 *gymnastics instructors* (minimum age 18) at $1600–$2200 per season ▶ 2 *ice hockey counselors* (minimum age 18) at $1600–$2200 per season ▶ 2 *lacrosse counselors* (minimum age 19) at $1600–$2200 per season ▶ 7 *nurses* (minimum age 22) at $3500 per season ▶ 2 *paddling counselors* (minimum age 18) at $1600–$2200 per season ▶ 3 *photography instructors* (minimum age 18) at $1600–$2200 per season ▶ 2 *piano/music instructors* (minimum age 19) at $1600–$2200 per season ▶ 6 *riding (English) counselors* (minimum age 19) at $1600–$2200 per season ▶ 2 *roller hockey counselors* (minimum age 18) at $1600–$2200 per season ▶ 3 *sailboarding counselors* (minimum age 18) at $1600–$2200 per season ▶ 7 *sailing counselors* (minimum age 18) at $1600–$2200 per season ▶ 12 *swimming counselors* (minimum age 18) at $1600–$2200 per season ▶ 18 *tennis counselors* (minimum age 18) at $2200 per season ▶ 10 *waterskiing counselors* (minimum age 18) at $1600–$2200 per season. Applicants must submit formal organization application. International applicants accepted; must apply through a recognized agency.

Benefits and Preemployment Training Free housing, free meals, formal training, willing to provide letters of recommendation, on-the-job training, willing to complete paperwork for educational credit, willing to act as a professional reference, and travel reimbursement. Preemployment training is required and includes accident prevention and safety, first aid, CPR, interpersonal skills, leadership skills.

Contact Jeremy Sollinger, Associate Director, Camp Laurel, Box 661, Alpine, New Jersey 07620. Telephone: 800-327-3509. Fax: 201-750-0665. E-mail: summer@camplaurel.com. World Wide Web: http://www.camplaurel.com. Contact by e-mail, fax, mail, phone, or through World Wide Web site. Application deadline: continuous.

CAMP LAUREL SOUTH

48 LAUREL ROAD
CASCO, MAINE 04015

General Information Family-oriented, coed, residential camp in Maine. Operates two 4-week sessions offering a variety of land and water sports, theater, arts, adventure, riding, and much more. Established in 1921. 120-acre facility located 24 miles from Portland. Features: freshwater, sandy-bottom lake; 8 hardcourt tennis courts; extensive staff lounge/cafe; wooded setting; top-notch program facilities; family atmosphere.

Profile of Summer Employees Total number: 170; typical ages: 19–50. 50% men; 50% women; 2% high school students; 85% college students; 8% non-U.S. citizens; 5% local applicants. Nonsmokers preferred.

Employment Information Openings are from June 16 to August 17. Jobs available: ▶ *adventure/ropes course instructors* at $1500 and up per season ▶ *aerobics instructor* at $1500 and up per season ▶ *archery instructors* at $1500 and up per season ▶ *arts and crafts instructors* at $1500 and up per season ▶ *baseball instructors* at $1500 and up per season ▶ *basketball instructors* at $1500 and up per season ▶ *campus leaders* at $2500 and up per season ▶ *ceramics instructors* at $1500 and up per season ▶ *dance instructors* at $1500 and up per season ▶ *field hockey instructor* at $1500 and up per season ▶ *fishing instructor* at $1500 and up per season ▶ *fitness instructors* at $1500 and up per season ▶ *football instructors* at $1500 and up per season ▶ *golf instructor* at $1500 and up per season ▶ *gymnastics instructors* at $1500 and up per season ▶ *horseback riding (English) instructors* at $1500 and up per season ▶ *lacrosse instructor* at $1500 and up per season ▶ *maintenance staff* at $1500 and up per season ▶ *nature counselor* at $1500 and up per season ▶ *nurses* at $3000 and up per season ▶ *office staff* at $1500 and up per season ▶ *photography instructors* at $1500 and up per season ▶ *piano player* at $1500 and up per season ▶ *program heads* at $2000 and up per season ▶ *riflery instructor* at $1500 and up per season ▶ *rocketry instructor* at $1500 and up per season ▶ *sailing instructors* at $1500 and up per season ▶ *soccer instructors* at $1500 and up per season ▶ *special programs coordinator* at $2000 and up per season ▶ *street/roller hockey instructors* at $1500 and up per season ▶ *swimming instructors* at $1500 and up per season ▶ *tennis instructors* at $1500 and up per season ▶ *theater staff* at $1500 and up per season ▶ *volleyball instructor* at $1500 and up per season ▶ *waterski instructors* at $1500 and up per season ▶ *windsurfing instructors* at $1500 and up per season. Applicants must submit formal organization application, three personal references. An in-person interview is recommended, but a telephone interview is acceptable. International applicants accepted; must apply through a recognized agency.

Benefits and Preemployment Training Free housing, free meals, formal training, willing to provide letters of recommendation, on-the-job training, willing to complete paperwork for educational credit, willing to act as a professional reference, travel reimbursement, and laundry service. Preemployment training is required and includes accident prevention and safety, interpersonal skills, leadership skills, teamwork training.

Contact Roger Christian, Director, Camp Laurel South, PO Box 14130, Gainesville, Florida 32604. Telephone: 888-528-7357. Fax: 352-331-0014. E-mail: fun@camplaurelsouth.com. World Wide Web: http://www.camplaurelsouth.com. Contact by e-mail, fax, mail, phone, or through World Wide Web site. Application deadline: applications are accepted September 15 to June 15.

CAMP MATOAKA FOR GIRLS

1 GREAT PLACE
SMITHFIELD, MAINE 04978-1288

General Information Residential camp serving 275 girls with a variety of activities. Established in 1951. 150-acre facility located 9 miles from Waterville. Features: 1½ miles of shore frontage; large gymnasium; heated 25-meter swimming pool; 3 waterslides 200 feet each; professional waterski program; full bathrooms in cabins.

Profile of Summer Employees Total number: 150; typical ages: 20–24. 20% men; 80% women; 3% minorities; 10% high school students; 45% college students; 2% retirees; 30% non-U.S. citizens; 10% local applicants. Nonsmokers required.

Employment Information Openings are from June 14 to August 20. Jobs available: ▶ 3 *English equitation instructors* (minimum age 19) with high skill level and horsemanship certification at $1100–$2000 per season ▶ 6 *arts and crafts instructors* (minimum age 19) with a major in fine arts at $1000–$1200 per season ▶ 2 *dance instructors* (minimum age 19) with a major in dance/movement and aerobics instructor experience at $1100–$1200 per season ▶ 3 *drama/music instructors* (minimum age 19) with a major in theater/drama at $1100–$1300 per season ▶ 3 *gymnastics instructors* (minimum age 19) with previous coaching/instructing and college team experience at $1200–$1400 per season ▶ 4 *land sports instructors* (minimum age 19) with a major in physical education or health/recreation at $1000–$1300 per season ▶ 5–10 *office administration* (minimum age 20) with organizational skills and computer skills at $2500–$3500 per season ▶ 2 *photographers* (minimum age 19) with major in photography at $1100–$1300 per season ▶ 1 *pianist/accompanist* (minimum age 19) with ability to sight read at $1100–$1600 per season ▶ 2 *ropes course instructors* (minimum age 23) with Project Adventure or Outward Bound certification at $1500–$2500 per season ▶ 2 *sewing instructors* (minimum age 19) with a major in home economics at $1200 per season ▶ 6 *ski instructors* (minimum age 19) with high skill level at $1100–$1500 per season ▶ 6 *small craft instructors* (minimum age 19) with Red Cross, CPR, and lifeguard certification at $1200–$1400 per season ▶ 6 *swimming instructors* (minimum age 19) with WSI certification at $1100–$1300 per season ▶ 6 *tennis instructors* (minimum age 19) with teaching and college team experience at $1000–$1400 per season ▶ 4 *trip instructors* (minimum age 21) with valid driver's license and experience in the field at $1200–$1400 per season ▶ 7 *video/radio personnel* (minimum age 19) with major in video/radio/communication at $1150–$1400 per season. Applicants must submit formal organization application, resume, two personal references, two letters of recommendation. An in-person interview is recommended, but a telephone interview is acceptable. International applicants accepted; must apply through a recognized agency.

Benefits and Preemployment Training Free housing, free meals, possible full-time employment, willing to provide letters of recommendation, willing to complete paperwork for educational credit, willing to act as a professional reference, and travel reimbursement. Preemployment training is required and includes accident prevention and safety, first aid, CPR, interpersonal skills, leadership skills.

Contact Mr. Michael Nathanson, Director/Owner, Camp Matoaka for Girls, 8751 Horseshoe Lane, Boca Raton, Florida 33496. Telephone: 800-MATOAKA. Fax: 561-488-6386. E-mail: matoaka@matoaka.com. World Wide Web: http://www.matoaka.com. Contact by e-mail, fax, mail, phone, or through World Wide Web site. Application deadline: continuous.

CAMP MICAH

11 MOOSE COVE LODGE ROAD
BRIDGTON, MAINE 04009

General Information A coed Jewish, overnight summer camp offering a full range of camp activities including team, individual, and waterfront sports, arts, multimedia, ropes, wilderness, hiking, and more. Established in 2001. 253-acre facility located 25 miles from Portland. Features: freshwater lake; wooded setting in mountains; 10 tennis courts, hockey court; 3 basketball courts; skate park; brand new facility in 2001.

Profile of Summer Employees Total number: 100; typical ages: 19–30. 50% men; 50% women; 1% minorities; 1% high school students; 70% college students; 25% non-U.S. citizens; 25% local applicants. Nonsmokers preferred.

Employment Information Openings are from June 18 to August 16. Jobs available: ▶ 10–70 *cabin counselors with particular specialties* (minimum age 18) with experience working with children and teaching an activity; salary based on experience. Applicants must submit a formal organization application, personal reference. An in-person interview is recommended, but a telephone interview is acceptable.

Benefits and Preemployment Training Free housing, free meals, willing to provide letters of recommendation, on-the-job training, willing to complete paperwork for educational credit, and willing to act as a professional reference. Preemployment training is required and includes 1 week of staff training prior to summer employment.

Contact Mark Lipof, Director, Camp Micah, 11 Hammond Pond Parkway #2, Chestnut Hill, Massachusetts 02467. Telephone: 617-244-6540. Fax: 617-277-7108. E-mail: markl@campmicah.com. World Wide Web: http://www.campmicah.com. Contact by e-mail, fax, mail, phone, or through World Wide Web site. Application deadline: continuous.

CAMP MODIN

MODIN WAY
BELGRADE, MAINE 04917

General Information Privately owned Jewish camp in New England serving 325 international campers. Established in 1922. 50-acre facility located 60 miles from Portland. Features: 13,000-square foot indoor recreation center; rollerblading; climbing tower and zip line; state-of-the art waterfront; overnight camping trips; specialized program for teens.

Profile of Summer Employees Total number: 813,110; typical ages: 18–28. 50% men; 50% women; 100% college students; 30% non-U.S. citizens. Nonsmokers required.

Employment Information Openings are from June 22 to August 24. Jobs available: ▶ 3–4 *arts and crafts instructors* with teaching experience in numerous areas at $1500–$2500 per season ▶ 20–30 *athletics instructors* with experience in field at $1500–$2500 per season ▶ 2–3 *fitness instructors* with experience in field at $1500–$2500 per season ▶ 40–50 *general counselors* with experience at $1300–$2500 per season ▶ 2–3 *gymnastics instructors* with experience in field at $1500–$2500 per season ▶ 4–5 *music, theater, and dance instructors* with experience in the field at $1500–$2500 per season ▶ 2 *photography instructors* with experience in the field at $1500–$2500 per season ▶ 4 *registered nurses* with RN or LPN and experience in the field at $3000–$4000 per season ▶ 2–3 *riflery/archery instructors* with experience and/or certification at $1500–$2500 per season ▶ 8–10 *swimming instructors* with WSI certification (minimum) and experience in the field at $1300–$2500 per season ▶ 4–6 *tennis instructors* with coaching experience at $1500–$2500 per season ▶ 10–15 *tripping/ropes/outdoor pursuits instructors* with certification and/or experience at $1500–$2500 per season ▶ 10–12 *waterskiing/sailing instructors* with experience in the field at $1500–$2500 per season. Applicants must submit formal organization application, three letters of recommendation. A telephone interview is required. International applicants accepted; must apply through a recognized agency.

Benefits and Preemployment Training Free housing, free meals, formal training, willing to provide letters of recommendation, on-the-job training, willing to complete paperwork for educational credit, willing to act as a professional reference, and travel reimbursement. Preemployment training is required and includes accident prevention and safety, interpersonal skills, leadership skills.

Contact Howard Salzberg, Director, Camp Modin, 401 East 80th Street, Suite 28EF, New York, New York 10021. Telephone: 212-570-1600. Fax: 212-570-1677. E-mail: modin@modin.com. World Wide Web: http://www.modin.com. Contact by e-mail, fax, mail, phone, or through World Wide Web site. Application deadline: continuous.

CAMP PONDICHERRY

RR 2, BOX 588
BRIDGTON, MAINE 04009

General Information Residential camp serving 144 girls ages 7–17 per session; season includes three 2-week sessions and one week of pre-camp. Established in 1971. 700-acre facility located 45 miles from Portland. Features: freshwater lake; platform tents; wooded setting; view of White Mountains; food service; program center.

Profile of Summer Employees Total number: 40; typical ages: 18–42. 1% men; 99% women; 5% minorities; 1% high school students; 90% college students; 30% non-U.S. citizens; 50% local applicants. Nonsmokers preferred.

Employment Information Openings are from June 20 to August 20. Spring break, winter break, and year-round positions also offered. Jobs available: ▶ 1 *assistant camp director* (minimum age 21) with degree and administrative experience; valid driver's license at $2800–$3000 per season ▶ 18 *assistant unit leaders* (minimum age 18) with experience working with children at $1785–$1850 per season ▶ 1 *business manager* (minimum age 21) with skills in money management and valid driver's license at $1800–$2000 per season ▶ 1 *camp steward* (minimum age 18) at $1800–$2000 per season ▶ 1 *counselor-in-training director* (minimum age 21) with experience working with older girls at $2000–$2800 per season ▶ 1 *health supervisor* (minimum age 21) with RN, LPN, or EMT license at $2520–$3000 per season ▶ 3 *kitchen helpers* (minimum age 16) with a positive attitude; team-oriented at $1600–$1700 per season ▶ 1 *kitchen steward* (minimum age 21) with ability to supervise kitchen helpers and packout at $1800–$2100 per season ▶ 1 *pack-out person* (minimum age 16) with organizational skills and detail-oriented at $1600–$1800 per season ▶ 4 *program consultants* (minimum age 21) with experience in designated field (dance, arts and crafts, sports, games, and nature) at $1840–$2300 per season ▶ 6 *unit leaders* (minimum age 21) with leadership ability and experience working with children at $1850–$2200 per season ▶ 6 *waterfront assistants* (minimum age 18) with current lifeguard, first aid, and CPR certification at $1800–$2100 per season ▶ 1 *waterfront director* (minimum age 21) with certification in first aid, CPR, lifeguard training, and waterfront administration experience at $2420–$2900 per season. Applicants must submit formal organization application, three personal references. An in-person interview is recommended, but a telephone interview is acceptable. International applicants accepted; must apply through a recognized agency.

Benefits and Preemployment Training Free housing, free meals, formal training, health insurance, willing to provide letters of recommendation, on-the-job training, willing to complete paperwork for educational credit, willing to act as a professional reference, opportunity to attend seminars/workshops, and travel reimbursement. Preemployment training is required and includes accident prevention and safety, first aid, CPR, interpersonal skills, leadership skills, lifeguard instruction and small craft safety.

Contact Tracey Graffam, Camp Director/Program Manager, Camp Pondicherry, PO Box 9421, South Portland, Maine 04116-9421. Telephone: 207-772-1177. Fax: 207-874-2646. E-mail: traceyg@kgsc.org. World Wide Web: http://www.kgsc.org. Contact by fax, mail, or phone. Application deadline: continuous.

CAMP RUNOIA

POINT ROAD
BELGRADE LAKES, MAINE 04918

General Information Residential camp for girls ages 7–17. Traditional program offering waterfront, riding, outdoor living skills, and more. Established in 1907. 88-acre facility located 12 miles from Augusta. Features: location at the end of a rural road; 128-square mile freshwater lake; clear lake water; mixture of woods and fields; clay tennis courts; stables.

Profile of Summer Employees Total number: 43; typical ages: 20–28. 5% men; 95% women; 5% minorities; 65% college students; 5% retirees; 15% non-U.S. citizens; 25% local applicants. Nonsmokers required.

Employment Information Openings are from June 13 to August 14. Jobs available: ▶ 1 *canoeing instructor* (minimum age 19) with lifeguard (or equivalent), first aid, CPR, and/or small watercraft certification at $1400–$2000 per season ▶ 1 *photography instructor* (minimum age 19) with basic darkroom skills and composition theory at $1400–$2000 per season ▶ 2 *sailing instructors* (minimum age 19) with lifeguard (or equivalent), first aid, CPR, and/or small watercraft certification at $1400–$2000 per season ▶ 2 *target sports (archery and riflery) instructors* (minimum age 19) with American Archery Association and National Riflery Association certification (or equivalent) at $1400–$2000 per season ▶ 1 *tennis instructor* (minimum age 19) with documented experience at $1400–$2000 per season. Applicants must submit formal organization application, three personal references. An in-person interview is recommended, but a telephone interview is acceptable. International applicants accepted; must apply through a recognized agency.

Benefits and Preemployment Training Free housing, free meals, formal training, willing to provide letters of recommendation, names of contacts, on-the-job training, willing to complete paperwork for educational credit, willing to act as a professional reference, opportunity to attend seminars/workshops, and travel allowance. Preemployment training is required and includes accident prevention and safety, first aid, CPR, interpersonal skills, leadership skills.

Contact Pamela N. Cobb, Director, Camp Runoia, 56 Jackson Street, Cambridge, Massachusetts 02140. Telephone: 617-547-4676. Fax: 617-661-1964. E-mail: runoia@citysource.com. World Wide Web: http://www.runoia.com. Contact by e-mail, fax, mail, phone, or through World Wide Web site. Application deadline: continuous.

CAMP SKYLEMAR

NAPLES, MAINE 04055

General Information Sports-oriented seven-week program for boys ages 8–16. Established in 1948. 200-acre facility located 30 miles from Portland. Features: freshwater lake; location in the White Mountains; 8 tennis courts; golf course; wooded setting; numerous athletic fields.

Profile of Summer Employees Total number: 70; typical ages: 18–30. 90% college students; 5% non-U.S. citizens; 5% local applicants. Nonsmokers required.

Employment Information Openings are from June 22 to August 15. Jobs available: ▶ 2 *arts and crafts instructors* (minimum age 18) with experience in the field at $1500–$2200 per season ▶ 2 *basketball instructors* (minimum age 18) with experience in the field at $1500–$2200 per season ▶ 2 *boating and skiing instructors* (minimum age 18) with small craft certification at $1500–$2200 per season ▶ 15 *general sports counselors* (minimum age 18) with experience in the field at $1500–$2200 per season ▶ 2 *golf instructors* (minimum age 18) with experience in the field at $1500–$2200 per season ▶ 3 *lifeguards* (minimum age 18) with certification at $1500–$2200 per season ▶ 1 *riflery instructor* (minimum age 18) with NRA instructor certification at $1500–$2200 per season ▶ 4 *ropes course leaders* (minimum age 18) with experience in the field at $1500–$2200 per season ▶ 4 *swimming instructors* (minimum age 18) with Red Cross lifeguard and WSI certification at $1500–$2200 per season ▶ 4 *tennis counselors* (minimum age 18) with experience in the field at $1500–$2200 per season ▶ 2 *trip counselors* (minimum age 18) with experience in the field at $1500–$2200 per season. Applicants must submit a formal organization application, five personal references. An in-person interview is recommended, but a telephone interview is acceptable.

Benefits and Preemployment Training Free housing, free meals, formal training, willing to provide letters of recommendation, on-the-job training, willing to complete paperwork for educational credit, willing to act as a professional reference, opportunity to attend seminars/workshops, and travel reimbursement. Preemployment training is required and includes accident prevention and safety, interpersonal skills, leadership skills.

Contact Arleen Shepherd, Director, Camp Skylemar, 2331 Old Court Road, Unit 310, Baltimore, Maryland 21208. Telephone: 410-337-9697. Fax: 410-337-5250. E-mail: campskylemar@aol.com. World Wide Web: http://www.campskylemar.com. Contact by e-mail, fax, mail, phone, or through World Wide Web site. Application deadline: continuous.

CAMP TAPAWINGO

ROUTE 93
SWEDEN, MAINE 04040

General Information Residential private girls camp offering a 7½-week program to 170 campers with a focus on developing self-confidence and independence in a caring environment. Established in 1919. 200-acre facility located 50 miles from Portland. Features: private lake; foothills of the White Mountains; 8 tennis courts; sports fields and courts; bunks with running water and electricity; main lodge and dining room.

Profile of Summer Employees Total number: 70; typical ages: 19–30. 10% men; 90% women; 1% minorities; 80% college students; 8% non-U.S. citizens; 1% local applicants. Nonsmokers required.

Employment Information Openings are from June 15 to August 14. Jobs available: ▶ 2 *art instructors* at $1650 per season ▶ 2 *canoeing instructors* (minimum age 19) with lifeguard certification and instructor rating at $1650–$1900 per season ▶ 1 *ceramics instructor* with teaching experience (preferred) at $1700–$1800 per season ▶ 2 *dramatics instructors* (minimum age 19) at $1650–$1700 per season ▶ 2 *gymnastics instructors* (minimum age 19) with experience in the field at $1650 per season ▶ 5–8 *landsports instructors* (minimum age 19) with college-level experience and ability to teach one or more of the following: softball, lacrosse, field hockey, basketball, volleyball, soccer at $1650–$1800 per season ▶ 1 *photography instructor* (minimum age 19) with knowledge of black-and-white photography and developing at $1650 per season ▶ 1 *piano accompanist* with sight-reading and transposing ability at $1800 per season ▶ 2 *ropes instructors* (minimum age 19) with first aid, CPR, and instructor certification at $1650–$1800 per season ▶ 2 *sailboard/sailing instructors* (minimum age 19) with lifeguard certification and instructor rating at $1650 per season ▶ 1 *stained glass instructor* at $1700–$1800 per season ▶ 8 *swimming instructors* (minimum age 19) with WSI and lifeguard certification at $1650–$1800 per season ▶ 5 *tennis instructors* (minimum age 19) with college-level experience at $1650–$1800 per season ▶ 6 *trip leaders* (minimum age 21) with lifeguard certification at $1750–$1800 per season ▶ 1 *waterskiing instructor* (minimum age 19) with lifeguard certification and instructor rating at $1650–$1800 per season. Applicants must submit a formal organization application, three personal references. A telephone interview is required. International applicants accepted.

Benefits and Preemployment Training Free housing, free meals, willing to provide letters of recommendation, on-the-job training, willing to complete paperwork for educational credit, willing to act as a professional reference, and laundry service. Preemployment training is required and includes accident prevention and safety, CPR, interpersonal skills, leadership skills, child development.

Contact Ms. Jane Lichtman, Director, Camp Tapawingo, PO Box 248, Maplewood, New Jersey 07040. Telephone: 973-275-1139. Fax: 973-275-1182. E-mail: camptap@aol.com. World Wide Web: http://www.camptapawingo.com. Contact by e-mail, fax, mail, phone, or through World Wide Web site. Application deadline: continuous.

CAMP WAWENOCK

33 CAMP WAWENOCK ROAD
RAYMOND, MAINE 04071-6824

General Information Residential camp serving 110 campers ages 8–16, all of whom attend for the full 7-week season. Features traditional camp experience with emphasis on human relationships and personal development. Established in 1910. 100-acre facility located 26 miles from Portland. Features: natural sand beach; freshwater lake; cabins; stables and paddocks; 4 tennis courts; wooded setting.

Profile of Summer Employees Total number: 50; typical ages: 18–21. 5% men; 95% women; 3% minorities; 5% high school students; 95% college students; 1% retirees; 10% non-U.S. citizens; 3% local applicants. Nonsmokers required.

Employment Information Openings are from June 15 to August 15. Jobs available: ▶ 1 *riding instructor* (minimum age 19) with certification or documented experience at $1000–$1400 per season ▶ 1 *riflery instructor* (minimum age 19) with instructor certification at $1000–$1400 per season ▶ 2 *swimming instructors* (minimum age 19) with WSI certification at $900–$1300 per season. Applicants must submit formal organization application, resume, three personal references. An in-person interview is recommended, but a telephone interview is acceptable. International applicants accepted; must apply through a recognized agency.

Benefits and Preemployment Training Free housing, free meals, willing to provide letters of recommendation, on-the-job training, willing to complete paperwork for educational credit, willing to act as a professional reference, opportunity to attend seminars/workshops, travel reimbursement, and laundry service. Preemployment training is required and includes accident prevention and safety, first aid, CPR, interpersonal skills, leadership skills.

Contact June W. Gray, Director/Owner, Camp Wawenock, 33 Camp Wawenock Road, Raymond,

Maine 04071-6824. Telephone: 207-655-4657. Contact by mail or phone. Application deadline: June 15.

CAMP WAZIYATAH
530 MILL HILL ROAD
WATERFORD, MAINE 04088

General Information Traditional residential camp serving 200 campers in two-, three-, four-, and seven-week sessions featuring junior and teen programs. Established in 1922. 150-acre facility located 51 miles from Portland. Features: sparkling lake; on-site stables; beautiful barn theater; 10 tennis courts; 50-foot climbing tower; charming rustic cabins.
Profile of Summer Employees Total number: 100; typical ages: 19–62. 50% men; 50% women; 5% minorities; 60% college students; 2% retirees; 30% non-U.S. citizens; 3% local applicants. Nonsmokers required.
Employment Information Openings are from June 1 to September 1. Jobs available: ▶ 3–6 *English riding instructors* (minimum age 20) with certification in field at $1400–$2500 per season ▶ 3 *administrative/office staff* (minimum age 21) with fast-paced previous office experience at $1600–$3000 per season ▶ 1 *archery instructor* (minimum age 21) with certification in field at $1400–$2500 per season ▶ 3 *arts and crafts instructors* (minimum age 19) with experience in the field at $1400–$2500 per season ▶ 1 *baseball/softball instructor* (minimum age 19) with experience in the field at $1400–$2500 per season ▶ 1 *canoe instructor* (minimum age 19) with certification in field at $1400–$2500 per season ▶ 1 *photo instructor* (minimum age 20) with professional training and experience at $1400–$2500 per season ▶ 1 *pianist/accompanist* (minimum age 20) with facile Broadway style at $1400–$2500 per season ▶ 2 *rifle instructors* (minimum age 21) with certification in field at $1400–$2500 per season ▶ 1 *sailing instructor* (minimum age 19) with Red Cross sailing certification at $1400–$2500 per season ▶ 6–10 *swimming instructors* (minimum age 19) with LGT/WSI certification at $1400–$2500 per season ▶ 6 *tennis instructors* (minimum age 19) at $1400–$2500 per season ▶ 2 *theater personnel* (minimum age 19) with experience in the field at $1400–$2500 per season ▶ 2 *trip leaders* (minimum age 21) with CPR, first aid, lifeguard, WFR, Maine Guide, EMT certification, and experience at $1400–$2500 per season ▶ 1 *video instructor* (minimum age 20) with professional training and experience at $1400–$2500 per season ▶ 4–6 *waterskiing instructors* (minimum age 21) with LGT and experience as a boat driver/ski instructor at $1400–$2500 per season ▶ 1 *windsurfing instructor* (minimum age 19) with Red Cross sailing, small craft, and LGT certification at $1400–$2500 per season. Applicants must submit formal organization application, resume, two personal references, two letters of recommendation. An in-person interview is recommended, but a telephone interview is acceptable. International applicants accepted; must obtain own visa, apply through a recognized agency.
Benefits and Preemployment Training Free housing, free meals, formal training, willing to provide letters of recommendation, on-the-job training, willing to complete paperwork for educational credit, willing to act as a professional reference, opportunity to attend seminars/workshops, and travel reimbursement. Preemployment training is required and includes accident prevention and safety, first aid, CPR, interpersonal skills, leadership skills.
Contact Kerns Family, Directors, Camp Waziyatah, 19 Vose Lane, East Walpole, Massachusetts 02032. Telephone: 508-668-9758. Fax: 508-668-2665. E-mail: info@wazi.com. World Wide Web: http://www.wazi.com. Contact by e-mail, fax, mail, phone, or through World Wide Web site. Application deadline: continuous.

CAMP WEKEELA
RFD 1, BOX 275, ROUTE 219
CANTON, MAINE 04221

General Information Residential traditional coeducational camp serving 290 campers with an emphasis on sports, water sports, and arts. Established in 1922. 150-acre facility located 20 miles from Lewiston. Features: freshwater lake; wooded setting; 10 tennis courts; multiple athletic fields; gymnasium; extensive waterfront.

Profile of Summer Employees Total number: 120; typical ages: 20–65. 50% men; 50% women; 84% college students; 1% retirees; 10% non-U.S. citizens; 5% local applicants. Nonsmokers required.

Employment Information Openings are from June 15 to August 22. Jobs available: ▶ *ceramics staff members* (minimum age 20) at $1200–$1600 per season ▶ *creative arts staff members* (minimum age 20) at $1200–$1600 per season ▶ 1 *department program head* (minimum age 24) with management skills as well as knowledge of program area at $2300–$3000 per season ▶ 3 *group leaders* (minimum age 23) with college degree; must oversee counselors and campers at $2000–$2500 per season ▶ *guitar instructors* (minimum age 20) at $1200–$1600 per season ▶ *gymnastics staff members* (minimum age 20) at $1200–$1600 per season ▶ *land sports staff members (tennis)* (minimum age 20) at $1200–$1600 per season ▶ *piano/music staff members* (minimum age 20) at $1200–$1600 per season ▶ *pioneering staff members* (minimum age 20) at $1200–$1600 per season ▶ *radio staff members* (minimum age 20) at $1200–$1500 per season ▶ *ropes instructors* (minimum age 20) at $1200–$1600 per season ▶ *tennis staff members* (minimum age 20) at $1200–$1600 per season ▶ *theatrical arts staff members* (minimum age 20) at $1200–$1500 per season ▶ *video/photo staff members* (minimum age 20) at $1200–$1500 per season ▶ *waterfront staff members* (minimum age 20) at $1200–$1600 per season ▶ *waterskiing staff members* (minimum age 20) at $1200–$1800 per season ▶ *woodworking staff members* (minimum age 20) at $1200–$1600 per season. Applicants must submit formal organization application, resume, portfolio, three personal references, three letters of recommendation. An in-person interview is recommended, but a telephone interview is acceptable. International applicants accepted; must apply through a recognized agency.

Benefits and Preemployment Training Free housing, free meals, formal training, on-the-job training, willing to complete paperwork for educational credit, and travel reimbursement. Preemployment training is required and includes accident prevention and safety, first aid, CPR, interpersonal skills, leadership skills.

Contact Eric Scoblionko, Director, Camp Wekeela, 2807C Delmar Drive, Columbus, Ohio 43209. Telephone: 614-253-3177. Fax: 614-253-3661. E-mail: wekeela1@aol.com. World Wide Web: http://www.campwekeela.com. Contact by e-mail, fax, mail, phone, or through World Wide Web site. Application deadline: continuous.

CAMP WINNEBAGO

KENTS HILL, MAINE

General Information Residential camp serving 155 boys for four- and eight-week sessions. Established in 1919. 350-acre facility located 17 miles from Augusta. Features: 3½-mile freshwater lake; wooded setting; 7 tennis courts; extensive waterfront program; campers from 13 countries and 20 states.

Profile of Summer Employees Total number: 75; typical ages: 19–60. 90% men; 10% women; 10% minorities; 60% college students; 15% non-U.S. citizens; 15% local applicants. Nonsmokers required.

Employment Information Openings are from June 17 to August 19. Jobs available: ▶ 2 *archery instructors* with certification in field; experience instructing archery preferred at $1200–$2500 per season ▶ 2 *arts and crafts instructors* (minimum age 19) with experience in clay, woodwork, weaving, or other crafts; teaching experience preferred at $1200–$2500 per season ▶ 4 *athletics instructors* (minimum age 19) with coaching experience preferred; competitive experience acceptable at $1200–$2500 per season ▶ 3 *camping skills instructors* (minimum age 19) with outdoor camping skills at $1200–$2500 per season ▶ 1 *nature instructor* (minimum age 19) with ability to relate the natural environment to children at $1200–$2500 per season ▶ 1 *newspaper instructor* (minimum age 19) with college or high school newspaper experience preferred at $1200–

$2500 per season ▶ 2 *photography instructors* (minimum age 19) with experience in photography or teaching at $1200–$2500 per season ▶ 1 *piano accompanist* (minimum age 19) with knowledge of show music at $1200–$2500 per season ▶ 2 *riflery instructors* with certification in field; experience instructing riflery preferred at $1200–$2500 per season ▶ 4 *swimming instructors* (minimum age 19) with WSI or lifeguard certification at $1200–$2500 per season ▶ 4 *tennis instructors* (minimum age 19) with coaching experience preferred; competitive playing experience acceptable at $1200–$2500 per season ▶ 2 *theater instructors* (minimum age 19) with theater experience; experience directing children preferred at $1200–$2500 per season ▶ 1 *videography instructor* (minimum age 19) with facility in use of video camera and ability to script shows at $1200–$2500 per season ▶ 2 *waterskiing instructors* (minimum age 19) with waterskiing and boat driving experience; teaching experience preferred at $1200–$2500 per season. Applicants must submit formal organization application, two personal references, two letters of recommendation. An in-person interview is recommended, but a telephone interview is acceptable. International applicants accepted; must apply through a recognized agency.

Benefits and Preemployment Training Free housing, free meals, willing to provide letters of recommendation, willing to complete paperwork for educational credit, willing to act as a professional reference, travel reimbursement, and health insurance at cost. Preemployment training is required and includes accident prevention and safety, first aid, interpersonal skills, leadership skills.

Contact Andy Lilienthal, Director, Camp Winnebago, 3816 36th Avenue South, Minneapolis, Minnesota 55406. Telephone: 612-276-0891. Fax: 612-724-6005. E-mail: unkandycw@aol.com. World Wide Web: http://www.campwinnebago.com. Contact by e-mail, fax, mail, phone, or through World Wide Web site. Application deadline: continuous.

FOREST ACRES CAMP FOR GIRLS

FRYEBURG, MAINE 04037

General Information Residential camp for 125 girls ages 6 to 16 for seven weeks. Established in 1927. 100-acre facility located 150 miles from Boston, Massachusetts. Features: heated Olympic-size pool; 6 tennis courts; indoor gym; lake area; White Mountains; many fields.

Profile of Summer Employees Total number: 60; typical age: 25. 2% men; 98% women; 50% college students; 2% retirees; 10% non-U.S. citizens; 10% local applicants. Nonsmokers preferred.

Employment Information Openings are from June 1 to August 16. Jobs available: ▶ 3 *arts and crafts instructors* (minimum age 19) at $1000–$1800 per season ▶ 3 *gymnastics instructors* (minimum age 19) at $1000–$1800 per season ▶ 3–5 *sailing and waterskiing instructors* at $1200–$2500 per season ▶ 3–5 *swimming instructors* with certification in field at $1000–$1800 per season ▶ 4 *tennis instructors* at $1200–$2500 per season ▶ 4 *unit leaders/administrators* (minimum age 22) at $1500–$2000 per season. Applicants must submit formal organization application, resume, three personal references. An in-person interview is recommended, but a telephone interview is acceptable. International applicants accepted; must apply through a recognized agency.

Benefits and Preemployment Training Free housing, free meals, formal training, willing to provide letters of recommendation, on-the-job training, willing to act as a professional reference, and opportunity to attend seminars/workshops. Preemployment training is required and includes accident prevention and safety, interpersonal skills, leadership skills.

Contact Lisa Newman, Directors, Forest Acres Camp for Girls, 2914 Medinah, Weston, Florida 33332. Telephone: 904-385-3545. E-mail: campdad@gate.net. World Wide Web: http://www.forestacres.com. Contact by mail or phone. Application deadline: continuous.

HIDDEN VALLEY CAMP
HIDDEN VALLEY CAMP ROAD
FREEDOM, MAINE 04941

General Information Residential, international, noncompetitive camp offering two 4-week sessions to 270 campers. Established in 1948. 350-acre facility located 80 miles from Portland. Features: spring-fed private lake; miles of wooded trails; modern, fully equipped art studios; adventure ropes course; heated pool.

Profile of Summer Employees Total number: 90; typical age: 23. 40% men; 60% women; 10% minorities; 5% high school students; 40% college students; 3% retirees; 20% non-U.S. citizens; 10% local applicants. Nonsmokers required.

Employment Information Openings are from June 1 to August 25. Jobs available: ▶ 10 *English riding instructors* with experience in the field at $1000–$1400 per season ▶ 4 *animal care personnel* with experience in the field at $1000–$1400 per season ▶ 5 *dance instructors* with experience in the field at $1000–$1400 per season ▶ 3 *guitar/music staff* at $1000–$1400 per season ▶ 2 *gymnastics instructors* at $1000–$1400 per season ▶ 2 *outdoor living staff* with experience in the field at $1000–$1500 per season ▶ 2 *outdoor travel leaders* with experience in the field at $1000–$1500 per season ▶ 2 *pottery instructors* at $1000–$1400 per season ▶ 6 *ropes instructors* with experience in the field at $1000–$1400 per season ▶ 2 *soccer instructors* at $1000–$1400 per season ▶ 3 *stained glass instructors* at $1000–$1400 per season ▶ 10 *swimming instructors* with WSI/lifeguard certification at $1000–$1400 per season. Applicants must submit formal organization application, letter of interest, resume, three personal references, letter of recommendation. An in-person interview is recommended, but a telephone interview is acceptable. International applicants accepted; must apply through a recognized agency.

Benefits and Preemployment Training Free housing, free meals, formal training, willing to provide letters of recommendation, on-the-job training, willing to complete paperwork for educational credit, and willing to act as a professional reference. Preemployment training is required.

Contact Meg Kassen, Co-Director/Owner, Hidden Valley Camp, RR 1, Box 2360, Freedom, Maine 04941. Telephone: 207-342-5177. Fax: 207-342-5685. E-mail: summer@hiddenvalleycamp.com. World Wide Web: http://www.hiddenvalleycamp.com. Contact by e-mail, fax, mail, phone, or through World Wide Web site. Application deadline: continuous.

IDLEASE AND SHORELANDS GUEST RESORT
PO BOX 3035
KENNEBUNK, MAINE 04043

General Information Resort serving visitors to scenic Kennebunkport. Established in 1967. 4-acre facility located 2 miles from Kennebunkport. Features: wooded country setting; close to sandy beach; near fishing river; family-oriented.

Profile of Summer Employees Total number: 8; typical ages: 20–25. 100% women; 30% high school students; 60% college students; 50% non-U.S. citizens; 50% local applicants. Nonsmokers required.

Employment Information Openings are from May 1 to October 31. Jobs available: ▶ 1 *assistant manager/housekeeper* with ability to perform general duties, desk work, scheduling, and supervise hourly help (must be a French-speaking college student or college teacher and be able to work from May to September); females only at $175–$200 per week ▶ 4 *housekeeping associates* with ability to stay from June to October (should be college or high school student or teacher); females only at $150–$200 per week. Applicants must submit letter of interest, resume. International applicants accepted; must obtain own visa, obtain own working papers, apply through a recognized agency.

Benefits and Preemployment Training Free housing, willing to provide letters of recommendation, on-the-job training, and willing to complete paperwork for educational credit.

Contact Sonja Haag-Ducharme, Owner, Idlease and Shorelands Guest Resort, PO Box 3035,

Kennebunk, Maine 04043. E-mail: idlease@mail.vrmedia.com. World Wide Web: http://www.idlease.com. Contact by e-mail or mail. Application deadline: April 15.

INDIAN ACRES CAMP FOR BOYS

FRYEBURG, MAINE 04037

General Information Residential camp for 125 boys ages 6–16. Established in 1924. 100-acre facility located 150 miles from Boston, Massachusetts. Features: heated Olympic-size pool; 6 tennis courts; indoor gym; lake area; location in the White Mountains; many fields for soccer and baseball.

Profile of Summer Employees Total number: 60; typical ages: 24–26. 98% men; 2% women; 50% college students; 2% retirees; 10% non-U.S. citizens; 10% local applicants. Nonsmokers preferred.

Employment Information Openings are from June 1 to August 16. Jobs available: ▶ 4 *archery and riflery instructors* (minimum age 19) at $1000–$1800 per season ▶ *basketball, baseball, hockey, and soccer instructors* (minimum age 19) at $1000–$1800 per season ▶ 3–5 *sailing and skiing instructors and lifeguards* (minimum age 19) at $1000–$1800 per season ▶ 3–5 *swimming instructors* (minimum age 19) with certification at $1000–$1800 per season ▶ *tennis instructors* (minimum age 19) at $1000–$1800 per season ▶ 4 *unit leaders, administrators, and teachers* (minimum age 22) at $1500–$2000 per season. Applicants must submit formal organization application, resume, three personal references. An in-person interview is recommended, but a telephone interview is acceptable. International applicants accepted; must apply through a recognized agency.

Benefits and Preemployment Training Free housing, free meals, formal training, willing to provide letters of recommendation, on-the-job training, willing to act as a professional reference, and opportunity to attend seminars/workshops. Preemployment training is required and includes accident prevention and safety, interpersonal skills, leadership skills.

Contact Lisa Newman, Director, Indian Acres Camp for Boys, 2914 Medinah, Weston, Florida 33332. Telephone: 954-385-3545. E-mail: campdad@gate.net. World Wide Web: http://www.indianacres.com. Contact by e-mail, mail, phone, or through World Wide Web site. Application deadline: continuous.

KAMP KOHUT

151 KOHUT ROAD
OXFORD, MAINE 04270

General Information Residential camp serving 175 girls and 175 boys with traditional activities in 2 four-week sessions. Focuses on single-gender classes at one campus facility. Established in 1907. 115-acre facility located 38 miles from Portland. Features: large freshwater lake; beautiful wooded setting; top-notch facilities; excellent waterfront program; large adventure and tripping program; 1 hour from Maine coast and White Mountains.

Profile of Summer Employees Total number: 100; typical ages: 20–24. 50% men; 50% women; 1% minorities; 73% college students; 2% retirees; 25% non-U.S. citizens; 5% local applicants. Nonsmokers required.

Employment Information Openings are from June 10 to August 17. Jobs available: ▶ 90 *activity specialists* (minimum age 19) with enthusiasm, friendliness, energy, and reliability at $1500–$3000 per season. Applicants must submit formal organization application, three personal references. A telephone interview is required. International applicants accepted; must apply through a recognized agency.

Benefits and Preemployment Training Free housing, free meals, formal training, health insurance, willing to provide letters of recommendation, on-the-job training, willing to complete paperwork for educational credit, willing to act as a professional reference, opportunity to attend seminars/workshops, and travel reimbursement. Preemployment training is required and includes accident prevention and safety, interpersonal skills, leadership skills.

Contact Lisa Tripler, Director, Kamp Kohut, Two Tall Pine Road, Cape Elizabeth, Maine 04107. Telephone: 207-767-2406. Fax: 207-767-0604. E-mail: kampkohut@aol.com. World Wide Web: http://www.kampkohut.com. Contact by e-mail, fax, mail, phone, or through World Wide Web site. Application deadline: continuous.

LONGACRE EXPEDITIONS, MAINE

UNITY, MAINE 04988

General Information Adventure travel program throughout Maine, New Hampshire, and into Canada, emphasizing group living skills, physical challenges, and fun. Longacre's challenging programs place equal emphasis on physical accomplishment and emotional growth. Established in 1981. Located 20 miles from Waterville.

Profile of Summer Employees Total number: 30; typical ages: 21–32. 50% men; 50% women; 10% minorities; 40% college students; 10% local applicants. Nonsmokers required.

Employment Information Openings are from June 15 to August 15. Jobs available: ▶ 20 *assistant trip leaders* (minimum age 21) with wilderness first aid, CPR, and good driving record at $150–$175 per week ▶ 1 *rock climbing instructor* (minimum age 21) with good driving record, wilderness first aid or WFR training, and CPR certification at $300–$450 per week ▶ 4 *support and logistics staff members* (minimum age 21) with good driving record and wilderness first aid and CPR certifications at $180–$240 per week. Applicants must submit a formal organization application, letter of interest, resume, three personal references. An in-person interview is recommended, but a telephone interview is acceptable. International applicants accepted; must obtain own visa, obtain own working papers.

Benefits and Preemployment Training Free housing, free meals, willing to provide letters of recommendation, on-the-job training, willing to complete paperwork for educational credit, willing to act as a professional reference, and pro-deal purchase program. Preemployment training is required and includes accident prevention and safety, interpersonal skills, leadership skills.

Contact Meredith Schuler, Director, Longacre Expeditions, Maine, 4030 Middle Ridge Road, Newport, Pennsylvania 17074-8110. Telephone: 717-567-6790. Fax: 717-567-3955. E-mail: merry@longacreexpeditions.com. World Wide Web: http://www.longacreexpeditions.com. Contact by e-mail, fax, mail, phone, or through World Wide Web site. Application deadline: continuous.

MAINE TEEN CAMP

481 BROWNFIELD ROAD
PORTER, MAINE 04068

General Information Residential coed camp for teenagers offering two sessions with 300 campers participating in each session. Established in 1985. 55-acre facility located 45 miles from Portland. Features: freshwater lake; wooded setting; 5 tennis courts; cabins; large main lodge; large ropes course.

Profile of Summer Employees Total number: 130; typical ages: 21–40. 47% men; 53% women; 10% minorities; 50% college students; 2% retirees; 30% non-U.S. citizens; 2% local applicants.

Employment Information Openings are from June 13 to August 17. Jobs available: ▶ 1 *ESL/ academics head coordinator* (minimum age 21) with teacher certification and an ESL course ▶ 1 *MIDI instructor* (minimum age 21) with experience and/or certification at $1300 per season ▶ 1–3 *arts instructors* (minimum age 21) with experience and/or certification at $1300 per season ▶ 2 *dance instructors* (minimum age 21) with experience and/or certification at $1300 per season ▶ 1 *drum instructor* (minimum age 21) with experience and/or certification at $1300 per season ▶ 1 *head of ropes* (minimum age 22) with relevant certifications at $1800–$2500 per season ▶ 1 *jewelry-crafting instructor* (minimum age 21) with experience and/or certification at

$1300 per season ▶ 1 *keyboard instructor* (minimum age 21) with experience and/or certification at $1300 per season ▶ 1–5 *land sports instructors* (minimum age 21) with experience and/or certification and ability to teach one or more of the following: soccer, basketball, baseball, field hockey, lacrosse, golf, volleyball, badminton at $1300 per season ▶ 2–3 *mountain biking instructors* (minimum age 21) with experience and/or certification at $1300 per season ▶ 2 *nurses* (minimum age 21) with RN or LPN preferred at $2000–$4000 per season ▶ 1 *photography head* (minimum age 21) with specific training and high level experience ▶ 4–10 *ropes instructors* (minimum age 21) with experience and/or certification at $1300 per season ▶ 2 *sailing/windsurfing instructors* (minimum age 21) with experience and/or certification at $1300 per season ▶ 1 *stained glass instructor* (minimum age 21) with skill and experience ▶ 1 *voice instructor* (minimum age 21) with experience and/or certification at $1300 per season ▶ 2 *waterskiing instructors* (minimum age 21) with experience and/or certification at $1300 per season. Applicants must submit formal organization application, 2-3 personal references or letters of recommendation. A telephone interview is required. International applicants accepted; must apply through a recognized agency.

Benefits and Preemployment Training Free housing, free meals, formal training, willing to provide letters of recommendation, names of contacts, on-the-job training, and staff cabin facility, staff lounge, and email access. Preemployment training is required and includes accident prevention and safety, first aid, CPR, interpersonal skills, leadership skills, lifeguard training, ropes course training.

Contact Bob Briskin, Director, Maine Teen Camp, 180 Upper Gulph Road, Radnor, Pennsylvania 19087. Telephone: 610-527-6759. Fax: 610-520-0182. E-mail: mtc@teencamp.com. World Wide Web: http://www.teencamp.com. Contact by e-mail, fax, phone, or through World Wide Web site. Application deadline: continuous.

NEW ENGLAND CAMPING ADVENTURES

PANTHER POND, PO BOX 160
RAYMOND, MAINE 04071

General Information Coed wilderness rafting and sailing programs for 120 campers that include backpacking, white-water canoe trips, rock climbing, ocean kayaking, mountain biking, ocean sailing, and wilderness adventure trips. 140-acre facility located 25 miles from Portland. Features: 2½ miles of shoreline; freshwater lake; acres of pine woods; small camp with family atmosphere.

Profile of Summer Employees Total number: 40. 50% men; 50% women; 15% minorities; 5% high school students; 80% college students; 5% non-U.S. citizens; 20% local applicants. Nonsmokers preferred.

Employment Information Openings are from June 15 to August 11. Jobs available: ▶ 4 *backpacking leaders* at $1400–$1800 per season ▶ 15–20 *camp counselors (crafts, sports, waterfront)* (minimum age 18) at $1200–$1650 per season ▶ 5 *canoe trip leaders* at $1400–$1800 per season ▶ 2 *rock climbing leaders* at $1300–$1800 per season ▶ 6 *sailing instructors* (minimum age 18) with ability to sail a 14-foot boat with 2 sails (FJ's) at $1250–$1800 per season. Applicants must submit a formal organization application, resume. International applicants accepted.

Benefits and Preemployment Training Free housing, free meals, formal training, willing to provide letters of recommendation, on-the-job training, willing to complete paperwork for educational credit, willing to act as a professional reference, and travel reimbursement.

Contact Ronald Furst, Director, New England Camping Adventures, 10 Scotland Bridge Road, York, Maine 03909. Telephone: 207-363-1773. Fax: 207-363-1773. E-mail: camphaw@nh.ultranet.com. Contact by e-mail, fax, mail, or phone. Application deadline: May 10.

OAKLAND HOUSE SEASIDE RESORT

435 HERRICK ROAD
BROOKSVILLE, MAINE 04617

General Information Rural, low-key family vacation resort and adults-only inn accommodating a combined total of approximately 75 guests. Established in 1889. 50-acre facility located 50 miles from Bangor. Features: 1/2-mile of ocean front with beach; freshwater lake; rowboats; hiking trails; 1 hour from Acadia National Park; recreation hall.

Profile of Summer Employees Total number: 35; typical ages: 18–50. 48% men; 52% women; 5% minorities; 52% college students; 22% non-U.S. citizens; 35% local applicants. Nonsmokers preferred.

Employment Information Openings are from May 15 to October 31. Jobs available: ▶ 1 *cabin service staff member* at $209–$300 per week ▶ 4 *culinary staff members* at $209–$249 per week ▶ 1 *host/hostess* at $3000–$5000 per season ▶ 4 *housekeepers* at $170–$400 per week ▶ 2 *maintenance and grounds staff members* at $209–$264 per week ▶ 1 *office receptionist* at $209–$249 per week ▶ 1–2 *sous chefs* (minimum age 21) at a negotiable salary with benefits ▶ 6 *waiters/waitresses* (minimum age 18) at $190–$425 per week. Applicants must submit formal organization application, letter of interest, resume, three personal references. A telephone interview is required. International applicants accepted; must apply through a recognized agency.

Benefits and Preemployment Training Housing at a cost, meals at a cost, on-the-job training, willing to complete paperwork for educational credit, willing to act as a professional reference, and beautiful location/multi-talented and multi-national staff. Preemployment training is required and includes accident prevention and safety, first aid, interpersonal skills, leadership skills, hospitality training, maintenance, skill development, culinary internships.

Contact James Littlefield, Owner, Oakland House Seaside Resort, 435 Herrick Road, Brooksville, Maine 04617. Fax: 207-359-9865. E-mail: jim@oaklandhouse.com. World Wide Web: http://www.oaklandhouse.com. Contact by e-mail, fax, mail, or through World Wide Web site. Application deadline: continuous.

THE SOUTHWESTERN COMPANY, MAINE

See The Southwestern Company on page 302 for complete description.

STUDENT CONSERVATION ASSOCIATION (SCA), MAINE

See Student Conservation Association (SCA), New Hampshire on page 209 for complete description.

WOHELO-LUTHER GULICK CAMPS

SOUTH CASCO, MAINE 04077

General Information Residential camp for girls on Sebago Lake emphasizing lifelong activities and personal growth. Established in 1907. 250-acre facility located 25 miles from Portland. Features: large lake; 27 sailboats; rustic cabins; beautiful sunsets; friendly people.

Profile of Summer Employees Total number: 65; typical ages: 18–25. 5% men; 95% women; 5% high school students; 75% college students; 2% retirees; 15% non-U.S. citizens; 3% local applicants. Nonsmokers preferred.

Employment Information Openings are from June 18 to August 30. Jobs available: ▶ *canoeing instructor* at $1100–$1400 per season ▶ 2 *dramatics instructors* at $1100–$1400 per season ▶ 2 *nature/ecology instructors* at $1100–$1400 per season ▶ 1 *pianist* at $1100–$1400 per season ▶ 1 *pottery instructor* at $1100–$1400 per season ▶ *sailing instructor* at $1100–$1400 per season ▶ 2 *swimming instructors* with WSI or LG certification at $1100–$1400 per season ▶ *tennis instructor* at $1100–$1400 per season. Applicants must submit formal organization application, resume, three letters of recommendation. An in-person interview is recommended, but a telephone interview is acceptable. International applicants accepted; must apply through a recognized agency.

Benefits and Preemployment Training Free housing, free meals, willing to provide letters of recommendation, on-the-job training, and willing to act as a professional reference. Preemployment training is required and includes accident prevention and safety, interpersonal skills, leadership skills.

Contact W. Davis Van Winkle, Director, Wohelo-Luther Gulick Camps, PO Box 39, South Casco, Maine 04077. Telephone: 207-655-4739. Fax: 207-655-2292. E-mail: staff@wohelo.com. World Wide Web: http://www.wohelo.com. Contact by e-mail, fax, mail, or phone. Application deadline: continuous.

MARYLAND

BLACKWATER NATIONAL WILDLIFE REFUGE

2145 KEY WALLACE DRIVE
CAMBRIDGE, MARYLAND 21613

General Information Non-profit government National Wildlife Refuge with visitor center and public use program. Established in 1933. 26,000-acre facility. Features: visitor center/exhibits; Wildlife Drive; 2 hiking trails; photoblind; 26,000 acres wildlife habitat; fresh water impoundment, Blackwater River.

Profile of Summer Employees Total number: 1–2; typical ages: 20–25. 100% college students. Nonsmokers preferred.

Employment Information Openings are from May to September. Jobs available: ▶ 1–2 *interns* knowledge of wildlife (preferred); people skills, computer skills, and a valid driver's license; $25 daily stipend. Applicants must submit resume, three personal references. An in-person interview is recommended, but a telephone interview is acceptable. International applicants accepted; must obtain own visa, obtain own working papers.

Benefits and Preemployment Training Free housing, willing to provide letters of recommendation, on-the-job training, willing to complete paperwork for educational credit, and willing to act as a professional reference.

Contact Maggie Briggs, Outdoor Recreation Planner, Blackwater National Wildlife Refuge. Telephone: 410-228-2677. Fax: 410-221-7738. E-mail: maggie_briggs@fws.gov. World Wide Web: http://www.blackwater.fws.gov/. Contact by e-mail, fax, mail, or phone. Application deadline: continuous.

CAMP AIRY FOR BOYS

14938 OLD CAMP AIRY ROAD
THURMONT, MARYLAND 21788

General Information Nonprofit residential camp serving 400 boys in each of four 2-week sessions or two 4-week sessions. Established in 1924. 450-acre facility located 50 miles from Washington, DC. Features: numerous ball fields; several craft facilities; outdoor living area with high and low element ropes courses; tennis courts and gym; theaters; comfortable bunk with counselor rooms.

Profile of Summer Employees Total number: 150; typical ages: 18–23. 95% men; 5% women; 2% minorities; 95% college students; 3% retirees; 20% non-U.S. citizens; 10% local applicants. Nonsmokers preferred.

Employment Information Openings are from June 18 to August 19. Jobs available: ▶ 2–4 *archery instructors (counselors)* (minimum age 18) with formal training and at least one year of college completed; NAA instructor certification preferred (we will locate classes and provide $400 bonus for successful completion) at $1,100 minimum per season with annual increments for returning staff ▶ 3–6 *arts and crafts instructors(counselors)* (minimum age 18) with formal training and at least one year of college completed; teaching experience preferred at $1,100 minimum per season with annual increments for returning staff ▶ 30 *athletics instructors (counselors)* (minimum age 18) with at least one year of college completed at $1,100 minimum per season with annual increments for returning staff ▶ 3–6 *ceramics instructors (counselors)* (minimum age 18) with formal training and at least one year of college completed; teaching experience preferred at $1,100 minimum per season with annual increments for returning staff ▶ 4 *drama instructors (counselors)* (minimum age 18) with at least one year of college completed at $1,100 minimum per season with annual increments for returning staff ▶ 1–2 *fencing instructors (counselors)* (minimum age 18) with formal training and at least one year of college completed; teaching experience preferred at $1,100 minimum per season with annual increments for returning staff ▶ 30 *general counselors* (minimum age 18) with at least one year of college completed at $1,100 minimum per season with annual increments for returning staff ▶ 5 *music instructors (counselors)* (minimum age 18) with one year of college completed and ability to teach one or more instruments (all types) at $1,100 minimum per season with annual increments for returning staff ▶ 2 *nature instructors (counselors)* (minimum age 18) with formal training and at least one year of college completed; teaching experience preferred at $1,100 minimum per season with annual increments for returning staff ▶ 12–15 *nurses* (minimum age 18) with RN (Maryland); flexible commitment of one to eight weeks at $250 per week or generous tuition discount for staff with children ▶ 10 *outdoor living instructors (counselors)* (minimum age 18) with one year of college completed and ability to teach rock climbing, rappelling, caving, survival training, and backpacking at $1,500 minimum per season with annual increments for returning staff ▶ 3–6 *photography instructors (counselors)* (minimum age 18) with formal training and at least one year of college completed; teaching experience preferred at $1,100 minimum per season with annual increments for returning staff ▶ 15 *swimming instructors (counselors)* (minimum age 18) with lifeguard training and one year of college completed; $400 bonus for WSI or LGI certification at $1,100 minimum per season with annual increments for returning staff. Applicants must submit formal organization application, two personal references, fingerprinting/background check to complete hiring process; international applicants apply through BUNAC. An in-person interview is recommended, but a telephone interview is acceptable. International applicants accepted; must apply through a recognized agency.

Benefits and Preemployment Training Free housing, free meals, formal training, willing to provide letters of recommendation, on-the-job training, willing to complete paperwork for educational credit, willing to act as a professional reference, travel reimbursement, and worker's compensation. Preemployment training is required and includes accident prevention and safety, interpersonal skills, leadership skills.

Contact Steve Goldklang, Assistant Director, Camp Airy for Boys, 5750 Park Heights Avenue, Baltimore, Maryland 21215. Telephone: 410-466-9010. Fax: 410-466-0560. E-mail: steve@airylouise.org. World Wide Web: http://www.airylouise.org. Contact by e-mail, fax, mail, phone, or through World Wide Web site. Application deadline: applications before April 15 are preferred.

CAMP CONOWINGO–GIRL SCOUTS OF CENTRAL MARYLAND

CONOWINGO, MARYLAND

General Information Nonprofit organization helping to enrich and work with every girl everywhere to develop her full individual potential. Established in 1955. 600-acre facility located

60 miles from Baltimore. Features: pool; pond and stream; wooded setting; rustic atmosphere; ropes course; playing surface.

Profile of Summer Employees Total number: 40; typical ages: 18–30. 1% men; 99% women; 10% high school students; 30% college students. Nonsmokers preferred.

Employment Information Openings are from June 15 to August 22. Jobs available: ▶ 1 *arts and crafts manager* (minimum age 21) with ability and basic knowledge to teach various arts and crafts at $1600–$2000 per season ▶ 1 *assistant camp director* (minimum age 23) with experience in resident camp setting at $2800–$3200 per season ▶ 6–8 *assistant counselors* (minimum age 18) skilled with children; enjoy outdoors at $1800–$2400 per season ▶ 6–8 *counselors* (minimum age 21) skilled with children, enjoy outdoors at $2500–$3000 per season ▶ 1 *nurse/health supervisor* (minimum age 23) with first aid and CPR certification by state of Maryland, license as registered nurse, nurse practitioner or physician's assistant at $5500–$6500 per season ▶ 1 *outdoor living skills manager* (minimum age 21) with ability to demonstrate and instruct campers in specialized fields at $1750–$2150 per season ▶ 1 *sports/games manager* (minimum age 21) with ability to organize and instruct girls ages 6 to 16 in various sports activities at $1600–$2000 per season. Applicants must submit formal organization application, resume, three personal references, background check and finger printing. An in-person interview is recommended, but a telephone interview is acceptable. International applicants accepted; must apply through a recognized agency.

Benefits and Preemployment Training Free housing, free meals, willing to provide letters of recommendation, willing to act as a professional reference, and laundry facilities. Preemployment training is required and includes accident prevention and safety, first aid, CPR, interpersonal skills, leadership skills.

Contact Adam Rubin, Outdoor Program Specialist, Camp Conowingo–Girl Scouts of Central Maryland, 4806 Seton Drive, Baltimore, Maryland 21215. Telephone: 410-358-9711 Ext. 237. Fax: 410-358-9918. E-mail: arubin@gscm.org. Contact by e-mail, fax, or phone. Application deadline: continuous.

CAMP SONSHINE
16819 NEW HAMPSHIRE AVENUE
SILVER SPRING, MARYLAND 20905

General Information Nonprofit Christian day camp for kids 4-16 years old. Activities include go-karts, paddleboats, crafts, nature, drama, swimming, and much more. Established in 1981. 60-acre facility located 10 miles from Washington, DC. Features: pond; woods; go-karts; paddleboats; ropes/climbing wall; sports.

Profile of Summer Employees Total number: 250; typical ages: 18–34. 30% men; 70% women; 80% college students; 13% non-U.S. citizens; 7% local applicants. Nonsmokers required.

Employment Information Openings are from June 18 to August 18. Jobs available: ▶ 40 *activity counselors (lifeguards, archery, drama, crafts, and go-karts)* (minimum age 18) at $1200 per season ▶ 50–100 *group counselors* (minimum age 18) at $1200 per season. Applicants must submit formal organization application, three personal references. A telephone interview is required. International applicants accepted; must apply through a recognized agency.

Benefits and Preemployment Training Free housing, free meals, willing to provide letters of recommendation, willing to complete paperwork for educational credit, willing to act as a professional reference, and travel reimbursement. Preemployment training is required and includes accident prevention and safety, interpersonal skills, leadership skills.

Contact Nathan Haas, Director, Camp Sonshine. Telephone: 888-883-2285. Fax: 301-989-7116. E-mail: staff@campsonshine.org. World Wide Web: http://www.campsonshine.org/campstaff.html. Contact by e-mail, mail, phone, or through World Wide Web site. Application deadline: continuous.

CAPITAL CAMPS
133 ROLLINS ROAD, UNIT 4
ROCKVILLE, MARYLAND 20852

General Information Residential kosher Jewish camp serving young teens. Established in 1990. 230-acre facility located 65 miles from Washington, DC. Features: tennis courts; lake; 2 Olympic-size swimming pools; wooded environment; ropes course; numerous sports facilities.
Profile of Summer Employees Total number: 150; typical ages: 17–30. 50% men; 50% women; 2% minorities; 10% high school students; 75% college students; 20% non-U.S. citizens; 10% local applicants. Nonsmokers preferred.
Employment Information Openings are from June 15 to August 20. Jobs available: ▶ *arts and crafts director* with art teaching background at $1200–$1500 per season ▶ *counselors* (minimum age 18) at $1100–$1500 per season ▶ *drama specialist* with ability to direct and produce a play at $1200–$1500 per season ▶ *nature specialist* with ropes course certification and outdoor living skills at $1200–$1500 per season ▶ *swimming instructors* with lifeguard training and WSI certification at $1100–$1200 per season ▶ *video specialist* with ability to produce camp videos at $1200–$1500 per season ▶ *waterfront director* with WSI certification and lifeguard training; pool operator preferred at $1500–$1800 per season. Applicants must submit formal organization application, three letters of recommendation. An in-person interview is recommended, but a telephone interview is acceptable. International applicants accepted; must apply through a recognized agency.
Benefits and Preemployment Training Free housing, free meals, formal training, willing to provide letters of recommendation, on-the-job training, willing to complete paperwork for educational credit, opportunity to attend seminars/workshops, and travel reimbursement. Preemployment training is required and includes accident prevention and safety, CPR, interpersonal skills, leadership skills, child development.
Contact Joe Finkelstein, Associate Director, Capital Camps, 133 Rollins Avenue, Unit 4, Rockville, Maryland 20852. Telephone: 301-468-2267. Fax: 301-468-1719. E-mail: joe@capitalcamps.org. World Wide Web: http://www.capitalcamps.org. Contact by e-mail, mail, phone, or through World Wide Web site. Application deadline: continuous.

CENTER FOR TALENTED YOUTH/JOHNS HOPKINS UNIVERSITY
2701 NORTH CHARLES STREET
BALTIMORE, MARYLAND 21218

General Information Organization that provides academically talented pre-college students the opportunity to take rigorous courses in mathematics, science, computer science, humanities, and writing at college campuses in the United States. Established in 1980. 50-acre facility. Features: university dormitories; libraries; athletic facilities; playing fields; small, quiet campuses.
Profile of Summer Employees Total number: 1,400; typical ages: 18–50. 50% men; 50% women; 10% minorities; 60% college students; 2% non-U.S. citizens; 10% local applicants.
Employment Information Openings are from June to August. Jobs available: ▶ 8 *academic counselors* with graduate training in counseling with 2 years counseling experience, familiarity with Attention Deficit Disorder, and experience in a boarding school or residential camp environment at $5000–$5400 per season ▶ 8 *academic deans* with graduate training in an academic discipline and teaching experience at $4400–$5400 per season ▶ 8 *deans of residential life* with master's degree preferred, 2 years residential administrative experience in a school or college, and counseling experience at $4400–$5400 per season ▶ 36 *health assistants* (minimum age 21) should be junior or senior in college or medical student; interested in medicine and health issues; CPR and first aid certified; valid driver's license at $2200 per season ▶ 100–120 *instructors* with BA or BS (master's degree preferred), experience with students in this age group, and leadership skills at $1800–$2700 per season ▶ 8 *office managers* with excellent office skills, bookkeeping experience, at least junior status in college; GPA 3.2 or higher at $3400–$3600 per

season ▶ 36 *office/general assistants* with office experience, at least one year of college, and 3.2 GPA at $2200 per season ▶ 400–450 *resident assistants* with experience as a college RA or as a camp counselor, GPA of 3.2 or higher, and experience in events planning at $2000 per season ▶ 8 *site directors* with master's degree preferred, teaching and administrative background, and leadership in an educational environment at $5400–$7400 per season ▶ 200–250 *teaching/laboratory assistants* with GPA of 3.2 or higher, strong interest in teaching, and experience with young people at $1800 per season. Applicants must submit formal organization application, letter of interest, resume, academic transcripts, letter of recommendation. A telephone interview is required. International applicants accepted; must obtain own working papers.

Benefits and Preemployment Training Free housing, free meals, willing to provide letters of recommendation, on-the-job training, willing to complete paperwork for educational credit, and willing to act as a professional reference. Preemployment training is required and includes accident prevention and safety, first aid, interpersonal skills, leadership skills.

Contact Simeon Brodsky, Coordinator for Academic Programs, Center for Talented Youth/Johns Hopkins University, 2701 North Charles Street, Baltimore, Maryland 21218. Telephone: 410-516-0053. Fax: 410-516-0093. E-mail: ctysummer@jhu.edu. World Wide Web: http://www.jhu.edu/gifted/ctysummer. Contact by e-mail, fax, mail, phone, or through World Wide Web site. Application deadline: printed deadline is January 30 but it is flexible; applications are accepted through June 1.

CENTER FOR TALENTED YOUTH/JOHNS HOPKINS UNIVERSITY–GARRISON FOREST SCHOOL

OWINGS MILLS, MARYLAND

See Center for Talented Youth/Johns Hopkins University on page 145 for complete description.

CENTER FOR TALENTED YOUTH/JOHNS HOPKINS UNIVERSITY–HOOD COLLEGE

FREDERICK, MARYLAND

See Center for Talented Youth/Johns Hopkins University on page 145 for complete description.

CENTER FOR TALENTED YOUTH/JOHNS HOPKINS UNIVERSITY–MARINE SCIENCES PROGRAM

BALTIMORE, MARYLAND

See Center for Talented Youth/Johns Hopkins University on page 145 for complete description.

CENTER FOR TALENTED YOUTH/JOHNS HOPKINS UNIVERSITY–SANDY SPRING FRIENDS SCHOOL

SANDY SPRING, MARYLAND

See Center for Talented Youth/Johns Hopkins University on page 145 for complete description.

CENTER FOR TALENTED YOUTH/JOHNS HOPKINS UNIVERSITY–ST. MARY'S COLLEGE

ST. MARY'S CITY, MARYLAND

See Center for Talented Youth/Johns Hopkins University on page 145 for complete description.

CENTER FOR TALENTED YOUTH/JOHNS HOPKINS UNIVERSITY–WASHINGTON COLLEGE

CHESTERTOWN, MARYLAND

See Center for Talented Youth/Johns Hopkins University on page 145 for complete description.

CYBERCAMPS–JOHNS HOPKINS UNIVERSITY

BALTIMORE, MARYLAND

See Cybercamps–University of Washington on page 335 for complete description.

CYBERCAMPS–UNIVERSITY OF MARYLAND

COLLEGE PARK, MARYLAND

See Cybercamps–University of Washington on page 335 for complete description.

ECHO HILL CAMP

13655 BLOOMINGNECK ROAD
WORTON, MARYLAND 21678

General Information Coeducational residential camp serving 140 campers per session in two-, four-, and eight-week sessions along with one-week postcamp sail and ski and fishing and crabbing camps. Established in 1915. 350-acre facility located 90 miles from Washington, DC. Features: Chesapeake Bay location.

Profile of Summer Employees Total number: 50; typical ages: 17–24. 55% men; 45% women; 2% minorities; 10% high school students; 70% college students; 10% non-U.S. citizens; 2% local applicants.

Employment Information Openings are from June 10 to August 30. Jobs available: ▶ *counselors* (minimum age 18) ▶ 2 *swimming instructors* with WSI and American Red Cross lifeguard certification at $600 per month. Applicants must submit formal organization application. International applicants accepted; must apply through a recognized agency.

Benefits and Preemployment Training Free housing, free meals, formal training, willing to provide letters of recommendation, on-the-job training, willing to complete paperwork for educational credit, willing to act as a professional reference, and opportunity to attend seminars/workshops. Preemployment training is required and includes accident prevention and safety, first aid, CPR, interpersonal skills, leadership skills.

Contact Peter Rice, Director, Echo Hill Camp, 13655 Bloomingneck Road, Worton, Maryland 21678. Telephone: 410-348-5303. Fax: 410-348-2010. E-mail: echohillcamp@hotmail.com. World Wide Web: http://www.echohillcamp.com. Contact by e-mail, mail, or phone. Application deadline: continuous.

THE SOUTHWESTERN COMPANY, MARYLAND

See The Southwestern Company on page 302 for complete description.

SPORTS INTERNATIONAL, INC.

12061 TECH ROAD
SILVER SPRING, MARYLAND 20904

General Information Privately owned company, organising and running youth football camps hosted by professional football players. Established in 1983. Located 15 miles from Washington, DC. Features: easy access to public transportation; beltway accessible.

Profile of Summer Employees Total number: 15; typical ages: 30–50. 95% men; 5% women; 1% high school students; 9% college students; 90% local applicants. Nonsmokers preferred.

Employment Information Openings are from January 1 to August 1. Spring break, winter break, and year-round positions also offered. Jobs available: ▶ *various positions* (minimum age 18) hourly salary dependent on position. Applicants must submit a formal organization applica-

tion, resume, personal reference. An in-person interview is recommended, but a telephone interview is acceptable.
Benefits and Preemployment Training Formal training, possible full-time employment, willing to provide letters of recommendation, on-the-job training, and willing to complete paperwork for educational credit.
Contact Josie Gahanm, Sports International, Inc. Telephone: 301-625-7713. Fax: 301-625-7723. E-mail: josieg36@hotmail.com. World Wide Web: http://www.footballcamps.com. Contact by e-mail, fax, mail, or phone. Application deadline: applications accepted from January to March.

SPORTS INTERNATIONAL–JOE KRIVAK (QUARTERBACK AND RECEIVING CAMP)
WESTMINSTER, MARYLAND
See Sports International, Inc. on page 147 for complete description.

SPORTS INTERNATIONAL–REDSKINS
WESTMINSTER, MARYLAND
See Sports International, Inc. on page 147 for complete description.

STUDENT CONSERVATION ASSOCIATION (SCA), MARYLAND
See Student Conservation Association (SCA), New Hampshire on page 209 for complete description.

WEST RIVER UNITED METHODIST CENTER
5100 CHALK POINT ROAD
CHURCHTON, MARYLAND 20733
General Information Residential camp on a mile-long waterfront near the Chesapeake Bay. Established in 1951. 45-acre facility located 15 miles from Annapolis. Features: diverse program; wooded setting; sailing and boating; lodges; one mile of waterfront; near Chesapeake Bay.
Profile of Summer Employees Total number: 25; typical ages: 17–24. 40% men; 60% women; 18% minorities; 12% high school students; 62% college students; 37% local applicants. Nonsmokers preferred.
Employment Information Openings are from June 1 to August 20. Jobs available: ▶ 2 *cooks* at $300–$400 per week ▶ 1 *head lifeguard* (minimum age 18) with WSI certification at $200–$250 per week ▶ 4 *kitchen aides* (minimum age 18) at $175–$200 per week ▶ 5 *lifeguards* (minimum age 18) with Red Cross lifeguard training at $200–$250 per week ▶ 2 *maintenance personnel* (minimum age 18) at $175–$200 per week ▶ 1 *nurse* (minimum age 20) with state RN license at $300–$400 per week ▶ 7 *program resource persons* (minimum age 18) with lifesaving training (preferred) at $200–$250 per week ▶ 1 *sailing instructor* (minimum age 18) with US Coast Guard or Red Cross sailing instructor certification or equivalent at $200–$250 per week. Applicants must submit formal organization application, letter of interest, resume, three personal references, criminal background check. An in-person interview is recommended, but a telephone interview is acceptable. International applicants accepted; must apply through a recognized agency.
Benefits and Preemployment Training Free housing, free meals, willing to provide letters of recommendation, on-the-job training, willing to complete paperwork for educational credit, and willing to act as a professional reference. Preemployment training is required and includes accident prevention and safety, interpersonal skills, leadership skills.
Contact Andrew Thornton, Manager, West River United Methodist Center, PO Box 429, Churchton, Maryland 20733. Telephone: 410-867-0991. Fax: 410-867-3741. E-mail: westrivercenter@starpower.net. World Wide Web: http://www.bwconf.org/camping. Contact by e-mail, fax, mail, or phone. Application deadline: continuous.

YMCA CAMP LETTS
4003 CAMP LETTS ROAD, PO BOX 208
EDGEWATER, MARYLAND 21037

General Information Residential camp serving 350 campers during one-week or 2-week sessions. Character development through sailing, horsemanship, low and high ropes programs, and fun. Established in 1906. 219-acre facility located 32 miles from Washington, DC. Features: 219-acre peninsula in the Chesapeake; large waterfront; stables with 2 instructional riding rings; high ropes and low ropes course; tennis and basketball courts; swimming pool.

Profile of Summer Employees Total number: 110; typical ages: 19–23. 50% men; 50% women; 20% minorities; 10% high school students; 80% college students; 1% retirees; 30% non-U.S. citizens; 25% local applicants. Nonsmokers required.

Employment Information Openings are from June 1 to August 30. Year-round positions also offered. Jobs available: ▶ 4 *adventure camp counselors* (minimum age 19) with outdoor experience (preferred), must be high/low ropes certified, Wilderness First Aid certified at $1700–$2000 per season ▶ 10 *assistant counselors* (minimum age 18) with First Aid and CPR certification; must be at least high school graduate at $1200–$1400 per season ▶ 1–10 *counselors* (minimum age 18) with First Aid and CPR certification at $1700–$2300 per season ▶ 6 *crew skippers (head counselors)* (minimum age 19) with supervisory experience, First Aid and CPR certification required at $1800–$2300 per season ▶ 1 *horsemanship director* (minimum age 19) should be college upperclassman or graduate with Pony Club background (preferred), CHA certification, and experience at $1800–$2300 per season ▶ 1 *horsemasters director* (minimum age 19) should be college upperclassman with experience at $1800–$2300 per season. Applicants must submit formal organization application, three personal references, three letters of recommendation. An in-person interview is recommended, but a telephone interview is acceptable. International applicants accepted; must apply through a recognized agency.

Benefits and Preemployment Training Free housing, free meals, possible full-time employment, willing to provide letters of recommendation, on-the-job training, willing to complete paperwork for educational credit, willing to act as a professional reference, and opportunity to attend seminars/workshops. Preemployment training is required and includes accident prevention and safety, first aid, CPR, interpersonal skills, leadership skills, skill training/certification (sailing, archery, horseback riding, canoeing, powerboating, waterskiing, ropes).

Contact Stephen J. Gruber, Senior Program Director, YMCA Camp Letts, PO Box 208, Edgewater, Maryland 21037. Telephone: 410-919-1400. Fax: 301-261-7336. E-mail: ymcacampletts@aol.com. World Wide Web: http://www.ymcawashdc.org. Contact by e-mail, fax, mail, or phone. Application deadline: continuous.

MASSACHUSETTS

BELVOIR TERRACE
80 CLIFFWOOD STREET
LENOX, MASSACHUSETTS 01240

General Information Residential camp serving 180 girls with a focus on fine and performing arts. The program provides specific services for the academically talented and the gifted. Established in 1954. 48-acre facility located 4 miles from Pittsfield. Features: mansion; 2 pools; 6 tennis courts; 5 modern dorms; 4 theaters; 4 dance studios; 16 art studios.

Profile of Summer Employees Total number: 90; typical ages: 25–40. 10% men; 90% women; 5% minorities; 10% college students; 5% non-U.S. citizens. Nonsmokers required.

Employment Information Openings are from June 16 to August 24. Jobs available: ▶ *ceramics or painting teacher* MFA at $2400 per season ▶ *theater teacher/director* (minimum age 22) with a graduate degree in theater and directing experience at $2400 per season. Applicants must submit formal organization application, letter of interest, resume, portfolio, three personal references, letter of recommendation. An in-person interview is recommended, but a telephone interview is acceptable. International applicants accepted; must apply through a recognized agency.
Benefits and Preemployment Training Free housing, free meals, willing to provide letters of recommendation, on-the-job training, willing to complete paperwork for educational credit, willing to act as a professional reference, opportunity to attend seminars/workshops, and travel reimbursement. Preemployment training is required and includes accident prevention and safety, first aid, CPR, interpersonal skills, leadership skills.
Contact Ms. Nancy S. Goldberg, Director, Belvoir Terrace, 101 West 79th Street, New York, New York 10024. Fax: 212-579-7282. E-mail: info@belvoirterrace.com. World Wide Web: http://www.belvoirterrace.com. Contact by e-mail, mail, or through World Wide Web site. Application deadline: continuous.

BONNIE CASTLE RIDING CAMP
574 BERNARDSTON ROAD
GREENFIELD, MASSACHUSETTS 01301

General Information Residential camp for girls ages 9-16 with three 2-week sessions. Established in 1982. 100-acre facility located 50 miles from Hartford, Connecticut. Features: swimming pool; 5 tennis courts; boarding school facilities; gymnasium; dance studio; ceramics studio.
Profile of Summer Employees Total number: 12; typical ages: 18–30. 100% women; 10% minorities; 10% high school students; 90% college students; 60% local applicants. Nonsmokers preferred.
Employment Information Openings are from June 25 to August 19. Jobs available: ▶ 2 *arts/photography instructors* (minimum age 20) with specific art media experience at $1100–$1800 per season ▶ 1 *camp nurse* with RN license and current CPR certification at $2700 per season ▶ 1 *dance instructor* (minimum age 20) at $1100–$1800 per season ▶ 1 *drama instructor* (minimum age 20) with theater/drama experience at $1100–$1800 per season ▶ 1–3 *riding instructors* (minimum age 20) with extensive Hunt Seat riding and showing experience at $1100–$1800 per season ▶ 1 *swimming instructor* (minimum age 20) with WSI and CPR certification at $1100–$1800 per season. Applicants must submit a formal organization application, letter of interest, resume, three personal references. An in-person interview is required. International applicants accepted.
Benefits and Preemployment Training Free housing, free meals, and willing to provide letters of recommendation. Preemployment training is required and includes accident prevention and safety, leadership skills.
Contact Karen E. Bertin, Director, Bonnie Castle Riding Camp, 574 Bernardston Road, Greenfield, Massachusetts 01301. Telephone: 413-774-2711. Fax: 413-772-2602. World Wide Web: http://www.sbschool.org. Contact by fax, mail, or phone. Application deadline: May 15.

BREWSTER DAY CAMP
3570 MAIN STREET
BREWSTER, MASSACHUSETTS 02631

General Information Fully inclusive day camp whose mission is to challenge, nurture, and support children and their families on Cape Cod. Established in 1981. 5-acre facility located 90 miles from Boston. Features: olympic pool; wooded 4.5 acres; sailing ponds; pavilions; playgrounds.
Profile of Summer Employees Total number: 95; typical ages: 17–64. 50% men; 50% women;

10% high school students; 40% college students; 5% non-U.S. citizens; 25% local applicants. Nonsmokers required.

Employment Information Openings are from June 15 to August 20. Jobs available: ▶ 10–40 *tent counselors/activity staff* (minimum age 17) at $2500–$5000 per season. Applicants must submit a formal organization application, letter of interest, resume, three personal references. An in-person interview is recommended, but a telephone interview is acceptable.

Benefits and Preemployment Training Formal training, possible full-time employment, willing to provide letters of recommendation, on-the-job training, willing to complete paperwork for educational credit, willing to act as a professional reference, and opportunity to attend seminars/ workshops. Preemployment training is required and includes accident prevention and safety, first aid, interpersonal skills, leadership skills.

Contact Miusa Galazzi, Director, Brewster Day Camp, 1406 Narragansett Boulevard, Cranston, Rhode Island 02905. Telephone: 888-396-CAMP. Fax: 401-461-4647. World Wide Web: http://www.brewsterdaycamp.com. Contact by e-mail, fax, mail, phone, or through World Wide Web site. Application deadline: continuous.

CAMP GOOD NEWS
ROUTE 130
FORESTDALE, MASSACHUSETTS 02644

General Information Coeducational residential and day camp serving 220 children ages 6–16. Established in 1935. 214-acre facility located 10 miles from Hyannis. Features: freshwater lake with sandy beach; wooded setting; 6 miles from ocean; 3 new tennis courts; tutoring center.

Profile of Summer Employees Total number: 80; typical ages: 18–45. 45% men; 55% women; 3% minorities; 1% high school students; 58% college students; 1% retirees; 2% non-U.S. citizens; 5% local applicants. Nonsmokers required.

Employment Information Openings are from June to August. Jobs available: ▶ 2 *arts and crafts instructors* (minimum age 25) with experience in the field at $1200–$1400 per season ▶ 35 *counselors* (minimum age 18) should be college student at $1500–$1800 per season ▶ 10 *kitchen staff members* (minimum age 18) at $1200 per season ▶ 2 *nurses* (minimum age 25) with RN of LPN at $1500 per season ▶ 1 *sports expert* (minimum age 19) at $1200–$1500 per season ▶ 1 *store manager* (minimum age 18) with driver's license at $1000–$1200 per season ▶ 1 *waterfront director* (minimum age 21) at $1500–$1800 per season. Applicants must submit a formal organization application, three personal references. An in-person interview is recommended, but a telephone interview is acceptable. International applicants accepted; must obtain own visa, obtain own working papers.

Benefits and Preemployment Training Free housing, free meals, on-the-job training, tuition assistance, and full campership in lieu of or with salary in some cases. Preemployment training is required and includes first aid, CPR, LGT, WSI.

Contact Faith Willard, Director, Camp Good News, PO Box 1295, Forestdale, Massachusetts 02644. Telephone: 508-477-9731. Fax: 508-477-8016. E-mail: office@campgoodnews.org. World Wide Web: http://www.campgoodnews.org. Contact by e-mail, fax, or mail. Application deadline: continuous.

CAMP NAWAKA
622 RESERVOIR ROAD
EAST OTIS, MASSACHUSETTS 01029

General Information Small non-profit resident camp located in Berkshires of Western Massachusetts. Traditional summer camp with swimming, boating, arts, athletics, and outdoor activities. Established in 1967. 130-acre facility located 25 miles from Springfield. Features: 20-acre freshwater pond; 180 forested acres; 2 tennis courts; archery range.

Profile of Summer Employees Total number: 35; typical ages: 17–25. 40% men; 60% women;

10% minorities; 10% high school students; 80% college students; 5% retirees; 50% local applicants. Nonsmokers required.

Employment Information Openings are from June 23 to August 19. Jobs available: ▶ 1 *CIT/LT Director* (minimum age 21) with experience in camp setting, working with teens at $2500–$3000 per season ▶ 1 *business manager* (minimum age 21) with basic experience with accounting at $2500–$3000 per season ▶ 1–3 *camp nurses* (minimum age 21) with RN license at $2500–$3000 per season ▶ 20 *counselors* (minimum age 18) with teaching skills in camp activities at $1600 per season ▶ 4 *department heads, area directors* (minimum age 21) with experience running camp activities at $2500–$3000 per season ▶ 1 *head cook/food service manager* (minimum age 21) with experience cooking, ordering and menu planning at $4500–$5000 per season ▶ 1 *program director/assistant director* (minimum age 25) with experience planning and running programs at $3000–$3250 per season ▶ 1 *senior camp director* (minimum age 21) with experience working with teens at $2500–$3000 per season ▶ 1 *unit coordinator* (minimum age 21) with experience supervising in a camp setting at $2500–$3000 per season. Applicants must submit formal organization application, three writing samples, three personal references. An in-person interview is recommended, but a telephone interview is acceptable. International applicants accepted; must apply through a recognized agency.

Benefits and Preemployment Training Free housing, free meals, formal training, willing to provide letters of recommendation, on-the-job training, willing to complete paperwork for educational credit, willing to act as a professional reference, and opportunity to attend seminars/workshops. Preemployment training is required and includes accident prevention and safety, first aid, CPR, interpersonal skills, leadership skills.

Contact Christopher Egan, Camp Director, Camp Nawaka, 108 Union Wharf, Boston, Massachusetts 02109. Telephone: 617-523-6006 Ext. 41. Fax: 617-523-6290. E-mail: egan@nawaka.org. World Wide Web: http://www.nawaka.org. Contact by e-mail. Application deadline: continuous.

CAMP TACONIC
770 NEW WINDSOR ROAD
HINSDALE, MASSACHUSETTS 01235

General Information Residential 7-week coed camp for 280 children offering top instruction in a wide range of program areas. Established in 1932. 250-acre facility located 10 miles from Pittsfield. Features: beautiful Berkshire Mountains; 2 heated swimming pools; 10 tennis courts; golf driving range; freshwater lake; ball fields and courts.

Profile of Summer Employees Total number: 140; typical ages: 19–25. 50% men; 50% women; 85% college students. Nonsmokers required.

Employment Information Openings are from June 16 to August 16. Jobs available: ▶ 16 *aquatics staff members (swimming, sailing, waterskiing, and boating)* with WSI certification for swimming at $1400–$2000 per season ▶ 10 *arts and crafts staff members (fine arts, ceramics, crafts, and silver jewelry)* at $1400–$4000 per season ▶ 14 *athletics staff members (team and individual sports)* at $1400–$2000 per season ▶ 2 *cooking instructors* with ability to teach cooking to campers at $1400–$2000 per season ▶ 12 *general counselors for 7-10 year olds* (must be a college sophomore) at $1400–$2000 per season ▶ 6 *media arts staff members (newspaper, photography, and video)* at $1400–$2000 per season ▶ 5 *outdoor adventure staff members (pioneering, climbing wall, and ropes course)* at $1400–$2000 per season ▶ 12 *tennis staff members* at $1400–$2000 per season ▶ 12 *theater arts staff members (dance, costume making, musical theater, and stagecraft)* at $1400–$2000 per season. Applicants must submit a formal organization application, three personal references. A telephone interview is required. International applicants accepted.

Benefits and Preemployment Training Free housing, free meals, formal training, willing to provide letters of recommendation, on-the-job training, willing to complete paperwork for educational credit, willing to act as a professional reference, and travel reimbursement.

Preemployment training is required and includes accident prevention and safety, first aid, CPR, interpersonal skills, leadership skills, low ropes/zipline, archery, lifeguard, WSI.
Contact Barbara Ezrol, Co-Director, Camp Taconic, 66 Chestnut Hill Lane, Briarcliff Manor, New York 10510. Telephone: 914-762-2820. Fax: 914-762-4437. E-mail: ctaconic@aol.com. World Wide Web: http://www.CampTaconic.com. Contact by e-mail, fax, mail, phone, or through World Wide Web site. Application deadline: continuous.

CAMP WATITOH

CENTER LAKE
BECKET, MASSACHUSETTS 01223

General Information Residential summer camp serving 200 children with a wide variety of land and water sports activities, including drama, nature, and trips to all Berkshire area attractions. Established in 1937. 85-acre facility located 130 miles from Boston. Features: mountain-top setting; attractive lakefront; noted cultural arts region; cabins with bathrooms; wide variety of athletic facilities.
Profile of Summer Employees Total number: 75; typical ages: 19–28. 50% men; 50% women; 85% college students; 10% non-U.S. citizens. Nonsmokers preferred.
Employment Information Openings are from June 22 to August 19. Jobs available: ▶ 3 *arts and crafts instructors* (minimum age 20) with experience preferred at $1500–$2500 per season ▶ *general sports instructor* (minimum age 19) must be completing first year of college and have some experience with sports at $1300–$1800 per season ▶ 2 *sailing instructors* (minimum age 20) with experience in open water sailing; competitive experience is helpful at $1400–$1800 per season ▶ 6 *swimming instructors* (minimum age 20) with WSI or LGT certification at $1400–$1800 per season ▶ 2 *waterskiing instructors* (minimum age 21) with teaching experience; able to slalom and trick ski at $1400–$1800 per season. Applicants must submit formal organization application, two letters of recommendation. International applicants accepted; must apply through a recognized agency.
Benefits and Preemployment Training Free housing, free meals, willing to provide letters of recommendation, on-the-job training, willing to complete paperwork for educational credit, willing to act as a professional reference, and travel reimbursement.
Contact William Hoch, Director, Camp Watitoh, 28 Sammis Lane, White Plains, New York 10605. Telephone: 914-428-1894. Fax: 914-428-1648. E-mail: watitoh@msn.com. World Wide Web: http://www.campwatitoh.com. Contact by mail, phone, or through World Wide Web site. Application deadline: continuous.

CAPE COD SEA CAMPS

PO BOX 1880
BREWSTER, MASSACHUSETTS 02631

General Information Residential camp serving 350 campers for 3½ or 7 weeks and a day camp serving 240 campers weekly. Established in 1922. 125-acre facility located 90 miles from Boston. Features: Cape Cod Bay; site on Cape's largest lake; 9 tennis courts; more than 40 sailboats; outdoor theater; photography lab.
Profile of Summer Employees Total number: 200; typical age: 20. 50% men; 50% women; 5% minorities; 80% college students; 5% non-U.S. citizens; 10% local applicants. Nonsmokers preferred.
Employment Information Openings are from June 20 to August 17. Jobs available: ▶ 3–6 *activity department heads* (minimum age 21) with CPR, first aid, and teaching certification at $2500–$3500 per season ▶ 10–40 *general counselors* (minimum age 19) with documented experience in camp activities; CPR, first aid certification at $1900–$2600 per season ▶ 2–5 *photography counselors* (minimum age 19) with CPR, first aid; should have taken photography courses and have experience developing pictures at $1800–$2200 per season ▶ 5–16 *sailing*

staff members (minimum age 19) with instruction and racing experience; CPR, first aid, small boat sailing, and small craft safety certification at $1800–$2400 per season ▶ 4–10 *swimming instructors* (minimum age 19) with WSI, LG certification at $1800–$2200 per season. Applicants must submit formal organization application, either three personal references or three letters of recommendation. An in-person interview is recommended, but a telephone interview is acceptable. International applicants accepted; must apply through a recognized agency.
Benefits and Preemployment Training Free housing, free meals, willing to provide letters of recommendation, on-the-job training, willing to complete paperwork for educational credit, and willing to act as a professional reference. Preemployment training is required and includes accident prevention and safety, first aid, CPR, interpersonal skills, leadership skills, certification courses: small boat sailing, lifeguard training, small craft water safety, archery and riflery instructor training, kayak clinic.
Contact Sherry Mernick, Associate Director, Cape Cod Sea Camps, PO Box 1880, Brewster, Massachusetts 02631. Telephone: 508-896-3451. Fax: 508-896-8272. E-mail: capecodsea@capecod.net. Contact by e-mail, fax, mail, or phone. Application deadline: continuous.

CENTER FOR TALENTED YOUTH/JOHNS HOPKINS UNIVERSITY–MOUNT HOLYOKE COLLEGE

SOUTH HADLEY, MASSACHUSETTS

See Center for Talented Youth/Johns Hopkins University on page 145 for complete description.

CHIMNEY CORNERS CAMP FOR GIRLS

748 HAMILTON ROAD
BECKET, MASSACHUSETTS 01223

General Information Residential YMCA camp serving 250 girls in each four-week session. Camp is international, and it promotes character development and personal growth. Established in 1931. 1,200-acre facility located 150 miles from Boston. Features: Berkshire Mountains; near cultural/historic points of interest; wooded setting; private, freshwater lake; tennis courts; horseback riding.
Profile of Summer Employees Total number: 125; typical ages: 16–30. 10% men; 90% women; 5% minorities; 25% high school students; 75% college students; 20% non-U.S. citizens; 1% local applicants. Nonsmokers preferred.
Employment Information Openings are from June 15 to August 18. Year-round positions also offered. Jobs available: ▶ 1 *carpenter* with construction experience preferred; at a negotiable salary ▶ 10–15 *counselors* (minimum age 18) at $1400–$1800 per season ▶ 3–6 *food service assistants* (minimum age 18) at $1800–$2500 per season ▶ *horseback riding instructors* at $1400–$2000 per season ▶ *lifeguards/swimming instructors* (minimum age 18) at $1400–$2500 per season ▶ 3 *nurses* with RN (preferred) or LPN license at $4000–$5000 per season ▶ *performing and creative arts staff* at $1400–$2200 per season ▶ 1 *program director* must be college graduate; see Web site for full description of job at $22500 per year ▶ 2–6 *sports instructors* (minimum age 18) at $1500–$1800 per season ▶ 1–3 *tennis coaches* (minimum age 18) with tennis skills and teaching experience at $1400–$2000 per season ▶ 2 *waterfront directors* (minimum age 21) with certification in WSI and lifeguard training or equivalent; will certify right candidate at $2000–$2500 per season ▶ 1–2 *woodworking instructors* (minimum age 18) at $1800–$2500 per season. Applicants must submit formal organization application, three personal references. An in-person interview is recommended, but a telephone interview is acceptable. International applicants accepted; must apply through a recognized agency.
Benefits and Preemployment Training Free housing, free meals, formal training, possible full-time employment, willing to provide letters of recommendation, names of contacts, on-the-job training, willing to complete paperwork for educational credit, willing to act as a professional reference, and opportunity to attend seminars/workshops.

Contact Shannon Donovan-Monti, Chimney Corners Camp Director, Chimney Corners Camp for Girls, 748 Hamilton Road, Becket, Massachusetts 01223. Telephone: 413-623-8991. Fax: 413-623-5890. E-mail: chimneycorners@bccymca.org. World Wide Web: http://www.bccymca.org. Contact by e-mail, fax, mail, phone, or through World Wide Web site. Application deadline: continuous.

CLARA BARTON CAMP
30 ENNIS ROAD
NORTH OXFORD, MASSACHUSETTS 01537

General Information The Barton Center for Diabetes Education (Clara Barton Camp). Established in 1932. 208-acre facility located 50 miles from Boston. Features: modern log cabins; challenge course; pool and pond; tennis courts; hiking trails; conference center.
Profile of Summer Employees Total number: 75; typical ages: 17–25. 5% men; 95% women; 15% minorities; 15% high school students; 75% college students; 20% non-U.S. citizens; 20% local applicants. Nonsmokers preferred.
Employment Information Openings are from June 1 to August 31. Jobs available: ▶ 30 *cabin counselors* (minimum age 18) with leadership in program activities, enthusiasm at $1440–$2350 per season ▶ 10 *camp nurses* with Massachusetts RN license, national board certification, experience with diabetes, CPR and first aid certificate at $2500–$5000 per season ▶ 1–5 *challenge course staff* (minimum age 18) documented challenge course experience at $2000–$3000 per season ▶ 5 *kitchen staff* (minimum age 18) with kitchen experience at $2500–$6000 per season ▶ 5 *travelling day camp staff* (minimum age 18) at $1440–$2000 per season ▶ 2 *waterfront directors* (minimum age 18) with lifeguarding, WSI, CPR, and first aid training; waterfront experience at $2000–$2800 per season. Applicants must submit formal organization application, resume, criminal background check, activity reference forms; 3 personal references/letters of recommendation. An in-person interview is recommended, but a telephone interview is acceptable. International applicants accepted; must apply through a recognized agency.
Benefits and Preemployment Training Free housing, free meals, health insurance, willing to provide letters of recommendation, willing to complete paperwork for educational credit, and willing to act as a professional reference. Preemployment training is required and includes accident prevention and safety, first aid, CPR, interpersonal skills, leadership skills, lifeguarding, ropes course.
Contact Brooke Beverly, Resident Camps Director, Clara Barton Camp, 30 Ennis Road, PO Box 356, North Oxford, Massachusetts 01537. Telephone: 508-987-3856. Fax: 508-987-2002. E-mail: brooke.beverly@bartoncenter.org. World Wide Web: http://www.bartoncenter.org. Contact by e-mail, fax, mail, phone, or through World Wide Web site. Application deadline: continuous.

COLLEGE GIFTED PROGRAMS
AMHERST COLLEGE
AMHERST, MASSACHUSETTS 01002-5000

General Information Residential educational academic summer camp for gifted and talented students in grades 4–11. Program blends in-depth academics with recreational and cultural activities. Established in 1984. 1,000-acre facility located 45 miles from Springfield. Features: dormitories; campus classroom facilities; campus recreational facilities include pool, tennis courts, and gym; campus library; beautiful campus setting.
Profile of Summer Employees Total number: 65; typical ages: 19–70. 50% men; 50% women; 30% minorities; 50% college students; 10% retirees; 10% non-U.S. citizens; 25% local applicants. Nonsmokers required.
Employment Information Openings are from June 26 to July 17. Jobs available: ▶ 30 *counselors* with two years of college completed and experience working with children at $900 to $1200 per 3-week session ▶ 4 *directors* with at least 5 years teaching/supervisory experience; master's degree required, doctorate preferred at $5000–$8000 per year ▶ 8 *housemasters/instructors*

(residential) with master's degree, teaching and supervisory experience at $2500 to $4500 per 3-week session ▶ 20 *instructors (non-residential)* with master's degree and teaching experience at $600 to $2500 per 3-week session ▶ 2 *nurses* with RN license; school experience preferred at $1300 per week. Applicants must submit formal organization application, resume, academic transcripts, two personal references, two letters of recommendation. An in-person interview is recommended, but a telephone interview is acceptable. International applicants accepted; must apply through a recognized agency.

Benefits and Preemployment Training Free housing, free meals, willing to provide letters of recommendation, willing to complete paperwork for educational credit, and willing to act as a professional reference. Preemployment training is required and includes accident prevention and safety, interpersonal skills, leadership skills, instructional strategies for gifted students.

Contact Charles Zeichner, Executive Director, College Gifted Programs, 120 Littleton Road, Suite 201, Parsippany, New Jersey 07054-1803. Telephone: 973-334-6991. Fax: 973-334-9756. E-mail: info@cgp-sig.com. World Wide Web: http://www.cgp-sig.com. Contact by e-mail, fax, mail, phone, or through World Wide Web site. Application deadline: continuous.

COLLEGE LIGHT OPERA COMPANY

HIGHFIELD THEATRE, PO DRAWER 906
FALMOUTH, MASSACHUSETTS 02541

General Information Residential summer-stock music theater for training undergraduate and graduate students. Established in 1969. 6-acre facility located 70 miles from Boston. Features: wooded setting on salt water; 100 yards from salt water beach.

Profile of Summer Employees Total number: 80; typical ages: 17–23. 50% men; 50% women; 5% minorities; 2% high school students; 80% college students; 2% local applicants.

Employment Information Openings are from June 5 to August 30. Jobs available: ▶ 1 *assistant business manager* with word processing skills, driver's license, and experience in the field at $1800 per season ▶ 2 *box office treasurers* with outgoing, friendly personality and driver's license at $1800 per season ▶ 1 *choreographer* with experience in the field at $2700 per season ▶ 2 *chorus masters* with piano experience at $1800 per season ▶ 1 *co-op work director* with driver's license and experience in the field of student co-op management at $3000–$4000 per season ▶ 1 *cook* with driver's license and experience in the field at $5000–$6000 per season ▶ 5 *costume crew* with experience in the field at $2000 per season ▶ 1 *costume designer* with driver's license and experience in the field at $4000 per season ▶ 18 *orchestra staff* with experience in the field at $1500 per season ▶ 2 *piano accompanists* with experience in the field at $1800 per season ▶ 1 *publicity director* with driver's license and car, word processing skills, and experience in the field at $1800 per season ▶ 1 *set designer/technical director* with driver's license and experience in the field at $4000 per season ▶ 6 *stage crew* with experience in the field at $2000 per season ▶ 32 *vocalists* salary is room and board with experience in the field. Applicants must submit a formal organization application, resume, two letters of recommendation, mandatory audio tape or CD audition for vocal and orchestra candidates. International applicants accepted; must obtain own visa, obtain own working papers.

Benefits and Preemployment Training Free housing, free meals, willing to provide letters of recommendation, on-the-job training, willing to complete paperwork for educational credit, and willing to act as a professional reference.

Contact Ursula P. Haslun, Producer, College Light Opera Company, 162 South Cedar Street, Oberlin, Ohio 44074. Telephone: 440-774-8485. Fax: 440-775-8642. E-mail: ursula.haslun@oberlin.edu. World Wide Web: http://www.collegelightopera.com. Contact by e-mail, fax, mail, phone, or through World Wide Web site. Application deadline: rolling admissions begin March 15 and continue until all positions are filled.

CRANE LAKE CAMP

STATE LINE ROAD

WEST STOCKBRIDGE, MASSACHUSETTS 01266

General Information Reform Jewish coeducational camp serving children ages 6–15 with traditional sports and a full cultural program. Established in 1890. 120-acre facility located 15 miles from Pittsfield. Features: springfed lake; all water sports; all land sports; in the Berkshires.

Profile of Summer Employees Total number: 130; typical ages: 18–24. 50% men; 50% women; 75% college students; 5% retirees; 25% non-U.S. citizens; 5% local applicants. Nonsmokers preferred.

Employment Information Openings are from June 15 to August 28. Jobs available: ▶ 2–4 *arts and crafts instructors* at $1200–$2000 per season ▶ 10–15 *athletics counselors* (minimum age 18) with a major in physical education or varsity athletics experience at $1200–$2000 per season ▶ 1–2 *dance staff* (minimum age 18) with teaching experience at $1200–$2000 per season ▶ 4 *doctors* must be a physician ▶ 40–60 *general counselors* (minimum age 18) high school graduate at $1200–$2500 per season ▶ 2–4 *guitar instructors* (minimum age 18) at $1200–$2000 per season ▶ 2–4 *gymnastics instructors* with experience in the field at $1200–$2000 per season ▶ 1–2 *nature instructors* (minimum age 18) at $1200–$2000 per season ▶ 3–4 *nurses* with Massachusetts RN license at $3000–$5000 per season ▶ 3–4 *painting/sketching/crafts/pottery instructors* (minimum age 18) at $1200–$2000 per season ▶ 1 *piano player* (minimum age 18) with ability to play by ear at $1200–$2000 per season ▶ 2–3 *pioneering/hiking instructors* (minimum age 18) at $1200–$2000 per season ▶ 6–9 *tennis instructors* (minimum age 18) with teaching experience at $1200–$2500 per season ▶ 6–12 *waterfront instructors* (minimum age 18) with small crafts certification and waterskiing, sailing, or canoeing experience at $1200–$2000 per season. Applicants must submit formal organization application, three personal references. An in-person interview is recommended, but a telephone interview is acceptable. International applicants accepted; must apply through a recognized agency.

Benefits and Preemployment Training Free housing, free meals, formal training, health insurance, willing to provide letters of recommendation, on-the-job training, willing to complete paperwork for educational credit, willing to act as a professional reference, and travel reimbursement.

Contact Herb May, Site Director, Crane Lake Camp, 633 3rd Avenue, New York, New York 10017. Telephone: 212-650-4208. Fax: 212-650-4139. E-mail: iluvcamp@aol.com. World Wide Web: http://www.cranelakecamp.com. Contact by e-mail, fax, mail, phone, or through World Wide Web site. Application deadline: continuous.

CYBERCAMPS–AMHERST COLLEGE

AMHERST, MASSACHUSETTS

See Cybercamps–University of Washington on page 335 for complete description.

CYBERCAMPS–BABSON COLLEGE

BABSON PARK, MASSACHUSETTS

See Cybercamps–University of Washington on page 335 for complete description.

CYBERCAMPS–BENTLEY COLLEGE

WALTHAM, MASSACHUSETTS

See Cybercamps–University of Washington on page 335 for complete description.

CYBERCAMPS–MERRIMACK COLLEGE

NORTH ANDOVER, MASSACHUSETTS

See Cybercamps–University of Washington on page 335 for complete description.

CYBERCAMPS–MIT

CAMBRIDGE, MASSACHUSETTS

See Cybercamps–University of Washington on page 335 for complete description.

4-H FARLEY OUTDOOR EDUCATION CENTER

615 ROUTE 130
MASHPEE, MASSACHUSETTS 02649

General Information Camp emphasizing overnight and day programs for boys and girls ages 4-15. There is limited mainstreaming of special needs children. Activities include nature, agriculture, outdoor living skills, arts, canoeing, kayaking, horseback riding, archery, swimming, snorkeling, and a ropes course. Established in 1934. 32-acre facility located 80 miles from Boston. Features: large freshwater lake; wooded setting; location on Cape Cod; close to ocean beaches; nearby historic sites; nearby entertainment options.

Profile of Summer Employees Total number: 35; typical ages: 18–26. 30% men; 70% women; 10% minorities; 80% college students; 20% non-U.S. citizens; 10% local applicants. Nonsmokers preferred.

Employment Information Openings are from June 23 to August 25. Spring break positions also offered. Jobs available: ▶ *archery instructors* (minimum age 18) with documented experience or certification at $220–$250 per week ▶ 5 *arts and craft counselors* (minimum age 18) at $220–$240 per week ▶ 1 *child care coordinator* (minimum age 24) with background in youth development at $300–$350 per week ▶ 30 *counselors* (minimum age 18) with specialized program skills and camping experience at $180–$230 per week ▶ 1 *health-care provider* (minimum age 24) with EMT, RN, or LPN license or special training in first aid at $400–$450 per week ▶ *kayaking and canoeing instructors* (minimum age 18) with documented experience or certification at $230–$250 per week ▶ 3 *kitchen staff members* (minimum age 18) at $240–$300 per week ▶ 8 *lifeguards* (minimum age 18) with LGT certification or equivalent and first aid/CPR at $240–$260 per week ▶ 5 *nature counselors* (minimum age 18) at $220–$240 per week ▶ *ropes instructor* (minimum age 20) with documented experience or certification at $250–$275 per week ▶ 3 *waterfront directors* (minimum age 21) with WSI certification and 6 weeks prior experience in a supervisory position at $300–$350 per week. Applicants must submit a formal organization application, three personal references, authorization for criminal background check. An in-person interview is required. International applicants accepted.

Benefits and Preemployment Training Free housing, free meals, formal training, health insurance, willing to provide letters of recommendation, on-the-job training, willing to complete paperwork for educational credit, willing to act as a professional reference, opportunity to attend seminars/workshops, and college credit via university. Preemployment training is required and includes accident prevention and safety, first aid, CPR, interpersonal skills, leadership skills, teaching skills and curricula.

Contact Mr. Michael Campbell, Executive Director, 4-H Farley Outdoor Education Center, 615 Route 130, Mashpee, Massachusetts 02649-2054. Fax: 508-539-0080. E-mail: office@campfarley.com. World Wide Web: http://www.campfarley.com. Contact by e-mail, fax, mail, or through World Wide Web site. Application deadline: continuous.

HORIZONS FOR YOUTH

121 LAKEVIEW STREET
SHARON, MASSACHUSETTS 02067

General Information Residential environmental education center that works with children from low-income families. Established in 1938.

Profile of Summer Employees Total number: 70; typical ages: 20–28. 40% men; 60% women; 20% minorities; 85% college students; 1% retirees; 20% non-U.S. citizens; 20% local applicants. Nonsmokers preferred.

Employment Information Openings are from June 7 to August 23. Year-round positions also offered. Jobs available: ▶ 1 *CIT director* (minimum age 21) with significant experience in working with disadvantaged teens; first aid/CPR certification preferred at $1600 per season ▶ 4 *activity specialists* (minimum age 21) with experience with disadvantaged children and in activity area; supervisory experience and first aid/CPR certification preferred at $1600 per season ▶ 1 *assistant cook* (minimum age 21 preferred) with cooking experience (quantity cooking experience preferred) at $275 per week ▶ 1 *cook* (minimum age 21 preferred) with supervisory and cooking experience; quantity cooking experience preferred at $350 per week ▶ 36 *counselors* (minimum age 18) with experience working with disadvantaged children; first aid/CPR certification preferred, American Red Cross certification required for lifeguards at $1400 per season ▶ 1 *driver* (minimum age 21) with valid driver's license and clean driving record; CPR/first aid certification preferred; experience with disadvantaged youth helpful at $1500 per season ▶ 4 *kitchen staff* (minimum age 20 preferred) with experience preferred in general kitchen skills; first aid/CPR certification preferred at $1100 per season ▶ 3 *maintenance staff members* (minimum age 20 preferred) with general skills including carpentry, painting, and landscaping; first aid/CPR certification preferred at $1100 per season ▶ 2 *nurses* (minimum age 21 preferred) with RN or LPN license or EMT, WFR, or WRA certification, current first aid/CPR certification, and relevant experience at a negotiable salary ▶ 4 *unit leaders* (minimum age 21) with supervisory and extensive experience with disadvantaged children; first aid/CPR certification preferred at $1800 per season ▶ 2 *waterfront directors* (minimum age 21) with American Red Cross CPR, LGT, WSI, and first aid certification, experience with disadvantaged children and supervisory experience at $1600 per season. Applicants must submit formal organization application, resume, two personal references, three letters of recommendation, criminal background check. An in-person interview is recommended, but a telephone interview is acceptable. International applicants accepted; must apply through a recognized agency.

Benefits and Preemployment Training Free housing, free meals, formal training, willing to provide letters of recommendation, on-the-job training, willing to complete paperwork for educational credit, willing to act as a professional reference, and opportunity to attend seminars/workshops. Preemployment training is required and includes accident prevention and safety, interpersonal skills, leadership skills.

Contact Allison McDonagh, Summer Program Director, Horizons for Youth, 121 Lakeview Street, Sharon, Massachusetts 02067. Telephone: 781-828-7550. Fax: 781-784-1287. E-mail: camp@hfy.org. World Wide Web: http://www.hfy.org. Contact by e-mail, fax, mail, phone, or through World Wide Web site. Application deadline: continuous.

LIGHTHOUSE INN, INC.

1 LIGHTHOUSE INN ROAD, PO BOX 128
WEST DENNIS, MASSACHUSETTS 02670

General Information Seasonal, oceanfront resort specializing in banquets, weddings, and group conferences in May, June, September, and October. July and August cater to social guests vacationing. Established in 1938. 9-acre facility located 80 miles from Boston. Features: oceanfront; swimming pool; tennis court; restaurant; private beach; children's program.

Profile of Summer Employees Total number: 100; typical ages: 19–28. 50% men; 50% women; 1% high school students; 15% college students; 10% local applicants.

Employment Information Openings are from May 15 to October 20. Jobs available: ▶ 5–10 *dining room staff* (minimum age 18) at $2.63 per hour plus tips. Applicants must submit formal organization application, resume, three personal references, two letters of recommendation, photograph. An in-person interview is recommended, but a telephone interview is acceptable. International applicants accepted; must obtain own visa, obtain own working papers, apply through a recognized agency.

Benefits and Preemployment Training Meals at a cost, willing to provide letters of recommendation, and willing to complete paperwork for educational credit.

Contact Bill Sherman, Food and Beverage Manager, Lighthouse Inn, Inc., 1 Lighthouse Inn

Road, PO Box 128, West Dennis, Massachusetts 02670. Telephone: 508-398-2244. Fax: 508-398-5658. E-mail: shoe@lighthouseinn.com. World Wide Web: http://www.lighthouseinn.com. Contact by e-mail, fax, mail, phone, or through World Wide Web site. Application deadline: continuous.

NORTH AMERICAN TRAILS

PO BOX 594
CARLISLE, MASSACHUSETTS 01741

General Information Cross country camping trips for teenagers, throughout North America, which focus on group dynamics in an outdoor setting. Predominately camping in full service campgrounds, with some nights on college campuses. Established in 1981. Features: national parks; whitewater rafting; day hikes; mountain biking; explore cities; camping.

Profile of Summer Employees Total number: 20; typical ages: 21–30. 50% men; 50% women; 20% college students; 80% local applicants. Nonsmokers required.

Employment Information Openings are from June 26 to August 15. Jobs available: ▶ 10–15 *counselors* (minimum age 21) with CPR/first aid certifications, driver's license, and previous experience with adolescents at $650–$950 per season ▶ 2 *food managers* (minimum age 21) with CPR/first aid certifications, driver's license, food preparation skills, and previous experience with adolescents at $1400 per season. Applicants must submit a formal organization application, letter of interest, resume, three personal references. An in-person interview is required.

Benefits and Preemployment Training Free housing, free meals, formal training, willing to provide letters of recommendation, names of contacts, on-the-job training, willing to complete paperwork for educational credit, and willing to act as a professional reference. Preemployment training is required and includes accident prevention and safety, interpersonal skills, leadership skills, procedures/logistics.

Contact Lori Pritchard, Director, North American Trails. Telephone: 978-371-2566. Fax: 978-287-0742. E-mail: lori@natrails.com. World Wide Web: http://www.natrails.com. Contact by e-mail, fax, mail, or through World Wide Web site. Application deadline: continuous.

NORTH SHORE MUSIC THEATRE

62 DUNHAM ROAD, PO BOX 62
BEVERLY, MASSACHUSETTS 01915–0062

General Information Musical theater with a six-show season of Broadway musicals as well as children's shows, concerts, and special events. Professional theater dedicated to the American musical and programs for young audiences, serving more than 300,000 patrons from March through December. Established in 1955. Located 20 miles from Boston. Features: 1800-seat arena theatre; celebrity concert series; on-site shop facilities; half hour north of Boston.

Profile of Summer Employees Total number: 100; typical ages: 18–25. 40% men; 60% women; 10% minorities; 70% college students; 20% local applicants.

Employment Information Openings are from April to December 23. Year-round positions also offered. Jobs available: ▶ 20 *technical theater interns* (minimum age 18) with college or summer stock experience in the field at $150–$200 per week ▶ 20 *technical theater staff members* with professional experience in the field at $275–$425 per week. Applicants must submit a letter of interest, resume. An in-person interview is required. International applicants accepted; must obtain own visa, obtain own working papers.

Benefits and Preemployment Training Housing at a cost, possible full-time employment, on-the-job training, willing to complete paperwork for educational credit, willing to act as a professional reference, and opportunity to attend seminars/workshops.

Contact Ali Sheehan Mignone, Associate Production Manager, North Shore Music Theatre, PO Box 62, Beverly, Massachusetts 01915–0062. Fax: 978-922-0768. World Wide Web: http://www.nsmt.org. Contact by fax or mail. Application deadline: continuous.

OFFENSE-DEFENSE GOLF CAMP, MASSACHUSETTS
THE WINCHENDON SCHOOL AND GOLF FACILITY
WINCHENDON, MASSACHUSETTS 01475

General Information Residential and day camp teaching golf to boys and girls ages 10–18. Established in 1992. 1,000-acre facility located 28 miles from Boston. Features: prep school dorms and cafeteria; putting green; 18-hole regulation golf course; golf range; 4 tennis courts; outdoor swimming pool; gymnasium.

Profile of Summer Employees Total number: 40; typical ages: 19–50. 80% men; 20% women; 10% minorities; 80% college students. Nonsmokers preferred.

Employment Information Openings are from July 1 to July 30. Jobs available: ▶ 1 *bus driver* (minimum age 21) with license to drive yellow school bus and CDL at $300–$350 per week ▶ 10 *general (non-golf) counselors* (minimum age 19) must like working with children at $275–$300 per week ▶ 10 *golf instructors* with college varsity, college coaching, PGA Pro (very low handicap players) status, or USGTA certification at $250–$350 per week ▶ *swimming counselors* (minimum age 19) with WSI certification at $300–$350 per week. A telephone interview is required. International applicants accepted; must obtain own visa.

Benefits and Preemployment Training Free housing, free meals, formal training, on-the-job training, and willing to complete paperwork for educational credit. Preemployment training is required and includes accident prevention and safety, first aid, CPR, interpersonal skills, leadership skills.

Contact Mike Meshken, President, Offense-Defense Golf Camp, Massachusetts, PO Box 6, Easton, Connecticut 06612. Telephone: 800-824-7336. Fax: 203-255-5666. World Wide Web: http://www.offensedefensegolf.com. Contact by phone. Application deadline: May 10.

SOUTH SHORE YMCA CAMPS
75 STOWE ROAD
SANDWICH, MASSACHUSETTS 02563

General Information Brother/sister residential camps on Cape Cod. Non-profit, YMCA traditional camps. Established in 1928. 400-acre facility located 65 miles from Boston. Features: freshwater lake; wooded setting; high/low ropes; horseback riding; tennis courts; basketball courts.

Profile of Summer Employees Total number: 165; typical ages: 18–28. 40% men; 60% women; 2% minorities; 10% high school students; 90% college students; 40% non-U.S. citizens; 5% local applicants.

Employment Information Openings are from June 21 to August 24. Jobs available: ▶ 76 *cabin counselors* (minimum age 18) at $150 per week ▶ 2 *cooks* (minimum age 21) at $300–$400 per week ▶ 3 *nurses* (minimum age 21) with RN and experience in the field at $400 per week ▶ 3 *office staff* (minimum age 18) at $150 per week ▶ 14 *specialists* (minimum age 21) with any appropriate specialized skills such as WSI, CPR, and first aid certification at $165 per week ▶ 16 *support staff (in kitchen, maintenance, and bathroom)* (minimum age 18) at $150 per week ▶ 8 *unit leaders* (minimum age 21) with leadership qualities at $165 per week ▶ 2 *van drivers/security staff* (minimum age 21) with driver's license for at least two years; first aid and CPR certification at $165 per week. Applicants must submit formal organization application, three personal references. An in-person interview is recommended, but a telephone interview is acceptable. International applicants accepted; must apply through a recognized agency.

Benefits and Preemployment Training Free housing, free meals, formal training, willing to provide letters of recommendation, on-the-job training, willing to complete paperwork for educational credit, and willing to act as a professional reference. Preemployment training is required and includes accident prevention and safety, first aid, interpersonal skills, leadership skills.

Contact Casey Tucci, Camp Director, South Shore YMCA Camps, 75 Stowe Road, Sandwich, Massachusetts 02563. Telephone: 508-428-2571. Fax: 508-420-3545. E-mail: ssymca@capecod.net. World Wide Web: http://www.ssymca.org. Contact by e-mail, fax, mail, phone, or through

World Wide Web site. Application deadline: continuous.

THE SOUTHWESTERN COMPANY, MASSACHUSETTS

See The Southwestern Company on page 302 for complete description.

SPORTS INTERNATIONAL–JOE KRIVAK (QUARTERBACK AND RECEIVING CAMP)

FITCHBURG, MASSACHUSETTS

See Sports International, Inc. on page 147 for complete description.

STUDENT CONSERVATION ASSOCIATION (SCA), MASSACHUSETTS

See Student Conservation Association (SCA), New Hampshire on page 209 for complete description.

STUDENT HOSTELING PROGRAM

1356 ASHFIELD ROAD, PO BOX 419
CONWAY, MASSACHUSETTS 01341

General Information Organization offering 1-8 week teenage bicycle touring trips through the countrysides and cultural centers of the US, Canada and Europe. Established in 1970. 60-acre facility located 25 miles from Northampton. Features: rural; wooded setting; camping; wildlife; very scenic.

Profile of Summer Employees Total number: 55; typical ages: 19–30. 50% men; 50% women; 100% college students. Nonsmokers preferred.

Employment Information Openings are from June 25 to August 25. Jobs available: ▶ 1 *assistant director* (minimum age 25) at $4000–$5000 per season ▶ 25–30 *assistant leaders* (minimum age 18) at $780–$1980 per season ▶ 25–30 *senior leaders* (minimum age 21) at $1040–$2640 per season. Applicants must submit a formal organization application, letter of interest, three personal references, three letters of recommendation. An in-person interview is required. International applicants accepted; must obtain own visa.

Benefits and Preemployment Training Free housing, free meals, formal training, willing to provide letters of recommendation, on-the-job training, willing to act as a professional reference, and travel reimbursement. Preemployment training is required and includes accident prevention and safety, leadership skills.

Contact Ted Lefkowitz, Director, Student Hosteling Program. Telephone: 800-343-6132. Fax: 413-369-4257. E-mail: shpbike@aol.com. World Wide Web: http://www.bicycletrips.com. Contact by e-mail, fax, mail, phone, or through World Wide Web site. Application deadline: May 12.

WILLIAMSTOWN THEATER FESTIVAL

1000 MAIN STREET, PO BOX 517
WILLIAMSTOWN, MASSACHUSETTS 01267

General Information Summer theater festival presenting productions of revivals of classics and new works by new and established playwrights. Established in 1953. Located 40 miles from Albany, New York. Features: Williams College campus; culturally rich area; idyllic New England town; 3 hours to New York City and Boston; fully equipped theater facility; beautiful Berkshires.

Profile of Summer Employees Total number: 60; typical ages: 17–35. 50% men; 50% women; 10% minorities; 1% high school students; 50% college students; 1% retirees; 1% non-U.S. citizens; 5% local applicants.

Employment Information Openings are from June 1 to September 1. Year-round positions also offered. Jobs available: ▶ 60 *Equity actors* at salary as per AEA contract ▶ 60–70 *acting apprentices* (minimum age 17) who pay fee of $3000 for room, board, and tuition (2002 rate)

▶ 50–70 *administrative and technical interns* with some experience in chosen field ▶ 12–16 *non-Equity actors* with advanced educational and/or professional acting experience (no salary) ▶ 60–70 *staff members* with advanced educational and/or professional experience at $50–$400 per week. Applicants must submit 2-3 personal references or 2-3 letters of recommendation; $30 processing fee (for apprentice applicants only). International applicants accepted; must obtain own visa, obtain own working papers.

Benefits and Preemployment Training Meals at a cost, willing to provide letters of recommendation, names of contacts, on-the-job training, willing to complete paperwork for educational credit, willing to act as a professional reference, opportunity to attend seminars/workshops, and housing free for staff, $500 for interns (2002 rate).

Contact Anne Lowrie, Company Manager, Williamstown Theater Festival, 229 West 42nd Street, #801, New York, New York 10036. Telephone: 212-395-9090. Fax: 212-395-9099. E-mail: alowrie@wtfestival.org. World Wide Web: http://www.wtfestival.org. Contact by e-mail, fax, mail, phone, or through World Wide Web site. Application deadline: March 29 for apprentice workshop; continuous for staff and interns.

YMCA CAMP LYNDON

117 STOWE ROAD
SANDWICH, MASSACHUSETTS 02563

General Information Day camp serving 400 children. Established in 1969. 80-acre facility located 45 miles from Boston. Features: freshwater lake; ropes course; outdoor school; wooded setting; boating program; diversified program.

Profile of Summer Employees Total number: 75–85; typical ages: 18–45. 40% men; 60% women; 2% minorities; 35% high school students; 55% college students; 10% non-U.S. citizens; 65% local applicants. Nonsmokers preferred.

Employment Information Openings are from June 24 to August 30. Year-round positions also offered. Jobs available: ▶ *age-specific unit directors* with certification or related experience with specific age group at $300–$450 per week ▶ 1 *archery specialist* with leadership experience in an archery program and archery certification at $270–$300 per week ▶ 3 *arts and crafts specialists* with teaching certification and experience in the field at $270–$300 per week ▶ 10 *boating instructors* with small craft or equivalent certification and sailing and canoeing experience at $270–$300 per week ▶ 60 *counselors* with youth experience at $270–$300 per week ▶ *dramatic arts specialist* with formal training and experience in the field at $270–$300 per week ▶ 2 *ropes/initiative specialists* with completion of course and experience in the field at $280–$340 per week ▶ *special populations one-to-one aide* (minimum age 18) must be Massachusetts resident familiar with ADA laws at $270–$300 per week ▶ 12 *swimming instructors* with LGT certification (minimum) at $270–$300 per week. Applicants must submit formal organization application, three personal references. An in-person interview is recommended, but a telephone interview is acceptable. International applicants accepted; must obtain own visa, obtain own working papers, apply through a recognized agency.

Benefits and Preemployment Training Formal training, on-the-job training, and willing to complete paperwork for educational credit. Preemployment training is required and includes accident prevention and safety, interpersonal skills, leadership skills.

Contact P. J. Richardson, Lyndon Center Director, YMCA Camp Lyndon, PO Box 188, West Barnstable, Massachusetts 02668. Telephone: 508-428-9251 Ext. 200. Fax: 508-362-5379. Contact by fax, mail, or phone. Application deadline: continuous.

A CHRISTIAN MINISTRY IN THE NATIONAL PARKS–MICHIGAN

See A Christian Ministry in the National Parks–Maine on page 122 for complete description.

AMERICAN YOUTH FOUNDATION–CAMP MINIWANCA

8845 WEST GARFIELD ROAD
SHELBY, MICHIGAN 49455

General Information Camp focusing on developing the leadership capacities of young people by helping them achieve their personal best, lead balanced lives, and serve others. Established in 1925. 360-acre facility located 80 miles from Grand Rapids. Features: 1 mile of Lake Michigan beach; Stoney Lake; wooded dunes; sand dunes; council circle at base of 2 dunes; open-air cabins and dormitories.

Profile of Summer Employees Total number: 200; typical ages: 18–60. 40% men; 60% women; 3% minorities; 10% high school students; 55% college students; 5% retirees; 8% non-U.S. citizens; 10% local applicants. Nonsmokers preferred.

Employment Information Openings are from January 1 to December 1. Spring break and year-round positions also offered. Jobs available: ▶ 1 *Four Trails program coordinator (year-round)* (minimum age 21) with WFR, CPR, first aid, and lifeguard certifications, current physical, TB test, and police background check at $2000–$3000 per month ▶ 1 *bike mechanic* (minimum age 18) with a current physical, TB test, and police background check at $300 per week ▶ 5 *building/grounds personnel* (minimum age 18) with some skill with tools and power equipment at $300 per week ▶ 90 *cabin leaders* (minimum age 18) should be college student or teacher at $175–$220 per week ▶ 6 *camp cleaning personnel* (minimum age 18) should be college student or retired person at $300 per week ▶ 4 *camp store staff members* (minimum age 18) should be college student or retired person at $275 per week ▶ 20 *central summer staff members* (minimum age 18) should be teachers or instructors at $200–$500 per week ▶ 2–4 *craft house staff members* (minimum age 18) should be college student or retired person at $250–$300 per week ▶ 2 *drivers* (minimum age 21) with a current physical, police background check, TB test, and a valid driver's license at $8.10 per hour ▶ *food/equipment manager* (minimum age 18) with CPR and first aid certifications, TB test, current physical, and police background checks at $250 per week ▶ 2–4 *health center staff* with EMT, RN, LPN or 2nd year RN students (BSN) at $500 per week ▶ 1 *logistics coordinator* (minimum age 18) with CPR and first aid certifications, TB test, current physical, and police background checks at $350 per week ▶ 1 *logistics specialist category A* (minimum age 21) with first aid and CPR certifications, current physical, TB test, police background check, and a valid driver's license at $270 per week ▶ 1 *logistics specialist category B* (minimum age 21) with CPR and first aid certifications, current physical, TB test, police background check, and a valid driver's license at $270 per week ▶ *logistics specialist category C* (minimum age 21) with CPR and first aid certifications, current physical, TB test, police background check, and a valid driver's license at $270 per week ▶ 2 *office staff members* (minimum age 18) should be college student or retired person at $250–$300 per week ▶ *secretary (Four Trails)* with a current physical, TB test, and police background check at $250 per week ▶ 2 *security personnel* (minimum age 21) at $300 per week ▶ 2 *trip coordinators categories A and B* (minimum age 21) with first aid and CPR certifications, current physical, TB test, and police background check at $350 per week ▶ 12 *trip leaders category A* (minimum age 18) with wilderness first aid, lifeguarding and CPR certifications, current physical, TB test, and police background check at $305–$350 per week ▶ 5–10 *trip leaders category B* (minimum age 18) with wilderness first aid, and lifeguarding/CPR certifications, current physical, TB test, and police background check at $295 per week ▶ 7 *trip leaders category C* (minimum age 18) with a current physical, CPR and first aid certifications, TB test, and police background check at $270 per week ▶ 1 *waterfront management* (minimum age 21) with LS/LGT/WSI and sailing and canoeing experience at $350 per week ▶ 2 *wood shop staff members* (minimum age 18) should be college student or retired person at $250–$300 per week ▶ 6 *year-round interns* (minimum age 20) with junior/senior status in college or college degree at $500 per month. Applicants must submit a formal organization application, letter of interest, resume, three personal references, three letters of recommendation. An in-person interview is recommended, but a telephone interview is acceptable. International applicants accepted.

Benefits and Preemployment Training Free housing, free meals, formal training, possible full-time employment, willing to provide letters of recommendation, on-the-job training, willing to complete paperwork for educational credit, willing to act as a professional reference, opportunity to attend seminars/workshops, travel reimbursement, and health insurance for interns. Preemployment training is required and includes accident prevention and safety, first aid, CPR, interpersonal skills, leadership skills, Wilderness First Responder, lifeguarding, WSI, high/low ropes challenge course/climbing tower.

Contact Jonathan Gilburg, Assistant to the Director, American Youth Foundation–Camp Miniwanca, 8845 West Garfield Road, Shelby, Michigan 49455. Telephone: 231-861-2262. Fax: 231-861-5244. E-mail: jon.gilburg@ayf.com. World Wide Web: http://www.ayf.com. Contact by e-mail, fax, mail, phone, or through World Wide Web site. Application deadline: May 31.

BAY CLIFF HEALTH CAMP

BIG BAY, MICHIGAN 49808

General Information Residential therapy camp serving 180 children with disabilities ages 3–17 during one 8-week session. Established in 1934. 170-acre facility located 323 miles from Milwaukee, Wisconsin. Features: outdoor setting; pool and beachfront.

Profile of Summer Employees Total number: 147; typical ages: 19–25. 30% men; 70% women; 5% minorities; 10% high school students; 50% college students; 2% retirees; 15% local applicants. Nonsmokers preferred.

Employment Information Openings are from June 13 to September 8. Jobs available: ▶ *arts and crafts aide* (minimum age 18) with interest in the field at $1200 per season ▶ 1 *arts and crafts instructor* with ability to plan and implement classes for all camp units, experience preferred at $2000 per season ▶ 1 *assistant cook* with experience in the field at $250–$300 per week ▶ 1 *baker* with experience at $2000 per season ▶ 50 *counselors* (minimum age 18) with one year of college completed (preferably in the study of special education, therapy, nursing, or human services) at $1600 per season ▶ 1 *dental assistant* with license at $1600 per season ▶ 1 *dental hygienist* with license at $2000 per season ▶ 12 *dining room aides* (minimum age 16) at $1000 per season ▶ *dining room supervisor* (minimum age 21) with experience in food management and supervision at $2000 per season ▶ 1 *head cook* at $350–$400 per week ▶ 3 *instructors for hearing impaired* with certification in field at $3000 per season ▶ 2 *instructors for visually impaired* with certification in the field at $3000 per season ▶ 3 *laundry/housekeeping personnel* (minimum age 18) at $1500 per season ▶ 2 *linen room personnel* (minimum age 18) at $1500 per season ▶ 4 *maintenance personnel* (minimum age 18) with experience at $1500–$2000 per season ▶ 1–2 *music therapists* with certification in field at $2600 per season ▶ 1 *nature instructor* with ability to plan and implement classes for all camp units, experience preferred at $2000 per season ▶ 3 *nurses* with RN or LPN license at $3000–$3500 per season ▶ 6 *occupational therapists* with certification in field at $3000 per season ▶ 5 *physical therapists* with certification in field at $3000 per season ▶ 1 *recreation instructor* with ability to plan and implement classes for all camp units, experience preferred at $2000 per season ▶ 8 *roving counselors* (minimum age 18) with one year of college completed (preferably in the study of special education, therapy, nursing, or human services) at $1600 per season ▶ 2 *secretaries* with good clerical skills and a pleasant, enthusiastic personality at $1400 per season ▶ 10 *speech therapists* with certification in field at $3000 per season ▶ 6 *student therapists* with formal school affiliation and ability to work with a supervising therapist at $600 per season ▶ 5 *unit leaders* (minimum age 22) with teaching experience and special education degree (preferred) at $2400 per season ▶ 4 *waterfront staff members* (minimum age 18) with WSI or lifeguard certification at $1600–$2000 per season ▶ *waterfront/pool supervisor* (minimum age 21) with certification, pool management and leadership experience at $2000 per season. Applicants must submit a formal organization application, 3-6 personal references. An in-person interview is recommended, but a telephone interview is acceptable.

Benefits and Preemployment Training Free housing, free meals, on-the-job training, willing to complete paperwork for educational credit, and travel reimbursement. Preemployment training is required and includes accident prevention and safety, first aid, interpersonal skills, camp policies.

Contact Tim Bennett, Camp Director, Bay Cliff Health Camp, 310 West Washington Street, Suite 300, Marquette, Michigan 49855. Telephone: 906-228-5770. Fax: 906-228-5769. E-mail: baycliffhc@aol.com. World Wide Web: http://www.baycliff.org. Contact by e-mail, mail, or phone. Application deadline: continuous.

BLACK RIVER FARM AND RANCH

5040 SHERIDAN LINE
CROSWELL, MICHIGAN 48422

General Information Residential camp serving 134 girls ages 7–15 in one- and two-week sessions with Western riding and vaulting program. Established in 1962. 300-acre facility located 80 miles from Detroit. Features: heated pool; 2 tennis courts; 65 horses; rural farm setting; 1/2 hour from Canada; 5 miles from Lake Huron and beach.

Profile of Summer Employees Total number: 60; typical ages: 16–24. 100% women; 20% high school students; 40% college students; 20% non-U.S. citizens; 20% local applicants. Nonsmokers required.

Employment Information Openings are from June 6 to August 30. Jobs available: ▶ 4–6 *kitchen staff* (minimum age 18) ▶ 1–3 *lifeguards/cabin counselors* (minimum age 18) with ARC-lifeguard or Bronze Medallion at $2000 per season ▶ 5 *riding instructors/cabin counselors* (minimum age 18) with teaching experience (preferred) at $2000 per season ▶ 1–2 *vaulting instructors/cabin counselors* (minimum age 18) with teaching experience (preferred) at $2000 per season. Applicants must submit formal organization application, resume, a total of 3 references and/or letters of recommendation. An in-person interview is recommended, but a telephone interview is acceptable. International applicants accepted; must apply through a recognized agency.

Benefits and Preemployment Training Free housing, free meals, formal training, willing to provide letters of recommendation, on-the-job training, willing to complete paperwork for educational credit, and willing to act as a professional reference. Preemployment training is required and includes accident prevention and safety, CPR, interpersonal skills, leadership skills.

Contact Meg Graham, Director, Black River Farm and Ranch, 5040 Sheridan Line, Croswell, Michigan 48422. Telephone: 810-679-2505. Fax: 810-679-3188. E-mail: brranch@greatlakes.net. World Wide Web: http://www.blackriverfarmandranch.com. Contact by e-mail, fax, mail, or phone. Application deadline: continuous.

BLUE LAKE FINE ARTS CAMP

300 EAST CRYSTAL LAKE ROAD
TWIN LAKE, MICHIGAN 49457

General Information Summer school of the arts serving over 4,500 junior high and high school students over an eight-week season. Established in 1966. 1,400-acre facility located 45 miles

from Grand Rapids. Features: wooded setting; on small lake; music shell seats 5,000; 3 athletic fields; 2 pools; in Manistee National Forest; over 270 cabins, structures, buildings, and facilities.
Profile of Summer Employees Total number: 600; typical ages: 19–45. 45% men; 55% women; 20% minorities; 60% college students; 5% retirees; 5% non-U.S. citizens; 15% local applicants. Nonsmokers preferred.
Employment Information Openings are from June 15 to August 30. Jobs available: ▶ 105 *cabin counselors* (minimum age 18) with one year of college and interest and/or experience in the fine arts at $1100–$2100 per season ▶ 4 *camp nurses* with RN or LPN license at $850 per 12-day session ▶ 1 *health lodge director* (minimum age 21) with First Responder or EMT certification; camp and administrative experience at $3000–$4000 per season ▶ 10 *health lodge staff members* (minimum age 19) with Red Cross Response to Emergencies, EMT, or First Responder certification at $1600–$2200 per season ▶ 4 *music library staff members* (minimum age 18) with clerical and/or music library experience at $6.50 per hour ▶ 3 *production assistants* (minimum age 18) with interest in gaining experience in backstage/arts production at $1500–$1700 per season ▶ 1 *production manager* (minimum age 21) with backstage, arts production, and supervisory experience at $3000–$4000 per season ▶ 1 *waterfront director* (minimum age 21) with WSI certification, American Red Cross lifeguard instructor certification, managerial, and supervisory experience at $3500–$4300 per season. Applicants must submit a formal organization application, three personal references, audition cassette for musical openings. A telephone interview is required. International applicants accepted; must obtain own visa, obtain own working papers.
Benefits and Preemployment Training Free housing, free meals, formal training, willing to provide letters of recommendation, on-the-job training, willing to complete paperwork for educational credit, willing to act as a professional reference, opportunity to attend seminars/workshops, and opportunities to perform in summer arts festival. Preemployment training is required and includes accident prevention and safety, first aid, CPR, interpersonal skills, leadership skills.
Contact Heidi Stansell, Camp Director, Blue Lake Fine Arts Camp, 300 East Crystal Lake Road, Twin Lake, Michigan 49457. Telephone: 231-894-1966. Fax: 231-893-5120. World Wide Web: http://www.bluelake.org. Contact by fax, mail, or phone. Application deadline: continuous.

CAMP FOWLER AT THE FOWLER CENTER
2315 HARMON LAKE ROAD
MAYVILLE, MICHIGAN 48744-9737

General Information Accessible outdoor recreation camp for children and adults with developmental disabilities promoting personal growth in those with special needs. Established in 1957. 202-acre facility located 90 miles from Detroit. Features: spring-fed lake; organic garden; equestrian stables; wheelchair-accessible nature trails; small animal barn; sports fields.
Profile of Summer Employees Total number: 75; typical ages: 18–30. 45% men; 55% women; 12% minorities; 3% high school students; 85% college students; 5% retirees; 5% non-U.S. citizens; 15% local applicants. Nonsmokers preferred.
Employment Information Openings are from May 15 to October 31. Spring break, winter break, and year-round positions also offered. Jobs available: ▶ 15–20 *counselors* must be highly motivated to work with special needs campers (will train) at $1900–$2300 per season ▶ 1 *creative arts instructor* with experience or desire to work with special needs campers at $1900–$2300 per season ▶ *horseback riding instructors* with NARHA or CHA certification and experience or desire to work with special needs campers at $1900–$2300 per season ▶ 1 *organic garden and barn instructor* with gardening experience and experience or desire to work with special needs campers at $1900–$2300 per season ▶ 1 *outdoor education instructor* with camping experience and desire to work with special needs campers at $1900–$2300 per season ▶ 1 *sports and recreation instructor* with experience or desire to work with special needs campers at $1900–$2300 per season ▶ *waterfront staff members* with lifeguard and WSI certification and

experience or desire to work with special needs campers at $1900–$2300 per season. Applicants must submit a formal organization application, three letters of recommendation, criminal background check. An in-person interview is required. International applicants accepted.

Benefits and Preemployment Training Free housing, free meals, formal training, possible full-time employment, willing to provide letters of recommendation, on-the-job training, willing to complete paperwork for educational credit, willing to act as a professional reference, and opportunity to attend seminars/workshops. Preemployment training is required and includes accident prevention and safety, first aid, CPR, interpersonal skills, leadership skills, direct care.

Contact Charles Morrison, Assistant Camp Director, Camp Fowler at The Fowler Center, 2315 Harmon Lake Road, Mayville, Michigan 48744-9737. Telephone: 989-673-2050. Fax: 989-673-6355. E-mail: camp@thefowlercenter.org. World Wide Web: http://www.thefowlercenter.org. Contact by e-mail, fax, mail, phone, or through World Wide Web site. Application deadline: continuous.

CAMP LOOKOUT
4410 LOOKOUT ROAD
FRANKFORT, MICHIGAN 49635

General Information Small, coeducational, loosely-structured residential camp that is noncompetitive and nonsectarian, emphasizing individual growth. Established in 1930. 10-acre facility located 30 miles from Traverse City. Features: large inland lake; proximity to National Lakeshore; Lake Michigan (sand dunes and a beach accessible only by boat); 10-acre island.

Profile of Summer Employees Total number: 15; typical ages: 19–35. 5% minorities; 20% high school students; 65% college students; 5% retirees; 15% non-U.S. citizens; 5% local applicants. Nonsmokers preferred.

Employment Information Openings are from June 15 to August 18. Jobs available: ▶ 1 *art specialist* (minimum age 19) with ability to organize art program (teacher preferred) at $1000–$2000 per season ▶ 1 *assistant director/program director* with ability to conduct programs for small and large groups at $1700–$4000 per season ▶ 1–2 *cooks* with experience at $1200–$3000 per season ▶ 8 *counselors* (minimum age 19) with lifesaving training and art, sailing, trip, and sports skills at $1100–$1700 per season ▶ 3 *junior counselors (high school students)* (minimum age 17) at $500–$700 per season ▶ 2 *nurses* with RN, LPN, or EMT license at $1200–$2500 per season ▶ *waterfront directors* with current LGT and WSI certification and experience at $1200–$2700 per season ▶ 3 *windsurfing instructors* (minimum age 19) with lifesaving training and experience in the field at $1100–$1700 per season. Applicants must submit formal organization application, resume. An in-person interview is recommended, but a telephone interview is acceptable. International applicants accepted; must obtain own visa, apply through a recognized agency.

Benefits and Preemployment Training Free housing, free meals, formal training, willing to provide letters of recommendation, and willing to complete paperwork for educational credit. Preemployment training is required and includes accident prevention and safety, first aid, CPR, interpersonal skills, leadership skills.

Contact David B. Reid, Director, Camp Lookout, 2768 South Shore Road East, Frankfort, Michigan 49635. Telephone: 231-352-7589. Fax: 231-352-6609. E-mail: xtalaire@benzie.com. World Wide Web: http://www.crystalairecamp.com. Contact by e-mail, fax, mail, or phone. Application deadline: continuous.

CAMP MAAS
4361 PERRYVILLE ROAD
ORTONVILLE, MICHIGAN 48462

General Information Residential camp and outdoor travel program to Alaska and western United States. Established in 1902. 1,500-acre facility located 45 miles from Detroit. Features:

wooded setting; lake for all water sports; swimming pool; horseback riding; 2 complete athletic fields and sports facilities; outdoor camping.

Profile of Summer Employees Total number: 400; typical ages: 18–25. 50% men; 50% women; 10% high school students; 80% college students; 40% non-U.S. citizens; 50% local applicants. Nonsmokers preferred.

Employment Information Openings are from June 18 to August 17. Jobs available: ▶ *clinic assistants* at $1500 per season ▶ *counselors* at $1000–$1500 per season ▶ *head nurse* at $3000–$5000 per season ▶ *song leader* (minimum age 18) at $2000–$3000 per season ▶ *specialists in all areas* at $1000–$1500 per season ▶ *supervisors in all areas* at $2000–$3500 per season. Applicants must submit formal organization application, three letters of recommendation. An in-person interview is recommended, but a telephone interview is acceptable. International applicants accepted; must apply through a recognized agency.

Benefits and Preemployment Training Free housing, free meals, willing to provide letters of recommendation, and willing to complete paperwork for educational credit. Preemployment training is required and includes first aid, CPR, interpersonal skills, leadership skills.

Contact Harvey Finkelberg, Executive Director, Camp Maas, 6735 Telegraph Road, Suite 380, Bloomfield Hills, Michigan 48301. Telephone: 248-647-1100. Fax: 248-647-1493. E-mail: tamarack@tamarackcamps.com. World Wide Web: http://www.tamarackcamps.com. Contact by e-mail, fax, mail, phone, or through World Wide Web site. Application deadline: continuous.

CAMP MAPLEHURST

12055 WARING ROAD
KEWADIN, MICHIGAN 49648

General Information Residential camp serving 120 campers per session. Wide variety of activities offered. Community spirit and development of decision-making abilities is encouraged among campers. Established in 1955. 400-acre facility located 18 miles from Traverse City. Features: private, freshwater lake; views of 7 lakes; wooded setting with open fields; 3 tennis courts; 2 waterfronts; cabins and main lodge.

Profile of Summer Employees Total number: 40; typical ages: 18–50. 50% men; 50% women; 5% high school students; 70% college students; 5% retirees; 10% non-U.S. citizens. Nonsmokers preferred.

Employment Information Openings are from June 15 to August 18. Jobs available: ▶ 2 *cooks* (minimum age 18) with food handler's card at $200–$400 per week ▶ 1 *nurse* (minimum age 21) with RN; experience with children preferred at $300–$400 per week ▶ 1 *sailing instructor* (minimum age 19) at $1000–$1500 per season ▶ 1 *scuba instructor* (minimum age 21) with teaching experience and instructor certification preferred at $1000–$1600 per season ▶ 4 *sports instructors* (minimum age 18) at $1000–$1500 per season ▶ 2 *swimming instructors* (minimum age 19) with WSI and lifeguard certification at $1000–$1600 per season ▶ 1 *tennis instructor* (minimum age 19) at $1000–$1500 per season. Applicants must submit formal organization application, three letters of recommendation. An in-person interview is recommended, but a telephone interview is acceptable. International applicants accepted; must apply through a recognized agency.

Benefits and Preemployment Training Free housing, free meals, formal training, willing to provide letters of recommendation, on-the-job training, willing to complete paperwork for educational credit, and willing to act as a professional reference. Preemployment training is required and includes accident prevention and safety, first aid, CPR, interpersonal skills, leadership skills.

Contact Laurence Cohn, Director, Camp Maplehurst, 1455 Quarton Road, Birmingham, Michigan 48009. Telephone: 248-647-2646. Fax: 248-647-6716. E-mail: campmaple@aol.com. World Wide Web: http://www.campmaplehurst.com. Contact by e-mail, fax, mail, or phone. Application deadline: continuous.

CAMP O'FAIR WINDS
3235 MCKEEN LAKE ROAD
COLUMBIAVILLE, MICHIGAN 48421

General Information Non-profit organization dedicated to providing girls with challenging outdoor programs; emphasis is placed on helping girls develop self-confidence, group communication skills, and independence. Established in 1930. 465-acre facility located 40 miles from Flint. Features: wooded setting; aquatic center with waterslide; low initiatives and high ropes course; freshwater lake; archery field; arts and crafts center.
Profile of Summer Employees Total number: 40; typical ages: 18–25. 1% men; 99% women; 10% minorities; 90% college students; 1% retirees; 30% non-U.S. citizens; 50% local applicants.
Employment Information Openings are from June 1 to August 15. Jobs available: ▶ 1 *aquatic supervisor* (minimum age 18) with strong communication skills, supervisory experience, lifeguard training, team player, experience working with children at $235 per week ▶ 1 *arts and craft director* (minimum age 18) with good teaching ability, strong leadership skills and experience teaching creative art projects to children at $220 per week ▶ 1 *assistant director* (minimum age 18) with supervisory experience, strong communication skills, team skills, and experience working at camps at $250 per week ▶ 1 *business manager* (minimum age 18) with good leadership skills, experience handling cash, good organization skills, and valid driver's license at $220 per week ▶ 1 *head cook* (minimum age 21) with experience in food preparation, menu planning, food safety, certification/degree preferred, supervisory experience, flexible attitude at $280 per week ▶ 1 *health supervisor* (minimum age 18) with RN or EMT certification, experience working with children at $225 per week ▶ 4 *kitchen aides* (minimum age 18) with experience in food handling, good team skills, positive attitude at $170 per week ▶ 4 *lifeguards* (minimum age 18) with lifeguard, first aid, CPR training, experience working with children, good leadership skills at $200 per week ▶ 1 *packout supervisor* (minimum age 18) with good communication skills, and knowledge of food handling procedures; must be licensed driver, and team player at $190 per week ▶ 1 *program director* (minimum age 18) with strong communication skills, camp experience, licensed driver, supervisory experience at $220 per week ▶ 1 *ropes/initiative director* (minimum age 18) with experience working with children, team player, strong leadership skills, moderate athletic ability, comfortable with heights at $225 per week ▶ 1 *smallcraft instructor* (minimum age 18) with lifeguard training, smallcraft experience, team player, experience working with children at $225 per week ▶ 1 *trip/overnight director* (minimum age 18) with good leadership skills, strong camping/outdoor skills, experience working with children, good organizational skills at $220 per week ▶ 20 *unit assistants* (minimum age 18) with experience with children, comfortable outdoors at $190 per week ▶ 8 *unit leaders* (minimum age 18) with strong communication skills, leadership ability, experience working with children at $210 per week. Applicants must submit formal organization application, three personal references, physical exam and TB test. An in-person interview is recommended, but a telephone interview is acceptable. International applicants accepted; must apply through a recognized agency.
Benefits and Preemployment Training Free housing, free meals, health insurance, on-the-job training, and willing to complete paperwork for educational credit. Preemployment training is required and includes first aid, CPR, lifeguard training, archery instructor training.
Contact Therese Plotz, Camp Director, Camp O'Fair Winds, 2029-C South Elms Road, Swartz Creek, Michigan 48473. Telephone: 800-482-6734. Fax: 810-230-0244. E-mail: tplotz@fwgsc.org. World Wide Web: http://www.gsfwc.org. Contact by e-mail, fax, phone, or through World Wide Web site. Application deadline: continuous.

CAMP WESTMINSTER
116 WESTMINSTER DRIVE
ROSCOMMON, MICHIGAN 48653

General Information Residential camp offering a unique combination of activities designed to promote a sense of responsibility and self-worth in a Christian community. Established in 1925.

40-acre facility located 200 miles from Detroit. Features: freshwater lake; wooded setting; climbing tower; high ropes course; 2 tennis courts; sailboat and canoe fleets.

Profile of Summer Employees Total number: 30; typical ages: 16–55. 50% men; 50% women; 30% minorities; 5% high school students; 90% college students; 5% retirees; 25% non-U.S. citizens; 5% local applicants. Nonsmokers required.

Employment Information Openings are from June 1 to August 15. Jobs available: ▶ 20 *counselors/program specialists* with specialized training at $125–$250 per week ▶ *kitchen staff* at $125–$500 per week ▶ 6 *lifeguards* with lifeguard training and CPR/first aid certification at $125–$250 per week ▶ 2 *program directors* at $250 per week ▶ 1 *registered nurse* at $200–$400 per week ▶ 6 *ropes course facilitators* with certification in field at $150–$250 per week ▶ 1 *waterfront director* with WSI certification at $150–$250 per week. Applicants must submit formal organization application, three personal references. An in-person interview is recommended, but a telephone interview is acceptable. International applicants accepted; must apply through a recognized agency.

Benefits and Preemployment Training Free housing, free meals, formal training, and on-the-job training. Preemployment training is required and includes accident prevention and safety, first aid, CPR, interpersonal skills, leadership skills, lifeguard training.

Contact Suzanne Getz Bates, Executive Director, Camp Westminster, 17567 Hubbell Avenue, Detroit, Michigan 48235. Telephone: 313-341-8969. Fax: 313-341-1514. E-mail: suzannebates@ureach.com. World Wide Web: http://www.campwestminster.com. Contact by e-mail, fax, mail, phone, or through World Wide Web site. Application deadline: continuous.

CEDAR LODGE

47000 52ND STREET
LAWRENCE, MICHIGAN 49064

General Information Residential coeducational camp serving 60 campers in a relaxed, loosely structured program with a special emphasis on horsemanship from the beginner to the show jumper. Established in 1964. 160-acre facility located 105 miles from Chicago, Illinois.

Profile of Summer Employees Typical age: 23. 25% men; 75% women; 95% college students; 5% retirees; 60% non-U.S. citizens; 5% local applicants. Nonsmokers required.

Employment Information Openings are from June to August. Jobs available: ▶ 1 *arts and crafts instructor* (minimum age 19) at $1000–$1200 per season ▶ 1 *biking/trip instructor* (minimum age 19) at $1000–$1200 per season ▶ 2 *kitchen assistants* (minimum age 18) at $1200–$1500 per season ▶ 1 *music/dance/drama instructor* (minimum age 19) at $1000–$1200 per season ▶ 2 *riding instructors* (minimum age 19) with English riding experience at $1000–$1500 per season ▶ 1 *sports instructor* (minimum age 19) at $1000–$1200 per season ▶ 2 *swimming instructors* (minimum age 21) with swimming experience at $1000–$1500 per season. Applicants must submit formal organization application, three personal references. A telephone interview is required. International applicants accepted; must apply through a recognized agency.

Benefits and Preemployment Training Free housing, free meals, formal training, willing to provide letters of recommendation, on-the-job training, and willing to complete paperwork for educational credit. Preemployment training is required and includes accident prevention and safety, first aid, CPR, leadership skills.

Contact Amy Edwards, Program Director, Cedar Lodge, PO Box 218, Lawrence, Michigan 49064. Telephone: 616-674-8071. Fax: 616-674-3143. E-mail: info@cedarlodge.com. World Wide Web: http://www.cedarlodge.com. Contact by e-mail, fax, mail, or phone. Application deadline: continuous.

CIRCLE PINES CENTER SUMMER CAMP

8650 MULLEN ROAD
DELTON, MICHIGAN 49046

General Information A small, coeducational, residential, multicultural camp for children ages 8–17 promoting peace, cooperation, and social justice. Established in 1938. 294-acre facility located 30 miles from Kalamazoo. Features: springfed lake; woodlands; meadows; organic garden; pre-Civil War farmhouse.

Profile of Summer Employees Total number: 24; typical ages: 20–23. 45% men; 55% women; 15% minorities; 40% college students; 5% retirees; 5% non-U.S. citizens; 5% local applicants. Nonsmokers preferred.

Employment Information Openings are from June 17 to August 12. Jobs available: ▶ 4 *cooks* with experience working with whole foods, large groups, and children at $1000 per season ▶ 12 *counselors* with experience with children and skills in leading activities at $1000 per season ▶ 1 *health officer* with RN, LPN, or EMT license or camp health officer training and experience at $1200–$1500 per season ▶ 1 *kitchen manager* (minimum age 18) with menu planning, supervisory, inventory and purchasing experience at $1000 per season ▶ 1 *maintenance staff member* must have maintenance skills and ability to work with children at $800 per season ▶ 1 *waterfront assistant* with CPR certificate plus lifeguard and first aid training at $1000 per season ▶ 1 *waterfront director* (minimum age 21) with CPR and lifeguard training/certification at $1000–$1200 per season. Applicants must submit a formal organization application, three personal references. An in-person interview is recommended, but a telephone interview is acceptable. International applicants accepted; must obtain own visa, obtain own working papers.

Benefits and Preemployment Training Free housing, free meals, on-the-job training, and willing to complete paperwork for educational credit.

Contact Traci Furman, Camp Director, Circle Pines Center Summer Camp, 8650 Mullen Road, Delton, Michigan 49046. Telephone: 616-623-5555. Fax: 616-623-9054. E-mail: circle@net-link.net. World Wide Web: http://www.circlepinescenter.org. Contact by e-mail, fax, mail, phone, or through World Wide Web site. Application deadline: continuous.

CRYSTALAIRE CAMP

2768 SOUTH SHORE ROAD EAST
FRANKFORT, MICHIGAN 49635

General Information Small, coeducational, loosely-structured residential camp that is noncompetitive and nonsectarian, emphasizing individual growth. Established in 1924. 145-acre facility located 30 miles from Traverse City. Features: large inland lake; proximity to National Lakeshore; Lake Michigan (sand dunes and beach accessible only by boat).

Profile of Summer Employees Total number: 45; typical ages: 19–28. 50% men; 50% women; 5% minorities; 20% high school students; 65% college students; 5% retirees; 15% non-U.S. citizens; 5% local applicants. Nonsmokers preferred.

Employment Information Openings are from June 15 to August 20. Jobs available: ▶ 1 *art specialist* (minimum age 19) with ability to organize art program (teacher preferred) at $1000–$2000 per season ▶ 1 *assistant director/program director* with ability to conduct programs for small and large groups at $1500–$4000 per season ▶ 2–3 *cooks* with experience at $1200–$3000 per season ▶ 14 *counselors* (minimum age 19) with lifesaving training; art, sailing, trip, and sports skills at $1100–$1700 per season ▶ 5 *junior counselors (high school students)* (minimum age 17) at $500–$900 per season ▶ 2 *nurses* with RN, LPN, or EMT license; will consider partial summer availability at $1200–$2200 per season ▶ 1 *riding instructor* (minimum age 19) with experience and ability to manage Western-style riding program at $1000–$1600 per season ▶ 3 *sailing/windsurfing instructors* (minimum age 19) with lifesaving training and experience in the field at $1000–$1800 per season ▶ *sports specialist* with experience in competitive and noncompetitive sports and games at $1000–$1500 per season ▶ 1 *stable helper* (minimum age 19) at $60–$150 per week ▶ 1 *trip coordinator* (minimum age 19) with ability to organize wilderness camping trips, train staff, and maintain bicycles, tents, and camping equipment at $1200–$2300 per season ▶ 2 *waterfront directors* with current LGT and WSI certification and experience at $1200–$2700 per season. Applicants must submit formal organization application, resume. An in-person interview is recommended, but a telephone interview is acceptable. International applicants accepted; must obtain own visa, apply through a recognized agency.

Benefits and Preemployment Training Free housing, free meals, formal training, willing to provide letters of recommendation, and willing to complete paperwork for educational credit. Preemployment training is required and includes accident prevention and safety, first aid, CPR, interpersonal skills, leadership skills.

Contact David B. Reid, Director, Crystalaire Camp, 2768 South Shore Road East, Frankfort, Michigan 49635. Telephone: 231-352-7589. Fax: 231-352-6609. E-mail: xtalaire@benzie.com. World Wide Web: http://www.crystalairecamp.com. Contact by e-mail, fax, mail, phone, or through World Wide Web site. Application deadline: continuous.

CYBERCAMPS–UNIVERSITY OF MICHIGAN

ANN ARBOR, MICHIGAN

See Cybercamps–University of Washington on page 335 for complete description.

CYO BOYS CAMP

1295 LAKESHORE ROAD
CARSONVILLE, MICHIGAN 48419

General Information CYO summer camps are open to boys ages 7½–16. The Pioneer Program is especially designed to meet the needs of experienced campers ages 14–16. Established in 1946. 70-acre facility located 90 miles from Detroit. Features: climbing wall; ropes course; lakeside setting; acres of woods and nature trails.

Profile of Summer Employees Total number: 40; typical ages: 17–25. 90% men; 10% women; 25% minorities; 45% high school students; 50% college students; 5% retirees.

Employment Information Openings are from June 17 to August 3. Jobs available: ▶ *archery director* (minimum age 18) at $900–$1000 per season ▶ *arts and crafts director* (minimum age 18) at $900–$1000 per season ▶ 10–15 *counselors-in-training* (minimum age 17) at $750 per season ▶ *group counselors/assistants* (minimum age 18) at $900–$1000 per season ▶ *nurse or health officer* (minimum age 21) with RN, LPN, or EMT with CPR training at $1400–$1600 per season ▶ *waterfront director/assistant* (minimum age 18) with WSI certification at $1100–$1400 per season. Applicants must submit formal organization application, three personal references. An in-person interview is recommended, but a telephone interview is acceptable. International applicants accepted; must obtain own visa, obtain own working papers, apply through a recognized agency.

Benefits and Preemployment Training Free housing, free meals, and on-the-job training. Preemployment training is required and includes accident prevention and safety, interpersonal skills, leadership skills.

Contact Caroline Krucker, Parish Services and Camps Director, CYO Boys Camp, 305 Michigan Avenue, 9th Floor, Detroit, Michigan 48266. Telephone: 313-963-7172. Fax: 313-963-7179. E-mail: ckrucker@cyodetroit.org. World Wide Web: http://www.cyocamps.org. Contact by e-mail, fax, mail, phone, or through World Wide Web site. Application deadline: continuous.

CYO GIRLS CAMP

1564 LAKESHORE ROAD
PORT SANILAC, MICHIGAN 48469

General Information CYO summer camps are open to girls ages 7½–16. The Pioneer Program is especially designed to meet the needs of experienced campers ages 14–16. Established in 1946. 30-acre facility located 90 miles from Detroit. Features: location on the shore of Lake Huron; with long sandy beaches; acres of woods and nature trails; climbing wall; high ropes course.

Profile of Summer Employees Total number: 40; typical ages: 17–25. 10% men; 90% women; 25% minorities; 40% high school students; 50% college students; 10% local applicants.

Employment Information Openings are from June 17 to August 3. Jobs available: ▶ 1 *archery director* (minimum age 21) at $800–$1000 per season ▶ 1 *arts and crafts director* (minimum

age 18) at $800–$900 per season ▶ 10–15 *counselors-in-training* (minimum age 17) at $750 per season ▶ 10 *group counselors/assistants* (minimum age 18) at $800–$1400 per season ▶ *nurse or health officer* (minimum age 21) with RN, LPN, EMT, or advanced first aid with CPR at $1400–$1600 per season ▶ 2 *waterfront directors/assistants* (minimum age 18) with WSI certification at $1000–$1200 per season. Applicants must submit a formal organization application, three personal references. An in-person interview is recommended, but a telephone interview is acceptable. International applicants accepted; must obtain own visa, obtain own working papers.
Benefits and Preemployment Training Free housing, free meals, health insurance, on-the-job training, and opportunity to attend seminars/workshops. Preemployment training is required and includes accident prevention and safety, interpersonal skills, leadership skills.
Contact Caroline Krucker, Parish Services and Camps Director, CYO Girls Camp, 305 Michigan Avenue, 9th Floor, Detroit, Michigan 48226. Telephone: 313-963-7172. Fax: 313-963-7179. E-mail: ckrucker@cyodetroit.org. World Wide Web: http://www.cyocamps.org. Contact by e-mail, fax, mail, phone, or through World Wide Web site. Application deadline: continuous.

DOUBLE JJ RESORT

PO BOX 94
ROTHBURY, MICHIGAN 49452

General Information Full service resort ranch with exclusive programming for adults, families, and children. Established in 1937. 1,500-acre facility located 20 miles from Muskegon. Features: horseback riding; championship 18-hole golf course; year-round activities; pools, spas, water slide; cabins, hotel and condominiums; snow tubing/dogsledding.
Profile of Summer Employees Total number: 300; typical ages: 18–30. 50% men; 50% women; 2% minorities; 5% high school students; 50% college students; 5% retirees; 8% non-U.S. citizens; 30% local applicants.
Employment Information Openings are from January 1 to December 31. Year-round positions also offered. Jobs available: ▶ 15 *children's counselors* (minimum age 18) at $150 per week ▶ 6 *cooks* (minimum age 18) with experience in the field at $200–$350 per week ▶ 10 *day care staff* (minimum age 18) at $150 per week ▶ 3 *dining room managers* (minimum age 18) with waiter/waitressing experience at $150–$220 per week ▶ 1 *disc jockey* (minimum age 18) with experience at $150–$200 per week ▶ 4 *dishwashers* (minimum age 18) at $150 per week ▶ 10 *golf course groundskeepers* (minimum age 18) at $150–$200 per week ▶ 10 *golf course personnel* (minimum age 18) with golfing knowledge and ability at $150 per week ▶ 15 *housekeepers* (minimum age 18) at $150–$200 per week ▶ 20 *lawn maintenance personnel* (minimum age 18) at $130–$200 per week ▶ 12 *lifeguards* (minimum age 18) with American Red Cross or Ellis lifeguard certification at $150–$200 per week ▶ 15 *office staff members* (minimum age 18) with computer experience and ability to answer phones and make reservations at $150 per week ▶ 10 *prep cooks/bakers* (minimum age 18) with experience at $150–$200 per week ▶ 12 *pro shop/gift shop staff members* (minimum age 18) at $150 per week ▶ 10 *snack bar/bar staff members* (minimum age 18) at $130 per week ▶ 9 *talented entertainers (guitarists, singers, pianists, and musicians)* (minimum age 18) with outgoing personality at $150–$200 per week ▶ 20 *waiters/waitresses* (minimum age 18) at $130 per week ▶ 10 *wranglers* (minimum age 18) with experience at $150–$220 per week. Applicants must submit formal organization application. An in-person interview is recommended, but a telephone interview is acceptable. International applicants accepted; must obtain own visa, obtain own working papers, apply through a recognized agency.
Benefits and Preemployment Training Free housing, free meals, possible full-time employment, willing to provide letters of recommendation, on-the-job training, willing to complete paperwork for educational credit, willing to act as a professional reference, and use of all resort amenities. Preemployment training is required and includes resort-wide orientation to familiarize employees with facility, procedures, and job description.
Contact Densie Angell, Human Resources, Double JJ Resort, PO Box 94, Rothbury, Michigan 49452. Telephone: 231-894-4444. Fax: 231-893-5355. E-mail: jobs@doublejj.com. World Wide

Web: http://www.doublejj.com. Contact by e-mail, fax, mail, phone, or through World Wide Web site. Application deadline: continuous.

INTERLOCHEN ARTS CAMP
4000 HIGHWAY M-137
INTERLOCHEN, MICHIGAN 49643

General Information America's first and foremost summer arts program for students age 8–18, offering instruction in creative writing, dance, music, theatre arts and visual arts. Established in 1928. 1,200-acre facility located 16 miles from Traverse City. Features: freshwater lakes; wooded setting; performance venues; ropes course; tennis court; basketball court.

Profile of Summer Employees Total number: 1,500; typical ages: 18–40. 40% men; 60% women; 20% minorities; 12% high school students; 70% college students; 12% retirees; 1% non-U.S. citizens; 5% local applicants.

Employment Information Openings are from June 8 to August 11. Jobs available: ▶ 16 *accompanists* must have BA degree at $1000–$1300 per season ▶ 13 *art assistants* (minimum age 18) art major at $900 per season ▶ 10 *audio services staff* (minimum age 18) at $900 per season ▶ 8 *box office staff* (minimum age 18) at $1000 per season ▶ 250 *cabin counselors* (minimum age 18) at $950–$1100 per season ▶ 6 *clerical staff* at $800 per season ▶ 12 *concert office staff* (minimum age 18) at $800 per season ▶ 5 *crafts instructors* (minimum age 18) at $800 per season ▶ 16 *music library staff* (minimum age 18) at $800 per season ▶ 25 *nurses* with Michigan license, RN, LPN at $13–$16 per hour ▶ 8 *physicians* primary care physicians preferred at $450 per week ▶ 6 *piano technicians* (minimum age 18) ▶ 14 *practice supervisors* (minimum age 18) at $1000 per season ▶ 8 *security staff* (minimum age 21) ▶ 3 *staff hall counselors* (minimum age 21) at $900 per season ▶ 36 *stage services staff* (minimum age 18) at $900 per season ▶ 2 *stage technicians/master electricians* with stage lighting and production experience at $900–$1500 per season ▶ 26 *theatre production staff* (minimum age 18) at $900–$1800 per season ▶ 8 *transportation drivers* (minimum age 21) at $900 per season ▶ 8 *waterfront staff* (minimum age 18) with current Red Cross lifeguard training at $950 per season. Applicants must submit a formal organization application, three letters of recommendation. International applicants accepted; must obtain own visa, obtain own working papers.

Benefits and Preemployment Training Free housing, free meals, willing to provide letters of recommendation, names of contacts, on-the-job training, willing to complete paperwork for educational credit, opportunity to attend seminars/workshops, and private lessons, playing in ensembles. Preemployment training is required and includes first aid, CPR, leadership skills.

Contact Grimaldo D. Robles, Coordinator, Seasonal Employment, Interlochen Arts Camp, Human Resources, PO Box 199, Interlochen, Michigan 49643. Telephone: 231-276-7337. Fax: 231-276-7850. E-mail: roblesgd@interlochen.k12.mi.us. World Wide Web: http://www.interlochen.org/. Contact by e-mail, fax, mail, phone, or through World Wide Web site. Application deadline: continuous.

MICHIGAN TECHNOLOGICAL UNIVERSITY SUMMER YOUTH PROGRAM
1400 TOWNSEND DRIVE
HOUGHTON, MICHIGAN 49931

General Information Summer program for students ages 12-18 in 70 explorations designed to introduce students to careers and knowledge (theater, engineering, pottery, and more), and give them a taste of residential college dorm life. Established in 1973. 120-acre facility located 250 miles from Green Bay, Wisconsin. Features: Lake Superior location; waterfalls; old growth forests; biking/hiking paths; Isle Royale; all university facilities.

Profile of Summer Employees Total number: 250; typical ages: 18–28. 50% men; 50% women; 20% minorities; 97% college students; 1% retirees; 30% non-U.S. citizens; 10% local applicants. Nonsmokers preferred.

Employment Information Openings are from June 8 to August 31. Jobs available: ▶ *counselors* (minimum age 18) must have completed one semester of college; at $220 per week plus room and board ▶ *teaching assistants* (minimum age 18) must have completed one year of college; paid at $200 per week. Applicants must submit formal organization application, two personal references. An in-person interview is recommended, but a telephone interview is acceptable. International applicants accepted; must obtain own visa, obtain own working papers, apply through a recognized agency.
Benefits and Preemployment Training Free housing, free meals, and on-the-job training. Preemployment training is required and includes accident prevention and safety, first aid, interpersonal skills, leadership skills.
Contact Cheryl Gherna, Youth Programs Secretary, Michigan Technological University Summer Youth Program, 1400 Townsend Drive, Houghton, Michigan 49931. Telephone: 906-487-2219. Fax: 906-487-3101. E-mail: yp@mtu.edu. World Wide Web: http://www.youthprograms.mtu.edu. Contact by e-mail, mail, or phone. Application deadline: applications are accepted December through April; most hiring complete by end of March.

THE SOUTHWESTERN COMPANY, MICHIGAN

See The Southwestern Company on page 302 for complete description.

STUDENT CONSERVATION ASSOCIATION (SCA), MICHIGAN

See Student Conservation Association (SCA), New Hampshire on page 209 for complete description.

SUMMER DISCOVERY AT MICHIGAN

UNIVERSITY OF MICHIGAN
ANN ARBOR, MICHIGAN 48109

General Information Precollege enrichment program for high school students at University of Michigan. Established in 1991. near Detroit. Features: sport facilities; beaches; mountains; lakes; major cities nearby; college towns.
Profile of Summer Employees Total number: 40; typical ages: 21–35. 45% men; 55% women; 10% minorities; 60% college students; 2% non-U.S. citizens. Nonsmokers required.
Employment Information Openings are from June 20 to August 25. Jobs available: ▶ 30 *resident counselors* (minimum age 21) with experience working with high school students/children at $200 per week. Applicants must submit a formal organization application, resume, three personal references. An in-person interview is required. International applicants accepted; must obtain own visa, obtain own working papers.
Benefits and Preemployment Training Free housing, free meals, possible full-time employment, on-the-job training, willing to complete paperwork for educational credit, willing to act as a professional reference, and travel reimbursement. Preemployment training is required and includes accident prevention and safety, CPR, leadership skills.
Contact Jason Walley, Admissions Director, Summer Discovery at Michigan, 1326 Old Northern Boulevard, Roslyn, New York 11576. Telephone: 516-621-3939. Fax: 516-625-3438. E-mail: staff@summerfun.com. World Wide Web: http://www.summerfun.com. Contact by e-mail, fax, mail, phone, or through World Wide Web site. Application deadline: continuous.

AUDUBON CENTER OF THE NORTH WOODS

PO BOX 530
SANDSTONE, MINNESOTA 55072

General Information Environmental education center that stresses the positive relationship between people and nature. Programs combine natural history, outdoor skills, and ethics and serve youth, college, and adult audiences. Established in 1968. 535-acre facility located 100 miles from Minneapolis. Features: freshwater lake; red pine forest; maple forest; high ropes challenge course; beaver pond and stream; raptor center.

Profile of Summer Employees Total number: 14; typical ages: 20–28. 50% men; 50% women; 10% minorities; 90% college students; 20% non-U.S. citizens; 10% local applicants. Nonsmokers preferred.

Employment Information Openings are from June 1 to August 30. Year-round positions also offered. Jobs available: ▶ 4 *environmental education staff members* (minimum age 20) with WSI and first aid certification at $250–$500 per month ▶ 1–2 *raptor rehabilitation/education staff members* (minimum age 20) at $250–$300 per month. Applicants must submit a letter of interest, resume, three letters of recommendation. An in-person interview is recommended, but a telephone interview is acceptable. International applicants accepted; must obtain own visa.

Benefits and Preemployment Training Free housing, free meals, willing to provide letters of recommendation, on-the-job training, willing to complete paperwork for educational credit, and willing to act as a professional reference. Preemployment training is required and includes accident prevention and safety, first aid, CPR, interpersonal skills, leadership skills.

Contact Adam Harju, Adventure Coordinator, Audubon Center of the North Woods. Telephone: 888-404-7743. Fax: 320-245-5272. E-mail: audubon1@audubon-center.org. World Wide Web: http://www.audubon-center.org. Contact by e-mail, phone, or through World Wide Web site. Application deadline: continuous.

CAMP BIRCHWOOD

6983 NORTH STEAMBOAT LAKE DRIVE
LAPORTE, MINNESOTA 56461

General Information Independently operated camp for girls offering a variety of recreational activities including horseback riding, sailing, tennis and more. Established in 1958. 260-acre facility located 200 miles from Minneapolis. Features: gorgeous lake; wooded property; small number of campers; riding trails; 2 riding arenas; lots of sailing.

Profile of Summer Employees Total number: 40; typical ages: 19–28. 100% women; 100% college students. Nonsmokers required.

Employment Information Openings are from June 1 to August 23. Jobs available: ▶ 25 *counselors/activity instructors* (minimum age 19) with first aid and CPR certification at $1800–$2000 per season ▶ 8 *support staff* (minimum age 18) with first aid and CPR certification at $1800–$2000 per season. Applicants must submit formal organization application, personal reference. An in-person interview is recommended, but a telephone interview is acceptable. International applicants accepted; must apply through a recognized agency.

Benefits and Preemployment Training Free housing, free meals, willing to provide letters of recommendation, on-the-job training, and willing to act as a professional reference. Preemployment training is required and includes accident prevention and safety, interpersonal skills, leadership skills.

Contact Terry Bredemus, Director/Owner, Camp Birchwood, 6983 North Steamboat Lake Drive, Laporte, Minnesota 56461. Telephone: 800-451-5270. Fax: 218-335-7866. E-mail: cbgwc@aol.com. World Wide Web: http://www.campbirchwood.com. Contact by e-mail, fax, mail, phone, or through World Wide Web site. Application deadline: continuous.

CAMP BUCKSKIN

9830 FREDRICKSON LANE
ELY, MINNESOTA 55731

General Information Residential camp offering two 30-day sessions for youths with academic and/or social skills difficulties (learning disabilities, Attention Deficit Disorder, and related difficulties). Established in 1959. 165-acre facility located 80 miles from Duluth. Features: freshwater lake; wooded setting; library; hiking trails; cabins; dining hall.

Profile of Summer Employees Total number: 70; typical ages: 19–25. 50% men; 50% women; 5% minorities; 10% high school students; 80% college students; 10% non-U.S. citizens; 10% local applicants. Nonsmokers preferred.

Employment Information Openings are from June 1 to August 25. Jobs available: ▶ 3 *counselors/archery instructors* (minimum age 18) with experience and certification from such organizations as the National Archery Association at $1600–$2500 per season ▶ 6 *counselors/arts and crafts instructors* (minimum age 18) with creativity and ability to teach at $1600–$2500 per season ▶ 10 *counselors/canoeing instructors* (minimum age 18) with lifeguard training, standard first aid, and CPR (preferred) at $1600–$2500 per season ▶ 6 *counselors/nature and environment instructors* (minimum age 18) with experience and certification in programs such as NOLS and Nature Quest (preferred) at $1600–$2500 per season ▶ 3 *counselors/riflery instructors* (minimum age 18) with gun and range safety training with the National Rifle Association, military, or similar agency (preferred) at $1600–$2500 per season ▶ 8 *counselors/swimming instructors* (minimum age 19) with WSI certification, lifeguard training, standard first aid, and CPR (preferred) at $1600–$2500 per season ▶ 5 *kitchen assistants* (minimum age 16) with positive attitude and ability to work with others at $1350–$1900 per season ▶ 2 *nurses* with RN license (preferred), or LPN license ▶ 2 *office assistants* (minimum age 16) with good typing and phone skills (computer experience a plus) at $1350–$2100 per season ▶ 8 *reading teachers* with license in elementary or secondary education or special education certification (preferred) at $1750–$2800 per season ▶ 8 *trip counselors* with lifeguard, CPR, and standard first aid training at $1650–$2800 per season. Applicants must submit formal organization application, writing sample, three personal references. An in-person interview is recommended, but a telephone interview is acceptable. International applicants accepted; must apply through a recognized agency.

Benefits and Preemployment Training Free housing, free meals, formal training, possible full-time employment, willing to provide letters of recommendation, names of contacts, on-the-job training, willing to complete paperwork for educational credit, willing to act as a professional reference, opportunity to attend seminars/workshops, and travel reimbursement. Preemployment training is required and includes accident prevention and safety, interpersonal skills, leadership skills, seminars relate to ADHD/learning disabilities, behavior management, teaching methodologies, and social skills goal setting, certification in Crisis Prevention Institute's Non-violent Physical Crisis Intervention.

Contact Thomas Bauer, Director, Camp Buckskin, 8700 West 36th Street, Suite 6W, St. Louis Park, Minnesota 55426-3936. Telephone: 952-930-3544. Fax: 952-938-6996. E-mail: buckskin@spacestar.net. World Wide Web: http://www.campbuckskin.com. Contact by e-mail, fax, mail, phone, or through World Wide Web site. Application deadline: continuous.

CAMP CHIPPEWA FOUNDATION

CASS LAKE, MINNESOTA 56633

General Information Residential camp for 60 boys offering land and water activities including extensive Canadian fishing, canoe, and kayak tripping. Established in 1935. 88-acre facility located 250 miles from Minneapolis. Features: isthmus between 2 lakes; one mile of shoreline; island fishing lodge in Ontario; location in Chippewa National Forest; 3 tennis courts.

Profile of Summer Employees Total number: 30; typical ages: 19–45. 95% men; 5% women; 5% minorities; 5% high school students; 65% college students; 10% non-U.S. citizens; 5% local applicants. Nonsmokers required.

Employment Information Openings are from June 10 to August 12. Jobs available: ▶ *NRA rifle instructor* (minimum age 19) with NRA certification at $1200–$1400 per season ▶ *archery instructor* (minimum age 19) at $1200–$1400 per season ▶ *general cabin counselors* (minimum age 19) at $1100–$1500 per season ▶ *sailing instructor* (minimum age 19) at $1200–$2200 per season ▶ *swimming instructor* (minimum age 19) with Red Cross WSI certification at $1200–$1800 per season. Applicants must submit formal organization application, three personal references. An in-person interview is recommended, but a telephone interview is acceptable. International applicants accepted; must apply through a recognized agency.

Benefits and Preemployment Training Free housing, free meals, formal training, health insurance, names of contacts, on-the-job training, and travel reimbursement. Preemployment training is required and includes accident prevention and safety, interpersonal skills, leadership skills.

Contact Michael Thompson, Director, Camp Chippewa Foundation, 15 East 5th Street, Suite 4022, Tulsa, Oklahoma 74103. Telephone: 800-262-1544. Fax: 918-582-7896. E-mail: mike@campchippewa.com. World Wide Web: http://www.campchippewa.com. Contact by e-mail, fax, mail, phone, or through World Wide Web site. Application deadline: continuous.

CAMP COURAGE

8046 83RD STREET, NW
MAPLE LAKE, MINNESOTA 55358

General Information Programs offered for physically disabled children and adults, including adventure camping for the deaf and speech therapy for speech/language-impaired children. Established in 1955. 300-acre facility located 50 miles from Minneapolis. Features: pool; gymnasium; tennis courts; lake; horses; accessible site.

Profile of Summer Employees Total number: 120; typical ages: 18–50. 50% men; 50% women; 8% minorities; 10% high school students; 80% college students; 1% retirees; 8% non-U.S. citizens; 60% local applicants.

Employment Information Openings are from June 1 to August 20. Year-round positions also offered. Jobs available: ▶ 6 *cooks* at $9 per hour ▶ 36 *counselors* at $165–$200 per week ▶ 3 *nurses* with RN, LPN, or GN license at $500–$600 per week ▶ 20 *program specialists* with appropriate certification for area at $150–$175 per week ▶ 3 *program specialists (crafts)* with certification or experience in the field at $165–$200 per week ▶ 3 *program specialists (photography)* with certification or experience in the field at $165–$225 per week ▶ 14 *speech clinicians* with MS in speech pathology/communications disorders (BA acceptable at lower pay rate) at $335–$455 per week ▶ 6 *waterfront personnel* with lifeguard certification at $165–$210 per week. Applicants must submit formal organization application, two personal references or two letters of recommendation. An in-person interview is recommended, but a telephone interview is acceptable. International applicants accepted; must obtain own visa, obtain own working papers, apply through a recognized agency.

Benefits and Preemployment Training Free housing, free meals, formal training, health insurance, willing to provide letters of recommendation, on-the-job training, willing to complete paperwork for educational credit, willing to act as a professional reference, opportunity to attend seminars/workshops, travel reimbursement, and tuition assistance. Preemployment training is

required and includes accident prevention and safety, first aid, CPR, interpersonal skills, leadership skills, camp skills.
Contact Roger Upcraft, Program Manager, Camp Courage, 8046 83rd Street, NW, Maple Lake, Minnesota 55358. Telephone: 320-963-3121. Fax: 320-963-3698. E-mail: camping@mtn.org. World Wide Web: http://www.lkdllink.net/~ccourage. Contact by e-mail, fax, mail, phone, or through World Wide Web site. Application deadline: continuous.

CAMP LINCOLN FOR BOYS/CAMP LAKE HUBERT FOR GIRLS

LAKE HUBERT, MINNESOTA 56459

General Information Separate boys and girls camps offering 30 land and water activities, staff from around the world, one- to four-week sessions for ages 8 to 17. Established in 1909. 800-acre facility located 140 miles from Minneapolis. Features: 800 acres; boys and girls camps; mile of lakeshore; 30 land water activities; log cabins; 150 fun staff.
Profile of Summer Employees Total number: 155; typical ages: 19–42. 50% men; 50% women; 5% minorities; 80% college students; 2% retirees; 15% non-U.S. citizens; 15% local applicants. Nonsmokers required.
Employment Information Openings are from June 3 to August 29. Jobs available: ▶ 6–10 *activity directors* (minimum age 20) with experience and ability to teach one or more of the following: sports, riflery, archery, campcraft, riding, windsurfing, arts and crafts, karate, sailing, high ropes, climbing wall at $1700–$2700 per season ▶ 2–4 *cooks, bakers* (minimum age 21) with food service experience at $1800–$3000 per season ▶ 10–20 *counselors* (minimum age 19) with some experience working with young people at $1600–$2500 per season ▶ 1–2 *drivers* (minimum age 21) with Class B driver's license, clean driving record, and ability to complete training course at $1700–$2200 per season ▶ 6–10 *general food service staff members* (minimum age 19) at $1600–$2500 per season ▶ 8–15 *head counselors* (minimum age 21) with leadership experience at $1750–$2700 per season ▶ 2–4 *nurses* (minimum age 21) with LPN, RN at $250–$375 per week ▶ 3–5 *office staff members* with computer experience at $1700–$2900 per season ▶ 2–4 *trip leaders* (minimum age 21) with lifeguard training, CPR, first aid, canoe and pack experience at $1700–$2500 per season. Applicants must submit formal organization application, three personal references. An in-person interview is recommended, but a telephone interview is acceptable. International applicants accepted; must apply through a recognized agency.
Benefits and Preemployment Training Free housing, free meals, formal training, willing to provide letters of recommendation, on-the-job training, willing to complete paperwork for educational credit, and travel reimbursement. Preemployment training is required and includes accident prevention and safety, interpersonal skills, leadership skills, lifeguard training.
Contact Ruggs Cote, Director, Camp Lincoln for Boys/Camp Lake Hubert for Girls, 10179 Crosstown Circle, Eden Prairie, Minnesota 55344. Telephone: 800-242-1909. Fax: 952-922-7149. E-mail: home@lincoln-lakehubert.com. World Wide Web: http://www.lincoln-lakehubert.com. Contact by e-mail, fax, mail, or phone. Application deadline: continuous.

CAMP NEW HOPE

53035 LAKE AVENUE
MCGREGOR, MINNESOTA 55760

General Information Nonprofit organization that provides recreation and leisure opportunities to individuals with developmental disabilities. Established in 1968. 40-acre facility located 70 miles from Duluth. Features: freshwater lake; wooded setting; peaceful; modern and rustic facilities.
Profile of Summer Employees Total number: 40; typical ages: 16–26. 20% men; 80% women.
Employment Information Openings are from May 20 to August 25. Jobs available: ▶ 1 *arts*

and crafts specialist (minimum age 18) at $195–$215 per week ▶ 2 *camp nurses* (minimum age 21) with current LPN or RN license in Minnesota at $350–$600 per week ▶ 18 *counselors* (minimum age 16) at $195–$205 per week ▶ 1 *music specialist* (minimum age 18) with experience in music therapy at $195–$215 per week ▶ 1 *nature specialist* with interest in nature and/or environmental education ▶ 1 *nurse* with RN certification ▶ 1 *recreation specialist* (minimum age 18) at $195–$215 per week ▶ 2 *waterfront lifeguards* (minimum age 18) with current lifeguard certification at $215–$230 per week ▶ 1 *waterfront specialist* with WSI, lifeguard, CPR, and first aid training. Applicants must submit formal organization application, three personal references. An in-person interview is recommended, but a telephone interview is acceptable. International applicants accepted; must apply through a recognized agency.

Benefits and Preemployment Training Free housing, free meals, willing to provide letters of recommendation, names of contacts, on-the-job training, willing to complete paperwork for educational credit, willing to act as a professional reference, and tuition assistance. Preemployment training is required and includes accident prevention and safety, first aid, CPR, interpersonal skills, leadership skills, therapeutic intervention, disability awareness.

Contact Director, Camp New Hope. Telephone: 218-426-3560. Fax: 218-426-3560. E-mail: cnewhope@lcp2.net. World Wide Web: http://www.campnewhopemn.org. Contact by e-mail, fax, mail, phone, or through World Wide Web site. Application deadline: continuous.

CAMP THUNDERBIRD FOR BOYS

20758 COUNTY ROAD 9
BEMIDJI, MINNESOTA 56601

General Information Residential camp serving 200 boys from forty U.S. cities and five other countries. Established in 1946. 700-acre facility located 12 miles from Bemidji. Features: 7½ miles of sand beach shoreline; 700 pristine acres of property; strong waterfront activities; climbing wall; tennis courts; Western riding program.

Profile of Summer Employees Total number: 100; typical ages: 19–60. 55% men; 45% women; 5% minorities; 12% high school students; 60% college students; 1% retirees; 10% non-U.S. citizens; 1% local applicants. Nonsmokers preferred.

Employment Information Openings are from June 1 to August 21. Jobs available: ▶ 1 *arts and crafts specialist* with experience as an art teacher or student status preferred (completion of junior year in college required); salary negotiable ▶ 40 *cabin counselors* with freshman year of college completed, experience working with children, high-energy, caring attitude, ability to assist or teach in several camp activities, and outdoor orientation; salary negotiable ▶ 2 *horseback specialists* with experience in Western riding, completion of junior year of college; and CHA or HSA certification preferred, but will send to clinic for certification; salary negotiable ▶ 10 *kitchen personnel* (minimum age 19) with ability to assist with kitchen operations, food preparation, dishwashing, and cleanup and one year of college completed; salary negotiable ▶ 2 *nurses* with RN or LPN license at $400 and up per week ▶ 2 *office personnel* (minimum age 19) with bookkeeping and computer knowledge, ability to handle camper/staff cash accounts, sophomore year of college completed, and average or above-average typing skills; salary negotiable ▶ 1 *program director* with experience encompassing staff supervision and direct leadership of children in outdoor recreation/camp activities and college degree; salary negotiable ▶ 1 *riflery instructor* with certification and teaching experience (required); salary negotiable ▶ 1 *sailing instructor* with sailing and lifeguard certification; salary negotiable ▶ 6 *swimming instructors* with WSI, lifeguard, and CPR certification; teaching experience (preferred); salary negotiable ▶ 1 *trip director* with experience in diverse kinds of wilderness trips and equipment use, and college degree; salary negotiable ▶ 4 *unit directors* (minimum age 23) with experience encompassing staff supervision and direct leadership of children in outdoor recreation/camp activities and college degree; salary negotiable ▶ 1 *waterfront director* with WSI, first aid, CPR, and lifeguard certification; college degree and knowledge of various water sports; salary negotiable ▶ 15 *wilderness and trip leaders* (minimum age 21) with certifications in CPR, lifeguard, and advanced first aid (must be comfortable and confident living in the wilderness) at $1200–$1800 per season. Applicants must submit formal organization application, three personal references. An in-person interview is recommended, but a telephone interview is acceptable. International applicants accepted; must apply through a recognized agency.

Benefits and Preemployment Training Free housing, free meals, willing to provide letters of recommendation, on-the-job training, willing to complete paperwork for educational credit, willing to act as a professional reference, opportunity to attend seminars/workshops, and travel reimbursement. Preemployment training is required and includes accident prevention and safety, first aid, CPR, interpersonal skills, leadership skills, with WSI, lifeguard training.

Contact Carol A. Sigoloff, Director, Camp Thunderbird for Boys, 941 Gardenview Office Parkway, St. Louis, Missouri 63141. Telephone: 314-567-3167. Fax: 314-567-7218. E-mail: tbirdcamp@primary.net. Contact by e-mail, fax, mail, or phone. Application deadline: continuous.

CAMP THUNDERBIRD FOR GIRLS

20758 COUNTY ROAD 9
BEMIDJI, MINNESOTA 56601

General Information Residential camp serving 150 girls from forty U.S. cities and five other countries. Established in 1970. 700-acre facility located 12 miles from Bemidji. Features: 7½ miles of sand beach shoreline; 700 pristine acres of property; extensive waterfront program and equipment; English riding program; gymnastic program; tennis courts.

Profile of Summer Employees Total number: 100; typical ages: 19–60. 10% men; 90% women; 5% minorities; 12% high school students; 60% college students; 1% retirees; 10% non-U.S. citizens; 1% local applicants. Nonsmokers preferred.

Employment Information Openings are from June 1 to August 21. Jobs available: ▶ 1 *arts and crafts specialist* with experience as an art teacher or art student preferred; (completion of junior year in college required); salary negotiable ▶ 2 *horseback specialists* with experience in English Hunt Seat specialty; junior year of college completed; CHA or HSA certification preferred, but will send to clinic for certification; salary negotiable ▶ 10 *kitchen personnel* (minimum age 19) with ability to assist with kitchen operations, food preparation, dishwashing, and cleanup; one year of college completed; salary negotiable ▶ 2 *nurses* with RN or LPN at $400 and up per week ▶ 2 *office personnel* (minimum age 19) with bookkeeping and computer knowledge; ability to handle camper/staff cash accounts; average or above-average typing skills; sophomore year of college completed; salary negotiable ▶ 1 *program director* with experience encompassing staff supervision and direct leadership of children in outdoor recreation/camp activities; college graduate; salary negotiable ▶ 1 *sailing instructor* with sailing and lifeguard certification; salary negotiable ▶ 6 *swimming instructors* with WSI, lifeguard, and CPR certification; teaching experience (preferred); salary negotiable ▶ 1 *trip director* with experience in diverse kinds of wilderness trips and equipment use; college graduate; salary negotiable ▶ 3 *unit directors* (minimum age 23) with experience encompassing staff supervision and direct leadership of children in outdoor recreation/camp activities; college graduate; salary negotiable ▶ 1 *waterfront director* with WSI, first aid, lifeguard, and CPR certification; college degree, and knowledge of various water sports; salary negotiable ▶ 10 *wilderness and trip leaders* (minimum age 21) with certifications in CPR, lifeguard, and advanced first aid (must be comfortable and confident living in the wilderness) at $1200–$1800 per season. Applicants must submit formal organization application, three personal references. An in-person interview is recommended, but a telephone interview is acceptable. International applicants accepted; must apply through a recognized agency.

Benefits and Preemployment Training Free housing, free meals, willing to provide letters of recommendation, on-the-job training, willing to complete paperwork for educational credit, willing to act as a professional reference, opportunity to attend seminars/workshops, and travel reimbursement. Preemployment training is required and includes accident prevention and safety, first aid, CPR, interpersonal skills, leadership skills, WSI, lifeguard training.

Contact Carol A. Sigoloff, Director, Camp Thunderbird for Girls, 941 Gardenview Office Parkway, St. Louis, Missouri 63141. Telephone: 314-567-3167. Fax: 314-567-7218. E-mail: tbirdcamp@primary.net. Contact by e-mail, fax, mail, or phone. Application deadline: continuous.

CYBERCAMPS–UNIVERSITY OF MINNESOTA

MINNEAPOLIS, MINNESOTA

See Cybercamps–University of Washington on page 335 for complete description.

DEEP PORTAGE CONSERVATION RESERVE

2197 NATURE CENTER DRIVE, NW
HACKENSACK, MINNESOTA 56452

General Information 6000-acre forest and conservation education center that conducts programs in environmental education. Established in 1973. 6,307-acre facility located 50 miles from Brainerd. Features: rolling, wooded glacial hills; 10 lakes; bogs; streams; large modern dormitory.
Profile of Summer Employees Total number: 16; typical ages: 18–25. 50% men; 50% women; 10% minorities; 10% high school students; 70% college students; 10% non-U.S. citizens.
Employment Information Openings are from June 5 to August 25. Jobs available: ▶ 10 *instructors/camp counselors* with college training in related fields at $175–$225 per week. Applicants must submit a letter of interest, resume, three personal references. A telephone interview is required. International applicants accepted; must obtain own visa, obtain own working papers.
Benefits and Preemployment Training Free housing, free meals, formal training, and on-the-job training.
Contact Dale Yerger, Executive Director, Deep Portage Conservation Reserve, 2197 Nature Center Drive, NW, Hackensack, Minnesota 56452. Telephone: 218-682-2325. Fax: 218-682-3121. E-mail: portage@uslink.net. World Wide Web: http://www.deep-portage.org. Contact by e-mail, fax, mail, phone, or through World Wide Web site. Application deadline: continuous.

FRIENDSHIP VENTURES/CAMP FRIENDSHIP

10509 108TH STREET, NW
ANNANDALE, MINNESOTA 55302

General Information Residential camp serving children and adults with developmental disabilities. Established in 1964. 115-acre facility located 60 miles from Minneapolis. Features: wooded setting; large waterfront; challenege course; cabins.
Profile of Summer Employees Total number: 150; typical ages: 16–25. 25% men; 75% women; 5% minorities; 15% high school students; 85% college students; 10% non-U.S. citizens; 20% local applicants.
Employment Information Openings are from May 29 to September 1. Year-round positions also offered. Jobs available: ▶ 5 *adventure/recreation specialists* with preference for current major in recreation, physical education, or adaptive physical recreation and leadership skills involving group activities at $125–$165 per week ▶ 2 *arts and crafts specialists* with preference for current major in therapeutic recreation, occupational therapy, or art education/therapy or experience planning and implementing arts and crafts activities/projects at $125–$165 per week ▶ 1 *camping specialist* with tent camping and outdoor experience and environmental education knowledge at $125–$165 per week ▶ 1 *canteen/camp store manager* with record-keeping skills at $125–$165 per week ▶ 60 *counselors* at $125–$165 per week ▶ 1 *dietary specialist* with experience in food service area with an emphasis on special diets at $125–$165 per week ▶ 2 *dining hall workers* experience working in food service or dining hall areas; at a negotiable salary ▶ 12 *junior counselors* (minimum age 16) with physical and emotional strength, mental alertness, creativity, flexibility, and high school student status (successful volunteer experience may be substituted for the age requirement) at $90–$100 per week ▶ 2 *laundry/housekeeping*

staff members at a negotiable salary ▶ 2 *music specialists* with preference for current major in music, music therapy, or special education and experience planning and implementing activities at $125–$165 per week ▶ 4 *nurses* with RN, LPN, or GN license or BSN degree; at a negotiable salary ▶ 2 *office support staff* with computer, typing, phone, and filing experience at $125–$165 per week ▶ 1 *outdoor specialist* with preference for current major in an environmental, outdoor, or education field at $125–$165 per week ▶ 1 *public relations assistant* with current major in journalism, photography, or related field and experience with a 35mm camera at $125–$165 per week ▶ 1 *waterfront director* with WSI and lifeguard certification at $150–$180 per week ▶ 4 *waterfront lifeguards* with WSI and lifeguard certification (preferred) at $125–$165 per week ▶ 3 *weekend counselors* with physical strength, mental alertness, and at least one year of college completed; at $150 per weekend. Applicants must submit formal organization application, 2 personal references or 2 letters of recommendation. An in-person interview is recommended, but a telephone interview is acceptable. International applicants accepted; must apply through a recognized agency.

Benefits and Preemployment Training Free housing, free meals, formal training, on-the-job training, willing to complete paperwork for educational credit, and scholarships available. Preemployment training is required and includes accident prevention and safety, first aid, CPR, interpersonal skills, leadership skills.

Contact Maria Schugel, Program Manager, Friendship Ventures/Camp Friendship, 10509 108th Street, NW, Annandale, Minnesota 55302. Telephone: 320-274-8376. Fax: 320-274-3238. E-mail: fv@friendshipventures.org. World Wide Web: http://www.friendshipventures.org. Contact by e-mail, fax, mail, or phone. Application deadline: continuous.

FRIENDSHIP VENTURES/EDEN WOOD CAMP

10509 108TH STREET, NW
ANNANDALE, MINNESOTA 55302

General Information Residential and day camp serving children and adults with developmental disabilities. Established in 1958. 12-acre facility located 15 miles from Minneapolis. Features: wooded setting; walking trails; cabins/dormitory; close to lakes area; challenge course.

Profile of Summer Employees Total number: 35; typical ages: 16–25. 25% men; 75% women; 5% minorities; 15% high school students; 85% college students; 10% non-U.S. citizens; 20% local applicants.

Employment Information Openings are from May 26 to September 1. Year-round positions also offered. Jobs available: ▶ 1 *arts and crafts specialist* with preference for current major in therapeutic recreation, occupational therapy, or art education/therapy or experience planning and implementing arts and crafts activities/projects at $165–$225 per week ▶ 30 *counselors* (minimum age 16) at $165–$225 per week ▶ 1 *creative movement/drama specialist* with experience in the performing arts field at $165–$200 per week ▶ 1 *dining hall staff worker* with experience in food service/dining hall area; at a negotiable salary ▶ 6 *junior counselors* (minimum age 16) with physical and emotional strength, mental alertness, creativity, flexibility, and high school student status (successful volunteer experience may be substituted for the age requirement) at $100 per week ▶ 2 *laundry/housekeeping staff members* (minimum age 18) at $165–$200 per week ▶ 2 *lifeguards* with WSI and lifeguard certification (preferred) at $165–$225 per week ▶ 1 *music specialist* with preference for major in music, music therapy, or special education and experience planning and implementing activities at $165–$200 per week ▶ 2 *nurses* with RN, LPN, GN license or BSN degree; at a negotiable salary ▶ 1 *office support staff* with computer, typing, phone, and filing experience at $165–$200 per week ▶ 1 *outdoor specialist* with preference for current major in environmental, outdoor, or education field at $165–$200 per week ▶ 1 *recreation specialist* with preference for current major in recreation, physical education, or adaptive physical recreation and leadership skills involving group activities at $165–$200 per week ▶ 6 *travel leaders* (minimum age 21) with leadership skills and valid driver's license at $20–$35 per day ▶ 10 *weekend counselors* with physical strength, mental alertness, and at least one year of college completed at $165 to $200 per weekend. Applicants must submit formal organization application, two personal references, letter of recommendation. An in-person interview is recommended, but a telephone interview is acceptable. International applicants accepted; must apply through a recognized agency.

Benefits and Preemployment Training Free housing, free meals, formal training, willing to provide letters of recommendation, on-the-job training, willing to complete paperwork for educational credit, willing to act as a professional reference, and academic scholarship. Preemployment training is required and includes accident prevention and safety, first aid, CPR, interpersonal skills, leadership skills.

Contact Maria Schugel, Program Manager, Friendship Ventures/Eden Wood Camp, 10509 108th Street, NW, Annandale, Minnesota 55302. Telephone: 952-852-0101. Fax: 952-852-0123. E-mail: jobs@friendshipventures.org. World Wide Web: http://www.friendshipventures.org. Contact by e-mail, fax, mail, phone, or through World Wide Web site. Application deadline: continuous.

GRAND VIEW LODGE GOLF AND TENNIS CLUB

23521 NOKOMIS AVENUE
NISSWA, MINNESOTA 56468

General Information Resort that caters to families and business conventions and operates public golf courses in Minnesota. Established in 1914. 1,300-acre facility located 150 miles from Minneapolis. Features: tennis courts; golf; beautiful lake for swimming, fishing, and waterskiing; wooded areas; indoor pool.

Profile of Summer Employees Total number: 500; typical ages: 16–25. 45% men; 55% women; 10% minorities; 20% high school students; 50% college students; 10% retirees; 20% non-U.S. citizens; 20% local applicants.

Employment Information Openings are from April 15 to November 1. Jobs available: ▶ 5 *bartenders* (minimum age 18) with experience in the field at $175–$220 per week ▶ 5 *beach staff members* (minimum age 16) with knowledge of boats and motors at $190–$240 per week ▶ 3 *children's program instructors* (minimum age 17) with CPR certification at $190–$240 per week ▶ 25 *dining room wait staff* (minimum age 18) at $200–$260 per week ▶ 10 *golf course maintenance staff* with knowledge of equipment at $225–$280 per week ▶ 5 *golf shop staff* with golf background and merchandise skills at $225–$280 per week ▶ 15 *housekeepers* (minimum age 15) at $210–$260 per week ▶ 3 *skilled front desk staff* (minimum age 18) at $185–$240 per week. Applicants must submit resume. An in-person interview is recommended, but a telephone interview is acceptable. International applicants accepted; must obtain own visa.

Benefits and Preemployment Training Housing at a cost, meals at a cost, formal training, willing to provide letters of recommendation, on-the-job training, and willing to complete paperwork for educational credit. Preemployment training is required and includes accident prevention and safety, leadership skills.

Contact Jan Kummet, Human Resources, Grand View Lodge Golf and Tennis Club, 23521 Nokomis Avenue, Nisswa, Minnesota 56468. Telephone: 218-963-2234. Fax: 218-963-0261. E-mail: work@grandviewlodge.com. World Wide Web: http://www.grandviewlodge.com. Contact by e-mail, fax, mail, phone, or through World Wide Web site. Application deadline: continuous.

LAKE HUBERT TENNIS CAMP

BOX 1308
LAKE HUBERT, MINNESOTA 56459

General Information Seven-day tennis camps featuring five hours of court time instruction daily for all skill levels; 12 courts for 36 campers. Established in 1973. 750-acre facility located 15 miles from Brainerd. Features: 12 outdoor courts; true camp setting; waterfront.

Profile of Summer Employees Total number: 15; typical ages: 19–45. 50% men; 50% women; 75% college students. Nonsmokers required.

Employment Information Openings are from June 6 to August 28. Jobs available: ▶ 6 *cabin* *counselors* (minimum age 19) at $175–$200 per week ▶ 10 *tennis instructors* (minimum age 19) with experience in the field at $200–$350 per week ▶ 2 *waterfront staff* (minimum age 21) with lifeguard training at $200–$250 per week. Applicants must submit formal organization application, three personal references. An in-person interview is recommended, but a telephone interview is acceptable. International applicants accepted; must apply through a recognized agency.

Benefits and Preemployment Training Free housing, free meals, formal training, willing to provide letters of recommendation, and travel reimbursement.

Contact Sam Cote, Director, Lake Hubert Tennis Camp, 10179 Crosstown Circle, Eden Prairie, Minnesota 55344. Telephone: 800-242-1909. Fax: 952-922-7149. E-mail: home@lincoln-lakehubert.com. World Wide Web: http://www.lincoln-lakehubert.com. Contact by e-mail, mail, phone, or through World Wide Web site. Application deadline: continuous.

MENOGYN–YMCA WILDERNESS ADVENTURES

55 MENOGYN TRAIL
GRAND MARAIS, MINNESOTA 55604

General Information Wilderness camp specializing in canoeing, backpacking, and rock-climbing trips in wilderness areas of North America. Established in 1922. 80-acre facility located 180 miles from Duluth. Features: 2,000,000 acres of wilderness; freshwater lakes; mountain hiking; rustic wilderness base camp; rock climbing; boundary waters canoe area.

Profile of Summer Employees Total number: 56; typical ages: 20–35. 50% men; 50% women; 5% minorities; 90% college students; 5% non-U.S. citizens; 75% local applicants. Nonsmokers required.

Employment Information Openings are from June to August 30. Jobs available: ▶ 1 *cook* (minimum age 20) with experience in the field and references at $6–$9 per hour ▶ 3–120 *in-camp staff members* with CPR, first aid, and lifeguard training at $140–$203 per week ▶ 1 *nurse* with current Minnesota license at $1200–$2000 per season ▶ 24–36 *trail counselors* (minimum age 19) with CPR, first aid, and lifeguard training at $140–$189 per week. Applicants must submit a formal organization application, three personal references. An in-person interview is recommended, but a telephone interview is acceptable. International applicants accepted.

Benefits and Preemployment Training Free housing, free meals, formal training, willing to provide letters of recommendation, on-the-job training, willing to complete paperwork for educational credit, and willing to act as a professional reference. Preemployment training is required and includes accident prevention and safety, first aid, CPR, interpersonal skills, leadership skills.

Contact Paul Danicic, Camp Director, Menogyn–YMCA Wilderness Adventures, 4 West Rustic Lodge Avenue, Minneapolis, Minnesota 55409. Telephone: 612-821-2905. Fax: 612-823-2482. E-mail: info@campmenogyn.org. World Wide Web: http://www.campmenogyn.org. Contact by e-mail, fax, mail, phone, or through World Wide Web site. Application deadline: April 30.

NELSON'S RESORT

7632 NELSON ROAD
CRANE LAKE, MINNESOTA 55725

General Information Family resort with conventions in the fall. Established in 1931. 84-acre facility located 70 miles from Virginia. Features: freshwater lake; wooded setting; proximity to Voyageurs National Park; near Boundary Water Canoe Area; Canadian Border Waters.

Profile of Summer Employees Total number: 30; typical ages: 18–40. 44% men; 56% women; 25% college students; 2% retirees; 1% non-U.S. citizens; 6% local applicants.

Employment Information Openings are from May 1 to October 15. Jobs available: ▶ 1–2 *bartenders* at $800–$1000 per month ▶ 1 *bellperson* at $800–$900 per month ▶ 5 *cabin staff members* at $800–$900 per month ▶ 3 *dock attendants* at $800–$900 per month ▶ 3 *kitchen helpers* at $800–$900 per month ▶ 1 *store clerk* at $800–$900 per month ▶ 6 *waiters/waitresses* at $800–$900 per month. Applicants must submit a formal organization application.

Benefits and Preemployment Training Meals at a cost, free housing, willing to provide letters of recommendation, and on-the-job training.

Contact Jerry Pohlman, Co-owner, Nelson's Resort, 7632 Nelson Road, Crane Lake, Minnesota 55725. Telephone: 218-993-2295. Fax: 218-993-2242. E-mail: nelsons@citlink.net. World Wide Web: http://www.nelsonresort.com. Contact by e-mail, fax, mail, phone, or through World Wide Web site. Application deadline: continuous.

SINGING HILLS GIRL SCOUT CAMP AND CANNON VALLEY DAY CAMPS

49496 193RD AVENUE
WATERVILLE, MINNESOTA 56096

General Information Residential camp serving 88 girls (grades 4–12) weekly, and day camp serving 60–100 girls (grades 2–5) weekly; day camps held at several sites. 160-acre facility located 30 miles from Minneapolis/St. Paul. Features: rustic setting; clean and clear lake; wooded area.

Profile of Summer Employees Total number: 20; typical ages: 16–65. 100% women; 10% high school students; 70% college students; 10% retirees; 10% non-U.S. citizens; 90% local applicants.

Employment Information Openings are from June 4 to August 4. Jobs available: ▶ 2 *cooks* (minimum age 16) with experience in group cooking and menu planning at $1750 per season ▶ 12 *general counselors* (minimum age 18) with love of working with kids and love of the outdoors at $1500–$1700 per season ▶ 1 *health supervisor* (minimum age 18) CPR/first aid/ EMT or Registered Nurse/Physician or Nursing student at $1800–$2000 per season ▶ 1 *unit leader* (minimum age 20) with leadership skills at $1700 per season ▶ 1 *waterfront director* with lifeguard training at $1800 per season. Applicants must submit formal organization application, three personal references. An in-person interview is recommended, but a telephone interview is acceptable. International applicants accepted; must apply through a recognized agency.

Benefits and Preemployment Training Free housing, free meals, formal training, health insurance, and on-the-job training. Preemployment training is required and includes accident prevention and safety, first aid, CPR, interpersonal skills, leadership skills.

Contact Jennifer Tschida, Camp Director, Singing Hills Girl Scout Camp and Cannon Valley Day Camps, PO Box 61, Northfield, Minnesota 55057. Telephone: 507-645-6603. Fax: 507-645-6605. E-mail: jennifert@gsccv.org. World Wide Web: http://www.gsccv.org. Contact by e-mail, fax, mail, phone, or through World Wide Web site. Application deadline: continuous.

THE SOUTHWESTERN COMPANY, MINNESOTA

See The Southwestern Company on page 302 for complete description.

SPORTS INTERNATIONAL–VIKINGS

ST. PAUL, MINNESOTA

See Sports International, Inc. on page 147 for complete description.

STRAW HAT PLAYERS

CENTER FOR THE ARTS–MINNESOTA STATE UNIVERSITY MOORHEAD
MOORHEAD, MINNESOTA 56563

General Information Summer stock theater producing four shows in a nine-week season. Established in 1963. 20-acre facility located near Fargo, North Dakota. Features: 900-seat proscenium theater; 350-seat thrust theater; scene shops, costume shops, and dance studio; access to library, pool, athletic center; largest metropolitan area between Minneapolis and Seattle.

Profile of Summer Employees Total number: 60; typical ages: 22–50. 40% men; 60% women; 5% minorities; 10% high school students; 80% college students; 40% local applicants.

Employment Information Openings are from May 26 to July 26. Jobs available: ▶ 40 *acting company members* (minimum age 17) must be high school junior or senior (minimum) at

$100–$180 per week ▶ 3 *costume stitchers* at $100–$250 per week. Applicants must submit formal organization application, letter of interest, resume, videotape. An in-person interview is required. International applicants accepted; must obtain own visa, obtain own working papers, apply through a recognized agency.

Benefits and Preemployment Training Meals at a cost, free housing, formal training, on-the-job training, willing to complete paperwork for educational credit, and tuition assistance.

Contact Jim Bartruff, Director of Theater, Straw Hat Players, Minnesota State University Moorhead, Moorhead, Minnesota 56563. Telephone: 218-236-4616. Fax: 218-236-4612. E-mail: bartruff@mnstate.edu. World Wide Web: http://www.mnstate.edu. Contact by e-mail, fax, mail, or through World Wide Web site. Application deadline: April 15.

STUDENT CONSERVATION ASSOCIATION (SCA), MINNESOTA

See Student Conservation Association (SCA), New Hampshire on page 209 for complete description.

VALLEYFAIR FAMILY AMUSEMENT PARK

1 VALLEYFAIR DRIVE
SHAKOPEE, MINNESOTA 55379

General Information Family amusement park offering a variety of entertainment attractions. Established in 1976. 90-acre facility located 20 miles from Minneapolis/St. Paul. Features: 5 roller coasters; waterpark; adventure golf and go karts; Berenstain Bear Country; Imax theater; live entertainment.

Profile of Summer Employees Total number: 1,600; typical ages: 16–22. 50% men; 50% women; 10% minorities; 40% high school students; 45% college students; 1% retirees; 10% non-U.S. citizens; 4% local applicants.

Employment Information Openings are from May 1 to September 30. Jobs available: ▶ 30 *accounting clerks/tellers* (minimum age 18) ▶ 40 *admissions cashiers* (minimum age 18) ▶ 270 *food hosts/hostesses* (minimum age 16) at $6.95 per hour ▶ 140 *game attendants* (minimum age 16) at $6.95 per hour ▶ 30 *lifeguards* (minimum age 16) with Ellis and Associates certification (training provided) ▶ 90 *merchandise attendants* (minimum age 16) at $6.95 per hour ▶ 25 *park-service attendants* (minimum age 18) at $7.75 per hour ▶ 280 *ride hosts/hostesses* (minimum age 18) at $7.75 per hour ▶ 28 *security officers/EMT's* (minimum age 18) with Emergency Medical Technician certification for some positions ▶ 40 *ticket takers* (minimum age 16). Applicants must submit formal organization application. International applicants accepted; must obtain own visa, obtain own working papers, apply through a recognized agency.

Benefits and Preemployment Training Housing at a cost, willing to provide letters of recommendation, on-the-job training, willing to complete paperwork for educational credit, and willing to act as a professional reference. Preemployment training is required and includes accident prevention and safety, first aid, CPR, leadership skills, guest service training.

Contact Human Resources, Valleyfair Family Amusement Park. Telephone: 952-496-5359. Fax: 952-496-5267. E-mail: jobs@valleyfair.com. World Wide Web: http://www.valleyfair.com. Contact by e-mail, fax, mail, phone, or through World Wide Web site. Application deadline: applications open from January 1 until jobs are filled (preferred deadline, April 1).

WILDERNESS DANCE CAMP

9807 NICOLLET AVENUE SOUTH
BLOOMINGTON, MINNESOTA 55420

General Information Resident camp teaching; ballet, tap, jazz, modern, and musical theatre. Established in 1997. Located 1 mile from Bemidji. Features: wooded setting; freshwater lake; swimming pool; recreation center; dormitories.

Profile of Summer Employees Total number: 15; typical age: 21. 10% men; 90% women; 15%

minorities; 15% high school students; 25% college students; 15% retirees; 15% non-U.S. citizens; 15% local applicants. Nonsmokers required.

Employment Information Openings are from July 20 to August 17. Jobs available: ▶ 1–4 *camp nurse* (minimum age 22) nursing experience; additional knowledge of sports injuries; salary varies with qualifications ▶ 10–40 *counselors* (minimum age 19) interest in kids, enjoyment of dance at $100–$200 per week. Applicants must submit letter of interest, resume, academic transcripts, three personal references, three letters of recommendation, criminal background check. An in-person interview is recommended, but a telephone interview is acceptable. International applicants accepted; must obtain own visa, obtain own working papers, apply through a recognized agency.

Benefits and Preemployment Training Free housing, free meals, willing to provide letters of recommendation, willing to complete paperwork for educational credit, willing to act as a professional reference, and opportunity to attend seminars/workshops. Preemployment training is required and includes accident prevention and safety, first aid, CPR, interpersonal skills, leadership skills.

Contact Chandra Saign, Director, Wilderness Dance Camp. Telephone: 952-884-6009. E-mail: info@dancecamp.org. World Wide Web: http://www.dancecamp.org. Contact by e-mail, mail, or phone. Application deadline: continuous.

YMCA CAMP PEPIN

434 MAIN STREET
RED WING, MINNESOTA 55066

General Information Youth camp serving over 800 campers; specialty programs include riding camp, adventure camp, theater camp, and CIT and LIT training sessions. Established in 1935. 40-acre facility located 60 miles from Minneapolis. Features: freshwater lake; bluff setting; canoe trips; camping/hiking; rock climbing; ropes course.

Profile of Summer Employees Total number: 35; typical ages: 18–24. 45% men; 55% women; 15% minorities; 90% college students; 15% non-U.S. citizens; 20% local applicants. Nonsmokers preferred.

Employment Information Openings are from June 12 to August 14. Year-round positions also offered. Jobs available: ▶ 1 *CIT/LDP counselor* (minimum age 19) with experience in teen programming at $155–$185 per week ▶ *adventure director* (minimum age 21) with wilderness skills at $150–$185 per week ▶ 1 *arts and crafts instructor* (minimum age 19) at $155–$185 per week ▶ 1–5 *counselors* (minimum age 19) at $145–$175 per week ▶ *health director* (minimum age 21) with RN or EMT license at $195–$245 per week ▶ 1 *program director* (minimum age 21) with previous program experience at $195–$235 per week ▶ 1 *ropes/trips director* (minimum age 21) with previous ropes course work at $155–$175 per week ▶ 2 *unit leaders/senior counselors* (minimum age 21) at $155–$185 per week ▶ *waterfront director* (minimum age 21) with CPR, LGT, and WSI certifications at $160–$195 per week. Applicants must submit formal organization application, three personal references. An in-person interview is recommended, but a telephone interview is acceptable. International applicants accepted; must apply through a recognized agency.

Benefits and Preemployment Training Free housing, free meals, formal training, willing to provide letters of recommendation, on-the-job training, willing to complete paperwork for educational credit, willing to act as a professional reference, and opportunity to attend seminars/workshops. Preemployment training is required and includes accident prevention and safety, interpersonal skills, leadership skills.

Contact Clint Knox, Camp Director, YMCA Camp Pepin, 434 Main Street, Red Wing, Minnesota 55066. Telephone: 651-388-4724. Fax: 651-388-5340. E-mail: camppepin@hotmail.com. World Wide Web: http://www.redwingymca.org. Contact by e-mail, fax, mail, phone, or through World Wide Web site. Application deadline: April 15.

MISSISSIPPI

CAMP STANISLAUS

304 SOUTH BEACH BOULEVARD
BAY ST. LOUIS, MISSISSIPPI 39520

General Information Camp Stanislaus is a traditional camp for boys with a carefully supervised and structured environment which enables a boy to succeed daily in a variety of recreational and learning pursuits. Established in 1928. 25-acre facility located 60 miles from New Orleans, Louisiana. Features: 1000 foot pier; white, sandy beaches; Gulf of Mexico; Jouron River; air conditioned dormitory; 3 tennis courts.

Profile of Summer Employees Total number: 65; typical ages: 16–75. 90% men; 10% women; 5% minorities; 15% high school students; 40% college students; 1% retirees; 1% non-U.S. citizens; 50% local applicants. Nonsmokers preferred.

Employment Information Openings are from May 15 to July 26. Jobs available: ▶ 1–2 *archery instructor* (minimum age 20) with leadership ability, self-motivation, and ability to instruct boys in the fundamentals of archery at $1300–$3000 per season ▶ *computer staff* (minimum age 18) Web design, e-mail, Pagemaker, Word, positive role model, leader, self-motivated at $1500–$2500 per season ▶ 1–28 *counselors* (minimum age 18) self-motivated leader and positive role model at $1300–$3000 per season ▶ 1–12 *counselors in training (CIT)* (minimum age 16) self-motivated leader and positive role model at $800–$1000 per season ▶ 1–6 *sailing instructors* (minimum age 16) self-motivated leader with ability to teach sailing on sunfish, catamarans, and harpoons at $700–$3000 per season ▶ 1–8 *skiing instructors* (minimum age 18) with ability to instruct water skiing, wake boarding, knee boarding; a self-motivated leader and role model at $1300–$3000 per season. Applicants must submit formal organization application, two personal references. An in-person interview is recommended, but a telephone interview is acceptable. International applicants accepted; must apply through a recognized agency.

Benefits and Preemployment Training Free housing, free meals, formal training, willing to provide letters of recommendation, on-the-job training, willing to complete paperwork for educational credit, willing to act as a professional reference, and access to weight room and other facilities including water skiing. Preemployment training is required and includes accident prevention and safety, first aid, CPR, interpersonal skills, leadership skills, lifeguard training, dealing with undesirable behaviors, sailing, skiing, communication.

Contact Michael J. Reso, Camp Director, Camp Stanislaus. Telephone: 228-467-9057 Ext. 235. Fax: 228-466-2972. E-mail: mreso@ststan.com. World Wide Web: http://www.campstanislaus.com. Contact by e-mail, fax, mail, or phone. Application deadline: continuous.

MARINE LIFE OCEANARIUM

JOSEPH T. JONES PARK, HIGHWAY 90
GULFPORT, MISSISSIPPI 39501

General Information Oceanarium with dolphins, sea lions, sharks, rays, giant sea turtles, exotic birds, and more. Established in 1956. 25-acre facility located 60 miles from New Orleans, Louisiana. Features: location on Gulf Coast; diving; boating; gift shop; snack bar; gravity ship.

Profile of Summer Employees Total number: 50; typical ages: 15–20. 66% men; 33% women; 40% high school students; 10% college students; 50% local applicants.

Employment Information Openings are from May 20 to September 20. Jobs available: ▶ *operations department staff, divers* (minimum age 18) with scuba certification at $150 per week ▶ 2–5 *operations department staff, fish sellers* (minimum age 15) at $150 per week. Applicants

must submit a formal organization application, letter of interest. An in-person interview is recommended, but a telephone interview is acceptable.
Benefits and Preemployment Training Formal training, possible full-time employment, willing to provide letters of recommendation, names of contacts, on-the-job training, willing to complete paperwork for educational credit, and willing to act as a professional reference.
Contact Jeffrey Siegel, Operations Manager/Education Director, Marine Life Oceanarium, PO Box 4078, Gulfport, Mississippi 39502. Fax: 228-863-3673. E-mail: jefdolfin@aol.com. World Wide Web: http://www.dolphinsrus.com. Contact by e-mail, mail, or through World Wide Web site. Application deadline: continuous.

THE SOUTHWESTERN COMPANY, MISSISSIPPI

See The Southwestern Company on page 302 for complete description.

STUDENT CONSERVATION ASSOCIATION (SCA), MISSISSIPPI

See Student Conservation Association (SCA), New Hampshire on page 209 for complete description.

MISSOURI

CAMP SABRA

ROCKY MOUNT, MISSOURI 65072

General Information Residential coed summer camping facility of St. Louis Jewish Community Center serving boys, girls, and teens entering grades 3-10 with complete waterfront and land activity program. Established in 1938. 960-acre facility located 10 miles from Eldon. Features: 3½ miles of private shoreline; large fleet of ski and sailboats; 12 miles of horseback riding trails; 3 lighted tennis courts; summer theater; 960 tree-shaded acres.
Profile of Summer Employees Total number: 130; typical ages: 18–22. 50% men; 50% women; 20% high school students; 75% college students; 10% non-U.S. citizens; 5% local applicants. Nonsmokers preferred.
Employment Information Openings are from June 2 to August 4. Jobs available: ▶ 10–20 *counselors* (minimum age 17) with experience preferred at $1000 and up per season ▶ 2 *female unit head programmers* (minimum age 21) with experience with 6th-8th grade children and supervision at $2000 per season (additional salary for experience) ▶ *ropes course director* (minimum age 21) at $2500 per season ▶ 4–5 *ropes course specialists* (minimum age 17) with experience with climbing tower, low ropes courses, and high ropes courses at $1000 and up per season ▶ 20–30 *specialists* (minimum age 17) with LGT for waterfront staff and experience in specialty required at $1000 and up per season. Applicants must submit formal organization application, three personal references. An in-person interview is recommended, but a telephone interview is acceptable. International applicants accepted; must apply through a recognized agency.
Benefits and Preemployment Training Free housing and free meals. Preemployment training is required and includes accident prevention and safety, first aid, CPR, interpersonal skills, leadership skills.
Contact Randy Comensky, Director, Camp Sabra, 16801 Baxter Road, Chesterfield, Missouri 63005. Telephone: 314-442-3426 Ext. 3426. Fax: 314-442-3404. E-mail: rcomensky@jccstl.org.

World Wide Web: http://www.campsabra.com. Contact by e-mail, fax, mail, phone, or through World Wide Web site. Application deadline: continuous.

CYBERCAMPS–WASHINGTON UNIVERSITY

ST. LOUIS, MISSOURI

See Cybercamps–University of Washington on page 335 for complete description.

THE SOUTHWESTERN COMPANY, MISSOURI

See The Southwestern Company on page 302 for complete description.

STIVERS STAFFING SERVICES–MISSOURI

See Stivers Staffing Services–Illinois on page 110 for complete description.

STUDENT CONSERVATION ASSOCIATION (SCA), MISSOURI

See Student Conservation Association (SCA), New Hampshire on page 209 for complete description.

TRAILS WILDERNESS SCHOOL

5 WHITE GATE LANE
ST. LOUIS, MISSOURI 63124-1905

General Information Wilderness adventure summer program for ages 12 and up; campers learn outdoor skills in WY, AK, Pacific NW, MO and Mexico; activities include backpacking, rock climbing, kayaking, canoeing, surfing, skiing and snowboarding. Established in 1994. Located 15 miles from Jackson, Wyoming. Features: base camp in Jackson Hole, WY; Grand Teton National Park; scenic views; wilderness setting; evening campfires; 10 minutes from airport.
Profile of Summer Employees Total number: 30; typical age: 29. 50% men; 50% women; 10% college students; 5% non-U.S. citizens; 10% local applicants. Nonsmokers required.
Employment Information Openings are from May 1 to August 31. Jobs available: ▶ 1–2 *drovers* (minimum age 21) clean driving record at $180–$250 per week ▶ 8–20 *instructors* (minimum age 25) backpacking, surfing, rock climbing at $180–$350 per week ▶ 1–2 *wizards* (minimum age 21) clean driving record at $180–$300 per week. Applicants must submit formal organization application, letter of interest, resume, three letters of recommendation, five personal references. International applicants accepted; must apply through a recognized agency.
Benefits and Preemployment Training Free housing, free meals, possible full-time employment, willing to provide letters of recommendation, names of contacts, willing to complete paperwork for educational credit, and willing to act as a professional reference. Preemployment training is required and includes accident prevention and safety, interpersonal skills, leadership skills, wilderness specific travel.
Contact Whigger Mullins, Director, Trails Wilderness School. Telephone: 314-994-9308. Fax: 314-994-9307. E-mail: info@trailsws.com. World Wide Web: http://www.trailsws.com. Contact by e-mail, mail, phone, or through World Wide Web site. Application deadline: continuous.

WORLDS OF FUN/OCEANS OF FUN

4545 WORLD OF FUN AVENUE
KANSAS CITY, MISSOURI 64161

General Information Amusement park. Established in 1973. 170-acre facility. Features: Mamba-roller coaster; 4 roller coasters; 5 restaurants; 6 live entertainment shows; water rides; rip cord.
Profile of Summer Employees Total number: 2,000; typical age: 14. 40% men; 60% women; 60% high school students; 25% college students; 15% retirees.
Employment Information Openings are from February 28 to October 31. Spring break posi-

tions also offered. Jobs available: ▶ 400–450 *food operations staff* (minimum age 14) at $6 to $8 per hour plus bonus ▶ 125–175 *games staff* (minimum age 14) at $6 to $8 per hour plus bonus ▶ 25–50 *grounds personnel* (minimum age 15) at $6 to $8 per hour plus bonus ▶ *lifeguards* (minimum age 16) at $6 to $8 per hour plus bonus ▶ 125–175 *merchandise staff* (minimum age 14) at $6 to $8 per hour plus bonus ▶ 300–350 *ride operations staff* (minimum age 16) at $6 to $8 per hour plus bonus ▶ *ticket sellers* (minimum age 16) at $6 to $8 per hour plus bonus. Applicants must submit a formal organization application, three personal references, resume for internships. An in-person interview is required.

Benefits and Preemployment Training On-the-job training and discounted meals, housing allowance.

Contact Brent A. Barr, Employment Manager, Worlds of Fun/Oceans of Fun. Telephone: 816-454-4545. Fax: 816-303-5012. E-mail: wofhr@worldsoffun.com. World Wide Web: http://www.worldsoffun.com. Contact by fax, mail, phone, or through World Wide Web site. Application deadline: continuous.

MONTANA

A CHRISTIAN MINISTRY IN THE NATIONAL PARKS–MONTANA

See A Christian Ministry in the National Parks–Maine on page 122 for complete description.

BEST WESTERN BUCKS T-4 LODGE OF BIG SKY

PO BOX 160279
BIG SKY, MONTANA 59716

General Information 74-unit Best Western Lodge serving skiers, outdoor enthusiasts, and visitors to Yellowstone National Park. Established in 1972. 20-acre facility located 40 miles from Bozeman. Features: Yellowstone National Park; Big Sky Resort; Gallatin River; mountain setting; whitewater rafting; horseback riding.

Profile of Summer Employees Total number: 60; typical ages: 19–25. 50% men; 50% women; 10% minorities; 5% high school students; 20% college students; 5% retirees; 60% non-U.S. citizens; 20% local applicants.

Employment Information Openings are from May 21 to November 1. Year-round positions also offered. Jobs available: ▶ 10 *cooks* at $5–$8 per hour ▶ 8 *dishwashers* at $6 per hour ▶ 5 *front desk staff* with computer and typing skills at $7–$10 per hour ▶ 10 *housekeeping staff* at $6–$7 per hour ▶ 25 *waitstaff* at $5 per hour. Applicants must submit formal organization application. An in-person interview is recommended, but a telephone interview is acceptable. International applicants accepted; must obtain own visa, obtain own working papers, apply through a recognized agency.

Benefits and Preemployment Training Housing at a cost, meals at a cost, possible full-time employment, willing to provide letters of recommendation, on-the-job training, and willing to act as a professional reference.

Contact Jayne Menzel, Hotel Manager, Best Western Bucks T-4 Lodge of Big Sky, PO Box 160279, Big Sky, Montana 59716. Telephone: 406-995-4111. Fax: 406-995-2191. E-mail: buckst4@mcn.net. World Wide Web: http://www.buckst4.com. Contact by e-mail, mail, phone, or through World Wide Web site. Application deadline: continuous.

BIG SKY RESORT
PO BOX 160001
BIG SKY, MONTANA 59716

General Information Winter and summer resort attracting both families and conventions. Established in 1976. 10,000-acre facility located 45 miles from Bozeman. Features: full-service resort facilities; Rocky Mountain setting; golf course.

Profile of Summer Employees Total number: 400; typical ages: 19–27. 50% men; 50% women; 5% minorities; 5% high school students; 40% college students; 20% non-U.S. citizens; 30% local applicants.

Employment Information Openings are from June 1 to October 7. Year-round positions also offered. Jobs available: ▶ *bartender* (minimum age 18) with previous bartending experience ▶ 5–10 *bell porters* (minimum age 18) with good customer service skills at $5.15 per hour plus tips ▶ 5–10 *bussers* (minimum age 18) at $5.55 per hour plus tips ▶ *concierge staff* (minimum age 18) with strong customer service skills at $6.75 per hour ▶ 10–20 *cooks* (minimum age 18) with cooking experience preferred at $7.50–$10 per hour ▶ *dishwashers* (minimum age 18) at $7 per hour ▶ 10–20 *food and beverage positions* (minimum age 18) ▶ 5–10 *front desk personnel* (minimum age 18) with good customer service skills at $7.50 per hour ▶ *golf pro-shop staff/starters* (minimum age 18) ▶ *hosts/hostesses* (minimum age 18) at $6 per hour ▶ 10–20 *housekeepers* (minimum age 18) ▶ 3 *housekeeping dispatchers* (minimum age 18) at $7 per hour ▶ *laundry staff* (minimum age 18) at $7 per hour ▶ *public area/janitorial attendants* (minimum age 18) at $7 per hour ▶ 5–10 *retail sales personnel* (minimum age 18) retail experience (preferred) at $6.75 per hour ▶ *room inspectors* (minimum age 18) with supervisory skills and an eye for detail at $8.15 per hour ▶ *ticket sales/lift operators (winter season)* (minimum age 18) ▶ 20–30 *waitstaff* (minimum age 18) with food service experience required at $5.15 per hour plus tips. Applicants must submit formal organization application, two letters of recommendation. A telephone interview is required. International applicants accepted; must apply through a recognized agency.

Benefits and Preemployment Training Housing at a cost, meals at a cost, possible full-time employment, on-the-job training, and lodging discounts for family. Preemployment training is required and includes accident prevention and safety.

Contact Velvet Williams, Human Resources, Big Sky Resort, c/o Human Resources, PO Box 160001, Big Sky, Montana 59716. Telephone: 406-995-5812. Fax: 406-995-5001. E-mail: vwilliams@bigskyresort.com. World Wide Web: http://www.bigskyresort.com. Contact by e-mail, fax, mail, phone, or through World Wide Web site. Application deadline: continuous.

CHRISTIKON
1108 24TH STREET WEST
BILLINGS, MONTANA 59102-3810

General Information Serving all on behalf of area ELCA Lutherans. Christikon offers residential, backpack and Creation Care programs in the Rocky Mountains near Yellowstone National Park. Established in 1951. 67-acre facility. Features: mountain wilderness setting.

Profile of Summer Employees Total number: 32; typical ages: 19–29. 50% men; 50% women; 4% minorities; 85% college students; 20% local applicants. Nonsmokers preferred.

Employment Information Openings are from June 1 to August 15. Jobs available: ▶ 21 *counselors* (minimum age 19) at $1850 per season ▶ 2 *forestry stewards* (minimum age 19) at $1850 per season ▶ 1 *head cook* (minimum age 19) at $1850 per season ▶ 1 *health care manager* (minimum age 19) at $1850 per season ▶ 1 *maintenance supervisor* (minimum age 21) at $1850 per season ▶ 1 *secretary* (minimum age 19) at $1850 per season ▶ 1 *trails room coordinator* (minimum age 19) at $1850 per season. Applicants must submit a formal organization application, three personal references. An in-person interview is recommended, but a telephone interview is acceptable.

Benefits and Preemployment Training Free housing, free meals, formal training, health insurance, willing to provide letters of recommendation, on-the-job training, willing to complete paperwork for educational credit, and willing to act as a professional reference. Preemployment training is required and includes accident prevention and safety, first aid, CPR, interpersonal skills, leadership skills, program development skills.

Contact Bob Quam, Pastor/Director, Christikon. Telephone: 406-656-1969. Fax: 406-656-1969. E-mail: christikon@aol.com. World Wide Web: http://www.christikon.org. Contact by e-mail, mail, phone, or through World Wide Web site. Application deadline: continuous.

LAZY K BAR RANCH
PO BOX 1550
BIG TIMBER, MONTANA 59011

General Information One-hundred-seventeen-year-old operating cattle and horse ranch that has welcomed selected guests for 81 summers. Established in 1887. 22,000-acre facility located 107 miles from Billings-Bozeman. Features: river; hot tub; mountains; lakes; timber; seclusion.

Profile of Summer Employees Total number: 15–18; typical ages: 16–25. 40% men; 60% women; 1% minorities; 45% high school students; 40% college students; 5% retirees; 5% non-U.S. citizens; 5% local applicants. Nonsmokers preferred.

Employment Information Openings are from June 10 to September 10. Jobs available: ▶ 1 *children's wrangler (female)* with extensive childcare experience and horse expertise at $600 per month ▶ 1 *chore person* (minimum age 16) with experience with milk cows at $550 per month ▶ 1 *dishwasher* (minimum age 17) at $550 per month ▶ 1 *head cook* (minimum age 20) with ability to cook for 40-45 people and experience in the field at $1500–$2000 per month ▶ 3 *housekeepers/laundry workers* (minimum age 16) with housekeeping and laundry experience at $550 per month ▶ 1 *second cook/baker* (minimum age 18) with baking experience at $650–$800 per month ▶ 1 *split-shift worker* (minimum age 20) with experience in cooking, baking, cleaning, waiting tables, and laundry at $575 per month ▶ 1 *storekeeper* (minimum age 18) with attention to detail at $540 per month ▶ 3 *waiters/waitresses* (minimum age 16) with serving experience at $550 per month ▶ 1 *winter caretaker* with desire for solitude and experience with chainsaws and other tools (position available from September 12 to June 12) at $500 per month ▶ 3 *wranglers* (minimum age 17) with extensive experience in the field at $600 per month. Applicants must submit formal organization application, resume, three letters of recommendation, photo. An in-person interview is recommended, but a telephone interview is acceptable. International applicants accepted; must obtain own visa, obtain own working papers, apply through a recognized agency.

Benefits and Preemployment Training Free housing, free meals, willing to provide letters of recommendation, on-the-job training, willing to complete paperwork for educational credit, and willing to act as a professional reference.

Contact Carol Kirby, Partner, Lazy K Bar Ranch, Box 1181, Big Timber, Montana 59011. Telephone: 406-932-4449. Fax: 406-932-4844. E-mail: kirby@mcn.net. World Wide Web: http://www.lazykbar.net. Contact by e-mail, mail, or through World Wide Web site. Application deadline: May 30.

THE RESORT AT GLACIER, ST. MARY LODGE
GLACIER NATIONAL PARK
ST. MARY, MONTANA 59417

General Information One of Montana's noted full-service high country resorts. Established in 1932. 100-acre facility located 90 miles from Kalispell. Features: mountain setting; updated rustic physical setting; small town atmosphere; 900 miles of hiking trails; exceptional staff.

Profile of Summer Employees Total number: 180; typical ages: 19–24. 40% men; 60% women; 2% minorities; 3% high school students; 80% college students; 3% retirees; 2% non-U.S. citizens; 10% local applicants. Nonsmokers preferred.

Employment Information Openings are from May 1 to October 15. Jobs available: ▶ 4 *accounting/secretarial staff members* with experience in the field at $996 per month ▶ 6 *bartenders/cocktail servers* with experience at $918 per month ▶ 5 *clerical staff members* at $996 per month ▶ 11 *deli cooks* at $996 per month ▶ 14 *dishwashing/kitchen personnel* at $996 per month ▶ 4 *front desk clerks* at $996 per month ▶ 5 *gas station attendants* at $996 per month ▶ 10 *gift shop clerks* with experience at $996 per month ▶ 6 *hosts/buspersons* at $918 per month ▶ 15 *housekeepers* at $996 per month ▶ 10 *maintenance personnel* at $996 per month ▶ 12 *pantry/fry cooks* with experience at $996 per month ▶ 4 *pizza parlor staff members* at $996 per month ▶ 3 *sporting-goods clerks* at $996 per month ▶ 9 *supermarket staff members* at $996 per month ▶ 26 *waiters/waitresses* with experience at $893 per month. Applicants must submit formal organization application, three personal references. An in-person interview is recommended, but a telephone interview is acceptable. International applicants accepted; must obtain own visa, obtain own working papers, apply through a recognized agency.

Benefits and Preemployment Training Housing at a cost, meals at a cost, on-the-job training, willing to complete paperwork for educational credit, willing to act as a professional reference, and employee discounts. Preemployment training is required and includes accident prevention and safety, interpersonal skills, leadership skills.

Contact Rocky Black, Resort Manager, The Resort at Glacier, St. Mary Lodge, PO Box 1808, Sun Valley, Idaho 83353. Telephone: 208-726-6279. Fax: 208-726-6282. E-mail: jobs@glcpark.com. World Wide Web: http://www.glcpark.com. Contact by e-mail, fax, mail, phone, or through World Wide Web site. Application deadline: continuous.

63 RANCH
PO BOX 979
LIVINGSTON, MONTANA 59047

General Information Working cattle and dude ranch operating from June through September with capacity for 30 guests. Ranch specializes in teaching horseback riding on all levels. Established in 1929. 2,000-acre facility located 50 miles from Bozeman. Features: Gallatin National Forest; Absaroka—Bear Tooth Wilderness; Yellowstone National Park; Yellowstone River; 5 mountain ranges; where the mountains meet the prairie.

Profile of Summer Employees Total number: 20; typical ages: 18–70. 47% men; 53% women; 5% high school students; 20% college students; 45% retirees; 10% local applicants. Nonsmokers required.

Employment Information Openings are from June 1 to September 15. Jobs available: ▶ 6–8 *cabin cleaners, dishwashers, and dining room servers* (minimum age 18) with first aid and CPR certifications at $800–$1000 per month ▶ 1 *head cook* (minimum age 18) with health certificate, first aid, CPR, and ability to run a kitchen and cook for 50 people at $1700–$2200 per month ▶ 1 *kitchen helper* (minimum age 18) with first aid, CPR, and health certificate at $800 per month ▶ 1 *second cook* (minimum age 18) with first aid, CPR, health certificate, and experience at $1000–$1500 per month. Applicants must submit a formal organization application, letter of interest, three work references with phone numbers. An in-person interview is recommended, but a telephone interview is acceptable. International applicants accepted.

Benefits and Preemployment Training Free housing, free meals, willing to provide letters of recommendation, on-the-job training, and opportunity to attend seminars/workshops. Preemployment training is required and includes accident prevention and safety, first aid, CPR, job skills.

Contact Sandra C. Cahill, President, 63 Ranch, PO Box 979-P, Livingston, Montana 59047. Telephone: 406-222-0570. Fax: 406-222-9446. E-mail: sixty3ranch@mcn.net. World Wide Web: http://www.63ranch.com. Contact by e-mail, fax, mail, phone, or through World Wide Web site. Application deadline: continuous.

THE SOUTHWESTERN COMPANY, MONTANA

See The Southwestern Company on page 302 for complete description.

STUDENT CONSERVATION ASSOCIATION (SCA), MONTANA

See Student Conservation Association (SCA), New Hampshire on page 209 for complete description.

SWEET GRASS RANCH

460 REIN LANE
BIG TIMBER, MONTANA 59011

General Information Working cattle ranch that accepts 20 guests to live ranch life. Established in 1965. 20,000-acre facility located 120 miles from Billings. Features: mountains; stream for fishing; horseback riding; working ranch experience; guests from around the world.

Profile of Summer Employees Total number: 10; typical ages: 20–30. 50% men; 50% women; 100% college students; 25% local applicants. Nonsmokers preferred.

Employment Information Openings are from June 1 to September 10. Jobs available: ▶ 2 *cabin staff members* (minimum age 19) with organizational and interpersonal skills, and attention to cleanliness and detail at $850 per month plus room, board, and tips ▶ 2 *cooks* (minimum age 19) with group cooking experience and love of cooking; experience or training as a baker/cook; attention to detail and ability to work well with others at $1000-$1500 per month plus room, board, and tips ▶ 1 *swingshift worker* (minimum age 19) with organizational and interpersonal skills; attention to cleanliness and detail; experience with group cooking; experience or training as a baker/cook; and ability to work well with others at $850 per month, plus room, board, and tips. Applicants must submit a formal organization application, resume, personal reference, two letters of recommendation. A telephone interview is required. International applicants accepted; must obtain own visa, obtain own working papers.

Benefits and Preemployment Training Free housing, free meals, willing to provide letters of recommendation, on-the-job training, willing to complete paperwork for educational credit, and willing to act as a professional reference.

Contact Shelly Carroccia, Owner, Sweet Grass Ranch. Telephone: 406-537-4477. Fax: 406-537-4477. E-mail: sweetgrass@mcn.net. World Wide Web: http://www.sweetgrassranch.com. Contact by e-mail, mail, or phone. Application deadline: April 30.

NEBRASKA

CALVIN CREST CAMP, RETREAT, AND CONFERENCE CENTER

2870 COUNTY ROAD 13
FREMONT, NEBRASKA 68025

General Information Church-affiliated camp and conference/retreat facility serving approximately 800 campers annually. Established in 1958. 255-acre facility located 5 miles from Fremont. Features: swimming pool; low ropes challenge course; tennis court; frisbee golf course.

Profile of Summer Employees Total number: 30; typical ages: 16–21. 50% men; 50% women; 20% high school students; 50% college students; 30% retirees; 80% local applicants. Nonsmokers preferred.

Employment Information Openings are from June 1 to August 15. Jobs available: ▶ 14 *core counselors* (minimum age 19) at $1040 per season ▶ 2–4 *food service staff members* (minimum age 16) at $5.40–$6.25 per hour ▶ 1–2 *housekeeping staff members* (minimum age 16) at

$5.40–$6 per hour ▶ 3 *lifeguards* (minimum age 18) with Red Cross lifeguard training at $130–$150 per week ▶ 2 *wranglers* (minimum age 19) with wrangler certification at $900 per season. Applicants must submit three personal references, two letters of recommendation. An in-person interview is recommended, but a telephone interview is acceptable.
Benefits and Preemployment Training Free housing, free meals, willing to provide letters of recommendation, on-the-job training, willing to complete paperwork for educational credit, and willing to act as a professional reference. Preemployment training is required and includes accident prevention and safety, first aid, CPR, interpersonal skills, leadership skills.
Contact Lynne Morton, Program Director, Calvin Crest Camp, Retreat, and Conference Center, 2870 County Road 13, Fremont, Nebraska 68025. Telephone: 402-628-6455. Fax: 402-628-8255. E-mail: calvin_crest@alltel.net. World Wide Web: http://www.calvincrest.org. Contact by e-mail, fax, mail, or phone. Application deadline: continuous.

THE SOUTHWESTERN COMPANY, NEBRASKA

See The Southwestern Company on page 302 for complete description.

STUDENT CONSERVATION ASSOCIATION (SCA), NEBRASKA

See Student Conservation Association (SCA), New Hampshire on page 209 for complete description.

NEVADA

CAMP WASIU II

605 WASHINGTON STREET
RENO, NEVADA 89503

General Information Resident camp of the Girl Scouts of the Sierra Nevada. Established in 1912. 40-acre facility. Features: wooded Sierra Nevada mountains; platform tents; pool; canoeing; horseback riding; dining hall.
Profile of Summer Employees Total number: 40; typical ages: 18–30. 100% women; 5% minorities; 80% college students; 10% non-U.S. citizens; 30% local applicants.
Employment Information Openings are from January 1 to June 1. Jobs available: ▶ 1 *assistant cook* (minimum age 18) some kitchen experience and organization at $60–$70 per day ▶ 1 *business manager* (minimum age 21) with leadership skills, business procedures, valid California or Nevada driver's license at $40–$50 per day ▶ 1 *canoe instructor* (minimum age 18) with experience working with children, prior canoeing experience, canoeing certificate at $35–$40 per day ▶ 1 *counselor-in-training director* (minimum age 21) with leadership skills, supervisory experience, prior camp experience, experience working with children, communication skills at $40 per day ▶ 1 *environmental education/archery instructor* (minimum age 18) with experience working with children, communication and organization skills at $35 per day ▶ 1 *head caretaker* (minimum age 21) with experience in plumbing, electrical, carpentry, vehicle maintenance, pool maintenance at $80–$90 per day ▶ 1 *head cook* (minimum age 21) kitchen supervision menu prep, food handlers certificate, prep for 100 or more people at $80–$90 per day ▶ 1 *health supervisor* (minimum age 21) with California state license as a physician or registered nurse, communication skills at $80–$90 per day ▶ 3 *lifeguards* (minimum age 18) with teamwork skills, American Red Cross Lifeguard Training, first aid and CPR certification at $35–$45 per

day ▶ 1 *maintenance assistant* (minimum age 18) with valid driver's license, must be hard-working individual at $35–$40 per day ▶ 1 *program director* (minimum age 21) with camp experience, leadership skills, California or Nevada driver's license, communication skills at $40–$50 per day ▶ 15 *unit counselors* (minimum age 18) with experience working with children at $30–$40 per day ▶ 6 *unit leaders* (minimum age 21) with leadership skills, supervisory experience at $35–$45 per day ▶ 1 *waterfront director* (minimum age 21) with lifeguarding and supervisory experience, Red Cross Advanced Lifeguard Training, first aid and CPR certification at $40–$50 per day. Applicants must submit formal organization application, three personal references. An in-person interview is recommended, but a telephone interview is acceptable. International applicants accepted; must apply through a recognized agency.

Benefits and Preemployment Training Free housing, free meals, health insurance, willing to provide letters of recommendation, on-the-job training, willing to complete paperwork for educational credit, and willing to act as a professional reference. Preemployment training is required and includes accident prevention and safety, interpersonal skills, leadership skills.

Contact Frances Brown, Camp Director, Camp Wasiu II, 605 Washington Street, Reno, Nevada 89503. Telephone: 775-322-0642. Fax: 775-322-0701. E-mail: fbrown@gssn.org. World Wide Web: http://www.gssn.org. Contact by e-mail, fax, mail, phone, or through World Wide Web site. Application deadline: continuous.

THE SOUTHWESTERN COMPANY, NEVADA

See The Southwestern Company on page 302 for complete description.

STUDENT CONSERVATION ASSOCIATION (SCA), NEVADA

See Student Conservation Association (SCA), New Hampshire on page 209 for complete description.

NEW HAMPSHIRE

AMERICAN YOUTH FOUNDATION–CAMP MERROWVISTA

147 CANAAN ROAD
CENTER TUFTONBORO, NEW HAMPSHIRE 03816

General Information Coed residential program for students ages 8–16. The focus is on leadership development and includes general program activities for students ages 8–12 and extended backpacking, canoeing, and cycling for students ages 13–16. Established in 1925. 600-acre facility located 140 miles from Boston, Massachusetts. Features: freshwater lake; beautiful mountains; trails leave right from camp into mountains; rustic, wooded setting.

Profile of Summer Employees Total number: 85; typical ages: 18–65. 50% men; 50% women; 2% minorities; 5% high school students; 60% college students; 3% non-U.S. citizens. Nonsmokers required.

Employment Information Openings are from June 15 to August 23. Winter break and year-round positions also offered. Jobs available: ▶ 1 *arts and crafts coordinator* (minimum age 18, 21 preferred) with crafts knowledge at $1800–$2000 per season ▶ 1 *bike mechanic* (minimum age 18, 21 preferred) with experience repairing and assembling touring bicycles, instruction of touring road safety, and bike maintenance at $2000–$2500 per season ▶ 1–4 *kitchen staff* *members* (minimum age 18, 21 preferred) with desire to pursue culinary arts as a career at $1200–$2500 per season ▶ 1 *naturalist* (minimum 18, 21 preferred) with experience teaching environmental activities; live animal experience preferred at $1200–$1800 per season ▶ 1 *nurse* (minimum age 21) with RN eligibility for New Hampshire license at $400–$550 per week ▶ 1 *office staff member* (minimum age 18, 21 preferred) with computer skills at $1800–$2200 per season ▶ 1 *outcamping equipment coordinator* (minimum age 18, 21 preferred) with ability to perform repair, inventory, check-out/check-in of backpacking and canoeing equipment; some driving of passenger vans required at $1800–$2000 per season ▶ 1 *outcamping food coordinator* (minimum age 18, 21 preferred) with an interest in outdoor education at $1800–$2000 per season ▶ *program directors* (minimum age 21) with supervisory experience at $3000–$4000 per season ▶ 1–3 *sailing instructors* (minimum age 18) with experience sailing Laser I and Laser II boats and lifeguard certification at $1800–$2000 per season ▶ 12 *trip leaders* (minimum age 21) with experience leading trips, WFR, lifeguard, and CPR/first aid training preferred at $215–$315 per week ▶ 20 *village leaders* (minimum age 18) with WSI and lifeguard certification, CPR/first aid training preferred at $180–$280 per week ▶ 2 *waterfront staff members* (minimum age 21) with WSI and lifeguard certification required at $1800–$3000 per season. Applicants must submit formal organization application, three personal references, trip resume outlining outdoor experiences for trip leading. A telephone interview is required. International applicants accepted; must apply through a recognized agency.

Benefits and Preemployment Training Free housing, free meals, formal training, willing to provide letters of recommendation, on-the-job training, willing to complete paperwork for educational credit, and willing to act as a professional reference. Preemployment training is required and includes accident prevention and safety, first aid, interpersonal skills, leadership skills, Wilderness First Responder training.

Contact Heather R. Kiley, Director of Camp Programs, American Youth Foundation–Camp Merrowvista, 147 Canaan Road, Center Tuftonboro, New Hampshire 03816. Telephone: 603-539-6607. Fax: 603-539-7504. E-mail: heather.kiley@ayf.com. World Wide Web: http://www.ayf.com. Contact by e-mail, fax, mail, phone, or through World Wide Web site. Application deadline: continuous.

BROOKWOODS FOR BOYS/DEER RUN FOR GIRLS

CHESTNUT COVE ROAD
ALTON, NEW HAMPSHIRE 03809

General Information Residential religious camps serving 300 campers in two- and four-week sessions. Established in 1944. 300-acre facility located 100 miles from Boston, Massachusetts. Features: freshwater lake (26 miles across).

Profile of Summer Employees Total number: 115; typical ages: 18–55. 50% men; 50% women; 10% minorities; 10% high school students; 90% college students; 10% non-U.S. citizens; 20% local applicants. Nonsmokers required.

Employment Information Openings are from June 18 to August 22. Year-round positions also offered. Jobs available: ▶ 20 *general counselors* with minimum one year of college completed at $2000 per season ▶ 3 *riding instructors* with CHA certification at $1750 per season ▶ 2 *riflery instructors* with NRA certification at $2000 per season ▶ 4 *trip staff members* (minimum age 21) with CPR and first aid certification; must be over 21 to drive 15-passenger van at $2200 per season. Applicants must submit formal organization application, three personal references. An in-person interview is recommended, but a telephone interview is acceptable. International applicants accepted; must apply through a recognized agency.

Benefits and Preemployment Training Free housing, free meals, formal training, willing to provide letters of recommendation, on-the-job training, willing to complete paperwork for educational credit, and willing to act as a professional reference. Preemployment training is required and includes accident prevention and safety, interpersonal skills, leadership skills.

Contact Bob Strodel, Executive Director, Brookwoods for Boys/Deer Run for Girls, Chestnut

Cove Road, Alton, New Hampshire 03809. Telephone: 603-875-3600. Fax: 603-875-4606. E-mail: brook@worldpath.net. World Wide Web: http://www.brookwoods.org. Contact by e-mail, fax, mail, phone, or through World Wide Web site. Application deadline: continuous.

CAMP ADVENCHUR

ROUTE 11, PO BOX 321
ALTON BAY, NEW HAMPSHIRE 03810

General Information Nonprofit Christian camp that provides an outdoor setting with a variety of activities for ages 6-16. Established in 1950. 95-acre facility located 100 miles from Manchester.

Profile of Summer Employees Total number: 30; typical ages: 16–35. 50% men; 50% women; 49% high school students; 50% college students; 1% non-U.S. citizens. Nonsmokers required.

Employment Information Openings are from June 16 to August 17. Jobs available: ▶ 1–2 *camp cooks* (minimum age 18) experienced in cooking for large groups of people at $150–$250 per week ▶ 24 *junior counselors* (minimum age 16) at $65–$75 per week ▶ 24 *senior counselors* (minimum age 18) at $150 per week ▶ 1–2 *waterfront directors* (minimum age 18) with WSI certification at $200 per week ▶ 1–2 *wilderness counselors* (minimum age 18) familiar with backpacking and wilderness skills at $150 per week. Applicants must submit a formal organization application, three personal references, voluntary disclosure form, health form, sexual harassment agreement, staff questionnaire. A telephone interview is required. International applicants accepted; must obtain own visa.

Benefits and Preemployment Training Free housing, free meals, formal training, health insurance, willing to provide letters of recommendation, on-the-job training, willing to complete paperwork for educational credit, and willing to act as a professional reference. Preemployment training is required and includes accident prevention and safety, first aid, CPR, interpersonal skills, leadership skills.

Contact Darla Rupert, Human Resources Manager, Camp Advenchur. Telephone: 603-875-6161. Fax: 603-875-0664. E-mail: campadvenchur@aol.com. World Wide Web: http://www.abccc.org/camp_advenchur.htm. Contact by e-mail, fax, mail, phone, or through World Wide Web site. Application deadline: continuous.

CAMP DEERWOOD

HOLDERNESS, NEW HAMPSHIRE 03245

General Information Residential camp serving 130 boys for seven weeks. Established in 1945. 88-acre facility located 100 miles from Boston, Massachusetts. Features: freshwater lake; woods; 4 tennis courts; blacksmith shop.

Profile of Summer Employees Total number: 50; typical ages: 17–30. 96% men; 4% women; 20% high school students; 60% college students; 5% retirees; 10% non-U.S. citizens; 5% local applicants. Nonsmokers required.

Employment Information Openings are from June 20 to August 15. Jobs available: ▶ 1 *ceramics instructor* at $1600–$3000 per season ▶ *general counselors* with WSI/lifeguard certification preferred (waterfront staff only) at $1200–$2500 per season ▶ *swimming instructors* with WSI/lifeguard certification at $1200–$2500 per season ▶ 2 *trip leaders* (minimum age 21) at $2000–$3000 per season. Applicants must submit a formal organization application, letter of interest, two letters of recommendation or personal references. An in-person interview is recommended, but a telephone interview is acceptable. International applicants accepted.

Benefits and Preemployment Training Free housing, free meals, willing to provide letters of recommendation, on-the-job training, willing to complete paperwork for educational credit, willing to act as a professional reference, opportunity to attend seminars/workshops, and tuition assistance. Preemployment training is required and includes accident prevention and safety, first aid, CPR, interpersonal skills, leadership skills.

Contact Tommy Thomsen, Director, Camp Deerwood, Box 188, Holderness, New Hampshire

03245. Telephone: 603-279-4237. Contact by mail or phone. Application deadline: February 1.

CAMP PEMIGEWASSETT
ROUTE 25A
WENTWORTH, NEW HAMPSHIRE 03282

General Information Traditional residential camp for 170 boys ages 8–15. A broad range of activities including sports, hiking, nature study, dramatics, and art in a 7-week session. Established in 1908. 600-acre facility located 75 miles from Manchester. Features: private lake; 7 tennis courts; 3 baseball fields; 2 soccer/lacrosse fields; fully equipped woodshop; superb nature facility.
Profile of Summer Employees Total number: 75; typical ages: 17–60. 90% men; 10% women; 5% minorities; 20% high school students; 40% college students; 8% retirees; 8% non-U.S. citizens; 10% local applicants. Nonsmokers required.
Employment Information Openings are from June 21 to August 16. Jobs available: ▶ *assistant counselors* (minimum age 17) with Red Cross CPR certification preferred at $1100–$1200 per season ▶ *cabin counselors/instructors* (minimum age 18) with Red Cross first aid and CPR certification preferred; minimum of one year of college completed at $1300–$1600 per season ▶ *cabin counselors/swimming instructors* (minimum age 18) with Red Cross WSI certification; minimum of one year of college completed at $1300–$1600 per season ▶ *kitchen workers* (minimum age 16) at $1100–$1400 per season. Applicants must submit formal organization application, letter of interest, three personal references. An in-person interview is required. International applicants accepted; must apply through a recognized agency.
Benefits and Preemployment Training Free housing, free meals, formal training, and on-the-job training. Preemployment training is required and includes accident prevention and safety, interpersonal skills, leadership skills.
Contact Robert Grabill, Director, Camp Pemigewassett, 25 Rayton Road, Hanover, New Hampshire 03755. Telephone: 603-643-8055. Fax: 603-643-9601. E-mail: robert.grabill@valley.net. World Wide Web: http://www.camppemi.com. Contact by e-mail, fax, mail, or phone. Application deadline: continuous.

CAMP ROBIN HOOD FOR BOYS AND GIRLS
65 ROBIN HOOD LANE
FREEDOM, NEW HAMPSHIRE 03836

General Information Residential camp serving 280 boys and girls ages 7–16 for 4-, 6-, and 8-week sessions. Established in 1927. 210-acre facility located 60 miles from Portland, Maine. Features: freshwater lake; wooded setting; extensive athletic fields; cabins with electricity and bathrooms; beautiful stables and riding facilities; lighted tennis, basketball, and volleyball courts.
Profile of Summer Employees Total number: 140; typical ages: 18–60. 60% men; 40% women; 3% minorities; 15% high school students; 70% college students; 20% non-U.S. citizens. Nonsmokers preferred.
Employment Information Openings are from June 18 to August 16. Jobs available: ▶ 1 *archery instructor* (minimum age 19) with experience in the field at $1000–$1400 per season ▶ 1 *ceramics instructor* (minimum age 19) with experience with wheel and kiln at $1000–$1500 per season ▶ 2 *crafts instructors* (minimum age 19) with experience in the field at $1000–$1500 per season ▶ 1 *dance instructor* (minimum age 19) at $1000–$1200 per season ▶ 10 *general counselors* (minimum age 19) at $850–$1000 per season ▶ 1 *gymnastics instructor* (minimum age 19) with experience in the field at $1000–$1500 per season ▶ 10 *kitchen/pantry staff* (minimum age 17) at $800–$1500 per season ▶ 2 *maintenance staff* (minimum age 19) with general carpentry skills at $1000–$1500 per season ▶ 2 *nurses* with RN certification at $3000–$3500 per season ▶ 3 *riding instructors* (minimum age 19) with English riding/teaching experience at $1000–$1500 per season ▶ 3 *sailing and canoeing instructors* (minimum age 19) with experience in the field at $1000–$1400 per season ▶ 2 *secretaries* (minimum age 18) with

computer skills at $900–$1500 per season ▶ 8 *sports coaches* (minimum age 19) with experience in the field at $1000–$1500 per season ▶ 4 *swimming instructors* (minimum age 19) with WSI certification, lifeguard training, or Bronze Medallion at $1000–$1500 per season ▶ 1 *tennis director* (minimum age 20) with teaching and program directing experience at $2500–$3500 per season ▶ 5 *tennis instructors* (minimum age 18) with playing and/or teaching experience at $1000–$1800 per season ▶ 3 *waterskiing instructors/boat drivers* (minimum age 19) with experience in the field at $850–$1400 per season ▶ 1 *woodworking instructor* (minimum age 19) with skills with power tools at $1000–$1500 per season. Applicants must submit formal organization application, three personal references. An in-person interview is recommended, but a telephone interview is acceptable. International applicants accepted; must apply through a recognized agency.

Benefits and Preemployment Training Free housing, free meals, formal training, willing to provide letters of recommendation, on-the-job training, and willing to complete paperwork for educational credit. Preemployment training is required and includes accident prevention and safety, first aid, CPR, interpersonal skills, leadership skills, group dynamics.

Contact John Klein, Director, Camp Robin Hood for Boys and Girls, 344 Thistle Trail, Mayfield Heights, Ohio 44124. Telephone: 440-646-1911. Fax: 440-646-1972. E-mail: robinhdnh@aol.com. World Wide Web: http://www.camprobinhood.com. Contact by e-mail, fax, mail, phone, or through World Wide Web site. Application deadline: continuous.

CAMP TEVYA

BROOKLINE, NEW HAMPSHIRE 03033

General Information Jewish coeducational cultural camp serving 325 campers. 650-acre facility located 50 miles from Boston, Massachusetts. Features: freshwater lake; 8 tennis courts; wooded setting.

Profile of Summer Employees Total number: 85–100; typical ages: 18–23. 50% men; 50% women; 16% high school students; 82% college students; 2% non-U.S. citizens. Nonsmokers preferred.

Employment Information Openings are from June 19 to August 16. Jobs available: ▶ *archery instructor* at $1500–$1900 per season ▶ *arts and crafts head* at $2000–$3000 per season ▶ 2–5 *arts and crafts instructors* at $1350–$1800 per season ▶ *athletics head* at $2000–$3000 per season ▶ *athletics staff* at $1350–$1800 per season ▶ *canoe instructors* at $1350–$2000 per season ▶ *drama head* at $2000–$3000 per season ▶ *music head* at $2000–$3000 per season ▶ *photography head* at $1350–$2000 per season ▶ *sailing instructors* at $1350–$2000 per season ▶ *swimming head* at $2000–$2500 per season ▶ *swimming instructors* at $1350–$2000 per season ▶ *waterskiing head* at $2000–$3000 per season. Applicants must submit formal organization application, personal reference, three letters of recommendation. An in-person interview is recommended, but a telephone interview is acceptable. International applicants accepted; must obtain own visa, obtain own working papers, apply through a recognized agency.

Benefits and Preemployment Training Free housing, free meals, formal training, on-the-job training, and willing to complete paperwork for educational credit. Preemployment training is required and includes accident prevention and safety, CPR, interpersonal skills, leadership skills.

Contact Pearl Lourie, Executive Director, Camp Tevya, 30 Main Street, Ashland, Massachusetts 01701. Telephone: 508-881-1002. Fax: 508-881-1006. World Wide Web: http://www.cohencamps.com. Contact by fax, mail, phone, or through World Wide Web site. Application deadline: continuous.

CAMP TOHKOMEUPOG

EAST MADISON, NEW HAMPSHIRE 03849

General Information Residential camp accommodating 120 boys ages 6–16 and featuring sports, mountain and canoe camping trips, and adventure program including ropes course and rock climbing. Established in 1932. 1,000-acre facility located 50 miles from Portland, Maine. Features: freshwater lake; 5 tennis courts; near White Mountain National Forest; 1000 acres; climbing wall- ropes course; street hockey rink.

Profile of Summer Employees Total number: 35; typical ages: 17–65. 95% men; 5% women; 5% minorities; 10% high school students; 50% college students; 5% retirees; 10% non-U.S. citizens; 85% local applicants. Nonsmokers preferred.

Employment Information Openings are from June 21 to August 17. Winter break positions also offered. Jobs available: ▶ 1 *archery instructor* (minimum age 20) at $1300–$1800 per season ▶ 4 *cabin counselors* (minimum age 20) with CPR, lifeguard, and first aid training at $700–$1400 per season ▶ *kitchen helper* (minimum age 18) at $2000–$3000 per season ▶ 1 *registered nurse* (minimum age 25) with RN license at $300–$400 per week ▶ 1 *rock climbing instructor and trip leader* (minimum age 22) at $250–$275 per week. Applicants must submit formal organization application, resume, three personal references, two letters of recommendation. An in-person interview is recommended, but a telephone interview is acceptable. International applicants accepted; must obtain own visa, obtain own working papers, apply through a recognized agency.

Benefits and Preemployment Training Free housing, free meals, formal training, willing to provide letters of recommendation, on-the-job training, and opportunity to attend seminars/workshops. Preemployment training is required and includes accident prevention and safety, first aid, CPR, interpersonal skills, leadership skills.

Contact Andrew Mahoney, Director, Camp Tohkomeupog, HC 63, Box 40, East Madison, New Hampshire 03849. Telephone: 603-367-8362. Fax: 603-367-8664. E-mail: tohko@tohko.com. World Wide Web: http://www.tohko.com. Contact by e-mail, fax, mail, or phone. Application deadline: continuous.

CAMP WALT WHITMAN

1000 CAPE MOONSHINE ROAD
PIERMONT, NEW HAMPSHIRE 03779

General Information Coeducational residential camp serving 390 campers and offering a strong general program. Established in 1948. 300-acre facility located 110 miles from Boston, Massachusetts. Features: freshwater lake; heated swimming pool; 11 clay tennis courts; multi sports complex; 3 arts studios; wooded, mountain setting.

Profile of Summer Employees Total number: 220; typical ages: 18–30. 50% men; 50% women; 75% college students; 2% retirees; 10% non-U.S. citizens. Nonsmokers required.

Employment Information Openings are from June 20 to August 19. Jobs available: ▶ 3 *art/woodshop instructors* (minimum age 20) with experience at $1300–$2500 per season ▶ 1 *arts and crafts staff* (minimum age 19) with experience at $1500–$3000 per season ▶ 2 *dance/gymnastics instructors* (minimum age 19) with experience at $1200–$1800 per season ▶ 20–30 *general counselors* (minimum age 19) with experience at $1100–$1600 per season ▶ 3 *hiking and camping specialists* (minimum age 20) with experience at $1300–$1800 per season ▶ 6 *kitchen and maintenance personnel* (minimum age 20) with experience at $1200–$2500 per season ▶ 1 *radio station manager* (minimum age 19) with experience at $1200–$1500 per season ▶ 3 *sailing, canoeing, and windsurfing instructors* (minimum age 19) with experience at $1300–$2000 per season ▶ 6 *sports coaches* (minimum age 20) with experience in the field at $1400–$2000 per season ▶ 6 *swimming instructors* (minimum age 19) with WSI and LG certification at $1300–$2000 per season ▶ 6 *tennis instructors* (minimum age 19) with experience at $1300–$2000 per season ▶ 2 *water skiing instructors* (minimum age 19) with experience at $1300–$2000 per season. Applicants must submit formal organization application, three personal references. A telephone interview is required. International applicants accepted; must apply through a recognized agency.

Benefits and Preemployment Training Free housing, free meals, formal training, willing to provide letters of recommendation, on-the-job training, willing to complete paperwork for educational credit, willing to act as a professional reference, opportunity to attend seminars/ workshops, travel reimbursement, and leadership and management training. Preemployment training is required and includes accident prevention and safety, first aid, CPR, interpersonal skills, leadership skills.

Contact Jancy Dorfman, Director, Camp Walt Whitman, PO Box 938, Bedford, New York 10506. Telephone: 800-657-8282. Fax: 914-234-5487. E-mail: staff@campwalt.com. World Wide Web: http://www.campwalt.com. Contact by e-mail, fax, mail, phone, or through World Wide Web site. Application deadline: continuous.

CHENOA

BRIMSTONE CORNER ROAD
ANTRIM, NEW HAMPSHIRE 03440

General Information Girl Scout residential camp serving 175 girls ages 6–16 in one- and two-week sessions, emphasizing girl decision-making and leadership development. Established in 1994. 300-acre facility located 80 miles from Boston, Massachusetts. Features: freshwater lake; wooded area; all new buildings; beaver pond.

Profile of Summer Employees Total number: 70; typical ages: 18–35. 1% men; 99% women; 2% minorities; 50% college students; 15% non-U.S. citizens; 15% local applicants. Nonsmokers preferred.

Employment Information Openings are from June 12 to August 22. Year-round positions also offered. Jobs available: ▶ 4 *cooks* (minimum age 18) with experience in quantity cooking at $2400–$4000 per season ▶ 1 *nurse* (minimum age 21) with RN, LPN or EMT at $3500–$5500 per season ▶ 2–3 *program specialists* (minimum age 18) with experience teaching groups of children and ability to lead programs in science, math, diversity, and gender issues at $1500–$3200 per season ▶ 20–30 *unit counselors* (minimum age 18) with high school diploma and experience working with groups of children at $1500–$2800 per season ▶ 4–6 *waterfront assistants* (minimum age 18) with WSI, LGT certification at $1500–$2400 per season ▶ 1 *waterfront director* (minimum age 21) with WSI, LGT certification at $2500–$3500 per season. Applicants must submit formal organization application, resume, three personal references. An in-person interview is recommended, but a telephone interview is acceptable. International applicants accepted; must apply through a recognized agency.

Benefits and Preemployment Training Free housing, free meals, formal training, health insurance, willing to provide letters of recommendation, on-the-job training, willing to complete paperwork for educational credit, willing to act as a professional reference, and opportunity to attend seminars/workshops. Preemployment training is required and includes accident prevention and safety, first aid, CPR, interpersonal skills, leadership skills, program skills.

Contact Missy Long, Camp Director, Chenoa, SWGSC, 8 Perimeter Road, Manchester, New Hampshire 03103. Telephone: 800-654-1270. Fax: 603-627-4169. E-mail: mlong@swgirlscouts.org. World Wide Web: http://www.swgirlscouts.org. Contact by e-mail, fax, mail, phone, or through World Wide Web site. Application deadline: continuous.

COLD RIVER CAMP, A.M.C.

HCR BOX 221
CENTER CONWAY, NEW HAMPSHIRE 03813

General Information Family camp for hiking and outdoor activities in White Mountain National Forest owned by Appalachian Mountain Club. Established in 1919. 135-acre facility located 65 miles from Portland, Maine. Features: mountain setting; rustic setting; individual cabins; excellent meals; organized hikes; mountain streams.

Profile of Summer Employees Total number: 14; typical ages: 18–23. 50% men; 50% women; 20% high school students; 80% college students; 10% retirees; 30% non-U.S. citizens; 10% local applicants. Nonsmokers preferred.

Employment Information Openings are from June 22 to August 31. Jobs available: ▶ 8 *crew* (minimum age 18) at $2200 per season ▶ 2 *kitchen positions* (minimum age 18) with food preparation experience at $2800–$3800 per season. Applicants must submit formal organization application, letter of interest, three personal references, three letters of recommendation. An in-person interview is recommended, but a telephone interview is acceptable. International applicants accepted; must apply through a recognized agency.
Benefits and Preemployment Training Free housing, free meals, willing to provide letters of recommendation, and willing to act as a professional reference.
Contact Bill Waste, Manager, Cold River Camp, A.M.C., 69 Washburn Hill Road, Lyme, New Hampshire 03768. Telephone: 603-795-4440. E-mail: bill.waste@valley.net. World Wide Web: http://www.outdoors.org. Contact by e-mail, mail, phone, or through World Wide Web site. Application deadline: January 31.

GENEVA POINT CENTER
MOULTONBORO, NEW HAMPSHIRE 03254

General Information Ecumenical conference center hosting groups and Elderhostel. Established in 1919. 200-acre facility located 40 miles from Concord. Features: freshwater lake; 200 acres; located in lakes region of New Hampshire; near White Mountains.
Profile of Summer Employees Total number: 30–40; typical ages: 18–24. 50% men; 50% women; 5% minorities; 20% college students; 25% retirees; 45% non-U.S. citizens; 5% local applicants. Nonsmokers required.
Employment Information Openings are from May 13 to October 19. Jobs available: ▶ 4–6 *dining room staff* at $170–$206 per week ▶ 6–8 *general kitchen staff* at $170–$206 per week ▶ 3–6 *housekeepers* at $170–$206 per week ▶ 5–6 *lifeguards* at $200–$220 per week. Applicants must submit formal organization application, three personal references, three letters of recommendation. A telephone interview is required. International applicants accepted; must apply through a recognized agency.
Benefits and Preemployment Training Free housing, free meals, on-the-job training, and opportunity to attend seminars/workshops. Preemployment training is required and includes accident prevention and safety.
Contact Tom MacKay, Operations Manager, Geneva Point Center, HCR 62, Box 469, Center Harbor, New Hampshire 03226. Telephone: 603-253-4366. Fax: 603-253-4883. E-mail: geneva@genevapoint.org. Contact by e-mail or phone. Application deadline: continuous.

INTERLOCKEN INTERNATIONAL SUMMER CAMP
RR 2, BOX 165
HILLSBORO, NEW HAMPSHIRE 03244

General Information Creative, noncompetitive international summer camp offering a wide range of activities to 180 campers per session from the United States and around the world. Established in 1961. 1,000-acre facility located 100 miles from Boston, Massachusetts. Features: several freshwater lakes; wooded setting; architect-designed buildings; rope swing and lake launch; red pine forest; starry sky.
Profile of Summer Employees Total number: 60; typical ages: 20–28. 50% men; 50% women; 20% minorities; 50% college students; 20% non-U.S. citizens. Nonsmokers required.
Employment Information Openings are from June 15 to August 24. Jobs available: ▶ 4 *applied arts staff members* with experience in the field ▶ 2 *environmental education staff members* with experience in the field ▶ 4 *music staff members* with experience in the field ▶ 4 *performing arts staff members* with experience in the field ▶ 4 *sports staff members* with experience in the field ▶ 4 *waterfront instructors* with experience in the field ▶ 6 *wilderness staff members* with experience in the field. Applicants must submit formal organization application, letter of interest, resume, three personal references. An in-person interview is recommended, but a telephone

interview is acceptable. International applicants accepted; must apply through a recognized agency.

Benefits and Preemployment Training Free housing, free meals, willing to provide letters of recommendation, on-the-job training, and willing to act as a professional reference. Preemployment training is required and includes accident prevention and safety, first aid, CPR, interpersonal skills, leadership skills, lifeguard training.

Contact Mr. Rick Davis, Staffing Director, Interlocken International Summer Camp, RR 2, Box 165, Hillsboro, New Hampshire 03244. Telephone: 603-478-3166. Fax: 603-478-5260. E-mail: rick@interlocken.org. World Wide Web: http://www.interlocken.org. Contact by e-mail, fax, mail, or through World Wide Web site. Application deadline: continuous.

INTERLOCKEN TRAVEL PROGRAMS

RR 2, BOX 165
HILLSBORO, NEW HAMPSHIRE 03244

General Information Experientially-based domestic and international small group travel programs that focus on performing arts, adventure/wilderness, community service, language, leadership training, adventure cycling, and environment. Travel programs are an outgrowth of the Interlocken International Summer Camp. Established in 1967. 1,000-acre facility located 100 miles from Boston, Massachusetts.

Profile of Summer Employees Total number: 30; typical ages: 24–35. 50% men; 50% women; 20% minorities; 20% non-U.S. citizens. Nonsmokers required.

Employment Information Openings are from June 12 to August 22. Jobs available: ▶ 12 *adventure/wilderness leaders* (minimum age 24) with WFR certification, and experience leading high school students at $1500–$2400 per season ▶ 6 *cycling leaders* (minimum age 24) with experience working with high school age students at $1500–$2400 per season ▶ 4 *leadership training leaders* (minimum age 24) with residential camp background and experience teaching leadership training at $1500–$2400 per season ▶ 6 *performing arts leaders* (minimum age 24) with background in physical theatre and experience teaching teenagers at $1500–$2400 per season ▶ 35 *travel leaders* (minimum age 24) with experience working with high school age students at $1500–$2400 per season. Applicants must submit formal organization application, letter of interest, resume, three letters of recommendation. An in-person interview is recommended, but a telephone interview is acceptable. International applicants accepted; must apply through a recognized agency.

Benefits and Preemployment Training Free housing, free meals, formal training, willing to provide letters of recommendation, willing to complete paperwork for educational credit, willing to act as a professional reference, opportunity to attend seminars/workshops, and travel reimbursement. Preemployment training is required and includes accident prevention and safety, first aid, CPR, interpersonal skills, leadership skills, lifeguard training.

Contact Mr. Rick Davis, Staffing Director, Interlocken Travel Programs, RR 2, Box 165, Hillsboro, New Hampshire 03244. Telephone: 603-478-3166. Fax: 603-478-5260. E-mail: rick@interlocken.org. World Wide Web: http://www.interlocken.org. Contact by e-mail, fax, mail, or through World Wide Web site. Application deadline: continuous.

ROAD'S END FARM HORSEMANSHIP CAMP

JACKSON HILL ROAD
CHESTERFIELD, NEW HAMPSHIRE 03443-0197

General Information Residential camp program serving 60 girls ages 8–16 who love horses, English pleasure riding, and the noncompetitive atmosphere of a family-owned horse farm at the end of a quiet dirt road. Sessions vary from 2 to 8 weeks in length. Established in 1958. 505-acre facility located 95 miles from Boston, Massachusetts. Features: family atmosphere; noncompetitive philosophy; 50 saddle horses; scenic and secluded setting; freshwater lake; 20 miles of private bridlepaths.

Profile of Summer Employees Total number: 26; typical ages: 19–40. 100% women; 10% minorities; 80% college students; 10% non-U.S. citizens. Nonsmokers required.

Employment Information Openings are from June 1 to August 17. Jobs available: ▶ 1 *camp nurse* (minimum age 22) with LPN or RN license at $4000–$5000 per season ▶ 1 *canoeing instructor* (minimum age 19) with Red Cross credentials and experience in the field at $3000–$3500 per season ▶ 1–2 *cooks* (minimum age 25) at $5000 per season ▶ 4–6 *lead riders* (minimum age 19) English-style equestrian competence and experience at $3000–$3500 per season ▶ 4 *lifeguards* (minimum age 19) with Red Cross credentials and experience in the field at $3000–$3500 per season ▶ 1 *prep cook* (minimum age 22) at $4000 per season ▶ 4–6 *riding instructors* (minimum age 19) with Pony Club, CHA, or BHS credentials or some very good experience at $3000–$3500 per season ▶ 3 *swimming instructors* (minimum age 19) with WSI certification and experience in the field at $3000–$3500 per season. Applicants must submit formal organization application, three personal references. An in-person interview is recommended, but a telephone interview is acceptable. International applicants accepted; must apply through a recognized agency.

Benefits and Preemployment Training Free housing, free meals, willing to provide letters of recommendation, on-the-job training, and willing to act as a professional reference. Preemployment training is required and includes accident prevention and safety, interpersonal skills, leadership skills.

Contact Tom Woodman, Director, Road's End Farm Horsemanship Camp, PO Box 197, Chesterfield, New Hampshire 03443-0197. Telephone: 603-363-4900. Fax: 603-363-4949. World Wide Web: http://www.roadsendfarm.com. Contact by fax, mail, or phone. Application deadline: continuous.

ROCKYWOLD-DEEPHAVEN CAMPS, INC. (RDC)

PINEHURST ROAD, PO BOX B
HOLDERNESS, NEW HAMPSHIRE 03245

General Information Family vacation camp providing guests with a unique family living experience offering rustic simplicity, high-quality services, and a natural setting. Established in 1897. 115-acre facility located 50 miles from Concord. Features: Squam Lake; location on the southern edge of White Mountain National Forest; 8 clay tennis courts; hiking and mountain bike trails leading from the property; old-fashioned ice boxes and fire places in each cottage; ballfield and basketball courts.

Profile of Summer Employees Total number: 90–100; typical ages: 18–25. 50% men; 50% women; 5% minorities; 4% high school students; 70% college students; 1% retirees; 45% non-U.S. citizens; 10% local applicants. Nonsmokers required.

Employment Information Openings are from May 15 to October 7. Jobs available: ▶ 20–25 *food service personnel* (minimum age 18) with a positive and flexible attitude and high work standards at $6–$9 per hour ▶ 10–12 *grounds/maintenance personnel* (minimum age 18) with experience in soft-surface tennis court maintenance and carpentry at $6–$6.50 per hour ▶ 22–24 *housekeeping personnel* (minimum age 18) with a positive and flexible attitude and high work standards at $6–$6.50 per hour ▶ 6–8 *office staff members* (minimum age 18) with word-processing and money handling skills and experience working with the public at $6.20–$6.50 per hour ▶ 5–7 *recreation staff members* (minimum age 18) with experience in tennis, water sports, outdoor recreation, crafts, and working with various age groups at $235–$260 per week. Applicants must submit formal organization application, three personal references, 3 recommendation forms. An in-person interview is recommended, but a telephone interview is acceptable. International applicants accepted; must apply through a recognized agency.

Benefits and Preemployment Training Free housing, free meals, willing to provide letters of recommendation, on-the-job training, willing to complete paperwork for educational credit,

willing to act as a professional reference, and opportunity to attend seminars/workshops.
Contact Ann Rampulla, General Manager, Rockywold–Deephaven Camps, Inc. (RDC), PO Box B, Holderness, New Hampshire 03245. Telephone: 603-968-3313. Fax: 603-968-3438. E-mail: rdc@lr.net. World Wide Web: http://www.rdcsquam.com. Contact by e-mail, fax, mail, phone, or through World Wide Web site. Application deadline: February 15.

THE SOUTHWESTERN COMPANY, NEW HAMPSHIRE

See The Southwestern Company on page 302 for complete description.

STUDENT CONSERVATION ASSOCIATION (SCA), NEW HAMPSHIRE

689 RIVER ROAD, PO BOX 550
CHARLESTOWN, NEW HAMPSHIRE 03603

General Information Nonprofit organization that places interns year-round in expense-paid conservation projects in national parks, forests, and wildlife refuges nationwide. Established in 1957. 20-acre facility located 120 miles from Hartford, Connecticut. Features: national parks; mountains; lakes and rivers; wooded setting/forests; historic sites; national landmarks.
Profile of Summer Employees Total number: 75; typical ages: 16–30. 45% men; 55% women; 15% minorities; 30% high school students; 70% college students; 5% retirees; 5% non-U.S. citizens; 5% local applicants.
Employment Information Openings are from January to December. Year-round positions also offered. Jobs available: ▶ 1200–1600 *conservation interns* (minimum age 18) with high school diploma; housing, travel, insurance, education awards available at $50–$160 per week ▶ 150–200 *high school crew leaders* (minimum age 21) with experience working with high school students; travel, training, and room and board included at $1360–$2360 per season ▶ 650 *high school trail crew members (volunteer)* (must be 15 to 19 years of age), interested in outdoors and service ▶ 100–150 *residential trails/education interns* (minimum age 18) with an interest in outdoors and working with children at $60 per week. Applicants must submit a formal organization application, additional requirements on searchable database at Web site; two personal references or two letters of recommendation; $20 processing fee ($40 for international applicants). A telephone interview is required. International applicants accepted; must obtain own visa.
Benefits and Preemployment Training Free housing, free meals, formal training, health insurance, names of contacts, on-the-job training, willing to complete paperwork for educational credit, opportunity to attend seminars/workshops, travel reimbursement, and tuition assistance. Preemployment training is required and includes accident prevention and safety, first aid, CPR, interpersonal skills, leadership skills, wilderness work skills, WFA, WFR.
Contact Recruitment Department, Student Conservation Association (SCA), New Hampshire. Telephone: 603-543-1700. Fax: 603-543-1828. E-mail: internships@sca-inc.org. World Wide Web: http://www.sca-inc.org. Contact by e-mail, fax, mail, phone, or through World Wide Web site. Application deadline: continuous.

THE WHALE'S TALE WATER PARK

ROUTE 3 NORTH
LINCOLN, NEW HAMPSHIRE 03251

General Information Water park with more than 10 wet and dry attractions. Established in 1985. 17-acre facility located 100 miles from Boston, Massachusetts. Features: 6 water slides; wave pool; children's play area; lazy river; volleyball courts; great mountain views.
Profile of Summer Employees Total number: 80; typical ages: 16–25. 48% men; 52% women; 60% high school students; 10% college students; 30% local applicants.
Employment Information Openings are from June 1 to September 1. Jobs available: ▶ 10–20 *food service staff* (minimum age 16) at $6–$10 per hour ▶ 10–20 *lifeguards* (minimum age 16)

with ARC certification at $6–$10 per hour ▶ 5–10 *sales staff* (minimum age 16) with money handling and customer service skills at $6–$8 per hour. Applicants must submit a formal organization application, on-line application. An in-person interview is recommended, but a telephone interview is acceptable. International applicants accepted.

Benefits and Preemployment Training Meals at a cost, willing to provide letters of recommendation, on-the-job training, willing to complete paperwork for educational credit, and willing to act as a professional reference. Preemployment training is required and includes accident prevention and safety, first aid, interpersonal skills, leadership skills.

Contact Jeb Boyd, General Manager, The Whale's Tale Water Park, PO Box 67, Lincoln, New Hampshire 03251. Telephone: 603-745-8810. Fax: 603-745-6958. E-mail: wtwp@together.net. World Wide Web: http://www.whalestalewaterpark.com. Contact by e-mail, fax, or mail. Application deadline: continuous.

YMCA CAMP LINCOLN
PO BOX 729, 67 BALL ROAD
KINGSTON, NEW HAMPSHIRE 03848

General Information YMCA Camp Lincoln is a year-round coed camp that offers girls and boys the opportunity to grow through engaging programs involving travel, nature, community development, and fun. Established in 1926. 75-acre facility located 40 miles from Boston, Massachusetts. Features: freshwater lake; beautiful cabins; close to ocean; close to mountains; excellent climbing wall/high ropes; great sports fields.

Profile of Summer Employees Total number: 120; typical ages: 16–26. 40% men; 60% women; 5% minorities; 60% high school students; 30% college students; 2% retirees; 5% non-U.S. citizens; 90% local applicants. Nonsmokers required.

Employment Information Openings are from June 15 to August 25. Jobs available: ▶ 1–4 *adventure trip leaders* (minimum age 21) at $3000–$4000 per season ▶ 1–30 *general counselors* (minimum age 16) at $2000–$3000 per season ▶ 1–15 *program specialists* (minimum age 18) at $2500–$3500 per season. Applicants must submit formal organization application, two personal references. An in-person interview is recommended, but a telephone interview is acceptable. International applicants accepted; must obtain own visa, obtain own working papers, apply through a recognized agency.

Benefits and Preemployment Training Free housing, free meals, possible full-time employment, willing to provide letters of recommendation, on-the-job training, willing to complete paperwork for educational credit, willing to act as a professional reference, and opportunity to attend seminars/workshops. Preemployment training is required and includes accident prevention and safety, first aid, CPR, interpersonal skills, leadership skills, lifeguard training.

Contact Eric Tucker, Director, YMCA Camp Lincoln, PO Box 729, Kingston, New Hampshire 03848. Telephone: 603-642-3361. Fax: 603-642-4340. E-mail: eric@ymcacamplincoln.com. World Wide Web: http://www.ymcacamplincoln.com. Contact by e-mail or through World Wide Web site. Application deadline: continuous.

YOGI BEAR'S JELLYSTONE PARK
ROUTE 132N, PO BOX 1926
ASHLAND, NEW HAMPSHIRE 03217

General Information Family fun resort and campground offering day trips, overnights, and weekend vacations in a trailer, log cabin rental, or campsite. Theme park with planned daily activities for all ages. Established in 1978. 40-acre facility located 30 miles from Concord. Features: sandy-bottomed river; pool and hot tub; hayrides; movies; snack bar; mini golf; large general store.

Profile of Summer Employees Total number: 50; typical ages: 16–69. 50% men; 50% women; 10% minorities; 10% high school students; 20% college students; 20% retirees; 20% non-U.S. citizens; 20% local applicants. Nonsmokers preferred.

Employment Information Openings are from April to October. Year-round positions also offered. Jobs available: ▶ 3 *food service staff* (minimum age 18) with salary starting at minimum wage ▶ 10 *general operations and maintenance staff* (minimum age 16) with salary starting at minimum wage ▶ 14 *housekeepers* (minimum age 16) with salary starting at minimum wage ▶ 3–4 *recreation directors* (minimum age 16) with salary starting at minimum wage ▶ 2–3 *reservationists* (minimum age 16) with computer experience preferred; salary starting at minimum wage ▶ 2–3 *store clerks* (minimum age 16) with salary starting at minimum wage. Applicants must submit formal organization application, letter of interest, resume, three personal references, two letters of recommendation. An in-person interview is recommended, but a telephone interview is acceptable. International applicants accepted; must obtain own visa, obtain own working papers, apply through a recognized agency.

Benefits and Preemployment Training Free housing, possible full-time employment, willing to provide letters of recommendation, on-the-job training, willing to complete paperwork for educational credit, and willing to act as a professional reference.

Contact Rachel Capps, Personnel Director, Yogi Bear's Jellystone Park, PO Box 1926, Ashland, New Hampshire 03217. Fax: 603-968-7349. E-mail: yogi@jellystonenh.com. World Wide Web: http://www.jellystonenh.com. Contact by e-mail, fax, or mail. Application deadline: continuous.

NEW JERSEY

APPEL FARM ARTS AND MUSIC CENTER

457 SHIRLEY ROAD
ELMER, NEW JERSEY 08318

General Information Arts and music camp for children with programs in music, dance, theater, fine arts, photography and video. Campers and staff form a non-competitive, nurturing artistic community. Established in 1960. 170-acre facility located 25 miles from Philadelphia, Pennsylvania. Features: tennis courts; swimming pool; new dining hall, fine arts building, and teaching spaces; rural setting near a major metropolitan area; beach 50 minutes away.

Profile of Summer Employees Total number: 95; typical ages: 20–35. 40% men; 60% women; 20% minorities; 15% college students; 20% non-U.S. citizens; 10% local applicants. Nonsmokers required.

Employment Information Openings are from June 16 to August 23. Jobs available: ▶ 10 *art instructors* (minimum age 20) with extensive experience in painting, drawing, printmaking, sculpture, weaving, and ceramics at $1600–$2000 per season ▶ 1 *community-outreach coordinator* (minimum age 20) with organizational ability and office work experience at $1600–$2000 per season ▶ 3 *dance instructors* (minimum age 20) with experience and expert knowledge of modern, jazz, and ballet dancing at $1600–$2000 per season ▶ 10 *music instructors* (minimum age 20) with extensive experience in woodwinds, piano, strings, percussion, voice, brass, electronic music, and rock at $1600–$2000 per season ▶ 5 *photography instructors* (minimum age 20) with experience in the field at $1600–$2000 per season ▶ 2 *registered nurses* (minimum age 20) with RN license, NJ certification preferred ▶ 3 *sports staff members* (minimum age 20) with experience in tennis and noncompetitive sports at $1400 per season ▶ 4 *swimming instructors* (minimum age 20) with Red Cross lifeguard training or WSI certification and Bronze Medallion at $1600–$2000 per season ▶ 5 *technical theater personnel* (minimum age 20) with experience in stagecraft, set design, costumes, and lighting at $1600–$2200 per season ▶ 10 *theater instructors* (minimum age 20) with directing experience at $1600–$2000 per season ▶ 3 *video instructors* (minimum age 20) with experience in the field at $1600–$2000 per season. Applicants must submit resume, three personal references, performance audio tapes, slides of present work. An in-person interview is recommended, but a telephone interview is acceptable. International applicants accepted.

Benefits and Preemployment Training Free housing, free meals, formal training, willing to provide letters of recommendation, on-the-job training, willing to complete paperwork for educational credit, willing to act as a professional reference, and opportunity to attend seminars/workshops.

Contact Matt Sisson, Camp Director, Appel Farm Arts and Music Center, PO Box 888, Elmer, New Jersey 08318. Telephone: 856-358-2472. Fax: 856-358-6513. E-mail: appelcamp@aol.com. World Wide Web: http://www.appelfarm.org. Contact through World Wide Web site. Application deadline: continuous.

CAMP LOU HENRY HOOVER
961 WEST SHORE DRIVE
MIDDLEVILLE, NEW JERSEY 07855

General Information Nonprofit girl scout camp that focuses on providing girls with a wide range of activities. Established in 1953. 328-acre facility located 15 miles from Newton. Features: waterfront; wooded area; tents facilities; multipurpose building; canoe/hike trips.

Profile of Summer Employees Total number: 60; typical ages: 16–32. 2% men; 98% women; 10% minorities; 30% high school students; 40% college students; 20% non-U.S. citizens; 10% local applicants. Nonsmokers preferred.

Employment Information Openings are from June 30 to August 20. Jobs available: ▶ 20–30 *counselors* (minimum age 18) at $1000–$3000 per season ▶ 2–4 *head cook/kitchen staff* (minimum age 18) at $800–$3000 per season ▶ 2–6 *waterfront staff* (minimum age 18) at $800–$2000 per season. Applicants must submit formal organization application, three personal references. An in-person interview is recommended, but a telephone interview is acceptable. International applicants accepted; must apply through a recognized agency.

Benefits and Preemployment Training Free housing, free meals, formal training, willing to provide letters of recommendation, on-the-job training, willing to complete paperwork for educational credit, and willing to act as a professional reference. Preemployment training is required and includes accident prevention and safety, first aid, CPR, interpersonal skills, leadership skills.

Contact Deborah Hooke, Director, Camp Lou Henry Hoover, 201 Grove Street East, Westfield, New Jersey 07090. Telephone: 908-232-3236 Ext. 1226. Fax: 908-232-2140. E-mail: hookie@ix.netcom.com. Contact by e-mail or phone. Application deadline: continuous.

CAMP RIVERBEND
116 HILLCREST ROAD
WARREN TOWNSHIP, NEW JERSEY 07059

General Information Family-owned day camp, with emphasis on fun and participation, not competition; offering swimming, crafts, sports and nature. Established in 1963. 30-acre facility located 5 miles from Summit. Features: 4 heated outdoor pools; on bank of Passaic River; woods and fields; roller rink with roof; modern gym and auditorium; separate pre-school area.

Profile of Summer Employees Total number: 200; typical ages: 18–30. 50% men; 50% women; 10% minorities; 50% college students; 100% local applicants. Nonsmokers preferred.

Employment Information Openings are from June to August. Jobs available: ▶ 1 *athletic director* with experience in sports, athletics, physical education, and recreation ▶ 1 *camp crafts staff* with experience in outdoor living, scouting, and camping lore ▶ 1 *group head counselor* with teaching experience/certification, and understanding and enjoyment of children ▶ 1 *low ropes specialist* with experience in low ropes. Applicants must submit a formal organization application, three personal references. An in-person interview is required.

Benefits and Preemployment Training Formal training, willing to provide letters of recommendation, on-the-job training, willing to complete paperwork for educational credit, willing to act as a professional reference, opportunity to attend seminars/workshops, and finder's fee, perfect attendance bonus. Preemployment training is required and includes accident prevention and safety, first aid, CPR, interpersonal skills.
Contact Miriam Peretsman, Program Director, Camp Riverbend, 116 Hillcrest Road, Warren Township, New Jersey 07059. Telephone: 908-580-CAMP. Fax: 908-647-2435. E-mail: rvrbnd1@aol.com. World Wide Web: http://www.campriverbend.bunk1.com. Contact by e-mail, fax, mail, phone, or through World Wide Web site. Application deadline: continuous.

COLLEGE GIFTED PROGRAMS
DREW UNIVERSITY
MADISON, NEW JERSEY 07940

General Information Residential educational academic summer camp for gifted and talented students in grades 4-11. Program blends in-depth academics with recreational and cultural activities. Established in 1984. 186-acre facility located 20 miles from New York, New York. Features: dormitories; campus classroom facilities; campus recreational facilities include pool, tennis courts, and gym; campus library; beautiful college setting.
Profile of Summer Employees Total number: 65; typical ages: 19–70. 50% men; 50% women; 30% minorities; 50% college students; 10% retirees; 10% non-U.S. citizens; 25% local applicants. Nonsmokers required.
Employment Information Openings are from June 26 to July 17. Jobs available: ▶ 30 *counselors* with two years of college completed and experience working with children at $900 to $1200 per 3-week session ▶ 4 *directors* with at least 5 years teaching/supervisory experience; master's degree required, doctorate preferred at $5000–$8000 per year ▶ 6 *housemasters/instructors (residential)* with master's degree, teaching and supervisory experience at $2500 to $4500 per 3-week session ▶ 20 *instructors (non-residential)* with master's degree and teaching experience at $600 to $2500 per 3-week session ▶ 2 *nurses* with RN license; school experience preferred at $1300 per week. Applicants must submit formal organization application, resume, academic transcripts, two personal references, two letters of recommendation. An in-person interview is recommended, but a telephone interview is acceptable. International applicants accepted; must apply through a recognized agency.
Benefits and Preemployment Training Free housing, free meals, willing to provide letters of recommendation, willing to complete paperwork for educational credit, and willing to act as a professional reference. Preemployment training is required and includes accident prevention and safety, interpersonal skills, leadership skills, instructional strategies for gifted students.
Contact Charles Zeichner, Executive Director, College Gifted Programs, 120 Littleton Road, Suite 201, Parsippany, New Jersey 07054-1803. Telephone: 973-334-6991. Fax: 973-334-9756. E-mail: info@cgp-sig.com. World Wide Web: http://www.cgp-sig.com. Contact by e-mail, fax, mail, phone, or through World Wide Web site. Application deadline: continuous.

CYBERCAMPS–FDU MADISON
MADISON, NEW JERSEY

See Cybercamps–University of Washington on page 335 for complete description.

CYBERCAMPS–RIDER UNIVERSITY
LAWRENCEVILLE, NEW JERSEY

See Cybercamps–University of Washington on page 335 for complete description.

DWIGHT-ENGLEWOOD SCHOOL

315 EAST PALISADE AVENUE
ENGLEWOOD, NEW JERSEY 07631-0489

General Information Summer school providing a variety of opportunities for students from public, parochial and independent schools through a combination of advancement, introduction, and enrichment courses in all academic disciplines, in the arts, and in sports, allowing for diversity of study. Established in 1889. Affiliated with National Association of Independent Schools, Secondary School Admission Test Board. 30-acre facility located 3 miles from New York, New York. Features: 5 tennis courts; nature sanctuary; theatre; state-of-the-art lower school; library.

Profile of Summer Employees Total number: 120; typical ages: 16–24. 50% men; 50% women; 50% minorities; 65% high school students; 25% college students; 10% local applicants.

Employment Information Openings are from June 17 to August 2. Jobs available: ▶ 10–15 *counselors* (minimum age 16) at $1600–$2100 per season ▶ 2–3 *science lab assistants* (minimum age 16) with knowledge of science at $1400–$1600 per season ▶ 4–8 *sports clinicians* (minimum age 16) with knowledge of a variety of sports at $1300–$1800 per season. Applicants must submit resume, three personal references, letter of recommendation. An in-person interview is required. International applicants accepted; must obtain own visa, obtain own working papers.

Benefits and Preemployment Training Possible full-time employment, willing to provide letters of recommendation, on-the-job training, willing to complete paperwork for educational credit, willing to act as a professional reference, and free meals or meals at cost (possible). Preemployment training is required and includes accident prevention and safety, interpersonal skills, leadership skills.

Contact Mark A. Schultz, Summer School Principal, Dwight-Englewood School. Telephone: 201-569-9500 Ext. 3501. Fax: 201-568-9451. E-mail: schultm@d-e.org. World Wide Web: http://www.d-e.org. Contact by e-mail. Application deadline: continuous.

EASTER SEALS CAMP MERRY HEART

21 O'BRIAN ROAD
HACKETTSTOWN, NEW JERSEY 07840

General Information Residential camp for persons with a disability ages 5–60, day camp for nondisabled children ages 5–12, and Travel Recreation Experiences in Camping (TREC) program for persons with a disability, ages 18-35. Established in 1949. 121-acre facility located 50 miles from New York, New York. Features: woodlands; freshwater lake; cabins; pool; tennis court/volleyball court; accessible facility.

Profile of Summer Employees Total number: 55; typical ages: 16–60. 50% men; 50% women; 25% minorities; 10% high school students; 75% college students; 25% non-U.S. citizens; 10% local applicants. Nonsmokers preferred.

Employment Information Openings are from June 9 to August 28. Jobs available: ▶ 1 *boating specialist* (minimum age 21) with small craft and first aid certifications and CPR at $1200–$1300 per season ▶ 2 *cooks* (minimum age 21) with knowledge of cooking for groups at $3600–$4800 per season ▶ 20 *counselors (female)* (minimum age 18) should be college students with education backgrounds at $1100–$1200 per season ▶ 20 *counselors (male)* (minimum age 18) should be college students with education backgrounds at $1100–$1200 per season ▶ 1 *nature specialist* (minimum age 21) with ecology background at $1200–$1300 per season ▶ 2 *nurses* with experience and NJ state RN license, first aid, and CPR certification at $3600–$4800 per season ▶ 1 *program specialist* (minimum age 19) with experience in the field at $1600–$2500 per season ▶ 1 *recreation specialist* (minimum age 21) with therapeutic background at $1200–$1300 per season ▶ 1 *swimming instructor* (minimum age 21) with CPR, first aid, lifeguard certification, experience, teaching ability, and WSI at $1200–$1300 per season. Applicants must submit formal organization application, three personal references, three letters of recommendation. An in-person interview is recommended, but a telephone interview is acceptable. International applicants accepted; must apply through a recognized agency.

Benefits and Preemployment Training Free housing, free meals, formal training, willing to provide letters of recommendation, on-the-job training, and willing to complete paperwork for educational credit. Preemployment training is required and includes accident prevention and safety, interpersonal skills, leadership skills, how to work with people with disabilities.

Contact Alex Humanick, Director, Easter Seals Camp Merry Heart, 21 O'Brien Road, Hackettstown, New Jersey 07840. Telephone: 908-852-3896. Fax: 908-852-9263. E-mail: ahumanick@nj.easter-seals.org. World Wide Web: http://www.eastersealsnj.org. Contact by fax, mail, or phone. Application deadline: continuous.

FAIRVIEW LAKE ENVIRONMENTAL TRIP

1035 FAIRVIEW LAKE ROAD
NEWTON, NEW JERSEY 07860

General Information Facility offering discovery and challenge trips to enhance an appreciation of the natural environment while fostering skills in communication, cooperation, and trust through physical challenges. Established in 1915. 600-acre facility located 60 miles from New York, New York. Features: 110-acre glacial lake; 20 minute walk to the Appalachian Trail; 500 acres of woods; adjoined to Delaware Water Gap National Recreation Area; camp dormitory housing; many species of endangered wildlife.

Profile of Summer Employees Total number: 110; typical ages: 17–30. 50% men; 50% women; 10% minorities; 50% college students; 10% non-U.S. citizens; 30% local applicants. Nonsmokers preferred.

Employment Information Openings are from June 15 to August 15. Year-round positions also offered. Jobs available: ▶ 25 *general counselors* (minimum age 18) with love of children and the outdoors, excellent character references and interpersonal skills at $125–$175 per week ▶ 3 *trip counselors* (minimum age 21) with lifeguard training, first aid, and CPR certification, love of nature and adventure at $180–$275 per week ▶ 3 *unit leaders* (minimum age 21) with same skills and requirements as counselors plus maturity, leadership, and supervisory skills at $190–$250 per week. Applicants must submit formal organization application, three personal references. An in-person interview is recommended, but a telephone interview is acceptable. International applicants accepted; must apply through a recognized agency.

Benefits and Preemployment Training Free housing, free meals, possible full-time employment, on-the-job training, willing to complete paperwork for educational credit, and willing to act as a professional reference. Preemployment training is required and includes accident prevention and safety, first aid, CPR, interpersonal skills, leadership skills, child abuse prevention, sexual harassment prevention, YMCA orientation.

Contact Marc Koch, Director, Fairview Lake Environmental Trip, 1035 Fairview Lake Road, Newton, New Jersey 07860. Telephone: 973-383-9282. Fax: 973-383-6386. E-mail: marckoch@starband.net. World Wide Web: http://www.fairviewlake.org. Contact by e-mail or phone. Application deadline: continuous.

FAIRVIEW LAKE YMCA CAMP

1035 FAIRVIEW LAKE ROAD
NEWTON, NEW JERSEY 07860

General Information Coed residential camp serving 275 campers. Emphasis is on improving self-esteem through creativity and/or physical challenges. Large sports, drama, and outdoor adventure programs offered. Established in 1915. 600-acre facility located 65 miles from New York, New York. Features: mile long freshwater lake; Appalachian Trail borders camp; climbing tower; 2 waterfronts; modern cabins; fine arts programs.

Profile of Summer Employees Total number: 75; typical ages: 18–35. 40% men; 60% women; 25% minorities; 10% high school students; 85% college students; 5% retirees; 10% non-U.S. citizens; 5% local applicants. Nonsmokers preferred.

Employment Information Openings are from June 16 to August 10. Year-round positions also offered. Jobs available: ▶ 60 *counselors* (minimum age 18) with experience working with children, program skills; EMT licensure highly valued but not required at $1000–$1400 per season ▶ 1 *drama director* (minimum age 18) at $1400–$1800 per season ▶ 1–4 *nurses* with RN and NJ state license at $250–$650 per week ▶ 1–3 *support staff* (minimum age 20) with maintenance/housekeeping skills at $1000–$2000 per season ▶ 1–2 *teen leadership directors* (minimum age 21) with relative experience at $1800–$2500 per season ▶ 1–3 *trip leaders* (minimum age 21) with lifeguard certification and experience working with children at $1200–$1800 per season ▶ 1–2 *waterfront directors* (minimum age 21) with lifeguard certification, first aid/CPR, management experience at $1800–$2500 per season. Applicants must submit formal organization application, three personal references. An in-person interview is recommended, but a telephone interview is acceptable. International applicants accepted; must obtain own visa, obtain own working papers, apply through a recognized agency.

Benefits and Preemployment Training Free housing, free meals, formal training, possible full-time employment, willing to provide letters of recommendation, on-the-job training, willing to complete paperwork for educational credit, willing to act as a professional reference, opportunity to attend seminars/workshops, and travel reimbursement. Preemployment training is required and includes accident prevention and safety, interpersonal skills, leadership skills, lifeguard training.

Contact Marc Koch, Summer Camp Director, Fairview Lake YMCA Camp, 1035 Fairview Lake Road, Newton, New Jersey 07860. Telephone: 973-383-9282. Fax: 973-383-6386. E-mail: marckoch@starband.net. World Wide Web: http://www.fairviewlake.org. Contact by e-mail, fax, mail, phone, or through World Wide Web site. Application deadline: continuous.

FELLOWSHIP DEACONRY, INC. (DAY CAMP SUNSHINE AND FELLOWSHIP CONFERENCE CENTER)

3575 VALLEY ROAD
LIBERTY CORNER, NEW JERSEY 07938

General Information Children's day camp and adult conference center that provides a program to meet the spiritual and physical needs of all participants by providing the study of God's word, rest, and recreation in a Christian community. Established in 1933. 50-acre facility located 40 miles from New York, New York. Features: location surrounded by beautiful Watchung Mountains; well-stocked Christian bookstore/gift shop; 2 swimming pools; pond for canoeing; historic areas with sightseeing attractions; miniature golf course; tennis courts.

Profile of Summer Employees Total number: 60–100; typical age: 20. 45% men; 55% women; 10% minorities; 20% high school students; 60% college students; 10% non-U.S. citizens; 25% local applicants. Nonsmokers required.

Employment Information Openings are from June 15 to September 10. Year-round positions also offered. Jobs available: ▶ 20–30 *counselors* (minimum age 18) at $250–$300 per week ▶ 10 *counselors-in-training* (minimum age 16) at $140–$200 per week ▶ 2 *housekeeping staff* (minimum age 16) at $140–$270 per week ▶ 2 *kitchen crew* at $140–$200 per week ▶ 5–8 *lifeguards* with Red Cross advanced lifesaving and CPR/first aid certifications at $160–$300 per week ▶ 1–2 *pantry person* (minimum age 16) at $200–$280 per week ▶ 5–8 *waitresses* (minimum age 15) at $90–$280 per week. Applicants must submit formal organization application, letter of interest, resume, two personal references, letter of recommendation. An in-person interview is recommended, but a telephone interview is acceptable. International applicants accepted; must apply through a recognized agency.

Benefits and Preemployment Training Free housing, free meals, possible full-time employment, on-the-job training, and laundry facilities. Preemployment training is required and includes interpersonal skills, general Christian living.

Contact Rita Krohn, Directing Deaconess, Fellowship Deaconry, Inc. (Day Camp Sunshine and Fellowship Conference Center), PO Box 204, Liberty Corner, New Jersey 07938-0204. Telephone:

908-647-1777. Fax: 908-647-4117. E-mail: deaconry@fellowshipdeaconry.org. World Wide Web: http://www.fellowshipdeaconry.org. Contact by e-mail, fax, mail, or phone. Application deadline: May 15.

LINDLEY G. COOK 4-H CAMP

100A STRUBLE ROAD
BRANCHVILLE, NEW JERSEY 07826

General Information Residential camp facility with a weekly capacity of 150 campers ages 9–16. Established in 1951. 108-acre facility located 65 miles from New York, New York. Features: freshwater lake; located in a state forest; cabins; shooting sports areas; indoor teaching areas; mountain setting.

Profile of Summer Employees Total number: 30; typical ages: 18–60. 40% men; 60% women; 10% minorities; 5% high school students; 95% college students; 1% retirees; 10% non-U.S. citizens; 10% local applicants. Nonsmokers preferred.

Employment Information Openings are from June 18 to August 12. Winter break positions also offered. Jobs available: ▶ 1 *CIT director* (minimum age 21) with camp experience at $300–$400 per week ▶ 1 *arts and crafts director* (minimum age 21) with experience at $250–$350 per week ▶ 2 *assistant cooks* (minimum age 18) with food preparation experience at $220–$300 per week ▶ 2 *boating/canoeing instructors/counselors* (minimum age 18) with lifeguard certification and experience in the field at $225–$270 per week ▶ 6 *cabin counselors* (minimum age 18) at $200–$270 per week ▶ 1 *chef* (minimum age 21) with kitchen, ordering, and supervisory experience at $300–$400 per week ▶ 1 *cook* (minimum age 18) with experience in the field at $275–$350 per week ▶ 2 *health directors* (minimum age 21) EMT or RN at $360–$450 per week ▶ 2 *lifeguards/counselors* (minimum age 18) with certification in field at $225–$270 per week ▶ 1 *outdoor education director* (minimum age 21) with experience working with youth at $250–$350 per week ▶ 1 *outdoor living skills director* (minimum age 21) with experience in field at $250–$350 per week ▶ 1 *shooting sports director* (minimum age 21) at $270–$350 per week ▶ 1 *waterfront supervisor* (minimum age 21) with lifeguard certification at $280–$350 per week. Applicants must submit formal organization application, three personal references. An in-person interview is recommended, but a telephone interview is acceptable. International applicants accepted; must obtain own visa, obtain own working papers, apply through a recognized agency.

Benefits and Preemployment Training Free housing, free meals, formal training, willing to provide letters of recommendation, on-the-job training, willing to complete paperwork for educational credit, and willing to act as a professional reference. Preemployment training is required and includes accident prevention and safety, first aid, CPR, interpersonal skills, leadership skills, conflict resolution.

Contact James Tavares, Director, Lindley G. Cook 4-H Camp, 100A Struble Road, Branchville, New Jersey 07826. Telephone: 973-948-3550. Fax: 973-948-0735. E-mail: 4hcamp@aesop.rutgers.edu. World Wide Web: http://nj4h.rutgers.edu/camp. Contact by e-mail, fax, mail, phone, or through World Wide Web site. Application deadline: continuous.

PRESBYTERIAN CAMP JOHNSONBURG

PO BOX 475
JOHNSONBURG, NEW JERSEY 07046

General Information Presbyterian camp that runs a seven week summer program focusing on faith development in a small group coed setting. 400-acre facility located 50 miles from New York, New York. Features: springfed lake; swimming pool; highropes course; team building course; archery range; recreation center.

Profile of Summer Employees Total number: 120; typical ages: 16–24. 50% men; 50% women.

Employment Information Openings are from June 14 to August 24. Jobs available: ▶ 1 *adventure director* (minimum age 21) with WFA, lifeguard certification at $250 per week ▶ 5–10 *summer* *counselors* (minimum age 18) at $165–$195 per week ▶ 1 *waterfront director* (minimum age 21) with lifeguard certification, waterfront experience at $250 per week. Applicants must submit formal organization application, personal reference. An in-person interview is recommended, but a telephone interview is acceptable. International applicants accepted; must apply through a recognized agency.

Benefits and Preemployment Training Free housing, free meals, formal training, willing to provide letters of recommendation, and willing to act as a professional reference. Preemployment training is required and includes accident prevention and safety, interpersonal skills, leadership skills.

Contact Douglas Norrie, Assistant Program Director, Presbyterian Camp Johnsonburg. Telephone: 908-852-2349. Fax: 908-852-0045. E-mail: norrideb@yahoo.com. World Wide Web: http://www.camjburg.org. Contact by e-mail or phone. Application deadline: May 1.

REIN TEEN TOURS

30 GALESI DRIVE
WAYNE, NEW JERSEY 07470

General Information Company specializing in teen travel during the summer. Established in 1985. Located 18 miles from New York, New York.

Profile of Summer Employees Total number: 6; typical ages: 21–35. 40% men; 60% women; 80% college students; 20% local applicants. Nonsmokers required.

Employment Information Openings are from June 20 to August 20. Jobs available: ▶ *counselors* (minimum age 21) at $100 per week ▶ *counselors/cooks* (minimum age 21) at $225 per week. Applicants must submit a formal organization application, two personal references. An in-person interview is required.

Benefits and Preemployment Training Free housing, free meals, and willing to provide letters of recommendation. Preemployment training is required and includes accident prevention and safety, interpersonal skills, leadership skills.

Contact Chris Vicari, Director, Rein Teen Tours. Telephone: 800-831-1313. Fax: 973-785-4268. E-mail: chris@reinteentours.com. World Wide Web: http://www.reinteentours.com. Contact by e-mail or phone. Application deadline: May 31.

SOMERSET COUNTY PARK COMMISSION ENVIRONMENTAL EDUCATION CENTER

190 LORD STIRLING ROAD
BASKING RIDGE, NEW JERSEY 07920

General Information Environmental education center/park providing leisure and learning opportunities for the public, schools, and scouting groups. Established in 1971. 430-acre facility located 15 miles from Morristown. Features: ponds; forests; fields; hiking trails; observation blinds; observation towers.

Profile of Summer Employees Total number: 15; typical ages: 19–24. 50% men; 50% women; 10% high school students; 90% college students. Nonsmokers preferred.

Employment Information Openings are from June 10 to August 24. Jobs available: ▶ 3–4 *maintenance crew* (minimum age 19) with CPR/first aid preferred; college graduate or upperclassman with outdoor skills, trail and general maintenance skills, and ability to use hand tools at $7.65 per hour ▶ 7 *seasonal naturalist assistants* (minimum age 19) with CPR, first aid, and LGT preferred; college graduate or upperclassman with summer camp, student teaching, or similar volunteer experience at $8.80 per hour. Applicants must submit a formal organization application, letter of interest, resume, driver's license. An in-person interview is recommended, but a telephone interview is acceptable.

Benefits and Preemployment Training Possible full-time employment, willing to provide letters of recommendation, names of contacts, on-the-job training, willing to complete paperwork for educational credit, and willing to act as a professional reference.

Contact Kurt Bender, Environmental Science Supervisor, Somerset County Park Commission Environmental Education Center. Telephone: 908-766-2489 Ext. 332. E-mail: kbbender@parks.co.somerset.nj.us. World Wide Web: http://www.park.co.somerset.nj.us. Contact by e-mail, mail, phone, or through World Wide Web site. Application deadline: May 15.

THE SOUTHWESTERN COMPANY, NEW JERSEY

See The Southwestern Company on page 302 for complete description.

STONY BROOK-MILLSTONE WATERSHED ASSOCIATION-ENVIRONMENTAL EDUCATION DAY CAMP

31 TITUS MILL ROAD
PENNINGTON, NEW JERSEY 08534

General Information Environmental education day camp conducting one- and two-week programs. Established in 1949. 785-acre facility located 9 miles from Trenton. Features: nature center; butterfly house; woodlands and rolling fields; 8 miles of trails; freshwater pond.
Profile of Summer Employees Total number: 21; typical ages: 16–36. 40% men; 60% women; 10% minorities; 10% high school students; 50% college students; 100% local applicants. Nonsmokers preferred.
Employment Information Openings are from June 24 to August 16. Year-round positions also offered. Jobs available: ▶ 2 *camp group leaders* with experience in camp setting, teaching, and ecology at $3200 per season ▶ 4 *camp interns* with experience or interest in camps, teaching, and ecology at $2000 per season ▶ 2 *camp naturalists* with extensive knowledge of local ecology at $2500 per season ▶ 2 *teachers/naturalists* with experience in nature center or environmental education at $2200 per season. Applicants must submit a letter of interest, resume, two personal references, letter of recommendation. An in-person interview is recommended, but a telephone interview is acceptable. International applicants accepted.
Benefits and Preemployment Training Formal training, willing to provide letters of recommendation, on-the-job training, willing to complete paperwork for educational credit, and willing to act as a professional reference. Preemployment training is required and includes accident prevention and safety, first aid, CPR, interpersonal skills, leadership skills.
Contact Rick Lear, Program Coordinator, Stony Brook-Millstone Watershed Association-Environmental Education Day Camp, 31 Titus Mill Road, Pennington, New Jersey 08534. Telephone: 609-737-7592. Fax: 609-737-3075. E-mail: rlear@thewatershed.org. World Wide Web: http://www.thewatershed.org. Contact by e-mail, fax, mail, or phone. Application deadline: April 15.

STUDENT CONSERVATION ASSOCIATION (SCA), NEW JERSEY

See Student Conservation Association (SCA), New Hampshire on page 209 for complete description.

TOMAHAWK LAKE WATER PARK

TOMAHAWK TRAIL, PO BOX 109
SPARTA, NEW JERSEY 07871-0109

General Information Swimming and picnicking park with water rides, boating, mini-golf, ball fields, arcade, snackbar, and a beer garden; open to the public between Memorial Day weekend and Labor Day weekend. Established in 1952. 150-acre facility located 50 miles from New York, New York. Features: freshwater lake; large white sand beach; shaded picnic groves; 6 water slides; boat rides; catered picnic facilities.
Profile of Summer Employees Total number: 80–100; typical ages: 16–25. 50% men; 50%

women; 2% minorities; 30% high school students; 30% college students; 10% retirees; 20% non-U.S. citizens; 10% local applicants. Nonsmokers preferred.

Employment Information Openings are from May 25 to September 16. Jobs available: ▶ 2 *bartenders* (minimum age 18) at $5.15 per hour; tips are additional income ▶ 9–12 *food service staff (snack bars)* (minimum age 16) with food handler training at $5.50–$6 per hour ▶ 3–4 *front office assistants* (minimum age 19) first aid/CPR training on-site required; college degree or full-time, year-round work experience preferred at $7.50–$10 per hour ▶ 3–4 *front office attendants* (minimum age 19) on-site first aid/CPR training advised; paid at $7.50–$7.75 per hour ▶ 10–20 *junior waterpark attendants* (minimum age 14) at $5.25 per hour ▶ 10–20 *lifeguards (shallow water)* (minimum age 15) with National Pool and Waterpark lifeguard license (training available) at $6.25–$6.75 per hour ▶ 15–25 *lifeguards (special facilities)* (minimum age 16) with completion of on-site National Pool and Waterpark lifeguard training at $7.25–$7.75 per hour ▶ 10–20 *parking attendants* (minimum age 16) first aid/CPR training on-site at $5.75–$6.25 per hour ▶ *retail sales attendant* (minimum age 19) with CPR and first aid training at $7.50 per hour ▶ 15–17 *ride dispatchers (water rides)* (minimum age 17) with on-site training in first aid and CPR; National Pool and Waterpark lifeguard license offered; paid at $6–$6.50 per hour. Applicants must submit formal organization application, working papers if under 18, cover letter and resume (from foreign applicants). An in-person interview is recommended, but a telephone interview is acceptable. International applicants accepted; must obtain own visa, apply through a recognized agency.

Benefits and Preemployment Training Housing at a cost, meals at a cost, formal training, willing to provide letters of recommendation, on-the-job training, willing to complete paperwork for educational credit, willing to act as a professional reference, and use of facility for staff in good standing, complimentary water and lemonade. Preemployment training is required and includes accident prevention and safety, first aid, CPR, interpersonal skills, leadership skills, lifeguard training.

Contact June Wallace, General Manager, Tomahawk Lake Water Park, PO Box 109, Sparta, New Jersey 07871. Telephone: 973-398-7785. Fax: 973-398-5056. World Wide Web: http://www.tomahawklake.com. Contact by fax, mail, or phone. Application deadline: continuous.

YMCA CAMPS OCKANICKON AND MATOLLIONEQUAY

1303 STOKES ROAD
MEDFORD, NEW JERSEY 08055

General Information YMCA brother/sister summer resident camp with traditional activities, high ropes, low ropes, climbing wall, and multiple lakes in the scenic pine barrens of New Jersey. Established in 1906. 560-acre facility located 20 miles from Philadelphia, Pennsylvania. Features: aquatics; horsemanship; challenge course; creative arts; freshwater lakes; outdoor education.

Profile of Summer Employees Total number: 200; typical ages: 19–29. 50% men; 50% women; 15% minorities; 15% high school students; 65% college students; 20% non-U.S. citizens; 5% local applicants. Nonsmokers preferred.

Employment Information Openings are from May 1 to October 30. Spring break, winter break, and year-round positions also offered. Jobs available: ▶ 1–10 *activity directors* (minimum age 21) with experience in nature, sports, and arts and crafts at $1400–$1700 per season ▶ 1–60 *cabin counselors* (minimum age 19) with willingness to live in cabin with campers at $1300–$1500 per season ▶ 1–15 *lifeguard counselors* (minimum age 18) with current certifications at $1400–$1700 per season ▶ 1–2 *nurses* with RN or LPN registered with State of New Jersey at $3000–$4000 per season ▶ 1–5 *ropes instructors* (minimum age 19) with experience or training at $1500–$1800 per season ▶ 2–3 *trip and travel leaders* (minimum age 21) with lifeguard, wilderness, first responder certification at $1500–$2000 per season. Applicants must submit formal organization application, three personal references. An in-person interview is recommended, but a telephone interview is acceptable. International applicants accepted; must apply through a recognized agency.

Benefits and Preemployment Training Free housing, free meals, formal training, possible full-time employment, willing to provide letters of recommendation, names of contacts, on-the-job training, willing to complete paperwork for educational credit, willing to act as a professional reference, and travel reimbursement. Preemployment training is required and includes accident prevention and safety, first aid, CPR, interpersonal skills, leadership skills, asset-based training.

Contact Mr. Tom Rapine, Associate Executive Director, YMCA Camps Ockanickon and Matollionequay, 1303 Stokes Road, Medford, New Jersey 08055. Telephone: 609-654-8225. Fax: 609-654-8895. E-mail: tom@ycamp.org. World Wide Web: http://www.ycamp.org. Contact by e-mail, fax, mail, phone, or through World Wide Web site. Application deadline: continuous.

NEW MEXICO

FENTON RANCH
26473 HIGHWAY 126
JEMEZ SPRINGS, NEW MEXICO 87025

General Information Residential facility that houses the environmental education program for a private elementary school, Manzano Day School. Established in 1974. 5-acre facility located 80 miles from Albuquerque. Features: small pond; evergreen forests; small stream; nearby hot springs; wildflower meadows; red rock cliffs.

Profile of Summer Employees Total number: 3–5; typical ages: 16–26. 40% men; 60% women; 25% high school students; 50% college students; 25% local applicants. Nonsmokers preferred.

Employment Information Openings are from July to August. Year-round positions also offered. Jobs available: ▶ 2 *camp counselors* (minimum age 21) with first aid/CPR certification and experience with children, outdoor recreation, crafts, and games at $1000 per season ▶ 2 *junior counselors* (minimum age 15) with experience working with children, outdoor recreation, crafts, and games at $500 per season. Applicants must submit a formal organization application, letter of interest, resume, two personal references. An in-person interview is recommended, but a telephone interview is acceptable. International applicants accepted; must obtain own visa, obtain own working papers.

Benefits and Preemployment Training Free housing, free meals, willing to provide letters of recommendation, on-the-job training, willing to complete paperwork for educational credit, and willing to act as a professional reference. Preemployment training is required and includes accident prevention and safety, interpersonal skills, leadership skills, counselor training.

Contact Kestrel Mandras, Director, Fenton Ranch, 1801 Central Avenue, NW, Albuquerque, New Mexico 87104. Telephone: 505-243-6659. Fax: 505-243-4711. E-mail: km@mds.k12.nm.us. World Wide Web: http://www.mds.k12.nm.us/programs/fenton/fenton.html. Contact by e-mail, mail, or phone. Application deadline: continuous.

THE SOUTHWESTERN COMPANY, NEW MEXICO

See The Southwestern Company on page 302 for complete description.

STUDENT CONSERVATION ASSOCIATION (SCA), NEW MEXICO

See Student Conservation Association (SCA), New Hampshire on page 209 for complete description.

NEW YORK

AMERICAN CAMPING ASSOCIATION–NEW YORK SECTION

1375 BROADWAY, 4TH FLOOR
NEW YORK, NEW YORK 10018

General Information Community of camping professionals dedicated to enriching the lives of children and adults through the camp experience. The New York Section of the American Camping Association assists member camps in finding qualified staff. Overnight camps are located in New York, New Jersey, Connecticut, Pennsylvania, Massachusetts, New Hampshire, Maine, and Vermont. Features: freshwater lake; ropes course; climbing wall; tennis courts; arts/fine arts; horseback riding.

Profile of Summer Employees Total number: 12; typical ages: 17–30. 50% men; 50% women; 5% high school students; 85% college students. Nonsmokers preferred.

Employment Information Openings are from June 15 to August 25. Jobs available: ▶ *EMT staff members* with EMT certification ▶ *general counselors/group leaders* with a love of working with children and enjoyment of outdoor life ▶ *horseback riding instructors* ▶ *kitchen staff members* with chef/cook experience with large organizations ▶ *land sports instructors* with a love of working with children and enjoyment of outdoor life. Positions may be available in tennis, golf, team sports, archery, and/or gymnastics ▶ *maintenance staff members* ▶ *office/administrative staff members* ▶ *outdoor adventure instructors* with experience in ropes course, rock climbing, climbing wall ▶ *outdoor education instructors* ▶ *visual and performing arts staff members* with a love of working with children and enjoyment of outdoor life ▶ *water sports instructors* with a love of working with children and enjoyment of outdoor life ▶ *waterfront staff (lifeguards and WSI)* lifeguarding, water safety instruction, CPR and first aid certifications. Applicants must submit apply online at www.acampjob4u.org. International applicants accepted; must apply through a recognized agency.

Benefits and Preemployment Training Free housing, free meals, willing to provide letters of recommendation, on-the-job training, willing to complete paperwork for educational credit, willing to act as a professional reference, and travel reimbursement. Preemployment training is required and includes accident prevention and safety, interpersonal skills, leadership skills.

Contact Robin Katz, Director, Camp Staffing Services, American Camping Association–New York Section. Fax: 212-391-5207. E-mail: robin@aca-ny.org. World Wide Web: http://www.aca-ny.org. Contact through World Wide Web site. Application deadline: before mid-June is recommended.

BRANT LAKE CAMP

7586 STATE ROUTE 8
BRANT LAKE, NEW YORK 12815

General Information Eight-week high-tuition private residential camp for boys ages 7–15 with a capacity of 330 campers. Also 2 three-week sessions for 60 teenage girls in dance, arts, and sports, particularly tennis. Established in 1917. 95-acre facility located 70 miles from Albany. Features: 6 mile long freshwater lake; 16 tennis courts; 7 basketball courts; 4 baseball fields.

Profile of Summer Employees Total number: 150; typical ages: 19–40. 85% men; 15% women; 10% minorities; 5% high school students; 70% college students; 2% retirees; 20% non-U.S. citizens; 5% local applicants. Nonsmokers required.

Employment Information Openings are from June 5 to August 20. Jobs available: ▶ 9 *athletics specialists* must be college-age at $1400–$1800 per season ▶ 15 *general staff members* must be college-age at $1400–$1600 per season ▶ 2 *group heads/athletics directors* (minimum age 25) with experience teaching/coaching at $2000–$3200 per season ▶ 2 *swimming instructors* with lifeguard certification at $1400–$1800 per season ▶ 6 *waterfront staff members* with WSI certification/lifeguard training; must be college age at $1600–$2000 per season. Applicants must submit formal organization application, resume, three personal references, three letters of recommendation. A telephone interview is required. International applicants accepted; must apply through a recognized agency.

Benefits and Preemployment Training Free housing, free meals, willing to provide letters of recommendation, on-the-job training, willing to complete paperwork for educational credit, willing to act as a professional reference, and travel reimbursement. Preemployment training is required and includes accident prevention and safety, first aid, CPR, leadership skills.

Contact Richard Gersten, Director, Brant Lake Camp, 8 Colonial Court, Armonk, New York 10504. Telephone: 914-273-5401. Fax: 914-273-1587. E-mail: brantlakec@aol.com. World Wide Web: http://www.brantlake.com. Contact by e-mail, fax, mail, phone, or through World Wide Web site. Application deadline: continuous.

BROOKLYN BOTANIC GARDEN

1000 WASHINGTON AVENUE
BROOKLYN, NEW YORK 11225

General Information Non-profit botanic cultural institution serving the community and the world with horticultural display, education, science research, community outreach and conservation. Established in 1910. 52-acre facility. Features: 52 acres of gardens; horticultural library; science labs; herbarium; glasshouse complex; outdoor cafe.

Profile of Summer Employees Total number: 250; typical ages: 16–24. 35% men; 65% women; 60% high school students; 40% college students; 10% non-U.S. citizens.

Employment Information Openings are from June 1 to August 31. Jobs available: ▶ 10 *children's garden interns* (minimum age 19) with horticulture, agriculture education, biology background at $7 per hour ▶ 3 *junior botanist summer adventures interns* (minimum age 19) college student with science, education at $7 per hour ▶ 12 *junior instructors* (minimum age 15) initial 100 hours are volunteer. Applicants must submit formal organization application, letter of interest, resume. An in-person interview is recommended, but a telephone interview is acceptable. International applicants accepted; must obtain own visa, obtain own working papers, apply through a recognized agency.

Benefits and Preemployment Training On-the-job training and opportunity to attend seminars/workshops. Preemployment training is required and includes accident prevention and safety, interpersonal skills, leadership skills, gardening, lesson planning, botany.

Contact Romi Ige, Coordinator of Interpretation and Internships, Brooklyn Botanic Garden. Telephone: 718-623-7298. Fax: 718-622-7839. E-mail: romiige@bbg.org. World Wide Web: http://www.bbg.org. Contact by e-mail, phone, or through World Wide Web site. Application deadline: April 1.

CAMP HILLARD, INC.

26 ELIZABETH STREET
SCARSDALE, NEW YORK 10583

General Information Children's summer day camp. Established in 1929. 17-acre facility located 15 miles from New York. Features: 6 heated pools; 16 buildings; multiple fields and courts; many trees and shade; outdoor amphitheater; unique mini-golf course.

Profile of Summer Employees Total number: 300; typical ages: 18–30. 33% men; 67% women; 25% high school students; 50% college students.

Employment Information Openings are from June 26 to August 17. Jobs available: ▶ *creative and performing arts counselors* ▶ *general counselors* ▶ *sports counselors* ▶ *swim counselors*. Applicants must submit a formal organization application, three personal references. An in-person interview is required. International applicants accepted; must obtain own visa, obtain own working papers.

Benefits and Preemployment Training Willing to provide letters of recommendation, willing to complete paperwork for educational credit, and willing to act as a professional reference. Preemployment training is required and includes accident prevention and safety, first aid, CPR, interpersonal skills, leadership skills, role of camp counselor, camp's policies and procedures.

Contact Jim Libman, Director, Camp Hillard, Inc., Box 1226, Scarsdale, New York 10583. Telephone: 914-949-8857. Fax: 914-949-5843. E-mail: staff@camphillard.com. World Wide Web: http://www.camphillard.com. Contact by e-mail, fax, mail, phone, or through World Wide Web site. Application deadline: continuous.

CAMP HILLCROFT

BOX 5
BILLINGS, NEW YORK 12510

General Information Day camp serving 400 children ages 4–14 for 4–8 weeks. Established in 1950. 185-acre facility located 11 miles from Poughkeepsie. Features: 3 pools and a lake; creative workshops and studios; dance studio, theater, and music barn; outdoor adventure facilities; fields and courts for sports; farm and vegetable garden.

Profile of Summer Employees Total number: 150; typical ages: 20–35. 50% men; 50% women; 1% high school students; 50% college students; 25% non-U.S. citizens; 70% local applicants. Nonsmokers preferred.

Employment Information Openings are from June 27 to August 24. Jobs available: ▶ 1–2 *art and ceramics instructors* (minimum age 20) with BFA or MFA preferred and teaching experience at $1400–$1600 per season ▶ 2–4 *group leaders* (minimum age 22) with at least 2 years of college completed and leadership experience with children at $1400–$1800 per season ▶ *outdoor adventure instructors* (minimum age 20) with experience with ropes, climbing, and initiative games and compatibility with children at $1400–$1600 per season ▶ 1–2 *tennis and archery instructors* (minimum age 20) with experience with children at $1400–$1600 per season ▶ *waterfront staff members/lifeguards/instructors* (minimum age 20) with current lifeguard, WSI, first aid, and CPR certification at $1400–$1600 per season. Applicants must submit formal organization application, resume, three work-related references, personal interview with selected staff member in applicant's location. A telephone interview is required. International applicants accepted; must apply through a recognized agency.

Benefits and Preemployment Training Free housing, free meals, formal training, willing to provide letters of recommendation, on-the-job training, willing to complete paperwork for educational credit, and willing to act as a professional reference. Preemployment training is required and includes accident prevention and safety, first aid, CPR, interpersonal skills, leadership skills, lifeguard training.

Contact Sally Buttinger, Director, Camp Hillcroft. Telephone: 845-223-5826. Fax: 845-223-5280. E-mail: fun@camphillcroft.com. World Wide Web: http://www.camphillcroft.com. Contact by e-mail, fax, mail, phone, or through World Wide Web site. Application deadline: continuous.

CAMP HILLTOP
7825 COUNTY HIGHWAY 67
HANCOCK, NEW YORK 13783

General Information Traditional residential coed camp for campers ages 7-15. Established in 1924. 400-acre facility located 40 miles from Binghamton. Features: lake; pool; lighted tennis courts; beautiful wooded setting; 300-foot zip line; well-equipped horsebarn.

Profile of Summer Employees Total number: 80; typical ages: 19–28. 50% men; 50% women; 5% minorities; 60% college students; 30% non-U.S. citizens. Nonsmokers required.

Employment Information Openings are from June 20 to August 20. Jobs available: ▶ 3 *archery staff members* (minimum age 20) with archery certification at $1400–$2000 per season ▶ 5 *arts and crafts staff members* (minimum age 19) at $1400–$2000 per season ▶ 2 *computer staff members* (minimum age 19) at $1400–$2000 per season ▶ 12–14 *high/low ropes staff* (minimum age 19) with willingness to become certified at $1400–$2000 per season ▶ 3 *horseback riding staff members* (minimum age 20) at $1400–$2000 per season ▶ *lifeguards* with WSI certification at $1400–$2000 per season ▶ 4 *sports staff members* (minimum age 19) at $1400–$2000 per season ▶ 2 *tennis staff members* (minimum age 19) at $1400–$2000 per season ▶ 7 *waterfront staff members* (minimum age 19) with ARC lifeguard or WSI certification at $1400–$2000 per season. Applicants must submit formal organization application, three personal references, two letters of recommendation. An in-person interview is recommended, but a telephone interview is acceptable. International applicants accepted; must obtain own visa, apply through a recognized agency.

Benefits and Preemployment Training Free housing, free meals, willing to provide letters of recommendation, on-the-job training, willing to complete paperwork for educational credit, willing to act as a professional reference, opportunity to attend seminars/workshops, and travel reimbursement. Preemployment training is required and includes accident prevention and safety, first aid, CPR, interpersonal skills, leadership skills.

Contact William H. Young, Director, Camp Hilltop. Telephone: 607-637-5201. Fax: 607-637-2389. E-mail: hilltop@hancock.net. World Wide Web: http://www.camphilltop.com. Contact by e-mail, fax, mail, phone, or through World Wide Web site. Application deadline: continuous.

CAMP JEANNE D'ARC
154 GADWAY ROAD
MERRILL, NEW YORK 12955

General Information Residential camp for 120 girls ages 6–17 focusing on individual activities and personal achievement. Established in 1922. 230-acre facility located 30 miles from Plattsburgh. Features: location on 14-mile lake in Adirondack State Park; surrounded by woodlands; Swiss chalet-type cabins with fireplaces and indoor baths; mile-long 28-station fitness trail; 3 tennis courts.

Profile of Summer Employees Total number: 50; typical ages: 19–23. 5% men; 95% women; 10% minorities; 10% high school students; 75% college students; 20% non-U.S. citizens; 15% local applicants. Nonsmokers required.

Employment Information Openings are from June 24 to August 18. Jobs available: ▶ 1 *administrative assistant* (minimum age 19) with computer, organizational, and writing skills at $2000–$2500 per season ▶ 2 *arts and crafts instructors* (minimum age 19) at $1000–$1500 per season ▶ 1 *canoeing instructor* (minimum age 19) with current CPR (preferred) and LGT (training available) at $1000–$1500 per season ▶ 1 *dance instructor* (minimum age 19) at $1000–$1500 per season ▶ 1 *drama instructor* (minimum age 19) at $1000–$1500 per season ▶ 1 *music/guitar instructor* (minimum age 19) at $1000–$1500 per season ▶ 2 *nurses* with RN, EMT, or LPN; salary negotiable ▶ 5 *other land sports instructors* (minimum age 19) at $1000–$1500 per season ▶ 5 *other water sports instructors* (minimum age 19) with current CPR (preferred) and LGT (training available) at $1000–$1500 per season ▶ 2 *outdoor camping counselors* (minimum age 19) with current CPR (preferred) and RTE (training available) at

$1000–$1500 per season ▶ 3 *riding instructors* (minimum age 19) with CHA certification and RTE (training available) at $1000–$2000 per season ▶ 1 *riflery instructor* (minimum age 19) with NRA rifle instructor certification at $1000–$1500 per season ▶ 1 *sailing instructor* (minimum age 19) with current CPR (preferred) and LGT (training available) at $1000–$1500 per season ▶ 3 *swimming instructors* (minimum age 19) with WSI and American Red Cross lifeguard certification; current CPR (preferred) at $1000–$1500 per season ▶ 2 *tennis instructors* (minimum age 19) at $1000–$1500 per season ▶ 2 *waterskiing instructors* (minimum age 19) with LGT (training available) and boat driving experience at $1000–$1500 per season. Applicants must submit formal organization application, three personal references, three letters of recommendation. An in-person interview is recommended, but a telephone interview is acceptable. International applicants accepted; must apply through a recognized agency.

Benefits and Preemployment Training Free housing, free meals, willing to provide letters of recommendation, on-the-job training, willing to complete paperwork for educational credit, willing to act as a professional reference, opportunity to attend seminars/workshops, and travel reimbursement. Preemployment training is required and includes accident prevention and safety, first aid, CPR, interpersonal skills, leadership skills, RTE (responding to emergencies).

Contact Fran Bisselle, Director, Camp Jeanne d'Arc, 154 Gadway Road, Merrill, New York 12955. Telephone: 518-425-3311. Fax: 518-425-6673. E-mail: franb@campjeannedarc.com. World Wide Web: http://www.campjeannedarc.com. Contact by e-mail, fax, mail, phone, or through World Wide Web site. Application deadline: continuous.

CAMP JENED–A FACILITY OF THE UNITED CEREBRAL PALSY ASSOCIATION OF NEW YORK STATE

ADAMS ROAD
ROCK HILL, NEW YORK 12775

General Information Nonprofit residential vacationing facility for adults who have physical, intellectual and/or behavioral disabilities. Established in 1978. 150-acre facility located 90 miles from New York. Features: located in the Catskill Mountains; wheelchair accessible buildings; freshwater, well stocked lake; wheelchair accessible swimming pool; wheelchair accessible cooking and camping out facilities; 2 hours from New York City.

Profile of Summer Employees Total number: 165; typical ages: 21–23. 35% men; 65% women; 23% minorities; 90% college students; 61% non-U.S. citizens; 1% local applicants.

Employment Information Openings are from June 1 to August 26. Jobs available: ▶ 1 *cook* (minimum age 18) with ability to prepare meals for large groups; salary is negotiable ▶ 20 *counselors* (minimum age 18) at $1400 per season, plus room and board. Applicants must submit formal organization application, two letters of recommendation. A telephone interview is required. International applicants accepted; must apply through a recognized agency.

Benefits and Preemployment Training Free housing, free meals, willing to provide letters of recommendation, willing to complete paperwork for educational credit, willing to act as a professional reference, and partial travel reimbursement. Preemployment training is required and includes accident prevention and safety, interpersonal skills, leadership skills, skills to provide personal care.

Contact Michael Branam, Camp Director, Camp Jened–A Facility of the United Cerebral Palsy Association of New York State, PO Box 483, Rock Hull, New York 12775. Telephone: 914-434-2220. Fax: 914-434-2253. E-mail: jened@catskill.net. World Wide Web: http://www.campjened.org. Contact by e-mail, fax, mail, phone, or through World Wide Web site. Application deadline: continuous.

CAMP LAKELAND/JEWISH COMMUNITY CENTER OF GREATER BUFFALO, INC.

2640 NORTH FOREST ROAD
GETZVILLE, NEW YORK 14068

General Information Summer camp located on 733 acres of forested hills and meadows, bringing campers together in a magical setting, creating special friendships and living Jewish experiences to last a lifetime. Established in 1910. 733-acre facility located 2 miles from Franklinville. Features: canoeing, boating, kayaking; water skiing; climbing wall; in ground pool; mountain boarding; mountain bikes.

Profile of Summer Employees Total number: 100; typical ages: 17–26. 50% men; 50% women; 30% non-U.S. citizens.

Employment Information Openings are from June 14 to September 1. Jobs available: ▶ 75–100 *camp counselors* (minimum age 17) at $900–$4000 per season. Applicants must submit formal organization application, resume, letter of recommendation. An in-person interview is required. International applicants accepted; must apply through a recognized agency.

Benefits and Preemployment Training Free housing, free meals, willing to provide letters of recommendation, on-the-job training, and willing to complete paperwork for educational credit. Preemployment training is required and includes accident prevention and safety, interpersonal skills, leadership skills.

Contact David Miller, Camp Director, Camp Lakeland/Jewish Community Center of Greater Buffalo, Inc. Telephone: 716-688-4033. Fax: 716-688-3572. E-mail: summer@camplakeland.com. World Wide Web: http://www.camplakeland.com. Contact through World Wide Web site. Application deadline: continuous.

CAMP LOYALTOWN-AHRC

GLEN AVENUE
HUNTER, NEW YORK 12442-0316

General Information Summer residential recreational vacation camp for mentally retarded and developmentally disabled children and adults of all ages and functional levels. Established in 1947. 240-acre facility located 35 miles from Albany. Features: rolling tree-covered mountain; heated swimming pool; studios for ceramics, arts and crafts, and dance; lighted stage; indoor and outdoor athletic facilities; 32 cabins; modern infirmary; extensive program department.

Profile of Summer Employees Total number: 170; typical ages: 18–28. 50% men; 50% women; 20% minorities; 3% high school students; 90% college students; 60% non-U.S. citizens; 40% local applicants. Nonsmokers preferred.

Employment Information Openings are from June 13 to August 17. Jobs available: ▶ 2 *arts and crafts instructors* (minimum age 19) with experience presenting arts and crafts to the developmentally disabled at $2350 per season ▶ 1 *athletics instructor* (minimum age 19) with experience in the field at $2350 per season ▶ 80 *cabin counselors* (minimum age 18) with a major in special education or related field, (physical therapy, occupational therapy, psychology, or similar) at $2000 per season ▶ 1 *ceramics instructor* (minimum age 19) with experience in the field at $2350 per season ▶ 1 *cooking instructor* (minimum age 19) with experience in the field at $2350 per season ▶ 4 *cooks* with experience in quantity food preparation and nutrition ▶ 1 *dance instructor* (minimum age 19) with experience in the field at $2350 per season ▶ 1 *drama instructor* (minimum age 19) with experience in the field at $2350 per season ▶ 6 *kitchen assistants* (minimum age 18) at $1400–$1600 per season ▶ 4 *lifeguards* with ALS or WSI certification; experience preferred at $2350 per season ▶ 1 *music instructor* (minimum age 19) with experience in the field at $2350 per season ▶ 1 *nature instructor* (minimum age 19) with experience in the field at $2350 per season ▶ 4 *office staff members* (minimum age 19) with knowledge of office procedures and typing clerical skills; experience with WordPerfect, Word and Paradox database at $2350 per season ▶ 1 *recreation instructor* (minimum age 19) with experience in the field at $2350 per season ▶ 1 *sewing/fabric arts instructor* (minimum age 19) with experience in the field at $2350 per season ▶ 1 *waterfront director* (minimum age 21) with ALS and WSI certification at $2500 per season ▶ 1 *woodshop instructor* (minimum age 19) with experience in the field at $2350 per season. Applicants must submit formal organization application, letter of interest, resume, three personal references. An in-person interview is recommended, but a telephone interview is acceptable. International applicants accepted; must apply through a recognized agency.

Benefits and Preemployment Training Free housing, free meals, formal training, willing to provide letters of recommendation, on-the-job training, willing to complete paperwork for educational credit, and willing to act as a professional reference. Preemployment training is required and includes accident prevention and safety, interpersonal skills, leadership skills, education on working with various disability conditions.

Contact Paul H. Cullen, Director of Camping, Camp Loyaltown-AHRC, 115 East Bethpage Road, Plainview, New York 11803-4299. Telephone: 516-293-2016 Ext. 410. Fax: 516-719-8100. E-mail: camp@ahrc.org. World Wide Web: http://www.ahrc.org/camp.htm. Contact by e-mail, fax, mail, phone, or through World Wide Web site. Application deadline: continuous.

CAMP MICHIKAMAU–YMCA OF GREATER BERGEN COUNTY

BEAR MOUNTAIN, NEW YORK 10911

General Information Coed residential YMCA camp in rustic setting serving 110 campers ages 8–15. Features traditional camping, waterfront activities, arts and crafts, and outdoor activities. Established in 1927. 20-acre facility located 30 miles from New York. Features: freshwater lakes; wooded setting; rustic cabins; miles of hiking trails; basketball courts/low ropes; location in a state park.

Profile of Summer Employees Total number: 35; typical ages: 18–26. 60% men; 40% women; 20% high school students; 80% college students; 20% non-U.S. citizens; 80% local applicants. Nonsmokers preferred.

Employment Information Openings are from June 22 to August 22. Jobs available: ▶ 1 *arts and crafts director* (minimum age 20) at $1600–$2000 per season ▶ 20 *counselors* (minimum age 18) at $900–$1500 per season ▶ 5 *lifeguards/counselors* (minimum age 17) with American Red Cross lifeguard training at $900–$1800 per season ▶ 2 *nurses* (minimum age 20) with LPN, RN, or EMT license at $2000–$2800 per season ▶ 1–2 *waterfront directors* (minimum age 21) with WSI certification/lifeguard training at $2000–$2800 per season. Applicants must submit formal organization application, letter of interest, two letters of recommendation. An in-person interview is recommended, but a telephone interview is acceptable. International applicants accepted; must obtain own visa, apply through a recognized agency.

Benefits and Preemployment Training Free housing, free meals, willing to provide letters of recommendation, on-the-job training, willing to complete paperwork for educational credit, and willing to act as a professional reference. Preemployment training is required and includes accident prevention and safety, first aid, CPR, interpersonal skills, leadership skills.

Contact Ken Riscinti, Camping Director, Camp Michikamau–YMCA of Greater Bergen County, 360 Main Street, Hackensack, New Jersey 07601. Telephone: 201-487-6600. Fax: 201-487-4539. World Wide Web: http://www.ymcagbc.org. Contact by mail or phone. Application deadline: continuous.

CAMP MONROE

MONROE, NEW YORK 10950

General Information A well-structured, coed camp meeting the needs and interests of today's youth in a traditional Jewish camp setting. Established in 1941. 192-acre facility located 60 miles from New York. Features: swimming pool; freshwater lake; horseback riding trails and ring; 5 tennis courts; 2 hockey rinks; 2 indoor gyms.

Profile of Summer Employees Total number: 150; typical ages: 20–24. 50% men; 50% women; 10% high school students; 60% college students; 1% retirees; 30% non-U.S. citizens; 10% local applicants. Nonsmokers required.

Employment Information Openings are from June 20 to August 22. Jobs available: ▶ 2 *aerobics/dance instructors* (minimum age 21) with related teaching experience at $450–$1200 per season ▶ 1 *archery instructor* (minimum age 21) with experience in archery instruction at $450–$1200 per season ▶ 2 *boating lifeguards* (minimum age 21) with lifeguard certification at $450–$1200 per season ▶ 2–10 *general counselors* (minimum age 20) with experience working with children at $450–$1200 per season ▶ 1 *piano player* (minimum age 21) with ability to play for musical shows and to sight read and change keys easily to play with children as they sing at $450–$1200 per season ▶ 1 *tennis instructor* (minimum age 21) with relevant teaching experience at $450–$1200 per season ▶ 1 *videographer* (minimum age 21) with experience in the field at $450–$1200 per season. Applicants must submit formal organization application, letter of interest, three personal references, three letters of recommendation. An in-person interview is required. International applicants accepted; must apply through a recognized agency.

Benefits and Preemployment Training Free housing, free meals, formal training, willing to provide letters of recommendation, on-the-job training, willing to complete paperwork for educational credit, and willing to act as a professional reference. Preemployment training is required and includes accident prevention and safety, first aid, CPR, interpersonal skills, leadership skills.

Contact Stanley Felsinger, Director, Camp Monroe, PO Box 475, Monroe, New York 10950. Telephone: 845-782-8695. Fax: 845-782-2247. Contact by fax, mail, or phone. Application deadline: continuous.

CAMP OF THE WOODS
ROUTE 30
SPECULATOR, NEW YORK 12164

General Information Nonprofit Christian family resort serving over 1000 people each week and Christian girls camp, Tapawingo, serving 72 girls ages 9-17 per week, both in a mountain setting. Established in 1900. 120-acre facility located 80 miles from Albany. Features: 1500-foot beach; 1400-seat auditorium; 16-element challenge course; fantastic Chapel speakers and concerts; Adirondack Mountains; 2 gyms, 6 tennis courts, climbing wall.

Profile of Summer Employees Total number: 300; typical ages: 16–24. 45% men; 55% women; 5% minorities; 15% high school students; 75% college students; 2% retirees; 8% non-U.S. citizens; 2% local applicants. Nonsmokers required.

Employment Information Openings are from May 15 to September 7. Winter break and year-round positions also offered. Jobs available: ▶ 50 *counselors/teachers* (minimum age 17) with ability to provide leadership and programming for children in preschool through high school at $1250–$1800 per season ▶ 45 *food service personnel* (minimum age 18) at $1250–$2000 per season ▶ 10 *maintenance personnel* (minimum age 16) at $1400–$1600 per season ▶ 45 *musical performance staff members (instrumental/vocal; double as waitstaff)* (minimum age 17) at $2000–$2500 per season ▶ 3 *nurses* (minimum age 21) with RN, LPN, or EMT license at $2000–$2500 per season ▶ 10 *office/clerical staff members* (minimum age 18) at $1400–$1500 per season ▶ 50 *operational personnel (dishwashers, maintenance staff, and housekeepers)* (minimum age 16) at $1250–$3000 per season ▶ 12–15 *recreation leaders* (minimum age 17) with tennis, hiking, rafting, and team sports experience at $1500–$1800 per season ▶ 4 *soundroom technicians* (minimum age 18) with experience running sound at $1500–$2000 per season ▶ 15 *supervisors (all departments)* (minimum age 21) at $1750–$2100 per season ▶ 10 *waterfront staff members* (minimum age 17) with WSI certification (director), lifeguard training, and CPR training (staff) at $1400–$1600 per season. Applicants must submit formal organization application, three writing samples, two personal references, $5 processing fee (waived for international applicants). An in-person interview is recommended, but a telephone interview is acceptable.

International applicants accepted; must obtain own visa, obtain own working papers, apply through a recognized agency.
Benefits and Preemployment Training Free housing, free meals, formal training, possible full-time employment, willing to provide letters of recommendation, on-the-job training, willing to complete paperwork for educational credit, willing to act as a professional reference, opportunity to attend seminars/workshops, and tuition assistance. Preemployment training is required and includes first aid, CPR, leadership skills, lifeguarding, RTE, climbing wall, and challenge course.
Contact Andrew Mather, Personnel Director, Camp of the Woods, Route 30, Speculator, New York 12164. Telephone: 518-548-4311. Fax: 518-548-9751. E-mail: andym@camp-of-the-woods.org. World Wide Web: http://www.camp-of-the-woods.org. Contact by e-mail, fax, mail, phone, or through World Wide Web site. Application deadline: March 1.

CAMP REGIS, INC.
PO BOX 245
PAUL SMITHS, NEW YORK 12970

General Information Residential coed children's camp serving 280 campers ages 6–16. Established in 1946. 100-acre facility located 18 miles from Lake Placid. Features: majestic Adirondack lake setting; extensive waterfront (60 boats); 7 tennis courts; large theater, music room, and arts and crafts studio; wilderness trip program originating from our doorstep; chalet-type cabins with fireplaces and bathrooms.
Profile of Summer Employees Total number: 90; typical ages: 18–60. 50% men; 50% women; 20% minorities; 70% college students; 10% non-U.S. citizens; 10% local applicants. Nonsmokers required.
Employment Information Openings are from June 23 to August 25. Jobs available: ▶ 1 *archery instructor* with teaching experience preferred at $1400–$2200 per season ▶ 2 *arts and crafts instructors* with teaching experience preferred at $1400–$2600 per season ▶ 3 *athletics instructors* with broad knowledge of numerous sports required at $1400–$3500 per season ▶ 10 *cabin counselors for boys groups* (minimum age 19) with at least one year of college completed at $1400–$1800 per season ▶ 10 *cabin counselors for girls groups* (minimum age 19) with at least one year of college completed at $1400–$1800 per season ▶ 5 *cooks* at $1600–$4600 per season ▶ 1 *dance instructor* with teaching experience preferred at $1400–$2400 per season ▶ 3 *dishwashers* at $1200–$1600 per season ▶ 2 *dramatics instructors* with teaching and directing experience preferred at $1400–$3500 per season ▶ 1 *gymnastics instructor* with coaching experience required at $1400–$2400 per season ▶ 2 *healthcare workers* with RN, LPN or EMT required at $1200–$2000 per month ▶ 1 *in-camp nature/ecology instructor* with knowledge of animals and their care at $1400–$2400 per season ▶ 2 *laundry workers* at $1200–$1600 per season ▶ 1 *mountain biking instructor* with Red Cross, CPR, and first aid required (will provide training) at $1400–$2200 per season ▶ 1 *music instructor* whose main instrument is the piano at $1400–$2800 per season ▶ 1 *office worker/office manager* with computer/office machines experience preferred at $1400–$2500 per season ▶ 3 *pioneering/trips instructors* with Red Cross, CPR, and first aid required (will provide training) at $1400–$3000 per season ▶ 2 *program directors* with camp experience preferred at $1600–$4600 per season ▶ 2 *sailing and windsurfing instructors* at $1400–$3500 per season ▶ 3 *swimming instructors* with Red Cross, lifeguarding and CPR required at $1400–$3500 per season ▶ 3 *tennis instructors* at $1400–$3500 per season ▶ 4 *unit leaders/head counselors* with camp experience preferred at $1600–$4000 per season ▶ 2 *waterskiing instructors* with boat driving experience required at $1400–$2600 per season. Applicants must submit formal organization application, personal reference. An in-person interview is recommended, but a telephone interview is acceptable. International applicants accepted; must apply through a recognized agency.
Benefits and Preemployment Training Free housing, free meals, formal training, possible full-time employment, willing to provide letters of recommendation, on-the-job training, willing

to complete paperwork for educational credit, willing to act as a professional reference, opportunity to attend seminars/workshops, travel reimbursement, and tuition assistance. Preemployment training is required and includes accident prevention and safety, first aid, CPR, interpersonal skills, leadership skills.

Contact Michael Humes, Director, Camp Regis, Inc., 60 Lafayette Road West, Princeton, New Jersey 08540-2428. Telephone: 609-688-0368. Fax: 609-688-0369. E-mail: campregis@aol.com. World Wide Web: http://www.campregis-applejack.com. Contact by e-mail, fax, mail, phone, or through World Wide Web site. Application deadline: continuous.

CAMP SEVEN HILLS
10150 OLEAN ROAD
HOLLAND, NEW YORK 14080

General Information Residential Girl Scout camp serving 150–200 girls ages 6–17 offering one-week, two-week and mini-sessions which include challenge courses, horseback riding, and out-of-camp trips. Established in 1930. 610-acre facility located 42 miles from Buffalo. Features: ropes course; horse stables; pool; sports complex; hiking trails; farm area.

Profile of Summer Employees Total number: 60; typical ages: 18–24. 2% men; 98% women; 5% minorities; 10% high school students; 90% college students; 5% non-U.S. citizens; 95% local applicants. Nonsmokers preferred.

Employment Information Openings are from June 26 to August 18. Jobs available: ▶ 5 *activity counselors/unit assistants* (minimum age 18) with specialization in sports/recreation, nature, arts and crafts, drama, and campcraft at $1500 per season ▶ 1 *assistant camp director* (minimum age 20) with camping experience, knowledge of Girl Scout program, and experience supervising and training staff at $2300 per season ▶ 1 *assistant cook* (minimum age 20) with experience in food preparation for large groups and ability to meet deadlines at $2100 per season ▶ 1 *assistant waterfront director* (minimum age 18) with current lifeguard training and first aid, CPR certifications, and waterfront modual at $1650 per season ▶ 1 *boating instructor* (minimum age 18) with current lifeguard and CPR/BLS certification, certification in the fundamentals of canoeing and/or boating or will provide, and waterfront modual at $1500 per season ▶ 1 *camp aide* (minimum age 16) with ability to work with limited supervision at $1050 per season ▶ 1 *counselor-in-training director* (minimum age 20) with extensive Girl Scout camp experience and experience teaching older adolescents at $1600 per season ▶ 2 *dining hall managers* (minimum age 18) with ability to supervise operation and procedures of dining hall at $1650 per season ▶ 1 *handyperson* (minimum age 18) with knowledge of basic machinery, and some maintenance skills; position is full- or part-time at $1600 per season ▶ 1 *health supervisor* (minimum age 21) with RN, LPN, or physician's assistant at $3200 per season ▶ 7 *junior counselors* (minimum age 16) with camp experience and successful completion of CIT program preferred at $1100 per season ▶ 2 *kitchen aides* (minimum age 16) with ability to work under supervision and as a team player at $1050 per season ▶ 5 *lifeguards/unit assistants* (minimum age 17) with lifeguard certification, first aid, CPR, and waterfront modual at $1300 per season ▶ 1 *program director* (minimum age 20) with Girl Scout and camping background preferred and creativity at $2000 per season ▶ 1 *riding director* (minimum age 20) with Western and English riding ability, knowledge of horses, simple medications, and proper care, ability to manage horse program, and CHA certification preferred, but will provide at $1600 per season ▶ 5 *riding instructors/unit assistants* (minimum age 18) with Western and English riding ability and knowledge of simple horse medications at $1500 per season ▶ 4 *ropes course counselors/unit assistants* (minimum age 18) with Project Adventure/ropes course certification (will provide certification) and group dynamics experience at $1500 per season ▶ 1 *stable manager* (minimum age 18) with knowledge of barn management and equine care, experience in English and Western riding at $1500 per season ▶ 1 *store manager* (minimum age 18) with knowledge of bookkeeping and budgeting and ability to manage truck-shop operation; sales/office experience at $1900 per season ▶ 4 *trip counselors* (minimum age 18) with experience in backpacking, canoeing, and outdoor living at

$1600 per season ▶ 7 *unit assistants* (minimum age 18) with experience working with children and camping and Girl Scout background preferred at $1250 per season ▶ 7 *unit leaders* (minimum age 20) with camping and Girl Scout background preferred and experience working with children at $1600 per season ▶ 1 *waterfront director* (minimum age 21) with WSI and lifeguard certification; waterfront modual at $1900 per season. Applicants must submit formal organization application, three personal references. An in-person interview is recommended, but a telephone interview is acceptable. International applicants accepted; must apply through a recognized agency.

Benefits and Preemployment Training Free housing, free meals, health insurance, willing to provide letters of recommendation, on-the-job training, willing to complete paperwork for educational credit, and opportunity to attend seminars/workshops. Preemployment training is required and includes accident prevention and safety, first aid, CPR, interpersonal skills, leadership skills, child development/Girl Scout programming.

Contact Janet M. DePetrillo, Director of Outdoor Program, Camp Seven Hills, 70 Jewett Parkway, Buffalo, New York 14214. Telephone: 716-837-6400. Fax: 716-837-6407. E-mail: jdepetrillo@bflogirlscouts.org. World Wide Web: http://www.bflogirlscouts.org. Contact by e-mail, fax, mail, phone, or through World Wide Web site. Application deadline: July 4.

CAMP WALDEN NY

429 TROUT LAKE ROAD
DIAMOND POINT, NEW YORK 12824

General Information Co-ed residential camp for children 6–16 located in the Adirondacks of New York. Established in 1931. Located 50 miles from Albany. Features: lake; swimming pool; ropes challenge course; 2 roller hockey rinks; 5 new, lit tennis courts; wonderful and caring staff.

Profile of Summer Employees Total number: 100; typical ages: 17–35. 50% men; 50% women; 10% high school students; 90% college students; 30% non-U.S. citizens. Nonsmokers preferred.

Employment Information Openings are from June 18 to August 17. Jobs available: ▶ *activity specialists* (minimum age 17) negotiable salary ▶ *counselors* (minimum age 17) negotiable salary ▶ *head chef* (minimum age 25) with experience as a chef; negotiable salary ▶ *registered nurse* (minimum age 25) with RN experience; negotiable salary. Applicants must submit formal organization application, resume, three personal references. An in-person interview is recommended, but a telephone interview is acceptable. International applicants accepted; must apply through a recognized agency.

Benefits and Preemployment Training Free housing, free meals, willing to provide letters of recommendation, on-the-job training, and willing to act as a professional reference. Preemployment training is required and includes leadership skills.

Contact Robyn Spector, Director/Head Counselor, Camp Walden NY, 61 Peter Andrew Crescent, Thornhill, Ontario L4J 3E2. Fax: 905-771-1971. E-mail: spector@interlog.com. World Wide Web: http://www.campwalden.org. Contact by e-mail. Application deadline: continuous.

CENTER FOR TALENTED YOUTH/JOHNS HOPKINS UNIVERSITY–SIENA COLLEGE

LOUDONVILLE, NEW YORK

See Center for Talented Youth/Johns Hopkins University on page 145 for complete description.

CENTER FOR TALENTED YOUTH/JOHNS HOPKINS UNIVERSITY–SKIDMORE COLLEGE

SARATOGA SPRINGS, NEW YORK

See Center for Talented Youth/Johns Hopkins University on page 145 for complete description.

CHINGACHGOOK YMCA OUTDOOR CENTER

1872 PILOT KNOB ROAD
KATTSKILL BAY, NEW YORK 12844

General Information Outdoor, environmental, and adventure education center in the Adirondacks that teaches school children, college students, families, and adult groups. Established in 1913. 200-acre facility located 50 miles from Albany. Features: water skiing. sailing, canoeing; 200 acres of Adirondack forest; 30-element-high and low ropes course; 32 mile fresh water lake; brand new hike and trip center; beach front cabins.

Profile of Summer Employees Total number: 110; typical ages: 17–25. 50% men; 50% women; 5% minorities; 20% high school students; 75% college students; 15% non-U.S. citizens; 30% local applicants. Nonsmokers preferred.

Employment Information Openings are from June 10 to September 5. Spring break, winter break, and year-round positions also offered. Jobs available: ▶ 6 *adventure trip leaders* (minimum age 21) at $1200–$2000 per season ▶ 1 *boating specialist (sailing, canoeing, row boating, windsurfing)* (minimum age 21) lifeguard certification at $1300–$3000 per season ▶ 35 *counselors* at $1000–$1500 per season ▶ 45 *general camp staff members* (minimum age 16) at $500–$4500 per season ▶ 1 *waterfront director* (minimum age 21) with WSI and lifeguarding certification, supervision of waterfront operations: swimming, boating, skiing, special programs; skills in motorboat operation and waterfront maintenance at $3000–$4000 per season. Applicants must submit formal organization application, three personal references. An in-person interview is recommended, but a telephone interview is acceptable. International applicants accepted; must apply through a recognized agency.

Benefits and Preemployment Training Free housing, free meals, formal training, willing to provide letters of recommendation, on-the-job training, willing to complete paperwork for educational credit, and willing to act as a professional reference. Preemployment training is required and includes accident prevention and safety, first aid, CPR, interpersonal skills, leadership skills.

Contact George Binter, Executive Director, Chingachgook YMCA Outdoor Center, 1872 Pilot Knob Road, Kattskill Bay, New York 12844. Telephone: 518-656-9462. Fax: 518-656-9362. E-mail: troode@cdymca.org. World Wide Web: http://www.chingachgook.org. Contact by e-mail, fax, or phone. Application deadline: continuous.

COLLEGE GIFTED PROGRAMS

VASSAR COLLEGE
POUGHKEEPSIE, NEW YORK 12601

General Information Residential educational academic summer camp for gifted and talented students in grades 4-11. Program blends in-depth academics with recreational and cultural activities. Established in 1984. 1,000-acre facility located 70 miles from New York. Features: dormitories; campus classroom facilities; campus recreational facilities include pool, tennis courts, and gym; campus library; beautiful college setting.

Profile of Summer Employees Typical ages: 19–70. 40% men; 60% women; 30% minorities; 50% college students; 10% retirees; 10% non-U.S. citizens; 25% local applicants. Nonsmokers required.

Employment Information Openings are from July 3 to July 24. Jobs available: ▶ 45 *counselors* with two years of college completed and experience working with children at $900 to $1200 per 3-week session ▶ 4 *directors* with at least 5 years teaching/supervisory experience; master's degree required, doctorate preferred at $5000–$8000 per year ▶ 9 *housemasters/instructors (residential)* with master's degree, teaching and supervisory experience at $2500 to $4500 per 3-week session ▶ 20 *instructors (non-residential)* with master's degree and teaching experience at $600 to $2500 per 3-week session ▶ 2 *nurses* with RN license; school experience preferred at $1300 per week. Applicants must submit formal organization application, resume, academic transcripts, two personal references, two letters of recommendation. An in-person interview is recommended, but a telephone interview is acceptable. International applicants accepted; must apply through a recognized agency.

Benefits and Preemployment Training Free housing, free meals, willing to provide letters of recommendation, willing to complete paperwork for educational credit, and willing to act as a professional reference. Preemployment training is required and includes accident prevention and safety, interpersonal skills, leadership skills, instructional strategies for gifted students.

Contact Charles Zeichner, Executive Director, College Gifted Programs, 120 Littleton Road, Suite 201, Parsippany, New Jersey 07054-1803. Telephone: 973-334-6991. Fax: 973-334-9756. E-mail: info@cgp-sig.com. World Wide Web: http://www.cgp-sig.com. Contact by e-mail, fax, mail, phone, or through World Wide Web site. Application deadline: continuous.

CYBERCAMPS–ADELPHI UNIVERSITY

GARDEN CITY, NEW YORK

See Cybercamps–University of Washington on page 335 for complete description.

EASTERN EXCEL TENNIS

LONG ISLAND UNIVERSITY
BROOKVILLE, NEW YORK 11545

General Information Camp that trains children in playing all aspects of tennis, including competition and match play. Established in 1991. Located 25 miles from New York. Features: 37 tennis courts.

Profile of Summer Employees Total number: 25; typical ages: 18–35. 75% men; 25% women; 10% high school students; 60% college students; 5% non-U.S. citizens. Nonsmokers required.

Employment Information Openings are from June 24 to August 23. Jobs available: ▶ 5–15 *tennis instructors* (minimum age 18) with some teaching experience at $150–$300 per week. Applicants must submit a formal organization application, resume, three personal references. An in-person interview is recommended, but a telephone interview is acceptable. International applicants accepted; must obtain own visa.

Benefits and Preemployment Training Willing to provide letters of recommendation and on-the-job training. Preemployment training is required and includes accident prevention and safety, interpersonal skills.

Contact Lawrence Kleger, Owner, Eastern Excel Tennis, 38 Club Drive North, Jericho, New York 11753. Telephone: 516-938-6076. Fax: 516-827-0981. E-mail: lkleger@optonline.net. Contact by mail or phone. Application deadline: June 1.

ENCHANTED FOREST/WATER SAFARI AND OLD FORGE

3183 STATE ROUTE 38
OLD FORGE, NEW YORK 13420

General Information Amusement/theme/water park, campground, and family entertainment center. Established in 1956. 200-acre facility located 50 miles from Utica. Features: water rides; amusement park rides; circus shows; campground; camping cabins; go-carts.

Profile of Summer Employees Total number: 350; typical ages: 14–20. 50% men; 50% women; 5% minorities; 70% high school students; 30% college students; 5% retirees; 1% non-U.S. citizens; 10% local applicants. Nonsmokers preferred.

Employment Information Openings are from May to October. Jobs available: ▶ 10 *admissions staff* (minimum age 16) at $5.15 per hour ▶ 30 *food service personnel* (minimum age 14) at $5.15 per hour ▶ 10 *games attendants* (minimum age 14) at $5.15 per hour ▶ 20 *grounds crew/housekeeping staff* (minimum age 16) at $5.15 per hour ▶ 20 *lifeguards* (minimum age 15) with CPR/lifeguard certification at $6.50 per hour ▶ 10 *registration/reservations* (minimum age 16) at $6 per hour ▶ 20 *retail personnel* (minimum age 14) at $5.15 per hour ▶ 30 *ride operators* (minimum age 18) at $5.15 per hour ▶ 75 *water/amusement ride operators* (minimum age 14) at $5.15 per hour. Applicants must submit a formal organization application, two personal references. An in-person interview is required. International applicants accepted; must obtain own visa, obtain own working papers.

Benefits and Preemployment Training Housing at a cost, meals at a cost, formal training, willing to provide letters of recommendation, on-the-job training, willing to complete paperwork for educational credit, willing to act as a professional reference, and scholarships; parties; discounts. Preemployment training is required and includes first aid, CPR, interpersonal skills, leadership skills, training for lifeguards, guest relations.

Contact Peter Pepper, Human Resources Manager, Enchanted Forest/Water Safari and Old Forge, 3183 State Route 28, Old Forge, New York 13420. Telephone: 315-369-6145. Fax: 315-369-6400. E-mail: safari@telenet.net. World Wide Web: http://www.watersafari.com. Contact by e-mail, fax, mail, phone, or through World Wide Web site. Application deadline: continuous.

FIVE RIVERS CENTER

GAME FARM ROAD
DELMAR, NEW YORK 12054

General Information Environmental education center serving schools and families. Established in 1973. 330-acre facility located 10 miles from Albany. Features: natural setting; many ponds; wooded areas; open meadows; visitor center; picnic area.

Profile of Summer Employees Total number: 6–8; typical ages: 18–65. 50% men; 50% women; 10% minorities; 10% high school students; 30% college students; 30% retirees; 20% local applicants. Nonsmokers required.

Employment Information Openings are from January 1 to December 31. Jobs available: ▶ 2 *naturalist interns* (minimum age 18) with college-level study in natural sciences preferred at $200 per week. Applicants must submit formal organization application, resume, academic transcripts, three personal references. An in-person interview is recommended, but a telephone interview is acceptable. International applicants accepted; must obtain own visa, obtain own working papers.

Benefits and Preemployment Training Free housing, formal training, willing to provide letters of recommendation, on-the-job training, willing to complete paperwork for educational credit, willing to act as a professional reference, and opportunity to attend seminars/workshops.

Contact A. Sanchez, Senior Educator, Five Rivers Center, 56 Game Farm Road, Delmar, New York 12054. Telephone: 518-475-0291. Contact by mail or phone. Application deadline: continuous.

FOREST LAKE CAMP

FOREST LAKE ROAD, PO BOX 67
WARRENSBURG, NEW YORK 12885

General Information Residential brother/sister camp for 100 boys and 85 girls with private lake. Features general program of sports, hobbies, waterfront activities, wilderness trips, and riding. Established in 1926. 400-acre facility located 65 miles from Albany. Features: private lake; 400 acres; vistas; climbing tower; cabins with fireplaces; wooded setting.

Profile of Summer Employees Total number: 80; typical ages: 18–24. 50% men; 50% women; 10% minorities; 5% high school students; 75% college students; 10% non-U.S. citizens; 15% local applicants. Nonsmokers preferred.

Employment Information Openings are from June 24 to August 25. Jobs available: ▶ 1 *baseball coach* with high school varsity (minimum) playing experience at $1400–$2000 per season ▶ 1 *basketball coach* with minimum high school varsity playing experience at $1400–$2000 per season ▶ 3–8 *general counselors* (minimum age 18) at $1400–$2000 per season ▶ 4 *swimming instructors* (minimum age 18) with lifeguard, first aid, and CPR training at $1400–$2000 per season ▶ 2 *tennis coaches* with high school varsity (minimum) playing experience at $1400–$2000 per season ▶ 1–3 *trip leaders* (minimum age 21) with RTE and wilderness expertise at

$2000–$4000 per season. Applicants must submit formal organization application, resume, three personal references. An in-person interview is recommended, but a telephone interview is acceptable. International applicants accepted; must apply through a recognized agency.
Benefits and Preemployment Training Free housing, free meals, willing to provide letters of recommendation, on-the-job training, willing to act as a professional reference, travel reimbursement, and tuition assistance. Preemployment training is required and includes accident prevention and safety, first aid, CPR, interpersonal skills, leadership skills, RTE.
Contact Gary Confer, Director, Forest Lake Camp, Box 648, Oldwick, New Jersey 08858. Telephone: 908-534-9809. Fax: 908-534-8474. E-mail: gaconfer@aol.com. World Wide Web: http://www.forestlakecamp.com. Contact by e-mail, fax, mail, or phone. Application deadline: continuous.

FORRESTEL FARM CAMP
4536 SOUTH GRAVEL ROAD
MEDINA, NEW YORK 14103

General Information Coed residential camp serving 60 children ages 7–15 for four 2-week sessions. Established in 1981. 1,000-acre facility located 40 miles from Buffalo. Features: 800-acre working farm; freshwater pond; 3 miles of Oak Orchard Creek; elaborate stable; tennis court; wooded setting.
Profile of Summer Employees Total number: 20; typical ages: 19–25. 30% men; 70% women; 100% college students; 80% non-U.S. citizens; 20% local applicants. Nonsmokers required.
Employment Information Openings are from June 20 to August 20. Jobs available: ▶ 1 *arts and crafts instructor* (minimum age 19) with some experience in the field ▶ 4 *athletics instructors* (minimum age 19) with coaching and teaching experience in one of the following: soccer, volleyball, basketball, softball, lacrosse ▶ 2 *cooks* (minimum age 19) with experience in the field ▶ 4 *lifeguards* (minimum age 19) with Red Cross lifeguard or WSI certification ▶ 1 *naturalist/conservationist* (minimum age 19) with experience in the field; pay commensurate with experience ▶ 3 *outdoor adventure instructors (canoeing, hiking, mountain biking, fishing, archery, riflery, wall climbing, and orienteering)* (minimum age 19) with experience in the field ▶ 8 *riding instructors* (minimum age 19) with previous teaching experience recommended per season ▶ 2 *tennis instructors* (minimum age 19) with USTA coaching or teaching experience recommended. Applicants must submit formal organization application, two personal references, two letters of recommendation. An in-person interview is recommended, but a telephone interview is acceptable. International applicants accepted; must apply through a recognized agency.
Benefits and Preemployment Training Free housing, free meals, willing to provide letters of recommendation, on-the-job training, willing to complete paperwork for educational credit, willing to act as a professional reference, and travel reimbursement. Preemployment training is required and includes accident prevention and safety, first aid, CPR, interpersonal skills, leadership skills.
Contact Mary Herbert, Camp Owner/Director, Forrestel Farm Camp, 4536 South Gravel Road, Medina, New York 14103. Telephone: 585-798-2222. Fax: 585-798-2222. E-mail: camp@forrestelfarmcamp.com. World Wide Web: http://www.forrestelfarmcamp.com. Contact by e-mail, fax, mail, phone, or through World Wide Web site. Application deadline: application by March 1 is preferred.

FRENCH WOODS FESTIVAL OF THE PERFORMING ARTS
HANCOCK, NEW YORK 13783

General Information Private children's summer camp with individualized programming in performing and visual arts, sports, and more. Established in 1970. 600-acre facility located 40 miles from Binghamton. Features: private lake; heated pool; five theatres; large circus building; air conditioned dining room; ample recreational facilities.

Profile of Summer Employees Total number: 350; typical ages: 19–25. 45% men; 55% women; 5% minorities; 70% college students; 5% retirees; 50% non-U.S. citizens; 50% local applicants. Nonsmokers required.

Employment Information Openings are from June 20 to August 25. Jobs available: ▶ 8–10 *head counselors* (minimum age 23) with ability to supervise group of counselors and campers at $3000–$6000 per season ▶ 10–20 *program heads* (minimum age 25) with extensive background in program area at $2500–$5000 per season ▶ 175–225 *specialist counselors* (minimum age 18) with skill in a program area and ability to teach at $1400–$2400 per season. Applicants must submit formal organization application, resume, two personal references, two letters of recommendation. An in-person interview is recommended, but a telephone interview is acceptable. International applicants accepted; must apply through a recognized agency.

Benefits and Preemployment Training Free housing, free meals, willing to provide letters of recommendation, on-the-job training, willing to complete paperwork for educational credit, willing to act as a professional reference, and travel reimbursement. Preemployment training is required and includes accident prevention and safety, CPR, interpersonal skills, leadership skills.

Contact Beth Schaefer, Director, French Woods Festival of the Performing Arts, PO Box 770100, Coral Springs, Florida 33077. Telephone: 800-634-1703. Fax: 954-346-7564. E-mail: beth_s@frenchwoodscamp.com. World Wide Web: http://www.frenchwoods.com. Contact by e-mail, fax, mail, or phone. Application deadline: continuous.

THE FRESH AIR FUND

SHARPE RESERVATION, VAN WYCK LAKE ROAD
FISHKILL, NEW YORK 12524

General Information Five residential camps serving 3,000 inner-city children each summer. Established in 1877. 3,000-acre facility located 65 miles from New York.

Profile of Summer Employees Total number: 400; typical ages: 18–23. 55% men; 45% women; 35% minorities; 3% high school students; 90% college students; 15% non-U.S. citizens; 30% local applicants. Nonsmokers preferred.

Employment Information Openings are from June 15 to August 24. Jobs available: ▶ 5 *farmers* (minimum age 18) with course work in animal biology or experience working with livestock at $1700–$2100 per season ▶ 200 *general counselors* (minimum age 18) with some college and experience with children at $1700–$2100 per season ▶ 9 *nurses* with RN license and one year of nursing experience required at $6000–$7000 per season ▶ 2 *nutritionists* (minimum age 18) with cooking experience and course work in nutrition at $1700–$2100 per season ▶ 35 *program specialists* (minimum age 18) with ability to teach in one of the following specialties: photography, video, music, sewing, pioneering, nature, or arts and crafts at $1700–$2200 per season ▶ 6 *ropes course facilitators* (minimum age 19) with experience as an instructor or participant on high and/or low ropes course programs; facilitators will be trained and certified during orientation at $1700–$2100 per season ▶ 22 *village leaders* (minimum age 20) with residential camp employment experience required at $2100–$2600 per season ▶ 20 *waterfront assistants* (minimum age 18) with lifeguard training and CPR for the professional rescuer at $2100–$2400 per season ▶ 5 *waterfront directors* (minimum age 21) with lifeguard training and CPR for the professional rescuer; three years of waterfront experience required; WSI preferred at $2500–$3000 per season. Applicants must submit formal organization application. An in-person interview is recommended, but a telephone interview is acceptable. International applicants accepted; must apply through a recognized agency.

Benefits and Preemployment Training Free housing, free meals, formal training, willing to provide letters of recommendation, on-the-job training, willing to complete paperwork for educational credit, and travel reimbursement. Preemployment training is required and includes accident prevention and safety, first aid, CPR, leadership skills, lifeguard training.

Contact Thomas S. Karger, Deputy Executive Director, The Fresh Air Fund, 633 Third Avenue, New York, New York 10017. Telephone: 800-367-0003. Fax: 212-681-0147. E-mail: freshair@

freshair.org. World Wide Web: http://www.freshair.org. Contact by e-mail, fax, mail, phone, or through World Wide Web site. Application deadline: continuous.

GIRL SCOUTS–INDIAN HILLS COUNCIL, INC.

32 WEST STATE STREET
BINGHAMTON, NEW YORK 13902-2145

General Information Residential camp program at the Amahami Outdoor Center set on 450 acres and serving girls ages 6 to 18. Specialty programs include: swimming, arts and crafts, nature activities, leadership training, and outdoor adventure activities. Established in 1929. 450-acre facility. Features: freshwater lake; staff housing with kitchen; low ropes/high ropes course; wooded setting; kayaks.

Profile of Summer Employees Total number: 30–35; typical ages: 16–40. 20% men; 80% women; 5% minorities; 10% high school students; 50% college students; 35% local applicants. Nonsmokers required.

Employment Information Openings are from June 24 to August 24. Jobs available: ▶ 1 *business manager* (minimum age 21) with driver's license, business training at $2400–$2500 per season ▶ 1–2 *camp director/assistant director* (minimum age 21) with Bachelor's Degree or 24 weeks of administrative/supervisory experience at $4200–$5500 per season ▶ 1–2 *cooks* at $2800–$3500 per season ▶ 1 *health supervisor* (minimum age 21) Physician, RN, EMT, NP, or LPN with current first aid/CPR certification at $3000–$4000 per season ▶ 1–3 *kitchen assistants* (minimum age 16) willing to assist cooks at $1500–$2000 per season ▶ 3–5 *lifeguards* (minimum age 16) with lifeguard certification, waterfront lifeguard certification at $1800–$3500 per season ▶ 1 *sports director* (minimum age 21) with experience in physical education; CPR/first aid certification or ability to get it at $1000–$1500 per season ▶ 10–20 *unit assistants* (minimum age 17) with a love of working with children; previous work with kids preferred; a love of being outdoors at $1800–$2500 per season ▶ 1 *western riding director* (minimum age 21) with experience instructing western horseback riding at $3000–$3500 per season. Applicants must submit formal organization application, resume, three personal references. An in-person interview is recommended, but a telephone interview is acceptable. International applicants accepted; must apply through a recognized agency.

Benefits and Preemployment Training Free housing, free meals, formal training, possible full-time employment, health insurance, willing to provide letters of recommendation, on-the-job training, willing to complete paperwork for educational credit, willing to act as a professional reference, and opportunity to attend seminars/workshops. Preemployment training is required and includes accident prevention and safety, first aid, CPR, interpersonal skills, leadership skills, child abuse recognition.

Contact Camp Administrator, Girl Scouts–Indian Hills Council, Inc. Telephone: 607-724-6572. Fax: 607-724-6575. E-mail: gsihc@pronetisp.net. Contact by e-mail, fax, mail, or phone. Application deadline: continuous.

GOLDEN ACRES FARM AND RANCH RESORT

COUNTY ROAD 14
GILBOA, NEW YORK 12076

General Information Kosher family farm and ranch resort catering to young professional families with children. Established in 1950. 600-acre facility located 60 miles from Albany. Features: horseback riding stable; indoor and outdoor pools; Catskill Mountain location; tennis, volleyball, and paddleball courts; children's day camp; theater productions.

Profile of Summer Employees Total number: 100; typical age: 22. 40% men; 60% women; 10% minorities; 51% college students; 2% retirees; 30% non-U.S. citizens; 10% local applicants.

Employment Information Openings are from August 1 to September 7. Jobs available: ▶ 1 *baker* with experience at $600–$700 per week ▶ 1 *bartender/barmaid* (minimum age 21) with cash-handling references and experience at $200–$275 per week ▶ 3 *bellhops/maintenance* *personnel* with mechanical abilities and driver's license at $215–$250 per week ▶ 11 *chamber staff members* (minimum age 19) with clean and neat appearance at $215–$250 per week ▶ 1–2 *chefs* (minimum age 25) with experience in banquet cooking; kosher experience preferred at $500–$600 per week ▶ 13 *counselors* (minimum age 19) with experience at $215–$250 per week ▶ 1–2 *dining room managers* (minimum age 25) with supervisory and serving experience at $300–$350 per week ▶ 20 *food service assistants* (minimum age 19) with experience at $215–$250 per week ▶ 4 *front desk clerks* with computer, cash, and credit card experience at $215–$250 per week ▶ 1 *head housekeeper* (minimum age 20) with supervisory skills at $250–$350 per week ▶ 3 *nursery counselors* with experience at $215–$250 per week ▶ 1 *social director* (minimum age 21) with driver's license and experience in the field at $215–$250 per week ▶ 2 *swimming instructors* with American Red Cross lifesaving certification at $215–$250 per week ▶ 8 *wranglers* with experience at $215–$300 per week. Applicants must submit formal organization application, resume, two letters of recommendation, two employment references. International applicants accepted; must obtain own visa, obtain own working papers, apply through a recognized agency.

Benefits and Preemployment Training Free housing, free meals, willing to provide letters of recommendation, names of contacts, on-the-job training, willing to complete paperwork for educational credit, and willing to act as a professional reference. Preemployment training is required and includes food safety training.

Contact Patricia Gauthier, Golden Acres Farm and Ranch Resort, HCR 1, Box 53, Gilboa, New York 12076. Telephone: 607-588-7329. Fax: 607-588-6911. E-mail: goldenacresfarm@aol.com. World Wide Web: http://www.goldenacres.com. Contact by e-mail, mail, or phone. Application deadline: continuous.

GORDON KENT'S NEW ENGLAND TENNIS CAMP AT TRINITY-PAWLING SCHOOL

300 ROUTE 22
PAWLING, NEW YORK 12564

General Information Tennis camp located at Trinity-Pawling School in Pawling, New York, for 80 campers ages 9–17. Established in 1965. 150-acre facility located 20 miles from Danbury, Connecticut. Features: 12 tennis courts; school dorms; many athletic fields; beautiful campus; gymnasium.

Profile of Summer Employees Total number: 20; typical ages: 18–25. 60% men; 40% women; 10% minorities; 5% high school students; 90% college students; 20% non-U.S. citizens. Nonsmokers required.

Employment Information Openings are from June 23 to August 16. Jobs available: ▶ 5–10 *counselors/tennis instructors* with experience playing tennis (on school team), outgoing personality, and patience; at least one year of college completed at $1450–$2000 per season. Applicants must submit formal organization application, three personal references, three letters of recommendation. An in-person interview is recommended, but a telephone interview is acceptable. International applicants accepted; must apply through a recognized agency.

Benefits and Preemployment Training Free housing, free meals, possible full-time employment, willing to provide letters of recommendation, on-the-job training, willing to complete paperwork for educational credit, willing to act as a professional reference, and opportunity to attend seminars/workshops. Preemployment training is required and includes accident prevention and safety, interpersonal skills, leadership skills, tennis teaching skills.

Contact Gordon Kent, Owner/Director, Gordon Kent's New England Tennis Camp at Trinity-Pawling School, PO Box 143, Riverdale, New York 10471. Telephone: 800-528-2752. Fax: 212-750-3704. E-mail: netennis@aol.com. Contact by e-mail, fax, mail, or phone. Application deadline: continuous.

HILLSIDE OUTDOOR EDUCATION CENTER DAY AND TRIPPING CAMP

400 DOANSBURG ROAD
BREWSTER, NEW YORK 10509-0719

General Information Coed day and tripping camp serving approximately 225 children ages 5-15. Established in 1972. 150-acre facility located 60 miles from New York. Features: farm; high and low ropes course; climbing tower; natural playground; Croton River for canoeing; rural setting.

Profile of Summer Employees Total number: 40–50; typical ages: 15–35. 30% men; 70% women; 2% minorities; 1% high school students; 80% college students; 50% non-U.S. citizens; 25% local applicants. Nonsmokers required.

Employment Information Openings are from June 20 to August 29. Year-round positions also offered. Jobs available: ▶ 2–4 *adventure specialists* (minimum age 21) with experience leading ropes courses, climbing tower, caving, and canoeing at $250 per week ▶ 1 *archery instructor* (minimum age 21) with archery instructor certification at $250 per week ▶ 1 *arts and crafts instructor* (minimum age 20) with experience in the field at $250 per week ▶ 10–20 *general counselors* (minimum age 20) with experience teaching children at $175–$200 per week ▶ 8 *horseback riding instructors* (minimum age 20) with experience teaching riding and children at $175–$250 per week ▶ 2 *swimming instructors* (minimum age 20) with WSI certification and experience as pool director at $500–$650 per month. Applicants must submit formal organization application, letter of interest, resume, three letters of recommendation. An in-person interview is recommended, but a telephone interview is acceptable. International applicants accepted; must obtain own visa, apply through a recognized agency.

Benefits and Preemployment Training Free housing, free meals, formal training, possible full-time employment, and on-the-job training.

Contact Duncan Lester, Director, Hillside Outdoor Education Center Day and Tripping Camp. Telephone: 845-279-2995 Ext. 325. Fax: 845-279-3077. E-mail: hillside@greenchimneys.org. World Wide Web: http://www.greenchimneys.org. Contact by e-mail, fax, mail, phone, or through World Wide Web site. Application deadline: applications by May 1 are preferred.

INTRODUCTION TO INDEPENDENCE

NEW YORK INSTITUTE OF TECHNOLOGY
CENTRAL ISLIP, NEW YORK 11722

General Information Residential pre-college/independent living experience serving 30–45 moderately to severely learning disabled young adults ages 16–20. 600-acre facility located 40 miles from New York. Features: golf course; gymnasium; fitness center; bowling alley; university dormitories; library.

Profile of Summer Employees Total number: 25; typical ages: 21–50. 33% men; 67% women; 15% minorities; 15% college students. Nonsmokers preferred.

Employment Information Openings are from June 21 to August 15. Year-round positions also offered. Jobs available: ▶ *resident advisors* with special education, psychology, or social work background (graduate students) at $1100–$1300 per season. Applicants must submit a letter of interest, resume. An in-person interview is required.

Benefits and Preemployment Training Free housing, free meals, and on-the-job training. Preemployment training is required and includes interpersonal skills, leadership skills, discussion about learning disabilities.

Contact Lauri Alpern, Director, Introduction to Independence, PO Box 730, Central Islip, New York 11722. Telephone: 631-348-3354. Fax: 631-348-0437. Contact by fax, mail, or phone. Application deadline: continuous.

L.I. ADVENTURELAND
2245 ROUTE 110
EAST FARMINGDALE, NEW YORK 11735

General Information Amusement park with rides, games and restaurant facilities. Caters to a wide age range between April and October. Established in 1962. 10-acre facility located 35 miles from New York. Features: roller coaster; ferris wheel; merry-go-round; restaurant; arcade; log flume.

Profile of Summer Employees Total number: 500; typical ages: 14–24. 40% men; 60% women; 50% minorities; 65% high school students; 35% college students; 5% retirees; 5% non-U.S. citizens; 95% local applicants.

Employment Information Openings are from April 1 to October 31. Spring break positions also offered. Jobs available: ▶ 50 *concession stand staff* (minimum age 14) good math skills at $5.50–$6.50 per hour ▶ 60–80 *game attendants* (minimum age 14) at $5.50–$6.50 per hour ▶ 150–225 *ride operators* (minimum age 16) at $5.50–$6.50 per hour. Applicants must submit formal organization application. An in-person interview is required. International applicants accepted; must obtain own visa, apply through a recognized agency.

Benefits and Preemployment Training Housing at a cost, meals at a cost, willing to provide letters of recommendation, and willing to complete paperwork for educational credit. Preemployment training is required and includes accident prevention and safety, interpersonal skills.

Contact Paul Gentile, Personnel Manager, L.I. Adventureland, 2245 Route 110, East Farmingdale, New York 11735. Telephone: 631-694-6868. Fax: 631-694-6816. E-mail: paul@adventurelandfamilyfun.com. World Wide Web: http://www.adventurelandfamilyfun.com. Contact by e-mail, mail, phone, or through World Wide Web site. Application deadline: continuous.

MIDWAY PARK, INC.
ROUTE 430, PO BOX E
MAPLE SPRINGS, NEW YORK 14756

General Information Amusement kiddie park located on Chautauqua Lake with rides, go-karts, mini-golf, bumper boats, food, and arcade. Established in 1898. 26-acre facility located 12 miles from Jamestown. Features: on Chautauqua Lake; picnic grove; ride area; roller rink.

Profile of Summer Employees Total number: 100; typical ages: 16–25. 50% men; 50% women; 5% minorities; 30% high school students; 60% college students; 10% retirees; 95% local applicants. Nonsmokers preferred.

Employment Information Openings are from May 25 to September 8. Jobs available: ▶ 10 *arcade attendants* (minimum age 16) at $5.15 per hour ▶ 10 *food concession staff* (minimum age 16) at $5.15 per hour ▶ 30 *ride attendants* (minimum age 16) at $5.15 per hour. Applicants must submit a formal organization application, three personal references. An in-person interview is required.

Benefits and Preemployment Training Willing to provide letters of recommendation and on-the-job training. Preemployment training is required and includes accident prevention and safety.

Contact Robin DeLong, Office Manager, Midway Park, Inc., PO Box E, Maple Springs, New York 14756. Fax: 716-386-4700. Contact by mail. Application deadline: continuous.

92ND STREET Y CAMPS
1395 LEXINGTON AVENUE
NEW YORK, NEW YORK 10128

General Information Summer camps for children ages 5 to 15 that focus on building self-esteem and exposing children to the outdoors in a safe, comfortable environment. Established in 1880. 100-acre facility. Features: rope challenge course; athletic fields; art and ceramic centers; nature center; basketball courts; swimming pools.

Profile of Summer Employees Total number: 300; typical ages: 17–30. 50% men; 50% women;

20% minorities; 35% high school students; 50% college students; 5% non-U.S. citizens; 90% local applicants. Nonsmokers preferred.

Employment Information Openings are from June 18 to August 22. Jobs available: ▶ 25 *activity specialists (arts, sports, ropes, nature, music, karate)* (minimum age 19) at $2000–$4000 per season ▶ 5 *assistant directors* (minimum age 22) with supervisory and camp experience at $3000–$5500 per season ▶ 100 *camp counselors* (minimum age 17) at $1000–$2250 per season. Applicants must submit formal organization application, resume, two personal references. An in-person interview is required. International applicants accepted; must obtain own visa, apply through a recognized agency.

Benefits and Preemployment Training Willing to provide letters of recommendation, names of contacts, on-the-job training, willing to complete paperwork for educational credit, and willing to act as a professional reference. Preemployment training is required and includes accident prevention and safety, first aid, CPR, interpersonal skills, leadership skills.

Contact Steve Levin, Assistant Director, Camp Programs, 92nd Street Y Camps, 1395 Lexington Avenue, New York, New York 10128. Telephone: 212-415-5641. Fax: 212-415-5637. E-mail: slevin@92ndsty.org. World Wide Web: http://www.92ndsty.org. Contact by e-mail, fax, mail, or phone. Application deadline: June 15.

NORTH SHORE HOLIDAY HOUSE
74 HUNTINGTON ROAD
HUNTINGTON, NEW YORK 11743

General Information Residential camp serving girls from low-income homes. Established in 1914. 5-acre facility located 40 miles from New York.

Profile of Summer Employees Total number: 20; typical ages: 19–25. 100% women; 50% minorities; 80% college students; 33% non-U.S. citizens; 20% local applicants. Nonsmokers preferred.

Employment Information Openings are from June 25 to August 23. Jobs available: ▶ 1 *arts and crafts staff member* at $1000–$1500 per season ▶ 5 *bunk counselors* at $1000 per season ▶ *computer instructor* at $1000–$1500 per season ▶ 1 *dance staff member* at $1000–$1500 per season ▶ 1 *music staff member* at $1000–$1500 per season ▶ 1 *swimming instructor* with WSI and lifeguard certification at $1500 per season. Applicants must submit formal organization application, three letters of recommendation. An in-person interview is recommended, but a telephone interview is acceptable. International applicants accepted; must apply through a recognized agency.

Benefits and Preemployment Training Free housing, free meals, formal training, willing to provide letters of recommendation, on-the-job training, and willing to complete paperwork for educational credit. Preemployment training is required and includes accident prevention and safety, first aid, CPR, interpersonal skills, leadership skills.

Contact Michael Marinello, Director, North Shore Holiday House, 74 Huntington Road, Huntington, New York 11743. Telephone: 516-427-7630. Fax: 516-427-1185. Contact by fax, mail, or phone. Application deadline: continuous.

PECONIC DUNES CAMP
SOUNDVIEW AVENUE
PECONIC, NEW YORK 11958

General Information Residential and day camp emphasizing environmental and recreational activities including canoeing, archery, swimming, fishing, and arts and crafts. Established in 1931. 98-acre facility located 75 miles from New York. Features: private beach on Long Island Sound; mile-long spring-fed lake; biodiverse habitats.

Profile of Summer Employees Total number: 40; typical age: 20. 50% men; 50% women; 15% minorities; 90% college students; 10% local applicants. Nonsmokers preferred.

Employment Information Openings are from June 16 to August 19. Jobs available: ▶ 1 *assistant* *cook* at $250–$350 per week ▶ 1 *athletics director* at $300–$375 per week ▶ 4 *environmental educators* at $350 per week ▶ 1 *head cook* with mature, responsible personality (pay commensurate with experience) at $600 per week ▶ 3 *kitchen helpers* should be high school student with mature attitude at $175 per week ▶ 2 *maintenance personnel* with maturity and full knowledge of carpentry, plumbing, and electrical wiring at $150–$400 per week ▶ 1 *nurse* with RN license at $600–$630 per week ▶ 1 *outdoor educator* at $400 per week ▶ 1 *residential art director* at $375 per week ▶ 20 *senior counselors* should be college senior or graduate with experience at $285–$300 per week ▶ 1 *waterfront director* with WSI certification at $350 per week ▶ 4 *waterfront staff members* with lifesaving or WSI certification at $300–$325 per week. Applicants must submit a formal organization application, three personal references. An in-person interview is required.

Benefits and Preemployment Training Free housing, free meals, and laundry facilities. Preemployment training is required and includes accident prevention and safety, first aid, CPR, interpersonal skills, leadership skills.

Contact Carol Hassell, Administrative Assistant, Peconic Dunes Camp, PO Box 204, Peconic, New York 11958. Telephone: 631-765-5770. Fax: 631-765-0017. E-mail: peconicdunescamp@aol.com. Contact by e-mail or phone. Application deadline: continuous.

POINT O' PINES CAMP
7201 STATE ROUTE 8
BRANT LAKE, NEW YORK 12815-2236

General Information Eight-week traditional residential girls camp with professional sports instruction as well as arts, performing arts, and horsemanship for 300 campers; winter restaurant and wedding caterers. Established in 1957. 523-acre facility located 90 miles from Albany. Features: peninsula location; freshwater lake; surrounded by wooded mountains; 12 tennis courts (4 with lights); winterized bunks with full bathrooms; winterized dining room with fireplace.

Profile of Summer Employees Total number: 160; typical ages: 18–55. 10% men; 90% women; 10% minorities; 80% college students; 10% non-U.S. citizens; 5% local applicants. Nonsmokers preferred.

Employment Information Openings are from June 16 to August 17. Year-round positions also offered. Jobs available: ▶ 4 *English horseback riding instructors* with at least two years of teaching experience at $1200–$2500 per season ▶ 6 *arts and crafts staff members* with professional teaching experience and/or a major in art at $1000–$1500 per season ▶ 6 *athletics staff members* with experience as college team player or professional instructor at $1000–$1500 per season ▶ 2 *boating instructors* with experience in the field at $1000–$1500 per season ▶ *cleaning and kitchen help* with references and experience ▶ 1 *drama director* with experience in the field at $2500–$3000 per season ▶ 1 *drama technical person* with at least two years of experience in college or community theater at $1500–$2000 per season ▶ *drama-costume director* with sewing ability at $1000–$1600 per season ▶ *fitness and conditioning instructor* with extensive training, certification, and experience in the field at $1500–$2300 per season ▶ 6 *gymnastics/dance staff members* with experience as college team player or instructor at $1000–$1500 per season ▶ 1 *music director* with experience as piano accompanist for theater (must be able to transpose) at $1400–$2000 per season ▶ 3 *nurses* with RN certification and clinical experience at $3500–$4500 per season ▶ 4 *outdoor adventure staff members* with extensive training in safety and experience in the field at $1200–$1600 per season ▶ 2 *photography staff members* with college or professional experience at $1000–$1500 per season ▶ 3 *sailing instructors* with experience in the field at $1000–$1500 per season ▶ 14 *tennis staff members* with experience as college team player or professional instructor at $1000–$1500 per season ▶ 2 *video instructors* with at least two years of experience in operating equipment at $1500–$2000 per season ▶ 23 *waterfront staff members* with extensive water sports experience at $1100–$1600 per season ▶ 8 *waterskiing instructors* with experience in the field at $1000–$1500 per season ▶ 1 *year-round dining room manager for restaurant* (minimum age 22) with college

degree and experience in business management or hotel and resort management at $23000–$33000 per year. Applicants must submit a formal organization application, resume, three personal references. An in-person interview is recommended, but a telephone interview is acceptable. International applicants accepted.
Benefits and Preemployment Training Free housing, free meals, formal training, willing to provide letters of recommendation, on-the-job training, willing to complete paperwork for educational credit, willing to act as a professional reference, travel reimbursement, and free laundry service. Preemployment training is required and includes accident prevention and safety, first aid, CPR, leadership skills.
Contact Sherie Alden, Associate Director, Point O' Pines Camp, 7201 State Route 8, Brant Lake, New York 12815-2236. Telephone: 888-726-9908. Fax: 518-494-3489. E-mail: info@pointopines.com. World Wide Web: http://www.pointopines.com. Contact by e-mail, fax, mail, phone, or through World Wide Web site. Application deadline: continuous.

SAGAMORE INSTITUTE OF THE ADIRONDACKS

SAGAMORE ROAD, PO BOX 40
RAQUETTE LAKE, NEW YORK 13436-0040

General Information Sagamore Institute is a non-profit steward of a National Historic Landmark that offers residential programs and public tours promoting culture, nature, and their critical interdependence. Established in 1972. 19-acre facility located 50 miles from Utica. Features: freshwater lake; wooded, wilderness setting; National Historic Landmark of 27 buildings; wide range outdoor programs; history, culture, artisan crafts.
Profile of Summer Employees Total number: 26; typical ages: 20–25. 20% men; 80% women; 100% college students. Nonsmokers preferred.
Employment Information Openings are from June 10 to October 20. Jobs available: ▶ 3 *environmental outdoor education staff* (minimum age 19) with various outdoor skills, environmental interpretation, teaching experience at $150 per week ▶ 2–5 *historic interpretation staff* (minimum age 19) with American History background; strong communication skills at $150 per week ▶ 1 *manager* (minimum age 19) with retail sales, food preparation experience at $150 per week. Applicants must submit a letter of interest, resume, three personal references, 1 expository writing sample. An in-person interview is recommended, but a telephone interview is acceptable. International applicants accepted; must obtain own visa, obtain own working papers.
Benefits and Preemployment Training Free housing, free meals, willing to provide letters of recommendation, on-the-job training, willing to complete paperwork for educational credit, willing to act as a professional reference, and opportunity to attend seminars/workshops.
Contact Dr. Michael Wilson, Associate Director, Sagamore Institute of the Adirondacks, 9 Kiwassa Road, Saranoe Lake, New York 12983. Telephone: 518-891-1718. Fax: 518-891-2561. E-mail: mwilson@northnet.org. World Wide Web: http://www.sagamore.org. Contact by e-mail. Application deadline: April 15.

SAIL CARIBBEAN

79 CHURCH STREET
NORTHPORT, NEW YORK 11768

General Information Summer sailing and scuba diving program in the Caribbean for teens. Extensive water sports, island exploration, marine sciences, and cultural activities. Established in 1979. Located 60 miles from San Juan. Features: Caribbean Sea; island exploration; 51' yachts; windsurfers; kayaks; waterskiing; scuba diving; beach sports.
Profile of Summer Employees Total number: 50; typical ages: 20–30. 66% men; 34% women; 60% college students. Nonsmokers required.
Employment Information Openings are from June to August. Jobs available: ▶ 2 *ARC lifeguard instructors* (minimum age 20) with CPR/first aid ▶ 6 *PADI scuba instructors* (minimum age 20) with CPR/first aid ▶ 6 *assistant skippers* (minimum age 20) with CPR/first aid ▶ 2 *food*

supervisors (minimum age 20) with CPR/first aid ▶ 4 *marine biology teachers* (minimum age 20) with CPR/first aid ▶ 6 *skippers* (minimum age 20) with CPR/first aid; (US Sailing basic keelboat instructor for one position). Applicants must submit a letter of interest, resume, 3-5 personal references, an in-person interview is highly recommended. International applicants accepted; must obtain own visa.

Benefits and Preemployment Training Free housing, free meals, possible full-time employment, willing to provide letters of recommendation, on-the-job training, willing to act as a professional reference, and travel reimbursement. Preemployment training is required and includes accident prevention and safety, interpersonal skills, leadership skills.

Contact Michael D. Liese, Founder/Director, Sail Caribbean, 79 Church Street, Northport, New York 11768. Telephone: 800-321-0994. Fax: 516-754-3362. E-mail: info@sailcaribbean.com. World Wide Web: http://www.sailcaribbean.com. Contact by e-mail, fax, mail, phone, or through World Wide Web site. Application deadline: continuous.

THE SOUTHWESTERN COMPANY, NEW YORK

See The Southwestern Company on page 302 for complete description.

STAGEDOOR MANOR THEATRE AND DANCE CAMP

KARMEL ROAD
LOCH SHELDRAKE, NEW YORK 12759

General Information Residential coeducational camp serving 240 campers in performing arts. Established in 1974. 25-acre facility located 95 miles from New York. Features: dormitory style hotel; indoor-outdoor pools; 7 on-campus theatres; rural setting by lake; two and a half hours from New York City; excellent technical facilities.

Profile of Summer Employees Total number: 127; typical ages: 24–35. 40% men; 60% women; 5% minorities; 25% college students; 50% non-U.S. citizens; 20% local applicants. Nonsmokers preferred.

Employment Information Openings are from June 18 to August 27. Jobs available: ▶ 3 *lifeguards* (minimum age 21) ARC certification (will provide) at $2000 per season ▶ 2 *modeling instructors* (minimum age 21) with runway experience at $2000–$2500 per season ▶ 3 *nurses* (minimum age 21) with RN or LPN license at $2500–$3000 per season ▶ 6 *scenic designers* (minimum age 21) with theater experience at $2000–$2500 per season ▶ 10 *technicians* (minimum age 21) with theater experience at $1800–$2000 per season ▶ 2 *tennis counselors* (minimum age 21) with coaching experience at $1500–$1800 per season ▶ 4 *video counselors* (minimum age 21) with video experience at $1800–$2000 per season. Applicants must submit a letter of interest, resume, personal reference. A telephone interview is required. International applicants accepted.

Benefits and Preemployment Training Free housing, free meals, formal training, willing to provide letters of recommendation, names of contacts, on-the-job training, willing to complete paperwork for educational credit, willing to act as a professional reference, and opportunity to attend seminars/workshops. Preemployment training is required and includes accident prevention and safety, first aid, CPR, interpersonal skills, leadership skills.

Contact Konnie Kittrell, Production Director, Stagedoor Manor Theatre and Dance Camp, 651 Skyline Drive, Gatlinburg, Tennessee 37738. Fax: 865-436-3030. World Wide Web: http://www.stagedoormanor.com. Contact by fax or mail. Application deadline: May 15.

STUDENT CONSERVATION ASSOCIATION (SCA), NEW YORK

See Student Conservation Association (SCA), New Hampshire on page 209 for complete description.

SUMMER AT HAWTHORNE VALLEY FARM CAMP
327 CR 21C
GHENT, NEW YORK 12075

General Information A farm and nature camp experience for children ages 9 to 15 on a commercial biodynamic dairy farm. Established in 1972. 450-acre facility located 30 miles from Albany. Features: 450 acre working biodynamic dairy farm; market vegetable garden; wooded hiking trails; fresh water pond; health food store on premises.

Profile of Summer Employees Total number: 50; typical ages: 21–30. 25% men; 75% women; 1% minorities; 1% high school students; 97% college students; 1% local applicants. Nonsmokers required.

Employment Information Openings are from June 23 to August 17. Year-round positions also offered. Jobs available: ▶ 4 *boys dorm counselors* (minimum age 18) with experience working with groups of children, interpersonal skills at $1500 per season ▶ 2 *camp assistant cooks* cooking with whole grains for at least 75 people at $2000–$2250 per season ▶ 4 *counselors in training* (minimum age 17) who enjoy outdoor activities and working with children at $750 per season ▶ 4 *field camp counselors* (minimum age 21) with experience working with groups of children, interpersonal skills at $1700 per season ▶ 4 *girls dorm counselors* (minimum age 18) with experience working with groups of children, interpersonal skills at $1500 per season ▶ 3 *specialty counselors in arts and crafts, archery, games* (minimum age 18) with experience working with groups of children, interpersonal skills at $1500 per season. Applicants must submit a formal organization application, letter of interest, resume, three personal references. An in-person interview is recommended, but a telephone interview is acceptable.

Benefits and Preemployment Training Free housing, free meals, willing to provide letters of recommendation, willing to complete paperwork for educational credit, and willing to act as a professional reference.

Contact Nick Franceschelli, Director, Summer at Hawthorne Valley Farm Camp. Telephone: 518-672-4790. Fax: 518-672-7608. E-mail: vsp@taconic.net. Contact by e-mail, fax, mail, or phone. Application deadline: continuous.

TIMBER LAKE WEST
BURNT HILL ROAD
ROSCOE, NEW YORK 12776

General Information Residential camp serving 320 campers in a traditional four-week program. Established in 1988. 320-acre facility located 120 miles from New York. Features: lake; 2 heated pools; main lodge; 6 tennis courts; movie theater; indoor gym.

Profile of Summer Employees Total number: 180; typical ages: 18–23. 50% men; 50% women; 4% high school students; 75% college students; 15% non-U.S. citizens; 1% local applicants. Nonsmokers preferred.

Employment Information Openings are from June 23 to August 24. Jobs available: ▶ 15 *arts and crafts instructors* (minimum age 18) at $1600 to $2000 plus $200 for travel over 350 miles ▶ 3 *boating instructors* (minimum age 18) with lifeguard certification at $1600 to $2000 plus $200 for travel over 350 miles ▶ 70 *general counselors* (minimum age 18) at $1600 to $2000 per season and $200 for travel over 350 miles ▶ 8 *housekeeping/maintenance staff members* (minimum age 18) at $1750 per season ▶ 14 *kitchen staff members* (minimum age 18) at $1750 per season ▶ 6 *tennis instructors* (minimum age 18) at $1600-$2000 plus $200 for travel over 350 miles ▶ 6 *water safety instructors* (minimum age 18) with WSI, first aid, lifeguard, and CPR certification at $1850-$2250 plus $200 for travel over 350 miles. Applicants must submit formal organization application, two personal references, two letters of recommendation. An in-person interview is recommended, but a telephone interview is acceptable. International applicants accepted; must apply through a recognized agency.

Benefits and Preemployment Training Free housing, free meals, willing to provide letters of recommendation, names of contacts, on-the-job training, willing to complete paperwork for educational credit, willing to act as a professional reference, and travel reimbursement. Preemployment training is required and includes accident prevention and safety, first aid, CPR, interpersonal skills, leadership skills.

Contact Jennifer A. Quinn, Assistant Director, Timber Lake West, 85 Crescent Beach Road, Glen Cove, New York 11542. Telephone: 516-656-4210. Fax: 516-656-4215. E-mail: west@camptlc.com. World Wide Web: http://www.timberlakewest.com. Contact by e-mail, fax, mail, phone, or through World Wide Web site. Application deadline: continuous.

TRAILMARK OUTDOOR ADVENTURES

16 SCHUYLER ROAD
NYACK, NEW YORK 10960

General Information Travel adventure program in New England, the Northern Rockies, the Pacific Northwest, and Southwest Colorado and Mid-Atlantic. Established in 1985.

Profile of Summer Employees Total number: 50; typical ages: 21–32. 50% men; 50% women; 10% college students. Nonsmokers required.

Employment Information Openings are from June 17 to August 20. Jobs available: ▶ 50 *trip leaders* (minimum age 21) with first aid/CPR, lifeguarding preferred; good interpersonal skills and experience working with children at $100–$300 per week. Applicants must submit a formal organization application, letter of interest, resume, three personal references. A telephone interview is required.

Benefits and Preemployment Training Free housing, free meals, health insurance, willing to provide letters of recommendation, on-the-job training, willing to complete paperwork for educational credit, and willing to act as a professional reference. Preemployment training is required and includes accident prevention and safety, first aid, CPR, interpersonal skills, leadership skills, lifeguarding.

Contact Rusty Pedersen, Director, Trailmark Outdoor Adventures, 16 Schuyler Road, Nyack, New York 10960. Telephone: 800-229-0262. Fax: 845-348-0437. E-mail: staff@trailmark.com. World Wide Web: http://www.trailmark.com. Contact by e-mail, fax, phone, or through World Wide Web site. Application deadline: continuous.

TYLER HILL CAMP

ROUTE 371
TYLER HILL, NEW YORK 18469

General Information Residential coeducational camp for ages 8–16 features full sports program and traditional camp activities. Established in 1955. 220-acre facility located 100 miles from New York. Features: 9-hole golf course; 2 magnificent lakes; 12 tennis courts; modern wood-paneled cabins; indoor roller hockey and basketball; 15 arts and crafts shops.

Profile of Summer Employees Total number: 225; typical age: 18. 50% men; 50% women; 20% minorities; 3% high school students; 95% college students; 15% non-U.S. citizens; 5% local applicants. Nonsmokers required.

Employment Information Openings are from June 20 to August 19. Jobs available: ▶ *creative arts staff (aerobics, dance, piano, drama)* at $1600–$2000 per season ▶ *general counselors* (minimum age 18) at $1600–$2000 per season ▶ 1–3 *nurses* at $4000 per season ▶ *sports staff* (minimum age 18) at $1660–$2000 per season ▶ *waterfront staff* with first aid/CPR and WSI at $1600–$2000 per season. Applicants must submit formal organization application, letter of interest, resume, three personal references, three letters of recommendation. An in-person interview is recommended, but a telephone interview is acceptable. International applicants accepted; must apply through a recognized agency.

Benefits and Preemployment Training Free housing, free meals, formal training, possible full-time employment, willing to provide letters of recommendation, on-the-job training, willing to complete paperwork for educational credit, willing to act as a professional reference, opportunity to attend seminars/workshops, and travel reimbursement. Preemployment training is required and includes accident prevention and safety, interpersonal skills, leadership skills.

Contact Andy Siegel, Director, Tyler Hill Camp, 85 Crescent Beach Road, Glen Cove, New York 11542. Telephone: 516-656-4220. Fax: 516-656-4215. E-mail: tylerhill@camptlc.com. World Wide Web: http://www.camptlc.com. Contact by e-mail, fax, mail, phone, or through World Wide Web site. Application deadline: continuous.

WEISSMAN TEEN TOURS

517 ALMENA AVENUE
ARDSLEY, NEW YORK 10502-2127

General Information Owner-operated and escorted personalized activity oriented student travel program in the United States, Western Canada, and Europe. All deluxe and first class hotels and resorts. Established in 1974.

Profile of Summer Employees Total number: 14; typical ages: 21–29. 50% men; 50% women; 50% local applicants. Nonsmokers required.

Employment Information Openings are from June 29 to August 11. Year-round positions also offered. Jobs available: ▶ 7 *tour leaders-Europe* (minimum age 21) with proficiency in French and/or Italian, background in Art History (preferred), experience working with teenagers, CPR, and first aid at $100 per week ▶ 7 *tour leaders-U.S./Western Canada* (minimum age 21) with experience working with teenagers, CPR, and first aid at $100 per week. Applicants must submit a formal organization application, letter of interest, resume, three personal references, three letters of recommendation. An in-person interview is required. International applicants accepted; must obtain own visa, obtain own working papers.

Benefits and Preemployment Training Free housing, free meals, formal training, possible full-time employment, on-the-job training, willing to act as a professional reference, and first class travel. Preemployment training is required and includes accident prevention and safety, interpersonal skills, leadership skills.

Contact Ronee Weissman, Owner/Director, Weissman Teen Tours, 517 Almena Avenue, Ardsley, New York 10502. Telephone: 914-693-7575. Fax: 914-693-4807. E-mail: wtt@cloud9.net. World Wide Web: http://www.weissmantours.com. Contact by e-mail, fax, mail, phone, or through World Wide Web site. Application deadline: continuous.

WESTCOAST CONNECTION TRAVEL CAMP

154 EAST BOSTON POST ROAD
MAMARONECK, NEW YORK 10543

General Information Travel programs in the United States, western Canada, Europe, Australia, and Israel for students ages 13–18, including active teen tours and outdoor adventure trips. Established in 1982.

Profile of Summer Employees Total number: 160; typical ages: 21–35. 50% men; 50% women; 80% college students. Nonsmokers required.

Employment Information Openings are from June 20 to August 25. Jobs available: ▶ *tour staff members/leaders* (minimum age 20) with experience working with teens; driver's license (CDL for some trips); CPR, lifeguard, first aid, WSI, and lifeguard certification preferred at $75–$600 per week. Applicants must submit a formal organization application, three personal references. An in-person interview is required. International applicants accepted; must obtain own visa, obtain own working papers.

Benefits and Preemployment Training Free housing, free meals, formal training, possible full-time employment, willing to provide letters of recommendation, on-the-job training, willing to complete paperwork for educational credit, willing to act as a professional reference, opportunity to attend seminars/workshops, and travel reimbursement. Preemployment training is required and includes accident prevention and safety, first aid, interpersonal skills, leadership skills, organizational skills.

Contact Jason Tanner, Director, Westcoast Connection Travel Camp, 154 East Boston Post

Road, Mamaroneck, New York 10543. Telephone: 914-835-0699. Fax: 914-835-0798. E-mail: usa@westcoastconnection.com. World Wide Web: http://www.westcoastconnection.com. Contact by e-mail, fax, mail, phone, or through World Wide Web site. Application deadline: continuous.

YMCA CAMPING SERVICES–CAMPS GREENKILL/ MCALISTER/TALCOTT

300 BIG POND ROAD
HUGUENOT, NEW YORK 12746

General Information Two traditional residential summer camps and one year-round facility serving general population. Camp McAlister serves ages 6–11, Camp Talcott serves ages 11–15, and Camp Greenkill is home to specialized programs. Established in 1924. 1,000-acre facility located 90 miles from New York. Features: 3 freshwater lakes; 7 tennis courts; 5 basketball courts; new environmental education building and auditorium; wooded setting; 5 miles of hiking trails through all types of terrain.

Profile of Summer Employees Total number: 140; typical ages: 18–25. 50% men; 50% women; 30% minorities; 8% high school students; 60% college students; 35% non-U.S. citizens; 10% local applicants.

Employment Information Openings are from June 15 to August 23. Winter break and year-round positions also offered. Jobs available: ▶ 3 *aquatic directors* with WSI, LGT, CPR, Basic Life Support, and first aid certification at $210–$250 per week ▶ 30 *general counselors* at $150–$160 per week ▶ 2 *high ropes instructors* at $150–$160 per week ▶ 10 *kitchen staff members* at $150–$160 per week ▶ 4 *naturalists* (minimum age 18) with experience teaching nature activities at $220–$250 per week ▶ 2 *nurses* with RN or LPN certification at $400–$450 per week ▶ 6 *swimming instructors* with WSI certification at $150–$160 per week ▶ 12 *unit directors* with leadership and camp experience at $180–$200 per week. Applicants must submit formal organization application, three personal references, (cover letter and resume not required but recommended). A telephone interview is required. International applicants accepted; must apply through a recognized agency.

Benefits and Preemployment Training Free housing, free meals, formal training, possible full-time employment, on-the-job training, willing to complete paperwork for educational credit, opportunity to attend seminars/workshops, and possible partial travel reimbursement; children of camp nurses may attend overnight programs for free. Preemployment training is required and includes accident prevention and safety, first aid, CPR, interpersonal skills, leadership skills, lifeguarding, high ropes.

Contact Chris Scheuer, Director of Camping, YMCA Camping Services–Camps Greenkill/ McAlister/Talcott, 300 Big Pond Road, Huguenot, New York 12746. Telephone: 845-858-2200. Fax: 845-858-7823. E-mail: cscheuer@ymcanyc.org. World Wide Web: http://www.ymcanyc.org/ camps. Contact by e-mail, fax, mail, phone, or through World Wide Web site. Application deadline: continuous.

NORTH CAROLINA

A CHRISTIAN MINISTRY IN THE NATIONAL PARKS–NORTH CAROLINA

See A Christian Ministry in the National Parks–Maine on page 122 for complete description.

BIKINGX

ASHEVILLE, NORTH CAROLINA 28815

General Information Mountain biking and touring programs for 12 to 16 year-old students divided by age and ability; multi-adventure programs also offered.

Profile of Summer Employees Total number: 20; typical ages: 25–27. 60% men; 40% women. Nonsmokers required.

Employment Information Openings are from June 18 to August 18. Jobs available: ▶ 10–15 *trip leaders–mountain biking or touring* (minimum age 21) with a love of biking and working with students at $50 per day. Applicants must submit a formal organization application, letter of interest, resume. A telephone interview is required.

Benefits and Preemployment Training Free housing, formal training, willing to provide letters of recommendation, willing to complete paperwork for educational credit, and willing to act as a professional reference. Preemployment training is required and includes accident prevention and safety, first aid, interpersonal skills, leadership skills, biking policy and procedures.

Contact Director, BikingX, PO Box 9913, Asheville, North Carolina 28815. Telephone: 800-654-5957. Fax: 828-296-9960. E-mail: info@bikingx.com. World Wide Web: http://www.bikingx.com. Contact by e-mail or through World Wide Web site. Application deadline: continuous.

CAMP CHOSATONGA FOR BOYS

2500 MORGAN MILL ROAD
BREVARD, NORTH CAROLINA 28712

General Information Traditional residential summer camp in the Blue Ridge Mountains of North Carolina with wholesome, dedicated, trained staff which helps to develop lifetime friendships and skills, and a sister camp, Camp Kahdalea for Girls. Established in 1977. 210-acre facility located 25 miles from Asheville. Features: strong in-camp and wilderness programs; only 2 sessions per summer; lake; Christian ideals; 3:1 camper to staff ratio; surrounded on 3 sides by Pisgah National Forest.

Profile of Summer Employees Total number: 30; typical ages: 18–25. 100% men; 1% minorities; 100% college students. Nonsmokers preferred.

Employment Information Openings are from May 30 to August 15. Jobs available: ▶ 15–30 *counselors* (minimum age 18) with at least one year of college completed at $1000–$1300 per season. Applicants must submit a formal organization application, letter of interest, three personal references. A telephone interview is required. International applicants accepted; must obtain own visa, obtain own working papers.

Benefits and Preemployment Training Free housing, free meals, formal training, possible full-time employment, willing to provide letters of recommendation, on-the-job training, willing to complete paperwork for educational credit, and willing to act as a professional reference. Preemployment training is required and includes accident prevention and safety, first aid, CPR, interpersonal skills, leadership skills, wilderness first aid.

Contact Mr. David Trufant, Owner/Director, Camp Chosatonga for Boys. Telephone: 828-884-6834. Fax: 828-884-6834. E-mail: office@kahdalea.com. World Wide Web: http://www.chosatonga.com. Contact by e-mail, fax, mail, phone, or through World Wide Web site. Application deadline: continuous.

CAMP HIGH ROCKS

GREENVILLE HIGHWAY
CEDAR MOUNTAIN, NORTH CAROLINA 28718

General Information Small residential boys camp focusing on development of skills in a non-competitive environment. There is a strong emphasis on outdoor adventure programming with many off-site trips. Established in 1958. 1,100-acre facility located 8 miles from Brevard. Features: freshwater lake; 50-foot climbing tower; 3 tennis courts; 2 activity fields; 29-stall barn facility; wooded mountainous setting.

Profile of Summer Employees Total number: 65; typical ages: 19–26. 67% men; 33% women; 80% college students. Nonsmokers required.

Employment Information Openings are from June 4 to August 12. Jobs available: ▶ 2 *athletics/tennis instructors* at $200–$260 per week ▶ 6 *backpacking instructors* at $200–$260 per week ▶ 23 *cabin counselor/skill instructors* at $200–$260 per week ▶ 3 *crafts instructors* at $200–$260 per week ▶ 8 *horseback riding instructors* at $200–$260 per week ▶ 4 *mountain biking instructors* at $200–$260 per week ▶ 2 *pottery instructors* at $200–$260 per week ▶ 7 *rock climbing instructors* at $200–$260 per week ▶ 3 *ropes course facilitators* at $200–$260 per week ▶ 3 *swimming instructors* with WSI certification or lifeguard certification at $200–$260 per week ▶ 7 *white-water canoeing instructors* at $200–$260 per week. Applicants must submit formal organization application, three personal references. An in-person interview is recommended, but a telephone interview is acceptable. International applicants accepted; must apply through a recognized agency.

Benefits and Preemployment Training Free housing, free meals, willing to complete paperwork for educational credit, and opportunity to attend seminars/workshops. Preemployment training is required and includes accident prevention and safety, first aid, interpersonal skills, leadership skills, wilderness first aid, rock rescue, and white-water instructor.

Contact Henry Birdsong, Camp Director, Camp High Rocks, PO Box 210, Cedar Mountain, North Carolina 28718. Telephone: 828-885-2153. Fax: 828-884-4612. E-mail: mail@highrocks.com. World Wide Web: http://www.highrocks.com. Contact by e-mail, fax, mail, phone, or through World Wide Web site. Application deadline: continuous.

CAMP KAHDALEA FOR GIRLS
2500 MORGAN MILL ROAD
BREVARD, NORTH CAROLINA 28712

General Information Traditional residential summer camp in the Blue Ridge Mountains of North Carolina, with a wholesome, dedicated, trained staff that helps develop lifetime friendships and skills; brother camp is Camp Chosatonga (for boys). Established in 1962. 210-acre facility located 25 miles from Asheville. Features: strong in-camp and wilderness programs; only 2 sessions per summer; lake; Christian ideals; 3:1 camper to staff ratio; surrounded on 3 sides by Pisgah National Forest.

Profile of Summer Employees Total number: 55; typical ages: 18–25. 1% men; 99% women; 1% minorities; 100% college students. Nonsmokers preferred.

Employment Information Openings are from May 30 to August 15. Jobs available: ▶ 1–3 *barn management* (minimum age 20) with previous barn management and horseback riding teaching experience per season at $ 1,500 to $2,500 per season, negotiable based on experience ▶ 30–50 *counselors* (minimum age 18) with at least one year of college completed at $1000–$1300 per season ▶ 1–5 *kitchen help* (minimum age 18) with previous cooking experience at $1000–$1600 per month. Applicants must submit a formal organization application, letter of interest, three personal references. A telephone interview is required. International applicants accepted; must obtain own visa, obtain own working papers.

Benefits and Preemployment Training Free housing, free meals, formal training, possible full-time employment, willing to provide letters of recommendation, on-the-job training, willing to complete paperwork for educational credit, and willing to act as a professional reference. Preemployment training is required and includes accident prevention and safety, first aid, CPR, interpersonal skills, leadership skills, wilderness first aid.

Contact Anne Trufant, Owner/Director, Camp Kahdalea for Girls. Telephone: 828-884-6834. Fax: 828-884-6834. E-mail: office@kahdalea.com. World Wide Web: http://www.kahdalea.com. Contact by e-mail, fax, mail, phone, or through World Wide Web site. Application deadline: continuous.

CAMP KANATA YMCA
13524 CAMP KANATA ROAD
WAKE FOREST, NORTH CAROLINA 27587

General Information Coeducational residential YMCA camp for children ages 6–15. Established in 1954. 150-acre facility located 20 miles from Raleigh. Features: 2 lakes; 18 cabins; 2 ball fields; high/low ropes course; wooded setting; 7000-square foot gym.

Profile of Summer Employees Total number: 42; typical ages: 18–21. 50% men; 50% women; 2% minorities; 30% high school students; 70% college students; 4% non-U.S. citizens; 35% local applicants. Nonsmokers preferred.

Employment Information Openings are from June 1 to August 8. Jobs available: ▶ 1 *arts and crafts director* (minimum age 19) with experience in the field at $165 per week ▶ 37 *cabin counselors* (minimum age 18) with child work experience at $160–$180 per week ▶ 2 *nature instructors* (minimum age 18) at $160–$170 per week ▶ 1 *program director* (minimum age 20) with creativity and camp experience at $210–$240 per week ▶ 1 *ropes course director* (minimum age 21) with 2-3 years camp experience and ropes course training at $170–$190 per week ▶ 1 *staff-trainee director* (minimum age 21) with camp experience at $220–$240 per week ▶ 1 *summer assistant director* (minimum age 21) with past camp supervisory experience at $250–$300 per week ▶ 1 *waterfront director* (minimum age 21) with lifeguard, lake usage, and camp experience; WSI, lifeguard instructor, or YMCA certification at $210–$230 per week. Applicants must submit a formal organization application, four personal references, criminal background check, drug test. An in-person interview is recommended, but a telephone interview is acceptable.

Benefits and Preemployment Training Free housing, free meals, willing to provide letters of recommendation, on-the-job training, willing to complete paperwork for educational credit, and willing to act as a professional reference. Preemployment training is required and includes accident prevention and safety, first aid, CPR, interpersonal skills, leadership skills.

Contact Mr. Richard R. Hamilton, Director, Camp Kanata YMCA, 13524 Camp Kanata Road, Wake Forest, North Carolina 27587. Telephone: 919-556-2661. Fax: 919-556-9459. E-mail: campkanata@earthlink.net. World Wide Web: http://ymcacampkanata.org. Contact by e-mail, fax, mail, phone, or through World Wide Web site. Application deadline: continuous.

CAMP MERRIE-WOODE
100 MERRIE-WOODE ROAD
SAPPHIRE, NORTH CAROLINA 28774

General Information A residential girls summer camp dedicated to building self-esteem and confidence through traditional camp and high adventure activities. Established in 1919. 250-acre facility located 60 miles from Asheville. Features: location in mountains of Western North Carolina, 3500-foot elevation; 1-mile-long freshwater lake; covered riding arena; 3 tennis courts; gym; indoor climbing wall; rustic cabins.

Profile of Summer Employees Total number: 80; typical ages: 19–22. 10% men; 90% women; 80% college students. Nonsmokers preferred.

Employment Information Openings are from May 31 to August 11. Jobs available: ▶ *archery staff members* (minimum age 19) salary commensurate with age and experience beginning at $235 per week; all wages paid at the end of the season, but weekly advances may be drawn on request ▶ *arts/crafts staff members* (minimum age 19) salary commensurate with age and experience beginning at $235 per week; all wages paid at the end of the season, but weekly advances may be drawn on request ▶ *canoeing and kayaking staff members* (minimum age 19) with lifeguard/river rescue/first aid certification and experience; salary commensurate with age and experience beginning at $235 per week; all wages paid at the end of the season, but weekly advances may be drawn on request ▶ *ceramics staff members* (minimum age 19) with experience in the field; salary commensurate with age and experience beginning at $235 per week; all wages paid at the end of the season, but weekly advances may be drawn on request ▶ *land sports staff members* (minimum age 19) salary commensurate with age and experience beginning at $235 per week; all wages paid at the end of the season, but weekly advances may be drawn on request ▶ *mountaineering staff members* (minimum age 20) with experience in the field; salary commensurate with age and experience beginning at $235 per week; all wages paid at the end of the season, but weekly advances may be drawn on request ▶ *nature staff members* (minimum age 19) salary commensurate with age and experience beginning at $235 per week; all wages paid at the end of the season, but weekly advances may be drawn on request ▶ *performing arts staff members* (minimum age 19) with experience in the field salary commensurate with age and experience beginning at $235 per week; all wages paid at the end of the season, but weekly advances may be drawn on request ▶ *photographer/Web site update* with the ability to make daily updates to the camp's Web site with news and photos ▶ *photography staff members* (minimum age 19) with black and white dark room experience salary commensurate with age and experience beginning at $235 per week; all wages paid at the end of the season, but weekly advances may be drawn on request ▶ *riding staff members* (minimum age 19) with strong riding skills and technique; some barn work and grooming required; salary commensurate with age and experience beginning at $235 per week; all wages paid at the end of the season, but weekly advances may be drawn on request ▶ *rock climbing staff members* (minimum age 21) with strong leadership and organizational skills; orienteering, first aid, strong climbing and backpacking skills; college degree preferred for head position; salary commensurate with age and experience beginning at $235 per week; all wages paid at the end of the season, but weekly advances may be drawn on request ▶ *sailing staff members* (minimum age 19) with lifeguard certification and experience; salary commensurate with age and experience beginning at $235 per week; all wages paid at the end of the season, but weekly advances may be drawn on request ▶ *swimming staff members* (minimum age 19) with lifeguard and WSI certification; salary commensurate with age and experience beginning at $235 per week; all wages paid at the end of the season, but weekly advances may be drawn on request ▶ *tennis staff members* (minimum age 19) with experience; salary commensurate with age and experience beginning at $235 per week; all wages paid at the end of the season, but weekly advances may be drawn on request ▶ *weaving staff members* (minimum age 19) with experience weaving on floor looms salary commensurate with age and experience beginning at $235 per week; all wages paid at the end of the season, but weekly advances may be drawn on request ▶ *woodworking staff members* (minimum age 21) with experience in the field; salary commensurate with age and experience beginning at $235 per week; all wages paid at the end of the season, but weekly advances may be drawn on request. Applicants must submit formal organization application, three writing samples, three personal references. An in-person interview is recommended, but a telephone interview is acceptable. International applicants accepted; must apply through a recognized agency.

Benefits and Preemployment Training Free housing, free meals, willing to provide letters of recommendation, willing to complete paperwork for educational credit, willing to act as a professional reference, and opportunity to attend seminars/workshops. Preemployment training is required and includes accident prevention and safety, first aid, interpersonal skills, leadership skills.

Contact Ms. Laurie Strayhorn, Director, Camp Merrie-Woode, 100 Merrie-Woode Road, Sapphire, North Carolina 28774. Telephone: 828-743-3300. Fax: 828-743-5846. E-mail: laurie@merriewoode.com. World Wide Web: http://www.merriewoode.com. Contact by e-mail, mail, phone, or through World Wide Web site. Application deadline: continuous.

CAMP MERRI-MAC

1123 MONTREAT ROAD
BLACK MOUNTAIN, NORTH CAROLINA 28711

General Information Residential camp for girls. Established in 1950. 150-acre facility located 15 miles from Asheville. Features: private lake; 3 climbing walls; 3 tennis courts; outstanding facility.

Profile of Summer Employees Total number: 60; typical ages: 19–25. 5% men; 95% women;

5% high school students; 80% college students; 5% non-U.S. citizens; 10% local applicants. Nonsmokers required.

Employment Information Openings are from June 8 to August 10. Jobs available: ▶ 35 *counselors* with strong expertise and requisite certification in activity at $1450–$2000 per season ▶ *skilled activity instructors* with documented experience and certifications at $1000–$1500 per season. Applicants must submit a formal organization application, two personal references. An in-person interview is required. International applicants accepted.

Benefits and Preemployment Training Free housing, free meals, formal training, on-the-job training, willing to complete paperwork for educational credit, willing to act as a professional reference, and opportunity to attend seminars/workshops. Preemployment training is required and includes accident prevention and safety, first aid, CPR, interpersonal skills, leadership skills.

Contact Adam Boyd, Director, Camp Merri-Mac. Telephone: 828-669-8766. Fax: 828-669-6822. E-mail: adam@merri-mac.com. World Wide Web: http://www.merri-mac.com. Contact by phone or through World Wide Web site. Application deadline: continuous.

CAMP SKY RANCH, INC.

634 SKY RANCH ROAD
BLOWING ROCK, NORTH CAROLINA 28605-9738

General Information Coed private residential camp serving 114 mentally disabled children and adults in four 2-week sessions. Campers must be able to walk, dress, and feed themselves, as well as take care of their toilet needs. Established in 1948. 175-acre facility located 100 miles from Charlotte. Features: freshwater lake; mountain setting; heated swimming pool; cool nights; creeks.

Profile of Summer Employees Total number: 20; typical ages: 18–25. 45% men; 55% women; 10% minorities; 20% high school students; 80% college students; 15% local applicants. Nonsmokers preferred.

Employment Information Openings are from June 3 to July 20. Jobs available: ▶ 22 *counselors/activity leaders* at $120–$170 per week ▶ 2 *lifeguards* (minimum age 19) with lifeguard training at $120–$180 per week ▶ 1 *waterfront director* with Red Cross certification at $130–$190 per week. Applicants must submit a formal organization application, three personal references. An in-person interview is recommended, but a telephone interview is acceptable.

Benefits and Preemployment Training Free housing, free meals, willing to provide letters of recommendation, and willing to complete paperwork for educational credit. Preemployment training is required and includes interpersonal skills, working with special children.

Contact Jack L. Sharp, Director, Camp Sky Ranch, Inc., 634 Sky Ranch Road, Blowing Rock, North Carolina 28605-9738. Telephone: 828-264-8600. Fax: 828-265-2339. E-mail: jsharpl@triad.rr.com. Contact by e-mail, fax, mail, or phone. Application deadline: continuous.

CAMPS MONDAMIN AND GREEN COVE

TUXEDO, NORTH CAROLINA 28784

General Information Residential camps focusing on noncompetitive, lifetime, and outdoor skills with an emphasis on extended trips. Established in 1922. 800-acre facility located 6 miles from Hendersonville. Features: freshwater lake; location in mountains; 800 acres of trails; near Smoky Mountains; tennis courts; climbing tower; horseback riding facilities.

Profile of Summer Employees Total number: 175; typical ages: 19–30. 50% men; 50% women; 2% minorities; 60% college students; 5% retirees; 2% non-U.S. citizens; 5% local applicants. Nonsmokers required.

Employment Information Openings are from June 1 to August 18. Jobs available: ▶ 2 *crafts and games instructors* (minimum age 18) with archery and riflery experience at $1600–$2000 per season ▶ 4 *horseback riding instructors* (minimum age 18) with hunter-style riding and barn experience at $1600–$2500 per season ▶ 2 *mountain biking instructors* (minimum age 18) with camping experience and mechanical expertise at $1600–$2300 per season ▶ 6 *mountaineering* *instructors (hiking, rock climbing)* (minimum age 20) at $1600–$2300 per season ▶ 2 *sailing instructors* (minimum age 18) with experience at $1600–$2300 per season ▶ 4 *swimming instructors* (minimum age 18) with ARC lifeguard and WSI at $1600–$2300 per season ▶ 2 *tennis instructors* (minimum age 18) with experience at $1600–$2300 per season. Applicants must submit formal organization application, five personal references. An in-person interview is recommended, but a telephone interview is acceptable. International applicants accepted; must apply through a recognized agency.

Benefits and Preemployment Training Free housing, free meals, willing to provide letters of recommendation, on-the-job training, willing to complete paperwork for educational credit, willing to act as a professional reference, and opportunity to attend seminars/workshops. Preemployment training is required and includes accident prevention and safety, first aid, CPR, interpersonal skills, leadership skills, ARC lifeguard, WSI, WMA wilderness first aid, ARC first aid.

Contact Frank or Nancy Bell, Directors, Camps Mondamin and Green Cove, PO Box 8, Tuxedo, North Carolina 28784. Telephone: 828-693-7446. Fax: 828-696-8895. E-mail: mondamin@mondamin.com. World Wide Web: http://www.mondamin.com. Contact by e-mail, fax, mail, or phone. Application deadline: continuous.

CAMP TIMBERLAKE

1123 MONTREAT ROAD
BLACK MOUNTAIN, NORTH CAROLINA 28711

General Information A Christian camp for boys offering a traditional residential program with outstanding staff. Established in 1983. 150-acre facility located 16 miles from Asheville. Features: private lake; 3 tennis courts; 3 climbing walls; outstanding riding facility; ropes course; classic camp atmosphere.

Profile of Summer Employees Total number: 40; typical ages: 17–26. 5% women; 10% high school students; 85% college students; 1% retirees; 1% non-U.S. citizens; 5% local applicants. Nonsmokers required.

Employment Information Openings are from June 8 to August 10. Jobs available: ▶ *activity heads* (minimum age 20) with documented experience and certification at $1000–$1500 per season ▶ 35 *counselors* with strong expertise and requisite certification in activity at $1450–$2000 per season. Applicants must submit formal organization application, two personal references. An in-person interview is required. International applicants accepted; must apply through a recognized agency.

Benefits and Preemployment Training Free housing, free meals, formal training, willing to provide letters of recommendation, on-the-job training, willing to act as a professional reference, and opportunity to attend seminars/workshops. Preemployment training is required and includes accident prevention and safety, first aid, CPR, interpersonal skills, leadership skills, Christian discipleship.

Contact Adam Boyd, Director, Camp Timberlake. Telephone: 828-669-8766. Fax: 828-669-6822. E-mail: adam@camptimberlake.com. World Wide Web: http://www.camptimberlake.com. Contact by e-mail, phone, or through World Wide Web site. Application deadline: continuous.

CYBERCAMPS–NORTH CAROLINA STATE

RALEIGH, NORTH CAROLINA

See Cybercamps–University of Washington on page 335 for complete description.

CYBERCAMPS–UNC, GRANVILLE TOWERS

CHAPEL HILL, NORTH CAROLINA

See Cybercamps–University of Washington on page 335 for complete description.

DUKE YOUTH PROGRAMS–DUKE UNIVERSITY CONTINUING EDUCATION

203 BISHOP'S HOUSE, BOX 90702
DURHAM, NORTH CAROLINA 27708

General Information Five summer enrichment programs serving 650 middle and high school students. Established in 1982. 20 miles from Raleigh. Features: university campus.

Profile of Summer Employees Total number: 50; typical ages: 19–22. 40% men; 60% women; 50% college students. Nonsmokers preferred.

Employment Information Openings are from June 10 to August 10. Jobs available: ▶ 14–16 *residential counselors* (minimum age 19) 21 year-olds with good driving records preferred at $1800–$2200 per season. Applicants must submit a formal organization application, letter of interest, resume, two personal references, two letters of recommendation. An in-person interview is recommended, but a telephone interview is acceptable.

Benefits and Preemployment Training Free housing, free meals, formal training, willing to provide letters of recommendation, on-the-job training, and willing to act as a professional reference. Preemployment training is required and includes accident prevention and safety, first aid, interpersonal skills, van driving, programming.

Contact Kim Price, Program Director, Duke Youth Programs–Duke University Continuing Education, Box 90702, Durham, North Carolina 27708. Telephone: 919-684-5387. Fax: 919-681-8235. E-mail: kprice@duke.edu. World Wide Web: http://www.learnmore.duke.edu/youth. Contact by e-mail, mail, or phone. Application deadline: February 15.

EAGLE'S NEST CAMP

43 HART ROAD
PISGAH FOREST, NORTH CAROLINA 28768

General Information Residential camp serving 185 campers in three 3-week sessions. Experiential education for young people, promoting the natural world and the betterment of human character. Specializes in wilderness adventure and the arts. Established in 1927. 40-acre facility located 30 miles from Asheville. Features: freshwater lakes; tennis courts; open air cabins with hot and cold running water; high ropes course; wooded setting; 12-stall barn and horses.

Profile of Summer Employees Total number: 80; typical ages: 19–26. 50% men; 50% women; 1% minorities; 80% college students; 3% non-U.S. citizens; 1% local applicants. Nonsmokers required.

Employment Information Openings are from May 15 to August 19. Year-round positions also offered. Jobs available: ▶ 5–8 *arts instructors* (minimum age 19) with creativity, teaching experience, CPR, and basic first aid certification at $160–$250 per week ▶ 5–8 *athletics instructors* (minimum age 19) with CPR, first aid, and experience working with children at $160–$250 per week ▶ 6–8 *canoeing instructors* (minimum age 19) with experience or American Canoe Association Instructor, CPR, and basic first aid certification at $160–$250 per week ▶ 4 *horseback instructors* (minimum age 19) with CPR and basic first aid certification and experience in the field at $160–$250 per week ▶ *kitchen staff* (minimum age 18) with experience in whole foods cooking at $160–$250 per week ▶ *medical staff members* should be RN, NP, PA or MD with CPR certification at $200 to $300 per week or tuition exchange for camper ▶ 6–10 *rock climbing instructors* (minimum age 19) with CPR and basic first aid (minimum) and experience in the field at $160–$300 per week ▶ 4–6 *swimming instructors* (minimum age 19) with WSI, LGT, CPR, and basic first aid certification; teaching and/or lifeguarding experience at $160–$250 per week ▶ 10 *wilderness instructors* (minimum age 19) with wilderness first aid, CPR, basic first aid certification and experience leading groups in the field at $160–$300 per week. Applicants must submit formal organization application, two personal references, personal statement (with application). A telephone interview is required. International applicants accepted; must apply through a recognized agency.

Benefits and Preemployment Training Free housing, free meals, formal training, possible full-time employment, willing to provide letters of recommendation, on-the-job training, willing to complete paperwork for educational credit, willing to act as a professional reference, and opportunity to attend seminars/workshops. Preemployment training is required and includes accident prevention and safety, interpersonal skills, leadership skills.

Contact Ms. Noni Waite-Kucera, Summer Director, Eagle's Nest Camp, 633 Summit Street, Winston-Salem, North Carolina 27101. Telephone: 336-761-1040. Fax: 336-727-0030. E-mail: noni@enf.org. World Wide Web: http://www.enf.org. Contact by e-mail, mail, or phone. Application deadline: continuous.

KEYSTONE CAMP

CASHIERS VALLEY ROAD
BREVARD, NORTH CAROLINA 28712

General Information A camp for girls (ages 7–17) offering programs in horsemanship, daily horseback riding, tennis, land sports, water sports on two lakes, gymnastics, rock climbing, and hiking in Pisgah National Forest. Established in 1916. 80-acre facility located 30 miles from Asheville. Features: 2 lakes; climbing wall; 4 tennis courts; low ropes course; 3 riding rings; beautiful wooded setting.

Profile of Summer Employees Total number: 35; typical ages: 18–30. 10% men; 90% women; 20% minorities; 100% college students; 30% non-U.S. citizens. Nonsmokers preferred.

Employment Information Openings are from June 1 to August 10. Jobs available: ▶ 1 *aerobics instructor* (minimum age 18) at $1530–$2500 per season ▶ 1 *archery instructor* (minimum age 18) at $1530–$2500 per season ▶ 3 *art instructors* (minimum age 18) at $1530–$2500 per season ▶ 1 *badminton instructor* (minimum age 18) at $1530–$2500 per season ▶ 2 *canoeing instructors* (minimum age 18) with lifeguard certification at $1530–$2500 per season ▶ 1 *dance instructor* (minimum age 18) at $1530–$2500 per season ▶ *dramatics instructor* (minimum age 18) at $1530–$2500 per season ▶ 3 *hiking and camping instructors* (minimum age 18) at $1530–$2500 per season ▶ *nature instructor* (minimum age 18) at $1530–$2500 per season ▶ *riding instructor* (minimum age 18) at $1530–$2500 per season ▶ 1 *riflery instructor* (minimum age 18) at $1530–$2500 per season ▶ 2 *rock climbing instructors* (minimum age 18) at $1530–$2500 per season ▶ *stable helper* (minimum age 18) at $1530–$2500 per season ▶ *swimming instructor* (minimum age 18) with WSI and/or lifeguard certification at $1530–$2500 per season ▶ 2–3 *tennis instructors* (minimum age 18) at $1530–$2500 per season ▶ 1 *trip staff director* (minimum age 18) at $1530–$3000 per season ▶ *various sports instructors* (minimum age 18) at $1530–$2500 per season. Applicants must submit formal organization application, two personal references. An in-person interview is recommended, but a telephone interview is acceptable. International applicants accepted; must apply through a recognized agency.

Benefits and Preemployment Training Free housing, free meals, formal training, willing to provide letters of recommendation, on-the-job training, willing to complete paperwork for educational credit, willing to act as a professional reference, and opportunity to attend seminars/ workshops. Preemployment training is required and includes accident prevention and safety, first aid, CPR, interpersonal skills, leadership skills.

Contact Ms. Mary Boyd, Associate Director, Keystone Camp, PO Box 829, Brevard, North Carolina 28712. Telephone: 828-884-9125. Fax: 828-883-8234. E-mail: mary@keystonecamp.com. World Wide Web: http://www.keystonecamp.com. Contact by e-mail, fax, mail, phone, or through World Wide Web site. Application deadline: continuous.

NORTH CAROLINA UNITED METHODIST OUTDOOR AND CAMPING MINISTRIES

1307 GLENWOOD AVENUE
RALEIGH, NORTH CAROLINA 27605

General Information Three campsites located in eastern North Carolina providing camping and outdoor experiences in an atmosphere of Christian faith. Established in 1948. 1,000-acre facility.

Profile of Summer Employees Total number: 150; typical ages: 18–25. 40% men; 60% women; 20% minorities; 10% high school students; 90% college students. Nonsmokers preferred.

Employment Information Openings are from May to August. Jobs available: ▶ *arts and crafts instructors* at $190–$210 per week ▶ *cabin counselors* at $190–$210 per week ▶ *lifeguards* at $190–$210 per week ▶ *naturalists* at $190–$210 per week ▶ *sailing staff members/canoeing instructors* at $190–$210 per week. Applicants must submit formal organization application, three personal references. An in-person interview is recommended, but a telephone interview is acceptable. International applicants accepted; must apply through a recognized agency.

Benefits and Preemployment Training Free housing, free meals, health insurance, willing to provide letters of recommendation, on-the-job training, and willing to act as a professional reference. Preemployment training is required and includes accident prevention and safety, first aid, CPR, interpersonal skills, leadership skills.

Contact Wray Stephens, Director, Camping Ministries, North Carolina United Methodist Outdoor and Camping Ministries, PO Box 10955, Raleigh, North Carolina 27605. Telephone: 919-832-9560. Fax: 919-832-9588. World Wide Web: http://www.ncumcamps.org. Application deadline: March 1.

PARAMOUNT'S CAROWINDS

14523 CAROWINDS BOULEVARD
CHARLOTTE, NORTH CAROLINA 28273

General Information Theme park entertaining close to 2 million guests each season with rides, shows, concerts, food, and games. Seasonal operation March through October. Established in 1972. 360-acre facility. Features: Top Gun Steel roller coaster; division of Viacom International; newly expanded waterpark; 10 roller coasters; 3-D action adventure; haunted mansion.

Profile of Summer Employees Total number: 2,000; typical ages: 15–80. 49% men; 51% women; 50% minorities; 35% high school students; 27% college students; 9% retirees; 1% non-U.S. citizens; 28% local applicants.

Employment Information Openings are from March 1 to October 31. Jobs available: ▶ 300–500 *food and beverage associates* (minimum age 16) with neat appearance and outgoing personality at $6–$8 per hour ▶ 50–150 *lifeguards* (minimum age 18) with free training and certification provided at $7–$9 per hour ▶ 500–600 *merchandise, games, and admissions associates* (minimum age 16) with neat appearance and outgoing personality at $6–$7 per hour ▶ 300–500 *ride operators* (minimum age 18) with neat appearance and outgoing personality at $6–$8 per hour. Applicants must submit formal organization application. An in-person interview is required. International applicants accepted; must apply through a recognized agency.

Benefits and Preemployment Training Health insurance, on-the-job training, willing to complete paperwork for educational credit, opportunity to attend seminars/workshops, travel reimbursement, and internships and cooperative education programs available.

Contact Paramount's Carowinds, Paramount's Carowinds, Employment Office, PO Box 410289, Charlotte, North Carolina 28241-0289. Telephone: 704-587-9006. Fax: 704-587-9101. World Wide Web: http://www.carowinds.com. Contact by mail, phone, or through World Wide Web site. Application deadline: continuous.

ROCKBROOK CAMP
HIGHWAY 276
BREVARD, NORTH CAROLINA 28712

General Information Residential camp serving girls ages 6–16, promoting independence in a non-competitive environment. Camp has two-, three-, and four-week sessions. Established in 1921. 185-acre facility located 30 miles from Asheville. Features: 1 freshwater lake; wooded setting; 6 tennis courts; climbing wall; Alpine Tower; on-site pottery studio.

Profile of Summer Employees Total number: 70; typical ages: 20–30. 8% men; 92% women; 8% minorities; 3% high school students; 75% college students; 2% retirees; 8% non-U.S. citizens; 8% local applicants. Nonsmokers required.

Employment Information Openings are from May 27 to August 12. Jobs available: ▶ 50 *cabin counselors (women only)* (minimum age 19) with CPR/first aid certification at $200 plus per week ▶ 2–4 *raft and canoeing guides* at $200 plus per week ▶ 6 *registered nurses (women only)* with RN license at $450 per week ▶ 2 *riding instructors (women only)* at $200 per week ▶ 2 *rock climbers* at $150–$200 per week. Applicants must submit formal organization application, three personal references. An in-person interview is recommended, but a telephone interview is acceptable. International applicants accepted; must obtain own visa, obtain own working papers, apply through a recognized agency.

Benefits and Preemployment Training Free housing, free meals, willing to provide letters of recommendation, on-the-job training, willing to act as a professional reference, and laundry. Preemployment training is required and includes accident prevention and safety, interpersonal skills, leadership skills.

Contact Charlotte Page, Associate Director, Rockbrook Camp, PO Box 792, Brevard, North Carolina 28712. Telephone: 828-884-6151. Fax: 828-884-6459. E-mail: rockbrook@citcom.net. World Wide Web: http://www.rockbrookcamp.com. Contact by e-mail, fax, mail, phone, or through World Wide Web site. Application deadline: continuous.

RUBIN'S OSCEOLA LAKE INN
PO BOX 2258
HENDERSONVILLE, NORTH CAROLINA 28793

General Information Summer resort hotel with 80 rooms, serving 3 meals daily. Established in 1941. 12-acre facility. Located 1 mile from . Features: lake; wooded setting; tennis; shuffleboard; putting green; ping-pong.

Profile of Summer Employees Total number: 30; typical ages: 18–50. 50% men; 50% women; 25% minorities; 25% college students; 25% non-U.S. citizens; 25% local applicants. Nonsmokers preferred.

Employment Information Openings are from June to October. Jobs available: ▶ 3 *bellhops* (minimum age 18) ▶ 6 *buspersons* (minimum age 18) ▶ 1 *chauffeur* (minimum age 20) ▶ 4 *desk clerks* (minimum age 18) ▶ 6 *housekeeping personnel* (minimum age 18) ▶ 3 *kitchen aides* (minimum age 18) ▶ 1 *secretary* (minimum age 18) with typing and computer skills ▶ 6 *waiters/waitresses* (minimum age 18). Applicants must submit resume, two personal references, two letters of recommendation. International applicants accepted; must obtain own visa, obtain own working papers, apply through a recognized agency.

Benefits and Preemployment Training Housing at a cost, meals at a cost, possible full-time employment, and on-the-job training.

Contact Stuart Rubin, Owner/Manager, Rubin's Osceola Lake Inn, 5005 Collins Avenue, PH7, Miami Beach, Florida 33140. Telephone: 305-865-6015. Contact by mail or phone. Application deadline: continuous.

THE SOUTHWESTERN COMPANY, NORTH CAROLINA

See The Southwestern Company on page 302 for complete description.

SPORTS INTERNATIONAL–JOE KRIVAK (QUARTERBACK AND RECEIVING CAMP)

SALISBURY, NORTH CAROLINA

See Sports International, Inc. on page 147 for complete description.

SPORTS INTERNATIONAL–PANTHERS

SALISBURY, NORTH CAROLINA

See Sports International, Inc. on page 147 for complete description.

STUDENT CONSERVATION ASSOCIATION (SCA), NORTH CAROLINA

See Student Conservation Association (SCA), New Hampshire on page 209 for complete description.

YMCA CAMP HANES

1225 CAMP HANES ROAD
KING, NORTH CAROLINA 27021

General Information Residential camp serving 205 campers weekly. Established in 1927. 400-acre facility located 17 miles from Winston-Salem. Features: mountainside location; swimming pool and waterpark; 2 small lakes; gymnasium; large high ropes course; large playing fields.

Profile of Summer Employees Total number: 60; typical ages: 17–24. 50% men; 50% women; 10% minorities; 5% high school students; 90% college students; 15% non-U.S. citizens; 70% local applicants. Nonsmokers required.

Employment Information Openings are from May 25 to August 5. Year-round positions also offered. Jobs available: ▶ 5 *adventure trip leaders* (minimum age 18) with wilderness first aid at $190–$220 per week ▶ 36 *cabin counselors* (minimum age 16) at $110–$210 per week ▶ 2 *counselor-in-training directors* (minimum age 21) with at least one year of college at $220–$250 per week ▶ 2 *equestrian directors* (minimum age 21) with riding experience at $220–$250 per week ▶ 2 *registered nurses* (minimum age 21) with RN degree at $250–$300 per week ▶ 1 *waterfront director* (minimum age 21) with WSI certification at $220–$250 per week. Applicants must submit formal organization application, three personal references. An in-person interview is recommended, but a telephone interview is acceptable. International applicants accepted; must apply through a recognized agency.

Benefits and Preemployment Training Free housing, free meals, possible full-time employment, willing to provide letters of recommendation, on-the-job training, willing to complete paperwork for educational credit, and willing to act as a professional reference. Preemployment training is required and includes accident prevention and safety, first aid, CPR, interpersonal skills, leadership skills, blood-borne pathogens information, lifeguard training.

Contact Patrick Kelly, Associate Executive Director, YMCA Camp Hanes, 1225 Camp Hanes Road, King, North Carolina 27021. Telephone: 336-983-3131. Fax: 336-983-4624. E-mail: fun@camphanes.org. World Wide Web: http://www.camphanes.org. Contact by e-mail, fax, mail, phone, or through World Wide Web site. Application deadline: continuous.

NORTH DAKOTA

A CHRISTIAN MINISTRY IN THE NATIONAL PARKS–NORTH DAKOTA

See A Christian Ministry in the National Parks–Maine on page 122 for complete description.

INTERNATIONAL MUSIC CAMP

INTERNATIONAL PEACE GARDEN
DUNSEITH, NORTH DAKOTA 58329

General Information Residential camp serving 500 students per week in 24 different arts programs. Established in 1956. 120-acre facility located 117 miles from Minot. Features: wooded setting in a state park; 2,000-seat concert hall.

Profile of Summer Employees Total number: 225; typical ages: 18–65. 50% men; 50% women; 5% minorities; 35% college students; 5% retirees; 10% non-U.S. citizens; 20% local applicants. Nonsmokers preferred.

Employment Information Openings are from June 1 to July 30. Jobs available: ▶ 11 *concessioners/housekeepers/maintenance persons* (minimum age 18) at $200–$250 per week ▶ 6 *cooks* (minimum age 18) with cooking experience at $200–$250 per week ▶ 20 *deans/counselors* (minimum age 21) college seniors or graduates at $200–$250 per week ▶ 4 *dishwashers* (minimum age 18) at $200 per week ▶ 1 *first aid technician* (minimum age 21) with CPR, first aid certification; RN or LPN license at $250 per week ▶ 4 *music librarians* (minimum age 18) with instrumental knowledge at $200 per week ▶ 6 *secretaries* (minimum age 18) with ability to type 50 wpm and knowledge of computers at $200 per week. Applicants must submit a formal organization application, letter of interest, resume, three letters of recommendation. An in-person interview is recommended, but a telephone interview is acceptable. International applicants accepted; must obtain own visa, obtain own working papers.

Benefits and Preemployment Training Free housing, free meals, willing to provide letters of recommendation, names of contacts, on-the-job training, willing to act as a professional reference, opportunity to attend seminars/workshops, and private music lessons at no cost. Preemployment training is required and includes accident prevention and safety, interpersonal skills, leadership skills.

Contact Joseph T. Alme, Camp Director, International Music Camp, 1725 11th Street, SW, Minot, North Dakota 58701. Telephone: 701-838-8472. Fax: 701-838-8472. E-mail: info@internationalmusiccamp.com. World Wide Web: http://www.internationalmusiccamp.com. Contact by e-mail, fax, or mail. Application deadline: continuous.

THE SOUTHWESTERN COMPANY, NORTH DAKOTA

See The Southwestern Company on page 302 for complete description.

STUDENT CONSERVATION ASSOCIATION (SCA), NORTH DAKOTA

See Student Conservation Association (SCA), New Hampshire on page 209 for complete description.

OHIO

CAMP ECHOING HILLS
36272 COUNTY ROAD 79
WARSAW, OHIO 43844

General Information Camp experience for 650 mentally and physically disabled campers of all ages. Full camping program with highest standards of care for special population campers. Established in 1966. 72-acre facility located 60 miles from Columbus. Features: wooded setting; lake; go-carts; wilderness camping.

Profile of Summer Employees Total number: 40; typical ages: 19–23. 35% men; 65% women; 20% minorities; 20% high school students; 70% college students; 10% non-U.S. citizens. Nonsmokers required.

Employment Information Openings are from June 1 to August 9. Jobs available: ▶ *assistant nurses* (minimum age 21) at $200–$300 per week ▶ 40 *counselors* (minimum age 18) at $175–$250 per week ▶ 20–25 *support staff members* (minimum age 16) at $175–$250 per week. Applicants must submit formal organization application, three personal references, three letters of recommendation. An in-person interview is recommended, but a telephone interview is acceptable. International applicants accepted; must obtain own visa, obtain own working papers, apply through a recognized agency.

Benefits and Preemployment Training Free housing, free meals, possible full-time employment, willing to provide letters of recommendation, on-the-job training, willing to complete paperwork for educational credit, and willing to act as a professional reference. Preemployment training is required and includes accident prevention and safety, first aid, interpersonal skills, leadership skills, caregiving for disabled population.

Contact Shaker Samuel, Camp Administrator, Camp Echoing Hills, 36272 County Road 79, Warsaw, Ohio 43844. Telephone: 740-327-2311. Fax: 740-327-6371. E-mail: campechohl@aol.com. World Wide Web: http://www.echoinghillsvillage.org. Contact by e-mail, fax, mail, or phone. Application deadline: continuous.

CAMP LIBBEY/GIRL SCOUTS OF MAUMEE VALLEY COUNCIL
DEFIANCE, OHIO

General Information Year-round residential facility serving girls, schools, and conference groups. 350-acre facility.

Employment Information Openings are from June to August 15. Jobs available: ▶ 3 *assistant cooks* (minimum age 18) with experience in quantity cooking and baking, teamwork skills, creative at $1980–$2340 per season ▶ 1 *business manager* (minimum age 21) with computer skills, good driving record, valid driver's license, people skills, money handling skills at $2400–$2800 per season ▶ 15 *counselors* (minimum age 18) with teamwork skills, outdoor skills, people skills at $1260–$1980 per season ▶ 4 *counselors/horseback riding instructors* (minimum age 18) with riding and teaching experience, outdoor skills, teamwork skills at $1440–$2160 per season ▶ 4 *counselors/lifeguards* (minimum age 18) with teamwork skills, lifeguard certification, outdoor skills at $1440–$2160 per season ▶ 1 *head cook* (minimum age 21) with kitchen management skills, quantity cooking and supervisory skills at $2800–$3200 per season ▶ 1 *naturalist* (minimum age 18) with experience/training in natural science or environmental studies, outdoor skills, teamwork skills, desire to work with youth at $2200–$2600 per season ▶ 1

waterfront director (minimum age 21) with WSI certification, supervisory experience at $3000–$3400 per season. Applicants must submit a formal organization application, three personal references. An in-person interview is recommended, but a telephone interview is acceptable.
Benefits and Preemployment Training Free housing, free meals, willing to complete paperwork for educational credit, and internet and laundry service. Preemployment training is required and includes first aid, CPR.
Contact Christy Gustin, Camp Manager, Camp Libbey/Girl Scouts of Maumee Valley Council, 28325 State Route 281, Defiance, Ohio 43512. Telephone: 419-784-5888. Fax: 419-782-9408. E-mail: clibbey@mvgsc.org. World Wide Web: http://www.mvgsc.org. Contact by e-mail, fax, mail, phone, or through World Wide Web site. Application deadline: continuous.

CAMP O'BANNON
9688 BUTLER ROAD, NE
NEWARK, OHIO 43055

General Information Residential camp serving children ages 9–14 with the goal of increasing self-esteem. Established in 1922. 169-acre facility located 40 miles from Columbus. Features: main camp; outpost camp; 2 high ropes courses.
Profile of Summer Employees Total number: 22; typical ages: 19–22. 40% men; 60% women; 20% high school students; 80% college students. Nonsmokers preferred.
Employment Information Openings are from June 8 to August 14. Jobs available: ▶ 1 *arts and crafts counselor* with one year of college at $1200–$1400 per season ▶ 1 *assistant cook* at $900–$1400 per season ▶ 8 *cabin counselors* with one year of college at $1200–$1400 per season ▶ *camp director* with college degree (preferred) at $1800 per season ▶ 1 *cook* with ability to cook for 65 or more people at $1500–$1800 per season ▶ 1 *lifeguard* with WSI certification (preferred) at $1200–$1400 per season ▶ 1 *maintenance counselor* at $1000–$1200 per season ▶ 1 *nature counselor* with one year of college at $1200–$1400 per season ▶ 1 *nurse* with RN license at $1400 per season ▶ 3 *outpost counselors* with one year of college at $1200–$1400 per season ▶ 1 *outpost director* with 2 years of college at $1500–$1800 per season ▶ 1 *program director* with 2 years of college at $1500 per season. Applicants must submit a formal organization application, three personal references, three letters of recommendation. An in-person interview is recommended, but a telephone interview is acceptable. International applicants accepted; must obtain own visa, obtain own working papers.
Benefits and Preemployment Training Free housing, free meals, health insurance, willing to provide letters of recommendation, names of contacts, on-the-job training, willing to complete paperwork for educational credit, and willing to act as a professional reference. Preemployment training is required.
Contact Ted Cobb, Camp Director, Camp O'Bannon. Telephone: 614-345-8295. Fax: 614-349-5093. Contact by mail or phone. Application deadline: continuous.

CAMP ROOSEVELT FOR BOYS/FIREBIRD FOR GIRLS
4141 DUBLIN ROAD
BOWERSTON, OHIO 44695

General Information Residential camp serving 60 campers per season. Established in 1918. 150-acre facility located 45 miles from Akron. Features: lake; tennis; golf; all water sports; land sports; English riding.
Profile of Summer Employees Total number: 40; typical ages: 19–30. 40% men; 60% women; 5% minorities; 80% college students; 10% non-U.S. citizens. Nonsmokers required.
Employment Information Openings are from June 15 to August 16. Jobs available: ▶ *English riding staff members* at $1600–$1800 per season ▶ *archery staff members* (minimum age 19) at $1600–$1800 per season ▶ *riflery staff members* at $1600–$1800 per season ▶ 2 *swimming instructors* (minimum age 19) with WSI, lifeguard, or equivalent certification at $1600–$2000

per season ▶ *tennis staff members* (minimum age 19) at $1600–$1800 per season. Applicants must submit formal organization application, letter of interest, three personal references, three letters of recommendation. An in-person interview is recommended, but a telephone interview is acceptable. International applicants accepted; must apply through a recognized agency.

Benefits and Preemployment Training Free housing, free meals, willing to provide letters of recommendation, on-the-job training, willing to complete paperwork for educational credit, travel reimbursement, and tuition assistance. Preemployment training is required and includes accident prevention and safety, CPR, leadership skills.

Contact W. V. Lorimer, Owner/Director, Camp Roosevelt for Boys/Firebird for Girls, 2814 Perry Park Road, Perry, Ohio 44081. Telephone: 440-259-2901. Fax: 440-259-2901. E-mail: rooseybird@earthlink.net. Contact by mail. Application deadline: May 1.

CEDAR POINT

1 CEDAR POINT DRIVE
SANDUSKY, OHIO 44870-5259

General Information Amusement/theme park with 68 rides, 4 resort hotels, a campground, go karts, ripcord, mini golf, and a water park. Established in 1870. 364-acre facility located 60 miles from Cleveland. Features: 15 roller coasters; 364-acre park; 4 hotels; mile-long sandy beach; adjacent waterpark; campground.

Profile of Summer Employees Total number: 4,000; typical ages: 18–85. 40% men; 60% women; 20% high school students; 60% college students; 20% retirees; 30% non-U.S. citizens.

Employment Information Openings are from May 1 to October 10. Jobs available: ▶ 450–500 *games/arcades staff* (minimum age 18 if housing is required) at $6.25 per hour plus bonus ▶ 450–500 *hotel housekeeping staff* (minimum age 18 if housing is required) at $6.25 per hour plus bonus ▶ 1500 *quick service workers, restaurant staff* (minimum age 18 if housing is required) at $6.25 per hour plus bonus ▶ 850–900 *ride operators* (minimum age 18) at $6.25 per hour plus bonus ▶ 450–500 *sales associates* (minimum age 18 if housing is required) at $6.25 per hour plus bonus. Applicants must submit formal organization application, online application. An in-person interview is recommended, but a telephone interview is acceptable. International applicants accepted; must obtain own visa, obtain own working papers, apply through a recognized agency.

Benefits and Preemployment Training Housing at a cost, meals at a cost, on-the-job training, willing to complete paperwork for educational credit, and employee activities program. Preemployment training is required and includes accident prevention and safety, first aid, CPR, interpersonal skills, leadership skills, diversity, sexual harassment awareness training.

Contact Amanda Rose-Royer, Assistant Director of Human Resources, Cedar Point, PO Box 5006, Sandusky, Ohio 44870. Telephone: 800-668-JOBS. Fax: 419-627-2163. World Wide Web: http://www.cedarpoint.com. Contact by mail, phone, or through World Wide Web site. Application deadline: August 1.

COLLEGE GIFTED PROGRAMS

DENISON UNIVERSITY
GRANVILLE, OHIO 43023

General Information Residential educational academic summer camp for gifted and talented students in grades 4-11. Program blends in-depth academics with recreational and cultural activities. Established in 1984. 1,200-acre facility located 30 miles from Columbus. Features: dormitories; campus classroom facilities; campus recreational facilities include pool, tennis courts, and gym; campus library; beautiful college setting.

Profile of Summer Employees Total number: 64; typical ages: 19–70. 50% men; 50% women; 30% minorities; 50% college students; 10% retirees; 10% non-U.S. citizens; 25% local applicants. Nonsmokers required.

Employment Information Openings are from July 24 to August 14. Jobs available: ▶ 24 *counselors* with two years of college completed and experience working with children at $900 to $1200 per 3-week session ▶ 4 *directors* with at least 5 years teaching/supervisory experience; master's degree required, doctorate preferred at $5000–$8000 per year ▶ 6 *housemasters/ instructors (residential)* with master's degree, teaching and supervisory experience at $2500 to $4500 per 3-week session ▶ 20 *instructors (non-residential)* with master's degree and teaching experience at $600 to $2500 per 3-week session ▶ 2 *nurses* with RN license; school experience preferred at $1300 per week. Applicants must submit formal organization application, resume, academic transcripts, two personal references, two letters of recommendation. An in-person interview is recommended, but a telephone interview is acceptable. International applicants accepted; must apply through a recognized agency.

Benefits and Preemployment Training Free housing, free meals, willing to provide letters of recommendation, willing to complete paperwork for educational credit, and willing to act as a professional reference. Preemployment training is required and includes accident prevention and safety, interpersonal skills, leadership skills, instructional strategies for gifted students.

Contact Charles Zeichner, Executive Director, College Gifted Programs, 120 Littleton Road, Suite 201, Parsippany, New Jersey 07054-1803. Telephone: 973-334-6991. Fax: 973-334-9756. E-mail: info@cgp-sig.com. World Wide Web: http://www.cgp-sig.com. Contact by e-mail, fax, mail, phone, or through World Wide Web site. Application deadline: continuous.

FRIENDS MUSIC CAMP

61830 SANDY RIDGE ROAD
BARNESVILLE, OHIO 43713

General Information Residential camp offering musical instruction to 75 10- to 18-year-olds featuring private music lessons, orchestra, band, jazz, chorus, and musical theater. Established in 1980. 30-acre facility located 30 miles from Wheeling, West Virginia. Features: boarding school dormitories; soccer fields; boarding school main building; woods, rolling hills.

Profile of Summer Employees Total number: 20; typical ages: 18–67. 50% men; 50% women; 5% minorities; 50% college students; 10% retirees; 5% non-U.S. citizens. Nonsmokers required.

Employment Information Openings are from July 9 to August 8. Jobs available: ▶ 1–2 *counselors* (minimum age 19) with leadership skills and experience at $1000 per season ▶ 4–10 *musical instructors* (minimum age 18) with experience in the field at $1000 per season. Applicants must submit a letter of interest, resume, three personal references. An in-person interview is recommended, but a telephone interview is acceptable. International applicants accepted.

Benefits and Preemployment Training Free housing, free meals, willing to provide letters of recommendation, on-the-job training, and travel reimbursement. Preemployment training is required and includes leadership skills.

Contact Peg Champney, Director, Friends Music Camp, PO Box 427, Yellow Springs, Ohio 45387. Telephone: 937-767-1311. Fax: 937-767-2254. E-mail: musicfmc@yahoo.com. World Wide Web: http://www.quaker.org/friends-music-camp/. Contact by e-mail, mail, or phone. Application deadline: continuous.

GIRL SCOUT CAMP MOLLY LOUMAN

LUCASVILLE, OHIO 45648

General Information Girl Scout residential camp that serves campers ages 7-16. General activities include swimming, cookouts, horseback riding, and archery. Specialized activities include adventure travel: backpacking, river canoeing, river rafting, and rappelling. Established in 1929. 160-acre facility located 20 miles from Portsmouth. Features: wooded setting; lake access; use of surrounding public lands; modern, air-conditioned dining hall; staff lodge (air-conditioned); stables.

Profile of Summer Employees Total number: 50; typical ages: 18–25. 4% men; 96% women;

5% minorities; 1% high school students; 80% college students; 1% retirees; 8% non-U.S. citizens; 15% local applicants. Nonsmokers preferred.

Employment Information Openings are from June 15 to August 18. Jobs available: ▶ 2–5 *cooks and kitchen support staff* (minimum age 18) with experience cooking for large groups at $1800–$3200 per season ▶ 4–10 *general counselors* (minimum age 18) with human relations skills and camping skills at $1800–$2025 per season ▶ 1–2 *horseback riding instructors* (minimum age 18) with western riding skills and camping skills at $1800 per season ▶ 1–2 *lifeguards* (minimum age 18) with good swimming skills; certification/training may be provided at $1800 per season. Applicants must submit formal organization application, three personal references, BCI fingerprint check. An in-person interview is recommended, but a telephone interview is acceptable. International applicants accepted; must apply through a recognized agency.

Benefits and Preemployment Training Free housing, free meals, formal training, willing to provide letters of recommendation, on-the-job training, willing to complete paperwork for educational credit, willing to act as a professional reference, and opportunity to attend seminars/ workshops. Preemployment training is required and includes accident prevention and safety, first aid, CPR, interpersonal skills, leadership skills.

Contact Becky Foreman, Camp Director, Girl Scout Camp Molly Louman, 1700 Water Mark Drive, Columbus, Ohio 43215. Telephone: 614-487-8101 Ext. 857. Fax: 614-487-8199. E-mail: becky@sealofohio.org. Contact by e-mail, fax, or phone. Application deadline: continuous.

HIDDEN HOLLOW CAMP

5127 OPOSSUM RUN ROAD
BELLVILLE, OHIO 44813-9134

General Information Traditional residential camp serving boys and girls ages 8-15 with activities such as swimming, nature hikes, trail rides, arts and crafts, archery, tennis, woodworking, dramatics, and pond canoeing. Established in 1940. 620-acre facility located 12 miles from Mansfield. Features: pond; wooded setting; Sky High Lodge with beautiful view; 2 tennis courts; 3 heated dorms and 11 cabins; observatory.

Profile of Summer Employees Total number: 30; typical ages: 16–24. 50% men; 50% women; 20% minorities; 49% high school students; 51% college students; 85% local applicants. Nonsmokers preferred.

Employment Information Openings are from June 25 to August 8. Jobs available: ▶ 15–25 *camp counselors* (minimum age 16) with lifeguarding and CPR certification preferred at $165–$220 per week. Applicants must submit a formal organization application, three personal references. An in-person interview is required.

Benefits and Preemployment Training Free housing and free meals.

Contact Thelda J. Dillon, Director, Hidden Hollow Camp, 380 North Mulberry Street, Mansfield, Ohio 44902. Fax: 419-522-2166. Contact by mail. Application deadline: April 1.

THE SOUTHWESTERN COMPANY, OHIO

See The Southwestern Company on page 302 for complete description.

STOIBER ENTERPRISES

BOX 240, DELAWARE AVENUE
PUT-IN-BAY, OHIO 43456

General Information Restaurants, 2 taverns, and 3 gift shops located on an island in Lake Erie serving customers April-October. Established in 1948. Located 60 miles from Cleveland. Features: freshwater lake; safe dormitory; volleyball; nightlife; cycling; family atmosphere.

Profile of Summer Employees Total number: 85; typical ages: 18–25. 40% men; 60% women; 1% minorities; 75% college students; 20% non-U.S. citizens; 5% local applicants.

Employment Information Openings are from April 1 to November 1. Jobs available: ▶ 2–4 *janitorial staff* (minimum age 18) with cleaning experience preferred at $7–$9 per hour ▶ 10–12 *retail clerks* (minimum age 18) at $6–$6.50 per hour ▶ 3–4 *short order cooks* (minimum age 18) with line cooking experience at $6–$6.50 per hour ▶ 18–20 *waitstaff* (minimum age 19) with experience at $3 per hour. Applicants must submit formal organization application. An in-person interview is recommended, but a telephone interview is acceptable. International applicants accepted; must apply through a recognized agency.

Benefits and Preemployment Training Housing at a cost, meals at a cost, willing to provide letters of recommendation, on-the-job training, and willing to complete paperwork for educational credit.

Contact June Stoiber, Owner, Stoiber Enterprises, Box 240, Put-In-Bay, Ohio 43456. Telephone: 419-285-4741. Fax: 419-285-2718. E-mail: jobs@frostys.com. World Wide Web: http://www.frostys.com. Contact by e-mail, fax, mail, phone, or through World Wide Web site. Application deadline: most hiring is done between March 15 and July 1.

STUDENT CONSERVATION ASSOCIATION (SCA), OHIO

See Student Conservation Association (SCA), New Hampshire on page 209 for complete description.

WRIGHT STATE UNIVERSITY PRE-COLLEGE PROGRAMS

3640 COLONEL GLENN HIGHWAY
DAYTON, OHIO 45435-0001

General Information Residential academic enrichment program for motivated students in grades 7-12. Established in 1990. Features: university setting; running/walking trails; campus recreation; university dormitories.

Profile of Summer Employees Total number: 20; typical ages: 19–22. 50% men; 50% women; 100% college students.

Employment Information Openings are from June to August. Jobs available: ▶ 5–10 *residential assistants* (minimum age 19) with experience working in camp setting at $250–$400 per week. Applicants must submit a letter of interest, resume.

Benefits and Preemployment Training Free housing, free meals, willing to provide letters of recommendation, willing to act as a professional reference, opportunity to attend seminars/workshops, and college credit. Preemployment training is required and includes accident prevention and safety, first aid, CPR, interpersonal skills, leadership skills.

Contact Chris S. Hoffman, Program Coordinator, Wright State University Pre-College Programs, E041 Student Union, 3640 Colonel Glenn Highway, Dayton, Ohio 45435-0001. Telephone: 937-775-3135. Fax: 937-775-4883. E-mail: chris.hoffman@wright.edu. World Wide Web: http://www.wright.edu/academics/precollege. Contact by e-mail, mail, phone, or through World Wide Web site. Application deadline: continuous.

YMCA CAMP TIPPECANOE

81300 YMCA ROAD
TIPPECANOE, OHIO 44699

General Information Residential camp serving 80–120 campers per week, with an emphasis on horsemanship, waterfront activities, and the natural world. Established in 1958. 1,100-acre facility located 55 miles from Canton. Features: 3 barns with riding rings; year-round conference center; wooded setting; foothills; primitive lake; miles of trails to hike and ride.

Profile of Summer Employees Total number: 35; typical ages: 18–42. 50% men; 50% women; 5% minorities; 2% high school students; 73% college students; 10% non-U.S. citizens; 10% local applicants. Nonsmokers preferred.

Employment Information Openings are from May 27 to August 20. Jobs available: ▶ 1 *assistant equestrian director* with riding instructor certification (preferably CHA) at $150–$200 per week ▶ 1 *assistant registrar* (minimum age 18) with customer service and computer skills at $160–

$200 per week ▶ 12 *cabin counselors* (minimum age 18) with caring demeanor and sensitivity to needs of campers at $155–$200 per week ▶ 1 *health director* (minimum age 18) with RN or EMT license at $200–$225 per week ▶ 2 *lifeguards/waterfront staff members* (minimum age 18) with WSI or equivalent, boating, or lifeguard certification at $160–$200 per week ▶ 2 *nature/crafts coordinators* (minimum age 18) with knowledge and experience at $160–$200 per week ▶ 1 *program director* (minimum age 21) with ability to plan, lead, and discipline at $210–$250 per week ▶ 2 *ranger counselors* (minimum age 19) with outdoor living skills at $155–$200 per week ▶ 4 *riding instructors* (minimum age 18) with CHA certification or equivalent at $145–$200 per week ▶ 2–4 *teen counselors* (minimum age 19) with ability to relate to and lead teenagers at $155–$200 per week ▶ 2–3 *village coordinators* (minimum age 19) with ability to plan, lead, and discipline at $170–$200 per week. Applicants must submit formal organization application, three personal references, background check, fingerprints. An in-person interview is recommended, but a telephone interview is acceptable. International applicants accepted; must obtain own visa, obtain own working papers, apply through a recognized agency.

Benefits and Preemployment Training Free housing, free meals, formal training, willing to provide letters of recommendation, on-the-job training, willing to complete paperwork for educational credit, willing to act as a professional reference, and opportunity to attend seminars/workshops. Preemployment training is optional and includes accident prevention and safety, first aid, CPR, interpersonal skills, leadership skills, child abuse detection, blood borne pathogens informational workshops.

Contact Jami Eager, Program Director, YMCA Camp Tippecanoe, 81300 YMCA Road, Tippecanoe, Ohio 44699. Telephone: 740-922-0679. Fax: 740-922-1152. E-mail: ycamptippe@aol.com. World Wide Web: http://ymcastark.org. Contact by e-mail, fax, mail, or phone. Application deadline: continuous.

OKLAHOMA

CAMP RED ROCK

ROUTE 1, BOX 110B
BINGER, OKLAHOMA 73009

General Information Residential camp serving weekly 150 Girl Scouts ages 6–17. Offers general camping, Western horse riding, swimming, archery, rappelling, crafts, low ropes course, and outdoor skills. Established in 1959. 285-acre facility located 60 miles from Oklahoma City. Features: canyon dividing the camp; wooded setting; swimming pool with diving board; sandstone rock outcroppings; dining hall seating 170 family style; cabins and platform tents sleeping 4 each.

Profile of Summer Employees Total number: 22; typical ages: 18–25. 3% men; 97% women; 14% minorities; 27% high school students; 18% college students; 18% non-U.S. citizens; 23% local applicants.

Employment Information Openings are from June 2 to July 24. Jobs available: ▶ 1 *assistant camp director* (minimum age 21) with management and supervisory experience with outdoor and camp programs at $200–$250 per week ▶ 1 *assistant cook* (minimum age 17) should have familiarity with kitchen operation at $150–$200 per week ▶ 1 *business manager* (minimum age 21) with knowledge of bookkeeping and office procedures; must have current driver's license at $180–$230 per week ▶ 1 *head cook* (minimum age 21) with food service skills for large groups and ability to purchase and plan within a budget at $200–$250 per week ▶ 1 *health supervisor* (minimum age 21) with RN, LPN, or EMT license, ability to adapt to camp life, and knowledge of emotional and physical needs of campers at $200–$250 per week ▶ 1 *pool assistant/lifeguard* (minimum age 17) with current ARC lifeguard certification at $150–$200 per week ▶ 1 *pool director* (minimum age 21) with WSI or equivalent certification, lifeguard certification, ability to teach, and knowledge of pool maintenance at $200–$250 per week ▶ 1–3 *program instructors* (minimum age 17) with ability to plan and implement all camp activities, craft experience, archery or ropes course certification or experience at $150–$200 per week ▶ 1 *riding director* (minimum age 21) with extensive riding experience and supervisory skills with knowledge and ability to teach Western riding; vaulting knowledge a plus; at $200–$250 per week ▶ 2 *riding instructors* (minimum age 17) with teaching skills, experience with horses, and Western riding. Vaulting knowledge a plus at $150–$200 per week ▶ 7 *unit assistants* (minimum age 17) with experience working with youth, leadership ability, and able to teach activities to campers at $135–$150 per week ▶ 6 *unit leaders* (minimum age 21) with supervisory and leadership skills, experience working with youth, and outdoor program at $150–$200 per week. Applicants must submit formal organization application, three personal references. An in-person interview is recommended, but a telephone interview is acceptable. International applicants accepted; must obtain own visa, obtain own working papers, apply through a recognized agency.

Benefits and Preemployment Training Free housing, free meals, formal training, willing to provide letters of recommendation, on-the-job training, willing to complete paperwork for educational credit, and willing to act as a professional reference. Preemployment training is required and includes accident prevention and safety, first aid, CPR, interpersonal skills, leadership skills, archery NAA certification.

Contact Eva Ryan, Camp Director, Camp Red Rock, 121 Northeast 50th Street, Oklahoma City, Oklahoma 73105. Telephone: 405-528-3535 Ext. 115. Fax: 405-528-4475. E-mail: eva@redlandscouncil.org. Contact by e-mail, fax, mail, or phone. Application deadline: continuous.

THE SOUTHWESTERN COMPANY, OKLAHOMA

See The Southwestern Company on page 302 for complete description.

STUDENT CONSERVATION ASSOCIATION (SCA), OKLAHOMA

See Student Conservation Association (SCA), New Hampshire on page 209 for complete description.

OREGON

A CHRISTIAN MINISTRY IN THE NATIONAL PARKS–OREGON

See A Christian Ministry in the National Parks–Maine on page 122 for complete description.

B'NAI B'RITH CAMP

NEOTSU, OREGON

General Information A complete Jewish camping experience for youth grades 2-11, on the scenic Oregon coast; activities include: athletics, arts and crafts, ropes challenge course, nature, aquatics, Shabbat celebration, trips, and much more. Established in 1921. 14-acre facility located

80 miles from Portland. Features: lakefront; heated pool; ropes challenge course; conference center; heated cabins; tennis courts.

Profile of Summer Employees Total number: 85; typical ages: 17–60. 50% men; 50% women; 90% minorities; 20% high school students; 30% college students; 25% non-U.S. citizens; 76% local applicants. Nonsmokers required.

Employment Information Openings are from October 1 to June 15. Jobs available: ▶ 1 *Jewish enrichment director* (minimum age 21) with experience with Jewish studies, first aid/CPR certification, teaching skills, desire to work with children; salary dependent on experience ▶ 2 *LIT directors* (minimum age 21) with leadership and teaching skills, experience working with children at $1200–$1600 per season ▶ 1 *aquatics director* (minimum age 21) with water craft instructor certification, lifeguard certification, CPR and first aid certification, supervisory skills at $1200–$1600 per season ▶ 1 *arts and crafts director* (minimum age 20) with two years training and experience in arts and crafts curriculum, teamwork skills, organization skills at $1000–$1500 per season ▶ 1 *athletic director* (minimum age 20) with teaching skills, training and experience in athletics activities and management, outdoor skills at $1000–$1500 per season ▶ 1 *camp bookkeeper* (minimum age 20) with degree in accounting, computer skills, problem solving skills, teamwork skills, valid driver's license, first aid and CPR certification; salary dependent on experience ▶ 3 *cooks* (minimum age 18) with experience as cook or assistant cook, food handler's card, first aid/CPR certification, Kosher cooking and food service, experience cooking for large groups at $1800–$2500 per season ▶ 1 *creative arts director* (minimum age 20) with two years training and experience in teaching and delivering creative arts and programs and curriculum at $1000–$1500 per season ▶ 1 *dining hall manager* (minimum age 20) with food handler's card, first aid/CPR certification, experience in camp setting at $1000–$1300 per season ▶ 4 *dishwashers/kitchen helpers* (minimum age 17) with food handler's card, first aid/CPR certification, desire to work in camp kitchen at $600–$900 per season ▶ *food service manager/head chef* (minimum age 21) with experience in camp or institutional food service setting, registered dietician, first aid/CPR certification, food handler's card and kosher cooking; salary dependent on experience ▶ 1 *health care assistant* (minimum age 18) with first aid/CPR certification, experience working with children at $1000–$1300 per season ▶ 15 *junior counselors* (minimum age 17) with experience working with youth, first aid/CPR certification at $600–$900 per season ▶ 1 *music director* (minimum age 20) with two years training and experience teaching music programs and curriculum, experience working with children at $1000–$1500 per season ▶ 1 *nature director* with two years training and experience teaching outdoor skills and environmental studies, first aid/CPR certification at $1000–$1500 per season ▶ 2 *office assistants* (minimum age 18) with office experience, teamwork skills, valid driver's license and good driving record, first aid/CPR certification at $600–$900 per season ▶ 1 *program director* (minimum age 21) with leadership experience, love of outdoors, supervisory skills, first aid/CPR certification; salary dependent on experience ▶ 1 *programming coordinator* (minimum age 18) with first aid/CPR certification, creative, teaching skills at $1000–$1400 per season ▶ 1 *ropes course director* (minimum age 20) with training and experience with adventure ropes course programs, CPR/first aid certification, experience working with children, outdoor skills at $1000–$1600 per season ▶ 2 *roving counselors* (minimum age 20) with previous experience working with children in an overnight camp or educational setting, CPR/first aid certification at $1000–$1200 per season ▶ 15 *senior counselors* (minimum age 19) with first aid/CPR certification, prior experience working with youth in overnight camp or educational setting at $900–$1400 per season ▶ 3 *unit heads* (minimum age 21) with prior camp staff experience, supervisory skills, CPR and first aid certification, experience working with children and adults at $1200–$2000 per season. Applicants must submit formal organization application, three personal references, three letters of recommendation. An in-person interview is recommended, but a telephone interview is acceptable. International applicants accepted; must apply through a recognized agency.

Benefits and Preemployment Training Free housing, free meals, formal training, possible

full-time employment, willing to provide letters of recommendation, names of contacts, on-the-job training, willing to complete paperwork for educational credit, and willing to act as a professional reference. Preemployment training is required and includes accident prevention and safety, interpersonal skills, leadership skills.
Contact Michelle Koplan, Camp Director, B'nai B'rith Camp, 6651 SW Capitol Highway, Portland, Oregon 97219. Telephone: 503-244-0111. Fax: 503-245-4233. E-mail: bbcamp@oregonjcc.org. World Wide Web: http://www.bbcamp.org. Contact by e-mail, phone, or through World Wide Web site. Application deadline: continuous.

CYBERCAMPS–LEWIS AND CLARK COLLEGE

PORTLAND, OREGON

See Cybercamps–University of Washington on page 335 for complete description.

LONGACRE EXPEDITIONS, OREGON

OREGON

General Information Adventure travel program in Oregon emphasizing group living skills, fun, and physical challenges. Programs place equal emphasis on physical accomplishment and emotional growth. Established in 1981. near Portland.
Profile of Summer Employees Total number: 30; typical ages: 21–35. 50% men; 50% women; 10% minorities; 40% college students. Nonsmokers required.
Employment Information Openings are from June 15 to August 1. Jobs available: ▶ 8 *assistant trip leaders* (minimum age 21) with good driving record, WFR, and CPR at $252–$300 per week ▶ 3 *support and logistics staff members* (minimum age 21) with good driving record, WFR, and CPR at $180–$300 per week. Applicants must submit a formal organization application, letter of interest, resume, three personal references, letter(s) of recommendation. An in-person interview is recommended, but a telephone interview is acceptable. International applicants accepted; must obtain own visa, obtain own working papers.
Benefits and Preemployment Training Free housing, free meals, willing to provide letters of recommendation, on-the-job training, willing to complete paperwork for educational credit, willing to act as a professional reference, and pro-deal purchase program. Preemployment training is required and includes accident prevention and safety, interpersonal skills, leadership skills.
Contact Meredith Schuler, Director, Longacre Expeditions, Oregon, 4030 Middle Ridge Road, Newport, Pennsylvania 17074-8110. Telephone: 717-567-6790. Fax: 717-567-3955. E-mail: longacre@longacreexpeditions.com. World Wide Web: http://www.longacreexpeditions.com. Contact by e-mail, fax, mail, phone, or through World Wide Web site. Application deadline: continuous.

MEADOWOOD SPRINGS SPEECH AND HEARING CAMP

330 SE EMIGRANT AVENUE
PENDLETON, OREGON 97801-0030

General Information A 38-year-old non-profit organization that provides a summer camp for children 6 to 16 years of age with speech and hearing disorders. Established in 1964. 143-acre facility located 240 miles from Portland. Features: mountains; wildlife; outdoor camp setting; nature hiking; swimming pool; unique facility.
Profile of Summer Employees Total number: 50–70; typical ages: 18–50. 30% men; 70% women; 1% minorities; 1% high school students; 70% college students; 1% non-U.S. citizens; 27% local applicants.
Employment Information Openings are from July 1 to August 1. Jobs available: ▶ 8 *activities staff* (minimum age 18) in art, crafts, sports, nature, aquatics at $1000 per month ▶ 17–21 *cabin counselors* (minimum age 18) with ability to provide instruction in daily living skills and reside

in unit with campers at $1000 per month ▶ 30–36 *clinical staff* speech-language education/interpreting; paid at $1800–$2200 per month. Applicants must submit a formal organization application, letter of interest, resume, personal reference, two letters of recommendation, academic transcripts (for student clinicians only). A telephone interview is required. International applicants accepted; must obtain own visa, obtain own working papers.
Benefits and Preemployment Training Free housing, free meals, willing to provide letters of recommendation, and willing to complete paperwork for educational credit.
Contact Rhonda Hack, Executive Administrator, Meadowood Springs Speech and Hearing Camp. Telephone: 541-276-2752. Fax: 541-276-7227. E-mail: meadowood@oregontrail.net. World Wide Web: http://www.meadowoodsprings.com. Contact by e-mail, fax, mail, phone, or through World Wide Web site. Application deadline: April 15; official deadline is 4/15 however applications will be accepted until positions filled.

NORTHWEST YOUTH CORPS
2621 AUGUSTA STREET
EUGENE, OREGON 97403

General Information Mobile, non-residential conservation corps program. Staff are responsible for daily activities (work project, camp operations, and environmental relations) for a crew of 10 high school age youth. Established in 1983.
Profile of Summer Employees Total number: 45; typical ages: 20–30. 65% men; 35% women; 10% minorities; 70% college students; 40% local applicants.
Employment Information Openings are from April 15 to October 15. Jobs available: ▶ 30–45 *field staff* (minimum age 20) with wilderness first aid and CPR; previous leadership/wilderness experience at $70–$78 per day. Applicants must submit a formal organization application, letter of interest, resume, four personal references. An in-person interview is recommended, but a telephone interview is acceptable. International applicants accepted; must obtain own visa, obtain own working papers.
Benefits and Preemployment Training Free housing, free meals, formal training, possible full-time employment, willing to provide letters of recommendation, on-the-job training, willing to complete paperwork for educational credit, and willing to act as a professional reference. Preemployment training is required and includes accident prevention and safety, interpersonal skills, leadership skills, program operation and technical project skills.
Contact Corps Program Director, Northwest Youth Corps, 2621 Augusta Street, Eugene, Oregon 97403. Telephone: 541-349-5055. Fax: 541-349-5060. E-mail: work@nwyouthcorps.org. World Wide Web: http://www.nwyouthcorps.org. Contact by e-mail, mail, or through World Wide Web site. Application deadline: continuous.

ROCK SPRINGS GUEST RANCH
64201 TYLER ROAD
BEND, OREGON 97701

General Information Dude ranch with riding, youth program. Established in 1969. 580-acre facility located 180 miles from Portland. Features: riding stables; pool; trout pond; 2 tennis courts; youth center; rural setting.
Profile of Summer Employees Total number: 45; typical ages: 18–22. 34% men; 66% women; 25% high school students; 70% college students; 5% local applicants.
Employment Information Openings are from June 10 to August 30. Year-round positions also offered. Jobs available: ▶ 9 *wranglers* (minimum age 18) with strong horsemanship and interpersonal skills at $1130 per month plus bonus ▶ 5 *youth counselors* (minimum age 18) with genuine interest in and experience with children at $1130 per month plus bonus. Applicants must submit a formal organization application, three personal references. An in-person interview is recommended, but a telephone interview is acceptable. International applicants accepted; must obtain own visa, obtain own working papers.

Benefits and Preemployment Training Housing at a cost, free meals, possible full-time employment, willing to provide letters of recommendation, on-the-job training, willing to complete paperwork for educational credit, and willing to act as a professional reference. Preemployment training is required and includes accident prevention and safety, interpersonal skills, training specific to operation.

Contact Eva Gill, Controller, Rock Springs Guest Ranch, 64201 Tyler Road, Bend, Oregon 97701. Telephone: 541-382-1957. Fax: 541-382-7774. E-mail: eva@rocksprings.com. World Wide Web: http://www.rocksprings.com. Contact by e-mail, fax, mail, phone, or through World Wide Web site. Application deadline: continuous.

THE SOUTHWESTERN COMPANY, OREGON

See The Southwestern Company on page 302 for complete description.

STUDENT CONSERVATION ASSOCIATION (SCA), OREGON

See Student Conservation Association (SCA), New Hampshire on page 209 for complete description.

YWCA CAMP WESTWIND

7495 NORTH FRASER ROAD
OTIS, OREGON 97368

General Information Coeducational residential camp with traditional activities for children ages 7–18 and adults. Established in 1936. 500-acre facility located 90 miles from Portland. Features: oceanfront; river; 5 ecosystems.

Profile of Summer Employees Total number: 40; typical ages: 18–22. 30% men; 70% women; 4% minorities; 2% high school students; 97% college students; 2% non-U.S. citizens; 40% local applicants. Nonsmokers required.

Employment Information Openings are from June 17 to September 1. Jobs available: ▶ 2 *kitchen aides* (minimum age 16) with food handlers certification at $1200–$1300 per season ▶ 1 *nature/marine science specialist* with CPR/first aid certification and knowledge of natural wildlife habitat at $165 per week ▶ 1 *waterfront director* (minimum age 21) with lifeguarding and CPR/first aid certification, and small craft instructor status at $165 per week. Applicants must submit formal organization application, two personal references, police check form. An in-person interview is recommended, but a telephone interview is acceptable. International applicants accepted; must apply through a recognized agency.

Benefits and Preemployment Training Free housing, free meals, formal training, willing to provide letters of recommendation, on-the-job training, willing to complete paperwork for educational credit, and willing to act as a professional reference. Preemployment training is required and includes accident prevention and safety, interpersonal skills, leadership skills, child management, programming.

Contact Kim Wilson, Camp Director, YWCA Camp Westwind, 1111 Southwest Tenth Avenue, Portland, Oregon 97205. Telephone: 503-294-7472. Fax: 503-721-1751. E-mail: kimw@ywca-pdx.org. Contact by e-mail, fax, mail, or phone. Application deadline: continuous.

PENNSYLVANIA

BLUE BELL DAY CAMP

PO BOX 184
BLUE BELL, PENNSYLVANIA 19422

General Information Sports and adventure day camp for boys with emphasis on instruction and lesson plans. Established in 1946. 41-acre facility located 15 miles from Philadephia. Features: 10 acres of playing fields; 30 acres of woods; boating pond.

Profile of Summer Employees Total number: 50; typical ages: 23–63. 90% men; 10% women; 4% retirees; 100% local applicants. Nonsmokers preferred.

Employment Information Openings are from June 24 to August 16. Jobs available: ▶ 15–20 *day camp specialists* (minimum age 21) must be proficient in specialty at $375–$450 per week. Applicants must submit resume. An in-person interview is required. International applicants accepted; must obtain own working papers.

Benefits and Preemployment Training Willing to provide letters of recommendation and willing to act as a professional reference. Preemployment training is required and includes general staff orientation.

Contact John Harris, Director, Blue Bell Day Camp. Telephone: 215-646-1897. Fax: 610-584-3577. E-mail: john@bluebellcamp.com. World Wide Web: http://www.bluebellcamp.com. Contact by e-mail, fax, mail, or phone. Application deadline: continuous.

CAMP AMERICA DAY CAMP

341 LOWER STATE ROAD
CHALFONT, PENNSYLVANIA 18914

General Information Summer day camp for children ages 2¼ to 14 offers 4-, 6-, and 8-week sessions that include transportation, lunch, and the option for extended hours. Established in 1967. 42-acre facility located 20 miles from Philadelphia. Features: challenge course (ropes and wall); 6 tennis courts; 4 swimming pools; pond for boating and fishing; indoor soccer stadium; softplay facility.

Profile of Summer Employees Total number: 85; typical ages: 15–30. 45% men; 55% women; 1% minorities; 20% high school students; 20% college students; 7% non-U.S. citizens; 93% local applicants. Nonsmokers preferred.

Employment Information Openings are from June to August. Jobs available: ▶ *athletics instructors* (minimum age 19) with driver's license and car and ability to plan and implement athletics program ▶ *ceramics instructors* (minimum age 19) with driver's license and car and ability to plan and implement ceramics program ▶ 2–3 *challenge/ropes course instructors* (minimum age 19) with driver's license and car and ability to run an adventure program ▶ 6–12 *general counselors* (minimum age 19) with driver's license and car ▶ 2 *go-kart instuctors* (minimum age 19) with driver's license and car ▶ *gymnastics instructors* (minimum age 19) with driver's license and car and ability to plan and implement gymnastics program ▶ 1–2 *nature instructors* (minimum age 19) with driver's license and car and ability to plan and implement nature program ▶ 8 *pool staff* (minimum age 19) with driver's license and car, WSI and lifeguard certification ▶ *tennis instructors* (minimum age 19) with driver's license and car and ability to plan and implement tennis program ▶ *woodshop instructors* (minimum age 19) with driver's license and car and ability to plan and implement woodshop program. Applicants must submit formal organization application, three personal references. An in-person interview is required. International applicants accepted; must apply through a recognized agency.

Benefits and Preemployment Training Willing to provide letters of recommendation and daily lunch provided. Preemployment training is required and includes accident prevention and safety, interpersonal skills, leadership skills.
Contact Norma Levin, Director, Camp America Day Camp, PO Box 737, Warington, Pennsylvania 18976. Telephone: 215-822-6313. E-mail: america@icdc.com. World Wide Web: http://www.camp-america.com. Contact by e-mail, mail, or phone. Application deadline: continuous.

CAMP CANADENSIS
LAKE ROAD
CANADENSIS, PENNSYLVANIA 18325

General Information Coeducational residential camp offering all activities in an eight-week program for children ages 7–16. Established in 1941. 1,000-acre facility located 90 miles from New York, New York. Features: 75-acre lake; 3 pools; 16 tennis courts; 13 miles of trails; modern cabins; excellent facilities and equipment.
Profile of Summer Employees Total number: 160; typical ages: 19–24. 50% men; 50% women; 90% college students; 10% non-U.S. citizens. Nonsmokers required.
Employment Information Openings are from May 1 to August 17. Spring break positions also offered. Jobs available: ▶ 2 *archery instructors* with experience; instructor certificate preferred at $1400–$1800 per season ▶ 7 *arts and crafts instructors* at $1400–$1800 per season ▶ 30–40 *athletics instructors* with team experience at $1400–$1800 per season ▶ 2–3 *cooking instructors* at $1400–$1800 per season ▶ 5–6 *drama instructors* with ability to direct shows at $1400–$1800 per season ▶ 50 *general counselors* at $1400–$1800 per season ▶ 4 *gymnastics instructors* with experience in the field at $1400–$1800 per season ▶ 3 *maintenance staff members* with grounds work experience at $1400–$1600 per season ▶ 4–5 *motorcycles trail riding staff* with riding experience at $1400–$1800 per season ▶ 2 *nature instructors* at $1400–$1800 per season ▶ 4–5 *nurses* with RN license at $3500–$4000 per season ▶ 4 *photography/newspaper instructors* with experience taking and developing pictures and writing at $1400–$1800 per season ▶ 2 *radio station staff* with radio experience at $1400–$1800 per season ▶ 7 *rafting/kayaking/scuba instructors* with experience in the field; lifeguard certification preferred at $1400–$1800 per season ▶ 8–12 *ropes course/climbing/low ropes instructors* with climbing experience at $1400–$1800 per season ▶ 8–10 *sailing/waterskiing/windsurfing/jetski instructors* with lifeguard certification at $1400–$1800 per season ▶ 7 *swimming instructors* with WSI and lifeguard certification at $1400–$1800 per season ▶ 14 *tennis instructors* with college team/coaching experience at $1400–$2000 per season. Applicants must submit formal organization application, resume, three personal references or three letters of recommendation. An in-person interview is recommended, but a telephone interview is acceptable. International applicants accepted; must apply through a recognized agency.
Benefits and Preemployment Training Free housing, free meals, willing to provide letters of recommendation, willing to complete paperwork for educational credit, and travel allowance. Preemployment training is required and includes accident prevention and safety, interpersonal skills, leadership skills, child care, problem solving.
Contact Steven Smilk, Director, Camp Canadensis, Box 182, Wyncote, Pennsylvania 19095. Telephone: 215-572-8222. Fax: 215-572-8298. E-mail: camp4you@canadensis.com. World Wide Web: http://www.canadensis.com. Contact by e-mail, fax, mail, phone, or through World Wide Web site. Application deadline: continuous.

CAMP CAYUGA
POCONO MOUNTAINS, NILES POND ROAD
HONESDALE, PENNSYLVANIA 18431

General Information Private coed, nonsectarian camp for children ages 5–15. Family operated since 1957. ACA accredited. Comprehensive facilities. Separate teen campus for ages 13–15.

Established in 1957. 350-acre facility located 110 miles from New York, New York. Features: modern cabins with bathrooms; 2 swimming pools; equestrian center with 25 horses; 10 tennis courts; 2 large gymnasiums with stages; separate teen campus for ages 13–15.

Profile of Summer Employees Total number: 135; typical ages: 19–55. 50% men; 50% women; 9% minorities; 98% college students; 2% retirees; 10% non-U.S. citizens; 2% local applicants. Nonsmokers preferred.

Employment Information Openings are from June 19 to August 19. Jobs available: ▶ 4–6 *Honda ATV quad-riding instructors* (minimum age 19) with experience riding ATV's and teaching children; at least one year of college completed at $2000 per season ▶ 2–3 *academic tutors and ESL instructors* (minimum age 19) with experience tutoring children; at least one year of college completed at $1800 per season ▶ 20–25 *activity specialists* (minimum age 19) with at least one year of college completed and experience playing and coaching children in one of the following activities: video camera, model rocketry, radio broadcasting, or roller skating/rollerblading at $2000 per season ▶ 4–6 *aerobics instructors* (minimum age 19) with experience in teaching aerobics to children, use of step-blocks at least one year of college completed at $2000 per season ▶ 6–8 *archery instructors* (minimum age 19) with National Archery Association certification preferred; experience teaching archery to children; at least one year of college completed at $2000 per season ▶ 2–3 *art directors* (minimum age 25) with state teacher's license preferred; experience teaching art to children; supervisory, organizational, and managerial skills necessary; kiln and pottery wheel operation knowledge at $2500 per season ▶ 10–12 *arts and crafts instructors* (minimum age 19) with experience teaching art to children; at least one year of college completed at $2000 per season ▶ 2–3 *athletics directors* (minimum age 25) with experience working with children in a sports environment; teachers and coaches preferred at $2500 per season ▶ 4–6 *basketball instructors* (minimum age 19) with experience playing basketball and coaching children; at least one year of college completed at $2000 per season ▶ 6–8 *canoeing and boating instructors* (minimum age 19) with American Red Cross lifeguard and American Canoeing Association certification preferred; experience canoeing and ability to instruct; at least one year of college completed at $2000 per season ▶ 10–12 *ceramics instructors/pottery instructors* (minimum age 19) experienced in kiln and pottery wheel operating and teaching ceramics to children; at least one year of college completed at $2000 per season ▶ 4–6 *chorus/singing instructors* (minimum age 19) with experience in chorus and ability to instruct; at least one year of college completed at $1800 per season ▶ 4–6 *dance instructors* (minimum age 19) with experience in ballet, jazz, and modern dance with teaching experience; at least one year of college completed at $2000 per season ▶ 6–8 *drama instructors* (minimum age 19) with theater experience including directing plays and improvisation; at least one year of college completed at $1800 per season ▶ 2–3 *evening activity directors* (minimum age 25) with experience in organizing and implementing activities; outgoing, good sense of humor, creative personality required at $2500 per season ▶ 4–6 *fishing instructors* (minimum age 19) with experience fishing and ability to instruct; at least one year of college completed at $1800 per season ▶ 10–12 *flying trapeze and circus instructors* (minimum age 19) with experience teaching or coaching children; at least one year of college completed; experience on the flying trapeze and circus skills; strong gymnastic skills helpful at $2000 per season ▶ 24–26 *food service staff (cooks, dining hall service, food prep)* (minimum age 20) with experience in quantity food production required; at least one year of college completed at $2500 per season ▶ 6–7 *golf instructors* (minimum age 19) with experience playing golf and coaching children; at least one year of college completed at $2000 per season ▶ 10–12 *gymnastics instructors* (minimum age 19) with experience on all gymnastics apparatus; experience teaching gymnastics preferred; at least one year of college completed at $2000 per season ▶ 4–6 *head counselors* (minimum age 30) with supervisory skills and experience working with children and young adults at $2500 per season ▶ 10–12 *horseback riding instructors* (minimum age 19) with CHA certification preferred; experience riding and caring for horses and stables; experience teaching children; at least one year of college completed at $2000 per season ▶ 2 *horsemanship directors* (minimum age 25) with CHA certification preferred; experience teaching equestrian skills to children; supervisory, organizational, and managerial skills necessary at $2000–$3000 per season ▶ 2–3 *intercamp tournament directors* (minimum age 25) with teacher's license preferred; experience working with children and young adults; strong organizational and scheduling skills necessary at $2500 per season ▶ 6–7 *lacrosse instructors* (minimum age 19) with experience playing lacrosse and coaching children; at least one year of college completed at $2000 per season ▶ 1–2 *lakefront directors* (minimum age 25) with American Red Cross lifeguard certification or equivalent required; experience instructing canoeing, sailing, and boating; supervisory and managerial skills necessary at $2000–$3000 per season ▶ 6–8 *martial arts instructors* (minimum age 19) with black belt in karate preferred; experience competing and teaching martial arts to children; at least one year of college completed at $2000 per season ▶ 4–6 *mountain biking instructors* (minimum age 19) with experience in biking and ability to instruct; at least one year of college completed at $2000 per season ▶ 2–4 *musical instruments instructors (keyboard, guitar, violin, trumpet, flute, etc)* (minimum age 19) with experience playing an instrument and ability to instruct; at least one year of college completed at $1800 per season ▶ 6 *nurses* (minimum age 25) with RN, LPN or EMT and experience working with children at $2000 per season ▶ 4–6 *office personnel* (minimum age 19) with experience working in a business office; good organizational skills, excellent telephone manner, and administration skills needed at $2000 per season ▶ 4–6 *petting zoo instructors* (minimum age 19) experience caring for animals (feeding, watering, grooming) at $2000 per season ▶ 2–4 *photography instructors* (minimum age 19) with experience taking photos, developing negatives, printing photos, darkroom procedures at $2000 per season ▶ 2–3 *program directors* (minimum age 30) with teaching/coaching license preferred; organizational and supervisory skills needed; experience in scheduling activities and staff at $2500 per season ▶ 1–2 *receptionists* (minimum age 21) with a good telephone manner, organizational skills, flexibility, pleasant personality at $2000 per season ▶ 4–6 *riflery instructors* (minimum age 20) with NRA instructor certification or equivalent preferred; experience with 22-caliber rifles; at least one year of college completed at $2000 per season ▶ 4–6 *roller hockey instructors* (minimum age 19) with experience as a player and hockey instructor/coach for children; at least one year of college completed at $2000 per season ▶ 8–10 *ropes course/ rock climbing instructors* (minimum age 19) with experience teaching rock climbing and zip line to children; professionally trained individuals; at least one year of college completed at $2000 per season ▶ 6–8 *sailing instructors* (minimum age 19) with American Red Cross sailing and lifeguard certification preferred; experience teaching sailing to children; at least one year of college completed at $2000 per season ▶ 2–4 *skateboarding instructors* (minimum age 19) with experience teaching skateboarding to children on half-pipe and street ramps at $2000 per season ▶ 4–6 *soccer instructors* (minimum age 19) with experience as a player and as an instructor/ coach for children; at least one year of college completed at $2000 per season ▶ 4–6 *softball/ baseball instructors* (minimum age 19) with experience as a player and softball/baseball instructor/ coach for children; at least one year of college completed at $2000 per season ▶ 12–14 *swimming instructors* (minimum age 19) with American Red Cross WSI and lifeguard certification or equivalent preferred; experience teaching swimming to children; at least one year of college completed at $2000 per season ▶ 35–40 *team sports instructors (soccer, frisbee, field hockey, softball, baseball)* (minimum age 19) with experience playing the sport and coaching children; at least one year of college completed at $2000 per season ▶ 12–14 *tennis instructors and certified tennis professional* (minimum age 19) with USTA license required for director position; experience playing and coaching tennis; at least one year of college completed at $2000 per season ▶ 1–2 *transportation directors* (minimum age 25) with driver's license and mechanical skills required; experience driving 15-passenger vans at $2500 per season ▶ 6–8 *volleyball instructors* (minimum age 19) with experience playing and coaching volleyball and at least one year of college completed at $1800 per season ▶ 1–2 *waterfront directors* (minimum age 25) with WSI and American Red Cross lifeguard certification or equivalent; pool management and maintenance skills; experience instructing children and supervisory skills at $2800 per season ▶ 4–6 *weight-*

lifting instructors (minimum age 19) with experience in weight training and ability to instruct; at least one year of college completed at $2000 per season ▶ 4–6 *windsurfing instructors* (minimum age 19) with American Red Cross lifeguard certification or equivalent preferred; experience teaching windsurfing to children; at least one year of college completed at $2000 per season ▶ 4–6 *wrestling instructors* (minimum age 19) with experience teaching wrestling to children; at least one year of college completed at $2000 per season. Applicants must submit formal organization application, three personal references, two letters of recommendation, copies of certifications, if applicable. A telephone interview is required. International applicants accepted; must apply through a recognized agency.

Benefits and Preemployment Training Free housing, free meals, formal training, willing to provide letters of recommendation, on-the-job training, willing to complete paperwork for educational credit, willing to act as a professional reference, opportunity to attend seminars/workshops, travel reimbursement, and 3-day all expenses-paid winter camp ski reunion; camp tuition is free for children of senior staff members; free weekly laundry service. Preemployment training is required and includes accident prevention and safety, first aid, CPR, interpersonal skills, leadership skills.

Contact Brian B. Buynak, Camp Director, Camp Cayuga, PO Box 151, Suite PSJ, Peapack, New Jersey 07977. Telephone: 800-422-9842. Fax: 908-470-1228. E-mail: info@campcayuga.com. World Wide Web: http://www.campcayuga.com. Contact by e-mail, fax, mail, phone, or through World Wide Web site. Application deadline: continuous.

CAMP CHEN-A-WANDA

THOMPSON, PENNSYLVANIA 18465

General Information Coeducational residential camp serving 400 campers for a 7½-week session. Established in 1939. 183-acre facility located 25 miles from Scranton. Features: heated Olympic-size pool; freshwater lake; indoor fitness center; indoor basketball court; 7 tennis courts; 3 soccer fields.

Profile of Summer Employees Total number: 150; typical ages: 19–24. 52% men; 48% women; 80% college students; 20% non-U.S. citizens. Nonsmokers preferred.

Employment Information Openings are from June 19 to August 17. Jobs available: ▶ 3 *arts and crafts specialists* (minimum age 19) at $600–$1800 per season ▶ 4 *baseball specialists* (minimum age 19) at $600–$1800 per season ▶ 4 *basketball specialists* (minimum age 19) at $600–$1800 per season ▶ 2 *go-cart/all terrain vehicle specialists* (minimum age 19) at $600–$1800 per season ▶ 1 *golf specialist* (minimum age 19) at $600–$1800 per season ▶ 2 *gymnastics specialists* (minimum age 19) at $600–$1800 per season ▶ 2 *lacrosse specialists* (minimum age 19) at $600–$1800 per season ▶ 2 *roller hockey specialists* (minimum age 19) at $600–$1800 per season ▶ 2–4 *ropes/rock climbing/rappelling specialists* (minimum age 19) at $700–$1800 per season ▶ 4 *soccer specialists* (minimum age 19) at $600–$1800 per season ▶ 2 *stage management/scenery staff members* (minimum age 19) at $600–$1800 per season ▶ 3 *tennis specialists* (minimum age 19) at $600–$1800 per season ▶ 2 *volleyball specialists* (minimum age 19) at $600–$1800 per season ▶ 10 *waterfront specialists (swimming, sailing, or waterskiing)* with WSI certification for swimming at $600–$1800 per season. Applicants must submit formal organization application, resume, two personal references, two letters of recommendation. A telephone interview is required. International applicants accepted; must apply through a recognized agency.

Benefits and Preemployment Training Free housing, free meals, willing to provide letters of recommendation, willing to complete paperwork for educational credit, and travel reimbursement. Preemployment training is required and includes accident prevention and safety, interpersonal skills, leadership skills.

Contact Morey Baldwin, Director, Camp Chen-A-Wanda, 8 Claverton Court, Dix Hills, New York 11747. Telephone: 888-268-6535. Fax: 631-643-0920. E-mail: cneier@aol.com. World

Wide Web: http://www.campchen-a-wanda.com. Contact by e-mail, fax, mail, phone, or through World Wide Web site. Application deadline: continuous.

CAMP HIDDEN FALLS
RR 2, BOX 720
DINGMAN'S FERRY, PENNSYLVANIA 18328

General Information Six-week nonprofit residential camp for girls ages 9-17. Established in 1912. 1,000-acre facility located 15 miles from Stroudsburg. Features: horseback riding; in-ground pool; lake for canoes and sail boats; forests; Delaware River nearby; waterfalls.

Profile of Summer Employees Total number: 45; typical ages: 18–25. 5% men; 95% women; 20% minorities; 10% high school students; 70% college students; 5% retirees; 10% non-U.S. citizens; 20% local applicants. Nonsmokers preferred.

Employment Information Openings are from June 9 to August 17. Jobs available: ▶ 14–16 *counselors* (minimum age 18) at $200–$240 per week ▶ 4–5 *lifeguards* (minimum age 18) with WSI, lifeguard training, first aid/CPR, or ability to get training at $210–$250 per week ▶ 4–5 *nature counselors* (minimum age 18) with experience in the field at $220–$240 per week ▶ *program specialists* (minimum age 21) with experience in the field at $220–$240 per week ▶ 4–5 *riding instructors* (minimum age 18) with experience in the field at $210–$250 per week ▶ 1 *waterfront director* (minimum age 21) with supervisory experience and WSI or lifeguarding certification at $280–$320 per week. Applicants must submit formal organization application, three personal references, letter of recommendation. An in-person interview is recommended, but a telephone interview is acceptable. International applicants accepted; must apply through a recognized agency.

Benefits and Preemployment Training Free housing, free meals, formal training, possible full-time employment, health insurance, willing to provide letters of recommendation, on-the-job training, willing to complete paperwork for educational credit, willing to act as a professional reference, and opportunity to attend seminars/workshops. Preemployment training is required and includes accident prevention and safety, first aid, CPR, interpersonal skills, leadership skills, lifeguarding, archery, boating instruction.

Contact Ann Gillard, Camp Director, Camp Hidden Falls, PO Box 27540, Philadelphia, Pennsylvania 19118. Telephone: 866-564-2030 Ext. 263. Fax: 215-564-6953. E-mail: agillard@gssp.org. World Wide Web: http://www.gssp.org. Contact by e-mail, fax, mail, or phone. Application deadline: continuous.

CAMP LAUGHING WATERS
300 HEIDELBEITEL ROAD
GILBERTSVILLE, PENNSYLVANIA 19525

General Information Large residential camp serving girls, Girl Scout troops, families, and youth groups. Established in 1912. 533-acre facility located 40 miles from Philadelphia. Features: fully equipped kitchen and dining hall; Olympic-size pool; 2 tennis courts; basketball court; platform tents and cabins; large playing fields.

Profile of Summer Employees Total number: 35–40; typical ages: 18–23. 5% men; 95% women; 50% minorities; 2% high school students; 90% college students; 50% local applicants. Nonsmokers preferred.

Employment Information Openings are from June to August. Jobs available: ▶ 3–4 *activities specialists* (minimum age 21) with education and or experience in specialized activity; ability to develop schedules, plan activities, and share knowledge with staff and campers at $220–$265 per week ▶ 1 *assistant director* (minimum age 21) with knowledge and experience in camping and program planning, current driver's license and vehicle at $350–$400 per week ▶ 1 *business manager* (minimum age 21) with training in business and/or retail practices and current driver's license at $210–$250 per week ▶ 1–2 *cooks* (minimum age 18) with experience as a cook or assistant cook and knowledge of standards of food preparation, serving, and kitchen procedure at $280–$320 per week ▶ 1 *food service manager* (minimum age 21) with experience in large group food preparation, overall supervision of staff, kitchen, and food ordering at $350–$400 per week ▶ 1–2 *health supervisors/nurses* (minimum age 21) RN, LPN or EMT with Standard First Aid and CPR certifications and current driver's license at $350–$400 per week ▶ 2 *kitchen aides* (minimum age 15) with a desire to work in the food service area, good communication skills, and ability to accept supervision at $175–$215 per week ▶ 3–4 *lifeguards* (minimum age 18) with WSI, lifeguard training, first aid/CPR (training available) at $210–$250 per week ▶ 1 *program director* (minimum age 21) with program and/or camp experience and current driver's license at $300–$350 per week ▶ 1 *riding director* (minimum age 21) with experience in staff supervision and general horseback riding program or certification from organization with instructor training program; CHA certification (preferred) at $280–$320 per week ▶ 3–4 *riding instructors* (minimum age 18) with experience with horses and tack; ability to teach beginning to intermediate riding skills and/or experience working with horses, tack, and stable care at $210–$250 per week ▶ 14 *unit counselors* (minimum age 18) with experience working with youth, leadership ability, and ability to teach activities to campers at $200–$240 per week ▶ 7 *unit leaders* (minimum age 21) with skills in leadership, supervision, working with youth, and education or experience in outdoor program at $220–$265 per week ▶ 1 *waterfront director* (minimum age 21) with ARC lifeguard training or equivalent; at least 6 weeks of pool or waterfront experience at $280–$320 per week. Applicants must submit formal organization application, three personal references, child abuse history clearance (State of Pennsylvania). An in-person interview is recommended, but a telephone interview is acceptable. International applicants accepted; must apply through a recognized agency.

Benefits and Preemployment Training Free housing, free meals, willing to provide letters of recommendation, on-the-job training, willing to complete paperwork for educational credit, and laundry facilities; internship possibilities. Preemployment training is required and includes accident prevention and safety, first aid, CPR, interpersonal skills, leadership skills, lifeguarding and additional training.

Contact Cindy Sassi, Camp Director, Camp Laughing Waters, PO Box 27540, Philadelphia, Pennsylvania 19118. Telephone: 215-564-4657. Fax: 215-564-6953. E-mail: csassi@gssp.org. World Wide Web: http://www.gssp.org. Contact by e-mail, fax, mail, phone, or through World Wide Web site. Application deadline: continuous.

CAMP LINDENMERE

RR1, BOX 160A
HENRYVILLE, PENNSYLVANIA 18332

General Information Private residential summer camp for children ages 7-17. Established in 1997. 159-acre facility. Features: ropes course; trapeze; riding stages; swimming pool; lake; skateboard park.

Profile of Summer Employees Total number: 130; typical age: 22. 40% men; 60% women; 10% minorities; 30% college students; 50% non-U.S. citizens; 5% local applicants. Nonsmokers required.

Employment Information Openings are from May 30 to September 1. Jobs available: ▶ 40 *counselors/specialists in all areas* (minimum age 18) some experience in area at $1400–$2000 per season. Applicants must submit formal organization application, resume, two personal references, background check. An in-person interview is recommended, but a telephone interview is acceptable. International applicants accepted; must apply through a recognized agency.

Benefits and Preemployment Training Free housing, free meals, willing to provide letters of recommendation, names of contacts, willing to act as a professional reference, and travel reimbursement. Preemployment training is required and includes accident prevention and safety, first aid, CPR, interpersonal skills, leadership skills.

Contact Jerry Marcus, Director, Camp Lindenmere, PO Box 770086, Coral Springs, Florida

33077. Telephone: 954-255-1656. Fax: 208-723-3288. E-mail: admin@camplindenmere.com. World Wide Web: http://www.camplindenmere.com. Contact by e-mail, fax, mail, phone, or through World Wide Web site. Application deadline: continuous.

CAMP LOHIKAN IN THE POCONO MOUNTAINS
WALLERVILLE ROAD
LAKE COMO, PENNSYLVANIA 18437

General Information Traditional coed summer camp for campers 6 to 15 years old that features 65 daily activities, evening activities, special events, intercamp games, trips, and more. Established in 1957. 1,200-acre facility located 30 miles from Scranton. Features: private lake; swimming pool; 11 tennis courts; 30 horses; 7 sports fields; 14 arts workshops.
Profile of Summer Employees Total number: 200; typical ages: 19–60. 50% men; 50% women; 5% minorities; 83% college students; 2% retirees; 5% non-U.S. citizens; 5% local applicants. Nonsmokers required.
Employment Information Openings are from June 1 to September 30. Jobs available: ▶ 6 *canoeing instructors* (minimum age 19) at $1300–$2300 per season ▶ 12 *creative arts instructors* (minimum age 19) at $1300–$2300 per season ▶ 7 *gymnastics instructors* (minimum age 19) at $1300–$2300 per season ▶ 10 *horseback riding instructors* at $1400–$2400 per season ▶ 10 *lifeguards* (minimum age 19) at $1400–$2400 per season ▶ 5 *performing arts instructors* (minimum age 19) at $1300–$2300 per season ▶ 4 *pottery instructors* (minimum age 19) at $1300–$2300 per season ▶ 5 *rock climbing instructors* (minimum age 19) at $1400–$2400 per season ▶ 4 *ropes course instructors* (minimum age 19) at $1300–$2300 per season ▶ 6 *sailing instructors* (minimum age 19) at $1300–$2300 per season ▶ 3 *skateboarding instructors* (minimum age 19) at $1300–$2300 per season ▶ 10 *sports instructors* (minimum age 19) at $1300–$2200 per season ▶ 12 *tennis instructors* (minimum age 19) at $1300–$2300 per season ▶ 3 *woodworking instructors* (minimum age 19) at $1300–$2300 per season. Applicants must submit formal organization application, three personal references, three letters of recommendation. An in-person interview is recommended, but a telephone interview is acceptable. International applicants accepted; must apply through a recognized agency.
Benefits and Preemployment Training Free housing, free meals, formal training, possible full-time employment, willing to provide letters of recommendation, on-the-job training, willing to complete paperwork for educational credit, willing to act as a professional reference, and travel reimbursement. Preemployment training is required and includes accident prevention and safety, first aid, CPR, interpersonal skills, leadership skills.
Contact Ian Brassett, Staffing Director, Camp Lohikan in the Pocono Mountains, PO Box 189, Gladstone, New Jersey 07934. Telephone: 908-470-9317. Fax: 908-470-9319. E-mail: mail@lohikan.com. World Wide Web: http://www.lohikan.com. Contact by e-mail, fax, mail, phone, or through World Wide Web site. Application deadline: continuous.

CAMP NETIMUS
708 RAYMONDSKILL ROAD
MILFORD, PENNSYLVANIA 18337

General Information Residential girls camp with two-, four-, or eight-week sessions, offering over forty activities to help campers develop self-confidence and a positive self image; a caring, sharing environment. Established in 1930. 402-acre facility located 120 miles from New York, New York. Features: freshwater lake; wooded setting; hikes and trails; sports field; 2 riding rings; 17 cabins.
Profile of Summer Employees Total number: 90; typical ages: 18–80. 25% men; 75% women; 6% minorities; 10% high school students; 70% college students; 10% retirees; 50% non-U.S. citizens; 5% local applicants. Nonsmokers required.
Employment Information Openings are from June 12 to August 19. Jobs available: ▶ 1–2

archery instructors (minimum age 21) with first aid/CPR certification; NAA or equivalent certification and teaching experience at $1000–$2000 per season ▶ 2–3 *canoeing instructors* (minimum age 21) with lifeguard training, first aid, and CPR; ARX instructor or equivalent certification, teaching or similar experience at $1000–$2000 per season ▶ 2 *dance instructors (jazz, modern, tap, and ballet)* (minimum age 21) with instructor certification or equivalent experience as a teacher or similar position at $1000–$2000 per season ▶ 4 *fine arts instructors* (minimum age 21) with teaching or equivalent certification/experience at $1000–$2000 per season ▶ 2 *gymnastics instructors* (minimum age 21) with instructor certification or equivalent and teaching experience or equivalent at $1000–$2000 per season ▶ 5 *horseback riding instructors* (minimum age 21) with first aid/CPR certification; Pony Club, AII, British Horse Club Society certification; teaching or equivalent experience at $1000–$2000 per season ▶ 2 *jewelry/metalcraft instructors* (minimum age 21) with teaching or equivalent certification/experience at $1000–$2000 per season ▶ 3 *nurses* (minimum age 21) with RN license, CPR/FA certification, and experience at $2000–$3000 per season ▶ 3 *outdoor/environmental instructors* (minimum age 21) with teaching experience/certification or equivalent and WFA at $1000–$2000 per season ▶ 1–2 *riflery instructors* (minimum age 21) with first aid/CPR certification; NRA or equivalent certification and teaching experience at $1000–$2000 per season ▶ 3 *rock climbing instructors* (minimum age 21) with first aid/CPR preferred; instructor certification or equivalent; teaching or similar experience at $1000–$2000 per season ▶ 2 *sailing instructors* (minimum age 21) with lifeguard training, CPR/first aid; instructor certification or equivalent; teaching or similar experience, ARC small craft safety at $1000–$2000 per season ▶ 2 *stained glass instructors* (minimum age 21) with teaching certification/experience or equivalent at $1000–$2000 per season ▶ 4 *swimming instructors* (minimum age 21) with WSI certification, lifeguard training, first aid, CPR, or equivalent; teaching or similar experience at $1000–$2000 per season ▶ 1–3 *trip instructors* (minimum age 21) with first aid, CPR, and lifeguard training; OLS or equivalent certification and teaching/trip leading experience, WFA, canoe experience at $1000–$2000 per season ▶ 2 *waterskiing instructors* (minimum age 21) with lifeguard training, CPR, first aid; teaching/coaching certification and/or equivalent experience at $1000–$2000 per season ▶ 2 *woodworking instructors* (minimum age 21) with teaching experience/certification or equivalent at $1000–$2000 per season. Applicants must submit formal organization application, letter of interest, resume, three personal references, three letters of recommendation, background check. An in-person interview is recommended, but a telephone interview is acceptable. International applicants accepted; must obtain own visa, apply through a recognized agency.

Benefits and Preemployment Training Free housing, free meals, formal training, willing to provide letters of recommendation, on-the-job training, willing to complete paperwork for educational credit, willing to act as a professional reference, and opportunity to attend seminars/workshops. Preemployment training is required and includes accident prevention and safety, first aid, CPR, interpersonal skills, leadership skills, teaching skills, team building, children skills for cabin counseling and teaching.

Contact Widge Hazell, Assistant Director, Camp Netimus, 708 Raymondskill Road, Milford, Pennsylvania 18337. Telephone: 866-NETIMUS. Fax: 570-296-6128. E-mail: netimus@warwick.net. World Wide Web: http://www.netimus.com. Contact by e-mail, fax, mail, phone, or through World Wide Web site. Application deadline: May 31.

CAMP NOCK-A-MIXON

249 TRAUGERS CROSSING ROAD
KINTNERSVILLE, PENNSYLVANIA 18930

General Information All-around residential coeducational camp serving 380 youngsters ages 7–15 during a seven-week session. Established in 1938. 115-acre facility located 45 miles from Philadelphia. Features: 2 heated swimming pools; 4 covered athletic pavilions; 2 spring-fed lakes; 10 tennis courts; 230-yard golf driving range; 7 basketball courts.

Profile of Summer Employees Total number: 150; typical ages: 18–40. 55% men; 45% women;

10% high school students; 80% college students; 10% non-U.S. citizens. Nonsmokers required.
Employment Information Openings are from June 21 to August 15. Jobs available: ▶ *adventure course (ropes and climbing wall) teacher* at $1500–$2200 per season ▶ *athletic directors* at $1400–$3000 per season ▶ 1 *crafts director* at $1500–$2000 per season ▶ *division leaders* (minimum age 22) with college degree at $1800–$3000 per season ▶ 2 *drama directors* at $1200–$1800 per season ▶ 2 *general cleaning and grounds workers* at $1500–$1800 per season ▶ 60 *general counselors* must be high school graduates at $1000–$1500 per season ▶ 6 *kitchen staff members* at $1500–$1800 per season ▶ *nurses* with RN license at $2800–$3200 per season ▶ 30 *specialists and counselors* at $1000–$1500 per season ▶ 10 *swimming instructors* with WSI certification and/or lifeguard training at $1000–$2000 per season ▶ 6 *tennis counselors* at $1000–$1600 per season. Applicants must submit formal organization application, three personal references. An in-person interview is recommended, but a telephone interview is acceptable. International applicants accepted; must obtain own visa, obtain own working papers, apply through a recognized agency.
Benefits and Preemployment Training Free housing, free meals, formal training, willing to provide letters of recommendation, on-the-job training, willing to complete paperwork for educational credit, willing to act as a professional reference, opportunity to attend seminars/ workshops, and internship credits through colleges. Preemployment training is required and includes accident prevention and safety, first aid, CPR, interpersonal skills, leadership skills, ropes, climbing wall certification, lifeguard training.
Contact Mark Glaser, Director, Camp Nock-A-Mixon, 16 Gum Tree Lane, Lafayette Hill, Pennsylvania 19444. Telephone: 610-941-0128. Fax: 610-941-1307. E-mail: mglaser851@aol.com. World Wide Web: http://www.campnockamixon.com. Contact by e-mail, fax, mail, phone, or through World Wide Web site. Application deadline: prior to May 15 recommended.

CAMP WATONKA

HAWLEY, PENNSYLVANIA 18428

General Information Residential science camp for 120 boys offering hands-on experience in all areas of science combined with traditional camp activities. Established in 1963. 250-acre facility located 30 miles from Scranton. Features: lake; fishing stream; sports facilities; biking trails; hiking trails; modern buildings.
Profile of Summer Employees Total number: 60; typical ages: 20–40. 95% men; 5% women; 10% minorities; 5% high school students; 55% college students; 20% non-U.S. citizens; 10% local applicants. Nonsmokers required.
Employment Information Openings are from June 20 to August 20. Jobs available: ▶ *archery instructor* should be college student or graduate at $1800–$2500 per season ▶ 3 *arts and crafts staff members* at $1500–$2500 per season ▶ 15 *cabin counselors* should be college juniors or seniors at $1500–$2500 per season ▶ *editors* ▶ *magic instructor* should be college student or graduate at $2000–$3000 per season ▶ 3 *minibike riding instructors* with experience in the field at $1500–$3000 per season ▶ *photography instructor* should be college student or graduate at $1800–$2500 per season ▶ 8 *science instructors* should be college student or graduate at $2000–$3000 per season ▶ 8 *science supervisors* with teaching certification at $2500–$3500 per season ▶ 1 *waterfront director* with ARC certification at $2500–$3500 per season ▶ 5 *waterfront/water sports instructors* with ARC certification at $1500–$3000 per season ▶ 2 *woodworking instructors* with teaching certification at $2500–$3500 per season. Applicants must submit formal organization application, letter of interest, resume. An in-person interview is recommended, but a telephone interview is acceptable. International applicants accepted; must apply through a recognized agency.
Benefits and Preemployment Training Free housing, free meals, formal training, willing to provide letters of recommendation, on-the-job training, and willing to act as a professional reference. Preemployment training is required and includes accident prevention and safety, first aid, CPR, leadership skills.

Contact Donald P. Wacker, Director, Camp Watonka, PO Box 127, Hawley, Pennsylvania 18428. Telephone: 570-857-1401. World Wide Web: http://www.watonka.com. Contact by mail or phone. Application deadline: continuous.

CAMP WAYNE FOR BOYS

PRESTON PARK, PENNSYLVANIA 18455

General Information Private resident camp with sports instruction-focused program offering all land, water sports, and arts and crafts. Established in 1921. 400-acre facility located 40 miles from Binghamton. Features: freshwater lake; 12 tennis courts; 2 indoor gyms; swimming pool; 3 baseball fields; climbing tower/high ropes course.

Profile of Summer Employees Total number: 175; typical ages: 19–60. 75% men; 25% women; 5% minorities; 90% college students; 5% retirees; 20% non-U.S. citizens; 5% local applicants. Nonsmokers preferred.

Employment Information Openings are from June 19 to August 16. Jobs available: ▶ 60 *counselors* with a minimum of 1 year of college completed, paid at $1500–$2000 per season. Applicants must submit formal organization application, two letters of recommendation. An in-person interview is recommended, but a telephone interview is acceptable. International applicants accepted; must obtain own visa, apply through a recognized agency.

Benefits and Preemployment Training Free housing, free meals, willing to provide letters of recommendation, on-the-job training, willing to complete paperwork for educational credit, willing to act as a professional reference, and travel reimbursement. Preemployment training is required and includes accident prevention and safety, interpersonal skills, leadership skills.

Contact Peter Corpuel, Director, Camp Wayne for Boys, 55 Channel Drive, Port Washington, New York 11050. Telephone: 516-883-3007. Fax: 516-883-2985. E-mail: info@campwayne.com. World Wide Web: http://www.campwayne.com. Contact by e-mail, phone, or through World Wide Web site. Application deadline: continuous.

CAMP WESTMONT

ROUTE 370
POYNTELLE, PENNSYLVANIA 18454

General Information Residential camp offering all land and water sports, individual and team athletics, arts and crafts, drama and dance, woodworking and ceramics, and circus and gymnastics to 380 campers ages 6–16 for eight weeks. Established in 1980. 225-acre facility located 100 miles from New York, New York. Features: freshwater lake and olympic size pool; wooded setting; 8 tennis courts; 3 soccer fields and 4 baseball fields; flying and stationary trapeze; 2 hockey rinks.

Profile of Summer Employees Total number: 150; typical ages: 18–45. 50% men; 50% women; 5% minorities; 5% high school students; 85% college students; 2% retirees; 10% non-U.S. citizens; 5% local applicants. Nonsmokers required.

Employment Information Openings are from June 15 to August 21. Jobs available: ▶ 80–100 *general counselors* (minimum age 18) with camp experience and experience working with children (coaching, Scouts, or similar) at $1500–$2500 per season ▶ 6–12 *group leaders* (minimum age 25) with camp or teaching experience with children at $2500–$3000 per season ▶ 6–8 *tennis specialists* (minimum age 18) with experience playing and/or teaching tennis at $1500–$2500 per season ▶ 6–10 *waterfront specialists* (minimum age 18) with WSI/lifeguard certification and experience as a swimming instructor or lifeguard at $1500–$2500 per season. Applicants must submit formal organization application, letter of interest, resume, two personal references, two letters of recommendation, photo and copy of proof of age. An in-person interview is recommended, but a telephone interview is acceptable. International applicants accepted; must obtain own visa, apply through a recognized agency.

Benefits and Preemployment Training Free housing, free meals, willing to provide letters of

recommendation, on-the-job training, willing to act as a professional reference, and travel reimbursement. Preemployment training is required and includes accident prevention and safety, interpersonal skills, leadership skills.
Contact Jack Pinsky, Owner/Director, Camp Westmont, 14 Squirrel Drive, East Rockaway, New York 11518. Telephone: 516-599-2963. Fax: 516-599-1979. E-mail: campwestmt@aol.com. World Wide Web: http://www.campwestmont.com. Contact by e-mail, fax, mail, phone, or through World Wide Web site. Application deadline: continuous.

CENTER FOR TALENTED YOUTH/JOHNS HOPKINS UNIVERSITY–DICKINSON COLLEGE

CARLISLE, PENNSYLVANIA

See Center for Talented Youth/Johns Hopkins University on page 145 for complete description.

CENTER FOR TALENTED YOUTH/JOHNS HOPKINS UNIVERSITY–FRANKLIN AND MARSHALL COLLEGE

LANCASTER, PENNSYLVANIA

See Center for Talented Youth/Johns Hopkins University on page 145 for complete description.

CENTER FOR TALENTED YOUTH/JOHNS HOPKINS UNIVERSITY–MORAVIAN COLLEGE

BETHLEHEM, PENNSYLVANIA

See Center for Talented Youth/Johns Hopkins University on page 145 for complete description.

COLLEGE GIFTED PROGRAMS

BRYN MAWR COLLEGE
BRYN MAWR, PENNSYLVANIA 19010

General Information Residential educational academic summer camp for gifted and talented students in grades 4-11. Program blends in-depth academics with recreational and cultural activities. Established in 1984. 135-acre facility located 11 miles from Philadelphia. Features: dormitories; campus classroom facilities; campus recreational facilities include pool, tennis courts, and gym; campus library; beautiful college setting.
Profile of Summer Employees Total number: 70; typical ages: 19–70. 50% men; 50% women; 30% minorities; 50% college students; 10% retirees; 10% non-U.S. citizens; 25% local applicants. Nonsmokers required.
Employment Information Openings are from July 24 to August 14. Jobs available: ▶ 35 *counselors* with two years of college completed and experience working with children at $900 to $1200 per 3-week session ▶ 4 *directors* with at least 5 years teaching/supervisory experience; master's degree required, doctorate preferred at $5000–$8000 per year ▶ 7 *housemasters/instructors (residential)* with master's degree, teaching and supervisory experience at $2500 to $4500 per 3-week session ▶ 20 *instructors (non-residential)* with master's degree and teaching experience at $600 to $2500 per 3-week session ▶ 2 *nurses* with RN license; school experience preferred at $1300 per week. Applicants must submit formal organization application, resume, academic transcripts, two personal references, two letters of recommendation. An in-person interview is recommended, but a telephone interview is acceptable. International applicants accepted; must apply through a recognized agency.
Benefits and Preemployment Training Free housing, free meals, willing to provide letters of recommendation, willing to complete paperwork for educational credit, and willing to act as a professional reference. Preemployment training is required and includes accident prevention and

safety, interpersonal skills, leadership skills, instructional strategies for gifted students.
Contact Charles Zeichner, Executive Director, College Gifted Programs, 120 Littleton Road, Suite 201, Parsippany, New Jersey 07054-1803. Telephone: 973-334-6991. Fax: 973-334-9756. E-mail: info@cgp-sig.com. World Wide Web: http://www.cgp-sig.com. Contact by e-mail, fax, mail, phone, or through World Wide Web site. Application deadline: continuous.

COLLEGE SETTLEMENT OF PHILADELPHIA

600 WITMER ROAD
HORSHAM, PENNSYLVANIA 19044

General Information Residential and day camp serving mostly economically disadvantaged youths ages 7–14 from the Philadelphia metropolitan area. Established in 1922. 235-acre facility located 15 miles from Philadelphia. Features: small lake/pond; low ropes/high ropes course; 2 pools; lighted hard-top for tennis and sports; 6 cabins and large house/dormitory; full-service dining hall.
Profile of Summer Employees Total number: 65; typical ages: 16–30. 50% men; 50% women; 20% minorities; 10% high school students; 80% college students; 20% non-U.S. citizens; 10% local applicants. Nonsmokers preferred.
Employment Information Openings are from June 1 to August 25. Year-round positions also offered. Jobs available: ▶ 2 *adventure staff* (minimum age 21) with experience in climbing and canoeing (preferred), driver's license at $2000–$3000 per season ▶ 26 *cabin counselors* (minimum age 19) with desire to have fun at camp with great kids at $1800–$2000 per season ▶ 2–4 *environmentalists* (minimum age 21) with driver's license (preferred) and background in teaching/sciences at $2000 per season ▶ 3–4 *pool directors* (minimum age 21) with WSI and LGT certification (training available) at $2000 per season ▶ 2 *provisions coordinators* (minimum age 21) with driver's license at $2000 per season ▶ 3 *trip leaders* (minimum age 21) with driver's license and experience (preferred), training provided at $3000 per season ▶ 3 *unit leaders* (minimum age 21) with supervisory experience (preferred) at $3000 per season. Applicants must submit formal organization application, letter of interest, resume, three personal references. An in-person interview is recommended, but a telephone interview is acceptable. International applicants accepted; must apply through a recognized agency.
Benefits and Preemployment Training Free housing, free meals, formal training, possible full-time employment, willing to provide letters of recommendation, on-the-job training, willing to complete paperwork for educational credit, willing to act as a professional reference, and possible certification training for archery, boating, lifeguard, and conflict resolution/counseling.
Contact Karyn McGee, Director of Resident Programs, College Settlement of Philadelphia, 600 Witmer Road, Horsham, Pennsylvania 19044. Telephone: 215-542-7974. Fax: 215-542-7457. E-mail: camps@i-bob.com. World Wide Web: http://www.collegesettlement.org. Contact by e-mail, fax, mail, phone, or through World Wide Web site. Application deadline: application by April 15th is preferred.

CYBERCAMPS–BRYN MAWR COLLEGE

PHILADELPHIA, PENNSYLVANIA

See Cybercamps–University of Washington on page 335 for complete description.

DORNEY PARK AND WILDWATER KINGDOM

3830 DORNEY PARK ROAD
ALLENTOWN, PENNSYLVANIA 18104

General Information Amusement park featuring more than 100 rides and attractions, including 4 roller coasters and a waterpark. Established in 1860. 200-acre facility located 50 miles from Philadelphia. Features: 5 designated children's areas; 11 water slides; wave pool; 1921 antique wooden Dentzel carousel; daily live entertainment.
Profile of Summer Employees Total number: 2,500.

Employment Information Openings are from May 1 to October 15. Jobs available: ▶ 350 *food hosts and hostesses* ▶ 100 *game attendants* ▶ 200 *lifeguards* ▶ 180 *merchandise clerks* ▶ 350 *ride operators* ▶ *security staff*. Applicants must submit formal organization application. An in-person interview is required. International applicants accepted; must apply through a recognized agency.

Benefits and Preemployment Training On-the-job training, willing to complete paperwork for educational credit, and scholarships available. Preemployment training is required and includes CPR.

Contact Eileen Minninger, Personnel Manager, Dorney Park and Wildwater Kingdom, 3830 Dorney Park Road, Allentown, Pennsylvania 18104. Telephone: 610-391-7752. Contact by mail or phone. Application deadline: continuous.

FORESITE SPORTS, INC.

632 GERMANTOWN PIKE
LAFAYETTE HILL, PENNSYLVANIA 19444

General Information Organization dedicated to fostering a love of golf by providing beginner and intermediate golfers with the opportunity to learn the fundamental skills of the game. Established in 1998. Located 10 miles from Philadelphia. Features: golf course or range.

Profile of Summer Employees Total number: 10; typical ages: 16–35. 70% men; 30% women; 20% high school students; 50% college students; 90% local applicants. Nonsmokers preferred.

Employment Information Openings are from June to August. Jobs available: ▶ 1–2 *camp counselors* (minimum age 16) at $8–$10 per hour ▶ 10–15 *golf instructors* (minimum age 18) at $10–$15 per hour. Applicants must submit a formal organization application, resume. An in-person interview is recommended, but a telephone interview is acceptable. International applicants accepted; must obtain own visa, obtain own working papers.

Benefits and Preemployment Training Possible full-time employment, willing to provide letters of recommendation, on-the-job training, willing to complete paperwork for educational credit, willing to act as a professional reference, and travel reimbursement. Preemployment training is required and includes interpersonal skills, leadership skills, golf skills.

Contact James Nam, Foresite Sports, Inc. Telephone: 610-825-2441. Fax: 610-825-2681. E-mail: info@forsitesports.com. World Wide Web: http://foresitesports.com. Contact by phone. Application deadline: continuous.

FORT NECESSITY NATIONAL BATTLEFIELD

1 WASHINGTON PARKWAY
FARMINGTON, PENNSYLVANIA 15437

General Information George Washington's first command and battlefield commemorating the opening battle of the French and Indian War and westward expansion along the National Road. Established in 1931. 903-acre facility located 70 miles from Pittsburgh. Features: reconstructed fort and battlefield; visitor center; 19th Century tavern; picnic area; grave site of General Braddock; skirmish site, Jumonville Glen.

Profile of Summer Employees Total number: 2; typical ages: 22–65. 75% men; 25% women; 25% minorities; 50% college students; 25% retirees.

Employment Information Openings are from June 1 to August 25. Jobs available: ▶ 1–2 *interpretive park rangers* (minimum age 18) with public speaking experience and interest in history at $10–$11 per hour. Applicants must submit a formal organization application.

Benefits and Preemployment Training Housing at a cost, formal training, willing to provide letters of recommendation, on-the-job training, willing to complete paperwork for educational credit, and willing to act as a professional reference.

Contact Brian S. Reedy, Supervisory Park Ranger, Fort Necessity National Battlefield, 1 Washington Parkway, Farmington, Pennsylvania 15437. Telephone: 724-329-5512. Fax: 724-329-8682. E-mail: brian_reedy@nps.gov. World Wide Web: http://www.nps.gov/fone. Contact by e-mail, fax, mail, phone, or through World Wide Web site. Application deadline: January 15.

JUMONVILLE
887 JUMONVILLE ROAD
HOPWOOD, PENNSYLVANIA 15445

General Information Residential Christian camp serving 250–300 persons of all age levels per week. Established in 1941. 281-acre facility located 50 miles from Pittsburgh. Features: 60-foot tall steel cross; high- and low-elements ropes course; adventure center; campus like setting; mountain location; excellent sports facilities.

Profile of Summer Employees Total number: 45; typical ages: 16–25. 50% men; 50% women; 5% minorities; 10% high school students; 90% college students; 5% non-U.S. citizens; 10% local applicants. Nonsmokers required.

Employment Information Openings are from May 15 to August 25. Jobs available: ▶ 1 *adventure program coordinator* (minimum age 19) at $210 per week ▶ 2 *adventure staff members* (minimum age 18) at $192 per week ▶ 1 *business manager/truck driver* at $210 per week ▶ 2 *cookout staff members* at $210 per week ▶ 5–8 *counselors* (minimum age 18) at $192 per week ▶ 2 *dining room staff members* at $192 per week ▶ 4 *dishroom staff members* at $210 per week ▶ 1 *health-care staff member* with paramedic, LPN, or RN license at $192 per week ▶ 1 *information technology coordinator* at $210 per week ▶ 2 *kitchen helpers* at $192 per week ▶ 2 *lifeguards* with certification at $192 per week ▶ 3–4 *multimedia specialists and internet staff* at $192 per week ▶ 2 *multipurpose floaters* at $192 per week ▶ 1 *office assistant/business manager* at $192 per week ▶ 2 *snack shop workers* at $192 per week. Applicants must submit formal organization application, three personal references. An in-person interview is required. International applicants accepted; must apply through a recognized agency.

Benefits and Preemployment Training Free housing, free meals, willing to provide letters of recommendation, on-the-job training, willing to complete paperwork for educational credit, and willing to act as a professional reference. Preemployment training is required and includes accident prevention and safety, first aid, CPR, interpersonal skills, leadership skills.

Contact Larry Beatty, President, Jumonville, 887 Jumonville Road, Hopwood, Pennsylvania 15445. Telephone: 724-439-4912. Fax: 724-439-1415. E-mail: info@jumonville.org. World Wide Web: http://www.jumonville.org. Contact by e-mail, fax, mail, phone, or through World Wide Web site. Application deadline: March 15.

KENNYWOOD PARK
4800 KENNYWOOD BOULEVARD
WEST MIFFLIN, PENNSYLVANIA 15122

General Information Amusement park servicing more than 1 million guests per season. Established in 1898. 40-acre facility located 7 miles from Pittsburgh. Features: roller coasters; cafe; lagoon; dark rides; pavilions; food concessions.

Profile of Summer Employees Total number: 1,500–1,600; typical ages: 16–26. 47% men; 53% women; 18% minorities; 20% high school students; 70% college students; 10% retirees; 100% local applicants.

Employment Information Openings are from April 15 to September 6. Jobs available: ▶ 1500 *team members (rides, games, and refreshments)* (minimum age 15) at $5.80 per hour. Applicants must submit a formal organization application, personal reference. An in-person interview is required.

Benefits and Preemployment Training Formal training and on-the-job training. Preemployment training is required and includes accident prevention and safety, interpersonal skills.

Contact Joe Barron, Human Resources Director, Kennywood Park, 4800 Kennywood Boulevard, West Mifflin, Pennsylvania 15122. Telephone: 412-461-0500 Ext. 106. Fax: 412-464-0719. Contact by fax, mail, or phone. Application deadline: continuous.

LONGACRE EXPEDITIONS
4030 MIDDLE RIDGE ROAD
NEWPORT, PENNSYLVANIA 17074-8110

General Information Adventure travel program in Pennsylvania for teenagers, emphasizing group living skills, physical challenges, and fun. Longacre's challenging programs place equal emphasis on physical accomplishment and emotional growth. Established in 1981. 35-acre facility located 35 miles from Harrisburg. Features: ropes course; climbing wall; wooded setting.
Profile of Summer Employees Total number: 30; typical ages: 21–32. 50% men; 50% women; 10% minorities; 40% college students; 10% local applicants. Nonsmokers required.
Employment Information Openings are from June 15 to August 15. Jobs available: ▶ 24 *assistant trip leaders* (minimum age 21) with good driving record, wilderness first aid, and CPR at $252–$300 per week ▶ 1 *caving instructor* (minimum age 21) with good driving record, wilderness first aid, and CPR at $300–$450 per week ▶ 1 *equipment manager* (minimum age 21) with good driving record, wilderness first aid, and CPR at $180–$240 per week ▶ 2 *rock climbing instructors* (minimum age 21) with wilderness first aid and CPR at $300–$450 per week ▶ 8 *support and logistics staff members* (minimum age 21) with good driving record, wilderness first aid, and CPR at $180–$240 per week. Applicants must submit a formal organization application, letter of interest, resume, three personal references. An in-person interview is recommended, but a telephone interview is acceptable. International applicants accepted; must obtain own visa, obtain own working papers.
Benefits and Preemployment Training Free housing, free meals, willing to provide letters of recommendation, on-the-job training, willing to complete paperwork for educational credit, willing to act as a professional reference, and pro-deal purchase program. Preemployment training is required and includes accident prevention and safety, interpersonal skills, leadership skills.
Contact Meredith Schuler, Director, Longacre Expeditions, 4030 Middle Ridge Road, Newport, Pennsylvania 17074-8110. Telephone: 717-567-6790. Fax: 717-567-3955. E-mail: longacre@longacreexpeditions.com. World Wide Web: http://www.longacreexpeditions.com. Contact by e-mail, fax, mail, phone, or through World Wide Web site. Application deadline: continuous.

SALVATION ARMY OF LOWER BUCKS
215 APPLETREE DRIVE
LEVITTOWN, PENNSYLVANIA 19055

General Information Community-based center that offers a full range of service and multigenerational programs. Established in 1865. 8-acre facility located 7 miles from Philadelphia. Features: air-conditioned facility; full-size gym; computer room; craft room; ballfield; church connected to building.
Profile of Summer Employees Total number: 10; typical ages: 18–25. 20% men; 80% women; 10% minorities; 10% high school students; 80% college students; 10% retirees; 90% local applicants. Nonsmokers preferred.
Employment Information Openings are from June 12 to August 30. Jobs available: ▶ 6–8 *day care counselors* (minimum age 17) with experience caring for children (babysitting, day care, or similar) at $6–$7 per hour ▶ 6–10 *summer camp counselors* (minimum age 18) with any type of childcare background and first aid/CPR (training provided) at $6–$7 per hour. Applicants must submit formal organization application, letter of interest, resume, academic transcripts, two personal references, two letters of recommendation. An in-person interview is required. International applicants accepted; must apply through a recognized agency.
Benefits and Preemployment Training Free meals, willing to provide letters of recommendation, willing to complete paperwork for educational credit, and willing to act as a professional reference. Preemployment training is required and includes accident prevention and safety, first aid, CPR, interpersonal skills, leadership skills.
Contact Maureen C. Carson, Community Programs Coordinator, Salvation Army of Lower

Bucks, Appletree Drive and Autumn Lane, Levittown, Pennsylvania 19055. Telephone: 215-945-0718. Fax: 215-945-0607. Contact by fax. Application deadline: January 20.

SHAVER'S CREEK ENVIRONMENTAL CENTER, PENNSYLVANIA STATE UNIVERSITY

508A KELLER BUILDING
UNIVERSITY PARK, PENNSYLVANIA 16802

General Information Center providing day and residential environmental education and outdoor adventure programming. Established in 1976. 7,000-acre facility located 13 miles from State College. Features: 20 birds of prey; team building low element course; 25 miles of hiking trails; herb and flower gardens; 72-acre lake; hands-on exhibits.

Profile of Summer Employees Total number: 15; typical ages: 20–30. 50% men; 50% women; 10% minorities; 90% college students; 25% non-U.S. citizens; 5% local applicants. Nonsmokers preferred.

Employment Information Openings are from June 3 to August 23. Year-round positions also offered. Jobs available: ▶ 4–6 *environmental education interns* at $150 per week. Applicants must submit formal organization application, resume, three letters of recommendation (international applicants only). A telephone interview is required. International applicants accepted; must apply through a recognized agency.

Benefits and Preemployment Training Free housing, formal training, willing to provide letters of recommendation, on-the-job training, willing to complete paperwork for educational credit, willing to act as a professional reference, and opportunity to attend seminars/workshops. Preemployment training is required and includes accident prevention and safety, first aid, CPR, interpersonal skills, leadership skills, animal handling.

Contact Doug Wentzel, Intern Coordinator, Shaver's Creek Environmental Center, Pennsylvania State University, 508A Keller Building, University Park, Pennsylvania 16802. Telephone: 814-863-2000. Fax: 814-865-2706. E-mail: shaverscreek@outreach.psu.edu. World Wide Web: http://www.shaverscreek.org. Contact by e-mail, fax, mail, phone, or through World Wide Web site. Application deadline: March 1.

SHELLY RIDGE DAY CAMP

330 MANOR ROAD
MIQUON, PENNSYLVANIA 19444

General Information Nine-week day camp for 200 girls ages 6–14. Established in 1912. 113-acre facility located 1 mile from Philadelphia. Features: swimming pool; hiking trails; natural environment; close to city of Philadelphia.

Profile of Summer Employees Total number: 60; typical ages: 15–60. 5% men; 95% women; 60% minorities; 10% high school students; 70% college students; 5% retirees; 100% local applicants. Nonsmokers preferred.

Employment Information Openings are from June 18 to August 14. Year-round positions also offered. Jobs available: ▶ *business manager* with experience in the field at $1800–$2400 per season ▶ *counselors* with first aid/CPR at $800–$1800 per season ▶ *lifeguards/swim instructors* with WSI or lifeguard training, first aid/CPR at $1200–$2000 per season. Applicants must submit formal organization application, three personal references, criminal background check (State of Pennsylvania). An in-person interview is recommended, but a telephone interview is acceptable. International applicants accepted; must apply through a recognized agency.

Benefits and Preemployment Training On-the-job training and willing to complete paperwork for educational credit. Preemployment training is required and includes accident prevention and safety, first aid, CPR, interpersonal skills, leadership skills.

Contact Rosemary Scanlon-Jacob, Program Director, Shelly Ridge Day Camp, Girl Scouts of Southeastern Pennsylvania, 330 Manor Road, Mignon, Pennsylvania 19144. Telephone: 215-564-4657. Fax: 215-564-6953. Contact by fax, mail, or phone. Application deadline: continuous.

SOUTH MOUNTAIN YMCA
PO BOX 147, 201 CUSHION PEAK ROAD
WERNERSVILLE, PENNSYLVANIA 19565

General Information A traditional coed summer camp with both day and resident programs operated by South Mountain YMCA. Established in 1948. 500-acre facility located 12 miles from Reading. Features: wooded setting; pool; tennis/basketball courts; staff lounge with email; laundry facilities; central to Philadelphia, New York City and Washington, D.C.
Profile of Summer Employees Total number: 100; typical ages: 17–28. 45% men; 55% women; 15% high school students; 85% college students; 25% non-U.S. citizens; 25% local applicants. Nonsmokers required.
Employment Information Openings are from June 4 to August 17. Jobs available: ▶ 1–100 *camp counselors* (minimum age 17) at $1200–$3000 per season. Applicants must submit formal organization application, three personal references, criminal background check (at organization's expense). An in-person interview is recommended, but a telephone interview is acceptable. International applicants accepted; must apply through a recognized agency.
Benefits and Preemployment Training Free housing, free meals, formal training, willing to provide letters of recommendation, names of contacts, willing to complete paperwork for educational credit, willing to act as a professional reference, and certification for certain activities (certified instructor in archery, riflery, horseback riding, lifeguarding). Preemployment training is required and includes accident prevention and safety, first aid, CPR, leadership skills.
Contact Lara Thomas, Director of Resident Camping, South Mountain YMCA. Telephone: 610-670-2267. Fax: 610-670-5010. E-mail: lthomas@smymca.org. World Wide Web: http://www.smymca.org. Contact by e-mail, fax, phone, or through World Wide Web site. Application deadline: continuous.

THE SOUTHWESTERN COMPANY, PENNSYLVANIA
See The Southwestern Company on page 302 for complete description.

SPORTS INTERNATIONAL–EAGLES
READING, PENNSYLVANIA
See Sports International, Inc. on page 147 for complete description.

SPORTS INTERNATIONAL–GIANTS
EAST STROUDSBURG, PENNSYLVANIA
See Sports International, Inc. on page 147 for complete description.

SPORTS INTERNATIONAL–JOE KRIVAK (QUARTERBACK AND RECEIVING CAMP)
SLIPPERY ROCK, PENNSYLVANIA
See Sports International, Inc. on page 147 for complete description.

SPORTS INTERNATIONAL–STEELERS
SLIPPERY ROCK, PENNSYLVANIA
See Sports International, Inc. on page 147 for complete description.

STIVERS STAFFING SERVICES–PENNSYLVANIA
See Stivers Staffing Services–Illinois on page 110 for complete description.

STREAMSIDE CAMP AND CONFERENCE CENTER
RURAL ROUTE 3, BOX 3307
STROUDSBURG, PENNSYLVANIA 18360

General Information Residential Christian camp with a focus on providing a quality camping experience for inner-city children, youth, and families. Established in 1942. 140-acre facility located 90 miles from Philadelphia. Features: boating and fishing ponds; outdoor swimming pool; wooded setting with hiking and horsetrails; comfortable rustic cabins; 300-foot waterslide; basketball and sand volleyball courts.

Profile of Summer Employees Total number: 60; typical ages: 15–25. 50% men; 50% women; 15% minorities; 25% high school students; 60% college students; 5% retirees; 10% non-U.S. citizens; 60% local applicants. Nonsmokers required.

Employment Information Openings are from June 7 to August 28. Year-round positions also offered. Jobs available: ▶ 20–26 *cabin counselors* (minimum age 18) at $150–$300 per week ▶ 1 *camp nurse* (minimum age 18) with minimum First Aid certifications at $150–$300 per week ▶ 2–4 *dining room workers* (minimum age 15) at $60–$120 per week ▶ 1–2 *horsemanship instructor/wranglers* (minimum age 18) with experience in working with horses at $150–$300 per week ▶ 4–6 *kitchen aides* (minimum age 15) with desire to learn at $60–$150 per week ▶ 1–2 *lifeguards* (minimum age 16) with lifeguard certification at $150–$300 per week ▶ 2–4 *maintenance team workers* (minimum age 15) at $60–$150 per week ▶ 1–2 *program specialists* (minimum age 18) with ability to teach and relate a specific area of expertise to the Christian daily life at $150–$300 per week ▶ 1–2 *water safety instructors* (minimum age 18) with WSI certification at $150–$300 per week. Applicants must submit formal organization application, three personal references. A telephone interview is required. International applicants accepted; must apply through a recognized agency.

Benefits and Preemployment Training Free housing, free meals, formal training, possible full-time employment, health insurance, willing to provide letters of recommendation, on-the-job training, willing to act as a professional reference, opportunity to attend seminars/workshops, travel reimbursement, and tuition assistance. Preemployment training is required and includes accident prevention and safety, first aid, CPR, interpersonal skills, leadership skills, lifeguard training.

Contact Dave Bouffard, Streamside Program Director, Streamside Camp and Conference Center, RR #3, Box 3307, Stroudsburg, Pennsylvania 18360. Telephone: 570-629-1902. Fax: 570-629-9650. E-mail: summerstaff@streamside.org. World Wide Web: http://www.streamside.org. Contact by e-mail, fax, mail, phone, or through World Wide Web site. Application deadline: continuous.

STUDENT CONSERVATION ASSOCIATION (SCA), PENNSYLVANIA

See Student Conservation Association (SCA), New Hampshire on page 209 for complete description.

SWARTHMORE TENNIS CAMP

500 COLLEGE AVENUE
SWARTHMORE, PENNSYLVANIA 19081

General Information Operates both a junior and adult camp for resident and day campers. 5 hours daily. Adults 3-day, 5-day, and weekend programs. Juniors 9–18, coed weekly and multiweek sessions. Established in 1981. 325-acre facility located 12 miles from Philadelphia. Features: wooded campus; tennis courts; swimming pool.

Profile of Summer Employees Total number: 12–14; typical ages: 19–40. 80% men; 20% women; 70% college students; 10% non-U.S. citizens. Nonsmokers required.

Employment Information Openings are from June 17 to August 9. Jobs available: ▶ 10 *tennis instructors* (minimum age 19) with collegiate tennis experience at $265–$285 per week. Applicants must submit a formal organization application, resume, three personal references. International applicants accepted.

Benefits and Preemployment Training Free housing and free meals. Preemployment training is required and includes interpersonal skills, leadership skills.

Contact Lois Broderick, President, Swarthmore Tennis Camp, 444 East 82nd Street, Suite 31D, New York, New York 10028. Telephone: 212-879-0225. Fax: 212-452-0816. E-mail: greatennis@

aol.com. Contact by e-mail, fax, mail, or phone. Application deadline: continuous.

WALDAMEER PARK, INC.
220 PENINSULA DRIVE
ERIE, PENNSYLVANIA 16505

General Information Amusement park and water park with rides, water slides, midway games, arcade, gift shops, refreshment stands, picnic/catering facilities and entertainment. Established in 1896. 42-acre facility located 90 miles from Cleveland, Ohio. Features: 16 major rides; 11 major water slides; kiddie rides and slides; midway games; food and gift shops; picnic shelters.
Profile of Summer Employees Total number: 400; typical ages: 14–22. 50% men; 50% women; 7% minorities; 70% high school students; 30% college students; 1% retirees; 1% non-U.S. citizens; 95% local applicants. Nonsmokers preferred.
Employment Information Openings are from May 1 to September 7. Jobs available: ▶ 15 *cashiers* (minimum age 18) ▶ 30 *food service personnel* (minimum age 16) ▶ 30 *games attendants* (minimum age 16) ▶ 30–40 *lifeguards* (minimum age 16) with first aid, CPR, and lifeguard certification ▶ 20 *picnic staff* (minimum age 18) ▶ 30–40 *ride operators* (minimum age 18). Applicants must submit a formal organization application, two personal references. An in-person interview is required. International applicants accepted; must obtain own visa, obtain own working papers.
Benefits and Preemployment Training Meals at a cost, willing to provide letters of recommendation, on-the-job training, willing to act as a professional reference, and use of amusement park facility. Preemployment training is required and includes accident prevention and safety, customer service skills.
Contact Steve Gorman, General Manager, Waldameer Park, Inc., PO Box 8308, Erie, Pennsylvania 16505. Fax: 814-835-7435. E-mail: info@waldameer.com. World Wide Web: http://www.waldameer.com. Contact by e-mail or mail. Application deadline: continuous.

YMCA CAMP FITCH
12600 ABLES ROAD
NORTH SPRINGFIELD, PENNSYLVANIA 16430

General Information Traditional residential camp serving 210 campers; special population camp serving 30–70 campers with special needs; specialty camps such as computer, running, and swimming camps serving 30 campers. Established in 1914. 450-acre facility located 15 miles from Erie. Features: location on Lake Erie; 4-acre inland lake; swimming pool; 450 wooded acres and horse trails; soccer and ball fields; many activity areas.
Profile of Summer Employees Total number: 120; typical ages: 17–60. 50% men; 50% women; 15% minorities; 35% high school students; 65% college students; 10% non-U.S. citizens; 60% local applicants. Nonsmokers preferred.
Employment Information Openings are from June 7 to August 31. Year-round positions also offered. Jobs available: ▶ 1–2 *kitchen stewards* (minimum age 19) with food service/cleaning experience at $150–$200 per week ▶ 4–6 *special population counselors* (minimum age 18) with camp counselor experience or experience with special populations at $120–$175 per week ▶ *summer camp counselors* (minimum age 18) at $120–$175 per week. Applicants must submit formal organization application, letter of interest, three personal references. An in-person interview is recommended, but a telephone interview is acceptable. International applicants accepted; must obtain own visa, obtain own working papers, apply through a recognized agency.
Benefits and Preemployment Training Free housing, free meals, formal training, willing to provide letters of recommendation, on-the-job training, willing to complete paperwork for educational credit, and opportunity to attend seminars/workshops. Preemployment training is required and includes accident prevention and safety, first aid, CPR, interpersonal skills, leadership skills.
Contact Bill Lyder, Executive Camp Director, YMCA Camp Fitch, 17 North Champion Street,

Youngstown, Ohio 44501-1287. Telephone: 330-744-8411. Fax: 330-744-8416. E-mail: campfitch@hotmail.com. World Wide Web: http://www.campfitch.com. Contact by e-mail, fax, mail, or phone. Application deadline: continuous.

RHODE ISLAND

CENTER FOR TALENTED YOUTH/JOHNS HOPKINS UNIVERSITY–ROGER WILLIAMS UNIVERSITY

BRISTOL, RHODE ISLAND

See Center for Talented Youth/Johns Hopkins University on page 145 for complete description.

CYBERCAMPS–BROWN UNIVERSITY

PROVIDENCE, RHODE ISLAND

See Cybercamps–University of Washington on page 335 for complete description.

THE SOUTHWESTERN COMPANY, RHODE ISLAND

See The Southwestern Company on page 302 for complete description.

SPORTS INTERNATIONAL–PATRIOTS

SMITHFIELD, RHODE ISLAND

See Sports International, Inc. on page 147 for complete description.

STUDENT CONSERVATION ASSOCIATION (SCA), RHODE ISLAND

See Student Conservation Association (SCA), New Hampshire on page 209 for complete description.

UNIVERSITY OF RHODE ISLAND SUMMER PROGRAMS

W. ALTON JONES CAMPUS, 401 VICTORY HIGHWAY
WEST GREENWICH, RHODE ISLAND 02817-2158

General Information Residential Earth Camp facility serving 100 campers in seven 1-week sessions focusing on nature awareness and conservation; expedition program for 40 teens in seven 1-week sessions includes backpacking, kayaking, canoeing, and rock-climbing. Farm and ecology day camp for ages 5–11 utilizes historic working farm and nature preserve. Established in 1962. 2,300-acre facility located 30 miles from Providence. Features: 75-acre lake; 2300-acre property; 40,000 acres of state forests; 10 miles of hiking trails; low ropes challenge course.

Profile of Summer Employees Total number: 50; typical ages: 14–29. 50% men; 50% women; 5% minorities; 10% high school students; 90% college students; 15% non-U.S. citizens; 50% local applicants. Nonsmokers preferred.

Employment Information Openings are from June 16 to August 15. Year-round positions also offered. Jobs available: ▶ 20 *Earth Camp/counselors* (minimum age 18) with CPR/first aid certification and experience working with children at $185–$240 per week ▶ 1 *animal and garden manager* with experience caring for farm animals and gardens at $250–$350 per week ▶ 1 *camp EMT or nurse assistant* (minimum age 20) student nurse with CPR/first aid certification; EMT preferred at $350–$375 per week ▶ 12 *day camp counselors* (minimum age 18) with

CPR/first aid certification and experience working with children at $300 per week ▶ 10–12 *field teachers/naturalists* (minimum age 21) with CPR/first aid certification; must have experience teaching children at $250 per week ▶ 2 *lifeguards* (minimum age 18) with driver's license, first aid, CPR, and lifeguard certification at $8–$12 per hour ▶ 10 *teen expedition leaders* (minimum age 21) with driver's license, CPR, first aid, and lifeguard certification; should have experience working with teens and/or outdoor skills at $200–$305 per week. Applicants must submit a formal organization application, letter of interest, resume, three personal references. A telephone interview is required. International applicants accepted.

Benefits and Preemployment Training Free housing, free meals, formal training, willing to provide letters of recommendation, on-the-job training, willing to complete paperwork for educational credit, and willing to act as a professional reference. Preemployment training is required and includes accident prevention and safety, first aid, CPR, interpersonal skills, leadership skills, lesson planning and teaching.

Contact John Jacques, Manager, Environmental Education Center, University of Rhode Island Summer Programs, 401 Victory Highway, West Greenwich, Rhode Island 02817-2158. Telephone: 401-397-3304 Ext. 6043. Fax: 401-397-3293. E-mail: urieec@etal.uri.edu. World Wide Web: http://www.uri.edu/ajc/eec. Contact by e-mail, fax, mail, phone, or through World Wide Web site. Application deadline: continuous.

SOUTH CAROLINA

BROADWAY AT THE BEACH

921 NORTH KINGS HIGHWAY
MYRTLE BEACH, SOUTH CAROLINA 29577

General Information Amusement, retail, shopping, and entertainment complex. Established in 1994. Located 100 miles from Columbia.

Profile of Summer Employees Total number: 75; typical age: 16. 50% men; 50% women; 75% high school students; 25% college students; 90% local applicants.

Employment Information Openings are from April to October. Spring break positions also offered. Jobs available: ▶ *cashiers* (minimum age 16) at $6.90 per hour ▶ *ride attendants* (minimum age 16) with ability to withstand sun at $6.90 per hour ▶ *snack cart cashiers* (minimum age 16) with ability to work outdoors at $6.90 per hour. Applicants must submit a formal organization application. An in-person interview is required.

Benefits and Preemployment Training Housing at a cost, meals at a cost, formal training, possible full-time employment, health insurance, on-the-job training, tuition assistance, and discounts to local company-owned amusement parks and golf. Preemployment training is required.

Contact Amanda Broderick, Human Resource Specialist, Broadway at the Beach. Telephone: 843-315-6005. Fax: 843-626-8461. E-mail: amanda.broderick@burroughs-chapin.com. World Wide Web: http://www.broadwayatthebeach.com. Contact by e-mail, fax, mail, or phone. Application deadline: continuous.

CAMP CHATUGA

291 CAMP CHATUGA ROAD
MOUNTAIN REST, SOUTH CAROLINA 29664

General Information Residential coeducational camp serving 165 campers per session in the heart of Sumter National Forest in the Blue Ridge Mountain foothills. Established in 1956.

60-acre facility located 125 miles from Atlanta, Georgia. Features: private lake; surrounded by national forest; football field; screened wood cabins; recreation hall; lodge.

Profile of Summer Employees Total number: 40–50; typical ages: 19–50. 50% men; 50% women; 10% minorities; 75% college students; 5% retirees; 20% non-U.S. citizens; 40% local applicants. Nonsmokers required.

Employment Information Openings are from June 1 to August 15. Jobs available: ▶ 1 *Western horseback riding director* (minimum age 21) with horse experience at $1500–$2500 per season ▶ 1–4 *camp "moms"* at $150 to $225 per week and tuition discounts for children ▶ 25 *counselors* (minimum age 19) at $1400–$2000 per season ▶ 1 *dining hall supervisor* (minimum age 21) with supervisory skills and interest in food service at $1500–$2000 per season ▶ 1–4 *health supervisors* (minimum age 21) with CPR/first aid certification, RN, BSN, MD, pediatric experience preferred at $200 per week and tuition discounts for children ▶ 1 *nanny* (minimum age 19) at $1500–$2000 per season ▶ 1 *waterfront director* (minimum age 21) with lifeguard certification required, WSI preferred at $1400–$2000 per season. Applicants must submit formal organization application, three personal references. A telephone interview is required. International applicants accepted; must obtain own visa, apply through a recognized agency.

Benefits and Preemployment Training Free housing, free meals, formal training, willing to provide letters of recommendation, names of contacts, on-the-job training, willing to complete paperwork for educational credit, willing to act as a professional reference, opportunity to attend seminars/workshops, and transportation to camp from airport, staff training certifications. Preemployment training is required and includes accident prevention and safety, first aid, CPR, interpersonal skills, leadership skills.

Contact Kelly Moxley, Director of Personnel, Camp Chatuga, 291 Camp Chatuga Road, Mountain Rest, South Carolina 29664. Telephone: 864-638-3728. Fax: 864-638-0898. E-mail: mail@campchatuga.com. World Wide Web: http://www.campchatuga.com. Contact by e-mail, fax, mail, phone, or through World Wide Web site. Application deadline: continuous.

THE CITADEL SUMMER CAMP

THE CITADEL, 171 MOULTRIE STREET
CHARLESTON, SOUTH CAROLINA 29409

General Information Structured sports-oriented residential camp for boys and girls ages 10 to 15. Located on the campus of The Citadel, Military College, Charleston, S.C. Approximately 250 campers/3-week section. Established in 1957. 200-acre facility. Features: college campus; boarding center; beach house; full athletic facilities; barracks dormitories.

Profile of Summer Employees Total number: 70; typical ages: 17–23. 85% men; 15% women; 30% high school students; 70% college students; 60% local applicants. Nonsmokers required.

Employment Information Openings are from January 15 to April 15. Jobs available: ▶ 6 *counselor in charge of quarters* (minimum age 19) at $500 per season ▶ 40 *counselors* (minimum age 17) at $850–$1350 per season. Applicants must submit a formal organization application, three personal references, (application available at Web site). An in-person interview is recommended, but a telephone interview is acceptable.

Benefits and Preemployment Training Free housing, free meals, health insurance, willing to provide letters of recommendation, and willing to act as a professional reference. Preemployment training is required and includes accident prevention and safety, first aid, interpersonal skills, leadership skills.

Contact Director, The Citadel Summer Camp, MSC 53-The Citadel, Charleston, South Carolina 29409. Telephone: 843-953-7120. Fax: 843-953-6803. E-mail: summercamp@citadel.edu. World Wide Web: http://www.citadel.edu/summercamp/. Contact by e-mail, fax, mail, or phone. Application deadline: continuous.

THE SOUTHWESTERN COMPANY, SOUTH CAROLINA

See The Southwestern Company on page 302 for complete description.

STUDENT CONSERVATION ASSOCIATION (SCA), SOUTH CAROLINA

See Student Conservation Association (SCA), New Hampshire on page 209 for complete description.

WILD DUNES RESORT

5757 PALM BOULEVARD
ISLE OF PALMS, SOUTH CAROLINA 29451

General Information Resort offering summer recreational programs for all age groups who are guests at the resort. Established in 1976. 1,700-acre facility located 15 miles from Charleston. Features: 2 18-hole golf courses; 17 Har-Tru tennis courts; 20 swimming pools; 3 miles of beach; marina; conference centers.

Profile of Summer Employees Total number: 700; typical ages: 19–24. 30% men; 70% women; 100% college students.

Employment Information Openings are from May 12 to September 10. Spring break and year-round positions also offered. Jobs available: ▶ 16–20 *recreation interns* with CPR certification, driver's license, and at least a junior in college at $200–$250 per month ▶ 1 *tennis intern* at $200–$250 per month. Applicants must submit a formal organization application, letter of interest, resume, three personal references, three letters of recommendation. An in-person interview is recommended, but a telephone interview is acceptable. International applicants accepted; must obtain own visa, obtain own working papers.

Benefits and Preemployment Training Meals at a cost, free housing, formal training, possible full-time employment, willing to provide letters of recommendation, names of contacts, on-the-job training, willing to complete paperwork for educational credit, willing to act as a professional reference, opportunity to attend seminars/workshops, and nationally accredited internship program. Preemployment training is required and includes accident prevention and safety, interpersonal skills, leadership skills.

Contact Kyle Markgraf, Recreation Manager, Wild Dunes Resort, 5757 Palmetto Boulevard, Isle of Palms, South Carolina 29451. Telephone: 843-886-2171. Fax: 843-886-2195. E-mail: kmarkgraf@wilddunes.com. World Wide Web: http://www.wilddunes.com. Contact by e-mail, fax, mail, phone, or through World Wide Web site. Application deadline: continuous.

SOUTH DAKOTA

A CHRISTIAN MINISTRY IN THE NATIONAL PARKS–SOUTH DAKOTA

See A Christian Ministry in the National Parks–Maine on page 122 for complete description.

AMERICAN PRESIDENTS RESORT

HIGHWAY 16A
CUSTER, SOUTH DAKOTA 57730

General Information Resort consisting of cabins, campground, and motel units rented nightly from mid-May to mid-September. Established in 1950. 50-acre facility located 40 miles from

Rapid City. Features: creek; pool/hot tub; volleyball; cabins; RV/tent sites; wooded setting.
Profile of Summer Employees Total number: 20. 20% men; 80% women; 35% high school students; 35% college students; 10% retirees; 50% local applicants. Nonsmokers preferred.
Employment Information Openings are from May 15 to September 15. Jobs available: ▶ 10 *desk clerks* at $5–$6 per hour ▶ 5 *laundry workers* at $6–$7 per hour ▶ 20 *maids* at $5–$6 per hour. International applicants accepted; must obtain own visa, obtain own working papers, apply through a recognized agency.
Benefits and Preemployment Training On-the-job training.
Contact Joan Kirschman, Manager, American Presidents Resort, PO Box 446, Custer, South Dakota 57730. Telephone: 605-673-3373. Fax: 605-673-3449. Contact by fax, mail, or phone. Application deadline: May 1.

CUSTER STATE PARK RESORT COMPANY

HC 83, BOX 74
CUSTER, SOUTH DAKOTA 57730

General Information Operator of 4 resorts offering services such as lodging, dining, groceries, gas, and souvenirs and gifts as well as activities that include trail rides, jeep tours, and cookouts. Established in 1989. 73,000-acre facility located 25 miles from Rapid City. Features: wooded setting; freshwater lakes; hiking trails; buffalo safari jeep tours; guided horseback rides; hayride/ chuckwagon cookouts.
Profile of Summer Employees Total number: 300; typical ages: 18–65. 35% men; 65% women; 15% minorities; 10% high school students; 50% college students; 20% retirees; 1% non-U.S. citizens; 20% local applicants. Nonsmokers preferred.
Employment Information Openings are from May 1 to October 15. Jobs available: ▶ 5 *bartenders* (minimum age 21) at $700–$900 per month ▶ 4–6 *bookkeepers* (minimum age 21) at $900–$1200 per month ▶ 15–25 *cook's assistants* (minimum age 18) at $700–$900 per month ▶ 10 *cooks/chefs* (minimum age 18) with ServSafe certification and experience required at $1000–$2000 per month ▶ 18 *dishwashers/buspersons* (minimum age 16) at $700–$800 per month ▶ 17–20 *front desk/reservations personnel* (minimum age 18) at $750–$950 per month ▶ 5–8 *hosts/hostesses* (minimum age 18) at $800–$900 per month ▶ 50–60 *housekeeping personnel* (minimum age 16) at $700–$850 per month ▶ 5–12 *jeep drivers* (minimum age 21) with clean driving record and CPR certification at $750–$900 per month ▶ 8–25 *kitchen/food preparation personnel* (minimum age 18) at $700–$800 per month ▶ 6–8 *maintenance personnel* (minimum age 21) at $900–$1200 per month ▶ 12 *manager trainees* (minimum age 21) with desire to learn the resort business at $1200–$1400 per month ▶ 35–50 *sales clerks* (minimum age 18) at $700–$900 per month ▶ 45–50 *waitpersons* (minimum age 18) at $600–$750 per month ▶ 8–14 *wranglers* (minimum age 18) at $800–$1000 per month. Applicants must submit formal organization application, resume, three personal references, photo. An in-person interview is recommended, but a telephone interview is acceptable. International applicants accepted; must obtain own visa, obtain own working papers, apply through a recognized agency.
Benefits and Preemployment Training Formal training, possible full-time employment, willing to provide letters of recommendation, on-the-job training, willing to complete paperwork for educational credit, willing to act as a professional reference, opportunity to attend seminars/ workshops, tuition assistance, and room and board are available as part of total compensation package. Preemployment training is required and includes accident prevention and safety, first aid, CPR, specific job training.
Contact Phil Lampert, President, Custer State Park Resort Company, HC 83, Box 74, Custer, South Dakota 57730. Telephone: 605-255-4772. Fax: 605-255-4706. E-mail: e-mail@custerresorts.com. Contact by e-mail, fax, mail, or phone. Application deadline: continuous.

MT. RUSHMORE CONCESSIONS
PO BOX 178
KEYSTONE, SOUTH DAKOTA 57751

General Information Authorized National Park concessionaire. Established in 1951. 25-acre facility located 25 miles from Rapid City. Features: beautiful Black Hills; camping; fishing; hiking; Custer State Park; Badlands National Park.

Profile of Summer Employees Total number: 160; typical ages: 18–70. 50% men; 50% women; 15% minorities; 2% high school students; 80% college students; 20% retirees; 2% non-U.S. citizens. Nonsmokers preferred.

Employment Information Openings are from April 15 to October 15. Jobs available: ▶ 75 *food attendants* (minimum age 18) at $6.25 per hour ▶ 75 *gift shop attendants* (minimum age 18) at $6 per hour. Applicants must submit formal organization application. International applicants accepted; must obtain own visa, obtain own working papers, apply through a recognized agency.

Benefits and Preemployment Training Housing at a cost, meals at a cost, possible full-time employment, on-the-job training, and willing to act as a professional reference. Preemployment training is required and includes accident prevention and safety, interpersonal skills.

Contact Christina McClanahan, Human Resource Manager, Mt. Rushmore Concessions, PO Box 178, Keystone, South Dakota 57751. Telephone: 605-574-2515. Fax: 605-574-2495. E-mail: cmcclanahan@amfaepnr.com. World Wide Web: http://www.coolworks.com/showme/rushmore. Contact by e-mail, fax, mail, phone, or through World Wide Web site. Application deadline: continuous.

THE SOUTHWESTERN COMPANY, SOUTH DAKOTA
See The Southwestern Company on page 302 for complete description.

STUDENT CONSERVATION ASSOCIATION (SCA), SOUTH DAKOTA
See Student Conservation Association (SCA), New Hampshire on page 209 for complete description.

TENNESSEE

A CHRISTIAN MINISTRY IN THE NATIONAL PARKS–TENNESSEE
See A Christian Ministry in the National Parks–Maine on page 122 for complete description.

CAMP NAKANAWA
1084 CAMP NAKANAWA ROAD
CROSSVILLE, TENNESSEE 38571-2146

General Information For profit, private organization offering a variety of sports and activities to help young ladies gain confidence and reach their potential in a positive and fun-filled natural environment. Established in 1920. 1,200-acre facility located near Nashville. Features: freshwater lake, 150 acres; 11 tennis courts; wooded setting; 24 horses owned by camp; climbing tower with zipline; 6-10 person war canoes.

Profile of Summer Employees Total number: 120; typical age: 19. 3% men; 97% women; 80%

college students; 14% retirees; 6% non-U.S. citizens. Nonsmokers preferred.

Employment Information Openings are from June 9 to July 28. Jobs available: ▶ 100 *general counselors and activity instructors* (minimum age 18) love of children and experience in one or more activities offered at $200–$250 per week ▶ 1 *head counselor/instructor for glee club and drama* (minimum age 20) play piano, organize, and produce musical performance at $300–$400 per week. Applicants must submit formal organization application, three personal references. An in-person interview is recommended, but a telephone interview is acceptable. International applicants accepted; must apply through a recognized agency.

Benefits and Preemployment Training Free housing, free meals, willing to provide letters of recommendation, on-the-job training, willing to complete paperwork for educational credit, willing to act as a professional reference, and opportunity to attend seminars/workshops. Preemployment training is required and includes accident prevention and safety, interpersonal skills, leadership skills, climbing wall certification class.

Contact Ann Perron, Owner/Director, Camp Nakanawa. Telephone: 931-277-3711. E-mail: campnalc@tnaccess.com. Contact by e-mail, mail, or phone. Application deadline: continuous.

CHEROKEE ADVENTURES WHITEWATER RAFTING

2000 JONESBOROUGH ROAD
ERWIN, TENNESSEE 37650-9524

General Information Guided rafting and mountain-biking trips; also ropes course emphasizing team building and camping. Established in 1979. 50-acre facility located 17 miles from Johnson City. Features: located on a river; wooded setting; volleyball courts.

Profile of Summer Employees Total number: 35–40; typical ages: 21–25. 60% men; 40% women; 40% college students; 2% non-U.S. citizens; 58% local applicants. Nonsmokers preferred.

Employment Information Openings are from May to October. Year-round positions also offered. Jobs available: ▶ 1–2 *cook* (minimum age 18) with prior experience as a line or grill cook for 6 months minimum at $6–$8.50 per hour ▶ 1–2 *dishwasher* (minimum age 18) at $5.25–$6.50 per hour ▶ 1–4 *food prep, cooks/cleaning staff members* (minimum age 19) with ability to prepare lunches and perform general cleaning at $5.25–$6.50 per hour ▶ 1–3 *raft guides* (minimum age 18) with responsible, outgoing personalities and Red Cross first aid/CPR certification (salary begins after training completed) at $400–$600 per month ▶ 3 *reservationists/general office personnel* (minimum age 19) with good phone manner and the ability to type 40 wpm at $5.25–$6.50 per hour ▶ 1–3 *servers/waitstaff* (minimum age 18) at $2.35 per hour plus tips with a minimum of $5.15. Applicants must submit a formal organization application, three personal references. International applicants accepted; must obtain own visa, obtain own working papers.

Benefits and Preemployment Training Housing at a cost, meals at a cost, willing to provide letters of recommendation, on-the-job training, and willing to act as a professional reference. Preemployment training is optional and includes first aid, CPR, leadership skills.

Contact Dennis I. Nedelman, President, Cherokee Adventures Whitewater Rafting, 2000 Jonesborough Road, Erwin, Tennessee 37650-9524. Telephone: 423-743-7733. Fax: 423-743-5400. E-mail: ca2raft@usit.net. Contact by e-mail, fax, mail, or phone. Application deadline: continuous.

GIRL SCOUT CAMP SYCAMORE HILLS

2020 GIRL SCOUT ROAD
ASHLAND CITY, TENNESSEE 37015

General Information ACA-accredited residential camp serving 175 girls per session with swimming, canoeing, archery, arts and crafts, ropes and rappelling, horseback programs, and trip and travel programs. Established in 1912. 742-acre facility located 35 miles from Nashville. Features: equestrian center; high ropes course; rappel bluffs; pool; creek with canoeing; arts and crafts facility.

Profile of Summer Employees Total number: 62; typical ages: 18–23. 1% men; 99% women; 85% college students; 10% local applicants. Nonsmokers preferred.

Employment Information Openings are from May 30 to July 25. Jobs available: ▶ *CIT director* (minimum age 20) female with previous resident camp experience (preferred); ability to work with teenagers and to provide positive leadership experiences at $175–$225 per week ▶ 1 *administrative assistant* (minimum age 16) at $100–$150 per week ▶ 1 *archery counselor* (minimum age 18) with archery or target sports experience as a participant or facilitator (preferred); ability to manage a safe archery program (certification training available) at $150–$200 per week ▶ 1 *arts and crafts counselor* (minimum age 17) with experience in the field preferred at $150–$200 per week ▶ 1 *business manager* (minimum age 21) with valid driver's license and money management skills at $250–$300 per week ▶ 1 *canoe counselor* (minimum age 18) female with canoe experience (certification course provided) at $150–$200 per week ▶ *cooks* (minimum age 18) at $250–$300 per week ▶ 8 *equestrian counselors* (minimum age 18) with experience in the field and CHA certification (training available) at $150–$200 per week ▶ 1 *food supervisor* (minimum age 21) with food management experience at $400–$800 per week ▶ 1 *healthcare assistant* (minimum age 18) female with first aid and CPR certification; nursing students or experienced healthcare professional (preferred) at $200–$300 per week ▶ 1 *healthcare supervisor* (minimum age 21) female with RN or EMT certification (preferred); nursing students considered; valid driver's license at $400–$700 per week ▶ *kitchen staff* (minimum age 16) with ability to lift 25 pounds; no experience required at $200–$275 per week ▶ 1 *music counselor* (minimum age 19) female with appreciation of music, dance, and theatre at $150–$225 per week ▶ 1 *nature counselor* (minimum age 19) female with appreciation of nature at $150–$225 per week ▶ 1 *program director* (minimum age 21) with valid driver's license; supervisory and camp experience required at $250–$300 per week ▶ 1 *ropes counselor* (minimum age 18) with high/low ropes and rappelling experience as participant or facilitator (preferred) at $150–$200 per week ▶ 1 *ropes director* (minimum age 20) with experience as participant or supervisor required; ability to keep record and coordinate weekly schedules; supervisory experience preferred; training available at $175–$225 per week ▶ 25 *unit counselors* (minimum age 17) female with ability to assume responsibility for daily safety, entertainment and care of campers at $150–$200 per week ▶ 9 *unit leaders* (minimum age 19) female with ability to supervise, keep schedules, provide safe, fun, timely activities at $175–$225 per week ▶ 3 *waterfront counselors* (minimum age 16) female with lifeguard certification (training available) at $150–$200 per week ▶ 1 *waterfront director* (minimum age 19) female with lifeguard and WSI certification (training available for experienced swimmers); supervisory experience (preferred); ability to keep records and coordinate weekly schedules; must have pool maintenance and lifeguarding experience at $175–$225 per week. Applicants must submit formal organization application, three personal references. An in-person interview is recommended, but a telephone interview is acceptable. International applicants accepted; must apply through a recognized agency.

Benefits and Preemployment Training Free housing, free meals, willing to provide letters of recommendation, on-the-job training, willing to complete paperwork for educational credit, willing to act as a professional reference, and accident insurance. Preemployment training is required and includes accident prevention and safety, first aid, CPR, interpersonal skills, leadership skills.

Contact Amy Reesman, Camp Director, Girl Scout Camp Sycamore Hills, 2020 Girl Scout Road, Ashland City, Tennessee 37015. Telephone: 800-395-5318. Fax: 615-792-7395. E-mail: gscouts@edge.net. Contact by e-mail, fax, mail, or phone. Application deadline: continuous.

GIRL SCOUT CAMP TANNASSIE

ROUTE 4, BOX 4174
TULLAHOMA, TENNESSEE 37388

General Information Residential summer camp where girls enjoy swimming, canoeing, sailing, waterskiing, snorkeling, arts and crafts, and traditional Girl Scout programs. Established in 1912.

37-acre facility located 60 miles from Chattanooga. Features: freshwater lake.

Profile of Summer Employees Total number: 12; typical ages: 18–23. 100% women; 90% college students; 5% non-U.S. citizens; 5% local applicants. Nonsmokers preferred.

Employment Information Openings are from June 13 to July 31. Jobs available: ▶ *business manager* (minimum age 21) female with money management skills and valid driver's license at $250–$300 per week ▶ *camp director* female with experience in youth camping and camp program, especially waterfront at $400–$500 per week ▶ *food service manager* with previous food experience and ability to lift 25 pounds at $300–$500 per week ▶ *health care manager* must be currently enrolled in nursing school or an EMT, with first aid and CPR training; experience with children and young adults (preferred) at $300–$400 per week ▶ *program specialists* female with team adventure experience and archery experience as participant or facilitator (preferred); ability to manage a safe archery range (training/certification provided); experience with camp crafts at $175–$225 per week ▶ 1 *sailing instructor* female with certification (preferred) and experience at $150–$200 per week ▶ *small craft instructor* female with certification (preferred), and experience at $150–$200 per week ▶ *unit counselors* female with ability to assume responsibility for daily safety, entertainment, and care of campers at $150–$200 per week ▶ *unit leaders* female with ability to supervise, keep schedules, provide safe, fun, timely activities at $175–$225 per week ▶ *waterfront counselors* (minimum age 19) female with certification; comfortable supervising lake, staff, and campers during free swim, water skiing, and tubing at $150–$200 per week ▶ 1 *waterfront director* female with certification and experience at $175–$225 per week. Applicants must submit formal organization application, three personal references. An in-person interview is recommended, but a telephone interview is acceptable. International applicants accepted; must apply through a recognized agency.

Benefits and Preemployment Training Free housing, free meals, health insurance, willing to provide letters of recommendation, on-the-job training, willing to complete paperwork for educational credit, willing to act as a professional reference, and accident insurance. Preemployment training is required and includes accident prevention and safety, first aid, CPR, interpersonal skills, leadership skills.

Contact Amy Reesman, Camp Director, Girl Scout Camp Tannassie, 2020 Girl Scout Road, Ashland City, Tennessee 37015. Telephone: 800-395-5318. Fax: 615-792-7395. E-mail: gscouts@edge.net. Contact by e-mail, fax, mail, or phone. Application deadline: continuous.

THE SOUTHWESTERN COMPANY

2451 ATRIUM WAY
NASHVILLE, TENNESSEE 37214

General Information Summer work program for college students selling educational books and software. Positions as independent contractors are available in all 50 states. Established in 1855.

Profile of Summer Employees Total number: 750; typical ages: 18–24. 55% men; 45% women; 100% college students.

Employment Information Openings are from April 25 to October 1. Jobs available: ▶ 4000 *sales-dealer in Southwestern products* (minimum age 18) must be relocatable and have summer free; commission salary. Applicants must submit Signed Dealer Agreement and Letter of Credit. An in-person interview is required. International applicants accepted; must obtain own visa, apply through a recognized agency.

Benefits and Preemployment Training Formal training, possible full-time employment, willing to provide letters of recommendation, on-the-job training, willing to complete paperwork for educational credit, willing to act as a professional reference, and opportunity to attend seminars/workshops. Preemployment training is required and includes accident prevention and safety, interpersonal skills, leadership skills.

Contact Trey Campbell, Public Relations and Sales Promotional Manager, The Southwestern Company. Telephone: 615-391-2801. Fax: 615-391-2703. E-mail: trey.campbell@southwestern.

com. World Wide Web: http://www.southwestern.com. Contact by e-mail or phone. Application deadline: June 15.

STUDENT CONSERVATION ASSOCIATION (SCA), TENNESSEE

See Student Conservation Association (SCA), New Hampshire on page 209 for complete description.

TEXAS

A CHRISTIAN MINISTRY IN THE NATIONAL PARKS–TEXAS

See A Christian Ministry in the National Parks–Maine on page 122 for complete description.

ASTRO-ART AMUSEMENTS

9603 PENNINGTON LANE
MISSOURI CITY, TEXAS 77459

General Information Operates face-painting, hair-wraps, temporary tattoos, painted-parasols, caricature, and other concessions at major theme parks in Texas. Established in 1982. 200-acre facility located near Houston. Features: Six Flags Over Texas; Six Flags Houston; Six Flags Fiesta Texas; rides; thrills; fun.

Profile of Summer Employees Total number: 60; typical ages: 16–26. 50% men; 50% women; 50% minorities; 40% high school students; 40% college students; 5% retirees; 2% non-U.S. citizens; 13% local applicants.

Employment Information Openings are from February 1 to October 1. Spring break and year-round positions also offered. Jobs available: ▶ 15–20 *"name on rice" jewelry vendor* (minimum age 16) with ability to write on a grain of rice in clean, concise printing at 26-30% of sales and profitshare/bonus ▶ 5–10 *balloon vendors* (minimum age 16) with superior interpersonal skills, smiles at 26-30% of sales and profitshare/bonus ▶ 15–20 *face-painters and caricaturists* (minimum age 16) with artistic skills at 26-30% of sales and profit share/bonus ▶ 15–20 *hair-wraps* (minimum age 16) with skillful and strong fingers at 26-30% of sales and profit share/bonus. Applicants must submit a formal organization application, portfolio, two personal references, proof of age, proof of eligibility to work in the United States. An in-person interview is required. International applicants accepted; must obtain own visa, obtain own working papers.

Benefits and Preemployment Training Meals at a cost, formal training, possible full-time employment, willing to provide letters of recommendation, on-the-job training, willing to complete paperwork for educational credit, willing to act as a professional reference, opportunity to attend seminars/workshops, and Six Flags seasonal employee benefits/tickets. Preemployment training is required and includes accident prevention and safety, interpersonal skills, leadership skills, artistic development and training.

Contact David Jennings, Owner, Astro-Art Amusements, 9001 Kirby Drive, Retail Department, Houston, Texas 77054. E-mail: djennings@entouchonline.net. Contact by e-mail or mail. Application deadline: continuous.

AUSTIN NATURE AND SCIENCE CENTER

301 NATURE CENTER DRIVE
AUSTIN, TEXAS 78746

General Information Living museum with 150 orphaned/injured animals and a focus on outdoor/environmental education including recycling, plants, animals, astronomy, caving, climbing, canoeing, archery, aquatic studies and swimming. Established in 1962. 80-acre facility. Features: pond; animals; 70 acres hiking preserve; on major Austin lake; swimming in local springs; central to many state parks.

Profile of Summer Employees Total number: 41; typical ages: 18–30. 13% men; 87% women; 10% minorities; 100% college students.

Employment Information Openings are from May 15 to August 9. Jobs available: ▶ 24 *summer counselors* (minimum age 18) with desire to work with children at $6.56 per hour. Applicants must submit a formal organization application, three personal references. An in-person interview is recommended, but a telephone interview is acceptable.

Benefits and Preemployment Training Possible full-time employment, willing to provide letters of recommendation, on-the-job training, willing to complete paperwork for educational credit, and willing to act as a professional reference. Preemployment training is required and includes accident prevention and safety, first aid, CPR, interpersonal skills, leadership skills, animal handling, driving safety.

Contact Shannon Kennedy, Public Programs Coordinator, Austin Nature and Science Center. Telephone: 512-327-8181. Fax: 512-327-8745. E-mail: shannon.kennedy@ci.austin.tx.us. World Wide Web: http://www.cityofaustin.org/nature-science. Contact by e-mail, mail, or phone. Application deadline: continuous.

CAMP BALCONES SPRINGS

104 BALCONES SPRINGS DRIVE
MARBLE FALLS, TEXAS 78654

General Information Christian residential camp offering sports, ropes course, outdoor, fine arts, and water sports to 230 young boys and girls ages 8–15 every week in the Texas hill country. Established in 1993. 300-acre facility located 45 miles from Austin. Features: one mile of lakefront; 10-acre private lake; 140-acre wilderness; air-conditioned cabins; wooded hills; abundant wildlife.

Profile of Summer Employees Total number: 120; typical ages: 19–23. 50% men; 50% women; 6% minorities; 2% non-U.S. citizens; 2% local applicants. Nonsmokers required.

Employment Information Openings are from May 25 to August 15. Jobs available: ▶ *archery/riflery instructors* with NRA and NAA certification and experience in the field at $1450–$1500 per season ▶ *arts and crafts instructors* with art background at $1450–$1500 per season ▶ *backpacking staff* with strong wilderness experience and one year of college or equivalent at $1450–$1500 per season ▶ *cabin leaders* at $1450–$1500 per season ▶ *horseback instructors* with English or Western riding experience at $1450–$1500 per season ▶ *mountain climbing staff* with climbing experience (free or sport) and one year of college or equivalent at $1450–$1500 per season ▶ *sailing/windsurfing instructors* with experience at $1450–$1500 per season ▶ *sports instructors* with strong experience in particular specialty sport required at $1450–$1500 per season ▶ *swimming instructors* with WSI and lifeguarding experience at $1450–$1500 per season. Applicants must submit a formal organization application, three personal references. An in-person interview is recommended, but a telephone interview is acceptable. International applicants accepted; must obtain own visa.

Benefits and Preemployment Training Free housing, free meals, formal training, and on-the-job training. Preemployment training is required and includes accident prevention and safety, first aid, CPR, interpersonal skills, leadership skills, specialized departmental training.

Contact Brian Manhart, Assistant Director, Camp Balcones Springs, 104 Balcones Springs Drive, Marble Falls, Texas 78654. Telephone: 800-485-5151. Fax: 830-693-6478. E-mail:

bmanhart@campbalconessprings.com. World Wide Web: http://www.campbalconessprings.com. Contact by e-mail, fax, mail, or phone. Application deadline: March 15.

CAMP FERN

1046 CAMP ROAD
MARSHALL, TEXAS 75672-1411

General Information Residential camp providing fun, adventure, learning, self-esteem development, and lasting friendships. Established in 1934. 100-acre facility. Located 9 miles from . Features: lake; wooded setting; log cabins; English horseback riding; Red Cross swimming; water skiing; tennis; golf; archery; riflery; trampoline; nature; campcrafts; team sports.

Profile of Summer Employees Total number: 75; typical age: 19. 50% men; 50% women; 100% college students. Nonsmokers required.

Employment Information Openings are from May 26 to August 10. Jobs available: ▶ *tennis staff members* at $125–$150 per week ▶ *waterfront staff members* with WSI, lifeguard, and CPR certification at $125–$150 per week. Applicants must submit a formal organization application, resume. An in-person interview is recommended, but a telephone interview is acceptable. International applicants accepted; must obtain own visa, obtain own working papers.

Benefits and Preemployment Training Free housing, free meals, on-the-job training, and laundry facilities. Preemployment training is required and includes accident prevention and safety, interpersonal skills, leadership skills.

Contact Margaret R. Thompson, Director, Camp Fern, 1040 Camp Road, Marshall, Texas 75672-1411. Telephone: 903-935-5420. Fax: 903-935-6372. E-mail: info@campfern.com. World Wide Web: http://www.campfern.com. Contact by e-mail, fax, mail, phone, or through World Wide Web site. Application deadline: April 1.

CAMP LA JUNTA

HIGHWAY 39 WEST
HUNT, TEXAS 78024

General Information Private residential camp with a focus on individual lifetime activities serving 200 boys in 2- or 4-week terms. Established in 1928. 200-acre facility located 75 miles from San Antonio. Features: spring-fed river; modern stone cabins; hill country setting.

Profile of Summer Employees Total number: 75; typical ages: 17–25. 90% men; 10% women; 5% minorities; 100% college students; 5% non-U.S. citizens; 25% local applicants. Nonsmokers required.

Employment Information Openings are from June 1 to August 5. Jobs available: ▶ *junior counselors* (minimum age 18) at $500–$650 per month ▶ *senior counselors* (minimum age 20) at $650–$750 per month. Applicants must submit formal organization application, three personal references. An in-person interview is recommended, but a telephone interview is acceptable. International applicants accepted; must apply through a recognized agency.

Benefits and Preemployment Training Free housing, free meals, formal training, health insurance, willing to provide letters of recommendation, on-the-job training, willing to complete paperwork for educational credit, willing to act as a professional reference, and travel reimbursement.

Contact Blake W. Smith, Director, Camp La Junta, PO Box 136, Hunt, Texas 78024. Telephone: 830-238-4621. Fax: 830-238-4888. E-mail: lajunta@ktc.com. World Wide Web: http://www.lajunta.com. Contact by e-mail, fax, mail, phone, or through World Wide Web site. Application deadline: continuous.

CAMP LOMA LINDA FOR GIRLS

MO RANCH, HC 1, BOX 158
HUNT, TEXAS 78024

General Information Residential camp serving girls ages 10-15 in two 3-week sessions. Established in 1977. 434-acre facility located 80 miles from San Antonio. Features: freshwater

river; dormitory housing; Christian camp; water slide; horseback riding; nature studies.
Profile of Summer Employees Total number: 120; typical ages: 18–28. 50% men; 50% women; 10% high school students; 85% college students; 5% local applicants. Nonsmokers preferred.
Employment Information Openings are from May 31 to September 6. Year-round positions also offered. Jobs available: ▶ 6–12 *counselors/instructors* (minimum age 21) with Christian faith at $1000–$1500 per month. Applicants must submit formal organization application, resume, two personal references. An in-person interview is recommended, but a telephone interview is acceptable. International applicants accepted; must obtain own visa, obtain own working papers, apply through a recognized agency.
Benefits and Preemployment Training Free housing, free meals, possible full-time employment, willing to provide letters of recommendation, on-the-job training, willing to complete paperwork for educational credit, and willing to act as a professional reference. Preemployment training is required and includes accident prevention and safety, first aid, CPR, interpersonal skills, leadership skills.
Contact Jami Ferris, Director of Human Resources, Camp Loma Linda for Girls, Route 1, Box 158, Hunt, Texas 78024. Telephone: 800-460-4401. Fax: 830-238-4832. E-mail: hr@moranch.com. World Wide Web: http://www.moranch.com. Contact by e-mail, fax, mail, phone, or through World Wide Web site. Application deadline: continuous.

CAMP RIO VISTA FOR BOYS
HIGHWAY 39 WEST
INGRAM, TEXAS 78025

General Information Private residential camp providing 100–150 boys, ages 6–16, with a fun-filled learning experience in a safe, wholesome environment. Established in 1921. 120-acre facility located 75 miles from San Antonio. Features: river; tennis courts; full-size gym; 3 softball fields; lighted football field; golf course.
Profile of Summer Employees Total number: 45; typical ages: 19–23. 100% men; 5% minorities; 10% high school students; 85% college students; 5% non-U.S. citizens; 2% local applicants. Nonsmokers preferred.
Employment Information Openings are from June 1 to August 2. Jobs available: ▶ 45 *cabin/activity counselors* (minimum age 18) with ability to be good role models and enjoy working with children at $155–$185 per week ▶ 10 *counselors/lifeguards* (minimum age 18) with lifeguard certification at $155–$185 per week ▶ 2 *nurses* with RN/LVN/EMT, experience with children, and field experience at $200–$250 per week. Applicants must submit formal organization application, three personal references, three letters of recommendation. An in-person interview is recommended, but a telephone interview is acceptable. International applicants accepted; must obtain own visa, obtain own working papers, apply through a recognized agency.
Benefits and Preemployment Training Free housing, free meals, formal training, health insurance, willing to provide letters of recommendation, on-the-job training, willing to complete paperwork for educational credit, willing to act as a professional reference, and travel reimbursement. Preemployment training is required and includes accident prevention and safety, first aid, CPR, interpersonal skills, leadership skills, child management, liability management.
Contact Mr. James Rice, Camp Director, Camp Rio Vista for Boys, HCR 78, Box 215, Ingram, Texas 78025. Telephone: 830-367-5353. Fax: 830-367-4044. E-mail: riovista@ktc.com. World Wide Web: http://www.vistacamps.com. Contact by e-mail, fax, mail, phone, or through World Wide Web site. Application deadline: May 10.

CAMP SIERRA VISTA FOR GIRLS
HIGHWAY 39 WEST
INGRAM, TEXAS 78025

General Information Private residential camp for girls ages 6–16. Provides a safe, wholesome, fun-filled, learning experience to 96 girls per term. Established in 1982. 120-acre facility located

75 miles from San Antonio. Features: 3/4 miles of riverfront; game fields; golf course; tennis courts; rock gymnasium; 30 activities.

Profile of Summer Employees Total number: 25; typical ages: 19–23. 100% women; 5% minorities; 10% high school students; 85% college students; 10% non-U.S. citizens; 5% local applicants. Nonsmokers preferred.

Employment Information Openings are from June 1 to August 2. Jobs available: ▶ 20–24 *cabin/activity counselors* (minimum age 18) with the ability to be good role models and who enjoy working with children at $155–$185 per week ▶ 2 *nurses* with LVN, RN, or EMT certification, experience with children, and field experience at $200–$250 per week ▶ 2 *office staff members* (minimum age 18) with good organizational skills and good telephone skills at $155–$185 per week ▶ 2 *swimming instructors* (minimum age 18) with lifeguard certification at $155–$185 per week. Applicants must submit formal organization application, three personal references, three letters of recommendation. An in-person interview is recommended, but a telephone interview is acceptable. International applicants accepted; must obtain own visa, obtain own working papers, apply through a recognized agency.

Benefits and Preemployment Training Free housing, free meals, formal training, health insurance, willing to provide letters of recommendation, on-the-job training, willing to complete paperwork for educational credit, willing to act as a professional reference, and travel reimbursement. Preemployment training is required and includes accident prevention and safety, first aid, CPR, interpersonal skills, leadership skills, child management, liability management.

Contact James Rice, Camp Director, Camp Sierra Vista for Girls, HCR 78, Box 215, Ingram, Texas 78025. Telephone: 830-367-5353. Fax: 830-367-4044. E-mail: riovista@ktc.com. World Wide Web: http://www.vistacamps.com. Contact by e-mail, fax, mail, phone, or through World Wide Web site. Application deadline: May 10.

CAMP STEWART FOR BOYS

HC 1, BOX 110
HUNT, TEXAS 78024-9714

General Information Traditional camp offering a fun, challenging program to 250 boys for fourteen- to twenty-eight-day programs. 522-acre facility located 65 miles from San Antonio.

Profile of Summer Employees 90% men; 10% women; 10% minorities; 86% college students; 10% non-U.S. citizens; 2% local applicants.

Employment Information Openings are from May 17 to August 17. Jobs available: ▶ 2 *archery instructors* with one year of college completed at $2000–$2500 per season ▶ 1 *band leader* with one year of college completed at $2000–$2500 per season ▶ 2 *challenge course instructors* with certification in field and one year of college completed at $2000–$2500 per season ▶ 2 *crafts instructors* with one year of college completed at $2000–$2500 per season ▶ 24 *general counselors* with leadership ability, good moral character, and one year of college completed at $2000–$2500 per season ▶ 12 *kitchen personnel* at $2000–$3000 per season ▶ 10 *riding instructors* with ability to take clinic at Stewart (required) and one year of college completed at $2000–$2500 per season ▶ 2 *riflery instructors* with NRA certification (may obtain at camp) and one year of college completed at $2000–$2500 per season ▶ 3 *rock climbing instructors* with certification in field (may obtain at camp) and one year of college completed at $2000–$2500 per season ▶ 2 *secretaries* with one year of college completed at $2000–$2500 per season ▶ 4 *sports personnel* with one year of college completed at $2000–$2500 per season ▶ 8 *swimming instructors* with WSI certification (may obtain at camp) and one year of college completed at $2000–$2500 per season ▶ 4 *tennis instructors* with one year of college completed at $2000–$2500 per season.

Benefits and Preemployment Training Free housing, free meals, health insurance, on-the-job training, and willing to complete paperwork for educational credit. Preemployment training is required and includes accident prevention and safety, first aid, CPR, interpersonal skills, leadership skills.

Contact Kathy C. Ragsdale, Co-Director, Camp Stewart for Boys, HC1, Box 110, Hunt, Texas 78024-9714. Telephone: 830-238-4670. Fax: 830-238-4737. E-mail: info@campstewart.com. World Wide Web: http://www.campstewart.com. Contact by e-mail, fax, mail, phone, or through World Wide Web site. Application deadline: April 1.

CAMP SUMMIT, INC.

ARGYLE, TEXAS

General Information A camp for children and adults with disabilities. Established in 1991.
Profile of Summer Employees Total number: 150.
Employment Information Openings are from May to August. Jobs available: ▶ 40 *camp counselors* with desire to work with people with disabilities at $150 per week ▶ 2 *challenge course activity directors* with Camp Summit course certification and experience working with development of personal goals through challenge center at $150 per week ▶ 2 *lifeguards* with WSI or other certification, knowledge of pool management, and ability to work with all ages at $150 per week ▶ 1 *nurse* with CPR/first aid certification, registered nurse experience working with diabetes and disabilities at $720 per week. Applicants must submit formal organization application, three personal references. An in-person interview is recommended, but a telephone interview is acceptable. International applicants accepted; must apply through a recognized agency.
Benefits and Preemployment Training Free housing, free meals, and laundry facilities. Preemployment training is required and includes accident prevention and safety, interpersonal skills, leadership skills.
Contact Brad Saxman, Assistant Camp Director, Camp Summit, Inc., 2915 LBJ Freeway, Suite 185, Dallas, Texas 75234. Telephone: 972-484-8900. Fax: 972-620-1945. World Wide Web: http://www.campsummittx.org. Contact by mail or through World Wide Web site. Application deadline: continuous.

CAMP WALDEMAR FOR GIRLS

HC 1, BOX 120
HUNT, TEXAS 78024

General Information Private residential skill-building girls camp offering sports, arts, and drama activities for girls ages 9 to 16. Established in 1926. 560-acre facility located 60 miles from San Antonio. Features: beautiful river; trees and hills; 8 tennis courts; 85 horses; buildings/cabins made of rock, tile, and cedar; 45 cabins.
Profile of Summer Employees Total number: 500; typical ages: 17–99. 100% women; 10% minorities; 2% high school students; 80% college students; 2% retirees; 2% non-U.S. citizens; 2% local applicants. Nonsmokers preferred.
Employment Information Openings are from May 27 to August 11. Jobs available: ▶ 5 *arts and crafts (ceramics, jewelry, and weaving) staff members* (minimum age 18) with ability to teach at $450–$700 per month ▶ 2 *fencing staff members* (minimum age 18) with college team playing experience and ability to teach at $450–$700 per month ▶ 5 *gymnastics staff members* (minimum age 18) with team experience at $450–$700 per month ▶ *nurse* ▶ 10 *riding teachers or wranglers* (minimum age 15) with English or Western equitation horsemanship and ability to teach or wrangle at $450–$700 per month ▶ 4–6 *rifle staff members* (minimum age 18) with ability to teach at $450–$700 per month ▶ 21 *swimming staff members* (minimum age 18) at $450–$700 per month ▶ 6 *tennis staff members* (minimum age 18) with varsity high school or college experience and ability to teach at $450–$700 per month. Applicants must submit formal organization application, three personal references. An in-person interview is recommended, but a telephone interview is acceptable. International applicants accepted; must apply through a recognized agency.
Benefits and Preemployment Training Free housing, free meals, formal training, willing to provide letters of recommendation, names of contacts, on-the-job training, willing to complete

paperwork for educational credit, willing to act as a professional reference, and travel reimbursement. Preemployment training is required and includes accident prevention and safety, first aid, CPR, interpersonal skills, leadership skills, lifeguarding, rifle instruction, and archery instruction.
Contact Meg Clark, Owner/Director, Camp Waldemar for Girls, HC 1, Box 120, Hunt, Texas 78024. Telephone: 830-238-4821. Fax: 830-238-4051. E-mail: info@waldemar.com. World Wide Web: http://www.waldemar.com. Contact by e-mail, fax, mail, or phone. Application deadline: continuous.

CYBERCAMPS–SOUTHERN METHODIST UNIVERSITY
DALLAS, TEXAS
See Cybercamps–University of Washington on page 335 for complete description.

CYBERCAMPS–UT AUSTIN
AUSTIN, TEXAS
See Cybercamps–University of Washington on page 335 for complete description.

KICKAPOO KAMP
216 HUMMINGBIRD LANE
KERRVILLE, TEXAS 78028
General Information Kickapoo Kamp is a private residential girls summer camp providing the following activities: horseback riding, water skiing, gymnastics, arts and crafts, cheerleading, riflery, archery, tennis, ping pong, tae-bo, fishing, drama, canoeing, flags, and aerobic dance. Established in 1925. 300-acre facility located 60 miles from San Antonio. Features: Texas hill country; spring-fed creek with lake; rustic cabins with individual bathrooms; horseback riding program (30 horses); lodge for dining; 2 open buildings for activities.
Profile of Summer Employees Total number: 26; typical ages: 18–23. 100% women; 100% college students. Nonsmokers preferred.
Employment Information Openings are from June 5 to August 3. Jobs available: ▶ 23 *staff counselors* (minimum age 18) must be able to teach an activity at $150 per week. Applicants must submit a formal organization application, three personal references, background check. An in-person interview is recommended, but a telephone interview is acceptable.
Benefits and Preemployment Training Free housing, free meals, willing to provide letters of recommendation, and willing to act as a professional reference. Preemployment training is required and includes accident prevention and safety, first aid, CPR, interpersonal skills, leadership skills.
Contact Laura Hodges, Director, Kickapoo Kamp, 10310 Quail Meadow, San Antonio, Texas 78230. Telephone: 210-690-8361. Fax: 210-690-5731. E-mail: hodges@kickapookamp.com. World Wide Web: http://www.kickapookamp.com. Contact by mail, phone, or through World Wide Web site. Application deadline: continuous.

LONGHORN TENNIS CAMP
IAW BELLMONT 718
AUSTIN, TEXAS 78712-1286
General Information Coed tennis camp for juniors ages 10–17. Provides group instruction, video tape analysis of strokes, mental and physical conditioning, private lessons, and team competition. Established in 1986. Features: 12 tennis courts; location at the University of Texas; directed by University of Texas men's and women's tennis coaches; 6 hours of tennis per day; additional recreational activities.
Profile of Summer Employees Total number: 20; typical age: 19. 60% men; 40% women; 50% college students. Nonsmokers required.
Employment Information Openings are from May to July. Jobs available: ▶ *tennis instructors/*

counselors (minimum age 19) with collegiate tennis and tennis teaching experience (physical education background, CPR, and first aid helpful) at $250–$300 per week. Applicants must submit a formal organization application, letter of interest, three personal references. An in-person interview is recommended, but a telephone interview is acceptable.
Benefits and Preemployment Training Free housing, free meals, on-the-job training, willing to complete paperwork for educational credit, and willing to act as a professional reference. Preemployment training is required and includes tennis teaching techniques.
Contact Bob Haugen, Coordinator, Longhorn Tennis Camp, IAW Bellmont 718, Austin, Texas 78712-1286. Telephone: 512-471-4404. Fax: 512-471-0794. E-mail: bhaugen@mail.utexas.edu. Contact by e-mail. Application deadline: continuous.

MO-RANCH SUMMER CAMPS
HC 1, BOX 158
HUNT, TEXAS 78024
General Information Residential camp serving boys and girls ages 8–16 in 1, 2, and 3-week sessions. Established in 1979. 434-acre facility located 80 miles from San Antonio. Features: freshwater river; water slide; dormitory; Christian camp; nature studies; horseback riding.
Profile of Summer Employees Total number: 20; typical ages: 18–24. 25% men; 75% women; 20% minorities; 100% college students. Nonsmokers required.
Employment Information Openings are from May 26 to August 6. Jobs available: ▶ 6–12 *counselors/instructors* (minimum age 18) with Christian faith at $150–$175 per week. Applicants must submit formal organization application, resume, three personal references. An in-person interview is recommended, but a telephone interview is acceptable. International applicants accepted; must obtain own visa, obtain own working papers, apply through a recognized agency.
Benefits and Preemployment Training Free housing, free meals, possible full-time employment, willing to provide letters of recommendation, on-the-job training, willing to complete paperwork for educational credit, willing to act as a professional reference, and travel reimbursement. Preemployment training is required and includes accident prevention and safety, first aid, CPR, interpersonal skills, leadership skills.
Contact Jami Ferris, Director of Human Resources, Mo-Ranch Summer Camps, HC 1, Box 158, Hunt, Texas 78024. Telephone: 800-460-4401. Fax: 830-238-4202. E-mail: hr@moranch.com. World Wide Web: http://www.moranch.com. Contact by e-mail, fax, mail, phone, or through World Wide Web site. Application deadline: continuous.

THE SOUTHWESTERN COMPANY, TEXAS
See The Southwestern Company on page 302 for complete description.

SPORTS INTERNATIONAL–COWBOYS
COMMERCE, TEXAS
See Sports International, Inc. on page 147 for complete description.

STUDENT CONSERVATION ASSOCIATION (SCA), TEXAS
See Student Conservation Association (SCA), New Hampshire on page 209 for complete description.

TAG/SOUTHERN METHODIST UNIVERSITY
PO BOX 750383
DALLAS, TEXAS 75275
General Information TAG is an academic, residential program for academically-able middle school students. Established in 1978. Features: beautiful campus; located in Dallas; air conditioned facilities; large library system.

Profile of Summer Employees Total number: 15; typical ages: 19–23. 50% men; 50% women; 100% college students. Nonsmokers preferred.

Employment Information Openings are from July 1 to August 1. Jobs available: ▶ 10–20 *residential assistants* (minimum age 19) at $700 per month. Applicants must submit a formal organization application, two personal references, two letters of recommendation. A telephone interview is required. International applicants accepted; must obtain own visa, obtain own working papers.

Benefits and Preemployment Training Free housing and free meals. Preemployment training is required and includes accident prevention and safety, first aid, interpersonal skills, leadership skills.

Contact Marilyn Swanson, Assistant Director, TAG/Southern Methodist University. Fax: 214-768-3147. E-mail: gifted@smu.edu. World Wide Web: http://www.smu.edu/tag. Contact by e-mail. Application deadline: April 1.

WESTERN PLAYLAND AMUSEMENT PARK

6900 DELTA
EL PASO, TEXAS 79905

General Information Amusement park with more than 30 rides, games, concession stands, and other attractions catering to families, school children, and corporations in the area. Established in 1960. 15-acre facility located 700 miles from Dallas. Features: roller coaster; 2 flume rides; racetrack and go-carts; kiddie area; 2 corporate party pavilions; 2 water slides.

Profile of Summer Employees Total number: 120–135; typical ages: 16–20. 50% men; 50% women; 98% minorities; 95% high school students; 5% college students; 25% non-U.S. citizens; 100% local applicants. Nonsmokers required.

Employment Information Openings are from March 1 to October 1. Year-round positions also offered. Jobs available: ▶ 100 *seasonal employees* (minimum age 16) at $5.15 per hour (starting wage). Applicants must submit a formal organization application, two personal references. An in-person interview is recommended, but a telephone interview is acceptable. International applicants accepted; must obtain own visa, obtain own working papers.

Benefits and Preemployment Training Formal training, willing to provide letters of recommendation, on-the-job training, and willing to act as a professional reference. Preemployment training is required and includes accident prevention and safety, first aid, interpersonal skills, leadership skills.

Contact Rudy Gandarilla, General Manager, Western Playland Amusement Park, 6900 Delta, El Paso, Texas 79905. Telephone: 915-772-3953 Ext. 16. Fax: 915-778-9821. E-mail: gandar7542@aol.com. World Wide Web: http://www.westernplayland.com. Contact by e-mail, mail, or phone. Application deadline: continuous.

UTAH

A CHRISTIAN MINISTRY IN THE NATIONAL PARKS–UTAH

See A Christian Ministry in the National Parks–Maine on page 122 for complete description.

KOSTOPULOS DREAM FOUNDATION/CAMP K
2500 EMIGRATION CANYON
SALT LAKE CITY, UTAH 84108

General Information Non-profit agency that provides therapeutic recreation and outdoor activities for people of all ages with disabilities. Established in 1967. 25-acre facility. Features: challenge course; horse stables; pool; campsites; fishing pond; teepee.

Profile of Summer Employees Total number: 40; typical ages: 19–24. 30% men; 70% women; 10% minorities; 10% high school students; 90% college students; 5% retirees; 15% non-U.S. citizens; 70% local applicants.

Employment Information Openings are from March 15 to June 15. Jobs available: ▶ 1 *camp cook* with food handlers permit; negotiable salary ▶ 12–20 *summer camp counselors* (minimum age 18) with experience with the disabled, or studying in related field (preferred) at $150–$175 per week. Applicants must submit formal organization application, two letters of recommendation. An in-person interview is recommended, but a telephone interview is acceptable. International applicants accepted; must apply through a recognized agency.

Benefits and Preemployment Training Free housing, free meals, formal training, possible full-time employment, willing to provide letters of recommendation, on-the-job training, willing to complete paperwork for educational credit, and willing to act as a professional reference. Preemployment training is required and includes accident prevention and safety, first aid, CPR, interpersonal skills, leadership skills, food handlers permit.

Contact Kevin McCulley, Program Director, Kostopulos Dream Foundation/Camp K. Telephone: 801-582-0700. Fax: 801-583-5176. E-mail: kevinmcc@campk.org. World Wide Web: http://www.campk.org. Contact by e-mail or phone. Application deadline: applications accepted from January to camp start (end of May).

SNOWBIRD SKI & SUMMER RESORT
7350 WASATCH BOULEVARD
SALT LAKE CITY, UTAH 84121

General Information Year-round ski and summer resort. Established in 1971. 2,500-acre facility located 12 miles from Salt Lake City. Features: cliff lodge/3 other hotels; tram; conference center; hiking; food and beverage restaurants; mountain biking.

Profile of Summer Employees Total number: 1,000; typical ages: 16–35. 60% men; 40% women; 10% minorities; 10% high school students; 30% college students; 50% local applicants.

Employment Information Openings are from January 1 to December 30. Year-round positions also offered. Jobs available: ▶ *banquet staff* at $5.75 per hour plus tips ▶ 15 *food service workers (room servers, buspersons, cooks, waitpersons, and dishwashers)* at salaries that vary depending on position ▶ *hotel staff (housekeepers, concierge, and desk manager)* at $5.25–$9 per hour. Applicants must submit formal organization application. An in-person interview is recommended, but a telephone interview is acceptable. International applicants accepted; must obtain own visa, obtain own working papers, apply through a recognized agency.

Benefits and Preemployment Training Meals at a cost, possible full-time employment, willing to complete paperwork for educational credit, and ski pass, EAP, transportation (bus). Preemployment training is required.

Contact Recruiting Office, Snowbird Ski & Summer Resort. Telephone: 801-947-8240. Fax: 801-947-8244. E-mail: employment@snowbird.com. World Wide Web: http://www.snowbird.com. Contact by e-mail, mail, phone, or through World Wide Web site. Application deadline: please see Web site for open position notification.

THE SOUTHWESTERN COMPANY, UTAH
See The Southwestern Company on page 302 for complete description.

STUDENT CONSERVATION ASSOCIATION (SCA), UTAH

See Student Conservation Association (SCA), New Hampshire on page 209 for complete description.

VERMONT

ALOHA FOUNDATION, INC.

2968 LAKE MOREY ROAD
FAIRLEE, VERMONT 05045-9400

General Information Nonprofit organization offering children's residential camps, day camp, youth wilderness trips, and traditional camp activities. Established in 1905. 1,000-acre facility located 20 miles from White River Junction. Features: wooded setting; freshwater lake waterfront; tennis courts; platform tents; washhouse with electricity and hot water; proximity to White and Green Mountains.

Profile of Summer Employees Total number: 325; typical ages: 21–50. 40% men; 60% women; 20% minorities; 5% high school students; 35% college students; 5% retirees; 25% non-U.S. citizens; 10% local applicants. Nonsmokers preferred.

Employment Information Openings are from June 15 to August 20. Jobs available: ▶ *summer camp counselors* (minimum age 18) at $750–$3000 per season. Applicants must submit formal organization application, three letters of recommendation. An in-person interview is recommended, but a telephone interview is acceptable. International applicants accepted; must apply through a recognized agency.

Benefits and Preemployment Training Free housing, free meals, formal training, possible full-time employment, willing to provide letters of recommendation, on-the-job training, and willing to act as a professional reference. Preemployment training is required and includes accident prevention and safety, first aid, CPR, interpersonal skills, leadership skills, lifeguard training.

Contact Ellen Bagley, Administrative Assistant, Aloha Foundation, Inc. Telephone: 802-333-3400. Fax: 802-333-3404. E-mail: ellen_bagley@alohafoundation.org. World Wide Web: http://www.alohafoundation.org. Contact by e-mail, fax, mail, phone, or through World Wide Web site. Application deadline: June 1.

THE BRIDGES FAMILY RESORT AND TENNIS CLUB

202 BRIDGES CIRCLE
WARREN, VERMONT 05674

General Information Tennis and condominium facility at major ski area in Vermont's Green Mountains. Established in 1970. 45-acre facility located 48 miles from Burlington. Features: 12 tennis courts; health club; wooded setting; 3 pools.

Profile of Summer Employees Total number: 50; typical ages: 18–25. 50% men; 50% women; 1% minorities; 5% high school students; 10% college students; 10% non-U.S. citizens; 64% local applicants.

Employment Information Openings are from June 11 to September 3. Year-round positions also offered. Jobs available: ▶ 1–7 *housekeeping staff* (minimum age 18) at $8–$8.50 per hour ▶ 1 *tennis desk/front desk staff* (minimum age 18) at $8–$8.50 per hour. Applicants must submit a formal organization application, letter of interest, resume. An in-person interview is recommended, but a telephone interview is acceptable. International applicants accepted; must obtain own visa.

Benefits and Preemployment Training Possible full-time employment, willing to provide letters of recommendation, on-the-job training, and willing to act as a professional reference.

Contact Jim Halavonich, General Manager, The Bridges Family Resort and Tennis Club, 202 Bridges Circle, Warren, Vermont 05674. Telephone: 802-583-2922. Fax: 802-583-1018. E-mail: bridges@madriver.com. World Wide Web: http://www.bridgesresort.com. Contact by e-mail, fax, mail, phone, or through World Wide Web site. Application deadline: continuous.

BURKLYN BALLET THEATRE
337 COLLEGE HILL, JOHNSON STATE COLLEGE
JOHNSON, VERMONT 05656

General Information Classical ballet workshop offers weekly performance opportunity to 136 boys and girls ages 12–20 in one 6-week program. Established in 1976. 100-acre facility located 35 miles from Burlington. Features: mountains; rural village; college campus; university dormitories; library; pool.

Profile of Summer Employees Total number: 20; typical ages: 20–75. 50% men; 50% women; 10% minorities; 25% college students; 1% retirees; 5% non-U.S. citizens. Nonsmokers preferred.

Employment Information Openings are from June 19 to August 3. Jobs available: ▶ 14 *counselors* (minimum age 20) with current professional dance contract or college dance major; salary may be program tuition, room, and board ▶ 1 *registered nurse* should be experienced licensed RN; salary may be child's tuition waiver ▶ 1 *technical director* (minimum age 25) with professional experience or college technical theater major at $100–$200 per week. Applicants must submit resume, in-person/video audition. International applicants accepted; must obtain own visa, obtain own working papers.

Benefits and Preemployment Training Free housing, free meals, formal training, willing to provide letters of recommendation, names of contacts, on-the-job training, willing to act as a professional reference, opportunity to attend seminars/workshops, and tuition assistance. Preemployment training is required and includes interpersonal skills, leadership skills.

Contact Angela Whitehill, Artistic Director, Burklyn Ballet Theatre, PO Box 907, Island Heights, New Jersey 08732. Fax: 732-288-2663. World Wide Web: http://www.burklynballet.com. Contact by fax or mail. Application deadline: April 15.

BURKLYN BALLET THEATRE II, THE CHILDREN'S PROGRAM
JOHNSON STATE COLLEGE
JOHNSON, VERMONT 05656

General Information Classical ballet workshop for 18 girls ages 8–11 in one 3-week session. Established in 1995. Located 35 miles from Burlington. Features: college campus; rural village; streams and mountains; library; 4 studios; pool.

Profile of Summer Employees Total number: 6; typical ages: 35–45. 100% women. Nonsmokers required.

Employment Information Jobs available: ▶ *registered nurse* should be experienced licensed RN at a negotiable salary which may be child's tuition waiver. Applicants must submit a formal organization application, letter of interest, resume, personal reference. An in-person interview is required. International applicants accepted; must obtain own visa, obtain own working papers.

Benefits and Preemployment Training Free housing, free meals, willing to provide letters of recommendation, on-the-job training, willing to act as a professional reference, opportunity to attend seminars/workshops, travel reimbursement, and tuition assistance. Preemployment training is required and includes interpersonal skills.

Contact Angela Whitehill, Artistic Director, Burklyn Ballet Theatre II, The Children's Program,

PO Box 907, Island Heights, New Jersey 08732. Telephone: 732-288-2660. Fax: 732-288-2663. Application deadline: March 15.

CAMP FARNSWORTH
ROUTE 113
THETFORD, VERMONT 05074

General Information Residential Girl Scout camp for girls ages 6–16 offering four 2-week sessions. Established in 1959. 300-acre facility located 150 miles from Boston, Massachusetts. Features: private lake; variety of terrain: woods, meadows, hills; 50-foot waterslide into lake; high ropes course.

Profile of Summer Employees Total number: 110; typical ages: 18–40. 1% men; 99% women; 5% minorities; 50% college students; 30% non-U.S. citizens; 20% local applicants. Nonsmokers preferred.

Employment Information Openings are from June 16 to August 22. Jobs available: ▶ 1 *adventure director* with experience instructing ropes course at $1800–$3200 per season ▶ 3 *arts assistants* (minimum age 18) with experience teaching in the field at $1500–$1800 per season ▶ 1 *arts director* with supervisory experience at $2400–$3200 per season ▶ 2 *cooks* with quantity cooking experience at $3000–$3800 per season ▶ 1 *counselor-in-training director* (minimum age 21) with camp supervisory experience at $1800–$2400 per season ▶ *driver/shopper* (minimum age 21) with driver's license at $1800–$2400 per season ▶ 1 *ecology director* with experience in the field at $1600–$2700 per season ▶ 2 *health directors* (minimum age 21) with RN, LPN, or EMT license at $2500–$4800 per season ▶ 1 *horseback riding director* (minimum age 21) with experience supervising English riding program at $2400–$3200 per season ▶ 4 *riding assistants* (minimum age 18) with instructor experience at $1400–$2400 per season ▶ 15–20 *unit assistants* (minimum age 18) with child supervisory experience and high school diploma at $1500–$1800 per season ▶ 12 *unit leaders* with high school diploma and experience supervising adults and working with groups of children at $1800–$2400 per season ▶ 8 *waterfront assistants* (minimum age 18) with Red Cross or YMCA lifeguard certification (WSI preferred) and experience teaching swimming at $1500–$2400 per season ▶ 1 *waterfront director* (minimum age 21) with WSI and LGT certification, supervisory experience and experience teaching swimming at $2400–$3200 per season. Applicants must submit formal organization application, three personal references. A telephone interview is required. International applicants accepted; must apply through a recognized agency.

Benefits and Preemployment Training Free housing, free meals, formal training, health insurance, willing to provide letters of recommendation, on-the-job training, willing to complete paperwork for educational credit, and willing to act as a professional reference. Preemployment training is required and includes accident prevention and safety, first aid, CPR, interpersonal skills, leadership skills, child development, camp program.

Contact Nancy Frankel, Camp Director, Camp Farnsworth, 8 Perimeter Road, Manchester, New Hampshire 03103. Telephone: 603-627-4158. Fax: 603-627-4169. E-mail: nfrankel@swgirlscouts.org. World Wide Web: http://www.swgirlscouts.org. Contact by e-mail, fax, mail, phone, or through World Wide Web site. Application deadline: continuous.

CAMP THOREAU-IN-VERMONT
ONE THOREAU WAY
THETFORD CENTER, VERMONT 05075-9601

General Information Interracial coeducational democratic community living for 140 campers and 64 staff members. Established in 1972. 380-acre facility located 25 miles from White River Junction. Features: rural environment; on-site riding facility; 4 clay tennis courts; campsite on 64-acre lake; hiking in nearby White and Green Mountains; fully equipped darkroom and video studio.

Profile of Summer Employees Total number: 65; typical ages: 17–35. 50% men; 50% women; 15% minorities; 8% high school students; 60% college students; 20% non-U.S. citizens; 10% local applicants. Nonsmokers preferred.

Employment Information Openings are from June 15 to August 22. Jobs available: ▶ 1 *counselor/newspaper person* with experience at $1400–$2200 per season ▶ 3 *counselors/arts and crafts instructors* with CPR/first aid certification and experience at $1500–$2400 per season ▶ 2 *counselors/drama instructors* with experience in the field at $1500–$2400 per season ▶ 2 *counselors/evening programs instructors* with experience and creativity to design activities for the entire camp at $1500–$2400 per season ▶ 2 *counselors/high-ropes instructors* with experience at $1500–$2400 per season ▶ 2 *counselors/hiking and outdoor living instructors* with experience, familiarity with area, CPR/first aid certification, and Wilderness First Responder or Wilderness EMT (preferred) at $1500–$2400 per season ▶ 12 *counselors/lifeguards* with LGT, CPR/FPR, and first aid certification at $1500–$2400 per season ▶ 2 *counselors/low-ropes instructors* with CPR/first aid certification and experience at $1500–$2400 per season ▶ 2 *counselors/martial arts and fencing instructors* with experience, belt and CPR/first aid certification; at $1500–$2400 per season ▶ 2 *counselors/nature (small animals) instructors* with CPR/first aid certification and experience at $1500–$2400 per season ▶ 2 *counselors/photography instructors* with CPR/first aid certification and experience at $1500–$2400 per season ▶ 4 *counselors/riding instructors* with CHA and CPR/first aid certification at $1500–$2400 per season ▶ 6 *counselors/small craft instructors* with LGT and canoeing/sailing/kayaking instructor certification at $1500–$2400 per season ▶ 4 *counselors/sports instructors* with CPR/first aid certification and experience at $1500–$2400 per season ▶ 8 *counselors/swimming instructors* with WSI, LGT, first aid, and CPR/FPR certification at $1600–$2500 per season ▶ 2 *counselors/top-rope rock climbing instructors* with experience at $1500–$2400 per season ▶ 2 *counselors/woodshop instructors* with CPR/first aid certification and experience at $1500–$2400 per season ▶ *maintenance staff* with experience at $1400–$2800 per season ▶ *nurses* with RN license, ability to obtain Vermont RN license, and CPR certification at $4500–$5500 per season ▶ 1 *office manager* with filing, simple bookkeeping, telephone and computer skills at $1300–$2500 per season. Applicants must submit formal organization application, letter of interest, personal reference, letter of recommendation. An in-person interview is recommended, but a telephone interview is acceptable. International applicants accepted; must apply through a recognized agency.

Benefits and Preemployment Training Free housing, free meals, health insurance, on-the-job training, willing to complete paperwork for educational credit, travel reimbursement, and laundry facilities; opportunity to work with diverse, multicultural staff in several different program areas. Preemployment training is required and includes program-specific skill development.

Contact Gregory H. Finger, Director, Camp Thoreau-In-Vermont, 157 Tillson Lake Road, Wallkill, New York 12589-3265. Telephone: 845-895-2974. Fax: 845-895-1281. E-mail: gfinger@frontiernet.net. World Wide Web: http://www.campthoreau-in-vermont.org. Contact by e-mail, phone, or through World Wide Web site. Application deadline: continuous.

CAMP THORPE, INC.
680 CAPEN HILL ROAD
GOSHEN, VERMONT 05733

General Information Summer residential camp that serves children and adults with special needs. Established in 1927. 171-acre facility located 70 miles from Burlington. Features: large pool; tennis court; pond; small stage; cabins; small farm.

Profile of Summer Employees Total number: 25; typical ages: 18–22. 40% men; 60% women; 10% high school students; 90% college students; 25% non-U.S. citizens; 75% local applicants. Nonsmokers preferred.

Employment Information Openings are from June 18 to August 10. Jobs available: ▶ 1 *camp nurse* with RN, LPN, or EMT license at $3000–$4000 per season ▶ 1 *cook* with previous experience at $3000–$4000 per season ▶ 12 *general counselors* (minimum age 17) with a desire to work with children and adults with special needs at $1500–$1600 per season ▶ 2 *head counselors* (minimum age 18) with two years of college completed at $1800–$2000 per season ▶ 2 *kitchen assistants* (minimum age 17) with previous experience at $200 per week ▶ 5 *specialists (art, nature, music, pool, and sports)* (minimum age 18) with one year of college completed at $1700–$1800 per season. Applicants must submit formal organization application, three personal references. An in-person interview is recommended, but a telephone interview is acceptable. International applicants accepted; must apply through a recognized agency.

Benefits and Preemployment Training Free housing, free meals, willing to provide letters of recommendation, on-the-job training, willing to complete paperwork for educational credit, and willing to act as a professional reference. Preemployment training is required and includes accident prevention and safety, first aid, CPR, interpersonal skills, leadership skills.

Contact Lyle P. Jepson, Director, Camp Thorpe, Inc., 680 Capen Hill Road, Goshen, Vermont 05733. Telephone: 802-247-6611. E-mail: mjep@sover.net. Contact by e-mail, mail, or phone. Application deadline: continuous.

CHALLENGE WILDERNESS CAMP FOR BOYS

480 ROARING BROOK ROAD
BRADFORD, VERMONT 05033

General Information Residential camp serving 45 boys ages 9–16 with outdoor skills and wilderness trips. Established in 1965. 650-acre facility located 26 miles from Hanover, New Hampshire. Features: 650-acre forest preserve; 15-acre trout-stocked private lake; adirondack shelters; blacksmith shop; playing fields.

Profile of Summer Employees Total number: 10–12; typical ages: 21–30. 100% men; 60% college students; 40% non-U.S. citizens. Nonsmokers required.

Employment Information Openings are from June 18 to August 25. Jobs available: ▶ 1 *blacksmithing instructor* (minimum age 21) with ability to be trained at $1600–$2500 per season ▶ 1 *fishing/fly-tying instructor* (minimum age 21) with trout specialty at $1600–$2500 per season ▶ 1 *food services director* (minimum age 21) with outdoorsman and cooking skills at $2000–$3000 per season ▶ 1 *kayak instructor* (minimum age 21) with ACA or BCU certification; LGT preferred at $1600–$2500 per season ▶ 1 *kitchen assistant* (minimum age 21) with outdoorsman skills at $1600–$2500 per season ▶ 1 *marksmanship instructor* (minimum age 21) with .22-caliber and military experience at $1600–$2500 per season ▶ 3 *rock climbing instructors* (minimum age 21) with one 5.10 lead plus two 5.9 seconds at $1600–$2500 per season ▶ 1 *waterfront director* with lifeguard training required; WSI preferred at $2000–$2500 per season ▶ 1 *woodworking instructor* (minimum age 21) with background in carpentry, woodwork, and cabinet-making at $1600–$2500 per season. Applicants must submit formal organization application, letter of interest, resume, three personal references. A telephone interview is required. International applicants accepted; must apply through a recognized agency.

Benefits and Preemployment Training Free housing, free meals, willing to provide letters of recommendation, on-the-job training, willing to complete paperwork for educational credit, willing to act as a professional reference, and outdoor leadership training. Preemployment training is required and includes accident prevention and safety, first aid, CPR, interpersonal skills, leadership skills, water safety rescue.

Contact Dr. J. Thayer, Director, Challenge Wilderness Camp for Boys, 300 Grove Street, #4, Rutland, Vermont 05701. Telephone: 800-832-HAWK. Fax: 802-786-0653. E-mail: rainest@sover.net. World Wide Web: http://www.challengewilderness.com. Contact by e-mail or phone. Application deadline: continuous.

FARM AND WILDERNESS CAMPS
263 FARM AND WILDERNESS ROAD
PLYMOUTH, VERMONT 05056

General Information 5 separate individual residential programs for boys/girls ages 9–17 offering diverse outdoor wilderness activities within Quaker-based communities. Also day camp for boys and girls ages 3–10. Established in 1939. 3,000-acre facility located 23 miles from Rutland. Features: freshwater lake; certified organic farm; Green Mountain National Forest; surrounded by 3000 acres of forest; farm animals; 3-sided cabins.

Profile of Summer Employees Total number: 200; typical ages: 19–24. 55% men; 45% women; 10% minorities; 5% high school students; 75% college students; 2% retirees; 2% non-U.S. citizens; 15% local applicants. Nonsmokers required.

Employment Information Openings are from June 9 to August 25. Year-round positions also offered. Jobs available: ▶ 18 *cooks* (minimum age 18) at $1800–$4000 per season ▶ 120–150 *counselors* (minimum age 18) at $1500–$2250 per season ▶ 5 *maintenance staff members* (minimum age 21) with carpentry and plumbing experience at $1350–$2250 per season ▶ 6 *nurses* (minimum age 21) with RN license or graduate nursing student status at $3000–$3500 per season ▶ 15 *swimming instructors* (minimum age 18) with LGT/WSI certification at $1350–$2250 per season. Applicants must submit formal organization application, three personal references. A telephone interview is required. International applicants accepted; must apply through a recognized agency.

Benefits and Preemployment Training Free housing, free meals, formal training, health insurance, willing to provide letters of recommendation, on-the-job training, willing to complete paperwork for educational credit, willing to act as a professional reference, and opportunity to attend seminars/workshops. Preemployment training is required and includes accident prevention and safety, first aid, CPR, interpersonal skills, leadership skills, outdoor skills.

Contact Gavin Boyles, Staff Counseling, Farm and Wilderness Camps. Telephone: 802-422-3761. Fax: 802-422-8660. E-mail: gavin@fandw.org. World Wide Web: http://www.fandw.org. Contact by e-mail, mail, phone, or through World Wide Web site. Application deadline: continuous.

KILLOOLEET
ROUTE 100
HANCOCK, VERMONT 05748-0070

General Information Full-season, noncompetitive, coeducational camp serving 100 campers ages 9–14 for 7 or more weeks. Emphasis is on developing techniques in group leadership and individual areas of expertise. Children specialize in a variety of sports and arts activities. Established in 1927. 300-acre facility located 35 miles from Rutland. Features: beautiful valley, streams and woods; flat campus and bicycles; freshwater lake; horses and riding program; all counselors go on hikes and overnight trips.

Profile of Summer Employees Total number: 45; typical ages: 18–30. 50% men; 50% women; 9% minorities; 12% high school students; 65% college students; 4% retirees; 20% non-U.S. citizens; 15% local applicants. Nonsmokers preferred.

Employment Information Openings are from June 20 to August 23. Jobs available: ▶ 1 *boating (canoeing, windsurfing) instructor* (minimum age 19) at $1200–$2000 per season ▶ 1 *drama counselor* (minimum age 18) with ability to direct a musical as well as teach improvisation/creative dramatics at $1400–$2300 per season ▶ 1 *electronics instructor* (minimum age 18) at $1400–$2200 per season ▶ 1 *fabric arts instructor* (minimum age 19) sewing skills needed; other fabric arts, such as weaving, knitting or crocheting are useful at $1400–$2200 per season ▶ 2 *horseback riding (English) instructors* (minimum age 19) with Pony Club or equivalent group teaching experience at $1400–$2500 per season ▶ *mountain biking/rock climbing/camping skills instructor* with teaching experience and other interests at $1400–$2200 per season ▶ 1–2 *music (folk, rhythm and blues/funk) instructors* with interest in working with camper bands, teaching individual lessons, and running group sings at $1400–$2500 per season

▶ 1 *music counselor* (minimum age 19) with ability to play piano for the camp musical and help campers with learning their songs (other activity skills desirable, too) at $1400–$2300 per season ▶ 1 *nature instructor* (minimum age 18) with teaching ideas using pond, fields, stream, and woods at $1400–$2200 per season ▶ 1 *secretary* (minimum age 18) with basic skills and enjoyment of working with children at $1400–$2500 per season ▶ 1 *shop counselor (woodworking or crafts)* (minimum age 19) at $1400–$2000 per season ▶ 2 *sports (individual and team) instructors* at $1400–$2200 per season ▶ 1–3 *swimming instructors* (minimum age 18) with current WSI and lifeguard certifications at $1500–$2200 per season ▶ 1 *video, filming, and editing instructor* (minimum age 19) with comfort with digital camera and editing systems at $1400–$2500 per season. Applicants must submit formal organization application, letter of interest, three personal references, brief biographical statement. An in-person interview is recommended, but a telephone interview is acceptable. International applicants accepted; must apply through a recognized agency.

Benefits and Preemployment Training Free housing, free meals, formal training, health insurance, willing to provide letters of recommendation, on-the-job training, willing to complete paperwork for educational credit, willing to act as a professional reference, opportunity to attend seminars/workshops, and partial travel reimbursement. Preemployment training is required and includes accident prevention and safety, first aid, CPR, interpersonal skills, leadership skills, wilderness first aid.

Contact Kate Spencer-Seeger, Director, Killooleet, 70 Trull Street, Somerville, Massachusetts 02145. Telephone: 617-666-1484. Fax: 617-666-0378. E-mail: camp05748@aol.com. World Wide Web: http://www.campjob.com/Killooleet/killooleet.htm. Contact by e-mail, fax, mail, phone, or through World Wide Web site. Application deadline: continuous.

LOCHEARN CAMP FOR GIRLS

LAKE FAIRLEE
POST MILLS, VERMONT 05058

General Information Private residential camp for girls ages 7–16 offering a comprehensive activity program with special emphasis on positive character development of children. Established in 1916. 51-acre facility located 150 miles from Boston, Massachusetts. Features: freshwater lake; wooded setting; lakeside cabins; gymnastics center; 5 tennis courts; 16- horse stable and riding facilities.

Profile of Summer Employees Total number: 75; typical ages: 18–26. 10% men; 90% women; 10% high school students; 80% college students; 10% retirees; 15% non-U.S. citizens. Nonsmokers required.

Employment Information Openings are from June 13 to August 23. Jobs available: ▶ 2 *English-style riding instructors* (minimum age 18) with experience in the field at $1700–$2100 per season ▶ 2 *canoeing instructors* (minimum age 18) with LGT certification or small crafts safety certification at $1600–$2100 per season ▶ 1 *diving instructor* (minimum age 18) with LGT certification at $1600–$2000 per season ▶ 5 *field sports instructors* (minimum age 18) at $1600–$2000 per season ▶ 3 *gymnastics instructors* (minimum age 18) with floor and full apparatus experience; coaching experience preferred at $1600–$2000 per season ▶ *head chef* (minimum age 26) with culinary training, prior experience in cooking, purchasing, and kitchen management at $7000–$9000 per season ▶ 3 *kitchen assistants* (minimum age 18) at $1600–$2000 per season ▶ 2 *leadership trainers* (minimum age 21) with experience in the field at $1700–$2100 per season ▶ 2 *outdoor adventure staff* (minimum age 21) with WFA/First Responder at $1600–$2100 per season ▶ 2 *performing arts instructors* (minimum age 18) with experience in the field at $1600–$2000 per season ▶ 2 *registered nurses* (minimum age 22) with RN (Vermont temporary license); CPR/first aid certification and pediatric experience at $3500–$4500 per season ▶ 2 *sailing instructors* (minimum age 18) with LGT or small crafts safety certification at $1600–$2000 per season ▶ 10 *studio arts instructors* (minimum age 18) at $1600–$2000 per season ▶ 2 *swimming instructors* (minimum age 18) with LGT/WSI certifica-

tion at $1600–$2000 per season ▶ 4 *tennis instructors* (minimum age 18) with coaching experience preferred at $1600–$2000 per season ▶ 2 *waterskiing instructors/boat drivers* (minimum age 18) with LGT certification or waterski instructors certification at $1700–$2100 per season. Applicants must submit formal organization application, three personal references. A telephone interview is required. International applicants accepted; must apply through a recognized agency.
Benefits and Preemployment Training Free housing, free meals, formal training, willing to provide letters of recommendation, on-the-job training, willing to complete paperwork for educational credit, willing to act as a professional reference, and travel reimbursement. Preemployment training is required and includes accident prevention and safety, interpersonal skills, leadership skills, character education, curriculum training, teacher/coach training.
Contact Rich Maxson, Owner/Director, Lochearn Camp for Girls, Camp Lochearn on Lake Fairlee, Post Mills, Vermont 05058. Telephone: 877-649-4151. Fax: 802-333-4856. E-mail: lochearn@earthlink.net. Contact by e-mail, fax, mail, or phone. Application deadline: continuous.

MOUNT SNOW
ROUTE 100
WEST DOVER, VERMONT 05356

General Information Major ski area. Summer operations include mountain biking, lift service for downhill bikers, kids camp, hotels, golf, golf school, hiking, bus tours, lift rides, schools for biking, 2 swimming pools, and lakes. Established in 1954. 1,000-acre facility located 50 miles from Albany, New York. Features: 2 swimming pools; 2 hotels; wooded setting; 3 lifts operational (summer); golf course (18 holes); climbing wall and in-line skate park.
Profile of Summer Employees Total number: 350; typical ages: 18–60. 70% men; 30% women; 10% high school students; 20% college students; 70% local applicants. Nonsmokers preferred.
Employment Information Openings are from May 31 to October 12. Spring break, winter break, and year-round positions also offered. Jobs available: ▶ *food and beverage staff* (minimum age 18) at $6.50 per hour ▶ *lift operators* (minimum age 18). Applicants must submit a formal organization application. An in-person interview is required. International applicants accepted; must obtain own visa.
Benefits and Preemployment Training Possible full-time employment, willing to provide letters of recommendation, on-the-job training, willing to complete paperwork for educational credit, and free golf/skiing depending on season, discounted bike rentals, use of bike trail network. Preemployment training is required and includes accident prevention and safety, interpersonal skills, leadership skills, guest service cross training.
Contact Charlie Romano, Recruiter/Trainer, Mount Snow, Human Resources, Route 100, West Dover, Vermont 05356. Telephone: 802-464-4221. Fax: 802-464-4135. E-mail: cromano@mountsnow.com. World Wide Web: http://www.mountsnow.com. Contact by e-mail, fax, phone, or through World Wide Web site. Application deadline: continuous.

POINT COUNTERPOINT CHAMBER MUSIC CAMP
LAKE DUNEMORE, VERMONT 05733

General Information Residential camp serving 50 string players and pianists for three-, four-, or seven-week sessions. Established in 1963. 2-acre facility located 50 miles from Burlington. Features: freshwater; mountains; small student body.
Profile of Summer Employees Total number: 22; typical ages: 19–40. 34% men; 66% women; 16% minorities; 33% college students; 16% non-U.S. citizens; 27% local applicants. Nonsmokers preferred.
Employment Information Openings are from June 18 to August 13. Jobs available: ▶ 1 *activities director* (minimum age 21) with interpersonal skills at $2400–$3000 per season ▶ 6 *activity counselors* (minimum age 19) with WSI, first aid, and CPR certification (preferred) at $1550–$1750 per season ▶ *cooks* with experience in the field at $2200–$6000 per season ▶ 8 *music*

staff members (4 violinists, 1 violist, 2 cellists, and 1 pianist) with performing and teaching experience at $2800–$3200 per season. Applicants must submit a formal organization application, resume, three personal references, audition tape for music faculty. A telephone interview is required. International applicants accepted; must obtain own visa, obtain own working papers.
Benefits and Preemployment Training Free housing, free meals, willing to provide letters of recommendation, and willing to act as a professional reference. Preemployment training is required and includes interpersonal skills, leadership skills.
Contact Paul Roby, Director, Point CounterPoint Chamber Music Camp, PO Box 3181, Terre Haute, Indiana 47803. Telephone: 812-877-3745. Fax: 812-877-2174. E-mail: pointcp@aol.com. World Wide Web: http://www.pointcp.com. Contact by e-mail, fax, mail, phone, or through World Wide Web site. Application deadline: continuous.

PUTNEY SUMMER PROGRAMS
ELM LEA FARM
PUTNEY, VERMONT 05346

General Information Residential program for 80 students in visual and performing arts, writing, and English as a Second Language. Established in 1987. 500-acre facility located 10 miles from Brattleboro. Features: superb arts facilities; working farm; residential cottages; computer lab; miles of biking/running trails; hilltop setting.
Profile of Summer Employees Total number: 45; typical ages: 21–32. 40% men; 60% women; 10% minorities; 30% college students; 10% non-U.S. citizens; 40% local applicants. Nonsmokers required.
Employment Information Openings are from June 25 to August 12. Jobs available: ▶ 12–15 *residential assistants* (minimum age 21) with experience in arts, music, writing, or English as a Second Language preferred; also residential and outdoor experience and first aid training at $1600 per season. Applicants must submit a formal organization application, letter of interest, resume, three personal references. An in-person interview is recommended, but a telephone interview is acceptable. International applicants accepted; must obtain own visa, obtain own working papers.
Benefits and Preemployment Training Free housing, free meals, formal training, on-the-job training, willing to act as a professional reference, and travel reimbursement. Preemployment training is required and includes accident prevention and safety, first aid, CPR, interpersonal skills, leadership skills.
Contact Tom Howe, Director, Summer Programs, Putney Summer Programs, The Putney School, Putney, Vermont 05346. Fax: 802-387-6216. E-mail: summer@putney.com. Contact by e-mail or mail. Application deadline: applications accepted from January 1 through March 15.

THE SOUTHWESTERN COMPANY, VERMONT
See The Southwestern Company on page 302 for complete description.

STUDENT CONSERVATION ASSOCIATION (SCA), VERMONT
See Student Conservation Association (SCA), New Hampshire on page 209 for complete description.

SUMMER DISCOVERY AT VERMONT
UNIVERSITY OF VERMONT
BURLINGTON, VERMONT 05401

General Information Precollege enrichment program for high school students at University of Vermont. Established in 1990. Features: sport facilities; beaches; mountains; lakes; major cities nearby; college towns.

Profile of Summer Employees Total number: 20; typical ages: 21–35. 10% minorities; 60% college students; 2% non-U.S. citizens. Nonsmokers required.
Employment Information Openings are from June 20 to August 25. Jobs available: ▶ 20 *resident counselors* (minimum age 21) with experience working with high school students/children at $200 per week. Applicants must submit a formal organization application, resume, three personal references. An in-person interview is required. International applicants accepted; must obtain own visa, obtain own working papers.
Benefits and Preemployment Training Free housing, free meals, possible full-time employment, on-the-job training, willing to complete paperwork for educational credit, willing to act as a professional reference, and travel reimbursement. Preemployment training is required and includes accident prevention and safety, CPR, leadership skills.
Contact Jason Walley, Admissions Director, Summer Discovery at Vermont, 1326 Old Northern Boulevard, Roslyn, New York 11576. Telephone: 516-621-3939. Fax: 516-625-3438. E-mail: staff@summerfun.com. World Wide Web: http://www.summerfun.com. Contact by e-mail, fax, phone, or through World Wide Web site. Application deadline: continuous.

VERMONT STATE PARKS DIVISION

103 SOUTH MAIN STREET
WATERBURY, VERMONT 05671

General Information Division that plans, maintains, operates, designs, and constructs a system of state parks. Established in 1924. Features: freshwater lakes; wooded settings; islands; beautiful views; 35 campgrounds; hundreds of miles of trails.
Profile of Summer Employees Total number: 200; typical ages: 16–75. 50% men; 50% women; 1% minorities; 15% high school students; 25% college students; 15% retirees; 44% local applicants. Nonsmokers preferred.
Employment Information Openings are from May 1 to October 15. Jobs available: ▶ 10–50 *park attendants* (minimum age 16) outstanding customer service skills, enjoy working with others; must work weekends at $7.32–$7.91 per hour ▶ 2–10 *park naturalists* (minimum age 20) outstanding customer service skills, extensive knowledge of Vermont's natural resources at $8.96–$9.62 per hour. Applicants must submit a formal organization application, letter of interest, resume, two letters of recommendation, 2-6 personal references. An in-person interview is recommended, but a telephone interview is acceptable. International applicants accepted; must obtain own visa, obtain own working papers.
Benefits and Preemployment Training Housing at a cost, willing to provide letters of recommendation, on-the-job training, willing to complete paperwork for educational credit, and willing to act as a professional reference.
Contact Mr. Larry T. Simino, Director of State Parks, Vermont State Parks Division. Fax: 802-244-1481. E-mail: parks@fpr.anr.state.vt.us. World Wide Web: http://www.vtstateparks.com. Contact by e-mail, fax, or mail. Application deadline: April 1.

WINDRIDGE TENNIS CAMP AT CRAFTSBURY COMMON

76 WINDRIDGE LANE
CRAFTSBURY COMMON, VERMONT 05827

General Information Residential coeducational camp serving 110 campers with an emphasis on tennis along with traditional camp activities. Owned by Windridge Tennis Camp, Inc. Established in 1973. 50-acre facility located 35 miles from Montpelier. Features: 16 tennis courts; private lake; lakeside cabins; sculling facilities; soccer fields; rural wooded setting.
Profile of Summer Employees Total number: 40; typical ages: 18–25. 50% men; 50% women; 10% minorities; 80% college students; 20% non-U.S. citizens; 10% local applicants. Nonsmokers required.
Employment Information Openings are from June 2 to August 23. Jobs available: ▶ 1 *archery*

instructor (minimum age 18) with American Archery Association Level-1 certification at $1900–$2500 per season ▶ 1 *arts and crafts instructor* (minimum age 18) at $1900–$2500 per season ▶ 3 *lifeguards* (minimum age 18) with LGT at $1900–$2500 per season ▶ 1 *mountain bike instructor* (minimum age 18) with riding and mechanical skills at $1900–$2500 per season ▶ 1 *photography instructor* (minimum age 18) at $1900–$2500 per season ▶ 1 *registered nurse* (minimum age 21) RN license at $500–$575 per week ▶ 2 *sailing instructors* (minimum age 18) with LGT at $1900–$2500 per season ▶ 3 *soccer instructors* (minimum age 18) at $1900–$2500 per season ▶ 12–16 *tennis instructors* (minimum age 18) with college or high school competitive experience at $1900–$2500 per season ▶ 1 *waterfront director* (minimum age 25) with LGT at $2000–$3000 per season. Applicants must submit formal organization application, three personal references. A telephone interview is required. International applicants accepted; must apply through a recognized agency.

Benefits and Preemployment Training Free housing, free meals, willing to provide letters of recommendation, on-the-job training, willing to complete paperwork for educational credit, and willing to act as a professional reference. Preemployment training is required and includes accident prevention and safety, first aid, CPR, interpersonal skills, leadership skills.

Contact Charles Witherell, Director, Windridge Tennis Camp at Craftsbury Common, PO Box 1298, Jeffersonville, Vermont 05464. Telephone: 802-644-6500. Fax: 802-644-6300. E-mail: windridgetenniscamps@pshift.com. World Wide Web: http://www.windridgetenniscamps.com. Contact by e-mail, fax, mail, or phone. Application deadline: continuous.

WINDRIDGE TENNIS CAMP AT TEELA-WOOKET, VERMONT

1215 ROXBURY ROAD
ROXBURY, VERMONT 05669

General Information Residential camp for boys and girls ages 9–15 specializing in tennis, riding, and soccer. Established in 1986. 235-acre facility located 55 miles from Burlington. Features: 21 clay tennis courts; 2 regulation soccer fields; 40-stall horse barn; rustic cabins; swimming pool; in-line hockey facility.

Profile of Summer Employees Total number: 70; typical ages: 18–24. 50% men; 50% women; 5% minorities; 5% high school students; 45% college students; 40% non-U.S. citizens; 10% local applicants. Nonsmokers required.

Employment Information Openings are from June 4 to August 22. Jobs available: ▶ 1–2 *activity specialists* (minimum age 18) with experience in mountain biking, in-line hockey, basketball, and team sports required at $1800–$2000 per season ▶ 1 *archery instructor* (minimum age 18) with experience preferred at $1800–$2000 per season ▶ 1 *childcare worker for staff children* (minimum age 18) with driver's license and ability to swim preferred at $1300–$2000 per season ▶ 1 *lifeguard* (minimum age 18) with Red Cross Lifeguard Training or equivalent at $1800–$2000 per season ▶ 1 *program director* (minimum age 21) with previous camp experience at $4000–$5000 per season ▶ 4–5 *riding instructors* (minimum age 18) with good riding skills and teaching experience at $1800–$2000 per season ▶ 18–23 *tennis instructors* (minimum age 18) with experience required and teaching experience preferred at $1800–$2000 per season. Applicants must submit formal organization application, resume, three personal references, three letters of recommendation. An in-person interview is recommended, but a telephone interview is acceptable. International applicants accepted; must apply through a recognized agency.

Benefits and Preemployment Training Free housing, free meals, willing to provide letters of recommendation, on-the-job training, willing to complete paperwork for educational credit, and travel reimbursement. Preemployment training is required and includes accident prevention and safety, first aid, CPR, interpersonal skills, leadership skills.

Contact Deb Fennell, Director, Windridge Tennis Camp at Teela-Wooket, Vermont, PO Box 1298, Jeffersonville, Vermont 05464. Telephone: 802-644-6500. Fax: 802-644-6300. E-mail: wcampsdeb@pshift.com. World Wide Web: http://www.windridgetenniscamps.com. Contact by e-mail, fax, mail, phone, or through World Wide Web site. Application deadline: continuous.

VIRGIN ISLANDS

LONGACRE EXPEDITIONS, VIRGIN ISLANDS

VIRGIN ISLANDS

General Information Adventure travel program in the Virgin Islands for teenagers, emphasizing group living skills and physical challenges. Established in 1981. near St. Thomas.
Profile of Summer Employees Total number: 6; typical ages: 23–30. 50% men; 50% women; 100% college students. Nonsmokers required.
Employment Information Openings are from June 15 to July 30. Jobs available: ▶ 3 *assistant leaders* (minimum age 21) with scuba certification, WFR, CPR, and lifeguard training at $252–$300 per week. Applicants must submit a formal organization application, three personal references. An in-person interview is recommended, but a telephone interview is acceptable. International applicants accepted; must obtain own visa, obtain own working papers.
Benefits and Preemployment Training Free housing, free meals, willing to provide letters of recommendation, on-the-job training, willing to complete paperwork for educational credit, willing to act as a professional reference, and pro-deal purchase program. Preemployment training is required and includes accident prevention and safety, interpersonal skills, leadership skills.
Contact Meredith Schuler, Director, Longacre Expeditions, Virgin Islands, 4030 Middle Ridge Road, Newport, Pennsylvania 17074-8110. Telephone: 717-567-6790. Fax: 717-567-3955. E-mail: longacre@longacreexpeditions.com. World Wide Web: http://www.longacreexpeditions.com. Contact by e-mail, fax, mail, phone, or through World Wide Web site. Application deadline: continuous.

VIRGINIA

A CHRISTIAN MINISTRY IN THE NATIONAL PARKS–VIRGINIA

See A Christian Ministry in the National Parks–Maine on page 122 for complete description.

CAMP CARYSBROOK

3500 CAMP CARYSBROOK ROAD
RINER, VIRGINIA 24149

General Information Traditional residential camp for girls ages 6-16 in two-, four-, six-, and eight-week sessions; 2 week equestrian camp in August. Established in 1923. 200-acre facility located 30 miles from Roanoke. Features: freshwater lake; mountains; wooded setting; cabins; 2 tennis courts; stables.
Profile of Summer Employees Total number: 30; typical ages: 18–25. 2% men; 98% women;

10% minorities; 90% college students; 10% non-U.S. citizens; 5% local applicants.

Employment Information Openings are from June to August. Jobs available: ▶ 1 *archery instructor* (minimum age 18) with experience in the field at $750–$1200 per season ▶ 2 *arts and crafts instructors* (minimum age 18) with experience in the field at $750–$1200 per season ▶ 1 *canoeing instructor* (minimum age 18) with Red Cross canoe and lifesaving certification at $750–$1500 per season ▶ 1 *climbing, rappelling, and caving instructor* (minimum age 21) with experience in the field at $750–$2000 per season ▶ 1 *dance instructor* (minimum age 18) with experience in the field at $750–$1200 per season ▶ 1 *drama instructor* (minimum age 18) with experience in the field at $750–$1200 per season ▶ 1 *ecology instructor* (minimum age 18) with experience in the field at $750–$1200 per season ▶ 1 *fencing instructor* (minimum age 18) with experience in the field at $750–$1200 per season ▶ 1 *outdoor living skills instructor* (minimum age 21) with experience in the field at $750–$1200 per season ▶ 1 *recreational sports staff member* (minimum age 18) with experience in the field at $750–$1200 per season ▶ 4 *riding instructors* (minimum age 18) with CHA, US Pony Club certification and/or experience in the field at $750–$2000 per season ▶ 3 *riflery instructors* (minimum age 18) with experience in the field at $750–$2000 per season ▶ 5 *swimming instructors* (minimum age 18) with WSI or lifesaving certification at $750–$2000 per season ▶ 2 *team sports staff members* (minimum age 18) with experience in the field at $750–$1200 per season ▶ 1 *tennis instructor* (minimum age 18) with experience in the field at $750–$1200 per season. Applicants must submit formal organization application, three personal references. An in-person interview is recommended, but a telephone interview is acceptable. International applicants accepted; must apply through a recognized agency.

Benefits and Preemployment Training Free housing, free meals, willing to provide letters of recommendation, names of contacts, on-the-job training, willing to complete paperwork for educational credit, willing to act as a professional reference, and opportunity to attend seminars/workshops. Preemployment training is required and includes accident prevention and safety, first aid, CPR, interpersonal skills, leadership skills.

Contact Rachel Baughman, Director, Camp Carysbrook, 3500 Camp Carysbrook Road, Riner, Virginia 24149. Telephone: 540-382-1670. E-mail: tmoose@aol.com. World Wide Web: http://www.campcarysbrook.com. Contact by e-mail, mail, phone, or through World Wide Web site. Application deadline: continuous.

CAMP FRIENDSHIP

PO BOX 145
PALMYRA, VIRGINIA 22963

General Information Residential camp with a traditional program, specialized equestrian program, golf, gymnastics, and tennis camps, and adventure trips for teens in one- and two-week sessions. Established in 1966. 730-acre facility located 25 miles from Charlottesville. Features: lake; junior Olympic-size pool; 2 gymnasiums; 80-stall stable; 60-event ropes course; 4 tennis courts.

Profile of Summer Employees Total number: 140; typical ages: 16–40. 50% men; 50% women; 5% minorities; 5% high school students; 50% college students; 15% non-U.S. citizens; 10% local applicants. Nonsmokers preferred.

Employment Information Openings are from June 1 to August 25. Year-round positions also offered. Jobs available: ▶ 1 *arts and crafts director* (minimum age 21) with skills and experience with variety of arts materials at $2000–$3000 per season ▶ 10 *challenge counselors* (minimum age 21) with outdoor skills, driver's license, and adventure skills (preferred) at $2000–$3000 per season ▶ 3 *drivers/maintenance personnel* (minimum age 21) with driver's license at $1200–$1400 per season ▶ 1 *general program staff* (minimum age 21) with camp experience (preferred); ability to lead camp activities at $2000–$3000 per season ▶ 25 *junior cabin counselors/instructors* (minimum age 16) with teaching skills at $75–$105 per week ▶ 11 *kitchen staff members* at $1000–$2000 per season ▶ 2 *nurses* with RN license at $2000–$4000 per season ▶ 4 *other support positions* (minimum age 16) ▶ 1 *performing arts director* (minimum age 21) with experience/background in performing arts at $2000–$3000 per season ▶ 1 *pool director* (minimum age 21) with WSI, lifeguard instructor certification, and experience supervising pool and lifeguards at $2000–$3000 per season ▶ 8 *riding counselors/instructors* with experience in the field at $1100–$2000 per season ▶ 35 *senior cabin counselors/instructors* (minimum age 19) with teaching skills in a program area at $1500–$2000 per season ▶ 1 *sports director* (minimum age 21) with experience in variety of sports required; teaching or coaching experience preferred at $2000–$3000 per season ▶ 1 *target sports director* (minimum age 21) with archery and riflery instructor's certification at $2000–$3000 per season ▶ 8 *village directors* with college degree and supervisory experience at $2000–$3000 per season ▶ 1 *waterfront director* (minimum age 21) with WSI and lifeguard instructor certification or small craft safety or other related certifications at $2000–$3000 per season. Applicants must submit formal organization application, three personal references, (contact for application forms or download from Web site). An in-person interview is recommended, but a telephone interview is acceptable. International applicants accepted; must apply through a recognized agency.

Benefits and Preemployment Training Free housing, free meals, formal training, possible full-time employment, willing to provide letters of recommendation, on-the-job training, willing to complete paperwork for educational credit, willing to act as a professional reference, and opportunity to attend seminars/workshops. Preemployment training is required and includes accident prevention and safety, first aid, CPR, interpersonal skills, leadership skills, specific activity instructor training.

Contact Director, Camp Friendship, PO Box 145, Palmyra, Virginia 22963. Telephone: 434-589-8950. Fax: 434-589-5880. E-mail: campstaff@campfriendship.com. World Wide Web: http://www.campfriendship.com. Contact by e-mail, fax, mail, phone, or through World Wide Web site. Application deadline: continuous.

CAMP HORIZONS
3586 HORIZONS WAY
HARRISONBURG, VIRGINIA 22802

General Information Summer residential camp for children ages 7-17. Teen adventure and traditional camp programs. Corporate training center and retreat center for schools, churches, and universities in the spring and fall. Established in 1983. 300-acre facility. Features: mountain setting; lake; pool; tennis courts; ropes course; modern cabins.

Profile of Summer Employees Total number: 100; typical ages: 19–45. 40% men; 60% women; 10% minorities; 90% college students; 40% non-U.S. citizens; 20% local applicants. Nonsmokers required.

Employment Information Openings are from June 1 to August 31. Year-round positions also offered. Jobs available: ▶ 20 *adventure counselors/adventure specialists* (minimum age 19) with skills in caving, rock climbing, canoeing, ropes course, and backpacking; CPR/first aid, valid driver's license, and good driving record at $1500–$1800 per season ▶ 2 *custodial/maintenance staff* (minimum age 19) with CPR/first aid certification at $1500–$1800 per season ▶ 6 *department heads* (minimum age 21) with bachelor's degree, experience and skills in education, administration, international education, and counseling; CPR/first aid, valid driver's license, and good driving record at $2200 per season ▶ 20 *general activities counselors* (minimum age 19) with first aid, CPR certification, and experience in any combination of the following: swimming, drama, model rocketry, caving, rock climbing, or sign language at $1500 per season ▶ 60 *general counselors* (minimum age 19) with CPR/first aid, valid driver's license, and good driving record at $1500 per season ▶ 4 *horseback riding counselors* (minimum age 19) with first aid, CPR certification, and knowledge of Western-style horseback riding at $1500 per season ▶ 5 *kitchen staff/cooks* (minimum age 19) with CPR/first aid certification at $1500–$1800 per season ▶ *registered nurse* (must reside at camp) at $500 per week ▶ 4 *village coordinators (unit leaders)* (minimum age 21) college graduate at $2200 per season ▶ 12 *waterfront counselors* (minimum age 19) with lifeguard, first aid, and CPR certification at $1500 per season. Applicants must submit formal organization application, two personal references, two letters of recommendation, medical form. An in-person interview is recommended, but a telephone interview is acceptable. International applicants accepted; must apply through a recognized agency.

Benefits and Preemployment Training Free housing, free meals, willing to provide letters of recommendation, on-the-job training, willing to complete paperwork for educational credit, and willing to act as a professional reference. Preemployment training is required and includes accident prevention and safety, first aid, CPR, interpersonal skills, leadership skills, ropes course training, lifeguarding.

Contact Ben Swartz, Camp Director, Camp Horizons, 3586 Horizons Way, Harrisonburg, Virginia 22802. Telephone: 540-896-7600. Fax: 540-896-5455. E-mail: camp@horizonsva.com. World Wide Web: http://www.camphorizonsva.com. Contact by e-mail, fax, phone, or through World Wide Web site. Application deadline: continuous.

CENTER FOR TALENTED YOUTH/JOHNS HOPKINS UNIVERSITY–ST. STEPHEN'S AND ST. AGNES SCHOOL

ALEXANDRIA, VIRGINIA

See Center for Talented Youth/Johns Hopkins University on page 145 for complete description.

CHEERIO ADVENTURES

754 FOX KNOB ROAD
MOUTH OF WILSON, VIRGINIA 24363

General Information Program in adventure tripping and wilderness travel serving campers ages 10-17. Established in 1982. 60-acre facility located 85 miles from Greensboro, North Carolina. Features: on New River; mixture of woodlands and fields; mountain setting; close proximity to many natural forests.

Profile of Summer Employees Total number: 20; typical ages: 19–25. 50% men; 50% women; 20% minorities; 90% college students. Nonsmokers required.

Employment Information Openings are from May 20 to August 3. Jobs available: ▶ 1 *food coordinator* (minimum age 21) with driver's license and experience in the field at $185–$250 per week ▶ 3 *skills coordinators* (minimum age 21) at $225–$260 per week ▶ 1 *transportation coordinator* (minimum age 21) with driver's license at $185–$225 per week ▶ 3 *trip guides* (minimum age 21) at $195–$250 per week ▶ 10 *trip leaders* (minimum age 19) at $185–$215 per week. Applicants must submit a formal organization application, four personal references. An in-person interview is recommended, but a telephone interview is acceptable. International applicants accepted; must obtain own visa.

Benefits and Preemployment Training Free housing, free meals, health insurance, willing to provide letters of recommendation, on-the-job training, willing to complete paperwork for educational credit, and willing to act as a professional reference. Preemployment training is required and includes accident prevention and safety, first aid, CPR, interpersonal skills, leadership skills, activity skills.

Contact Keith Russell, Director, Cheerio Adventures, 1430 Camp Cheerio Road, Glade Valley, North Carolina 23627. Telephone: 336-363-2604. Fax: 336-363-3671. E-mail: advcamp@aol.com. World Wide Web: http://www.campcheerio.org. Contact by e-mail, fax, mail, phone, or through World Wide Web site. Application deadline: continuous.

CHINCOTEAGUE NATIONAL WILDLIFE REFUGE

PO BOX 62, 8231 BEACH ROAD
CHINCOTEAGUE, VIRGINIA 23336

General Information National Wildlife Refuge providing habitat for migratory birds and various animals and educating refuge visitors. Established in 1943. 14,000-acre facility located 60 miles from Salisbury, Maryland. Features: housing provided; ocean; lighthouse; wildlife observation; endangered species.

Profile of Summer Employees Total number: 40; typical ages: 18–24. 30% men; 70% women; 90% college students; 10% local applicants.

Employment Information Openings are from April to December. Jobs available: ▶ *environmental education interns* with good oral and written communication skills at $100 per week ▶ *field research assistant/wildlife management interns* at $100 per week ▶ *interpretive interns* must be comfortable in front of big groups at $100 per week. Applicants must submit a letter of interest, resume. A telephone interview is required. International applicants accepted; must obtain own visa, obtain own working papers.

Benefits and Preemployment Training Free housing, willing to provide letters of recommendation, on-the-job training, willing to complete paperwork for educational credit, and willing to act as a professional reference.

Contact Geralyn Mireles, Volunteer Coordinator, Chincoteague National Wildlife Refuge. Telephone: 757-336-6122. Fax: 757-336-5273. E-mail: geralyn_mireles@fws.gov. World Wide Web: http://chinco.fws.gov. Contact by e-mail or mail. Application deadline: varies by internship.

CYBERCAMPS–GEORGE MASON UNIVERSITY

FAIRFAX, VIRGINIA

See Cybercamps–University of Washington on page 335 for complete description.

4 STAR SUMMER CAMPS AT THE UNIVERSITY OF VIRGINIA

CHARLOTTESVILLE, VIRGINIA 22905

General Information Residential camp that offers golf, tennis, and academic enrichment courses daily and other sporting events in the evenings. Programs are available for campers ages 9–18. Established in 1975. Located 100 miles from Washington, DC. Features: university facilities; 13 tennis courts; full athletic facilities.

Profile of Summer Employees Total number: 35; typical ages: 19–25. 60% men; 40% women; 10% minorities; 70% college students; 10% local applicants. Nonsmokers required.

Employment Information Openings are from June 24 to August 10. Jobs available: ▶ 1 *evening activities director/recreation director* (minimum age 19) with good organization and planning skills at $1800–$2250 per season ▶ 10 *general counselors* (minimum age 19) with ability to work with young people at $900–$1400 per season ▶ 15 *golf counselors* (minimum age 19) should be advanced-level player with ability to work with children at $900–$1875 per season ▶ 6 *resident advisors* (minimum age 20) with experience as a resident advisor at a college or university at $1500–$2600 per season ▶ 25 *tennis instructors* (minimum age 19) should be advanced-level players with some competitive experience; must be college students or older at $900–$1400 per season. Applicants must submit formal organization application, letter of interest, resume, three personal references, three letters of recommendation. An in-person interview is recommended, but a telephone interview is acceptable. International applicants accepted; must obtain own visa, obtain own working papers, apply through a recognized agency.

Benefits and Preemployment Training Free housing, free meals, willing to provide letters of recommendation, on-the-job training, willing to complete paperwork for educational credit, and willing to act as a professional reference. Preemployment training is required and includes first aid, interpersonal skills, leadership skills, teaching tennis training.

Contact Ann Grubbs, Assistant Director, 4 Star Summer Camps at the University of Virginia, PO Box 3387, Falls Church, Virginia 22043. Fax: 703-866-7775. E-mail: a.grubbs@4starcamps.com. World Wide Web: http://www.4starcamps.com. Contact by e-mail, fax, mail, or through World Wide Web site. Application deadline: continuous.

FREDERICKSBURG AND SPOTSYLVANIA NATIONAL MILITARY PARK
120 CHATHAM LANE
FREDERICKSBURG, VIRGINIA 22405

General Information Historic park preserving and interpreting four Civil War battlefields in the Fredericksburg area. Established in 1927. 7,340-acre facility located 50 miles from Washington, DC. Features: 4 Civil War battlefields; 2 visitor centers; historic structures; park housing; historical trails; book store.

Profile of Summer Employees Total number: 50; typical ages: 21–40. 50% men; 50% women; 20% minorities; 5% high school students; 40% college students; 5% retirees; 30% local applicants.

Employment Information Openings are from May 19 to September 1. Year-round positions also offered. Jobs available: ▶ 1–5 *park guides* (minimum age 18) with knowledge of the Civil War at $10.85–$12.14 per hour ▶ 1 *seasonal natural resource assistant* (minimum age 18) knowledge of GIS preferable at $10.85–$12.14 per hour ▶ 1–5 *visitor use assistants* (minimum age 18) with knowledge of the Civil War at $10.85–$12.14 per hour. Applicants must submit a formal organization application.

Benefits and Preemployment Training Housing at a cost, formal training, willing to provide letters of recommendation, on-the-job training, willing to complete paperwork for educational credit, and willing to act as a professional reference. Preemployment training is required and includes interpersonal skills, interpretive skills.

Contact Gregory A. Mertz, Supervisory Historian, Fredericksburg and Spotsylvania National Military Park, 120 Chatham Lane, Fredericksburg, Virginia 22405. Telephone: 540-373-6124. Fax: 540-654-5521. E-mail: greg_mertz@nps.gov. World Wide Web: http://www.nps.gov/frsp. Contact by e-mail or through World Wide Web site. Application deadline: applications are accepted as needed; generally every three months a position is announced and applications will be accepted for a one-week period.

LEGACY INTERNATIONAL'S GLOBAL YOUTH VILLAGE
1020 LEGACY DRIVE
BEDFORD, VIRGINIA 24523

General Information International youth training program in a camp setting that focuses on cross-cultural understanding and leadership training and offers workshops in conflict resolution, the arts, ESOL, international relations, and other programs. Established in 1979. 40-acre facility located 40 miles from Roanoke. Features: rural, wooded setting; stream; rock climbing site; pool; cabins with electricity; central bathhouses.

Profile of Summer Employees Total number: 25–30; typical ages: 22–45. 40% men; 60% women; 15% minorities; 10% college students; 30% non-U.S. citizens; 1% local applicants. Nonsmokers preferred.

Employment Information Openings are from July 1 to August 15. Jobs available: ▶ 1 *English as a Second Language instructor* (minimum age 21) must be native English speaker with classroom teaching experience at $1200 per season or on a volunteer basis ▶ 1 *adventure/outdoor skills instructor* (minimum age 21) with first aid and CPR certification and rock-climbing teaching experience (preferred) at $900 per season or on a volunteer basis ▶ 2 *art instructors* (minimum age 21) with experience in the field; one position requires ability to teach pottery using the wheel and kiln at up to $1,200 per season or on a volunteer basis ▶ 5–6 *counselors (female)* (minimum age 21) must have demonstrated professional youth work experience; at up to $1,200 per season or on a volunteer basis ▶ 3–4 *counselors (male)* (minimum age 21) must have demonstrated professional youth work experience at up to $1,200 per season or on a volunteer basis ▶ 1 *global issues instructor* (minimum age 21) with background and knowledge in international relations and teaching experience at $1,200 per season or on a volunteer basis ▶ 7 *kitchen staff members* (minimum age 19) at $1,200 per season or on a volunteer basis ▶ 1 *leadership instructor* (minimum age 21) with ability to teach skills such as event planning, setting priorities, and running meetings; experience in the field at up to $1,200 per season or on a volunteer basis ▶ 2–3 *lifeguards* (minimum age 21) with first aid, CPR, lifeguarding certification at up to $900 per season or on a volunteer basis ▶ 1 *program coordinator* (minimum age 21) with performing arts background (preferred) and very good organizational and motivational skills at $1,200 per season or on a volunteer basis ▶ 1 *sports and games coordinator* (minimum age 21) with ability to lead and guide large groups in various games and sports and familiarity with new games and noncompetitive sports at $900 per season or on a volunteer basis ▶ 1 *theater arts instructor* (minimum age 21) with improvisational theater experience and experience teaching youths at up to $1,200 per season or on a volunteer basis. Applicants must submit formal organization application, resume, 2-3 professional references with phone/fax numbers. A telephone interview is required. International applicants accepted; must obtain own visa, obtain own working papers, apply through a recognized agency.

Benefits and Preemployment Training Free housing, free meals, formal training, health insurance, willing to provide letters of recommendation, names of contacts, on-the-job training, willing to complete paperwork for educational credit, willing to act as a professional reference, and laundry service. Preemployment training is required and includes accident prevention and safety, first aid, CPR, interpersonal skills, leadership skills, cross-cultural communication, counselor training.

Contact Leila Baz, Co-Director,, Legacy International's Global Youth Village, 1020 Legacy Drive, Bedford, Virginia 24523. Fax: 540-297-1860. E-mail: staff@legacyintl.org. World Wide Web: http://www.globalyouthvillage.org. Contact by e-mail, fax, mail, or through World Wide Web site. Application deadline: June 1.

OAKLAND SCHOOL AND CAMP

BOYD TAVERN
KESWICK, VIRGINIA 22947

General Information Coed residential and day camp for 130 students ages 8-14 with learning disabilities or other academic difficulties. Established in 1950. 450-acre facility located 65 miles from Richmond. Features: riding ring and trails; swimming pool; 2 tennis courts; unique classrooms; gym and recreation center; hiking trails; streams.

Profile of Summer Employees Total number: 70; typical ages: 19–25. 50% men; 50% women; 10% minorities; 75% college students; 25% local applicants. Nonsmokers preferred.

Employment Information Openings are from June 10 to August 9. Year-round positions also offered. Jobs available: ▶ 3–5 *camp counselors* (minimum age 19) with experience working with children; residential camp experience preferred at $3000–$3400 per season ▶ 1 *swimming instructor* (minimum age 20) with lifesaving and WSI certification at $3000–$3400 per season ▶ 1–5 *teachers* with teacher certification, special education preferred at $3500-$4000 per 7 weeks. Applicants must submit a formal organization application, letter of interest, resume, two personal references, two letters of recommendation. An in-person interview is required.

Benefits and Preemployment Training Free housing, free meals, formal training, possible full-time employment, willing to provide letters of recommendation, and on-the-job training. Preemployment training is required and includes accident prevention and safety, first aid, CPR, interpersonal skills, leadership skills, recreational activity planning, behavior management.

Contact Ms. Carol Smieciuch, Director, Oakland School, Oakland School and Camp, Boyd Tavern, Keswick, Virginia 22947. Telephone: 434-293-9059. Fax: 434-296-8930. E-mail: csoakland@earthlink.net. World Wide Web: http://www.oaklandschool.net. Contact by e-mail, fax, mail, phone, or through World Wide Web site. Application deadline: continuous.

THE SOUTHWESTERN COMPANY, VIRGINIA

See The Southwestern Company on page 302 for complete description.

SPORTS INTERNATIONAL–REDSKINS

FAIRFAX, VIRGINIA

See Sports International, Inc. on page 147 for complete description.

STUDENT CONSERVATION ASSOCIATION (SCA), VIRGINIA

See Student Conservation Association (SCA), New Hampshire on page 209 for complete description.

WOODBERRY FOREST SUMMER SCHOOL

WOODBERRY STATION
WOODBERRY FOREST, VIRGINIA 22989

General Information Coeducational boarding school for approximately 200 students grades 8–12. Established in 1889. 1,000-acre facility located 30 miles from Charlottesville. Features: woodlands and river; 6 tennis courts; 4 athletic fields; computer labs/network; 2 pools; golf course.

Profile of Summer Employees Total number: 21; typical age: 21. 60% men; 40% women; 40% college students. Nonsmokers preferred.

Employment Information Openings are from June 17 to August 3. Jobs available: ▶ 21 *interns (math, science, English)* (minimum age 21) with three or four years of college (or recent graduate) at $1300 per season ▶ 30 *teachers (all subjects)* at $2500 per season. Applicants must submit letter of interest, resume, academic transcripts, two letters of recommendation. International applicants accepted; must obtain own visa.

Benefits and Preemployment Training Free housing, free meals, willing to provide letters of recommendation, on-the-job training, and willing to act as a professional reference.

Contact Director of Summer School, Woodberry Forest Summer School, Woodberry Forest School, Woodberry Forest, Virginia 22989. Telephone: 540-672-6047. Fax: 540-672-9076. E-mail: wfs_summer@woodberry.org. World Wide Web: http://www.woodberry.org. Contact by e-mail, fax, mail, or phone. Application deadline: February 1.

WASHINGTON

A CHRISTIAN MINISTRY IN THE NATIONAL PARKS–WASHINGTON

See A Christian Ministry in the National Parks–Maine on page 122 for complete description.

CAMP BERACHAH

19830 SOUTHEAST 328TH PLACE
AUBURN, WASHINGTON 98092

General Information Offers eleven day camps (150 campers each), 22 horse camps (24 campers each), junior and teen camp (300 campers each), resident camps, and soccer camp (200 campers). Established in 1973. 160-acre facility located 30 miles from Seattle. Features: wooded setting; indoor pool; large gym; mountain bikes; horses; climbing wall/high ropes course.

Profile of Summer Employees Total number: 120; typical ages: 17–28. 40% men; 60% women;

5% minorities; 30% high school students; 70% college students; 8% non-U.S. citizens; 30% local applicants. Nonsmokers required.

Employment Information Openings are from June 10 to August 31. Spring break, winter break, and year-round positions also offered. Jobs available: ▶ 1–2 *bus driver* (minimum age 21) at $9 per hour ▶ *climbing wall facilitator* (minimum age 18) at $125–$150 per week ▶ *counselors* (minimum age 18) 16 year-olds with CIT experience are also eligible; paid at $115–$140 per week ▶ 1 *crafts director* (minimum age 21) at $125–$150 per week ▶ 1 *high ropes course facilitator* (minimum age 18) at $125–$150 per week ▶ *horsemanship instructor/wrangler* at $900–$1500 per season ▶ *lifeguard* (minimum age 16) at $125–$150 per week ▶ *mountain bike leader* (minimum age 18) at $125–$150 per week ▶ 1 *nurse* (minimum age 21) at $125–$150 per week ▶ 1 *recreation director* (minimum age 21) at $125–$150 per week. Applicants must submit formal organization application, two personal references, two letters of recommendation. An in-person interview is recommended, but a telephone interview is acceptable. International applicants accepted; must obtain own visa, obtain own working papers, apply through a recognized agency.

Benefits and Preemployment Training Free housing, free meals, possible full-time employment, willing to provide letters of recommendation, on-the-job training, willing to complete paperwork for educational credit, willing to act as a professional reference, and college savings plan; college scholarships; contract completion bonus. Preemployment training is required and includes accident prevention and safety, first aid, CPR, interpersonal skills, leadership skills.

Contact James Richey, Program Director, Camp Berachah, 19830 Southeast 328th Place, Auburn, Washington 98092. Telephone: 253-939-0488. Fax: 253-833-7027. E-mail: staff@berachahcamp.org. World Wide Web: http://www.berachahcamp.org. Contact by e-mail, fax, mail, phone, or through World Wide Web site. Application deadline: continuous.

CAMP KIRBY

4734 SAMISH POINT ROAD
BOW, WASHINGTON 98232

General Information Non-profit youth-serving agency summer camp and environmental education center. Established in 1923. 47-acre facility located 25 miles from Bellingham. Features: 1.5 miles beachfront; Climbing tower; 40 acres of trails; beautiful rustic setting; tree houses and tipis; basketball courts.

Profile of Summer Employees Total number: 30; typical ages: 17–21. 30% men; 70% women; 25% minorities; 10% high school students; 90% college students; 5% retirees; 70% local applicants. Nonsmokers preferred.

Employment Information Openings are from June 20 to August 26. Jobs available: ▶ 1–2 *assistant directors* (minimum age 21) with experience with youth; experience supervising others at $1500–$2000 per season ▶ 4–5 *kitchen staff* (minimum age 16) with Washington food handlers permit at $1200–$2000 per season ▶ *lifeguards* with lifeguarding certification; must be high school graduate (minimum) at $1200–$1300 per season ▶ 25–30 *summer camp staff* with experience working with youth; must be high school graduate (minimum) at $1000–$2000 per season. Applicants must submit a formal organization application, personal references and letters of recommendation in any combination equal to 3. An in-person interview is recommended, but a telephone interview is acceptable. International applicants accepted; must obtain own visa, obtain own working papers.

Benefits and Preemployment Training Free housing, free meals, formal training, willing to provide letters of recommendation, on-the-job training, willing to complete paperwork for educational credit, and willing to act as a professional reference. Preemployment training is required and includes accident prevention and safety, interpersonal skills, leadership skills.

Contact Jenn Brown, Camp Director, Camp Kirby. Telephone: 360-766-6060. Fax: 360-733-5711. E-mail: tamarjb@aol.com. World Wide Web: http://www.campkirby.org. Contact by e-mail, mail, phone, or through World Wide Web site. Application deadline: continuous.

CAMP RIVER RANCH

33300 NORTHEAST 32ND STREET
CARNATION, WASHINGTON 98014

General Information Resident camp serving approximately 190 girls per session, ages 6–17, and offering a variety of programs including swimming, boating, crafts, environmental education, outdoor skills and outdoor cooking, as well as specialty programs in English and Western riding, biking, backpacking, leadership, and drama. Established in 1951. 430-acre facility located 30 miles from Seattle. Features: freshwater lake; wooded setting; river; climbing wall.

Profile of Summer Employees Total number: 70; typical ages: 17–35. 100% women; 5% minorities; 5% high school students; 80% college students; 10% non-U.S. citizens; 5% local applicants. Nonsmokers preferred.

Employment Information Openings are from June 15 to August 20. Jobs available: ▶ 20 *camp counselors* (minimum age 18) at $1500–$2000 per season ▶ 4 *program coordinators* (minimum age 21) with interest in or ability with horses, arts and nature, water and trips, leadership at $2400–$3000 per season ▶ 6 *program specialists* (minimum age 20) with interest in or ability with horses, arts, nature, waterfront, trips, leadership at $1700–$2200 per season. Applicants must submit formal organization application, three personal references. An in-person interview is recommended, but a telephone interview is acceptable. International applicants accepted; must apply through a recognized agency.

Benefits and Preemployment Training Free housing, free meals, health insurance, willing to provide letters of recommendation, on-the-job training, willing to complete paperwork for educational credit, and willing to act as a professional reference. Preemployment training is optional and includes first aid, CPR, leadership skills, small craft safety (boating), lifeguarding, wilderness first aid.

Contact Margie Culbertson, Camp Administrator, Camp River Ranch. Telephone: 800-878-4685. Fax: 425-333-6236. E-mail: margiemc@girlscoutstotem.org. World Wide Web: http://www.girlscoutstotem.org. Contact by e-mail, fax, mail, phone, or through World Wide Web site. Application deadline: continuous.

CAMP VOLASUCA

617 FIRST STREET
SULTAN, WASHINGTON 98294

General Information Non-profit organization with a camp program that serves underprivileged youth and people with disabilities. Established in 1941. 110-acre facility located near Seattle. Features: mini golf course; trampoline; challenge course and area for sports recreation; hiking/wooded area; campfire; craft room.

Profile of Summer Employees Total number: 6–60; typical ages: 18–24. 10% minorities; 30% high school students; 30% college students; 10% non-U.S. citizens; 20% local applicants.

Employment Information Openings are from June to August. Jobs available: ▶ 1 *assistant cook* with ability to assist in food preparation; no previous experience required at $1750–$2250 per season ▶ 20 *counselors* experienced working with youth/special needs (preferred) at $1750–$2250 per season ▶ 1 *crafts leader* with knowledge of arts and crafts activities and adaptations for special needs at $1750–$2250 per season ▶ 1 *head cook* with food handlers permit; ability to supervise and direct others at $2500–$3500 per season ▶ 2 *lead staff* with experience with camping industry, and/or experience with developmentally disabled at $2000–$2500 per season ▶ 1 *lifeguard* with current lifesaving validation from an accredited program; CPR certification at $1750–$2250 per season ▶ 1 *office assistant* with organizational and customer skills, phone skills, computer skills, experience with Office 97. Applicants must submit a formal organization application. International applicants accepted.

Benefits and Preemployment Training Free housing, free meals, and willing to provide letters of recommendation. Preemployment training is required and includes accident prevention and safety.

Contact Chris Shroy, Program Director, Camp Volasuca, PO Box 268, Sultan, Washington 98294. Telephone: 360-793-0646. Fax: 360-793-8919. E-mail: cshroy@voaww.org. Contact by e-mail, fax, mail, or phone. Application deadline: continuous.

CAMP ZANIKA LACHE/CAMP FIRE USA NCW COUNCIL

PO BOX 1734
WENATCHEE, WASHINGTON 98807

General Information ACA-accredited camp located on the shores of Lake Wenatchee in the Wenatchee National Forest: a wonderful setting for campers to enjoy water sports, mountain trails, rivers, forests and streams, great natural beauty and outdoor adventure. Established in 1932. 13-acre facility. Features: freshwater lake; mountain area; ropes/challenge course; forested area; rustic cabins.

Profile of Summer Employees Total number: 35; typical ages: 18–25. 35% men; 65% women; 1% minorities; 1% high school students; 95% college students; 1% non-U.S. citizens; 1% local applicants. Nonsmokers preferred.

Employment Information Openings are from June 11 to August 11. Jobs available: ▶ 1 *archery director* (minimum age 18) with knowledge of archery, instructor certification and/or college course, experience with children at $1175 per season ▶ 1 *arts and crafts director* (minimum age 18) with training and experience in arts and crafts, experience teaching children at $1175 per season ▶ 2 *assistant camp directors* (minimum age 21) with experience with children and/or bookkeeping, camp staff experience, supervisory experience, experience with camp programming, organizational skills at $1800 per season ▶ 1 *assistant cook* (minimum age 18) with experience cooking for large groups, Washington State food handlers permit at $1500 per season ▶ 15 *cabin counselors* (minimum age 18) with CPR and first aid training, experience working with children at $1100–$1150 per season ▶ 3 *dishwashers* (minimum age 16) with teamwork skills and Washington State food handler's permit at $900–$950 per season ▶ 1 *head cook* (minimum age 21) with CPR and first aid training, Washington State food handler's permit, and experience cooking and ordering for large groups at $2500 per season ▶ 2 *lifeguards* with Red Cross, WSI, or LT, CPR training, and lifeguard experience at $1175 per season ▶ 1 *maintenance person* (minimum age 21) with valid driver's license and ability to operate power and maintenance equipment safely at $2600 per season ▶ *nature director* (minimum age 18) with knowledge of natural science and outdoor environment, ability to teach children at $1175 per season ▶ 1 *ropes course director* (minimum age 18) with documentation or certification of skills and experience in ropes course operation, and experience working with children at $1500 per season ▶ 1 *tripping director* (minimum age 21) with valid driver's license and good driving record, wilderness first aid or woofer certification, basic first aid and CPR training, backcountry experience at $1500 per season ▶ 3 *unit directors* (minimum age 18) with camp counseling experience, youth program experience, supervisory experience, one to two years college experience, valid driver's license and good driving record at $1300 per season ▶ 1 *waterfront director* (minimum age 21) with WSI or LT certification, supervisory experience, current driver's license and good driving record, and CPR lake guard experience a plus at $1500 per season. Applicants must submit formal organization application, three personal references. An in-person interview is recommended, but a telephone interview is acceptable. International applicants accepted; must obtain own visa, obtain own working papers, apply through a recognized agency.

Benefits and Preemployment Training Free housing, free meals, health insurance, willing to provide letters of recommendation, on-the-job training, willing to complete paperwork for educational credit, and laundry facilities. Preemployment training is required and includes accident prevention and safety, interpersonal skills, leadership skills, training for position.

Contact Wendy Borden, Outdoor Programs Director, Camp Zanika Lache/Camp Fire USA NCW Council, PO Box 1734, Wenatchee, Washington 98807. Telephone: 509-663-1609. Fax: 509-664-3038. E-mail: camp4@crcwnet.com. World Wide Web: http://www.ncwcampfire.org.

Contact by e-mail, fax, mail, phone, or through World Wide Web site. Application deadline: continuous.

CYBERCAMPS–BELLEVUE COMMUNITY COLLEGE
BELLEVUE, WASHINGTON
See Cybercamps–University of Washington below for complete description.

CYBERCAMPS–UNIVERSITY OF PUGET SOUND
TACOMA, WASHINGTON
See Cybercamps–University of Washington below for complete description.

CYBERCAMPS–UNIVERSITY OF WASHINGTON
UNIVERSITY OF WASHINGTON
SEATTLE, WASHINGTON
General Information Technology education for kids ages 7-16 in a well-rounded camp environment. Cybercamps is located nationwide on college campuses. Established in 1997. Features: held on college campuses nationwide; overnight campers stay in the dorms; 1 computer for every camper; small class sizes; fun outdoor activities; project-oriented curriculum.
Profile of Summer Employees Total number: 250; typical ages: 18–35. 50% men; 50% women; 4% high school students; 96% college students; 90% local applicants. Nonsmokers preferred.
Employment Information Openings are from June 1 to August 30. Jobs available: ▶ 10–30 *assistant camp directors* (minimum age 21) with camp experience and/or Bachelor's degree at $500 per week ▶ 30–45 *camp directors* (minimum age 25) with camp experience and/or Bachelor's degree at $800 per week ▶ 200–250 *counselors* (minimum age 18) with experience with children and computers at $300 per week. Applicants must submit resume, three personal references, on-line application from Web site. An in-person interview is recommended, but a telephone interview is acceptable.
Benefits and Preemployment Training Free meals, formal training, willing to provide letters of recommendation, on-the-job training, willing to act as a professional reference, and possibility of free housing or housing at cost. Preemployment training is required and includes accident prevention and safety, interpersonal skills, leadership skills.
Contact Giant Campus/Cybercamps, Cybercamps–University of Washington, 720 Olive Way, Suite 1800, Seattle, Washington 98101. Fax: 206-442-4501. E-mail: summerjobs@cybercamps.net. World Wide Web: http://www.cybercamps.com. Contact by mail or through World Wide Web site. Application deadline: continuous.

CYBERCAMPS–UNIVERSITY OF WASHINGTON, BOTHELL
BOTHELL, WASHINGTON
See Cybercamps–University of Washington above for complete description.

ENCHANTED PARKS, INC.
36201 ENCHANTED PARKWAY SOUTH
FEDERAL WAY, WASHINGTON 98003
General Information Amusement/theme park with rides, food stands, and a water park. Established in 1977. 60-acre facility located 16 miles from Seattle. Features: roller coaster; 9 water slides; wavepool; 22 amusement rides; daily shows.
Profile of Summer Employees Total number: 800–1,000; typical ages: 16–24. 47% men; 53% women; 30% minorities; 60% high school students; 20% college students; 10% retirees; 5% non-U.S. citizens; 85% local applicants.
Employment Information Openings are from April 11 to October 31. Winter break positions also offered. Jobs available: ▶ 200–250 *lifeguards* (minimum age 16) with water park training

course at $7.05–$9 per hour ▶ 300–500 *park employees* (minimum age 16) at $7–$10 per hour. Applicants must submit a formal organization application, two personal references. An in-person interview is required. International applicants accepted.

Benefits and Preemployment Training Meals at a cost, possible full-time employment, health insurance, willing to provide letters of recommendation, on-the-job training, willing to complete paperwork for educational credit, willing to act as a professional reference, opportunity to attend seminars/workshops, and tuition assistance. Preemployment training is required and includes accident prevention and safety, first aid, CPR.

Contact Kimberly Zier, Human Resources Manager, Enchanted Parks, Inc., 36201 Enchanted Parkway South, Federal Way, Washington 98003. Telephone: 253-661-8027. Fax: 253-661-8065. E-mail: kzier@sftp.com. World Wide Web: http://www.sixflags.com. Contact by e-mail, fax, mail, phone, or through World Wide Web site. Application deadline: continuous.

GIRL SCOUTS PACIFIC PEAKS COUNCIL–CAMP ST. ALBANS

5326 LITTLEROCK ROAD, SW
TUMWATER, WASHINGTON 98512

General Information Resident camp for girls ages 7 to 17, providing program opportunities with arts and crafts, nature, horses, archery, or waterfront. Established in 1935. 414-acre facility located 15 miles from Bremerton. Features: rustic cabins/tents; viking boats; horse program; freshwater lake; ACA accreditation; wooded setting.

Profile of Summer Employees Total number: 55; typical ages: 18–22. 100% women; 3% minorities; 10% high school students; 90% college students; 80% local applicants.

Employment Information Openings are from June 15 to August 26. Jobs available: ▶ 1 *business manager and driver* (minimum age 21) with first aid/CPR certification, good driving record, basic office skills at $1900–$2100 per season ▶ 1 *camp health manager* (minimum age 21) must be registered professional in Washington with first aid training, registered nurse preferred at $2600–$2700 per season ▶ 1 *head cook/kitchen supervisor* (minimum age 21) with experience in large quantity cooking and ability to work within a limited budget required at $2600–$2700 per season ▶ 4–10 *program staff (lifeguards, riding staff, arts and crafts and nature specialists)* (minimum age 18) at $1500–$1800 per season ▶ 15–30 *unit leaders/counselors* (minimum age 18) with high school diploma or equivalent, first aid/CPR certification, and experience in camping preferred at $1500–$1800 per season. Applicants must submit formal organization application, three personal references. An in-person interview is recommended, but a telephone interview is acceptable. International applicants accepted; must apply through a recognized agency.

Benefits and Preemployment Training Free housing, free meals, formal training, willing to provide letters of recommendation, willing to complete paperwork for educational credit, willing to act as a professional reference, and health insurance, if job related.

Contact Michelle Van Alstine, Camp Director/Outreach Specialist, Girl Scouts Pacific Peaks Council–Camp St. Albans, 5326 Littlerock Road, SW, Tumwater, Washington 98512. Telephone: 360-943-0490. Fax: 360-943-8653. E-mail: mvanalstine@gsppc.org. World Wide Web: http://www.gsppc.org. Contact by e-mail, fax, mail, phone, or through World Wide Web site. Application deadline: continuous.

LONGACRE EXPEDITIONS, WASHINGTON

BELLINGHAM, WASHINGTON

General Information Adventure travel program throughout the Pacific Northwest including Washington, Oregon, and British Columbia. Challenging programs place equal emphasis on physical accomplishment and emotional growth. Established in 1981.

Profile of Summer Employees Total number: 30; typical ages: 21–28. 50% men; 50% women; 10% minorities; 40% college students; 30% local applicants. Nonsmokers required.

Employment Information Openings are from June 15 to August 10. Jobs available: ▶ 15 *assistant trip leaders* (minimum age 21) with good driving record, CPR, and WFR certification at $252–$300 per week ▶ 1 *mountaineering instructor* (minimum age 21) with WFR and CPR certification at $300–$400 per week ▶ 1 *rock climbing instructor* (minimum age 21) with good driving record, WFR, and CPR at $300–$400 per week ▶ 2 *sea kayaking instructors* (minimum age 21) with lifeguard training, CPR and WFR certification at $300–$400 per week ▶ 3 *support and logistics staff members* (minimum age 21) with good driving record, WFR, and CPR at $180–$240 per week. Applicants must submit a formal organization application, letter of interest, resume, three personal references. An in-person interview is recommended, but a telephone interview is acceptable. International applicants accepted; must obtain own visa, obtain own working papers.

Benefits and Preemployment Training Free housing, free meals, willing to provide letters of recommendation, on-the-job training, willing to complete paperwork for educational credit, willing to act as a professional reference, and pro-deal purchase program. Preemployment training is required and includes accident prevention and safety, interpersonal skills, leadership skills.

Contact Meredith Schuler, Director, Longacre Expeditions, Washington, 4030 Middle Ridge Road, Newport, Pennsylvania 17074-8110. Telephone: 717-567-6790. Fax: 717-567-3955. E-mail: longacre@longacreexpeditions.com. World Wide Web: http://www.longacreexpeditions.com. Contact by e-mail, fax, mail, phone, or through World Wide Web site. Application deadline: continuous.

MARROWSTONE MUSIC FESTIVAL

11065 5TH AVENUE, NE, SUITE A
SEATTLE, WASHINGTON 98125

General Information A three-week music festival set on the campus of Western Washington University in beautiful Bellingham, WA. Established in 1942. near Bellingham. Features: top-notch music facilities; music library; concert hall; Cascade Mountains; tennis courts; university dormitories.

Profile of Summer Employees Total number: 40; typical ages: 18–25. 50% men; 50% women; 25% minorities; 30% high school students; 70% college students. Nonsmokers preferred.

Employment Information Openings are from July 28 to August 18. Jobs available: ▶ 6–8 *camp counselors* (minimum age 18) with ability to work well with peers and younger students; responsible ▶ 6–12 *interns* (minimum age 18) at $100 per week ▶ *stage crew* (minimum age 13). Applicants must submit formal organization application, resume, Marrowstone application materials; $35-$40 fee for program costs. International applicants accepted; must obtain own visa, apply through a recognized agency.

Benefits and Preemployment Training Free housing, free meals, willing to provide letters of recommendation, willing to act as a professional reference, opportunity to attend seminars/workshops, and tuition assistance.

Contact Stuart Wolferman, Festival Coordinator, Marrowstone Music Festival. Telephone: 206-362-2300. Fax: 206-361-9254. E-mail: marrowstone@syso.org. World Wide Web: http://www.marrowstone.org. Contact by e-mail. Application deadline: rolling beginning November 1.

MT. RAINIER GUEST SERVICES

PO BOX 108
ASHFORD, WASHINGTON 98304

General Information Operates hotels, food services, and gift shops in Mt. Rainier National Park. Established in 1917. 244,000-acre facility located 100 miles from Tacoma. Features: old growth forests; wildlife; mountain meadows; glaciers; canyons; wilderness.

Profile of Summer Employees Total number: 240; typical ages: 18–75. 50% men; 50% women;

10% minorities; 50% college students; 10% retirees; 30% non-U.S. citizens; 10% local applicants. Nonsmokers preferred.

Employment Information Openings are from May to October. Jobs available: ▶ 20 *cook's helpers/pantry persons* (minimum age 18) with ability to perform prep work plus make salads and sandwiches at $7.25 per hour ▶ 10 *cooks* (minimum age 21) with fine dining cooking experience and ability to work in casual and fine dining restaurants at $8.25–$10.50 per hour ▶ 10 *desk clerks* (minimum age 18) with ability to register guests and handle cash at $7.25 per hour ▶ 30 *fast food attendants* (minimum age 18) with ability to take/fill orders, bus tables, and operate cash register at $6.90 per hour ▶ 20 *housekeeping staff members* (minimum age 18) with ability to clean guest rooms and hotel at $6.90–$7.50 per hour ▶ 5 *janitors (night and day)* (minimum age 18) with ability to clean halls, restrooms, windows, and carpets and empty garbage at $7.25–$9 per hour ▶ 5 *kitchen porters (night and day)* (minimum age 18) with ability to clean hoods, ovens, and floors and assist in dishwashing at $7.25–$8 per hour ▶ 30 *kitchen/utility personnel* (minimum age 18) at $7.25 per hour ▶ 20 *retail clerks* (minimum age 18) with ability to perform retail sales, stocking, and cleaning duties at $7.25 per hour. Applicants must submit formal organization application. International applicants accepted; must obtain own visa, obtain own working papers, apply through a recognized agency.

Benefits and Preemployment Training Housing at a cost, meals at a cost, and on-the-job training. Preemployment training is required and includes accident prevention and safety, CPR, wilderness preparedness.

Contact Sandra Miller, Personnel Manager, Mt. Rainier Guest Services, PO Box 108, Ashford, Washington 98304. Telephone: 360-569-2400 Ext. 119. Fax: 360-569-2770. World Wide Web: http://www.coolworks.com/rainier. Contact by fax, mail, phone, or through World Wide Web site. Application deadline: continuous.

THE SOUTHWESTERN COMPANY, WASHINGTON

See The Southwestern Company on page 302 for complete description.

STUDENT CONSERVATION ASSOCIATION (SCA), WASHINGTON

See Student Conservation Association (SCA), New Hampshire on page 209 for complete description.

YMCA CAMP SEYMOUR

9725 CRAMER ROAD KPN
GIG HARBOR, WASHINGTON 98329

General Information Summer camp offers in-camp overnight programs (youth entering 1st-8th grade); out-of-camp wilderness and caravan trip adventures (youth entering 8th-12th grade); and teen leadership experiences (youth entering 8th-12th grade). Established in 1905. 160-acre facility located 20 miles from Tacoma. Features: forested hills; 1/2-mile saltwater shoreline; ropes courses and climbing wall; outdoor pool; waterfront/dock; comfortable cabins.

Profile of Summer Employees Total number: 50; typical ages: 18–30. 45% men; 55% women; 10% minorities; 10% high school students; 45% college students; 5% non-U.S. citizens; 40% local applicants. Nonsmokers preferred.

Employment Information Openings are from June 18 to August 24. Jobs available: ▶ 1 *adventure areas director* (minimum age 20) with CPR, first aid, ropes course and/or climbing wall experience/certifications; lifeguard preferred at $30–$34 per day ▶ 12–14 *cabin leaders* (minimum age 18) with first aid and CPR certifications, prefer lifeguard certification, and some experience in the field at $18–$22 per day ▶ 1 *camp programs director* (minimum age 21) with first aid and CPR certifications, prefer lifeguard certification, and experience with summer camp programming at $32–$36 per day ▶ 1 *creative arts director* (minimum age 19) with first aid and CPR certification and relevant experience at $30–$34 per day ▶ 1 *health care director* with preference for

RN/LPN license in Washington state; minimum requirement is entering final year of degree at $36–$40 per day ▶ 1 *outfitter* (minimum age 21) with CPR, first aid, driver's license, good driving record, experience with packing and outfitting trips at $32–$36 per day ▶ 1 *pool director* (minimum age 20) with lifeguard certification, first aid, CPR, and experience in the field at $30–$34 per day ▶ 12–14 *senior cabin leaders* (minimum age 19) with first aid and CPR certifications, experience in the field; one year of college and lifeguard certification (preferred) at $25–$27 per day ▶ 1 *skills director* (minimum age 21) with CPR, first aid, experience with many program areas and skills, lifeguard preferred at $32–$36 per day ▶ 1 *target sports director* (minimum age 19) with CPR, first aid, experience/certifications in bb, riflery, and/or archery; lifeguard preferred at $30–$34 per day ▶ 4 *teen leaders* (minimum age 20) with CPR, wilderness first aid, safe driving record, and experience in field at $30–$34 per day ▶ 6 *trip leaders* (minimum age 19) with experience in the field; ability to lead bike, backpacking, canoe, or kayak trips; wilderness first aid and CPR certifications at $30–$38 per day ▶ 4 *unit directors* (minimum age 20) with CPR and first aid certification, experience in camping required at $32–$36 per day ▶ 2 *van driver/assistant outfitters* (minimum age 21) with driver's license, ability to drive trips to remote locations, assist with trip preparation at $28–$32 per day ▶ 1 *waterfront director* (minimum age 20) with lifeguard certification, first aid, CPR, and experience in the field at $30–$34 per day. Applicants must submit formal organization application, letter of interest, resume, three personal references, three professional references. An in-person interview is recommended, but a telephone interview is acceptable. International applicants accepted; must apply through a recognized agency.

Benefits and Preemployment Training Free housing, free meals, formal training, willing to provide letters of recommendation, on-the-job training, willing to complete paperwork for educational credit, and willing to act as a professional reference. Preemployment training is required and includes accident prevention and safety, interpersonal skills, leadership skills, working/communicating with children.

Contact Aaron Keating, Camping Director, YMCA Camp Seymour, 9725 Cramer Road KPN, Gig Harbor, Washington 98329. Telephone: 253-884-3392. Fax: 253-460-8897. E-mail: campseymour@ymcatacoma.org. World Wide Web: http://www.campseymour.org. Contact by e-mail, mail, or through World Wide Web site. Application deadline: continuous.

WEST VIRGINIA

CAMP RIM ROCK

YELLOW SPRING, WEST VIRGINIA 26865

General Information Residential camp serving 260 girls offering a strong general program and horseback riding, aquatics, and performing arts programs. Established in 1952. 600-acre facility located 90 miles from Washington, DC. Features: river runs through the property; mountains frame the camp; spacious modern stables with 65 horses; large amphitheatre and several pavilions; 2 in-ground pools; 2 tennis courts.

Profile of Summer Employees Total number: 80–90; typical ages: 18–30. 5% men; 95% women; 10% minorities; 75% college students; 1% retirees; 30% non-U.S. citizens; 5% local applicants. Nonsmokers required.

Employment Information Openings are from June 1 to August 16. Jobs available: ▶ 1–5 *archery instructor* (minimum age 19) with certification and/or experience at $200 per week (starting salary) ▶ *arts and crafts instructor* (minimum age 19) with skills in this field at $200 per week (starting salary) ▶ 1–2 *dance instructors* (minimum age 19) with skills in teaching dance and experience working with children at $200 per week (starting salary) ▶ 1–3 *drama instructors* (minimum age 19) with skills and experience in drama and working with children at $200 per week (starting salary) ▶ *drawing and painting instructor* (minimum age 19) with skills in this field at $200 per week (starting salary) ▶ 20 *general counselors* with ability to work with children at $200 per week (starting salary) ▶ 5 *landsports instructors* (minimum age 19) experience and ability to teach in one or more of the following: basketball, volleyball, tennis, archery, softball at $200 per week (starting salary) ▶ 2–3 *music instructors* (minimum age 19) experience and ability to teach one or more of the following: a cappella choir, percussion, recorder, guitar, dulcimer at $200 per week (starting salary) ▶ 2–6 *nurses* with RN (full season or partial season position available); at a negotiable salary; may work in exchange for daughter's tuition ▶ 12–15 *riding staff members* with teacher certification at $200 per week (starting salary) ▶ 5–8 *swimming counselors* (minimum age 19) with WSI certification and/or ability to teach; canoeing experience a plus at $200 per week (starting salary) ▶ 2 *tennis counselors* with experience in the field and working with children at $200 per week (starting salary). Applicants must submit formal organization application, three personal references. An in-person interview is recommended, but a telephone interview is acceptable. International applicants accepted; must apply through a recognized agency.

Benefits and Preemployment Training Free housing, free meals, formal training, willing to provide letters of recommendation, names of contacts, on-the-job training, willing to complete paperwork for educational credit, willing to act as a professional reference, travel reimbursement, and 24 hours off per week. Preemployment training is required and includes accident prevention and safety, first aid, CPR, interpersonal skills, leadership skills, program orientation, lifeguard certification, archery instructor certification, canoe instructor certification.

Contact Deborah Matheson, Director, Camp Rim Rock, Box 69, Yellow Spring, West Virginia 26865. Telephone: 800-662-4650. Fax: 304-856-3201. E-mail: office@camprimrock.com. World Wide Web: http://www.camprimrock.com. Contact by e-mail, fax, mail, phone, or through World Wide Web site. Application deadline: continuous.

CAMP TALL TIMBERS
ROUTE 1
HIGH VIEW, WEST VIRGINIA 26808

General Information Summer camp for children. Traditional program including 35 activities. Established in 1970. 112-acre facility located 20 miles from Winchester, Virginia. Features: 112 secluded acres; private lake; swimming pool; 4 tennis courts; basketball and roller hockey courts; athletic fields.

Profile of Summer Employees Total number: 50; typical ages: 19–25. 50% men; 50% women; 90% college students; 1% retirees; 10% non-U.S. citizens. Nonsmokers required.

Employment Information Openings are from June 15 to August 17. Jobs available: ▶ 10–20 *counselors* (minimum age 19) a desire to work with children and ability to assist with or teach an activity at $1200–$1600 per season. Applicants must submit formal organization application. An in-person interview is recommended, but a telephone interview is acceptable. International applicants accepted; must obtain own visa, obtain own working papers, apply through a recognized agency.

Benefits and Preemployment Training Free housing, free meals, possible full-time employment, willing to provide letters of recommendation, willing to complete paperwork for educational credit, willing to act as a professional reference, and travel reimbursement. Preemployment training is required and includes accident prevention and safety, first aid, CPR, interpersonal skills, leadership skills.

Contact Jerry Smith, Executive Director, Camp Tall Timbers, 11615 Fulham Street, Silver Spring, Maryland 20902-3080. Telephone: 301-649-5577. Fax: 301-681-6662. E-mail: funcamp@

aol.com. World Wide Web: http://www.camptalltimbers.com. Contact through World Wide Web site. Application deadline: continuous.

THE SOUTHWESTERN COMPANY, WEST VIRGINIA

See The Southwestern Company on page 302 for complete description.

STUDENT CONSERVATION ASSOCIATION (SCA), WEST VIRGINIA

See Student Conservation Association (SCA), New Hampshire on page 209 for complete description.

WISCONSIN

AURORA UNIVERSITY, LAKE GENEVA CAMPUS

PO BOX 210
WILLIAMS BAY, WISCONSIN 53191

General Information Educational conference center serving families, nonprofit organizations, and groups. Established in 1884. 300-acre facility located 45 miles from Milwaukee. Features: freshwater lake; wooded setting; 2 tennis courts; cabins; 1200 feet of lakefront; 3 piers.

Profile of Summer Employees Total number: 175; typical ages: 14–68. 40% men; 60% women; 60% high school students; 40% college students; 10% non-U.S. citizens. Nonsmokers preferred.

Employment Information Openings are from May 25 to September 9. Jobs available: ▶ 2 *arts and crafts staff members* (minimum age 18) at $7–$8 per hour ▶ 1–2 *conference center set-up crew* (minimum age 18) with driver's license and clean driving record at $6–$6.50 per hour ▶ 20–25 *food service workers* (minimum age 14) at $6–$6.50 per hour ▶ 3–4 *front desk workers* (minimum age 18) at $7–$8 per hour ▶ 5–6 *golf course staff members* (minimum age 18) at $6–$7 per hour ▶ 4–5 *lifeguards* (minimum age 16) with WSI certification, CPR, and advanced first aid at $7–$8 per hour ▶ 2–3 *preschool/day care staff members* (minimum age 18) at $7–$8 per hour ▶ 3–4 *snack shop clerks* at $5–$6 per hour. Applicants must submit formal organization application, letter of interest. International applicants accepted; must apply through a recognized agency.

Benefits and Preemployment Training Housing at a cost, meals at a cost, formal training, willing to provide letters of recommendation, on-the-job training, willing to complete paperwork for educational credit, and willing to act as a professional reference. Preemployment training is optional and includes first aid, CPR.

Contact Richard Miller, Director of Personnel, Aurora University, Lake Geneva Campus, PO Box 210, Williams Bay, Wisconsin 53191-0210. Telephone: 262-245-8508. Fax: 262-245-8505. E-mail: rmiller@aurora.edu. World Wide Web: http:////augeowms.org/. Contact by e-mail, fax, mail, or phone. Application deadline: continuous.

BIRCH TRAIL CAMP FOR GIRLS

PO BOX 527
MINONG, WISCONSIN 54859

General Information Residential camp serving 185 girls ages 8–15 in two 4-week sessions including extensive wilderness trips. Established in 1959. 310-acre facility located 55 miles from

Duluth, Minnesota. Features: freshwater lake; low and high ropes course; tournament water ski slalom course; wooded setting; 3-sided climbing tower; beautiful rustic area.
Profile of Summer Employees Total number: 90; typical ages: 17–40. 5% men; 95% women; 10% minorities; 10% high school students; 80% college students; 15% non-U.S. citizens; 5% local applicants. Nonsmokers preferred.
Employment Information Openings are from June 12 to August 13. Jobs available: ▶ 25–50 *cabin counselors* (minimum age 18) at $1300–$1900 per season ▶ 1–2 *caretaker's assistants* at $1350–$1750 per season ▶ *housekeepers* at $1350–$1750 per season ▶ *kitchen helpers* at $1350–$1750 per season ▶ 1–3 *nurses* (minimum age 21) with RN or LPN at $2150–$3500 per season ▶ 1–3 *swimming instructors* (minimum age 18) with LGT or WSI certification at $1300–$2000 per season ▶ 3–6 *wilderness trip leaders* (minimum age 21) with LGT certification; canoeing, backpacking, and climbing experience preferred at $1700–$2300 per season. Applicants must submit formal organization application. An in-person interview is recommended, but a telephone interview is acceptable. International applicants accepted; must apply through a recognized agency.
Benefits and Preemployment Training Free housing, free meals, formal training, health insurance, willing to provide letters of recommendation, on-the-job training, willing to complete paperwork for educational credit, willing to act as a professional reference, and travel reimbursement. Preemployment training is required and includes accident prevention and safety, first aid, CPR, interpersonal skills, leadership skills, wilderness skills.
Contact Richard Chernov, Owner/Director, Birch Trail Camp for Girls, PO Box 527, Minong, Wisconsin 54859. Fax: 715-466-2217. E-mail: brchtrail@aol.com. World Wide Web: http://www.birchtrail.com. Contact through World Wide Web site. Application deadline: May 1.

BOYD'S MASON LAKE RESORT

PO BOX 57
FIFIELD, WISCONSIN 54524

General Information American-plan family resort that rents 18 cabins, serves 3 meals daily, and performs daily maid service for up to 100 guests. Established in 1895. 2,600-acre facility located 250 miles from Madison. Features: 4 freshwater, spring-fed lakes; 2600 private acres; heavily forested, wooded setting; very secluded; miles of hiking/biking trails; very old resort with modern conveniences.
Profile of Summer Employees Total number: 30; typical ages: 17–60. 30% men; 70% women; 7% high school students; 15% college students; 10% retirees; 10% non-U.S. citizens; 75% local applicants. Nonsmokers preferred.
Employment Information Openings are from May 15 to October 15. Jobs available: ▶ 1 *children's recreation supervisor* (minimum age 18) with background in elementary education at $7 per hour ▶ 5 *dining room attendants* (minimum age 18) at $7–$10 per hour ▶ 1 *dishwasher* (minimum age 18) at $7–$10 per hour ▶ 2 *housekeepers* (minimum age 18) at $7 per hour ▶ 1 *pots and pans washer* (minimum age 18) at $7–$10 per hour ▶ 1 *receptionist* (minimum age 18) at $7 per hour ▶ 1 *swing cook* (minimum age 18) at $7–$10 per hour. Applicants must submit formal organization application, resume, two personal references. An in-person interview is recommended, but a telephone interview is acceptable. International applicants accepted; must obtain own visa, obtain own working papers, apply through a recognized agency.
Benefits and Preemployment Training Free housing, free meals, willing to provide letters of recommendation, on-the-job training, and outdoor recreational activities (boating, swimming, hiking).
Contact Richard Simon, Manager/Owner, Boyd's Mason Lake Resort, PO Box 57, Fifield, Wisconsin 54524. Telephone: 715-762-3469. Contact by mail or phone. Application deadline: continuous.

CAMP ALICE CHESTER–EAST TROY

EAST TROY, WISCONSIN

General Information Girl Scouts of Milwaukee area resident camp located on a beautiful lake in the woods of southern Wisconsin serving girls ages 8 to 15.

Employment Information Openings are from June to August. Jobs available: ▶ 3 *adventure trip staff* (minimum age 21) with high school diploma, camping experience, knowledge of Girl Scouts, desire for adventure at $1900–$2100 per season ▶ 1 *assistant director (camp operations)* (minimum age 21) with two-year degree, knowledge of Girl Scout program, ability to encourage creative thinking, willingness to lead girls in decision-making, team skills, communication skills, supervisory ability at $2200–$3200 per season ▶ 1 *business manager* (minimum age 21) with two-year degree preferably in business/education, knowledge of Girl Scout program and philosophy, creative thinking skills, ability to manage accounts and maintain inventory, team skills, communication skills, customer service experience at $2200–$2700 per season ▶ 16 *camp counselors* (minimum age 18) with flexibility, creativity, patience, stamina, communication skills, ability to live outdoors during summer, leadership initiative at $1800–$1900 per season ▶ 4 *lifeguards/counselors* (minimum age 16) with certificate, lakefront experience, attentive lifeguard certification, safety practices in camp environment, team skills, ability to work and live in summer camp at $2000–$2200 per season ▶ 1 *lifeguards/trip staff* (minimum age 21) with lifeguarding/smallcraft certification, leadership skills, team skills, ability to work in summer camp setting at $2200–$2300 per season ▶ 2 *program specialists* (minimum age 18) with ability to work and teach girls ages 8 and up; ability to deliver interesting and active programs; ability to live and work in outdoor camp setting at $1900–$2100 per season ▶ 1 *smallcraft instructor* (minimum age 18) with smallcraft instructor certification, ability to teach and encourage 8-14 year old girls, team skills, fun attitude, willingness to live and work in camp setting at $2000–$2200 per season. Applicants must submit a formal organization application, resume, three personal references. A telephone interview is required.

Benefits and Preemployment Training Free housing, free meals, health insurance, and paid training. Preemployment training is required and includes accident prevention and safety, first aid, CPR, interpersonal skills, leadership skills.

Contact Andrea Yanacheck, Camp Director, Camp Alice Chester–East Troy, 131 South 69th Street, Milwaukee, Wisconsin 53214. Telephone: 414-476-1050 Ext. 159. Fax: 414-476-5958. E-mail: ayanacheck@girlscoutsmilwaukee.org. World Wide Web: http://www.girlscoutsmilwaukee.org. Contact by fax, mail, or phone. Application deadline: continuous.

CAMP BIRCH KNOLL FOR GIRLS

EAGLE RIVER, WISCONSIN 54554

General Information Residential camp with 40 instructed activities for girls ages 8–16. Established in 1945. 400-acre facility located 250 miles from Milwaukee. Features: indoor gymnastics and dance center; 5 new tennis courts; on-site horseback riding arena; excellent art facilities; extensive waterfront equipment.

Profile of Summer Employees Total number: 50; typical ages: 18–22. 20% men; 80% women; 5% high school students; 70% college students; 5% local applicants. Nonsmokers required.

Employment Information Openings are from June 2 to August 13. Jobs available: ▶ 1 *cook* (minimum age 18) with experience in quantity cooking at $200–$400 per week ▶ 20 *counselors/instructors* (minimum age 17) must be high school graduate at $1800–$2400 per season ▶ 1 *gymnastics director* (minimum age 18) at $2000–$2500 per season ▶ 2 *registered nurses* with RN or LPN license at $3000–$3500 per season ▶ 1 *riding director* (minimum age 18) at $2500–$3500 per season ▶ 1 *swimming director* (minimum age 18) at $2000–$2500 per season ▶ 1 *tennis director* (minimum age 18) at $2000–$2500 per season. Applicants must submit a formal organization application, two personal references, two letters of recommendation. An in-person interview is recommended, but a telephone interview is acceptable.

Benefits and Preemployment Training Free housing, free meals, willing to provide letters of recommendation, on-the-job training, willing to complete paperwork for educational credit, willing to act as a professional reference, and laundry service. Preemployment training is required and includes accident prevention and safety, first aid, CPR, interpersonal skills, leadership skills.
Contact Gary Baier, Director, Camp Birch Knoll for Girls, PO Box 13, Stevens Point, Wisconsin 54481. Telephone: 800-843-2904. Fax: 715-341-4261. E-mail: cbkfun@aol.com. World Wide Web: http://www.birchknoll.com. Contact by e-mail, fax, mail, phone, or through World Wide Web site. Application deadline: May 1.

CAMP EDWARDS
N8901 ARMY LAKE ROAD
EAST TROY, WISCONSIN 53120

General Information Residential camp serving youth and families with six- and eleven-day sessions. Established in 1929. 132-acre facility located 45 miles from Milwaukee. Features: extensive freshwater lake frontage; 2 low ropes courses; 1/2 mile-elevated marsh boardwalk; 7 distinct ecosystems; full log amphitheater; lakefront viewing deck.
Profile of Summer Employees Total number: 50; typical ages: 17–24. 50% men; 50% women; 2% minorities; 10% high school students; 90% college students; 1% retirees; 1% non-U.S. citizens; 1% local applicants. Nonsmokers required.
Employment Information Openings are from June 7 to August 12. Year-round positions also offered. Jobs available: ▶ 1 *arts and crafts coordinator/cabin leader* (minimum age 21) at $150–$170 per week ▶ 16–20 *assistant cabin leaders* (minimum age 17) at $70 per week ▶ 1 *assistant leadership in development director* (minimum age 19) at $150–$175 per week ▶ 1 *assistant waterfront director* (minimum age 20) at $150–$175 per week ▶ 16–20 *cabin counselors* (minimum age 18) at $140–$150 per week ▶ 1 *health director* (minimum age 21) with WI RN license or EMT at $300–$350 per week ▶ 1 *leader in training director* (minimum age 21) at $175–$200 per week ▶ 1 *program associate* (minimum age 21) at $175–$200 per week ▶ 1 *program coordinator* (minimum age 21) at $175–$200 per week ▶ 1 *trips director* (minimum age 21) with lifeguarding, first aid, CPR at $175–$200 per week ▶ 1–2 *trips leaders* (minimum age 18) at $140–$150 per week ▶ 1 *unit leader* (minimum age 20) at $150–$180 per week ▶ 1 *waterfront director* (minimum age 21) with appropriate certifications at $175–$200 per week. Applicants must submit formal organization application, three personal references, two letters of recommendation. An in-person interview is recommended, but a telephone interview is acceptable. International applicants accepted; must apply through a recognized agency.
Benefits and Preemployment Training Free housing, free meals, willing to provide letters of recommendation, on-the-job training, willing to complete paperwork for educational credit, willing to act as a professional reference, opportunity to attend seminars/workshops, and laundry facilities. Preemployment training is required and includes CPR, leadership skills, optional Red Cross lifeguard and first aid training.
Contact Craig Steward, Camp Director, Camp Edwards, PO Box 16, East Troy, Wisconsin 53120. Telephone: 262-642-7466. Fax: 262-642-5108. E-mail: camped@netwurx.net. World Wide Web: http://www.campedwards.org. Contact by e-mail, fax, mail, or phone. Application deadline: continuous.

CAMP INTERLAKEN JCC
7050 OLD HIGHWAY 70
EAGLE RIVER, WISCONSIN 54521

General Information Residential Jewish coeducational camp serving 400 campers ages 8–16. Established in 1966. 110-acre facility located 250 miles from Milwaukee. Features: lakefront; ropes challenge course; lighted tennis courts; north woods setting; Judaic Resource Center; special teen camp program.

Profile of Summer Employees Total number: 95; typical ages: 18–22. 50% men; 50% women; 5% minorities; 90% college students; 5% non-U.S. citizens. Nonsmokers preferred.
Employment Information Openings are from June 18 to August 18. Jobs available: ▶ 1 *crafts instructor* with knowledge of ceramics, tie-dyeing, crafts, and painting preferred at $1200–$2000 per season ▶ 4 *kitchen stewards* (minimum age 21) with experience at $1500 per season ▶ *secretary* (minimum age 19) with experience at $1300–$1600 per season. Applicants must submit formal organization application, resume, three personal references. An in-person interview is recommended, but a telephone interview is acceptable. International applicants accepted; must apply through a recognized agency.
Benefits and Preemployment Training Free housing, free meals, willing to provide letters of recommendation, on-the-job training, willing to complete paperwork for educational credit, willing to act as a professional reference, opportunity to attend seminars/workshops, travel reimbursement, and internship opportunities available. Preemployment training is required and includes accident prevention and safety, first aid, CPR, interpersonal skills, leadership skills.
Contact Howard Wagan, Director, Camp Interlaken JCC, 6255 North Santa Monica, Milwaukee, Wisconsin 53217. Telephone: 414-967-8240. Fax: 414-964-0922. E-mail: ciljcc@execpc.com. World Wide Web: http://www.campinterlaken.org. Contact by e-mail, fax, or phone. Application deadline: continuous.

CAMP MANITO-WISH YMCA
PO BOX 246
BOULDER JUNCTION, WISCONSIN 54512

General Information Facility offering wilderness tripping, canoeing, kayaking, and backpacking for 220 campers ages 11–15 in a 3-week session. Traditional camp programs offer variety when campers are not on the trail. Established in 1919. 300-acre facility located 275 miles from Milwaukee. Features: freshwater lake; north woods setting; wilderness travel; challenge course; Manito-wish Leadership center.
Profile of Summer Employees Total number: 225; typical ages: 17–23. 50% men; 50% women; 15% high school students; 85% college students; 1% non-U.S. citizens; 1% local applicants. Nonsmokers preferred.
Employment Information Openings are from June 6 to October 31. Year-round positions also offered. Jobs available: ▶ 60 *assistant counselors* (minimum age 17) with LGT and first aid/CPR certification at $128–$140 per week ▶ 60 *cabin counselors/trip leaders* (minimum age 19) with LGT and first aid/CPR certification at $165–$170 per week ▶ 20–30 *program area staff* (minimum age 19) with first aid/CPR certification, lifeguard training in some cases at $165–$275 per week ▶ 1 *ropes course director* (minimum age 21) with ropes course certified training and experience in the field at $200–$275 per week ▶ 20 *wilderness trip leaders* (minimum age 19) with Wilderness First Responder certification (training available), CPR, and LGT at $190–$220 per week. Applicants must submit formal organization application, three personal references. An in-person interview is recommended, but a telephone interview is acceptable. International applicants accepted; must apply through a recognized agency.
Benefits and Preemployment Training Free housing, free meals, formal training, health insurance, willing to provide letters of recommendation, names of contacts, on-the-job training, willing to complete paperwork for educational credit, willing to act as a professional reference, opportunity to attend seminars/workshops, and internships. Preemployment training is optional and includes CPR, leadership skills, lifeguard training; wilderness first aid, challenge course training, wilderness trips.
Contact Jack Chamberlain, Summer Program Director, Camp Manito-wish YMCA, PO Box 246, Boulder Junction, Wisconsin 54512. Telephone: 715-385-2312. Fax: 715-385-2461. E-mail: jack.chamberlain@manito-wish.org. World Wide Web: http://www.manito-wish.org. Contact by e-mail, fax, mail, phone, or through World Wide Web site. Application deadline: continuous.

CAMP NEBAGAMON FOR BOYS
11451 CAMP NEBAGAMON DRIVE
LAKE NEBAGAMON, WISCONSIN 54849

General Information Residential boys camp for 240 campers from forty different communities and several countries. Established in 1929. 70-acre facility located 30 miles from Duluth, Minnesota. Features: 914-acre freshwater lake; nearby state forests; wooded campsite; proximity to Lake Superior and to Brule River.

Profile of Summer Employees Total number: 115; typical ages: 16–55. 80% men; 20% women; 5% minorities; 27% high school students; 40% college students; 10% non-U.S. citizens; 18% local applicants.

Employment Information Openings are from June 15 to August 15. Jobs available: ▶ 2 *cooks* with experience cooking for large groups at $200–$300 per week ▶ 2 *drivers* (minimum age 21) with clean driving record at $1400–$2400 per season ▶ 25 *junior cabin counselors* with skills in water and land sports, tennis, target skills, art, campcraft, and photography; 11th and 12th graders at $1000–$1050 per season ▶ 1 *nurse* with RN license at $200–$250 per week ▶ 2 *photography specialists* at $1500–$2200 per season ▶ 25 *senior cabin counselors* with skills in water and land sports, tennis, target skills, art, campcraft, and photography; must be college age at $1250–$1625 per season ▶ 2 *swimming instructors* with WSI or lifeguard certification at $1100–$2000 per season ▶ 2 *waterfront directors* (minimum age 21) with WSI or Red Cross lifeguard certification at $1800–$2600 per season. Applicants must submit formal organization application, three personal references. An in-person interview is required. International applicants accepted; must obtain own visa, obtain own working papers, apply through a recognized agency.

Benefits and Preemployment Training Free housing, free meals, formal training, willing to provide letters of recommendation, names of contacts, on-the-job training, willing to complete paperwork for educational credit, willing to act as a professional reference, opportunity to attend seminars/workshops, and travel reimbursement. Preemployment training is required and includes accident prevention and safety, first aid, CPR, interpersonal skills, leadership skills.

Contact Judy Wallenstein, Co-Director, Camp Nebagamon for Boys, 5237 North Lakewood, Chicago, Illinois 60640. Telephone: 773-271-9500. Fax: 773-271-9816. E-mail: cnebagamon@aol.com. World Wide Web: http://www.campnebagamon.com. Contact by e-mail, fax, mail, phone, or through World Wide Web site. Application deadline: continuous.

CAMPS WOODLAND AND TOWERING PINES
EAGLE RIVER, WISCONSIN 54521

General Information Residential camps on separate sites having four- or six-week seasons. Established in 1946. 400-acre facility located 22 miles from Rhinelander. Features: north woods and lakes; resort area.

Profile of Summer Employees Total number: 60; typical ages: 18–70. 60% men; 40% women; 5% high school students; 80% college students; 5% retirees; 5% non-U.S. citizens; 5% local applicants. Nonsmokers preferred.

Employment Information Openings are from June 17 to August 8. Year-round positions also offered. Jobs available: ▶ *cooks/assistant cooks* with experience at $200–$300 per week ▶ *crafts/Indian lore staff members* at $150–$250 per week ▶ *dishwashers* at $150–$200 per week ▶ *nurse* with RN license at $350–$450 per week ▶ *riflery/archery staff members* with NRA training at $150–$250 per week ▶ *swimming/small craft staff members* with WSI certification at $200–$250 per week ▶ *tennis/gymnastics staff members* at $150–$250 per week. Applicants must submit formal organization application, four personal references. A telephone interview is required. International applicants accepted; must obtain own visa, apply through a recognized agency.

Benefits and Preemployment Training Free housing, on-the-job training, willing to complete paperwork for educational credit, and travel reimbursement. Preemployment training is required and includes accident prevention and safety, first aid, CPR, interpersonal skills, leadership skills.

Contact John Jordan, Camps Woodland and Towering Pines, 242 Bristol Street, Northfield, Illinois 60093. Telephone: 847-446-7311. Fax: 847-446-7710. E-mail: towpines@aol.com. Contact by e-mail, fax, mail, or phone. Application deadline: continuous.

CENTRAL WISCONSIN ENVIRONMENTAL STATION/ UNIVERSITY OF WISCONSIN–STEVENS POINT

10186 COUNTY ROAD MM
AMHERST JUNCTION, WISCONSIN 54407

General Information Environmental station that provides a foundation for appreciation and understanding of the environment and develops the skills and attitudes needed to deal with present and future environmental problems. Established in 1975. 400-acre facility located 90 miles from Green Bay. Features: freshwater lake; wooded setting; log cabins; multi-purpose living/teaching building; challenge course.

Profile of Summer Employees Total number: 15; typical age: 18. 50% men; 50% women; 10% minorities; 10% high school students; 90% college students; 10% non-U.S. citizens; 60% local applicants. Nonsmokers preferred.

Employment Information Openings are from June 1 to August 24. Year-round positions also offered. Jobs available: ▶ *assistant summer program director* (minimum age 18) with first aid/CPR, driver's license, experience working with youth, and environmental education or related experience at $150–$180 per week ▶ *counselors/naturalists* (minimum age 18) with first aid/CPR certifications, driver's license, experience working with youth, and environmental education with related experience at $130–$150 per week ▶ *health lodge supervisor* (minimum age 18) with EMT, RN, or advanced first aid training at $140–$170 per week ▶ *summer program director* (minimum age 21) with first aid/CPR, driver's license; experience working with youth and supervising staff; environmental education or related experience at $200–$250 per week ▶ *tripping leaders* (minimum age 18) with first aid/CPR, driver's license, camping, backpacking, and youth leadership experience. at $150–$190 per week ▶ *waterfront director* (minimum age 18) with WSI, lifeguard certification, and driver's license at $135–$160 per week. Applicants must submit formal organization application. An in-person interview is recommended, but a telephone interview is acceptable. International applicants accepted; must obtain own visa, obtain own working papers, apply through a recognized agency.

Benefits and Preemployment Training Free housing, formal training, willing to provide letters of recommendation, on-the-job training, willing to complete paperwork for educational credit, willing to act as a professional reference, and free meals or meals at cost (possible). Preemployment training is required and includes accident prevention and safety, first aid, interpersonal skills, leadership skills, teaching skills.

Contact Rebecca Clarke, Program Manager, Central Wisconsin Environmental Station/University of Wisconsin–Stevens Point, 10186 County Road MM, Amherst Junction, Wisconsin 54407. Telephone: 715-824-2428. Fax: 715-824-3201. E-mail: bclarke@uwsp.edu. World Wide Web: http://www.uwsp.edu/cnr/cwes. Contact by e-mail, fax, phone, or through World Wide Web site. Application deadline: continuous.

CLEARWATER CAMP FOR GIRLS

7490 CLEARWATER ROAD
MINOCQUA, WISCONSIN 54548

General Information Traditional residential camp providing caring staff and camping experiences for girls ages 8–16. Established in 1933. 80-acre facility located 25 miles from Rhinelander. Features: 3600-acre headwaters lake; wooded setting; 5-acre island; historical buildings; footbridge from mainland to island.

Profile of Summer Employees Total number: 70; typical ages: 19–70. 2% men; 98% women;

1% minorities; 5% high school students; 85% college students; 1% retirees; 3% non-U.S. citizens; 5% local applicants. Nonsmokers required.

Employment Information Openings are from June 7 to August 12. Jobs available: ▶ 2 *English-style riding instructors* with first aid, CPR, CHA, or HSA certification and experience in the field at $2000–$4000 per season ▶ 1–2 *archery instructors* with archery certification preferred and experience in the field at $2000–$2500 per season ▶ 4–6 *canoeing instructors* with lifeguard or emergency water safety, CPR, and canoe certification (preferred) and experience in the field at $2000–$2600 per season ▶ 1–3 *cook and assistant cooks* with sanitation certification preferred and experience in the field at $4000–$6000 per season ▶ 2–4 *crafts instructors* with creativity and varied skills in weaving, pottery, and leather at $2000–$2600 per season ▶ 2 *drama instructors* with talent, ability to direct, and creativity at $2000–$2500 per season ▶ 10–25 *general counselors* (minimum age 19) with ability to assist or teach an activity, love for children, willingness and ability to assist youngsters, lifeguard, first aid, CPR certification, and good role modeling at $2000–$3000 per season ▶ 6 *kitchen staff members* (minimum age 16) with cheerful attitude and good work ethic at $1800–$2500 per season ▶ 6 *sailing instructors* with experience handling C scows, CPR/LGT certification, Red Cross sailing/USRA rating (preferred) at $2200–$2500 per season ▶ 2 *skilled tripping leaders* (minimum age 21) with Wilderness Water Safety and First Aid certification, CPR, and LGT at $2500–$3500 per season ▶ 5 *swimming instructors* with CPR, WSI or lifeguard certification at $2200–$2400 per season ▶ 2 *tennis instructors* with CPR certification and the ability to teach with enthusiasm at $2000–$4000 per season ▶ 2 *trip leaders* (minimum age 21) with campcraft, canoeing, and backpacking experience and first aid, CPR, and lifeguard or wilderness first aid/safety and Wilderness Water Safety at $2000–$4000 per season ▶ 2 *waterskiing instructors* with boat-driving experience, WSI or lifeguard certification, and waterski instructor course preferred at $2000–$2500 per season ▶ 1 *windsurfing instructor* with lifeguard and windsurfing instructor rating (preferred) at $2000–$2500 per season. Applicants must submit formal organization application, two personal references, three letters of recommendation. An in-person interview is recommended, but a telephone interview is acceptable. International applicants accepted; must obtain own visa, apply through a recognized agency.

Benefits and Preemployment Training Free housing, free meals, health insurance, willing to provide letters of recommendation, names of contacts, on-the-job training, willing to complete paperwork for educational credit, willing to act as a professional reference, opportunity to attend seminars/workshops, and possible travel reimbursements.

Contact Sunny Moore, Director, Clearwater Camp for Girls, 7490 Clearwater Road, Minocqua, Wisconsin 54548. Telephone: 800-399-5030. Fax: 715-356-3124. E-mail: clearwatercamp@newnorth.net. World Wide Web: http://www.clearwatercamp.com. Contact by e-mail, fax, mail, phone, or through World Wide Web site. Application deadline: continuous.

EASTER SEALS WISCONSIN
101 NOB HILL ROAD, SUITE 301
WISCONSIN DELLS, WISCONSIN 53713

General Information Nonprofit agency providing camping and recreation services to children and adults with disabilities. 400-acre facility located 55 miles from Madison. Features: wooded setting; swimming pool; near resort town; rope course.

Profile of Summer Employees Total number: 100; typical ages: 20–25. 40% men; 60% women; 10% minorities; 90% college students; 30% non-U.S. citizens; 5% local applicants. Nonsmokers preferred.

Employment Information Openings are from June 1 to August 10. Year-round positions also offered. Jobs available: ▶ 70 *counselors* (minimum age 18) with good communication skills at $185 per week ▶ 4 *kitchen aides* (minimum age 18) at $160 per week ▶ *nurse* (minimum age 21) with first aid training, knowledge of passing medications, seizures, catheterizations, suppositories, colostomy bags, and feeding tubes at $800 per week. Applicants must submit formal

organization application, resume, three personal references, criminal background check. A telephone interview is required. International applicants accepted; must apply through a recognized agency.
Benefits and Preemployment Training Free housing, free meals, formal training, willing to provide letters of recommendation, on-the-job training, willing to complete paperwork for educational credit, willing to act as a professional reference, and laundry facilities. Preemployment training is required and includes accident prevention and safety, first aid, CPR, interpersonal skills, leadership skills, lifeguarding, ropes course.
Contact Chris Hollar, Camp Director, Easter Seals Wisconsin. Telephone: 800-422-2324. Fax: 608-277-8333. E-mail: wawbeck@wi-easterseals.org. World Wide Web: http://www.wi-easterseals.org. Contact by e-mail, fax, mail, phone, or through World Wide Web site. Application deadline: continuous.

RED PINE CAMP FOR GIRLS
PO BOX 69
MINOCQUA, WISCONSIN 54548

General Information Private traditional camp providing individual attention for girls ages 6-16, enrolling 130 campers for two-, four-, and eight-week sessions. Established in 1937. 40-acre facility located 60 miles from Wausau. Features: only private property on 1200-acre freshwater lake; tennis courts; cabins; surrounded by state land; shower facilities.
Profile of Summer Employees Total number: 50–55; typical ages: 18–45. 10% men; 90% women; 80% college students; 10% non-U.S. citizens; 8% local applicants.
Employment Information Openings are from June 12 to August 16. Jobs available: ▶ 2–7 *English-style riding instructors or stable managers* (minimum age 18) with skill and love of horses and experience in the field at $1300–$2000 per season ▶ 2–10 *arts and crafts, gymnastics, aerobic jazz, cheerleading, and archery staff members* (minimum age 18) with skill and experience in combination of areas at $1200–$1500 per season ▶ 2–6 *canoeing staff members* with emergency and basic water safety (Red Cross) certification preferred, skill and experience in still waters, and knowledge of campcraft at $1200–$1800 per season ▶ *food service staff members* (minimum age 18) with experience in one or more of the following: cook, assistant to cook, general kitchen and dining room help at $1350–$2000 per season ▶ 2–3 *nurses* (minimum age 21) with RN, LPN, EMT or GN license (Wisconsin) at $1500–$2500 per season ▶ 1–2 *sailboarding staff members* (minimum age 18) with experience in the field; Red Cross certification preferred at $1200–$1800 per season ▶ 2–4 *sailing staff members* (minimum age 18) with swimming, LGT, and small craft certification preferred and skill in sailing Sunfish, Puffers, and Zumas at $1200–$1800 per season ▶ 6–9 *swimming instructors* (minimum age 18) with WSI, LGT, CPR, and first aid certification at $1200–$1800 per season ▶ 2–5 *tennis staff members* with high degree of skill and professional training preferred at $1200–$1800 per season. Applicants must submit formal organization application, resume, three personal references, three letters of recommendation. An in-person interview is recommended, but a telephone interview is acceptable. International applicants accepted; must obtain own visa, obtain own working papers, apply through a recognized agency.
Benefits and Preemployment Training Free housing, free meals, willing to provide letters of recommendation, on-the-job training, willing to complete paperwork for educational credit, willing to act as a professional reference, opportunity to attend seminars/workshops, travel reimbursement, and laundry service. Preemployment training is required and includes accident prevention and safety, first aid, CPR, interpersonal skills, leadership skills, archery and sailing workshops.
Contact Robin Thies, Co-director, Red Pine Camp for Girls, PO Box 69, Minocqua, Wisconsin 54548. Telephone: 715-356-4571. Fax: 715-356-1077. E-mail: redpinec@newnorth.net. World Wide Web: http://www.redpinecamp.com. Contact by e-mail, fax, mail, phone, or through World Wide Web site. Application deadline: continuous.

SALVATION ARMY WONDERLAND CAMP AND CONFERENCE CENTER

9241 CAMP LAKE ROAD, PO BOX 222
CAMP LAKE, WISCONSIN 53109-0222

General Information Residential Evangelical Christian camping program for Chicago-area Salvation Army, including camps for 120 low-income and at-risk young people for six 8-day sessions. Established in 1924. 145-acre facility located 45 miles from Milwaukee. Features: freshwater lake; upland forest; meadows and prairie; heated outdoor pool and diving tank; gym, tennis and volleyball courts; low ropes course.

Profile of Summer Employees Total number: 90–100; typical ages: 18–26. 50% men; 50% women; 30% minorities; 8% high school students; 90% college students; 2% retirees; 5% non-U.S. citizens; 10% local applicants. Nonsmokers required.

Employment Information Openings are from May 25 to August 14. Winter break positions also offered. Jobs available: ▶ 1 *aquatics assistant* (minimum age 20) with WSI and LTI certification (preferred); leadership ability and supervisory experience at $225–$235 per week ▶ 1 *aquatics director* (minimum age 22) with WSI and LTI certification (preferred); leadership ability and supervisory experience at $230–$250 per week ▶ 1 *arts and crafts director* (minimum age 20) with two years of college completed and experience working with children at $210–$220 per week ▶ 6 *boys counselors* (minimum age 19) with one year of college completed and experience working with children at $210–$220 per week ▶ 2 *cooks* (minimum age 20) with experience at $240–$280 per week ▶ 6 *girls counselors* (minimum age 19) with one year of college completed and experience working with children at $210–$220 per week ▶ 1 *health services assistant* (minimum age 20) with student nurse status or experience in nursing; ARC-PFR and first aid; experience working with children at $210–$220 per week ▶ *lifeguard/support counselor* (minimum age 19) with ARC-LGT (on-site training available) at $210–$220 per week ▶ 1 *nature director* (minimum age 20) with two years of college completed at $210–$220 per week ▶ 1–2 *nurses* (minimum age 22) with BSN or RN license with CPR training (USA certification), PFR, first aid, and experience working with children at $425–$450 per week ▶ 1 *pioneer director* (minimum age 20) with two years of college completed at $210–$220 per week ▶ 4 *program unit directors* (minimum age 20) with two years of college completed, experience working with children; leadership ability and organizational skills at $210–$220 per week ▶ 6–8 *support counselors* (minimum age 18) with one year of college required at $210–$220 per week. Applicants must submit formal organization application, three personal references, written interview, resume (optional). An in-person interview is recommended, but a telephone interview is acceptable. International applicants accepted; must apply through a recognized agency.

Benefits and Preemployment Training Free housing, free meals, formal training, willing to provide letters of recommendation, on-the-job training, willing to complete paperwork for educational credit, willing to act as a professional reference, and on-site certifications available.

Contact David Ditzler, Director of Camping Services, Salvation Army Wonderland Camp and Conference Center, 9241 Camp Lake Road, PO Box 222, Camp Lake, Wisconsin 53109-0222. Telephone: 262-889-4305 Ext. 304. Fax: 262-889-4307. E-mail: wonderland@techheadnet.com. World Wide Web: http://www.techheadnet.com/wonderland. Contact by e-mail, fax, mail, or phone. Application deadline: May 15.

THE SOUTHWESTERN COMPANY, WISCONSIN

See The Southwestern Company on page 302 for complete description.

STIVERS STAFFING SERVICES–WISCONSIN

See Stivers Staffing Services–Illinois on page 110 for complete description.

STUDENT CONSERVATION ASSOCIATION (SCA), WISCONSIN

See Student Conservation Association (SCA), New Hampshire on page 209 for complete description.

WOODSIDE RANCH RESORT

W4015 HIGHWAY 82
MAUSTON, WISCONSIN 53948

General Information Full-service American-plan dude ranch offering log cabins with fireplaces. Established in 1926. 1,200-acre facility located 70 miles from Madison. Features: 5-acre lake with island; buffalo herd; pine plantation; 800 acres of riding and hiking trails; volleyball, tennis, and mini golf; log cabins with fireplace.

Profile of Summer Employees Total number: 70; typical ages: 16–50. 40% men; 60% women; 5% minorities; 25% high school students; 25% college students; 5% non-U.S. citizens; 50% local applicants.

Employment Information Openings are from June 7 to September 7. Winter break positions also offered. Jobs available: ▶ 2 *bartenders/country store clerks* (minimum age 18, 21 preferred) with experience at $220–$240 per week ▶ 6 *food service personnel* (minimum age 18) at $210–$230 per week ▶ 1 *horse-drawn wagon teamster* (minimum age 21) with significant experience in the field at $240–$280 per week ▶ 2 *horse-trail guides* (minimum age 18) with experience in the field at $210–$240 per week ▶ 2 *housekeepers* (minimum age 18) at $220–$240 per week ▶ 1 *recreation director* with recreation experience; minimum age 18, 21 preferred at $250–$300 per week. Applicants must submit formal organization application, resume. An in-person interview is recommended, but a telephone interview is acceptable. International applicants accepted; must apply through a recognized agency.

Benefits and Preemployment Training Free housing, free meals, willing to provide letters of recommendation, on-the-job training, and use of most resort facilities off-duty.

Contact Carrie Donahue, Office Manager, Woodside Ranch Resort, W4015 Highway 82, Mauston, Wisconsin 53948. Telephone: 608-847-4275. Fax: 608-847-2630. E-mail: woodside@mwt.net. World Wide Web: http://www.woodsideranch.com. Contact by e-mail or mail. Application deadline: continuous.

YMCA CAMP U-NAH-LI-YA

13654 SOUTH SHORE DRIVE
SURING, WISCONSIN 54174

General Information YMCA camp offering outdoor environmental education and retreats for children grades 5–8 and a summer residential camp with trips. Established in 1937. 140-acre facility located 65 miles from Green Bay. Features: pine forest setting; climbing tower; high and low ropes course; 12 sleeping cabins; modern facilities; 600-acre lake.

Profile of Summer Employees Total number: 40; typical ages: 18–24. 40% men; 60% women; 1% minorities; 95% college students; 4% non-U.S. citizens. Nonsmokers preferred.

Employment Information Openings are from June 7 to August 16. Year-round positions also offered. Jobs available: ▶ 2–4 *outdoor environmental education instructors* (minimum age 21) with related degree (preferred) at $220–$245 per week ▶ 6–8 *resident counselors* (minimum age 18) with CPR/first aid and one year of college completed at $140–$155 per week ▶ 4 *tripping counselors* (minimum age 21) with CPR/first aid/lifeguarding at $165–$175 per week. Applicants must submit a letter of interest, resume, three personal references, personal statement. An in-person interview is recommended, but a telephone interview is acceptable. International applicants accepted; must obtain own visa.

Benefits and Preemployment Training Free housing, free meals, possible full-time employment, willing to provide letters of recommendation, names of contacts, on-the-job training, willing to act as a professional reference, opportunity to attend seminars/workshops, and use of all recreational equipment, one season full YMCA membership. Preemployment training is required and includes accident prevention and safety, first aid, CPR, interpersonal skills, leadership skills, lifeguard training.

Contact Kathleen McKee, Program Director, YMCA Camp U-Nah-Li-Ya, 13654 South Shore Drive, Suring, Wisconsin 54174. Telephone: 715-276-7116. Fax: 715-276-1701. E-mail: mckeeka@greenbayymca.org. World Wide Web: http://www.greenbayymca.org. Contact by e-mail, fax, mail, phone, or through World Wide Web site. Application deadline: continuous.

WYOMING

ABSAROKA MOUNTAIN LODGE

1231 NORTHFORK HIGHWAY
CODY, WYOMING 82414

General Information Mountain lodge located 12 miles from East Gate of Yellowstone National Park. Offering 16 log cabins; main lodge located along Gunbarrel Creek; lodging, dining, and horseback rides in the Absaroka Wilderness Area. Established in 1910. 10-acre facility. Features: mountain setting; creek through property; historic lodge and cabins; horseback riding; close to Yellowstone National Park.

Profile of Summer Employees Total number: 14; typical ages: 18–26. 50% men; 50% women; 20% high school students; 70% college students; 10% retirees; 5% non-U.S. citizens; 5% local applicants. Nonsmokers preferred.

Employment Information Openings are from May 1 to September 30. Jobs available: ▶ 1 *cook* (minimum age 18) with cooking experience required at $600–$1200 per month ▶ 4–6 *waiters/waitresses/cabin cleaners* (minimum age 18) with serving and some cleaning experience at $400–$500 per month ▶ 2–4 *wranglers* (minimum age 18) with horse experience (trail guiding, horse care, etc.) required at $400–$600 per month. Applicants must submit a letter of interest, resume, two personal references, two letters of recommendation. A telephone interview is required. International applicants accepted; must obtain own visa.

Benefits and Preemployment Training Free housing, free meals, willing to provide letters of recommendation, on-the-job training, willing to complete paperwork for educational credit, willing to act as a professional reference, and opportunity to partake in ranch activities and horseback riding.

Contact Patti Bates, Owner, Absaroka Mountain Lodge, 1231 Northfork Highway, Cody, Wyoming 82414. Telephone: 307-587-3963. E-mail: batesfam@frontiernet.net. World Wide Web: http://www.absarokamtlodge.com. Contact by e-mail, mail, phone, or through World Wide Web site. Application deadline: continuous.

A CHRISTIAN MINISTRY IN THE NATIONAL PARKS–WYOMING

See A Christian Ministry in the National Parks–Maine on page 122 for complete description.

ALPENHOF LODGE

BOX 288, 3255 WEST MCCOLLISTER AVENUE
TETON VILLAGE, WYOMING 83025

General Information Alpine-style resort lodge with 40 rooms providing clientele with personalized service. Established in 1988. 1-acre facility located 260 miles from Salt Lake City, Utah.

Features: mountains and rivers.

Profile of Summer Employees Total number: 85; typical ages: 20–25. 50% men; 50% women; 1% high school students; 50% college students; 10% non-U.S. citizens; 39% local applicants. Nonsmokers preferred.

Employment Information Openings are from May 20 to October 12. Year-round positions also offered. Jobs available: ▶ 3 *bellmen* with aptitude for greeting guests in a friendly manner, ability to assist with luggage, run errands, and do light maintenance work at $1040–$1200 per month ▶ 8 *dining room staff members (buspersons and waitstaff)* with tableside experience and wine knowledge at $275–$420 per month ▶ 3–5 *dishwashers* with ability to work quickly at $960–$1040 per month ▶ 8 *food waitstaff members* with interest in working with public and the ability to serve at $370 per month ▶ 2 *front desk clerks* at $9–$10 per hour ▶ 5 *housekeeping staff members* with ability to clean rooms and willingness to do hard work at $1040–$1100 per month ▶ 2–4 *prep or line cooks* with ability to cook in line and work quickly at $1120–$1600 per month. Applicants must submit a formal organization application. An in-person interview is required. International applicants accepted; must obtain own visa, obtain own working papers.

Benefits and Preemployment Training Housing at a cost, free meals, formal training, possible full-time employment, willing to provide letters of recommendation, on-the-job training, willing to complete paperwork for educational credit, and willing to act as a professional reference. Preemployment training is required and includes accident prevention and safety, interpersonal skills.

Contact Mark D. Johnson, Assistant General Manager, Alpenhof Lodge, PO Box 288, Teton Village, Wyoming 83025. Telephone: 307-733-3242. Fax: 307-739-1516. E-mail: mj@alpenhoflodge.com. Contact by e-mail, fax, or mail. Application deadline: continuous.

BILL CODY RANCH
2604 YELLOWSTONE HIGHWAY
CODY, WYOMING 82414

General Information Guest ranch catering to families with 14 cabins, cookouts, entertainment, daily horseback rides. Established in 1996. 8-acre facility located 135 miles from Billings, Montana. Features: national forest; 30 minutes from Yellowstone; 70 riding horses; white-water rafting; nightly entertainment; 30 minutes from Cody, Wyoming.

Profile of Summer Employees Total number: 20; typical ages: 18–25. 40% men; 60% women; 1% high school students; 90% college students; 2% local applicants. Nonsmokers preferred.

Employment Information Openings are from May 15 to September 30. Jobs available: ▶ 2 *cooks* with some culinary experience at $800–$1500 per month ▶ 5 *horse wranglers* (minimum age 18) with physical ability to perform required duties, valid driver's license, and a clean driving record, trailering experience a plus, must have horseback riding experience at $500–$700 per month ▶ 6 *housekeepers/waitstaff* at $450–$550 per month ▶ 2 *office assistants* at $600–$800 per month ▶ 1 *prep cook* at $600–$1000 per month. Applicants must submit formal organization application, resume, two personal references. A telephone interview is required. International applicants accepted; must apply through a recognized agency.

Benefits and Preemployment Training Free housing, free meals, willing to provide letters of recommendation, and on-the-job training.

Contact John Parsons, Co-Owner, Bill Cody Ranch, 2604 Yellowstone Highway, Cody, Wyoming 82414. Telephone: 307-587-6271. Fax: 307-587-6272. E-mail: billcody@billcodyranch.com. World Wide Web: http://www.billcodyranch.com. Contact by e-mail, fax, mail, phone, or through World Wide Web site. Application deadline: continuous.

COWBOY VILLAGE RESORT AT TOGWOTEE
PO BOX 91
MORAN, WYOMING 83013

General Information Mountain lodge serving a varied clientele. Established in 1923. 67-acre facility located 48 miles from Jackson Hole. Features: wooded setting; streams; views of Grand

Tetons; near Yellowstone.
Profile of Summer Employees Total number: 50–60; typical ages: 18–60. 60% men; 40% women; 5% high school students; 50% college students; 20% retirees; 5% non-U.S. citizens; 20% local applicants.
Employment Information Openings are from June 10 to September 30. Winter break and year-round positions also offered. Jobs available: ▶ 3 *bartenders* (minimum age 21) with an outgoing personality, desire to perform a thorough job, and experience in the field at $5 to $6 per hour plus gratuities ▶ 2 *convenience store clerks* (minimum age 21) with good math skills and an outgoing personality at $5.50–$6 per hour ▶ 3 *dishwashers* with ability to accomplish tasks neatly and quickly at $5.50–$6 per hour ▶ 8 *experienced saute and broiler line cooks* with neat and efficient work habits at $6–$9 per hour ▶ *front desk/reservations persons* with good math aptitude and an outgoing personality at $6–$6.50 per hour ▶ 2 *general laborers* with efficient work habits at $6–$8 per hour ▶ 9 *housekeepers* with neat appearance and efficient work habits at $5.50–$6 per hour ▶ 7 *waitstaff* (minimum age 18) with an outgoing personality and desire to perform a thorough job at $4.15 per hour plus gratuities. Applicants must submit formal organization application, three personal references. A telephone interview is required. International applicants accepted; must obtain own visa, obtain own working papers, apply through a recognized agency.
Benefits and Preemployment Training Housing at a cost, meals at a cost, possible full-time employment, willing to provide letters of recommendation, on-the-job training, willing to act as a professional reference, and discounts on horseback riding and other activities.
Contact Rebecca G. Horton, Human Resources Manager, Cowboy Village Resort at Togwotee. Telephone: 307-543-2847. Fax: 307-543-2391. E-mail: togwotee@rmisp. World Wide Web: http://www.coolworks.com/cowboyvillage/default.htm. Contact by e-mail, fax, mail, phone, or through World Wide Web site. Application deadline: continuous.

ELEPHANT HEAD LODGE
1170 YELLOWSTONE HIGHWAY
WAPITI, WYOMING 82450

General Information Guest ranch on eastern edge of Yellowstone National Park with lodging, meals, horseback riding, fishing, cookouts, and other activities. Established in 1910. 6-acre facility located 100 miles from Billings, Montana. Features: historic lodge and 12 log cabins; 25 riding horses; Shoshone river fishing; 80 miles from Grand Teton National Parks and 11 miles from Yellowstone National Park; horseback rides in Shoshone National Forest; abundant wildlife.
Profile of Summer Employees Total number: 10; typical ages: 19–22. 40% men; 60% women; 20% minorities; 10% high school students; 80% college students; 2% retirees; 10% non-U.S. citizens; 8% local applicants. Nonsmokers required.
Employment Information Openings are from May to September. Jobs available: ▶ 2 *cooks* (minimum age 18) with ability to plan and cook meals for crew, cook on outdoor grill, experience preferred at $650–$850 per month ▶ 2 *experienced wranglers* (minimum age 19) with valid driver's license and ability to drive a horse trailer at $750–$850 per month ▶ 2 *horse wranglers* (minimum age 19) with outgoing personality and physical ability to perform required duties at $650–$750 per month ▶ 5–7 *housekeepers/waitstaff* (minimum age 16) with interest in working with the public and an outgoing personality at $650–$750 per month. Applicants must submit resume, two personal references, letter of recommendation. A telephone interview is required. International applicants accepted; must obtain own visa, obtain own working papers, apply through a recognized agency.
Benefits and Preemployment Training Free housing, free meals, willing to provide letters of recommendation, on-the-job training, willing to complete paperwork for educational credit, willing to act as a professional reference, and laundry facilities, free horseback riding, river rafting, fly-fishing.
Contact Phil Lamb, Owner, Elephant Head Lodge, 1170 Yellowstone Highway, Wapiti, Wyoming

82450. Telephone: 307-587-3980. Fax: 307-527-7922. E-mail: vacation@elephantheadlodge.com. World Wide Web: http://www.elephantheadlodge.com. Contact by e-mail, fax, mail, or phone. Application deadline: continuous.

HATCHET MOTEL AND RESTAURANT

PO BOX 316
MORAN, WYOMING 83013

General Information Rustic log motel with 33 units, restaurant, gift shop, and gas station. Established in 1955. 8-acre facility located 35 miles from Jackson. Features: dormitories and employee dining; mountain surroundings; fishing; hiking; biking; near Grand Teton and Yellowstone; hot tub.

Profile of Summer Employees Total number: 27; typical ages: 18–25. 40% men; 60% women; 15% minorities; 15% high school students; 75% college students; 10% local applicants. Nonsmokers preferred.

Employment Information Openings are from May 15 to October 30. Year-round positions also offered. Jobs available: ▶ 4 *cooks (morning and evening shift)* (minimum age 18) at $7–$7.50 per hour ▶ 3 *desk attendants (morning and evening shift)* (minimum age 18) at $6–$6.25 per hour ▶ 3 *housekeeping staff members* (minimum age 18) at $6–$6.25 per hour ▶ 5 *kitchen helpers (morning and evening shift)* (minimum age 18) at $6–$6.25 per hour ▶ 1 *maintenance staff* (minimum age 20) at $6.50–$9 per hour ▶ 5 *waiters/waitresses (morning and evening shift)* (minimum age 18) at $3.05–$3.25 per hour ▶ 1 *yard maintenance person* (minimum age 18) at $6–$6.50 per hour. Applicants must submit a formal organization application, two personal references. A telephone interview is required. International applicants accepted; must obtain own visa, obtain own working papers.

Benefits and Preemployment Training Housing at a cost, meals at a cost, formal training, possible full-time employment, willing to provide letters of recommendation, on-the-job training, willing to complete paperwork for educational credit, and willing to act as a professional reference. Preemployment training is required and includes accident prevention and safety, interpersonal skills.

Contact Greg Smith, General Manager, Hatchet Motel and Restaurant. Telephone: 307-543-2413. Fax: 307-543-2034. E-mail: hatchet@rmisp.com. World Wide Web: http://www.hatchetmotel.com. Contact by e-mail, fax, mail, phone, or through World Wide Web site. Application deadline: continuous.

THE SOUTHWESTERN COMPANY, WYOMING

See The Southwestern Company on page 302 for complete description.

STUDENT CONSERVATION ASSOCIATION (SCA), WYOMING

See Student Conservation Association (SCA), New Hampshire on page 209 for complete description.

TETON VALLEY RANCH CAMP EDUCATION FOUNDATION

JACKSON HOLE, PO BOX 3968
JACKSON, WYOMING 83001

General Information Residential summer camp serving 125 boys or girls in separate 5-week sessions with Western horseback-riding and backpacking adventures. Features multi-day trips into the mountains and exciting in-camp activities. Established in 1939. Features: warm (68 degree) spring-fed pond; log cabin; spectacular mountain setting; working cattle ranch; surrounded by national park and forest.

Profile of Summer Employees Total number: 75; typical ages: 18–30. 50% men; 50% women; 5% minorities; 10% high school students; 70% college students; 10% retirees; 2% non-U.S. citizens; 10% local applicants. Nonsmokers preferred.

Employment Information Openings are from June 3 to August 25. Jobs available: ▶ 16–20 *boys cabin counselors* (minimum age 21) with first aid and CPR certification, outdoor skills, and experience working with children (position is first 5 weeks of summer) at $500–$800 per season ▶ 2 *crafts and nature discovery instructors* (minimum age 21) with CPR/first aid certification, knowledge of appropriate skills, and desire to work with children at $1300–$1400 per season ▶ 3 *dishwashers* (minimum age 18) at $1000–$1200 per season ▶ 16–20 *girls cabin counselors* (minimum age 21) with first aid and CPR certification, outdoor skills, and experience working with children (position is second 5 weeks of summer) at $500–$800 per season ▶ 1–3 *horse wranglers* (minimum age 21) with first aid, CPR, and experience instructing riding and safety; should be confident rider with knowledge of horses at $1200–$1800 per season ▶ 5 *kitchen staff members* (minimum age 18) with cooking and food service experience at $1100–$1500 per season ▶ 1 *lapidary instructor* (minimum age 21) with first aid/CPR certification and lapidary experience at $1300–$1400 per season ▶ 2 *laundry workers* (minimum age 18) at $1300–$1500 per season ▶ *maintenance staff members* (minimum age 18) at $1200–$1800 per season ▶ 4–6 *trip leaders (backpack)* (minimum age 21) with training and background in leadership, environmentally respective camping skills, and wilderness first aid certification at $1000–$1500 per season ▶ 2–3 *trip leaders (pack trip with horses)* (minimum age 21) with knowledge of horse situations, care, and camping leadership with children; excellent riding and precautionary skills; wilderness first aid certification at $1000–$1500 per season. Applicants must submit a formal organization application, letter of interest, resume, three personal references, three letters of recommendation, drivers record/criminal background check. An in-person interview is recommended, but a telephone interview is acceptable. International applicants accepted; must obtain own visa, obtain own working papers.

Benefits and Preemployment Training Free housing, free meals, on-the-job training, willing to complete paperwork for educational credit, and travel reimbursement. Preemployment training is required and includes accident prevention and safety, interpersonal skills, leadership skills.

Contact Ean Cuthbert, Director, Teton Valley Ranch Camp Education Foundation, PO Box 3968, Jackson, Wyoming 83001. Telephone: 307-733-2958. Fax: 307-733-2978. E-mail: mailbag@tvrcamp.org. World Wide Web: http://www.tvrcamp.org. Contact by e-mail, fax, mail, phone, or through World Wide Web site. Application deadline: continuous.

WILDERNESS VENTURES

PO BOX 2768
JACKSON HOLE, WYOMING 83001

General Information Organization devoted to leading teenagers on wilderness trips in national parks and forests in the American west and abroad. Established in 1973. Located 280 miles from Salt Lake City, Utah.

Profile of Summer Employees Total number: 110; typical ages: 21–31. 50% men; 50% women; 50% college students; 10% local applicants. Nonsmokers required.

Employment Information Openings are from June 16 to August 22. Jobs available: ▶ 50 *trip leaders* (minimum age 21) with valid driver's license, first aid, CPR at $1000–$2000 per season. Applicants must submit a formal organization application, letter of interest, resume, two letters of recommendation. A telephone interview is required. International applicants accepted; must obtain own visa, obtain own working papers.

Benefits and Preemployment Training Free housing, free meals, possible full-time employment, willing to provide letters of recommendation, willing to complete paperwork for educational credit, willing to act as a professional reference, and opportunity to attend seminars/workshops. Preemployment training is required and includes accident prevention and safety, interpersonal skills, leadership skills.

Contact Maury Wray, Personnel Coordinator, Wilderness Ventures. Telephone: 800-533-2281. Fax: 307-739-1934. E-mail: maury@wildernessventures.com. World Wide Web: http://www.wildernessventures.com. Contact by e-mail, fax, mail, phone, or through World Wide Web site. Application deadline: continuous.

YELLOWSTONE PARK SERVICE STATIONS
YELLOWSTONE NATIONAL PARK
YELLOWSTONE, WYOMING 82190

General Information Automotive service facilities and information service in Yellowstone National Park. Established in 1947. 2,200,000-acre facility located 90 miles from Bozeman, Montana. Features: geysers; lakes; waterfalls; hiking trails; grizzly bears, elk, wolves; mountaineering.

Profile of Summer Employees Total number: 75; typical ages: 18–24. 60% men; 40% women; 5% minorities; 80% college students; 5% retirees; 10% local applicants. Nonsmokers preferred.

Employment Information Openings are from May 12 to October 16. Jobs available: ▶ 3 *accounting clerks* (minimum age 18) with ability to operate 10-key adding machine by touch, plus computer and communication skills at $265 per week ▶ 18 *automobile mechanics* (minimum age 18) with ASE certification or current enrollment in an ASE program at $300–$380 per week ▶ 50 *service station attendants* (minimum age 18) with good interpersonal skills and desire to work outdoors at $260 per week ▶ 1 *warehouse helper* (minimum age 18) with good driving record and communication skills at $265 per week. Applicants must submit formal organization application, letter of interest. International applicants accepted; must obtain own visa, obtain own working papers, apply through a recognized agency.

Benefits and Preemployment Training Housing at a cost, meals at a cost, formal training, possible full-time employment, health insurance, willing to provide letters of recommendation, names of contacts, on-the-job training, willing to complete paperwork for educational credit, willing to act as a professional reference, and opportunity to attend seminars/workshops. Preemployment training is required and includes accident prevention and safety, leadership skills.

Contact Hal Broadhead, General Manager, Yellowstone Park Service Stations, PO Box 11, Department WDM, Gardiner, Montana 59030-0011. Telephone: 406-848-7333. Fax: 406-848-7731. E-mail: jobs@ypss.com. World Wide Web: http://www.coolworks.com/ypss/. Contact by e-mail, fax, mail, phone, or through World Wide Web site. Application deadline: June 1.

CALAWAY PARK
245033 RANGE ROAD 33
CALGARY, ALBERTA T3Z 2E9

General Information Amusement/theme park with rides, games, food services, merchandise and entertainment. Established in 1982. 70-acre facility located 6 miles from Calgary. Features: mountain view; roller coaster; campground; country setting; indoor theater; restaurants.

Profile of Summer Employees Total number: 500; typical ages: 14–70. 50% men; 50% women; 25% minorities; 70% high school students; 25% college students; 5% retirees; 100% non-U.S. citizens; 95% local applicants.

Employment Information Openings are from May 1 to October 15. Jobs available: ▶ 50–100 *food service staff and game operators* (minimum age 15) at Can$6.75 to Can$7.00 per hour

▶ 20–25 *merchandise/admissions staff* (minimum age 15) at Can $6.75 to Can $7.00 per hour ▶ 50–100 *ride operators* (minimum age 15) at Can $6.75 to Can $7.00 per hour. Applicants must submit a formal organization application, resume, letter of recommendation. An in-person interview is recommended, but a telephone interview is acceptable. International applicants accepted; must obtain own visa, obtain own working papers.

Benefits and Preemployment Training Formal training, possible full-time employment, willing to provide letters of recommendation, on-the-job training, willing to complete paperwork for educational credit, willing to act as a professional reference, and scholarship program; employee referral program. Preemployment training is required and includes leadership skills, guest service certification, technical training.

Contact Dawn Rappel, Human Resource Manager, Calaway Park. Telephone: 403-240-3822 Ext. 145. Fax: 403-242-3885. World Wide Web: http://www.calawaypark.com. Contact by fax, mail, or through World Wide Web site. Application deadline: continuous.

BRITISH COLUMBIA

CAMP ARTABAN
1058 RIDGEWOOD DRIVE
NORTH VANCOUVER, BRITISH COLUMBIA V7R 1H8

General Information Residential camp with Anglican Church affiliation offering traditional program to 100 boys and girls entering grades 3 through 11 in 7-day sessions. Family and specialty weekend adult camps are also offered. Established in 1923. 63-acre facility located 45 miles from Vancouver. Features: waterfront (salt water) on remote island location; swim tank; canoe and row boats; archery range; crafts log hut; outdoor chapel.

Profile of Summer Employees Total number: 18; typical ages: 17–25. 50% men; 50% women; 30% minorities; 20% high school students; 80% college students. Nonsmokers required.

Employment Information Openings are from June to August. Jobs available: ▶ 1 *chaplain* (minimum age 25) should be priest or theology student (Anglican/Episcopalian background preferred) able to work with children at Can$3000 per season ▶ 1 *first aid attendant* with occupational first aid certification/wilderness first aid or equivalent at CAN$3000 to CAN$5000 per season ▶ 1 *head cook* (minimum age 25) with supervisory experience and quantity cooking experience; salary negotiable ▶ 5–6 *kitchen staff members* (minimum age 17) at Can$2000 to Can$5000 per season ▶ 2 *maintenance staff members* (minimum age 17) at Can$2000 to Can$4000 per season ▶ 1 *registrar/expediter* (minimum age 18) must have a car and insurance; computer skills (Microsoft Office) and data entry skills (will train) at Can$10 per hour ▶ 2 *swimming staff members* (minimum age 18) with WSI and NLS certification at Can$2000 to Can$4000 per season. Applicants must submit a formal organization application, letter of interest, resume, personal reference, letter of recommendation. An in-person interview is recommended, but a telephone interview is acceptable. International applicants accepted; must obtain own working papers.

Benefits and Preemployment Training Free housing, free meals, willing to provide letters of recommendation, on-the-job training, and willing to complete paperwork for educational credit.

Contact Nancy Ferris, On-site Manager, Camp Artaban. Telephone: 604-980-0391. E-mail: office@campartaban.com. World Wide Web: http://www.campartaban.com. Contact by e-mail or mail. Application deadline: February 28.

EVANS LAKE FOREST EDUCATION CENTRE

PO BOX 1893
SQUAMISH, BRITISH COLUMBIA V0N 3G0

General Information Residential camp offering environmental education for children 8–11 years old (6-day camp), 10–14 years old (8-day camp) and 13-16 years old (8-day camp) with a capacity of 80 children. Established in 1997. 604-acre facility located 31 miles from Vancouver. Features: freshwater lake; 604-acre demonstration forest; swimming; boating; 15 kilometers of hiking trails; projects and activities to learn about the forest.

Profile of Summer Employees Total number: 40; typical ages: 17–55. 50% men; 50% women; 10% minorities; 60% high school students; 35% college students; 5% local applicants. Nonsmokers preferred.

Employment Information Openings are from July 1 to August 31. Jobs available: ▶ 16–25 *cabin leaders* (minimum age 17) with counselor training and outdoor experience and experience with children at Can$64 per day ▶ *instructor* (minimum age 19) with experience working with children and in outdoor education; occupational First Aid or Wilderness First Aid for Leaders at Can$95 per day ▶ 3–6 *lifeguards* (minimum age 19) with NLS certification and outdoor education experience at Can$95 per day. Applicants must submit a letter of interest, resume, two letters of recommendation. An in-person interview is required.

Benefits and Preemployment Training Free housing, free meals, willing to provide letters of recommendation, on-the-job training, and willing to act as a professional reference. Preemployment training is required and includes accident prevention and safety, interpersonal skills, leadership skills, child care program.

Contact Matt Thom, Operations Manager, Evans Lake Forest Education Centre, #101 1433 Rupert Street, North Vancouver, British Columbia V7J 1G1. Fax: 604-904-2260. Contact by fax or mail. Application deadline: continuous.

CAMP FRENDA

SEVENTH-DAY ADVENTIST CHURCH, RR #2
PORT CARLING, ONTARIO P0B 1J0

General Information Residential camp serving more than 100 children ages 8–16. 60-acre facility located 100 miles from Toronto. Features: freshwater lake.

Profile of Summer Employees Typical ages: 18–27. 50% men; 50% women; 20% minorities; 20% high school students; 80% college students; 1% retirees. Nonsmokers required.

Employment Information Openings are from June 21 to August 29. Jobs available: ▶ 1 *archery staff member* (minimum age 18) ▶ 1 *canoeing staff member* (minimum age 18) ▶ 1 *glass etching staff member* (minimum age 18) ▶ 3–4 *high ropes course instructors* (minimum age 18) ▶ 4 *horsemanship staff members* (minimum age 18) ▶ 2 *kitchen staff members* ▶ 2 *maintenance staff members* ▶ 2 *outdoor living skills staff members* (minimum age 18) ▶ 1 *photography staff member* (minimum age 18) ▶ 1 *radio broadcasting staff member* (minimum age 18) ▶ 1 *rappelling staff member* (minimum age 18) ▶ 1 *sailing staff member* (minimum age 18) ▶ 1 *silkscreening staff member* (minimum age 18) ▶ 5 *swimming staff members* (minimum age 18) ▶ 1 *tumbling staff member* (minimum age 18) ▶ 4 *waterskiing staff members* (minimum age 18) ▶ *windsurfing staff member*. Applicants must submit a formal organization application, three letters of recommendation, police background check. An in-person interview is recommended, but a telephone interview is acceptable. International applicants accepted.

Benefits and Preemployment Training Free housing, free meals, on-the-job training, willing to complete paperwork for educational credit, opportunity to attend seminars/workshops, and tuition assistance. Preemployment training is required and includes accident prevention and safety, first aid, CPR, interpersonal skills, leadership skills.
Contact Cyril Millett, Director, Camp Frenda, 1110 King Street East, Oshawa, Ontario L1H 1H8. Telephone: 905-571-1022. Fax: 905-571-5995. E-mail: cmillett@ont_sda.org. World Wide Web: http://www.campfrenda.com. Contact by e-mail, fax, mail, phone, or through World Wide Web site. Application deadline: February 30.

CAMP MANITOU-WABING
MCKELLAR, ONTARIO POG 1CO

General Information Residential camp for boys and girls ages 8 to 17 offering professional instruction and training in sports, arts, and outdoor adventure. Established in 1959. 200-acre facility located 20 miles from Parry Sound. Features: freshwater lake and river; wilderness setting; 12 tennis courts; creative arts and dance; golf; ropes course.
Profile of Summer Employees Total number: 175; typical ages: 19–40. 50% men; 50% women; 50% minorities; 10% high school students; 75% college students; 75% non-U.S. citizens; 50% local applicants.
Employment Information Openings are from June 25 to August 23. Jobs available: ▶ 100–120 *staff members* (minimum age 18) at Can$800 to Can$3000 per season. Applicants must submit a letter of interest, resume, 2-3 personal references. An in-person interview is recommended, but a telephone interview is acceptable. International applicants accepted; must obtain own visa.
Benefits and Preemployment Training Free housing, free meals, formal training, willing to provide letters of recommendation, on-the-job training, willing to complete paperwork for educational credit, and willing to act as a professional reference. Preemployment training is required and includes accident prevention and safety, first aid, CPR, interpersonal skills, leadership skills.
Contact Jeff Wilson, Camp Director, Camp Manitou-wabing, 2660 Yonge Street, 2nd Floor, Toronto, Ontario. Telephone: 416-322-5888. Fax: 416-322-3635. E-mail: camp@manitoucamp.com. World Wide Web: http://www.manitoucamp.com. Contact by e-mail, fax, mail, phone, or through World Wide Web site. Application deadline: June 15.

CAMP ROBIN HOOD
158 LIMESTONE CRESCENT
DOWNSVIEW, ONTARIO M3J 2S4

General Information Day camp serving 850 campers daily. Established in 1946. 50-acre facility located near Toronto. Features: 4 swimming pools; 1 canoe pond; many indoor areas; 4 baseball diamonds; 4 sports fields; large barn converted to theater.
Profile of Summer Employees Total number: 350; typical ages: 17–23. 40% men; 60% women; 5% minorities; 50% high school students; 50% college students; 100% local applicants.
Employment Information Openings are from July 2 to August 22. Jobs available: ▶ 100 *counselors* at Can$500 to Can$1200 per season ▶ 32 *section and specialty heads* at Can$2000 to Can$3000 per season ▶ 100 *specialty counselors* at Can$500 to Can$1200 per season. Applicants must submit a formal organization application, three personal references. An in-person interview is recommended, but a telephone interview is acceptable.
Benefits and Preemployment Training Formal training and on-the-job training. Preemployment training is required and includes accident prevention and safety, interpersonal skills, leadership skills.
Contact Patti Stulberg, Registrar, Camp Robin Hood, 158 Limestone Crescent, Downsview, Ontario M3J 2S4. Fax: 416-736-9971. E-mail: crh@camprh.com. World Wide Web: http://www.

camprh.com. Contact by e-mail, fax, or through World Wide Web site. Application deadline: continuous.

GANADAOWEH
RR#3
AYR, ONTARIO N0B 1E0

General Information Residential, day, and wilderness camping programs offering Christian education to 100 campers weekly. Established in 1982. 174-acre facility located 15 miles from Kitchener. Features: freshwater lake; wooded setting; 1 sports court; wildlife; high ropes course; pool.

Profile of Summer Employees Total number: 40; typical ages: 17–25. 40% men; 60% women; 10% minorities; 60% high school students; 35% college students; 95% local applicants. Nonsmokers required.

Employment Information Openings are from May 1 to August 31. Jobs available: ▶ 1 *administrative assistant* (minimum age 16) with computer and organizational skills at Can$180 to Can$190 per week ▶ 1 *camp nurse* (minimum age 19) should be student nurse at college or university, RN preferred at Can$210 per week ▶ 4 *cooks* (minimum age 16) with cooking experience (knowledge of nutrition preferred) at $Can180 to Can$200 per week ▶ 15 *counselors* (minimum age 16) with counselor training program completed at Can$190 to Can$260 per week ▶ 1 *head cook* (minimum age 19) with cooking experience and knowledge of nutrition at Can$180 to Can$200 per week ▶ 1 *high ropes instructor* (minimum age 18) with assistant high ropes instructor certification (minimum) at Can$180 to Can$200 per week ▶ 2 *lifeguards* (minimum age 16) with NLS; leaders and instructors preferred at Can$200 per week ▶ 1 *maintenance staff member* (minimum age 16) with cleaning/groundskeeping experience preferred at Can$180 to Can$190 per week ▶ 6 *outdoor ed-program instructors* (minimum age 18) with leadership and environmental knowledge at Can$190 to Can$200 per week ▶ 2 *program assistants* (minimum age 16) at Can$185 to Can$195 per week ▶ 1 *wilderness assistant director* (minimum age 19) with Bronze Cross, NLS, outtripping and leadership experience at Can$180 to Can$200 per week ▶ 1 *wilderness camp director* (minimum age 16) with NLS or Bronze Cross and leadership and outtripping experience at Can$190 to Can$200 per week. Applicants must submit a formal organization application, two personal references, letter of recommendation. An in-person interview is recommended, but a telephone interview is acceptable.

Benefits and Preemployment Training Free housing, free meals, formal training, willing to provide letters of recommendation, names of contacts, on-the-job training, willing to complete paperwork for educational credit, willing to act as a professional reference, and opportunity to attend seminars/workshops. Preemployment training is required and includes accident prevention and safety, first aid, interpersonal skills, leadership skills, Christian program/education development, special needs, child abuse disclosures.

Contact Maja Hipkin, Director, Ganadaoweh, RR 3, Ayr, Ontario N0B 1E0. Telephone: 519-632-7559. Fax: 519-632-9607. E-mail: camp@ganadaoweh.ca. World Wide Web: http://www.ganadaoweh.ca. Contact by e-mail, fax, mail, or phone. Application deadline: continuous.

NEW STRIDES DAY CAMP
ETOBICOKE CITY HALL, 399 THE WEST MALL
ETOBICOKE, ONTARIO M9C 2Y2

General Information The Adapted-Integrated service section provides resources and transition support to individuals with disabilities; also day camp serving 105 individuals with varying special needs. Established in 1977. 525-acre facility located 12 miles from Toronto. Features: sport fields; mini-golf; tennis courts; indoor swimming pool.

Profile of Summer Employees Total number: 12; typical ages: 18–26. 20% men; 80% women; 30% high school students; 70% college students; 90% local applicants. Nonsmokers preferred.

Employment Information Openings are from July to August. Jobs available: ▶ 1 *New Strides director* (minimum age 21) with experience working in camps/recreation and with special needs population; standard first aid/CPR certification; CPI and aquatics helpful at Can$9 to Can$10 per hour ▶ *Stepping Up, adult life skills and recreation programmer* (minimum age 20) with standard first aid/CPR certification (aquatic and CPI preferred) and driver's license; should have program planning and recreation experience with a wide range of age and ability within the special population community at Can$9 to Can$10 per hour ▶ 1 *community integration coordinator* (minimum age 21) with experience in camps/recreation/playgrounds and one-to-one experience with special needs children; standard first aid and CPR; CPI and aquatics helpful at Can$9 to Can$11 per hour ▶ 4–12 *leader positions* (minimum age 18) with standard first aid and CPR certification; background working with special needs individuals; aquatic skills helpful at Can$7 to Can$8 per hour. Applicants must submit a formal organization application, letter of interest, resume, two personal references, possible police checks in the future. An in-person interview is required.

Benefits and Preemployment Training Formal training, willing to provide letters of recommendation, names of contacts, on-the-job training, willing to complete paperwork for educational credit, willing to act as a professional reference, and opportunity to attend seminars/workshops. Preemployment training is required and includes accident prevention and safety, first aid, CPR, interpersonal skills, leadership skills.

Contact Miss Sarah Bumstead, Recreationist, Adapted/Integrated Services, New Strides Day Camp, 399 The West Mall, Etobicoke, Ontario M9C 2Y2. Telephone: 416-394-8533. Fax: 416-394-8935. World Wide Web: http://www.city.toronto.on.ca. Contact by mail or phone. Application deadline: March 15.

PICKERING COLLEGE SUMMER CAMPS

16945 BAYVIEW AVENUE
NEWMARKET, ONTARIO L34 4X2

General Information Nonprofit co-ed day and residential independent school, day camp, and summer ESL program camp with a general program and ESL from all over the world. Established in 1842. 42-acre facility located 12 miles from Toronto. Features: 100 plus person dormitory; hiking paths; playing fields; art studio; computer labs; dining hall.

Profile of Summer Employees Total number: 50; typical ages: 18–25. 40% men; 60% women; 12% high school students; 80% college students; 5% non-U.S. citizens; 8% local applicants. Nonsmokers required.

Employment Information Openings are from June 17 to August 24. Jobs available: ▶ 1 *computer instructor* (minimum age 21) with good knowledge of computers; good with children at $400 per week ▶ 1 *music and drama instructor* (minimum age 21) with experience and good skills for working with children at $400 per week. Applicants must submit a formal organization application, letter of interest, resume, two personal references. A telephone interview is required.

Benefits and Preemployment Training Free housing, free meals, formal training, health insurance, willing to provide letters of recommendation, on-the-job training, willing to act as a professional reference, and opportunity to attend seminars/workshops. Preemployment training is required and includes accident prevention and safety, first aid, CPR, interpersonal skills, leadership skills, skills for working with children.

Contact Michael Bakker, Director, Pickering College Summer Camps. Telephone: 877-895-1700. Fax: 905-895-9076. E-mail: mbakker@pickeringcollege.on.ca. World Wide Web: http://www.pickeringcollege.on.ca. Contact by e-mail, fax, or through World Wide Web site. Application deadline: continuous.

YMCA KITCHIKEWANA
PO BOX 71
HONEY HARBOUR, ONTARIO P0E 1E0

General Information YMCA Outdoor Education Center serving more than 750 school-age students during spring and fall sessions as well as summer program. Established in 1919. 15-acre facility located 50 miles from Barrie. Features: located on Georgian Bay; sandy beaches; rustic cabins; 30 foot climbing wall; outdoor chapel; low ropes/initiative course.

Profile of Summer Employees Total number: 64; typical ages: 17–22. 40% men; 60% women; 3% minorities; 55% high school students; 35% college students; 7% local applicants. Nonsmokers required.

Employment Information Openings are from March to September. Jobs available: ▶ 3–6 *counselors (male)* (minimum age 16) with NLS (National Lifesaving Award), standard first aid (minimum of Red Cross leaders), level C CPR, and instructor certification at Can$120 to Can$150 per week ▶ 1–2 *prep cooks* with Level C CPR and standard first aid certification at Can$200 per week ▶ 1–2 *site staff* (minimum age 17) with standard first aid and CPR certifications at Can$200 to Can$250. Applicants must submit a letter of interest, resume, three personal references, criminal reference check. An in-person interview is recommended, but a telephone interview is acceptable. International applicants accepted; must obtain own visa, obtain own working papers.

Benefits and Preemployment Training Free housing, free meals, on-the-job training, willing to act as a professional reference, and opportunity to attend seminars/workshops. Preemployment training is required and includes accident prevention and safety, interpersonal skills, leadership skills.

Contact Darryl McKenzie, Camp Director, YMCA Kitchikewana, Little Lake Park, PO Box 488, Midland, Ontario L4R 4L3. Telephone: 705-526-7828. Fax: 705-526-8735. E-mail: kitchi@csolve.net. World Wide Web: http://www.kitchi.com. Contact by e-mail, fax, mail, phone, or through World Wide Web site. Application deadline: prefer applications before January 15.

QUEBEC

CAMP NOMININGUE
1889 CHEMIN DES MESANGES
NOMININGUE, QUEBEC J0W 1R0

General Information Residential camp for 220 boys ages 7–15 providing a place to cultivate friendships, self-confidence, and a sense of achievement. Established in 1925. 400-acre facility located 120 miles from Montreal. Features: half mile of sandy beach; freshwater lake; 400 acres of woods and fields; 4 tennis courts.

Profile of Summer Employees Total number: 80; typical ages: 18–25. 99% men; 1% women; 15% minorities; 10% high school students; 70% college students; 1% retirees; 80% local applicants. Nonsmokers preferred.

Employment Information Openings are from June 22 to August 25. Year-round positions also offered. Jobs available: ▶ *TOESL instructors* (minimum age 18) must be current student or graduate in university ESL program at Can$210 per week ▶ *archery instructors* (minimum age 18) with CPR, first aid, and instructors certifications at Can$125 to Can$200 per week ▶ *athletics instructors* (minimum age 18) with CPR and first aid certifications at Can$125 to Can$200 per week ▶ *campcraft instructors* (minimum age 18) with CPR and first aid certifications at Can$125 to Can$200 per week ▶ *canoeing instructors* (minimum age 18) with CPR and first aid certifications at Can$125 to Can$200 per week ▶ 1–30 *general counselors* (minimum age 18) with CPR and first aid certifications at Can$125 to Can$200 per week ▶ *golf instructors* (minimum age 18) with CPR and first aid certifications at Can$125 to Can$200 per week ▶ 1–3 *kayaking instructors* (minimum age 18) with CPR and first aid certifications at Can$125 to Can$200 per week ▶ 1 *nature awareness instructor* (minimum age 18) with CPR and first aid certifications at Can$200 per week ▶ *orienteering instructors* (minimum age 18) with CPR and first aid certifications at Can$125 to Can$200 per week ▶ *riflery instructors* (minimum age 18) with CPR and first aid certifications at Can$125 to Can$200 per week ▶ 1–3 *sailing instructors* (minimum age 18) with CPR and first aid certifications and ability to operate motor boat at Can$200 per week ▶ *tennis instructors* (minimum age 18) with CPR and first aid certifications at Can$125 to Can$200 per week ▶ *theater instructors* (minimum age 18) with CPR and first aid certifications at Can$125 to Can$200 per week ▶ 1–3 *windsurfing instructors* (minimum age 18) with CPR and first aid certifications and ability to operate motor boat at Can$200 per week ▶ 1 *woodworking instructor* (minimum age 18) with CPR and first aid certification and ability to operate woodworking machinery at Can$200 per week. Applicants must submit a formal organization application, letter of interest, resume, three personal references. An in-person interview is recommended, but a telephone interview is acceptable. International applicants accepted; must obtain own visa.

Benefits and Preemployment Training Housing at a cost, meals at a cost, formal training, possible full-time employment, willing to provide letters of recommendation, on-the-job training, and willing to act as a professional reference. Preemployment training is required and includes accident prevention and safety, first aid, interpersonal skills, leadership skills.

Contact Grant McKenna, Executive Director, Camp Nominingue, 2700 rue Halpern, St. Laurent, Quebec H45 1R6. Telephone: 514-856-1333. Fax: 514-856-8001. E-mail: camp@axess.com. World Wide Web: http://www.nominingue.com. Contact by e-mail, fax, mail, phone, or through World Wide Web site. Application deadline: continuous.

STIVERS STAFFING SERVICES–CANADA

See Stivers Staffing Services–Illinois on page 110 for complete description.

BELIZE

LONGACRE EXPEDITIONS

Recreation Workers

General Information Adventure travel program in Belize for teenagers, emphasizing group living skills and physical challenges. Established in 1981. near Belize City, Belize.

Profile of Summer Employees Total number: 4; typical ages: 21–30. 50% men; 50% women; 1% minorities; 100% college students. Nonsmokers required.

Employment Information Openings are from June 15 to July 31. Jobs available: ▶ 2 *assistant leaders* (minimum age 21) with scuba certification, first aid or WFR, CPR, and lifeguard training at $252–$300 per week. Applicants must submit a formal organization application, three personal references. An in-person interview is recommended, but a telephone interview is acceptable. International applicants accepted; must obtain own visa, obtain own working papers.

Benefits and Preemployment Training Free housing, free meals, willing to provide letters of recommendation, on-the-job training, willing to act as a professional reference, and pro-deal purchase program. Preemployment training is required and includes accident prevention and safety, interpersonal skills, leadership skills.

Contact Meredith Schuler, Director, Longacre Expeditions, 4030 Middle Ridge Road, Newport, Pennsylvania 17074-8110. Telephone: 717-567-6790. Fax: 717-567-3955. E-mail: merry@longacreexpeditions.com. World Wide Web: http://www.longacreexpeditions.com. Contact by e-mail, fax, mail, phone, or through World Wide Web site. Application deadline: continuous.

FRANCE

BOMBARD BALLOON ADVENTURES

CHATEAU DE LABORDE
LABORDE AU CHATEAU, BEAUNE, FRANCE

General Information Bombard Balloon Adventures is a tour operator providing complete luxury travel programs blending daily hot-air ballooning with fine restaurants and hotels and personal visits to an international clientele. Established in 1977.

Profile of Summer Employees Total number: 10–20; typical ages: 18–25. 80% men; 20% women; 80% college students; 99% non-U.S. citizens. Nonsmokers preferred.

Employment Information Openings are from May 1 to November 1. Winter break positions also offered. Jobs available: ▶ 10–20 *hot-air balloon ground crew* (minimum age 18) with driver's license for at least one year; clean driving record; and minimum weight of 150 pounds. Applicants must submit a formal organization application, letter of interest, resume, photocopy of driver's license, ID photo, height, weight, and dates of availability. A telephone interview is required. International applicants accepted; must obtain own visa, obtain own working papers.

Benefits and Preemployment Training Free housing and free meals.

Contact Michael Lincicome, Bombard Balloon Adventures. Fax: 33-380-26-69-20. World Wide Web: http://www.bombardsociety.com/jobs. Contact by fax, mail, or through World Wide Web site. Application deadline: continuous.

U.S. VIRGIN ISLANDS

A CHRISTIAN MINISTRY IN THE NATIONAL PARKS–VIRGIN ISLANDS, WEST INDIES

See A Christian Ministry in the National Parks–Maine on page 122 for complete description.

STUDENT CONSERVATION ASSOCIATION (SCA), VIRGIN ISLANDS

See Student Conservation Association (SCA), New Hampshire on page 209 for complete description.

UNITED KINGDOM

GREENFORCE

11-15 BETTERTON STREET, COVENT GARDEN
LONDON, UNITED KINGDOM

General Information Nonprofit conservation organization that places individuals on environmental projects throughout the world. Also opportunities for long-term staff positions once volunteer phase is over. Established in 1996. Features: Africa; Amazon; Borneo; Fiji; United Kingdom; Bahamas.

Profile of Summer Employees Total number: 50; typical ages: 18–28. 50% men; 50% women; 25% high school students; 75% college students; 90% non-U.S. citizens.

Employment Information Openings are from January 1 to December 31. Spring break, winter break, and year-round positions also offered. Jobs available: ▶ 180–200 *research assistants* (minimum age 18). Applicants must submit a formal organization application, there is a fee of 2550 British pounds once hired to take part in the program. A telephone interview is required. International applicants accepted.

Benefits and Preemployment Training Free housing, free meals, formal training, possible full-time employment, health insurance, willing to provide letters of recommendation, on-the-job training, willing to complete paperwork for educational credit, willing to act as a professional reference, opportunity to attend seminars/workshops, and tuition assistance. Preemployment training is optional and includes accident prevention and safety, first aid, CPR, interpersonal skills, leadership skills, kit, map, or dive training subject to location.

Contact M. Jones, Director of Operations, Greenforce, 11-15 Betterton Street, London WC2H 9BP. Telephone: 207-470-8888. Fax: 207-470-8889. E-mail: greenforce@btinternet.com. World Wide Web: http://www.greenforce.com. Contact by e-mail, fax, mail, phone, or through World Wide Web site. Application deadline: continuous.

SUMMER DISCOVERY AT CAMBRIDGE

NEW HALL COLLEGE, CAMBRIDGE UNIVERSITY
CAMBRIDGE, UNITED KINGDOM

General Information Precollege enrichment program for high school students at Cambridge University in England. Established in 1987. Located 100 miles from London. Features: sport facilities; beaches; mountains; lakes; major cities nearby; college towns.

Profile of Summer Employees Total number: 20; typical ages: 23–35. 10% minorities; 30% college students. Nonsmokers required.

Employment Information Openings are from June 20 to August 25. Jobs available: ▶ 20 *resident counselors* (minimum age 23) with experience working with high school students/children at $150–$400 per week. Applicants must submit a formal organization application, resume, personal reference. An in-person interview is required. International applicants accepted; must obtain own visa, obtain own working papers.

Benefits and Preemployment Training Free housing, free meals, possible full-time employment, health insurance, willing to provide letters of recommendation, on-the-job training, willing to complete paperwork for educational credit, willing to act as a professional reference, and travel reimbursement. Preemployment training is required and includes accident prevention and safety, CPR, interpersonal skills, leadership skills.

Contact Jason Walley, Admissions Director, Summer Discovery at Cambridge, 1326 Old Northern Boulevard, Roslyn, New York 11576. Telephone: 516-621-3939. Fax: 516-625-3438. E-mail:

staff@summerfun.com. World Wide Web: http://www.summerfun.com. Contact by e-mail, fax, mail, phone, or through World Wide Web site. Application deadline: continuous.

CATEGORY INDEX

Accommodations and Food Services
Absaroka Mountain Lodge 352
Alpenhof Lodge 352
American Presidents Resort 297
Aurora University, Lake Geneva Campus 341
Bar NI Ranch 67
Best Western Bucks T-4 Lodge of Big Sky 193
Big Sky Resort 194
Bill Cody Ranch 353
Boyd's Mason Lake Resort 342
The Bridges Family Resort and Tennis Club 313
Cherokee Park Ranch 70
Colorado Trails Ranch 71
Cowboy Village Resort at Togwotee 353
Custer State Park Resort Company 298
Double JJ Resort 174
Drakesbad Guest Ranch 54
Drowsy Water Ranch 73
Elephant Head Lodge 354
Elk Mountain Ranch 74
Estes Valley Resorts 75
Geneva Point Center 206
Golden Acres Farm and Ranch Resort 238
Grand Canyon National Park Lodges 43
Grand View Lodge Golf and Tennis Club 185
Hatchet Motel and Restaurant 355
Hunewill Guest Ranch 58
Idlease and Shorelands Guest Resort 137
Katmailand Inc. 42
Lighthouse Inn, Inc. 159
Mt. Rainier Guest Services 337
Mt. Rushmore Concessions 299
Nelson's Resort 186
North Fork Guest Ranch 78
Oakland House Seaside Resort 141
Redfish Lake Lodge 106
The Resort at Glacier, St. Mary Lodge 195
Rock Springs Guest Ranch 272
Rocky Mountain Park Company (The Trail Ridge Store) 80
Rockywold–Deephaven Camps, Inc. (RDC) 208
Rubin's Osceola Lake Inn 259
63 Ranch 196
Snowbird Ski & Summer Resort 312
Stoiber Enterprises 266
Sunrise Resort 92
Tumbling River Ranch 83
Vail Resorts 83
Vista Verde Ranch 84
Wild Dunes Resort 297
Winter Park Resort 84
Woodside Ranch Resort 351
YMCA of the Rockies, Snow Mountain Ranch 86
Yosemite Concession Services Corporation 66

Agriculture, Forestry, Fishing, and Hunting
Mitchell Harvesting 116
Northwest Youth Corps 272

Ambulatory Health Care Services
American Red Cross National Headquarters 97

Amusement and Theme Parks
Adventure City 47
Astro-Art Amusements 303
Calaway Park 357
Cedar Point 264
Dorney Park and Wildwater Kingdom 286
Enchanted Forest/Water Safari and Old Forge 234
Enchanted Parks, Inc. 335
Funland 95
Kennywood Park 288
L.I. Adventureland 241
Midway Park, Inc. 241
Paramount's Carowinds 258
Sea World of Florida 100
Tomahawk Lake Water Park 219
Valleyfair Family Amusement Park 188
Viking Golf Theme & Waterpark 96
Waldameer Park, Inc. 293
Western Playland Amusement Park 311
The Whale's Tale Water Park 209
Worlds of Fun/Oceans of Fun 192

Business and Professional Organizations
Legacy International's Global Youth Village 329
Stivers Staffing Services–Illinois 110
YES TO JOBS 65

Educational Services
Audubon Center of the North Woods 177
Castilleja School 51
Center for American Archeology 109
Center for Talented Youth/Johns Hopkins University 145
Choate Rosemary Hall 91
Cybercamps–University of Washington 335
Duke Youth Programs–Duke University Continuing Education 256
Dwight-Englewood School 214
Elite Educational Institute 55
Idyllwild Arts Summer Program 59
Pickering College Summer Camps 362
Sagamore Institute of the Adirondacks 244
Stevenson School Summer Camp 63
Summer Discovery at UCLA 63
TAG/Southern Methodist University 310

Woodberry Forest Summer School 331
Wright State University Pre-College Programs 267

Nature Parks and Environmental Organizations
Acadia Corporation 121
Alaska State Parks Volunteer Program 40
Austin Nature and Science Center 304
Blackwater National Wildlife Refuge 142
Brooklyn Botanic Garden 223
Chincoteague National Wildlife Refuge 327
Chingachgook YMCA Outdoor Center 233
Deep Portage Conservation Reserve 183
Five Rivers Center 235
Fort Necessity National Battlefield 287
Fredericksburg and Spotsylvania National Military Park 329
Greenforce 366
Marine Life Oceanarium 190
Somerset County Park Commission Environmental Education Center 218
Student Conservation Association (SCA), New Hampshire 209

Performing Arts Companies
Burklyn Ballet Theatre 314
Burklyn Ballet Theatre II, The Children's Program 314
Central City Opera 68
College Light Opera Company 156
French Woods Festival of the Performing Arts 236
Marrowstone Music Festival 337
North Shore Music Theatre 160
Straw Hat Players 187
Williamstown Theater Festival 162

Professional, Scientific and Technical Services
Advatech Pacific, Inc. 46

Public Administration
Vermont State Parks Division 322

Recreation Industries
ActionQuest 98
Adventure Connection, Inc. 47
America & Pacific Tours, Inc. (A&P) 41
AmeriCan Adventures 48
Blazing Adventures 68
Bombard Balloon Adventures 365
Broadway at the Beach 295
Cherokee Adventures Whitewater Rafting 300
Echo Canyon River Expeditions 74
Epley's Whitewater Adventures 104
Fairview Lake Environmental Trip 215
Foresite Sports, Inc. 287
Hidden Creek Ranch 104
Interlocken Travel Programs 207
Lazy K Bar Ranch 195
Longacre Expeditions 289
Longacre Expeditions 364
Longacre Expeditions, Colorado 78
Longacre Expeditions, Hawaii 103
Longacre Expeditions, Maine 139
Longacre Expeditions, Oregon 271
Longacre Expeditions, Virgin Islands 324
Longacre Expeditions, Washington 336
Mount Snow 320
Mystic Saddle Ranch 105
North American Trails 160
Rein Teen Tours 218
Sail Caribbean 244
Saratoga Springs Picnic, Campgrounds, and Day Camp 61
Student Hosteling Program 162
Sweet Grass Ranch 197
Trailmark Outdoor Adventures 247
Trails Wilderness School 192
Weissman Teen Tours 248
Westcoast Connection Travel Camp 248
Wilderness Ventures 356

Recreational and Vacation Camps
Academy by the Sea/Camp Pacific 46
Alford Lake Camp 122
Aloha Foundation, Inc. 313
Alpine Conference Center 48
American Camping Association–New York Section 222
American Youth Foundation–Camp Merrowvista 199
American Youth Foundation–Camp Miniwanca 164
Anderson Western Colorado Camps, Ltd. 67
Appel Farm Arts and Music Center 211
Awosting and Chinqueka Camps 87
Bar 717 Ranch/Camp Trinity 49
Bassett-Martin Tennis Camp 49
Bay Cliff Health Camp 165
Bear Creek Aquatic Camp/Girl Scouts of Kentuckiana 117
Belvoir Terrace 149
BikingX 250
Birch Trail Camp for Girls 341
Black River Farm and Ranch 166
Blue Bell Day Camp 274
Blue Lake Fine Arts Camp 166
B'nai B'rith Camp 269
Bonnie Castle Riding Camp 150
Brant Lake Camp 222
Brewster Day Camp 150
Brookwoods for Boys/Deer Run for Girls 200
Buck's Rock Performing and Creative Arts Camp 88
Calvin Crest Camp, Retreat, and Conference Center 197
Camp Advenchur 201
Camp Agawam 123
Camp Airy for Boys 142
Camp Algonquin 107
Camp Alice Chester–East Troy 343
Camp America Day Camp 274
Camp Androscoggin 124
Camp Arcadia 124
Camp Artaban 358
Camp Balcones Springs 304
Camp Barney Medintz 101
Camp Berachah 331
Camp Birch Knoll for Girls 343
Camp Birchwood 177
Camp Blue Ridge 98
Camp Buckskin 178
Camp Canadensis 275
Camp Carysbrook 324
Camp Cayuga 275

Camp Cedar Point 107
Camp Chatuga 295
Camp Chen-A-Wanda 278
Camp Chippewa Foundation 179
Camp Chosatonga for Boys 250
Camp Conowingo–Girl Scouts of Central Maryland 143
Camp Courage 179
Camp Courageous of Iowa 115
Camp Deerwood 201
Camp Echoing Hills 262
Camp Edwards 344
Camp Encore-Coda for a Great Summer of Music, Sports, and Friends 125
Camp Farnsworth 315
Camp Fern 305
Camp Fire Camp Wi-Ta-Wentin 120
Camp Fowler at The Fowler Center 167
Camp Frenda 359
Camp Friendship 325
Camp Good News 151
Camp Harmon 0
Camp Hawthorne 126
Camp Hidden Falls 279
Camp High Rocks 250
Camp Hillard, Inc. 224
Camp Hillcroft 224
Camp Hilltop 225
Camp Horizons 326
Camp Interlaken JCC 344
Camp JCA Shalom 50
Camp Jeanne d'Arc 225
Camp Jened–A Facility of the United Cerebral Palsy Association of New York State 226
Camp Jewell YMCA 89
Camp Kahdalea for Girls 251
Camp Kanata YMCA 252
Camp Kirby 332
Camp La Jolla 50
Camp La Junta 305
Camp Lakeland/Jewish Community Center of Greater Buffalo, Inc. 227
Camp Lakota 51
Camp Laney for Boys 39
Camp Laughing Waters 279
Camp Laurel 127
Camp Laurel South 127
Camp Libbey/Girl Scouts of Maumee Valley Council 262
Camp Lincoln for Boys/Camp Lake Hubert for Girls 180
Camp Lindenmere 280
Camp Logan 111
Camp Lohikan in the Pocono Mountains 281
Camp Loma Linda for Girls 305
Camp Lookout 168
Camp Lou Henry Hoover 212
Camp Loyaltown-AHRC 227
Camp Maas 168
Camp Manitou-wabing 360
Camp Manito-wish YMCA 345
Camp Maplehurst 169
Camp Matoaka for Girls 128
Camp Merrie-Woode 252
Camp Merri-Mac 253
Camp Micah 129
Camp Michikamau–YMCA of Greater Bergen County 228
Camp Modin 130
Camp Monroe 228
Camp Nakanawa 299
Camp Nawaka 151
Camp Nebagamon for Boys 346
Camp Netimus 281
Camp New Hope 180
Camp Nock-A-Mixon 282
Camp Nominingue 363
Camp O'Bannon 263
Camp O'Fair Winds 170
Camp of the Woods 229
Camp Pemigewassett 202
Camp Pennyroyal/Girl Scouts of Kentuckiana 118
Camp Pondicherry 130
Camp Red Rock 268
Camp Regis, Inc. 230
Camp Rim Rock 339
Camp Rio Vista for Boys 306
Camp Riverbend 212
Camp River Ranch 333
Camp Robin Hood 360
Camp Robin Hood for Boys and Girls 202
Camp Roosevelt for Boys/Firebird for Girls 263
Camp Runoia 131
Camp Sabra 191
Camp Seven Hills 231
Camp Sierra Vista for Girls 306
Camp Skylemar 132
Camp Skyline 39
Camp Sky Ranch, Inc. 254
Camp Sloane YMCA, Inc. 89
Camps Mondamin and Green Cove 254
Camp Sonshine 144
Camp Stanislaus 190
Camp Stewart for Boys 307
Camp Summit, Inc. 308
Camps Woodland and Towering Pines 346
Camp Taconic 152
Camp Tall Timbers 340
Camp Tapawingo 108
Camp Tapawingo 132
Camp Tevya 203
Camp Thoreau-In-Vermont 315
Camp Thorpe, Inc. 316
Camp Thunderbird 99
Camp Thunderbird for Boys 181
Camp Thunderbird for Girls 182
Camp Timberlake 255
Camp Togowoods 41
Camp Tohkomeupog 203
Camp Volasuca 333
Camp Waldemar for Girls 308
Camp Walden NY 232
Camp Walt Whitman 204
Camp Washington 90
Camp Wasiu II 198
Camp Watitoh 153
Camp Watonka 283
Camp Wawenock 133
Camp Wayne for Boys 284
Camp Waziyatah 134
Camp Wekeela 134

Camp Westminster 170
Camp Westmont 284
Camp Winnebago 135
Camp Woodmen of the World 119
Camp Woodmont for Boys and Girls on Lookout Mountain 102
Camp Zanika Lache/Camp Fire USA NCW Council 334
Cape Cod Sea Camps 153
Capital Camps 145
Cedar Lodge 171
Center for Talented Youth/Johns Hopkins University–Dickinson College 285
Center for Talented Youth/Johns Hopkins University–Franklin and Marshall College 285
Center for Talented Youth/Johns Hopkins University–Garrison Forest School 146
Center for Talented Youth/Johns Hopkins University–Hood College 146
Center for Talented Youth/Johns Hopkins University–Loyola Marymount University 52
Center for Talented Youth/Johns Hopkins University–Marine Sciences Program 146
Center for Talented Youth/Johns Hopkins University–Mirman School 52
Center for Talented Youth/Johns Hopkins University–Moravian College 285
Center for Talented Youth/Johns Hopkins University–Mount Holyoke College 154
Center for Talented Youth/Johns Hopkins University–Pepperdine University 52
Center for Talented Youth/Johns Hopkins University–Roger Williams University 294
Center for Talented Youth/Johns Hopkins University–Sandy Spring Friends School 146
Center for Talented Youth/Johns Hopkins University–Skidmore College 232
Center for Talented Youth/Johns Hopkins University–Stanford University 52
Center for Talented Youth/Johns Hopkins University–University of California, Santa Cruz 52
Center for Talented Youth/Johns Hopkins University–Washington College 147
Central Wisconsin Environmental Station/University of Wisconsin–Stevens Point 347
Challenge Wilderness Camp for Boys 317
Channel 3 Kids Camp 91
Cheerio Adventures 327
Cheley Colorado Camps 69
Chenoa 205
Chesapeake Bay Girl Scout Council 94
Children's Beach House, Inc. 95
Chimney Corners Camp for Girls 154
Christikon 194
Circle Pines Center Summer Camp 171
The Citadel Summer Camp 296
Clara Barton Camp 155
Clearwater Camp for Girls 347
Cold River Camp, A.M.C. 205
College Gifted Programs 213
College Gifted Programs 155
College Gifted Programs 233
College Gifted Programs 285
College Gifted Programs 264
College Settlement of Philadelphia 286
The Colorado Mountain Ranch 70
Colvig Silver Camps 71
Crane Lake Camp 157
Cross Bar X Youth Ranch 72
Crystalaire Camp 172
Culver Summer Camps 112
CYO Boys Camp 173
CYO Girls Camp 173
Deer Hill Expeditions 72
Discovery Day Camp 109
Douglas Ranch Camps 53
Dudley Gallahue Valley Camps 113
Eagle Lake Camp–Colorado 74
Eagle's Nest Camp 256
Eastern Excel Tennis 234
Easter Seals Camp Harmon 55
Easter Seals Camp Merry Heart 214
Easter Seals Wisconsin 348
Echo Hill Camp 147
Emandal–A Farm on a River 55
Evans Lake Forest Education Centre 359
Fairview Lake YMCA Camp 215
Farm and Wilderness Camps 318
Fenton Ranch 221
Flying G Ranch 75
Flying G Ranch, Tomahawk Ranch–Girl Scouts Mile Hi Council 76
Forest Acres Camp for Girls 136
Forest Lake Camp 235
Forrestel Farm Camp 236
4-H Farley Outdoor Education Center 158
4 Star Summer Camps at the University of Virginia 328
The Fresh Air Fund 237
Friendship Ventures/Camp Friendship 183
Friendship Ventures/Eden Wood Camp 184
Friends Music Camp 265
Ganadaoweh 361
Geneva Glen Camp, Inc. 77
Girl Scout Camp Molly Louman 265
Girl Scout Camp Sycamore Hills 300
Girl Scout Camp Tanglefoot 115
Girl Scout Camp Tannassie 301
Girl Scouts–Indian Hills Council, Inc. 238
Girl Scouts of the San Fernando Valley 56
Girl Scouts of Tierra del Oro 56
Girl Scouts Pacific Peaks Council–Camp St. Albans 336
Gordon Kent's New England Tennis Camp at Trinity-Pawling School 239
Griffith Park Boys Camp 57
Hamlin Camps 58
Hidden Hollow Camp 266
Hidden Valley Camp 137
Hillside Outdoor Education Center Day and Tripping Camp 240
Horizons for Youth 158
Howe Military School Summer Camp 114
Indian Acres Camp for Boys 138
Interlochen Arts Camp 175
Interlocken International Summer Camp 206
International Music Camp 261
Introduction to Independence 240
Jameson Ranch Camp 59

Jumonville 288
Kamp Kohut 138
Keystone Camp 257
Kickapoo Kamp 309
Killooleet 318
Kostopulos Dream Foundation/Camp K 312
Lake Hubert Tennis Camp 185
Le Camp Français en Californie 60
Life Adventure Camp 119
Lindley G. Cook 4-H Camp 217
Lochearn Camp for Girls 319
Longhorn Tennis Camp 309
Maine Teen Camp 139
Meadowood Springs Speech and Hearing Camp 271
Menogyn–YMCA Wilderness Adventures 186
Michigan Technological University Summer Youth Program 175
Mo-Ranch Summer Camps 310
New England Camping Adventures 140
New Strides Day Camp 361
92nd Street Y Camps 241
Noark Girl Scout Camp 45
North Carolina United Methodist Outdoor and Camping Ministries 258
North Shore Holiday House 242
Oakland School and Camp 330
Offense-Defense Golf Camp, Massachusetts 161
Orme Summer Camp 44
Peconic Dunes Camp 242
Point CounterPoint Chamber Music Camp 320
Point O' Pines Camp 243
Poulter Colorado Camps 79
Presbyterian Camp Johnsonburg 217
Putney Summer Programs 321
Rawhide Ranch 60
Red Pine Camp for Girls 349
Road's End Farm Horsemanship Camp 207
Rockbrook Camp 259
Sabin-Mulloy-Garrison Tennis Camp 99
Salvation Army Wonderland Camp and Conference Center 350
Sanborn Western Camps 81
Santa Catalina School Summer Camp 61
Seacamp Association, Inc. 100
Shaffer's High Sierra Camp 62
Shaver's Creek Environmental Center, Pennsylvania State University 290
Shelly Ridge Day Camp 290
Singing Hills Girl Scout Camp and Cannon Valley Day Camps 187
SJ Ranch, Inc. 92
South Mountain YMCA 291
South Shore YMCA Camps 161
Sports International, Inc. 147
Stagedoor Manor Theatre and Dance Camp 245
Stony Brook-Millstone Watershed Association-Environmental Education Day Camp 219
Streamside Camp and Conference Center 291
Summer at Hawthorne Valley Farm Camp 246
Summer Discovery at Cambridge 366
Summer Discovery at Georgetown 97
Summer Discovery at Michigan 176
Summer Discovery at Vermont 321
Swarthmore Tennis Camp 292
TENNIS: EUROPE 93
Teton Valley Ranch Camp Education Foundation 355
Thunderbird Ranch 64
Timber Lake West 246
Tomahawk Ranch 82
Tyler Hill Camp 247
UCLA Bruin Tennis Camp 64
United Cerebral Palsy Association of Greater Hartford 94
University of Rhode Island Summer Programs 294
Walton's Grizzly Lodge Summer Camp 65
West River United Methodist Center 148
Wilderness Dance Camp 188
Windridge Tennis Camp at Craftsbury Common 322
Windridge Tennis Camp at Teela-Wooket, Vermont 323
Wohelo-Luther Gulick Camps 141
YMCA Camp Fitch 293
YMCA Camp Hanes 260
YMCA Camping Services–Camps Greenkill/McAlister/Talcott 249
YMCA Camp Letts 149
YMCA Camp Lincoln 210
YMCA Camp Lyndon 163
YMCA Camp Pepin 189
YMCA Camp Seymour 338
YMCA Camps Ockanickon and Matollionequay 220
YMCA Camp Surf 65
YMCA Camp Tippecanoe 267
YMCA Camp U-Nah-Li-Ya 351
YMCA Kitchikewana 363
YMCA of the Rockies–Camp Chief Ouray 85
YMCA of the Rockies Estes Park Center 85
Yogi Bear's Jellystone Park 210
YWCA Camp Westwind 273

Religious Organizations

A Christian Ministry in the National Parks–Maine 122
Fellowship Deaconry, Inc. (Day Camp Sunshine and Fellowship Conference Center) 216

Retail Trade

The Southwestern Company 302
Yellowstone Park Service Stations 357

Social Assistance

Rocky Mountain Village 80
Salvation Army of Lower Bucks 289
A Christian Ministry in the National Parks–Kentucky 117
Cybercamps–Babson College 157

EMPLOYER INDEX

Absaroka Mountain Lodge 352
Academy by the Sea/Camp Pacific 46
Acadia Corporation 121
A Christian Ministry in the National Parks (all locations) 122
ActionQuest 98
Advatech Pacific, Inc. 46
Adventure City 47
Adventure Connection, Inc. 47
Alaska State Parks Volunteer Program 40
Alford Lake Camp 122
Aloha Foundation, Inc. 313
Alpenhof Lodge 352
Alpine Conference Center 48
America & Pacific Tours, Inc. (A&P) 41
AmeriCan Adventures 48
American Camping Association–New York Section 222
American Presidents Resort 297
American Red Cross National Headquarters 97
American Youth Foundation–Camp Merrowvista 199
American Youth Foundation–Camp Miniwanca 164
Anderson Western Colorado Camps, Ltd. 67
Appel Farm Arts and Music Center 211
Astro-Art Amusements 303
Audubon Center of the North Woods 177
Aurora University, Lake Geneva Campus 341
Austin Nature and Science Center 304
Awosting and Chinqueka Camps 87
Bar NI Ranch 67
Bar 717 Ranch/Camp Trinity 49
Bassett-Martin Tennis Camp 49
Bay Cliff Health Camp 165
Bear Creek Aquatic Camp/Girl Scouts of Kentuckiana 117
Belvoir Terrace 149
Best Western Bucks T-4 Lodge of Big Sky 193
Big Sky Resort 194
BikingX 250
Bill Cody Ranch 353
Birch Trail Camp for Girls 341
Black River Farm and Ranch 166
Blackwater National Wildlife Refuge 142
Blazing Adventures 68
Blue Bell Day Camp 274
Blue Lake Fine Arts Camp 166
B'nai B'rith Camp 269
Bombard Balloon Adventures 365
Bonnie Castle Riding Camp 150
Boyd's Mason Lake Resort 342
Brant Lake Camp 222
Brewster Day Camp 150
The Bridges Family Resort and Tennis Club 313
Broadway at the Beach 295
Brooklyn Botanic Garden 223
Brookwoods for Boys/Deer Run for Girls 200
Buck's Rock Performing and Creative Arts Camp 88
Burklyn Ballet Theatre 314
Burklyn Ballet Theatre II, The Children's Program 314
Calaway Park 357
Calvin Crest Camp, Retreat, and Conference Center 197
Camp Advenchur 201
Camp Agawam 123
Camp Airy for Boys 142
Camp Algonquin 107
Camp Alice Chester–East Troy 343
Camp America Day Camp 274
Camp Androscoggin 124
Camp Arcadia 124
Camp Artaban 358
Camp Balcones Springs 304
Camp Barney Medintz 101
Camp Berachah 331
Camp Birch Knoll for Girls 343
Camp Birchwood 177
Camp Blue Ridge 98
Camp Buckskin 178
Camp Canadensis 275
Camp Carysbrook 324
Camp Cayuga 275
Camp Cedar Point 107
Camp Chatuga 295
Camp Chen-A-Wanda 278
Camp Chippewa Foundation 179
Camp Chosatonga for Boys 250
Camp Conowingo–Girl Scouts of Central Maryland 143
Camp Courage 179
Camp Courageous of Iowa 115
Camp Deerwood 201
Camp Echoing Hills 262
Camp Edwards 344
Camp Encore-Coda for a Great Summer of Music, Sports, and Friends 125
Camp Farnsworth 315
Camp Fern 305
Camp Fire Camp Wi-Ta-Wentin 120
Camp Fowler at The Fowler Center 167
Camp Frenda 359
Camp Friendship 325
Camp Good News 151
Camp Hawthorne 126
Camp Hidden Falls 279
Camp High Rocks 250
Camp Hillard, Inc. 224

Camp Hillcroft 224
Camp Hilltop 225
Camp Horizons 326
Camp Interlaken JCC 344
Camp JCA Shalom 50
Camp Jeanne d'Arc 225
Camp Jened–A Facility of the United Cerebral Palsy Association of New York State 226
Camp Jewell YMCA 89
Camp Kahdalea for Girls 251
Camp Kanata YMCA 252
Camp Kirby 332
Camp La Jolla 50
Camp La Junta 305
Camp Lakeland/Jewish Community Center of Greater Buffalo, Inc. 227
Camp Lakota 51
Camp Laney for Boys 39
Camp Laughing Waters 279
Camp Laurel 127
Camp Laurel South 127
Camp Libbey/Girl Scouts of Maumee Valley Council 262
Camp Lincoln for Boys/Camp Lake Hubert for Girls 180
Camp Lindenmere 280
Camp Logan 111
Camp Lohikan in the Pocono Mountains 281
Camp Loma Linda for Girls 305
Camp Lookout 168
Camp Lou Henry Hoover 212
Camp Loyaltown-AHRC 227
Camp Maas 168
Camp Manitou-wabing 360
Camp Manito-wish YMCA 345
Camp Maplehurst 169
Camp Matoaka for Girls 128
Camp Merrie-Woode 252
Camp Merri-Mac 253
Camp Micah 129
Camp Michikamau–YMCA of Greater Bergen County 228
Camp Modin 130
Camp Monroe 228
Camp Nakanawa 299
Camp Nawaka 151
Camp Nebagamon for Boys 346
Camp Netimus 281
Camp New Hope 180
Camp Nock-A-Mixon 282
Camp Nominingue 363
Camp O'Bannon 263
Camp O'Fair Winds 170
Camp of the Woods 229
Camp Pemigewassett 202
Camp Pennyroyal/Girl Scouts of Kentuckiana 118
Camp Pondicherry 130
Camp Red Rock 268
Camp Regis, Inc. 230
Camp Rim Rock 339
Camp Rio Vista for Boys 306
Camp Riverbend 212
Camp River Ranch 333
Camp Robin Hood 360
Camp Robin Hood for Boys and Girls 202
Camp Roosevelt for Boys/Firebird for Girls 263
Camp Runoia 131
Camp Sabra 191
Camp Seven Hills 231
Camp Sierra Vista for Girls 306
Camp Skylemar 132
Camp Skyline 39
Camp Sky Ranch, Inc. 254
Camp Sloane YMCA, Inc. 89
Camps Mondamin and Green Cove 254
Camp Sonshine 144
Camp Stanislaus 190
Camp Stewart for Boys 307
Camp Summit, Inc. 308
Camps Woodland and Towering Pines 346
Camp Taconic 152
Camp Tall Timbers 340
Camp Tapawingo 108
Camp Tapawingo 132
Camp Tevya 203
Camp Thoreau-In-Vermont 315
Camp Thorpe, Inc. 316
Camp Thunderbird 99
Camp Thunderbird for Boys 181
Camp Thunderbird for Girls 182
Camp Timberlake 255
Camp Togowoods 41
Camp Tohkomeupog 203
Camp Volasuca 333
Camp Waldemar for Girls 308
Camp Walden NY 232
Camp Walt Whitman 204
Camp Washington 90
Camp Wasiu II 198
Camp Watitoh 153
Camp Watonka 283
Camp Wawenock 133
Camp Wayne for Boys 284
Camp Waziyatah 134
Camp Wekeela 134
Camp Westminster 170
Camp Westmont 284
Camp Winnebago 135
Camp Woodmen of the World 119
Camp Woodmont for Boys and Girls on Lookout Mountain 102
Camp Zanika Lache/Camp Fire USA NCW Council 334
Cape Cod Sea Camps 153
Capital Camps 145
Castilleja School 51
Cedar Lodge 171
Cedar Point 264
Center for American Archeology 109
Center for Talented Youth/Johns Hopkins University (all locations) 145
Central City Opera 68
Central Wisconsin Environmental Station/University of Wisconsin–Stevens Point 347
Challenge Wilderness Camp for Boys 317
Channel 3 Kids Camp 91
Cheerio Adventures 327
Cheley Colorado Camps 69
Chenoa 205
Cherokee Adventures Whitewater Rafting 300

Cherokee Park Ranch 70
Chesapeake Bay Girl Scout Council 94
Children's Beach House, Inc. 95
Chimney Corners Camp for Girls 154
Chincoteague National Wildlife Refuge 327
Chingachgook YMCA Outdoor Center 233
Choate Rosemary Hall 91
Christikon 194
Circle Pines Center Summer Camp 171
The Citadel Summer Camp 296
Clara Barton Camp 155
Clearwater Camp for Girls 347
Cold River Camp, A.M.C. 205
College Gifted Programs 213
College Gifted Programs 155
College Gifted Programs 233
College Gifted Programs 285
College Gifted Programs 264
College Light Opera Company 156
College Settlement of Philadelphia 286
The Colorado Mountain Ranch 70
Colorado Trails Ranch 71
Colvig Silver Camps 71
Cowboy Village Resort at Togwotee 353
Crane Lake Camp 157
Cross Bar X Youth Ranch 72
Crystalaire Camp 172
Culver Summer Camps 112
Custer State Park Resort Company 298
Cybercamps–University of Washington (all locations) 335
CYO Boys Camp 173
CYO Girls Camp 173
Deep Portage Conservation Reserve 183
Deer Hill Expeditions 72
Discovery Day Camp 109
Dorney Park and Wildwater Kingdom 286
Double JJ Resort 174
Douglas Ranch Camps 53
Drakesbad Guest Ranch 54
Drowsy Water Ranch 73
Dudley Gallahue Valley Camps 113
Duke Youth Programs–Duke University Continuing Education 256
Dwight-Englewood School 214
Eagle Lake Camp–Colorado 74
Eagle's Nest Camp 256
Eastern Excel Tennis 234
Easter Seals Camp Harmon 55
Easter Seals Camp Merry Heart 214
Easter Seals Wisconsin 348
Echo Canyon River Expeditions 74
Echo Hill Camp 147
Elephant Head Lodge 354
Elite Educational Institute 55
Elk Mountain Ranch 74
Emandal–A Farm on a River 55
Enchanted Forest/Water Safari and Old Forge 234
Enchanted Parks, Inc. 335
Epley's Whitewater Adventures 104
Estes Valley Resorts 75
Evans Lake Forest Education Centre 359
Fairview Lake Environmental Trip 215
Fairview Lake YMCA Camp 215
Farm and Wilderness Camps 318
Fellowship Deaconry, Inc. (Day Camp Sunshine and Fellowship Conference Center) 216
Fenton Ranch 221
Five Rivers Center 235
Flying G Ranch 75
Flying G Ranch, Tomahawk Ranch–Girl Scouts Mile Hi Council 76
Foresite Sports, Inc. 287
Forest Acres Camp for Girls 136
Forest Lake Camp 235
Forrestel Farm Camp 236
Fort Necessity National Battlefield 287
4-H Farley Outdoor Education Center 158
4 Star Summer Camps at the University of Virginia 328
Fredericksburg and Spotsylvania National Military Park 329
French Woods Festival of the Performing Arts 236
The Fresh Air Fund 237
Friendship Ventures/Camp Friendship 183
Friendship Ventures/Eden Wood Camp 184
Friends Music Camp 265
Funland 95
Ganadaoweh 361
Geneva Glen Camp, Inc. 77
Geneva Point Center 206
Girl Scout Camp Molly Louman 265
Girl Scout Camp Sycamore Hills 300
Girl Scout Camp Tanglefoot 115
Girl Scout Camp Tannassie 301
Girl Scouts–Indian Hills Council, Inc. 238
Girl Scouts of the San Fernando Valley 56
Girl Scouts of Tierra del Oro 56
Girl Scouts Pacific Peaks Council–Camp St. Albans 336
Golden Acres Farm and Ranch Resort 238
Gordon Kent's New England Tennis Camp at Trinity-Pawling School 239
Grand Canyon National Park Lodges 43
Grand View Lodge Golf and Tennis Club 185
Greenforce 366
Griffith Park Boys Camp 57
Hamlin Camps 58
Hatchet Motel and Restaurant 355
Hidden Creek Ranch 104
Hidden Hollow Camp 266
Hidden Valley Camp 137
Hillside Outdoor Education Center Day and Tripping Camp 240
Horizons for Youth 158
Howe Military School Summer Camp 114
Hunewill Guest Ranch 58
Idlease and Shorelands Guest Resort 137
Idyllwild Arts Summer Program 59
Indian Acres Camp for Boys 138
Interlochen Arts Camp 175
Interlocken International Summer Camp 206
Interlocken Travel Programs 207
International Music Camp 261
Introduction to Independence 240
Jameson Ranch Camp 59
Jumonville 288
Kamp Kohut 138
Katmailand Inc. 42
Kennywood Park 288

Keystone Camp 257
Kickapoo Kamp 309
Killooleet 318
Kostopulos Dream Foundation/Camp K 312
Lake Hubert Tennis Camp 185
Lazy K Bar Ranch 195
Le Camp Français en Californie 60
Legacy International's Global Youth Village 329
L.I. Adventureland 241
Life Adventure Camp 119
Lighthouse Inn, Inc. 159
Lindley G. Cook 4-H Camp 217
Lochearn Camp for Girls 319
Longacre Expeditions 289
Longacre Expeditions 364
Longacre Expeditions, Colorado 78
Longacre Expeditions, Hawaii 103
Longacre Expeditions, Maine 139
Longacre Expeditions, Oregon 271
Longacre Expeditions, Virgin Islands 324
Longacre Expeditions, Washington 336
Longhorn Tennis Camp 309
Maine Teen Camp 139
Marine Life Oceanarium 190
Marrowstone Music Festival 337
Meadowood Springs Speech and Hearing Camp 271
Menogyn–YMCA Wilderness Adventures 186
Michigan Technological University Summer Youth Program 175
Midway Park, Inc. 241
Mitchell Harvesting 116
Mo-Ranch Summer Camps 310
Mt. Rainier Guest Services 337
Mt. Rushmore Concessions 299
Mount Snow 320
Mystic Saddle Ranch 105
Nelson's Resort 186
New England Camping Adventures 140
New Strides Day Camp 361
92nd Street Y Camps 241
Noark Girl Scout Camp 45
North American Trails 160
North Carolina United Methodist Outdoor and Camping Ministries 258
North Fork Guest Ranch 78
North Shore Holiday House 242
North Shore Music Theatre 160
Northwest Youth Corps 272
Oakland House Seaside Resort 141
Oakland School and Camp 330
Offense-Defense Golf Camp, Massachusetts 161
Orme Summer Camp 44
Paramount's Carowinds 258
Peconic Dunes Camp 242
Pickering College Summer Camps 362
Point CounterPoint Chamber Music Camp 320
Point O' Pines Camp 243
Poulter Colorado Camps 79
Presbyterian Camp Johnsonburg 217
Putney Summer Programs 321
Rawhide Ranch 60
Redfish Lake Lodge 106
Red Pine Camp for Girls 349
Rein Teen Tours 218
The Resort at Glacier, St. Mary Lodge 195
Road's End Farm Horsemanship Camp 207
Rockbrook Camp 259
Rock Springs Guest Ranch 272
Rocky Mountain Park Company (The Trail Ridge Store) 80
Rocky Mountain Village 80
Rockywold–Deephaven Camps, Inc. (RDC) 208
Rubin's Osceola Lake Inn 259
Sabin-Mulloy-Garrison Tennis Camp 99
Sagamore Institute of the Adirondacks 244
Sail Caribbean 244
Salvation Army of Lower Bucks 289
Salvation Army Wonderland Camp and Conference Center 350
Sanborn Western Camps 81
Santa Catalina School Summer Camp 61
Saratoga Springs Picnic, Campgrounds, and Day Camp 61
Seacamp Association, Inc. 100
Sea World of Florida 100
Shaffer's High Sierra Camp 62
Shaver's Creek Environmental Center, Pennsylvania State University 290
Shelly Ridge Day Camp 290
Singing Hills Girl Scout Camp and Cannon Valley Day Camps 187
63 Ranch 196
SJ Ranch, Inc. 92
Snowbird Ski & Summer Resort 312
Somerset County Park Commission Environmental Education Center 218
South Mountain YMCA 291
South Shore YMCA Camps 161
The Southwestern Company (all locations) 302
Sports International, Inc. (all locations) 147
Stagedoor Manor Theatre and Dance Camp 245
Stevenson School Summer Camp 63
Stivers Staffing Services (all locations) 110
Stoiber Enterprises 266
Stony Brook-Millstone Watershed Association-Environmental Education Day Camp 219
Straw Hat Players 187
Streamside Camp and Conference Center 291
Student Conservation Association (SCA) (all locations) 209
Student Hosteling Program 162
Summer at Hawthorne Valley Farm Camp 246
Summer Discovery at Cambridge 366
Summer Discovery at Georgetown 97
Summer Discovery at Michigan 176
Summer Discovery at UCLA 63
Summer Discovery at Vermont 321
Sunrise Resort 92
Swarthmore Tennis Camp 292
Sweet Grass Ranch 197
TAG/Southern Methodist University 310
TENNIS: EUROPE 93
Teton Valley Ranch Camp Education Foundation 355
Thunderbird Ranch 64
Timber Lake West 246
Tomahawk Lake Water Park 219

Tomahawk Ranch 82
Trailmark Outdoor Adventures 247
Trails Wilderness School 192
Tumbling River Ranch 83
Tyler Hill Camp 247
UCLA Bruin Tennis Camp 64
United Cerebral Palsy Association of Greater Hartford 94
University of Rhode Island Summer Programs 294
Vail Resorts 83
Valleyfair Family Amusement Park 188
Vermont State Parks Division 322
Viking Golf Theme & Waterpark 96
Vista Verde Ranch 84
Waldameer Park, Inc. 293
Walton's Grizzly Lodge Summer Camp 65
Weissman Teen Tours 248
Westcoast Connection Travel Camp 248
Western Playland Amusement Park 311
West River United Methodist Center 148
The Whale's Tale Water Park 209
Wild Dunes Resort 297
Wilderness Dance Camp 188
Wilderness Ventures 356
Williamstown Theater Festival 162
Windridge Tennis Camp at Craftsbury Common 322
Windridge Tennis Camp at Teela-Wooket, Vermont 323
Winter Park Resort 84
Wohelo-Luther Gulick Camps 141
Woodberry Forest Summer School 331
Woodside Ranch Resort 351
Worlds of Fun/Oceans of Fun 192
Wright State University Pre-College Programs 267
Yellowstone Park Service Stations 357
YES TO JOBS 65
YMCA Camp Fitch 293
YMCA Camp Hanes 260
YMCA Camping Services–Camps Greenkill/McAlister/Talcott 249
YMCA Camp Letts 149
YMCA Camp Lincoln 210
YMCA Camp Lyndon 163
YMCA Camp Pepin 189
YMCA Camp Seymour 338
YMCA Camps Ockanickon and Matollionequay 220
YMCA Camp Surf 65
YMCA Camp Tippecanoe 267
YMCA Camp U-Nah-Li-Ya 351
YMCA Kitchikewana 363
YMCA of the Rockies–Camp Chief Ouray 85
YMCA of the Rockies Estes Park Center 85
YMCA of the Rockies, Snow Mountain Ranch 86
Yogi Bear's Jellystone Park 210
Yosemite Concession Services Corporation 66
YWCA Camp Westwind 273

JOB TYPES INDEX

Accountants and Auditors, 42
Actors, 162, 187
Amusement and Recreation Attendants, 47, 83, 95, 96, 188, 192, 219, 234, 241, 258, 264, 286, 288, 293, 295, 311, 335, 357
Animal Service Workers, 45, 51, 54, 58, 67, 70, 71, 73, 74, 75, 78, 79, 83, 84, 104, 105, 111, 137, 174, 192, 195, 197, 238, 272, 298, 352, 353, 354, 355
Announcers, 127
Artists and Related Workers, 175, 303
Automotive Mechanics and Service Technicians, 67, 357
Baggage Porters and Bellhops, 186, 194, 238, 259, 352
Bakers, 67, 83, 104, 165, 238
Bartenders, 42, 106, 121, 185, 186, 194, 195, 219, 238, 298, 351, 353
Bicycle Repairers, 164, 199
Bookkeeping, Accounting, and Auditing Clerks, 41, 188, 269, 298, 357
Broadcast Technicians, 128, 134, 275, 359
Building Cleaning Workers, 165, 341
Bus Drivers, School, 42, 50, 70, 74, 161, 331
Captains, Mates, and Pilots of Water Vessels, 244
Carpenters, 154
Cashiers, 43, 54, 188, 195, 293, 295
Chefs and Head Cooks, 42, 45, 51, 58, 59, 67, 70, 73, 119, 121, 124, 151, 165, 170, 194, 195, 196, 198, 212, 217, 232, 238, 242, 262, 268, 319, 333, 334, 336, 358, 361
Child Care Workers, 83, 84, 104, 158, 174, 195, 289, 295, 323, 341
Clergy, 122, 358
Combined Food Preparation and Serving Workers, Including Fast Food, 67, 337
Communications and Media Workers, 59, 68, 87, 127, 134, 152, 156, 160, 162, 166, 174, 175, 211, 243, 245, 288, 337
Computer Programmers, 46
Computer Specialists, 80, 190, 225, 288
Concierges, 194
Conservation Scientists, 89, 199, 218, 236, 249, 258, 262, 322, 329, 366
Cooks, Institution and Cafeteria, 41, 43, 51, 54, 56, 58, 61, 66, 67, 69, 70, 72, 73, 74, 78, 79, 80, 81, 83, 99, 104, 105, 106, 113, 118, 119, 148, 156, 158, 161, 165, 168, 169, 171, 172, 174, 179, 180, 186, 187, 193, 194, 195, 196, 197, 198, 201, 205, 207, 214, 217, 218, 226, 227, 230, 231, 236, 238, 242, 246, 261, 262, 263, 265, 268, 269, 279, 288, 298, 300, 312, 315, 316, 318, 320, 333, 334, 337, 342, 343, 346, 347, 350, 352, 353, 354, 355, 361
Cooks, Short Order, 266
Counselors, 41, 44, 45, 46, 48, 49, 50, 51, 53, 55, 56, 57, 58, 59, 60, 61, 63, 64, 65, 67, 68, 69, 70, 71, 72, 73, 74, 75, 76, 77, 78, 79, 80, 81, 82, 83, 85, 86, 88, 89, 90, 91, 94, 95, 97, 99, 100, 101, 102, 104, 107, 108, 109, 111, 112, 113, 114, 115, 117, 118, 119, 120, 125, 127, 129, 130, 132, 140, 142, 143, 144, 145, 147, 149, 150, 151, 152, 153, 154, 155, 157, 158, 160, 161, 162, 163, 164, 165, 166, 167, 168, 170, 171, 172, 173, 174, 175, 176, 177, 178, 179, 180, 181, 183, 184, 185, 186, 187, 188, 189, 190, 191, 194, 197, 198, 200, 201, 202, 203, 204, 205, 210, 212, 213, 214, 215, 216, 217, 218, 219, 220, 221, 222, 224, 226, 227, 228, 229, 230, 231, 232, 233, 235, 236, 237, 238, 240, 241, 242, 246, 247, 249, 250, 251, 252, 253, 254, 255, 256, 258, 259, 260, 261, 262, 263, 264, 265, 266, 267, 268, 269, 271, 272, 274, 275, 279, 282, 283, 284, 285, 286, 287, 288, 289, 290, 291, 293, 294, 295, 296, 300, 301, 304, 305, 306, 307, 308, 310, 312, 313, 314, 315, 316, 318, 320, 321, 325, 326, 328, 329, 330, 331, 332, 333, 334, 335, 336, 337, 338, 339, 340, 341, 342, 343, 344, 345, 346, 347, 348, 350, 351, 355, 359, 360, 361, 363, 366
Counter Attendants, Cafeteria, Food Concession, and Coffee Shop, 47, 66, 80, 96, 100, 174, 192, 209, 219, 241, 264, 288, 341
Customer Service Representatives, Except Sales and Financial, 74, 110
Dancers and Choreographers, 156
Dental Assistants, 165
Dental Hygienists, 165
Dietetic Technicians, 183
Dietitians and Nutritionists, 50, 237
Dining Room and Cafeteria Attendants and Bartender Helpers, 43, 66, 88, 100, 106, 112, 121, 159, 165, 183, 184, 185, 194, 206, 259, 288, 291, 342
Dishwashers, 42, 73, 85, 100, 106, 174, 193, 194, 195, 230, 261, 269, 288, 298, 300, 334, 337, 342, 346, 352, 353, 355
Editors, 283
Education Administrators, 145
Electricians, 175
Emergency Medical Technicians and Paramedics, 74, 98, 222, 294, 358
Engineers, 46
Entertainment Attendants and Related Workers, 303
Executive Secretaries and Administrative Assistants, 46, 70, 75, 76, 82, 112, 225, 300, 361
Farming, Fishing, and Forestry Workers, 116
Farmworkers and Laborers, Crop, Nursery, and Greenhouse, 55, 237, 294

Farmworkers, Farm and Ranch Animals, 172, 231, 257
Fashion Designers, 243
Financial Specialists, 46
First-Line Supervisors/Managers of Clerical and Administrative Support Workers, 111, 145, 230, 315
First-Line Supervisors/Managers of Food Preparation and Serving Workers, 243, 352
First-Line Supervisors/Managers of Retail Store Workers, 80, 151, 183, 231
Food Preparation and Serving Workers, 47, 48, 55, 74, 83, 85, 86, 104, 107, 111, 115, 154, 180, 181, 194, 195, 197, 199, 208, 210, 229, 234, 238, 258, 275, 293, 299, 300, 312, 320, 341, 349, 351
Food Preparation Workers, 43, 49, 51, 53, 54, 56, 59, 66, 70, 71, 80, 83, 87, 88, 92, 99, 100, 104, 121, 130, 141, 148, 151, 155, 158, 161, 166, 170, 171, 174, 178, 182, 186, 196, 199, 202, 203, 204, 205, 206, 207, 216, 222, 227, 231, 238, 242, 243, 246, 249, 251, 256, 259, 273, 279, 282, 288, 291, 298, 300, 307, 316, 317, 319, 325, 326, 329, 332, 337, 341, 347, 348, 352, 353, 355, 358, 359, 363
Food Service Managers, 41, 42, 56, 80, 111, 119, 130, 160, 164, 165, 171, 174, 231, 238, 244, 269, 279, 293, 295, 301, 317, 327, 344
Foresters, 40, 194
Games of Chance Attendants, 241
Grounds Maintenance Workers, 42, 51, 54, 58, 67, 70, 71, 73, 74, 78, 80, 83, 85, 86, 87, 88, 104, 106, 127, 130, 141, 148, 158, 164, 165, 171, 185, 192, 195, 208, 210, 218, 222, 234, 242, 275, 282, 291, 298, 315, 318, 325, 341, 353, 355, 358, 359, 361
Health-Related Workers, 77, 87, 107, 112, 115, 145, 164, 166, 168, 171, 173, 230, 256, 269, 288, 291, 300, 350
Health Service Coordinators, 48, 65, 115, 143, 158, 194, 301, 336
Health Technologists and Technicians, 261
Hosts and Hostesses, Restaurant, Lounge, and Coffee Shop, 43, 66, 121, 141, 188, 194, 195, 286, 298
Hotel, Motel, and Resort Desk Clerks, 43, 66, 75, 86, 106, 185, 193, 194, 195, 210, 234, 238, 259, 297, 298, 300, 313, 337, 341, 352, 353, 355
Human Resources and Labor Relations Specialists, 86
Installation, Maintenance, and Repair Workers, 48
Interns, 65, 68, 72, 91, 97, 142, 160, 162, 164, 209, 219, 223, 235, 290, 297, 327, 331, 337
Janitors and Cleaners, Except Maids and Housekeeping Cleaners, 58, 66, 86, 194, 266, 326, 337
Laborers and Freight, Stock, and Material Movers, Hand, 80, 100, 357
Landscaping and Groundskeeping Laborers, 55, 58, 68, 100, 174
Laundry and Dry-Cleaning Workers, 87, 194, 230, 297, 355
Librarians, 68, 261
Library Technicians and Assistants, 166, 175
Lifeguards, Ski Patrol, and Other Recreational Protective Service Workers, 39, 41, 44, 48, 51, 56, 59, 61, 65, 66, 80, 85, 86, 88, 90, 92, 96, 100, 101, 107, 108, 111, 114, 115, 117, 118, 120, 130, 132, 134, 148, 154, 158, 165, 167, 170, 171, 174, 175, 179, 180, 183, 184, 185, 188, 192, 197, 198, 199, 205, 206, 207, 209, 212, 216, 217, 219, 220, 222, 224, 225, 227, 228, 229, 231, 234, 236, 237, 238, 242, 243, 245, 247, 254, 258, 262, 263, 265, 267, 268, 279, 281, 286, 288, 290, 291, 293, 294, 300, 301, 305, 306, 308, 315, 322, 323, 326, 329, 331, 332, 333, 334, 335, 341, 343, 350, 359, 361
Maids and Housekeeping Cleaners, 42, 43, 54, 58, 66, 67, 71, 73, 84, 85, 86, 92, 106, 121, 137, 141, 164, 165, 174, 183, 184, 185, 186, 193, 194, 195, 196, 197, 206, 208, 210, 215, 216, 229, 238, 246, 259, 261, 264, 297, 298, 312, 313, 337, 341, 342, 351, 352, 353, 354, 355
Maintenance and Repair Workers, 56, 76, 198, 202, 229, 231, 263, 334, 355
Managers and Administrators, 41, 42, 45, 50, 51, 56, 61, 62, 65, 68, 71, 74, 75, 76, 80, 82, 89, 90, 91, 94, 100, 107, 108, 109, 111, 113, 115, 117, 118, 120, 125, 127, 130, 134, 136, 137, 138, 143, 145, 149, 151, 153, 154, 155, 156, 158, 161, 162, 163, 164, 165, 166, 168, 170, 171, 172, 173, 175, 180, 181, 182, 183, 187, 189, 191, 194, 198, 199, 201, 202, 203, 204, 205, 209, 210, 212, 213, 215, 217, 220, 227, 228, 229, 230, 231, 233, 236, 237, 238, 241, 242, 244, 249, 251, 252, 254, 257, 260, 262, 263, 264, 267, 268, 269, 273, 275, 279, 282, 283, 285, 286, 288, 289, 290, 295, 298, 300, 301, 308, 315, 317, 320, 322, 323, 325, 326, 327, 329, 331, 332, 333, 334, 335, 336, 338, 343, 344, 346, 347, 350, 351, 360, 361
Medical and Health Services Managers, 41, 45, 51, 56, 75, 76, 82, 91, 108, 111, 113, 117, 119, 130, 166, 170, 187, 189, 198, 217, 231, 238, 267, 268, 279, 295, 300, 315, 338, 344, 347
Merchandise Displayers and Window Trimmers, 80
Motor Vehicle Operators, 42, 69, 158, 164, 175, 180, 298, 315, 346
Multi-Media Artists and Animators, 145
Musical Instrument Repairers and Tuners, 175
Music Directors and Composers, 243, 269, 307
Musicians and Singers, 50, 101, 122, 125, 127, 128, 132, 134, 135, 141, 156, 157, 168, 174, 175, 228, 229
Occupational Therapists, 165
Office and Administration Workers, 42, 74, 86, 100, 128, 134, 222, 267, 288, 333
Office Clerks, 48, 68, 69, 70, 73, 88, 92, 104, 110, 121, 122, 124, 127, 145, 161, 164, 174, 175, 178, 180, 181, 182, 183, 184, 195, 199, 208, 219, 227, 229, 269, 275, 306, 353
Parking Lot Attendants, 61, 80, 219
Performers and Entertainers, 39
Personal Care and Service Workers, 83
Photographers, 44, 65, 74, 100, 128, 228, 252
Physical Therapists, 165
Physicians, 157, 175
Procurement Clerks, 358

Producers and Directors, 101, 203, 215, 243, 282, 314
Protective Service Workers, 100
Public Relations Specialists, 68, 80, 156, 183
Receptionists and Information Clerks, 85, 110, 141, 275, 342
Recreation Workers, 48, 55, 61, 71, 72, 75, 78, 84, 85, 86, 96, 100, 103, 115, 130, 139, 147, 164, 170, 174, 180, 183, 185, 186, 190, 192, 194, 199, 208, 209, 214, 219, 222, 231, 252, 262, 271, 286, 288, 289, 304, 322, 324, 325, 329, 336, 338, 344, 345, 360, 361, 363, 364, 365
Registered Nurses, 50, 55, 67, 69, 71, 74, 77, 79, 80, 81, 85, 88, 90, 99, 100, 107, 124, 127, 130, 139, 142, 148, 150, 151, 154, 155, 157, 158, 161, 165, 166, 168, 169, 170, 172, 175, 178, 179, 180, 181, 182, 183, 184, 186, 188, 199, 202, 203, 205, 207, 211, 213, 214, 215, 220, 225, 228, 229, 232, 233, 237, 242, 243, 245, 247, 249, 259, 260, 262, 263, 264, 275, 281, 282, 285, 306, 308, 314, 315, 316, 318, 319, 322, 325, 326, 331, 339, 341, 343, 346, 348, 349, 350, 361
Residential Advisors, 85, 240, 328
Retail Salespersons, 42, 43, 48, 66, 68, 80, 86, 100, 106, 121, 164, 174, 185, 186, 188, 192, 194, 195, 209, 210, 219, 234, 264, 266, 286, 298, 299, 337, 353, 357
Sales Workers, 100, 190, 192, 194, 302
Secretaries (Except Legal, Medical, and Executive), 70, 83, 124, 164, 165, 194, 195, 202, 259, 261, 307, 318, 344
Security Guards, 161, 164, 175, 188, 286
Service Station Attendants, 106, 195, 357
Set and Exhibit Designers, 88, 156, 245, 278
Shipping, Receiving, and Traffic Clerks, 121
Social and Human Service Assistants, 163, 211, 361
Sound Engineering Technicians, 175, 229
Speech-Language Pathologists, 165, 179, 271
Sports and Physical Training Instructors and Coaches, 39, 42, 44, 45, 48, 49, 50, 53, 56, 59, 62, 64, 67, 68, 70, 75, 76, 78, 80, 81, 82, 83, 85, 87, 88, 89, 91, 92, 93, 94, 95, 98, 99, 101, 102, 107, 108, 111, 112, 113, 115, 117, 119, 120, 122, 123, 124, 125, 126, 127, 128, 130, 131, 132, 133, 134, 135, 136, 137, 138, 139, 140, 141, 142, 145, 147, 148, 150, 151, 152, 153, 154, 155, 157, 158, 161, 163, 166, 167, 168, 169, 170, 171, 172, 178, 179, 180, 181, 182, 183, 184, 185, 189, 190, 191, 192, 198, 199, 200, 201, 202, 203, 204, 206, 207, 210, 211, 212, 214, 217, 220, 222, 224, 225, 227, 228, 229, 230, 231, 233, 234, 235, 236, 237, 238, 239, 240, 242, 243, 244, 245, 246, 247, 249, 250, 252, 254, 256, 257, 258, 259, 260, 262, 263, 265, 267, 268, 269, 274, 275, 278, 279, 281, 282, 283, 284, 286, 287, 288, 289, 291, 292, 300, 301, 304, 305, 306, 307, 308, 309, 315, 317, 318, 319, 322, 323, 324, 325, 326, 328, 329, 330, 331, 334, 336, 338, 339, 341, 343, 345, 346, 347, 349, 350, 358, 359, 361, 363
Tailors, Dressmakers, and Custom Sewers, 68, 152, 156, 187
Taxi Drivers and Chauffeurs, 68, 259, 338
Teachers and Instructors, 39, 40, 46, 50, 53, 55, 56, 59, 60, 62, 70, 75, 76, 79, 80, 81, 82, 85, 86, 87, 88, 89, 91, 92, 94, 98, 99, 100, 101, 107, 109, 112, 113, 114, 115, 119, 122, 123, 124, 125, 126, 127, 128, 130, 131, 132, 134, 135, 136, 137, 138, 139, 141, 142, 145, 148, 149, 150, 151, 152, 153, 154, 155, 156, 157, 158, 161, 163, 164, 165, 167, 168, 170, 171, 172, 175, 177, 178, 179, 180, 181, 182, 183, 184, 185, 189, 191, 199, 201, 202, 203, 204, 205, 206, 207, 210, 211, 212, 213, 214, 215, 217, 219, 222, 223, 224, 225, 227, 230, 232, 233, 236, 237, 240, 241, 242, 243, 244, 245, 246, 247, 250, 252, 253, 254, 255, 256, 257, 258, 263, 264, 265, 267, 268, 269, 271, 273, 274, 275, 278, 279, 280, 281, 283, 285, 286, 291, 294, 299, 300, 301, 304, 307, 308, 309, 315, 316, 317, 318, 319, 320, 322, 324, 325, 327, 328, 329, 330, 331, 333, 336, 338, 339, 341, 343, 344, 346, 347, 349, 351, 355, 359, 360, 361, 362, 363
Therapists, 165
Tour Guides and Escorts, 41, 47, 48, 50, 56, 74, 80, 84, 89, 90, 100, 104, 105, 109, 122, 128, 132, 134, 137, 164, 180, 181, 182, 184, 199, 200, 201, 207, 215, 220, 235, 244, 247, 248, 250, 286, 287, 294, 327, 329, 338, 341, 344, 345, 347, 351, 355, 356
Transportation Workers, 83, 106, 186, 320, 351
Truck Drivers, Light/Delivery Services, 116
Ushers, Lobby Attendants, and Ticket Takers, 156, 175, 188
Waiters and Waitresses, 54, 58, 66, 70, 71, 74, 75, 78, 83, 84, 92, 100, 104, 106, 121, 141, 174, 186, 193, 194, 195, 216, 259, 266, 298, 300, 352, 353, 355